MW00527922

Racial Democracy and the Black Metropolis

Racial Democracy and the Black Metropolis

Housing Policy in Postwar Chicago

Preston H. Smith II

 University of Minnesota Press
Minneapolis
London

The University of Minnesota Press gratefully acknowledges financial assistance provided for the publication of this book from Mount Holyoke College.

Portions of chapters 3 and 8 appeared previously in Preston H. Smith II, "The Quest for Racial Democracy: Black Civic Ideology and Housing Interests in Postwar Chicago," *Journal of Urban History* 26, no. 2 (January 2000): 131–57, copyright 2000 Sage Publications, Inc. All rights reserved.

Copyright 2012 by the Regents of the University of Minnesota

All rights reserved. No part of this publication may be reproduced, stored in a retrieval system, or transmitted, in any form or by any means, electronic, mechanical, photocopying, recording, or otherwise, without the prior written permission of the publisher.

Published by the University of Minnesota Press
111 Third Avenue South, Suite 290
Minneapolis, MN 55401-2520
http://www.upress.umn.edu

Library of Congress Cataloging-in-Publication Data

Smith, Preston H.
　Racial democracy and the black metropolis : housing policy in postwar Chicago / Preston H. Smith II.
　Includes bibliographical references and index.
　ISBN 978-0-8166-3702-7 (hc : alk. paper) — ISBN 978-0-8166-3703-4 (pb : alk. paper)
　1. African Americans—Housing—Illinois—Chicago—History—20th century. 2. Home ownership—Illinois—Chicago—History—20th century. I. Title.

　HD7288.72.U52S65 2012
　363.5'99607307731109045—dc23   2011044239

Printed in the United States of America on acid-free paper

The University of Minnesota is an equal-opportunity educator and employer.

19 18 17 16 15 14 13 12   10 9 8 7 6 5 4 3 2 1

For my parents,
Preston H. Smith Sr. (1931–2010) and Mariam Graham Smith

Contents

Abbreviations

ASLL	American Savings and Loan League
ANP	Associated Negro Press
CAD	Council Against Discrimination
CEMV	Conference to End Mob Violence
CHA	Chicago Housing Authority
CHR	Mayor's Commission on Human Relations
CIO	Congress of Industrial Organizations
CLCC	Chicago Land Clearance Commission
CUL	Chicago Urban League
DSCUR	Division of Slum Clearance and Urban Redevelopment
FEPC	Fair Employment Practices Committee
FHA	Federal Housing Administration
FNMA	Federal National Mortgage Association
FNMB	Federal National Mortgage Bank
FPHA	Federal Public Housing Authority
HHFA	Housing and Home Finance Agency
HPKCC	Hyde Park-Kenwood Community Conference
LHC	Labor Housing Conference
MBA	Mortgage Bankers Association
MCRR	Mayor's Commission on Race Relations
MHPC	Metropolitan Housing and Planning Council
NAACP	National Association for the Advancement of Colored People
NAHB	National Association of Home Builders
NAREB	National Association of Real Estate Brokers
NCDH	National Committee Against Discrimination in Housing
NCNW	National Council of Negro Women
NHA	National Housing Agency
NNC	National Negro Congress
NNIA	National Negro Insurance Association
NUL	National Urban League
OPA	Office of Price Administration

PHA	Public Housing Administration
PWA	Public Works Administration
RRS	Racial Relations Service
SECC	South East Chicago Commission
SSPB	South Side Planning Board
UAW	United Auto Workers
UCEH	United Community for Emergency Housing
UPWA	United Packinghouse Workers of America
URA	Urban Renewal Administration
USHA	United States Housing Authority
USSLL	United States Savings and Loan League
VA	Veteran Administration
VHMCP	Voluntary Home Mortgage Credit Program

Introduction

In the introduction to the 1962 edition of St. Clair Drake and Horace R. Cayton's classic work *Black Metropolis*, the white sociologist Everett Hughes describes an outlying area of the black community as a "peaceful middle-class area of one-story brick bungalows and two-flat buildings, probably built for second or third generation Irish, Czechs or Poles. Men were washing their cars, mowing the lawn, or painting the back porch on that Saturday morning. Women were coming and going from the shops, or could be seen dusting in the front room. All at once, I saw that one industrious householder had a dark complexion. Then I saw that all were brown or black."[1] Four years later, St. Clair Drake describes a similar scene: "The power mower in the yard, the steak grill on the rear lawn, a well stocked library and equally well stocked bar in the rumpus room—these mark the homes of well-to-do Negroes living in the more desirable portions of the Black Belt. Many of them would flee to suburbia, too, if housing were available to Negroes there."[2] For black civic elites in Chicago and other major cities, these descriptions represented an intended outcome of the housing policies they had formulated, advocated, and endorsed during and after the Second World War. They were pleased that black homeowners resembled middle-class whites in their housing tastes and residential behavior. It was not a complete fulfillment of their vision for "more and better housing" for African Americans, but for these elites, it represented an important start.

By the 1960s, Drake, Hughes, and other social commentators had noticed not only the newer phenomenon of black middle-class neighborhoods but also the rapid growth of "Chicago's Negro slums."[3] While they all acknowledged this class disparity in African Americans' housing, they either celebrated the existence of middle-class housing as racial progress or, more likely, dismissed black upscale housing as merely a token achievement, given that most blacks lived in substandard housing units. These authors regarded these housing outcomes as an implicit critique of residential segregation rather than the result of a particular housing policy. The class disparity within black housing was either accepted as normal or interpreted through a racial lens—it represented either racial progress or token achievement. The inattention to the roles that the real estate industry, federal housing policy-makers, and black policy elites have played in creating housing inequality has made it difficult to adequately account for the class segregation in the black community that has unfolded throughout the twentieth and early twenty-first centuries.

The purpose of this book is to explore the ways in which African American reformers themselves contributed to class segregation in black communities in the postwar period. Though they were not the architects of the policies that produced housing inequalities, black leaders helped legitimate housing stratification by devoting inconsistent attention to the political-economic foundations of residential segregation. These black civic leaders in Chicago included Claude Barnett, owner of the Associated Negro Press and board member of Supreme Liberty Life, a black-owned insurance company; Horace R. Cayton, executive director of Parkway Community House, a multiservice center located in the Black Belt, and coauthor with St. Clair Drake of the classic *Black Metropolis*; Earl B. Dickerson, former alderman, president of the Chicago Urban League, and legal counsel for Supreme Liberty Life; Robert R. Taylor, chairman of the Chicago Housing Authority (CHA) board, secretary of Illinois Federal Savings & Loan, and manager of the Julius Rosenwald Michigan Boulevard Apartments; and Sidney R. Williams, executive director of the Chicago Urban League, 1947–55.

As a group, these leaders were generally male, well educated, and employed in white-collar professions, working, for example, as insurance executives, lawyers, and publishers. Due to both the political possibilities of the moment and their own class perspectives, African American reformers of the postwar era adhered to a class worldview that took economic inequality for granted. Standing atop the truncated social structure of the segregated Black Metropolis, black civic leaders lived in affluent enclaves within the Black Belt. And yet, they too were victims of housing discrimination. Motivated by their idiosyncratic interests and a sense of social responsibility, African American reformers would serve as both advocates and critics of federal and local housing policy. Many black civic leaders, moreover, would play multiple roles in both for-profit and nonprofit housing.

Though the elites examined in this study were based in Chicago, a number of them acquired national prominence through their work in government agencies and/or national civil rights organizations. Those not directly employed by the government or civil rights groups were nonetheless plugged into these sites of influence through personal and professional connections. Thus, in their response to and advocacy for housing policy, black civic leaders were bound together in a tightly knit community. Nationally, this network consisted of government officials, civil rights organizations, and black real estate trade associations. It included black policy elites who worked in direct policy positions within the federal government or in national civil rights organizations, such as Robert C. Weaver, an economist and former New Deal housing and labor official, and George Nesbitt, a Chicago-based regional racial relations officer for federal housing agencies. African American leaders in Chicago influenced policy through the connections with key federal government officials that they had acquired through successful mobilization as an interest group.

In the postwar era, the housing policies envisioned by African American elites were informed by an ideology I have termed *racial democracy.* Racial democracy meant equal access to housing aid and housing markets for racial minorities. This ideology had a more narrow scope than *social democracy*, which argued that citizens should have access to decent housing regardless of their ability to pay for it. Racial democratic ideology focused on challenging racial discrimination and segregation in housing policy and markets. Conversely, social democracy did not assume that simply removing racial barriers would result in access to good housing for working-class and poor blacks. Instead, adherents of social democracy wanted a direct attack on the class stratification in housing promoted by the real estate industry and endorsed by the federal government. Racial democracy accepted class inequality in housing for several reasons: It considered class stratification normal; it accepted class inequality temporarily while the ideology focused on racial disparities; or it held that the best way to attack class segregation was through opposing racial inequality. Whatever the rationale, acceptance of class stratification within the ideology of racial democracy did not serve the housing needs of the black popular classes well.

During the Great Depression and into World War II, social democracy gained currency in the Black Metropolis when black left-wing activists fought foreclosures, supported tenant rights, and promoted government housing.[4] As the postwar period progressed, black civic and policy elites distanced themselves from social democracy and increasingly accepted, even promoted, class stratification in housing. Their policy analysis and prescriptions mirrored federal housing policy that deemphasized providing public

housing to concentrate on facilitating urban redevelopment and constructing middle-class housing. Only social democracy could contend with the
postwar capitalism that had produced inadequate and unaffordable housing
for far too many working-class Americans. The conflicting trends in labor
and housing markets illustrate a central contradiction in American capitalism. In the labor market, capitalists sought to profit by keeping the wages
paid to their workers as low as possible. In housing markets, real estate capitalists built housing largely for the affluent because that market offered larger
profit margins. Thus many Americans could not afford the price of housing set by builders and mortgage lenders because their wages were too low,
resulting in the creation of an ill-housed working class.[5]

The contradictions that had plagued housing in the U.S. capitalist system
appeared to be resolved in the postwar period. The postwar boom, fueled by
military spending and international expansion into new markets, raised both
wages and profits. The rise in real incomes made housing more affordable for
many working-class citizens employed in growing economic sectors such as
the auto, steel, rubber, chemicals, and aircraft industries. The real incomes of
all workers increased 40 percent from 1947 to 1965. During roughly the same
time period, thirty million new housing units, mostly single-family homes
in the suburbs, were built. However, while the number of owner-occupied
units more than doubled from 1945 to 1960, the quantity of renter-occupied
housing units hardly increased at all. Middle-income households benefited,
but low-income families lost access to affordable and adequate housing. Poor
households were squeezed by a limited supply of cheap housing on the one
hand and, on the other, by the fact that the rising cost of standard housing outstripped their real income gains, leaving them "shelter-poor." At the
beginning of the Great Depression, twelve million households, or roughly 40
percent of the population, were shelter-poor. By 1970, the number of shelter-
poor households had risen to nineteen million, constituting 30 percent of
the population. Perhaps black civic leaders were caught up in the moment
of the postwar housing boom and noticed only racial disparities. However,
their failure to challenge the contradictions of labor and housing markets
under U.S. postwar capitalism meant they could never adequately confront
housing inequality for black working-class citizens.[6]

Over time, the debate among black civic leaders was less about the relative merits of social democracy versus racial democracy and more about
which of the different strains of racial democracy—integration or self-help—
would best inform their approach to housing policy.[7] Racial integration, the

predominant tendency during this period, promoted equal access to American institutions, including housing markets, for qualified black individuals. For housing policy, it meant promoting "open occupancy" so that eligible blacks would not be barred from public or private housing due to their race.[8]

Black self-help represented a subordinate tendency to antidiscrimination within the orbit of racial democratic ideology. Black self-help intended that African Americans should pool all their resources to support and develop (segregated) black institutions including black businesses, not for racial separation, but to establish a more powerful position in the United States' ethnic pluralist political economy. In terms of housing policy, self-help adherents preferred that the location of housing for blacks would be in an expanding ghetto rather than dispersed throughout the white population. Above all, self-help proponents supported black realtors, builders, and lenders to serve a burgeoning black housing market, wherever it was located, for group empowerment and private gain. Whether black civic elites followed integration or a self-help approach to racial democracy, they failed to address the housing needs of the vast majority of working-class blacks.

Even though black elites were not the most powerful actors in determining housing stratification, the housing policies they formulated or endorsed did contribute to class-segregated black housing markets. According to Arnold Hirsch, the most powerful actors were the white architects of housing and redevelopment policies that produced a "second ghetto" in Chicago and other cities.[9] Hirsch's important scholarship has highlighted the persistence of racial discrimination and segregation in metropolitan housing markets buttressed by government policy as something all black citizens seeking adequate housing had to confront. While the power of white business and political elites to determine the structure of metropolitan housing markets has been well researched, it is equally important to examine the complicity of the African American elites, who represented blacks' housing interests, to determine whether their actions, directly or indirectly, obstructed blacks' access to adequate and affordable housing.

Scholars who have uncovered the class bias of black elites, such as Andrew Wiese, still assert the decisive power of white elites by arguing that African Americans' opposition to racial constraints favored the middle-class segment of the black housing market rather than other strata. In other words, black housing activists pursued an antidiscrimination or civil rights housing policy that aided the blacks most able to take advantage of the new housing opportunities extracted from a reluctant state and a recalcitrant housing market.[10]

While this line of argument goes a long way toward explaining black elites' inability to formulate or pursue policy that better served working-class blacks' housing interests, it does not go far enough. In this view, class segregation in the black community is an unintended outcome of the actions of the black policy elites. The pursuit of civil rights is characterized as a path of least resistance, a strategic action taking advantage of a political opportunity afforded by the growing awareness of the contradictions of persistent racial disparities in a nominally democratic society.[11] The failure of black elites to pursue a social democratic housing agenda that would have aided the majority of poor and working-class blacks is blamed on an overdetermining cold-war environment that made such policies impossible. This argument assumes that black policy elites embraced a social democratic agenda of adequate and affordable housing for all citizens but were overruled by more powerful whites who determined the nation's housing policy agenda.[12] In this book, I argue instead that black civic leaders and policy elites had their own reasons for pursuing a racial politics that initially incorporated social democratic tenets, only to abandon the latter to accommodate a probusiness political economy.

Adopting the democratic rhetoric that was prevalent in the United States during and after the war against Fascism, African American policy elites chose to articulate their democratic claims mainly in a racial idiom. While a racial and a class critique constituted most black political formulations during the Depression and World War II, the class critique became increasingly muted after the war. As a result, black policy elites pursued a racial politics that did not simply have class implications—it also represented a *class* politics.[13] It sought to establish and solidify the power of black elites in representing the racial group's housing interests. In doing so, black policy elites pursued racial reform that was not up to the task of confronting the housing industry's class stratification. Thus, not only was the privilege of the black upper and middle strata in housing preserved, but also the black elites' reforms predictably failed to respond adequately to the housing needs of working-class and poor blacks. The fact that black elites had both racial *and* class interests highlighted their participation as multifaceted political actors in the postwar housing scene. It is my aim in this book to explore black civic and policy elites as fully developed political actors, both acting and reacting in an environment of constrained choices.

In the transition from the Great Depression to World War II, the relationship between the state and market was in flux. Racial democratic ideology proved to be malleable during this period. Earlier racial democracy served as a beachhead for social democracy, assuming that an attack on racial inequality would necessarily expand to an attack on class inequalities in housing policies. Later, after the war, this ideology increasingly endorsed government intervention in the private housing market *only* when it sought to correct racial discriminatory behavior or to promote racially integrated residential living. The consequence of this more limited democratic response by black housing reformers was that it left all other housing inequalities unaddressed. As time went on, black policy elites became more ambivalent about direct government intervention for class equality. This ambivalence can be traced, in part, to a strategic response to a conservative political environment bolstered by resurgent business power and accompanying anticommunism, but it was also informed by the class interests of black policy elites.

This study focuses on the motives of black civic leaders for supporting the policies they legitimated, rather than accepting their politics as purely a calculated response to a racist and conservative political environment. I do this for three reasons. First, it simply provides a more balanced account since political actors do not *only* respond to a powerful political environment. They also have interests that shape *how* they respond to that environment. Second, since state repression of egalitarian politics has been a consistent feature of the U.S. political economy, it cannot serve as a sufficient explanation for black policy elites' faltering embrace of social democracy in the postwar period. Third, if black reformers' class interests remain hidden by their racial politics, these interests will reemerge, unexpectedly, to undermine popular movements once the political environment has been pressured to entertain broad egalitarian claims, as in the 1960s. Arguably, black power activists' inability to shed the racial pluralist models of politics that reestablished the predominance of racial democracy contributed to their failure to develop a more thoroughgoing radical politics among the black population, rendering blacks unable to do their part to transform U.S. society.[14]

It is not my intention here to saddle African Americans with the burden of failing, single-handedly, to stem the reactionary postwar political tide. More powerful organized labor and white liberal forces made their own Faustian bargains with cold-war capitalism.[15] Rather, I argue that it is important to track the trajectory of postwar black politics to understand the distinct ways in which black elites negotiated their own pact with U.S. capitalism. African American policy elites' fight against racial discrimination and segregation was timely, important, and even noble at mid-twentieth century.

However, victory would have brought only a *partial* democratization, leaving unaddressed the housing needs of many moderate- and low-income African Americans. Success against racial discrimination did not guarantee success against class stratification. Unfortunately, black elites' myopic focus on racial discrimination and segregation, and their subsequent neglect of class stratification, would continue to inform a flawed approach to housing provision that even today leaves too many African Americans with inadequate and unaffordable shelter.

· · ·

This work is organized by chapters that examine different housing policies and actions in Chicago during and after World War II. Each chapter generally follows the chronological development of housing policies or housing-based political actions. The book also follows a broadly chronological approach, with the early chapters focusing on public housing during and after the war, and later chapters treating black middle-class housing markets and the black real estate industry in the 1950s.

Chapter 1 provides historical and ideological context by explaining the appeal of racial democracy to the postwar cohort of black civic leaders in Chicago. It also sets the stage for housing struggles by describing the wartime and postwar Chicago political economy. Chapters 2 and 3 focus on black policy elites and public housing policy. In chapter 2, I discuss the racial and social democratic reasons that black civic leaders embraced public housing. The analysis explores the black leaders' class critique of the real estate industry, assailing its lack of interest in providing adequate and affordable housing for all low-income citizens. Despite this class critique, black elites found racial democratic reasons equally or more compelling for supporting public housing, such as cultivating middle-class culture in the lowest economic stratum of the race. Chapter 3 outlines the opposition that black civic elites faced in Chicago from both the black bourgeoisie and white political officials for their support for public housing.

The next three chapters treat the politics of urban redevelopment policy as they affect African American citizens in Chicago. Chapter 4 explores the conflict that occurred between national black elites and a coalition of local black civic, neighborhood, and business leaders over slum clearance and urban redevelopment in Chicago. It highlights the inability of the opposition's predominant racial lens to adequately account for the class injuries suffered by working-class black tenants in land clearance. Chapter 5 focuses on black policy elites' efforts to reform the relocation policy that forced both black property owners and tenants to look for housing in a racial dual housing market. It was the plight of the displaced blacks who were ineligible for public housing that encouraged black policy elites to concentrate on the accessibility of private housing markets. Chapter 6 chronicles efforts by black civic and business elites to lead redevelopment of black middle-class neighborhoods in order to stand against the city's land-clearance onslaught but also to serve as a model community for the rest of Bronzeville. In this chapter, I begin to outline the role of black self-help ideology in black elites' housing advocacy.

Chapters 7 and 8 deal with black civic leaders' attempts to open new neighborhoods to African Americans and their response to whites' violent opposition. Chapter 7 explores the crisis of black civic leadership in Chicago over its failure to stop whites' violence against black citizens seeking housing in white neighborhoods. Chapter 8 discusses how black policy elites fought against race-restrictive covenants and created race-neutral occupancy standards that favored those blacks who had the income and class culture to reside in integrated middle-class neighborhoods.

The last two chapters focus on the efforts of black policy elites to encourage white and black private enterprise to provide housing for black Chicagoans. Chapter 9 examines the work of black civic leaders and white policy analysts who made the case that a viable black housing market existed in Chicago and other major cities, which could be profitably served by the housing industry. Chapter 10 investigates the makeup of the black real estate industry and that group's full embrace, along with that of black federal housing officials, of private enterprise as the legitimate provider of housing for U.S. citizens. This chapter elaborates on the self-help strain in racial democratic ideology and its tension with the integrationist tendency. Black civic and policy elites started out in the early postwar years criticizing the real estate industry on class and racial grounds. By the end of the 1950s, there was no trace of a class critique in their housing policy formulations; instead, they focused their political pressure on the federal and municipal government to promote market equality by correcting racial disparities

1

Black Civic Ideology and Political Economy in Postwar Chicago

All citizens of the United States suffered through the postwar housing crisis brought on by pent-up demand and little construction during World War II. The situation for African Americans, however, was worse. The mass migration of blacks to northern and western cities added more home seekers to communities that were already poorly housed. Furthermore, the fact that the newcomers were forced to fit within racially enforced boundaries increased the urgency of the housing situation. Housing conditions in the black community were so bad that the Chicago city council formed the Subcommittee on Negro Housing, chaired by Alderman Earl B. Dickerson in 1939. The subcommittee heard horror stories such as testimony about a building located at Mid-South Side, where five African American families, a total of twenty-four people, shared one toilet.[1] A year later, in his article on black housing, the sociologist Horace Cayton elaborated on the extent of overcrowding in segregated black neighborhoods. He found that between Thirty-Ninth and Fifty-Fifth Streets on the city's South Side, the average density of the black population was between 53,000 and 70,000 per square mile—twice that of the white population, which averaged between 34,000 and 37,000. Black civic elites largely attributed poor black housing conditions to racial segregation, which forced too many blacks to live in housing that was inadequate for their needs.

Black civic elites sought policy solutions to poor housing conditions from within a framework of racial democracy. Some of the core concepts in their racial democratic ideology—urban ecology, social disorganization, and ethnic pluralism—originated in the Chicago school of sociology, which had trained or influenced many black intellectuals, including E. Franklin Frazier, St. Clair Drake, Horace Cayton, Robert Weaver, and Richard Wright. Black civic reformers also drew ideas of political pluralism and modernization theory from the political science of that era. All these ideas informed the approach that black civic leaders brought to the black housing crisis.

Urban ecology explains the spatial organization of cities, specifically, the relationship between industrial, commercial, and residential spaces. Chicago school founders assumed that marketplace decisions drive urban growth and shape the configuration of urban spaces. Therefore, Chicago school sociologists did not question the residential segregation that resulted from market-based allocation of housing based on the ability to pay. When black intellectuals and civic elites imported urban ecological assumptions, they also adopted the idea of market-driven urban growth and its product, class segregation, as normal. They counterposed normal class segregation with an aberrant racial segregation that needed reforming.[2] This explains why racial segregation, not class-segmented housing markets, became the target of their housing reform activity.[3]

Equally important for black civic elites was the concept of *social disorganization*. Chicago school theorists explained social disorganization as a process whereby individuals who experience rapid social change, such as migration, engage in antisocial behavior and seem unable to maintain a conventional family structure. Since the concept described a process, the condition could be temporary, but the danger existed that it could become a permanent pathology. The evidence of social disorganization was provided by the disproportionate incidence of social problems such as juvenile delinquency, illegitimacy, and desertion, which over time came to be designated as causes of social disorganization. Black housing reformers embraced this understanding of social disorganization in the midst of the massive wartime and postwar migration of black Southerners to Chicago and other northern and western cities. While they were not confident that poor black migrants could adjust easily to Chicago, they blamed racial residential segregation for producing overcrowded and deteriorated housing conditions, which in turn caused social disorganization.[4]

The idea of social disorganization appealed to black civic leaders for a number of reasons. Since all African Americans were subject to racial segregation, for these black elites, social disorganization helped to explain why some succeeded in escaping poverty while others failed. Not only was it a convenient concept to explain class differences in the black community, but it also paid racial democratic dividends. Black policy elites could single out low-income blacks as the bearers of personal and family disorganization and thus contest whites who generalized pathology to blacks of all economic strata. In addition, since social disorganization was a process, it was subject to intervention. Black civic leaders could attack social disorganization in two ways: by confronting racial segregation that produced slum conditions and/or by correcting the values and behavior of working-class blacks in the segregated institutions that they managed. Black elites became invested in inculcating middle-class values into their poorer brethren so that once the racial barriers were lowered, the low-income stratum would have the cultural tools to take full advantage of an open housing market.

In addition to adopting the Chicago school concepts of urban ecology and social disorganization, black civic leaders embraced the idea of ethnic pluralism, the view that the U.S. population consists of racial and ethnic groups that make distinct cultural and economic contributions to American society. This sociological view dovetailed with a concurrent theory of pluralism promoted by political scientists, who contended that as long as individuals were attached to groups, they would have equal ability to work for their interests in an arena where the government distributed benefits and costs.[5] Political scientists began to see racial and ethnic groups as competing for power to compel public and private institutions to respond to their group's needs.[6] African Americans' mass migration to cities gave them electoral advantages that brought them into the New Deal coalition in the 1930s. African American policy elites assumed that they were participating in an ethnic pluralist political system that conferred special disadvantages to their race because racism was more persistent than ethnocentrism.[7]

Ethnic pluralism assumed that the group was the unit of political activity. Moreover, it theorized that each group needed a leadership cohort to best represent the interests of the group in the political system. The assumptions of elite leadership and a group basis for politics had parallels in *modernization theory*, which was formulated by social scientists attempting to explain the politics of newly independent nations in Asia and Africa. Modernization theory presumed that Third World countries would develop in a fashion approximating the liberal capitalist political economies of the West. Perhaps the tenet of the theory most relevant to this discussion is the idea that a strong middle class is important for the political and economic stability of developing countries. While the elite would provide political leadership, the middle class constituted their main public by developing the institutions of civil society including a private economy.[8]

Both the ideas of group-based politics and elite leadership coincided with African American civic leaders' political understanding. These elites assumed that by virtue of education, occupation, accomplishment, and class, they legitimately constituted the leadership of black Americans in the postwar period.

Since some commentators, including a few black policy elites, likened African Americans' situation in the postwar period to that of citizens of decolonizing societies, it is not a stretch to suggest that these elites applied modernization theory to their predicament.[9] In fact, black policy elites sought the "modernization" of African Americans as a race or racial group.

Black civic leaders assumed that, while a viable middle class was crucial for this task of modernization, the working class would not be left out. Contrary to the notion that elites sought only exclusive personal or class gains, their commitment to modernization was based on the notion that the material upgrade for the poor working majority was necessary for the whole group to advance.[10] A corollary task was a cultural upgrade, which meant correcting the habits of the black "lower classes," which the elites saw as holding back the modernizing project. Here is where they deployed the idea of social disorganization to better understand and explain how black migrants' premodern habits hampered their adjustment to urban industrial civilization. For black policy elites, modernization theory reinforced the idea that blacks constituted a political unit that needed leadership from their class.

In this chapter, I relate these concepts from the Chicago school of sociology and related social sciences to three developments in the ideology and material interests of African American elites in order to set up a larger examination of the elites' housing politics. The first section explores the anatomy of racial democracy as a reform ideology. In the next section, I examine the claims that black civic elites made for racial leadership. The last section outlines Chicago's postwar political economy, and the material stakes involved in the reconstruction of its inner-city neighborhoods for the city's progrowth coalition and its black elite. After World War II, black civic leaders presented the black community with a more conventional agenda than the social democratic one that black unionists and radicals had promoted earlier. In this chapter, I examine the underlying assumptions held by black elites that explain their more conservative approach to housing reform.

Racial Democracy as Black Civic Ideology

Postwar black civic elites built upon the sociological ideas from the Chicago school to develop an ideology of racial democracy. This ideological framework helped them analyze and propose policies intended to respond to the problems and challenges facing African Americans at that time. A major facet of this ideology was the belief that democracy in the United States was deeply flawed because it had not extended full political and civil rights to its largest racial minority.[11] At the same time, there was confidence that awarding legal rights to blacks was possible within the framework of a liberal democratic polity.[12] Black activists launched the Double-V campaign based on the idea that democracy needed to be won in the United States as much as it did in Europe and Asia. While not everyone shared this view, the admission that U.S. democracy suffered from racial deficits gradually took on new importance in the postwar era. Soon its racial policies were widely considered the only defect of U.S. democracy.[13]

The concept of racial democracy grew out of the generally perceived need to correct the racial disparities of U.S. democracy to restore it to health, a process and outcome that would confer on African Americans "first-class citizenship."[14] Civil rights was a form of racial democracy since it represented the extension of formal political rights and civil liberties to racial minorities. However, racial democracy went beyond civil rights, insisting that African Americans should have not only full political and civil rights but also equal access to all economic and social opportunities.[15] Becoming a first-class citizen meant not only being able to vote and receive equal treatment in public accommodations but also having nondiscriminatory access to adequate and quality schools, housing, jobs, and income. For some, civil rights advocacy denoted integration, but other advocates of racial democracy tolerated self-segregation if it achieved racial parity.[16] For African American policy elites, racial democracy meant equal treatment in the marketplace as well as by government.

Unlike the more limited racial democracy, social democracy attacked the broad inequality of U.S. society that stemmed from distribution of goods and services to a privileged few at the expense of a poor working majority.[17] During the 1930s, the same progressive forces promoted democratization along class and racial lines.[18] However, as U.S. society came increasingly under the sway of an organized and resurgent business class during the postwar period, the gains made by proponents of social democracy came under attack.[19] That attack came in the form of anticommunist rhetoric and the promotion of private enterprise. During this period, black elites who, like organized labor and liberals, found supporting social democracy to be politically risky abandoned it and devoted their attention and resources to pursuing a more circumscribed racial democracy.[20] Due to the malleability of racial democracy, its proponents were able to accommodate its goals and methods with the political compromises that accompanied the postwar political-economic restructuring of Chicago and other cities. The following sections explore the different components of racial democratic ideology, particularly how African American elites deployed it to serve their political interests.

The Primacy of Race

One of the consequences of separating social and racial democracy was the reemergence of "race" as the key analytical and prescriptive concept in black elite political thinking.[21] The primacy of race seemed obvious given the great and pervasive racial disparities in all aspects of postwar U.S. life. However, to understand the endurance of race as the key social category for black civic and political elites, the many reasons for its primacy in their ideology need to be uncovered. The primacy of race in racial democracy derived from three sources: (1) The growing acceptance that the racial inequities in the United States were the nation's only obstacle to achieving true democracy; (2) the association, in U.S. racist ideology, of black identity with lower-class traits, which meant that black class mobility, by severing that link, was racially progressive; and (3) the importance of racial consciousness and its link to individual achievement and group progress in black petit bourgeois thinking. All three factors combined to establish the primacy of race and to downplay the salience of class in black civic ideology.

A key element in establishing the primacy of race was the acceptance of racial democracy within liberal philanthropic, academic, and political circles marked by the 1944 publication of Gunnar Myrdal's *American Dilemma*. The emergence of this view, coupled with a growing anticommunism, discredited any serious attempt by the U.S. government to ensure equal distribution of income, housing, education, and health care to all its citizens.[22] Emphasis on the racial inequities in U.S. democracy has long been a staple of African American political thought, dating from at least as early as from Frederick Douglass and the Convention Movement.[23] Now this idea was adopted by leading racial liberals, and it would get "official" endorsement in 1947, with the publication of *To Secure These Rights*, by Harry Truman's Presidential Committee on Civil Rights.[24]

Paradoxically, the second factor that supported the primacy of race was the particular role that class played in the interpretation of racial equality. In the United States, the cognitive map of racism associated all African Americans with poverty and "lower-class traits" while linking whites with affluence and middle- and upper-class status.[25] Racial stereotypes associated such traits as laziness, stupidity, promiscuity, immorality, and profligacy with the lower class. In this environment, when black individuals managed against all odds to achieve upward mobility and adopt middle-class attributes, their achievements and very beings subverted widely held racist beliefs.[26] In this context, African Americans' upward class mobility was considered racial progress.[27]

Following this logic, middle-class blacks rationalized that if they could substitute their image as the archetype of the race, more racial equality was achievable.[28] This consideration explains the succession of racial uplift projects by black elites as they attempted to inject middle-class values and habits into black manual laborers and domestic servants. It also explains the ambivalence of poor blacks who accepted individual black achievements as symbols of racial pride but harbored suspicions that black middle-class gains came at their expense. In a segregated black public sphere dominated by black elite-owned and -run newspapers, schools, and churches, the voices that mattered were those of the black middle class, not those of working-class blacks.[29] Black upward mobility was not interpreted as class inequality or intraracial stratification; instead, it constituted evidence of racial democratization.

The last, and most influential, factor promoting the primacy of race was the new postwar black middle class of teachers, social workers, managers, and supervisors whose ideas and behavior conveyed the importance of racial self-consciousness. E. Franklin Frazier provided insight into the ethos of this postwar black middle class, aptly describing their belief system as being characterized by the interrelationship of morality, upward mobility, and racial consciousness.[30] He argued that middle-class African Americans were highly race conscious and that their racial consciousness incorporated values of moral respectability and upward mobility. Respectability was combined with moral discipline, which was needed to channel this black stratum's energies into productive activity such as educational and economic achievement that could facilitate their class ascension both materially and socially. Middle-class black parents expected their children not only to rise in the "Negro world" but also to prove their worth to whites by rising in the white world as well.[31]

This desire to rise in the white world should not be misinterpreted, however. The black middle class, like other middle classes, regarded its social esteem and moral code of conduct important for its acceptance by a higher class. Because this higher class was mostly white, their behavior has been mistakenly identified as *simply* assimilationist, if not a denial of their putative racial identity. In purely racialist terms, class ascension meant whitening an essential blackness. But a more complicated reading of black middle-class behavior appreciates their class aspirations on their own terms. To deny privileged blacks their class behavior is to misread a crucial component of their sense of themselves and their politics.

African American middle-class values of racial consciousness, moral respectability, and upward mobility combined to fuel and define racial progress.[32] Racial progress was measured by the growing number of black individuals who would qualify for middle-class status based on occupation, income, education, and behavior. In other words, racial-group mobility meant increasing the number of upper- and middle-class blacks to a proportion more closely resembling the white class structure.[33] In the estimation of middle-class blacks, and that of white society, the success of the black middle class became synonymous with racial progress.

These three factors were melded in the crucible of black class relationships. The African American middle class, like other middle strata, interpreted as immorality what it considered the inappropriate public behavior of the working class. Although the black middle class did not discount racial discrimination, they feared that a lack of moral discipline or personal disorganization made poor blacks unable to maintain regular employment and a suitable home, which contributed to their social unacceptability and stunted racial progress. In other words, middle-class blacks felt the black working class was really *lower* class in behavior and culture. The black middle class interpreted the apparent lack of moral discipline on the part of the black working class as demonstrating a lack of racial pride. Middle-class blacks knew that poor blacks' antisocial behavior reinforced whites' racist stereotypes, thus tarnishing their own carefully constructed class status.[34] They felt that many black wage earners and relief recipients, particularly migrants, were ignorant and needed the assistance of the "better classes" to set them on the right path of upward mobility and racial respectability.[35]

Individual black upward mobility was dependent on an achievement orientation fueled by racial self-confidence and facilitated by moral discipline. Racial consciousness convinced elites and a noisy stratum of black strivers that their individual and class achievements represented racial progress. Thus the role for politics was to attack institutional racial barriers that prevented potentially high-achieving black individuals from becoming upwardly mobile and so blocked the main engine of racial-group progress. In addition, this politics also needed a way to ensure that more black individuals were ready to achieve in a competitive, hostile white world. It meant that those blacks who did not exhibit the requisite moral discipline and racial consciousness needed to be resocialized in a reconstituted nuclear family protected by good housing and decent neighborhoods.[36]

The primacy of race as the central component of racial democracy stemmed from the use of class mobility to undercut racism, the reinforcement of racial consciousness through morality and mobility, and the liberal elite's recognition of the racial flaws of democracy. Each factor normalized conventional upward mobility and obscured the political economic factors that produced class and racial inequalities in American society. Though class was overshadowed by race, it remained a powerful, if hidden, force in shaping racial democracy as a class ideology. As much as racial democracy constituted a racial politics, it also represented a class politics masked by the equation of racial progress with normative middle-class achievement.

Pluralism, Modernization, and Class Leadership

In order for racial democracy to function as a political ideology, it needed concepts of agency, organization, and leadership that were compatible with the primacy of race. The primary political unit of racial democracy was the "race," or racial group. The nature of the political unit determined the form that leadership would take. Treating individual blacks as part of a racial group has been another staple of African American political thought. The idea of a unitary black agency was another recurrent theme in black political tracts of the time.[37] The establishment of a unitary black agency, subordinating individual or segmental needs, emanated from a predominantly elite response to African Americans' minority status in a racist polity. Since all blacks suffered some form of racial discrimination and segregation, what they had in common was their racial identity. Under this conception, blacks' minority status and common identity necessitated that all blacks act as one under an elite leadership.[38]

Racial unity was required, black elites reasoned, if African Americans hoped to counteract racial oppression. Unity was so crucial that intraracial differences—class, gender, region, ideology—were seen as secondary to race because racism was considered the chief reason for blacks' lack of rights and opportunities.[39] Theoretically, unifying around race would lead to the surmounting of political differences.[40] Of course, subordinating nonracial factors to race allowed those who enjoyed class, gender, and regional privileges or held conventional political views to go unchallenged and to dominate the conceptualization of unitary interests.[41] These elites rationalized their privileges by asserting that, since the social environment was so overdetermined by race, racial progress would benefit all members of the race regardless of intraracial differences.

This idea of a unitary black politics—notably, the conception of the racial group and the need for middle-class leadership—was buoyed by a pair of postwar social-scientific concepts. Both pluralism and modernization theory, outlined earlier, supported black elites' conception of racial-group politics and the need for elite leadership. Their arguments for unifying black interests under a racial banner were bolstered by the idea that the political system is constituted by interest groups that vie for power and influence in the government arena. Both pluralist and modernization theories required an elite to lead or represent each group. Black civic elites used social disorganization theory to discredit working-class blacks as unqualified for leadership while supporting their own leadership claims. The black bourgeoisie developed a conventional political understanding of the problems of and solutions to African Americans' plight. Conversely, black radicals and unionists using a social democratic framework addressed racial discrimination by confronting its political-economic foundations. For them, unlike black civic elites, racial inequality could not be successfully challenged without confronting the inequality that emanates from a capitalist political economy.

In its challenge to a racist environment, the ideology of racial democracy equated racial progress with normative middle-class achievement. Its ideas about racial-group agency and elite leadership were bolstered by postwar social science in the form of pluralism, modernization, and social disorganization theories. It will be important to see how these ideas constituted a black civic ideology in a dynamic political environment. The crucial test for this ideology was how it explained to its proponents—black policy and civic elites—what the problem was and how to solve it, as well as on what basis they could claim legitimate leadership against their rivals. Among the places where black civic elites operationalized this ideology was in the social and political economic context of postwar Chicago.

Black Civic Elites and Racial Leadership

Prior to World War II, black civic leaders had to withstand a radical challenge to their hegemony in Bronzeville. St. Clair Drake and Horace Cayton chronicle the rise of this radical politics in *Black Metropolis*. Blacks began to participate in mass popular action during Congress of Industrial

Organizations (CIO) organizing drives and protests against the effects of the Depression. Between 1935 and 1940, the CIO organized all the mass-production industries such as steel, automobile, meatpacking, and farm equipment. These new industrial unions organized large numbers of black workers during this time, and, in the process, according to Drake and Cayton, converted "Negro peasants" into proletarians.[42] CIO leadership registered their commitment to racial equality by promoting blacks for local union leadership as well as ending racial wage differentials. Blacks joined or at least supported the industrial unions partly because of the unions' "racial policy"—equal pay for equal work and nonsegregated working conditions. But their support for CIO unions also conveyed their belief that cooperation with white workers under a multiracial union leadership represented a useful vehicle for improving their income and working conditions.

Although the Communist Party in Chicago had more black members than most cities, the numbers were not large. The Communist Party, which spearheaded both CIO organizing and street protests, became well known and well liked in the Chicago black community for its militant defense of blacks' economic and civil rights.[43] For instance, the Communist-led unemployed councils created "flying squadrons" that returned evicted tenants' furniture and belongings to their homes right after the police deposited them into the streets. Unemployed councils also agitated on other issues such as racial discrimination and relief cuts while supporting social security, tenant rights, and government housing projects.[44]

According to Drake and Cayton, blacks supported the Communist Party because it provided them with a program of action and did not practice racial discrimination. The Communist Party played a crucial role along with black nationalists in discrediting the "safe leaders" of black middle-class organizations. The CIO, prompted by "a militant Communist minority," not only put black and white workers together to fight for union gains but also presented the issue of racial inequality to numerous white workers.[45] In addition to the CIO and the Communist Party, the National Negro Congress (NNC), founded in Chicago in 1936, sought to organize all existing black organizations to fight for social rights under a black left-wing leadership. Black leftists criticized the NAACP and the National Urban League (NUL) for their inattention to an "economic program" that would better represent working-class blacks' needs and interests during the Depression.

Black civic elites countered with the Council of Negro Organizations, which tried to adopt proletarian-style protests.[46] In addition, local chapters of the Urban League and the NAACP in Chicago felt they had to adopt "mass protest" methods such as marches, demonstrations, and mass meetings coupled with a militant racial rhetoric in order to remain legitimate to wage-earning blacks. Despite the change in tactics and rhetoric, black civic elites retained their conviction that they should lead the race and that policy analysis and prescriptions of black housing interests should be done primarily through a racial prism. They also believed that they needed a base among the black popular classes.[47]

After the disruptive 1930s, black middle-class leaders realized that the loyalty of the wage-earning blacks was still up for grabs. Drake and Cayton identify four political directions that working-class blacks might have taken after the war. The first two directions—black nationalist movements like the Nation of Islam or the Moorish Science Temple, and the communist movement—were largely rejected by most wage-earning blacks in the postwar period.[48] A third path involved participation in trade union activities, reflecting the influence of CIO unions. The final option entailed the pursuit of more mainstream avenues for upward mobility such as saving money, adopting middle-class consumption habits, seeking more education, and participating in ward politics. Because the postwar CIO purged its ranks of Communists and adopted a narrower political agenda, the third and fourth paths converged over time.

Most black workers, who followed a mainstream path of trade union and ward politics, did not make these choices in a vacuum. Undoubtedly, they were encouraged by the employment and income gains being made during and after the war, which economic prosperity and unionization facilitated. But they were also influenced by black elite-led segregated institutions like churches and schools, which credited these gains to the adoption of a conventional politics, except on racial questions.[49]

Like other social democrats, black radicals were in retreat after World War II. Competition for racial leadership mainly developed between reenergized black civic leaders who favored civil rights principles and black politicians who pursued more pragmatic interests and incremental gains. Congressman William Dawson created a "submachine" that governed the Black Belt under the aegis of the white-controlled Cook County Democratic Party organization.[50] Black machine politicians resented black civic leaders' "amateur" politics, which in their view featured irresponsible racial rhetoric. As professional politicians, they preferred to serve "the race" by doling out patronage jobs and favors to their black constituents in exchange for their vote. The fact that black elected officials, in contrast to civic leaders, contested for office gave them a nominal popular base among working-class black citizens. African American civic leaders who directed local civil rights organizations like the NAACP and the Urban League related to black wage earners either as members or as clients. In either case, their ties to a black popular base were more distant than those of elected black political leaders.[51]

Despite their competition, and unlike their radical counterparts, black civic and electoral leaders had in common a belief in elite leadership and the primacy of race. Black politicians, like all machine politicians, shied away from redistributive policies that threatened a capitalist political economy.[52] They rejected black civic elites' militancy, arguing that they would be better able to advance racial progress behind the scenes by assisting black professionals and business owners while providing mainly symbolic and limited material aid to black wage earners. Both liberal factions were threatened by a left-wing politics that organized black citizens to fight for broad egalitarian policy changes, including civil rights, and challenged the hold of the black middle class on racial leadership.

African American civic activists were convinced, and attempted to convince others, that civil rights would provide more political and economic opportunities for racial progress than the incremental gains of ward politics or the revolutionary goals of radical politics. They fused a militant leadership style onto a liberal politics that advocated individual upward mobility based on equal opportunities extracted by racial protest. The modest social democratic response to the Depression would give way, in the postwar period, to the predominantly racial democratic political agenda of black civic elites.

Black Incorporation in a Postindustrial Political Economy

In order for black civic elites to attract and retain the support of different black social strata, black men and women had to see real and potential gains in their income and housing. Just as important, they had to believe that those gains were achieved by following a civil rights and progrowth politics. Because of the employment and income gains realized during this period by the upwardly mobile black skilled and clerical workers constituting the core of the postwar black middle class, it was perhaps easier to convince this group that this agenda represented the best political path toward first-class citizenship. The black upper and middle strata represented a more active and immediate public to black civic leaders than did the large majority of wage-earning and relief-receiving blacks.

After the radical threat of the immediate postwar period had waned, black civic leaders did not envision wage-earning blacks participating in postwar politics beyond attending the occasional mass meeting at DuSable High School or a demonstration downtown over the latest racial affront. Poor and unskilled blacks did not play an influential role in shaping black civic leaders' postwar agenda. Black civic leaders assumed that the lower strata were politically mute, and they represented them that way to white government and business elites. The black professionals who vied for leadership assumed a custodial role when it came to representing the working majority of blacks. As far as they were concerned, low-income black citizens were members of the racial group and were presumed to be satisfied with any evidence of group progress, symbolic or material. This worked as long as group progress could point to potential, if not real, gains on the civil rights horizon for the lower rungs of Bronzeville's class structure. Key to black civic elites' leadership claims was their ability to deliver postwar goods such as adequate and affordable housing to most black strata, especially the attentive middle class. This would occur by opening up and extracting market opportunities and securing their fair share of government benefits.

Many blacks experienced rising incomes and greater occupational mobility in the postwar period. Nationally, African Americans' incomes nearly tripled during the 1940s and grew another 50 percent in the subsequent decade.[53] In Chicago, nonwhite workers' real wages grew 73 percent compared to 32 percent for white workers from 1940 to 1947.[54] Still, an average black worker in 1947 earned only 54 percent of the average white worker's income, a gap that remained virtually unchanged in 1962.[55]

Despite the racial disparities, the occupational distribution of blacks began to approach that of whites for the first time. However, the growth of the black middle class was not so much due to increased proportions of black professionals, businesspeople, or government managers within Chicago's black class structure. In Chicago, these elite occupations experienced limited growth, representing only 7 percent of all employed black men in 1960.[56] Black middle-class growth was largely due to the expansion of white-collar clerical work, especially among black women, and to the growth in the proportion of black foremen, supervisors, and craftsmen.[57] However, the greatest shift in black occupational structure was the decreasing proportion of black men and women in unskilled manual and domestic employment and the growing proportion employed as semiskilled factory operatives and clerical workers. Despite these real employment gains, however, 44.5 percent of black men and women remained restricted to unskilled work, unsteady employment, and low-wage jobs, compared to just 12.9 percent of white Americans in 1960.[58]

The limited growth of black professionals and managers before 1960 in Chicago explains this stratum's support for aggressive action through civil rights politics to ensure better rewards than they had experienced from simply servicing a growing black proletariat in the segregated Black Belt.[59] They backed a racial politics whose goal was to pry open new employment (including the public sector) and housing markets, directly promoting their professional and consumption interests and reflecting enhanced class status. The white- and blue-collar blacks who had recently joined the postwar middle class were attracted to a black civic agenda that they hoped would in time let them solidify their upward mobility by moving to brick bungalows in outlying neighborhoods in the city or southern suburbs and eventually open up new educational and economic opportunities for their children.

Civil Rights and Economic Progress

The economic progress experienced by semiskilled and skilled black workers both in Chicago and nationally began during World War II due to renewed migration, tight labor markets, wartime production demands, and tentative antidiscrimination policies by government. These gains also reflected pressure exerted by black interest-group organizations and new civil rights agencies. While natural increase played a role, a good deal of the growth in the size of the black population after 1940 stemmed from migration from the American South. Chicago's black population increased 77 percent, from 278,000 in 1940 to 492,000 in 1950, but experienced even more spectacular growth in the 1950s. By 1960, blacks numbered 813,000, representing an addition of more than half a million people since the beginning of World War II. This massive migration was stimulated by wartime labor demand in Chicago and other defense production centers across the nation. In Los Angeles, for instance, the black population more than doubled, from roughly 98,000 in 1940 to 212,000 in 1950.[60] Ten years later, the black population further increased to 335,000.[61]

In the early years of the war, blacks were excluded from defense employment. It was not until 1943 that the defense industry finally began the concerted hiring of blacks.[62] Not surprisingly, 1943 also marked a shift in federal policy. The federal government decided that it would not certify collective bargaining units unless they accepted racial minorities, and the War Labor Board outlawed racial wage differentials. Evidence of African Americans' delayed entrance into the defense industry was reflected in the fact that black workers' wartime production employment peaked in 1945, two years after that of white workers. By 1952, the Commission on Human Relations in Chicago noted that African Americans made up more than half the workers in the meatpacking industry and a large percentage in the steel industry. They were also employed in machine production, machine tools, farm equipment, automobiles, freight cars, and clothing.[63] While slower than men to get defense employment, many black women were able to leave domestic work, mainly to do other service work as waitresses, cooks, and hairdressers.[64] According to Drake and Cayton, black Chicagoans even gained lower-level managerial and clerical positions during the war.[65] In Chicago, blacks saw their share of metropolitan employment increase from almost 5 percent in 1940 to 11.7 percent at the end of the war.[66]

While wartime labor shortages were important in increasing black employment in the defense industry, occupational upgrades would have been unlikely without political pressure from black organizations like the NAACP, the NUL, the March on Washington Movement, and their local affiliates against discriminatory hiring and promotion practices.[67] In 1941, A. Philip Randolph, founder and president of the Brotherhood of Sleeping Car Porters union, threatened to organize fifty thousand blacks to march on Washington, D.C., to protest discrimination in the defense industry and armed forces. President Roosevelt responded by signing Executive Order 8802 outlawing discrimination in defense production and creating the Federal Employment Practices Committee (FEPC) to monitor hiring practices.[68]

The pressure from black political groups and the FEPC was responsible for lowering racial barriers, especially to skilled and white-collar employment.[69] In Chicago, Elmer Henderson, the African American director of the FEPC's regional office, with the support of CIO unionists, was able to integrate a number of defense plants in 1944.[70] The Dodge plant, one of the nation's largest, along with Campbell's Soup, Argo Corn, Illinois Bell Telephone, and the city's mass-transit companies, accepted black employees for the first time.[71] The Chicago Urban League placed blacks in six hundred different industries in 1943, with an official claiming, "Right now all employable Negroes either have or can find jobs."[72] African Americans integrated previously closed occupations as bus drivers, elevated train operators, store clerks, and restaurant servers.[73] Nonetheless, despite continued political pressure in 1943 and 1944, black women were less successful in getting sales jobs in downtown stores.[74] The campaign to desegregate public transportation met with greater success.[75] Overall, as the historian Andrew Kerstein has observed, the FEPC was especially successful in the Chicago area due to the combined efforts of local labor, civil rights, and government leaders to alter employment patterns.[76] The success of black civic organizations in lowering employment barriers contributed to their increased membership, especially among working-class blacks. Nationally, the NAACP increased its membership nearly tenfold from fifty-four thousand to more than five hundred thousand during World War II, "giving the organization its first mass base."[77]

Postindustrial Economy and Progrowth Coalitions

The United States emerged as a preeminent power after World War II, largely powered by the economic output of its large cities like Chicago. A 1942 Chicago Plan Commission study anticipated that the city would play a vital role in the postwar economy because it had become a centralized hub for different modes of transportation, allowing the city to distribute consumer goods to a national market.[78] But as in many northeastern and midwestern cities, economic output and fiscal stability in postwar Chicago were adversely affected by industrial decentralization and commercial blight. In the 1950s, manufacturing employment grew in suburbs at the expense of the central city.[79] Due to residential segregation, African Americans, for the most part, did not have the luxury of following well-paid jobs to the suburbs.[80]

Chicago's diversified base in an emerging "corporate-center" economy made it better able than comparable cities to withstand the "suburbanization of manufacturing." This economy featured new central-city institutions that took the place of industrial firms, including corporate headquarters, banks, and advanced corporate service firms in management consulting, law, accounting, advertising, and other professional fields, along with centrally located private, nonprofit organizations such as universities and hospitals.[81] Nonetheless, the loss of industrial jobs and tax revenue put more pressure on its corporate firms and commercial enterprises to compensate.

Business elites focused on the problem of commercial blight, which was magnified in the context of industrial decentralization. The profits and investments of these new economic institutions were more concentrated in

downtown property and retail sales than in industrial products, raising particular concern among business elites about the advancing areas of decay
and blight. City officials and business elites characterized blight as a process
of physical deterioration that destroys property values and lowers the quality
of urban life.[82] For real estate firms, landlords, and other property owners,
physical deterioration of buildings and the environment reduced what they
could charge for rent or earn via sale; often downtown property owners got
less revenue from their buildings but were subject to the same tax rates that
had been set during the prosperous 1920s.[83] With advancing suburbanization, business leaders in Chicago and other cities feared the decreasing use of
the downtown area for employment and shopping, a trend that particularly
troubled department-store owners. Office-building vacancies increased,
threatening the profits of many real estate firms. During the period in which
there was very little construction, some property owners opted to demolish
buildings and build much-needed parking lots.

Downtown business elites sought a way to reverse the tide of capital
relocating to other parts of the metropolitan area. Since everything on their
wish list entailed millions of dollars in capital investment, elites recognized
early in the post–World War II era that attaining their goals would take a
public–private partnership of downtown property owners, corporations,
and government officials.[84] City officials depended on downtown revenue
to support increasing municipal services, and they concluded that the
solvency of municipal government depended on the health of downtown
businesses. Business and public officials saw physical reconstruction of the
city's infrastructure as the key to halting blight and reversing the decline of
the central city.[85]

Political entrepreneurs, by using public capital to build public–private
coalitions to renew their cities, reshaped urban politics in the postwar era.
They built progrowth coalitions with real estate developers and builders,
banks, construction trades, merchants, corporate officials, professional planners, public administrators, and white and black civic leaders. Business and
real estate interests were willing to join these coalitions because they realized that in order for slum clearance and urban redevelopment to work, they
needed public authority and government aid. The electorate often had to
approve bonds in order to secure municipal financing for rebuilding.[86]

In Chicago's case, the progrowth coalition got its start under Mayor Martin Kennelly (1947–55) and matured under the long reign of Mayor Richard

J. Daley (1955–76). The historian Arnold Hirsch makes a compelling case that before Mayor Daley's reign the initiative for urban redevelopment emanated from real estate, banking, and commercial elites and not from political entrepreneurs.[87] By the time Daley came into office in 1955, the political framework for rebuilding had been put into place by activist business leaders. But with the arrival of Daley, Chicago became an atypical example of a progrowth coalition joined to a political machine.

To the extent that black Chicagoans joined the city's progrowth coalition, they did so as junior partners. Compared to other, more powerful white business elites and machine politicians, they were less able to advance their interests. Their lack of power, however, was relative, not absolute. They played a crucial role in electing Richard Daley in 1955 and 1963, and they reaped some benefits from participating in the electoral and governing coalitions in the city. Blacks were important to Chicago's progrowth coalition in two ways: Their votes were needed to pass bond issues required by state legislation, and it was their deteriorated neighborhoods that were targeted by slum clearance and redevelopment of central-city property. Dawson and other black machine politicians were responsible for delivering the votes for bond issues and for ensuring that black displacement did not slow down or stop the city's redevelopment plans.

Progrowth elites in Chicago were concerned about the potential for black civic leaders to inflame black citizens with militant racial rhetoric. In order to avoid racial violence, the city's elites were prepared to make limited concessions to the black community. So, in addition to incorporating black machine politicians, black civic elites were also absorbed into the coalition, serving on government commissions, redevelopment agencies, and civic planning organizations that informed and managed the slum clearance and redevelopment process.

For the most part, black civic elites endorsed the slum clearance and redevelopment objectives of public–private partnerships' goals. They felt slums menaced the health, morals, and housing of black citizens, and they hoped that new public and redeveloped housing would serve the housing needs of working-class and middle-class citizens. They also hoped that redevelopment would present professional and economic opportunities to the black professionals working in the real estate and housing fields. Black civic leaders cooperated, competed, and conflicted with white business and political elites in the use of federal aid and authority, seeking to route benefits mainly to the black real estate industry and black recipients of new housing and in so doing increase their political influence in both the Black and Midwest Metropolis.

African American civic leaders felt their ideology of racial democracy would help them gain that influence. Racial democracy, bolstered by notions of social disorganization, ethnic pluralism, and modernization theory, legitimized their claim for leadership and a passive political role for poor and working-class blacks. Having absorbed the assumptions that underlay Chicago school urban ecology, black policy elites targeted racial segregation for reform while they accepted class-segmented housing markets. This position shaped black civic elites' efforts to confront racial discrimination and segregation in housing policy and markets. During the postwar battles over urban land and its use, the material stakes were high. Unlike black radicals, black civic leaders did not dissent from the progrowth agenda put into place by white business and political elites. Not surprisingly, they opposed that agenda only when it undercut their aim of opening new housing opportunities for upwardly mobile blacks in integrated settings while preserving middle-class housing and eradicating slum housing in Bronzeville.

2

Racial Democracy and the Case for Public Housing

Of all the housing policies, public housing most closely embodied social democratic principles since it advocated for adequate housing for citizens regardless of their ability to pay. The way in which public housing policy was formulated and implemented, however, severely limited its ability to meet the shelter needs of society's most vulnerable. The opposition of the real estate industry to public housing is legendary. Yet shared assumptions and strategic mistakes by housing reformers, white and black, were equally responsible for the failure of public housing. These missteps stemmed from the public housers' embrace of slum clearance and urban redevelopment, hoping it would lead to the replacement of slums with modern housing and clean neighborhoods. In order to understand just how black civic reformers contributed to these missteps, we need to examine the reasons for the support of public housing in the first place.

In this chapter, I contend that this support stemmed from black reformers' commitment to racial democracy as much as from any fidelity to social democracy. The fact that both racial and social democratic goals could be met with a sound public housing policy was *not* a problem in itself. On the contrary, both forms of democracy often work well (and work best) in tandem. Nonetheless, failing to make analytical distinctions between the two policy rationales in a context in which one goal is sacrificed for the other can lead to policy catastrophe. As the postwar period progressed, black policy elites increasingly viewed their commitment to public housing within a racial democratic framework that considered slum clearance and urban redevelopment as complementary housing policies rather than as conflicting or competing policy priorities, which would have reflected a more social democratic interpretation. Social democracy, featuring class equality as a major goal, was fundamentally opposed to the bias toward the upper class that characterized urban redevelopment schemes. In the social democratic view, any reconstruction of the urban core should have been intended predominantly to provide affordable housing for current residents, not to provide housing and amenities to attract new urban gentry.[1]

Because the majority of African Americans were low income and the added freight of race exacerbated working-class blacks' material conditions, a class critique joined a racial one in black elite formulations at the time. As long as most blacks were in the low-income group, and as long as the real estate industry refused to build for low-income citizens and *all* blacks, social democratic and racial democratic concerns would continue to cohere in black policy analysis. However, after World War II, neither of these conditions would hold. More blacks were gaining better occupations and incomes, contributing to unprecedented class differentiation, and while the housing industry remained a bulwark of residential segregation, by the mid-1950s, it began paying attention to the black housing market.

In this chapter, I demonstrate black policy elites' support for public housing in Chicago and in national policy circles—and the racial and social democratic rationales for that support. Specifically, I delineate black elites' class and racial critique of the housing industry. Based on their critique, I explore how their support for public housing was based on their desire for black citizens to have access to modern housing and to reinforce normative residential behavior, both of which they saw as necessary for acquiring the property-based citizenship that became widespread after World War II.

Black Housing Crisis

On the eve of World War II, black Chicago as well as other black communities nationwide experienced a severe housing shortage. According to the 1940 Census, 55,157 residential units in Chicago were overcrowded, and 206,103 units were substandard, either with no private bath or needing major repairs.[2] In 1939, blacks occupied nearly 71,000 units, of which almost 60 percent were overcrowded, deteriorating, or both.[3] In Chicago, there were a number of investigations into black housing conditions before World War II, including Alderman Earl B. Dickerson's Subcommittee on Negro Housing in 1939;[4] city council and state senate hearings on rental increases in the black community in the spring of 1937; and the Citizen's Committee on Housing, which Horace Cayton chaired. All these investigations focused on how overcrowding, density, segregation, and exorbitant rents led to housing deterioration and neighborhood decline in black communities.

Horace Cayton defined the housing crisis facing a restive black community as one that encompassed a lack of space and a need for more housing units. He maintained that in the Black Belt, 200,000 people lived in an area that should accommodate only 150,000. In 1940, the most densely populated section of the black community was between Forty-Seventh and Fifty-First Streets, considered the center of the Black Metropolis. This section of town, dominated by four- and five-story apartment buildings, had a population density of 70,000, twice as dense as a comparable white residential district. Robert Taylor likened the population density, closer to 90,000 per square mile by his estimation, to that of Calcutta. With not enough housing units to go around, many black families were "doubling-up," Cayton reported.[5]

The problem of overcrowding and density was caused by mass migration, housing shortage, residential segregation, and exploitative rents. Between 1940 and 1944, the *Chicago Defender* claimed that the population of the Second Ward, in the heart of the Black Belt, had increased by 33,000, the largest increase of any ward in the city. At this time, the *Defender* surveyed the South Side for housing vacancies and did not find any. Frayser Lane of the Chicago Urban League (CUL) commented that the black community needed 50,000 housing units in 1938, noting that in recent years the shortage had grown "by leaps and bounds." During World War II, black migration to Chicago increased by 75,000, and now Bronzeville needed 100,000 housing units to meet earlier and current deficits.[6]

Though all of Chicago, and the nation for that matter, lacked housing, residential segregation exacerbated that need in the black community. Horace Cayton testified during the Dickerson-led hearings that inadequate housing for African Americans went back as far as 1910. He blamed restrictive covenants, which barred blacks from renting or buying dwellings in many white neighborhoods, for limiting the areas where blacks could live. According to Earl Dickerson, these white neighborhoods included vacant land that offered "logical" sites for new housing developments. Thus, residential segregation through restrictive covenants was a chief cause of blacks' housing shortage.[7]

Black Chicagoans lack of housing also stemmed from the combination of increased demolition with scant housing construction. In 1940, Cayton commented that there had not been a single instance since the Great Depression in which private capital had built new housing for blacks. Exacerbating the problem caused by the lack of new construction was the clearing of old substandard housing. Cayton observed that during the Depression the encroachment of business had caused the demolition of buildings in the deteriorated area north of Thirty-ninth Street. Much of this area, he maintained, was held by real estate developers for speculative purposes. In 1937, he quoted a Chicago Housing Authority (CHA) study calculating that the Black Belt had lost 2,700 dwelling units through demolitions. This estimate was made before the clearing of substandard housing that had preceded the construction of the Ida B. Wells federal housing project in 1941. Land clearance without rebuilding caused black citizens to suspect that clearing the slums was not the only motive behind urban redevelopment schemes.[8]

Not only were many African Americans living in unsanitary and dangerous conditions, but they had to pay a premium for these places. The Negro Housing hearings exposed the high rents that blacks had to pay for inadequate dwellings. One expert reported that black South Siders paid $30 per room, while people in the richest neighborhood in the city, the Gold Coast, paid only $22 to $27 per room. Almost ten years later, Robert Weaver reported, in his national study, that urban landowners still took advantage of the fact that blacks had fewer housing options to charge rents 50 percent higher than what whites paid for better housing. Despite the slumlike conditions where blacks resided, property values were high because of the area's proximity to downtown and Lake Michigan. The high cost of housing had two effects: First, it made it difficult for people take care of their property, since most of their money was used for paying their rent. Second, people took in boarders to help with the costs, which, according to black civic leaders, sometimes created or exacerbated overcrowding, lack of privacy, and immorality.[9]

Not surprisingly, overcrowded conditions led to housing deterioration and neighborhood decline. Throughout the Negro Housing hearings, Dickerson publicized the extent of black housing troubles, regularly condemning the city for not upgrading the health and safety of slum tenements in black districts.[10] Black Alderman Benjamin A. Grant of the Third Ward blamed the kitchenettes or one-room apartments for causing the overcrowding in his ward, contributing to a garbage-disposal problem. David E. Mackelman of the Metropolitan Housing Council, a civic planning organization, and Frayser Lane concurred that poor neighborhoods, many of them in the black community, experienced haphazard garbage collection. Both condemned a recent ruling by the Chicago Health Department that categorized kitchenettes as "lodgings," not apartments, allowing converted buildings to avoid stricter health regulations.[11] The *Chicago Defender*, the city's major black newspaper, covered the Dickerson-led hearings and outlined the sinister causes that produced poor housing conditions for black Chicagoans. The newspaper explained that exorbitant rent and the scarcity of adequate housing contributed to overcrowding, which accelerated property deterioration and threatened community health.[12] By 1940, the perennial housing shortage had reached crisis proportion, with the combination of demolition and the lack of new housing construction causing unprecedented levels of overcrowding and congestion in Bronzeville.

Black Elite Support for Public Housing

In the late 1930s, black policy elites in Washington, D.C., New York, and Chicago embraced public housing as the best possible solution to this crisis. Middle-class black housing reformers advocated for public housing from its legislative origins in 1934, to its renewal in 1937 and 1949. Nationally, civil rights organizations such as the National Association for the Advancement of Colored People (NAACP), the National Urban League (NUL), and the National Association of Negro Women (NANW) lobbied hard for public housing legislation including the 1949 Housing Act, which authorized sizeable public housing.

Office of Racial Relations

The origins of the Office of Racial Relations within federal housing agencies are intertwined with the development of public housing policy in 1937. The impetus for the office came from Chicagoan Robert Taylor while he was embroiled in the fight for the Ida B. Wells housing project in the city.[13] The Public Works Administration (PWA) Housing Division had designated the location of the Wells Homes in 1934. The Illinois State Housing Board, the Chicago Plan Commission, a committee of black civic leaders, and consultants from the University of Chicago had selected the site between Thirty-Ninth and Thirty-Seventh Streets, with South Parkway Avenue to the west and Cottage Grove Avenue as the eastern boundary. However, neighboring white property owners to the east and south wanted the site moved farther west to the less desirable real estate bordering Rock Island Railroad tracks (at Federal Street), the western border of the black ghetto. Their opposition delayed construction. Adding insult to injury, the demolition of impaired tenements on the site for the Wells Homes exacerbated blacks' chronic housing shortage. Black citizens engaged in mass protest over the delays in construction, but the contested project did not open until seven years later. Black civic and national elites considered the construction of Ida B. Wells federal housing project a major political victory for Black Chicagoans, who until then had not substantively participated in the public housing program in Chicago.[14]

Robert Taylor and Robert Weaver developed the groundwork for the Wells victory. Taylor, a well-known housing expert in Chicago, worked for both the Division of Defense Housing Coordination and the Office of the Administrator of the National Housing Agency during World War II.[15] He had been a board member of the Chicago Housing Authority (CHA) since 1937; in 1943, he became the first African American to chair the housing authority board of a major city. Weaver, a Harvard-trained economist and New Deal bureaucrat, had been an adviser on "Negro Affairs" in the Interior Department but later became consultant to the PWA Housing Division. The Office of Racial Relations was established when the Housing Division's programs were transferred to the United States Housing Authority (USHA) under the Wagner-Steagall Housing Act of 1937.[16]

Weaver became special assistant to the administrator of the USHA, in charge of the office. He brought along Corienne Robinson, his secretarial assistant in the Interior Department, and later recruited Frank S. Horne of New York as his associate director.[17] This office consisted of black housing professionals who acted as racial relations advisers to federal housing agency directors. Their job was to monitor the impact of housing policy on African Americans and other racial minorities.[18] Weaver interpreted the office's purpose as protecting the federal housing agencies from charges of racial discrimination. He determined that the best way to avoid this charge was to integrate racial minorities in all federal housing programs. Whenever programs were inaugurated or modified, racial relations advisers alerted the agency if the program had a negative impact on blacks and other racial minorities. Since African Americans were taxpaying citizens, black housing officials argued, they should receive equal benefits from the housing programs. The race relations advisers shrewdly represented black housing interests by portraying this work as "protecting" the racial reputation of the federal agencies.[19]

The Office of Racial Relations had four responsibilities: (1) It gathered statistics on the impact of slum clearance and public housing construction in black areas, (2) it planned and proposed sites in these areas, (3) it negotiated the agreements on black employment targets with local contractors, and (4) it was responsible for persuading blacks to support the proposed housing developments.[20] Many of these responsibilities would persist as the configuration of federal housing agencies evolved over the years.

Perhaps the most successful, though short-lived, program was the public employment policy, which Weaver formulated when he was consultant to the PWA Housing Division. Since the purpose of the New Deal housing policy was to provide employment as well as housing, Weaver made sure African Americans got their share of the jobs that were created. Black housing officials calculated the portion of the local labor market that blacks represented in order to determine their fair share of employment in public housing construction.[21] That percentage became the target number of blacks to be hired in the planning, design, and construction phases of public housing projects. During the Depression, black lawyers, architects, engineers, and skilled workers particularly welcomed the PWA Housing Division's policy since local housing authorities provided them with hard-to-find employment. Moreover, blacks usually filled the management and clerical positions of a public housing project designated for black occupancy. To Weaver, these job opportunities, especially for technical and white-collar workers, represented evidence that public housing policy would live up to democratic norms.[22] Because of this policy, by 1940 black workers had been paid over $1 million, with 20 percent going to skilled workers. Weaver admitted, however, that this policy was more effective in cities like Chicago, where blacks were knowledgeable and politically active.[23]

The Office of Racial Relations, created by national black housing experts, was the focal point of a housing policy network constituted by black federal housing officials, national civil rights organizations, and black civic leaders in localities like Chicago.[24] Initially, one of the important tasks carried out by racial relations advisers was to build a constituency among various black strata for the siting, construction, occupation, and management of public housing. These tasks were perhaps more difficult than was first assumed. They had to overcome the skepticism of some local black elites toward their claims of political influence. One black newspaper editor, for example, commented bluntly that the race relations advisers did not make policy. Despite their claims to the contrary, the editor argued, blacks would only be integrated into housing programs if the white housing agency director were a liberal.

Racial relations advisers were very aware of their limited influence, and by extension their legitimacy among local black elites and their black middle-class public. Black housing officials had to contend with racist or indifferent white federal housing agency directors and coworkers who were, at best, more interested in building housing unobstructed by considerations of racial fairness. At worst, these white officials either wanted to exclude blacks entirely or used federal policy to enforce segregation in cities or neighborhoods that had experienced racially mixed residential living. The racial relations office defined its "primary and only purpose" as defending the principles that compel the integration of African Americans into the privileges and responsibilities of American society. If these principles were "sacrificed," it was argued, then the office would only become an "apologist," and its effectiveness would be lost.[25]

Another obstacle was that black civic leaders were excluded from the local advisory committees that planned public housing projects. Their exclusion meant that they were not in a position to persuade black property owners to sell their land or to challenge the perceived indifference of low-income blacks. These difficulties resulted in few applications for occupancy and, in general, risked a lukewarm response to public housing in the black community. Without the participation of black civic leaders, black federal housing officials claimed, no one would educate low-income black families about their eligibility for public housing. They argued that poor black families did not realize that public housing was available to them since they were "conditioned" not to expect to receive any new housing.[26]

While it is true that public housing was a new benefit and that the first projects were often restricted to whites, this explanation stretches credulity after accounting for a black citizenry that was experienced at petitioning for New Deal state benefits. Black federal housing officials' interpretation reflects their expectation that policy implementation was dependent on local black elites playing a pivotal role in the acceptance of public housing policy among black citizens in cities across the country. They credited much of the success of the public housing program in black communities to black civic leaders' efforts. The officials argued that black civic leaders had been alert to the possibilities of the public housing program from the beginning; that, in fact, public housing had been initiated in response to their prodding in the first place. Since the early 1930s, black civic leaders had grown increasingly vigilant and vocal and rarely hesitated to make their interests known, according to racial relations advisers. The relationship between black racial relations advisers and local black civic leaders served as an important component of an emerging black housing policy network.

Throughout the postwar period, the approach of the Office of Racial Relations to other federal housing policies was governed by the same principles that informed their approach to public housing policy. The office maintained that all racial groups should have equal access to public housing in nonsegregated areas. Likewise, the public housing program should not reinforce residential segregation or displace blacks from desirable neighborhoods. The racial relations advisers determined that racial minorities, in particular, needed protection during the demolition and construction phases of the program. They evaluated the program by determining whether it would provide or deny housing to racial minorities. Beyond housing, they expected that black professionals and skilled workers would plan, construct, and manage new public housing developments designated for black occupancy. In general, racial relations advisers' role was to interpret federal housing programs to minorities while they communicated the perspectives and needs of racial minorities to these agencies.[27] In other words, the stance of the Office of Race Relations toward public housing policy was informed by racial democratic principles of racial parity and equal access for African American citizens. Civil rights organizations and local black civic leaders shared the same policy framework as their federal government counterparts.

Class Critique and the Material Benefits of Public Housing

Black policy elites' support for public housing encompassed both racial and class critiques of the white real estate industry. Robert Taylor explained that blacks' inadequate housing was caused by racial discrimination *and* low wages. Since most blacks were working class, Taylor reasoned, their lack of income meant they had fewer options in the private housing market. In this market, the lower a person's income, the worse the available housing; thus impoverished workers lived in inadequate and deteriorating tenements in the older parts of the city around the downtown areas. The only housing that wage-earning blacks could afford to rent was dilapidated and lacked modern facilities such as indoor toilets or central heating. The added burden of their racial identity meant that they were not welcomed in neighborhoods that had better conditions at affordable rents. Since African Americans were disproportionately low income and restricted to these older communities, they were trapped in a private market of slum tenements. The Dickerson-led Subcommittee on Negro Housing report commented that representatives of the private housing industry admitted that they did not gain profits building for low-income groups. Taylor was more emphatic, stating that private capital would never accommodate poor families.[28]

African American policy elites' answer to private capital's failure was government housing. They favored low-rent public housing as the solution to wage-earning blacks' housing woes. Taylor told the Dickerson subcommittee that government subsidy offered the only solution to the problem of adequately housing low-income people. Taylor argued that African Americans suffered from substandard housing more than any other group in Chicago. Therefore, they stood to gain the most from a government program that provided adequate housing to those relegated to the bottom of the private housing market. Taylor recognized that public provision to subsidize construction of adequate and affordable housing would "ultimately revolutionize" urban blacks' standard of living. Moreover, he claimed, "a soundly conceived and ably administered public housing program," more than any other social endeavor, promised immediate benefits to African Americans. Therefore, Taylor advocated that "the best leadership in the race" should embrace a public housing program.[29]

Robert Weaver, concurring with Taylor, outlined what those benefits would be for all low-income citizens, including blacks. In addition to larger living quarters and modern conveniences, public housing developments offered on-site health and welfare services at subsidized costs. Moreover, low-cost public housing would save blacks from paying exploitative rents for inadequate shelter. Weaver determined that prewar public housing offered Bronzeville residents the possibility of escaping slum living, gaining their first opportunity to live in decent, modern, and affordable housing.[30] Nor, in subsequent years, did Weaver's commitment to public housing wane. In the early 1950s, he found that, despite postwar economic gains, the majority of blacks were still unserved by private enterprise, which emphasized to Weaver the continued need for a federally subsidized low-rent housing program.[31]

According to Weaver and Taylor, two of the more influential black housing policy analysts, as long as blacks did not have the income for private housing, access to public housing was necessary and beneficial and should continue to be a part of a black housing agenda. Yet as the postwar period progressed, public housing occupied a less and less prominent place on that agenda. As the political environment became more conservative, black policy elites responded by promoting private housing through either redevelopment or building for the black middle-class market. They convinced themselves that rather than make direct, and potentially costly, appeals to social democracy, they were better off promoting the more palatable racial democracy. Racial parity achieved in this way would accommodate the housing needs of at least some working-class blacks.

Racial Democracy and the Moral Benefits of Public Housing

Social democratic ideology was not alone in recognizing most blacks' inability to afford adequate housing; racial democracy had similar concerns. Rather than seeing black poverty as mostly an individual or even a class problem, however, racial democracy identified the problem as one of the racial group. A material upgrade in housing for the lower echelon would, in their eyes, increase racial-group parity. And its benefits would not end there. Public housing was equally attractive to black policy and civic elites for its purported moral benefits. They recognized that public housing also gave their professional cohort the opportunity to shape black tenants' behavior and groom them for responsible citizenship. These elites' ambivalence about wage-earning blacks'—especially recent migrants'—readiness for modern residential living influenced this leadership class to use public housing as a site to modernize working-class blacks' residential habits and prepare them for first-class citizenship.

Slum Housing and Social Disorganization

As housing reformers who believed slums produced social disorganization, black elites were invested in the idea that good housing could bring order into the lives of poor black workers, especially new migrants. Many black civic elites had come of age during the Progressive Era and had imbibed the idea that social and physical environments shaped personal behavior. In their professional and political work, they deployed the Chicago school of sociology's ideas about social disorganization.[32] They believed that social disorganization resulted from the maladjustment that many new migrants experienced in their new urban environment. The fact that this new urban environment featured overcrowded housing without central heat and indoor plumbing exacerbated migrants' already difficult adjustment to a competitive, often hostile city. Horace Cayton typified the thinking of his colleagues when he explained that the "influence of environment" on communal conditions could be measured by "the amount of social disorganization which slums produce." While admitting that he could not prove that poor housing

causes juvenile delinquency, he pointed out that this and other social problems increase in overcrowded neighborhoods.[33] These housing reformers
banked on the idea that public housing, with increased light, sanitation, and
privacy, would contribute to solving social problems such as juvenile delinquency, illegitimacy, and desertion, which they attributed to the "disordered"
lives of working-class blacks.

Robert Taylor explained the role poor housing played in creating slums.
Taylor, like his colleagues, indicted absentee landlords for creating slum
conditions by not maintaining their rental properties and charging African Americans exploitative rents in segregated areas. The fact that trapped
black families spent so much of their income on rent meant less money was
available for other necessities such as food, clothing, or medicine, contributing to poor health and social conditions. These buildings would deteriorate
over time through a combination of overcrowding and lack of maintenance,
undermining the physical capacity of the rental housing. Complicit with
slumlords were the municipal departments with the authority to regulate
building and sanitation conditions. Their indifference to these conditions,
often due to corruption, racism, or both, allowed slumlords to operate with
impunity.[34]

Poverty and overcrowding produced stress on family and communal
relationships, causing individuals to engage in antisocial behavior such as
crime and delinquency. Taylor, like Cayton, located a disproportionate
amount of crime, delinquency, and disorder in overcrowded and blighted
neighborhoods in the urban center. Taylor adopted the Chicago school's
idea of spatial determinism in showing how social and health problems
were associated with physical geography. He also adopted the discourse of
social disorganization by criticizing slums for being "a menace to an organized community" and for causing "social instability." He noted, in addition,
numerous incidences of tuberculosis and other infectious diseases, not to
mention high infant mortality rates, in working-class black neighborhoods.[35]
Slum housing, he believed, threatened the moral and physical health of its
occupants.

Earl Dickerson and Horace Cayton narrowed the blame, indicting "kitchenettes" as the site of social disorganization. In addition to disease and
crime, they explained how immoral behavior was formed under the "vicious
conditions" of kitchenettes. The Dickerson report claimed that kitchenettes
victimized their inhabitants, making it impossible for the racial group to
improve its standard of living, to create a healthy community, or to produce

responsible citizens.[36] The report explained just how overcrowding, particularly in one-room kitchenettes, led to moral lapses. The lack of privacy creates a "forced intimacy" that denies "normal home-life" and creates an inevitable demoralization.[37] To dramatize the threat that kitchenettes posed to moral living, Cayton, in his important article "Negro Housing in Chicago," quoted a passage from Richard Wright's 1940 novel *Native Son*. The passage described how the close quarters in their family's one-room kitchenette forced Bigger Thomas and his brother to avert their eyes so that his mother and sister could dress and not feel ashamed.[38]

Middle-class black housing reformers feared that the overcrowded kitchenettes with their lack of privacy promoted inappropriate sexual behavior that led to illegitimacy and "broken families." Juvenile delinquency, gangs, and illegitimacy were blamed on "an unsatisfactory home environment." The Dickerson report expressed vividly how "crowded, stuffy, smelly, rat-infested" housing conditions stripped home environments of their ability to protect their inhabitants, especially children, against the debilitating conditions of the street. The report found it counterproductive to eliminate vice on the South Side, unless slum housing conditions that promoted vice were "remedied."[39] The report identified slum housing as the underlying cause of crime and social disorder.

According to African American policy elites, social disorder was not the only negative consequence of slum housing. Blighted housing created barriers to conventional socialization, which could in turn lead to political instability. A 1944 National Urban League (NUL) report warned that "slum residence breeds slum psychology." A black man could become "an unstable citizen" if he and his family were forced to live in an "unsafe and unsanitary" home. His behavior becomes "anti-social" because he is "frustrated and dogged" by the squalid conditions. The report implied that during the "oppressive summer months" these tensions could lead to violence.[40] The League shifted the focus from the inadequate home environment to the father's psychological makeup, his motives and influences, in order to understand why he would engage in such behavior.

Slum conditions affected not only the father's psychology but also the personal development of his children. Dickerson's report discussed how children growing up under blighted conditions faced a "stunted manhood and womanhood."[41] The lack of protection from slum housing prevented children from becoming fully formed adults, unable or unwilling to take on civic duties or to exercise their rights in a constructive manner. According to black civic leaders, slum conditions produced frustrated men, victimized women, and stunted children who were a threat not only to the segregated black community but to the nation as a whole. This was not an enviable position for a nation fighting a war or preparing for an uncertain postwar future, many black commentators noted. While black civic elites' warnings were meant for municipal and national officials, their words betrayed their own anxieties about the ability of working-class and migrant blacks to function in a democratic polity unless guided by forward-thinking elites.

Black civic leaders felt too vulnerable to voice directly their anxieties regarding low-income blacks' ability to maintain modern living standards. Given the racial climate, they could not be sure that such a criticism of any segment of African Americans would not be extended to all blacks. With this consideration in mind, they confronted the question posed by conservative opponents of public housing: Do bad tenants create poor housing conditions, or does deteriorated housing produce bad tenants? This cohort of black policy elites invariably chose the latter explanation. The National Urban League's housing officials argued that slum dwellers were the *victims*, not *creators*, of slum environments. Horace Cayton asked, "And why should we expect people who live under these conditions to be paragons of virtue?" Cayton acknowledged that slum dwellers could do a great deal for themselves, but without improvement in their social conditions, the public should not expect improvement in "their health, behavior and manners." The Dickerson report concluded, "regardless of race . . . vicious conditions produce vicious men."[42]

Underlying the causal question was an implied connection, feared by all black elites, between the inability of slum dwellers to live decently and racial inferiority. Weaver pointed out that the same logic underlay the argument that housing improvement would not change the slum dweller's habits because of their inability to do any better and that "Negroes are poor, ignorant, and underprivileged because they are naturally inferior."[43] These black analysts took the environmental position, in part because they felt *all* blacks' character was at stake in the conservative arguments that "bad tenants" created slum housing. They countered accusations of racial inferiority with evidence of spatial determinism, proving that slum housing and associated social problems had existed in the same districts that ethnic whites had previously occupied. Ultimately concerned that whites would generalize to all blacks the class behavior of low-income African Americans, black elites advanced the environmental position not so much to defend poor blacks' character as to particularize it and to portray it as amenable to positive reform.

Reginald Johnson, the NUL's chief housing official, following E. Franklin Frazier's line of argument in his pioneering study *The Negro Family in Chicago*, stated that racial characteristics alone could not account for slum conditions because not *all* blacks were poor and ignorant. He argued that the conditions of the slum were an "economic" not a racial question because increasing numbers of blacks living in or near the same slum neighborhoods had "homes [that] show all the care and beauty which reflect their economic and cultural level."[44] Johnson reasoned that if *some* blacks had the income and taste to create good homes, then it could not be their *race* alone that produces slums. Conversely, it must be a black resident's lack of income and training that caused slum living; without adequate income, he or she could not afford standard housing, and without middle-class culture, he or she might not know how to properly care for that home. Perhaps inadvertently, by identifying that some of these upscale homes were near slum neighborhoods, Johnson undermined the idea that slum conditions *alone* produced bad residential behavior. He shifted the focus from neighborhood and housing conditions to the income and culture of individual households. While Johnson's use of class distinctions among blacks invalidates the racial inferiority argument, it replaces the latter with an argument about working-class inferiority—identifying middle income and class culture as preconditions for good housing conditions.

Public Housing and Social Disorganization

If substandard housing creates antisocial behavior, then arguably good housing produces appropriate social behavior and molds better citizens. This fundamental belief was shared by black and white housing reformers. Black civic elites pursued public housing not only because of the immediate shelter needs of the black population but also because it offered a vehicle for reorganizing black working-class families. Adequate and affordable housing provided by the government, they believed, would give blacks the opportunity to show they could live decently in good housing. Robert Weaver's analysis made an explicit connection between environments, public housing, and strong citizenship. The theory behind public housing, he argued, was the idea that environments shape individuals. A good environment will produce a more developed person and a better citizen. Weaver knew that highlighting "environmental factors" and not innate abilities would "open new doors of opportunity and hope to colored Americans." It paved the way for housing programs not only to benefit numerous black families but also to represent an instrument of opportunity and hope.[45] Weaver articulated the environmental assumptions underlying public housing as he hammered home the connection between improved homes and productive citizenship.

Black housers' belief in environmental causality made them find large-scale public housing developments especially attractive. Large-scale developments were popular within the public housing movement in the 1930s and early 1940s because proponents felt that they protected their occupants from the surrounding slum conditions better than did smaller developments. In other words, large-scale projects kept the "worthy poor" away from less desirable slum dwellers. Ironically, the isolation of public housing projects, by the 1990s an object of much criticism, was initially seen as a virtue. Planners felt they were creating communities, not just constructing buildings. In addition to its social benefits, housing reformers argued that a large-scale project would reduce construction costs via economies of scale. Moreover, large projects were designed to buffer the residential community from dangerous traffic by eliminating through streets, using the land between the buildings instead for recreational space. High-rises were preferred because inner-city land was costly, and they maximized the open space for trees, shrubbery, and recreational activities. Robert Taylor, who studied European housing, was in favor of large-scale housing, as was Robert Weaver.[46] Their enthusiasm is understandable considering that larger projects meant more units available to an ill-housed population and increased the likelihood that the new project would approximate a separate and enclosed neighborhood. After all, Dickerson's Subcommittee on Negro Housing had recommended building ten public housing projects, all larger than the Ida B. Wells project in Chicago.[47]

Robert Taylor argued that public housing should be an important tool for creating better citizens, comparable to public education. The Dickerson report claimed that public housing projects had "already raised several thousand Chicago families from virtual outcasts to functioning citizens." Embracing the environmental assumptions underlying the public housing agenda, the report stated that the physical and social conditions of the habitat shaped "the individual's life-pattern, his outlook, his aspirations, his general ability to adjust and compete in a complex world."[48] Dickerson and his colleagues drew an explicit connection between the physical and social makeup of the housing and social adjustment in a competitive urban industrial society. Yet while black housing reformers extolled the impact of modern housing facilities on the moral and physical health of ordinary blacks, they did not think improved housing conditions alone would reverse the residual effects of "slum psychology" that had been bred in unsuspecting black workers.

Black policy elites argued that black housing managers would play a critical role in stamping out any residual slum psychology. This social purpose easily dovetailed with their ongoing concerns about finding employment opportunities for professional and upwardly mobile blacks. Black civic leaders expected that these scarce white-collar management positions in black-occupied public housing would go to their cohort. Management and clerical positions at public housing projects such as Ida B. Wells and Altgeld Gardens were considered plum jobs for a black middle class with few professional and white-collar opportunities. Competition for these jobs in Chicago and other large cites was intense, and candidates depended on recommendations from such black notables as Claude A. Barnett, the owner of Associated Negro Press and board director of Supreme Liberty Life Insurance Company in Chicago.[49] The Office of Racial Relations advisers in Washington, D.C., and national civil rights organizations monitored the placement of black professionals in public housing management positions throughout the country.[50] Beyond seizing a rare professional employment opportunity, public housing managers were tasked with the responsibility of making black tenancy in public housing successful.

Getting the right person for the job was considered critical by black housing reformers. In all their arguments for public housing, they stressed the importance of effective management. Taylor felt large-scale public housing would be successful if, among other things, it was "managed by a skilled and enlightened staff." Housing management was something Taylor knew very well since he served as manager of the Michigan Boulevard Garden Apartments until his death in 1957. Popularly known as "The Rosenwald," the private apartment building was named after its benefactor, Julius Rosenwald, co-owner of Sears, Roebuck & Co. and a philanthropist who supported black causes. The Rosenwald had housed the black upper and middle classes since its creation in 1929. By "enlightened," Taylor meant that while a black manager did not believe in racial inferiority, he or she did suspect low-income black tenants of being socially disorganized. He implied that black managers could criticize and reshape black tenant behavior without being considered racist. Taylor assumed that black tenants would be more likely to accept social instruction from a black manager than a white one. A pamphlet from the period instructed public housing managers on how to get tenants to commit to the maintenance of the building. The pamphlet warned the housing manager that tenants would exhibit "indifference and lack of training." These "handicapping factors" were "correctable," however, by "skillful Management" through the "sharing of maintenance responsibilities." These "corrective procedures" fostered pride in one's home and surroundings.[51] The charge of "lack of training" referred to Reginald Johnson's idea that residents need to have attained the right "cultural level" in order to appreciate the importance of maintaining property and optimal neighborhood conditions.

Management was vital because blacks' participation in public housing was an experiment in the eyes of the public at large. Weaver felt public housing could provide the setting to prove that stable, low-income blacks would consistently pay their rent and maintain their homes when government planned housing to meet their needs.[52] William Hill, a regional racial relations adviser based in Chicago, concurred. He argued that public housing was many African Americans' "first experience" living in modern housing or creating new communities with other black families. The public housing experience fostered not only responsible rent paying but also "greater consideration of their neighbors, and newer levels of community cooperation and participation."[53] The views of Robert Taylor, Robert Weaver, Horace Cayton, Earl Dickerson, and other black elites were shared by a black middle-class public that hoped that the experience of living in public housing with a black professional staff would induce habits that would eventually make poor black workers desirable tenants and neighbors in black neighborhoods. Despite these assurances, however, black middle-class stewardship did not necessarily assuage the anxieties of the black bourgeoisie when it came to siting public housing near their affluent homes. Public housing was acceptable as long as it performed its instructional duties some distance from affluent black neighborhoods.

Conclusion

Black policy elite support for public housing stemmed from many sources. In a period of severe housing shortage, only government promised at least a limited supply of modern units. In the late 1930s, public housing policy became an arena where black policy elites could legitimate their claims for racial leadership by delivering an important benefit to wage-earning and poor blacks who needed adequate and affordable housing. For a set of elites who sought modernization for their racial group, access to modern housing would be key. For those consigned to the bottom of the black class structure, it represented not only an increased standard of living but also potential upward mobility that would modify the pyramidal shape of that structure. Although upper- and middle-income blacks were expected to test the segregative barriers in labor and housing markets, this stratum alone could not lessen the racial gaps between its group and whites. Working-class blacks had a role to play in this postwar drama, even if they were neither the director nor the leading actors. Public housing would rescue them from slum housing and provide them with an environment conducive to learning conventional behavioral habits in order to spur their racial progress as hardworking and high-achieving citizens successfully competing in Chicago's industrial political economy.

As long as the majority of blacks fit within the low-income category, public housing would satisfy both social democratic and racial democratic tendencies within black civic ideology. While public housing met a social democratic standard of providing adequate housing to those who could least afford it, its main attraction to black elites stemmed from its ability to fulfill racial democratic goals. Racial parity in black participation in public housing construction, management, and tenancy provided one version of racial democratization. Race-conscious policymaking fit easily with later professions of color-blind principles of nonracial access to public housing in black elite policy formulations. Black policy elites advocated both positions, keeping in mind the end goal of getting black people more and better housing. Yet racial democratic goals were also fulfilled by ridding black Americans of the scourge of slum living. Slum housing and neighborhood conditions propagated antisocial behavior and a slum psychology, subverting the work ethic and racial pride necessary for individual achievement that served as a precondition for black elites' claims to democratic access to U.S. goods and services such as decent housing. Public housing could play an important role in creating those preconditions.

In their attempt to shape public housing policy, black policy elites met two significant obstacles. They had to overcome their own ambivalence toward the wage-earning blacks whom they sought to control in managed housing developments. This ambivalence was dramatized and exacerbated throughout the wartime and postwar period by the opposition of the black bourgeoisie to the siting of public housing near their affluent homes. Yet more powerful opponents—the white real estate industry, white homeowners, and white politicians—would also emerge to successfully block blacks' access to optimal sites for public housing and equal access to public housing units. If public housing was to fulfill its political goals, black civic elites had to overcome these obstacles.

3

Black Factions Contesting Public Housing

In the process of advocating for public housing, African American policy elites had to battle both white and black opponents. The white opponents—the real estate industry, local politicians, and anxious homeowners—were well known, powerful, and responsible for racializing public housing by largely restricting it to blacks in the ghetto. Not as easily identifiable, on the other hand, were black opponents, including the black upper and middle classes, who felt their hard-earned affluence threatened by the proximity of public housing. Although black civic leaders used both class and racial criteria to criticize affluent blacks' opposition, they stayed within the logic of racial democracy by cajoling or shaming affluent blacks into perform-ing their racial duty by supporting decent housing for working-class blacks. Their reluctance to convey an internal class critique resulted from a number of factors, not least their membership in the same class as the opponents of public housing. They shared the same assumptions about poor blacks, especially newcomers to the city, even though they saw public housing as a laboratory to reshape a black proletariat into citizens ready to help integrate American society. While these leaders did not agree that public housing threatened property values, they *were* invested in showcasing upscale black homes to counteract, in part, the racist assumption that blacks were unable to take care of their properties and adhere to middle-class decorum.

In the end, black civic elites rejected an explicit class critique of black public housing opponents, but by trying to marshal a racial democratic critique, they muddied the issue by absolving the black bourgeoisie of politi-cal responsibility and, ultimately, weakened their resolve against a more powerful white opponent.[1] By freighting public housing with the task of socialization, black civic leaders ensured that once public housing no longer functioned as a laboratory for producing better citizens, support from the black middle class would melt away. While public housing represented black policy elites' most substantial commitment to social democracy, it would be these internal contests and the policy elites' own ambivalence that would test that commitment during the postwar era. By relying on racial democratic rationales for public housing, black civic elites could not make the necessary case for it to a black public, thus weakening the public mandate for decent housing for all American citizens. In this chapter, I explore how black national and civic elites utilized racial and social democratic rationales when facing opposition to public housing outside and inside Bronzeville.

Black Civic Leaders and War Housing

During World War II, there was a shift in black civic elites' arguments for more and better housing for blacks in Chicago. Before the war, these leaders had emphasized both the low incomes and racial identities of wage-earning blacks as the reasons they had not received, but should receive, adequate housing. In a sense, they made their claim for improved housing on a charge of class exploitation and racial discrimination practiced by a predatory market and a complicit government. During the war, these elites could point not simply to their victimization but also to the sacrifice that African Americans were making for the war effort as an argument for their fair treatment. Before the war, black civic elites had lobbied all levels of government, typified by Earl Dickerson's Subcommittee on Negro Housing targeting state and local officials. Once the war began, they dealt with the federal government exclusively. Since these civic leaders were predisposed to seek racial democratic change through corrective government action, it made sense for them to make their claims to federal housing bureaucrats in the last days of the New Deal. At the time, many civic planning committees highlighted the current poor housing conditions of blacks and predicted their further decline after the war. The committee that perhaps best carried on the work of the Dickerson subcommittee during the war was the collection of black civic leaders who constituted the United Committee on Emergency Housing (UCEH).

Black Wartime Housing Crisis

Black Chicagoans, like their fellow citizens, were affected by the general causes of the housing shortage that the city experienced during and immediately after the war. There were four reasons for Chicago's housing shortage: (1) High marriage rates soon after the war expanded the number of families needing housing; (2) since 1940 many families that had been "doubled up" with other families sought their own housing; (3) building materials needed for enough home construction to meet consumer demand had been diverted to meet war production requirements; and (4) returning veterans needed to be housed. In addition to what white citizens had to contend with, black Chicagoans suffered more due to massive in-migration from the South and residential segregation that yielded severe overcrowding.

Blacks did gain more government housing during the war, but the amount provided paled in comparison to their needs. They gained access to three of the city's four newly constructed government projects. The federal government converted public housing, which was designated as "low-rent" under the terms of the 1937 Housing Act, to war housing.[2] Blacks gained access to the Frances Cabrini Homes on the Near North Side and Lawndale Gardens and Richard H. Brooks Houses on the West Side. The largest wartime housing project was Altgeld Gardens, with 1,500 units occupied by 7,000 tenants, all African American. Altgeld Gardens consisted of two-story buildings located in the low-density Far South Side–Lake Calumet industrial area. Constructed on an isolated site, it included many community facilities such as a shopping center, church, schools, public library, and a Board of Health station.[3]

Despite these gains, the shift from low-rent to war housing proved detrimental to blacks' housing needs. Not only were blacks more reliant on subsidized housing than whites because of their disproportionate poverty and difficulty securing adequate market-rate housing, but also their eligibility for defense housing was tied to initially inaccessible war production jobs.[4] Sometimes discrimination in one area would hurt blacks in another. For instance, war housing had to be located near war production facilities. Normally, defense employers recruited their workers from nearby communities, which typically were all white. If blacks were restricted from the residential areas near the plants, they would not be recruited for employment. Conversely, defense industries claimed that they could not hire blacks because there was no housing available for them in white-only defense areas.[5] The result of this double jeopardy was that blacks continued to suffer disproportionately from inadequate housing in Chicago and other large cities during wartime even when they could find employment.

During the war, as before it, black civic leaders claimed that the chief opposition to more public housing in the city came from large real estate firms. These leaders accused real estate interests of spreading racist propaganda to undermine the overall effort to gain good housing projects. They surmised that the real estate industry's opposition stemmed from the threat posed by public housing to the profits they gained from dividing large homes and apartments into one-room kitchenettes.[6] By 1940, real estate industry opposition had been successful in stopping the public housing production that had been authorized under the 1937 Housing Act. Black civic leaders were dismayed when they heard, in late 1943, that the National Housing Agency (NHA) planned to provide Chicago with 3,000 private housing units, of which a scant 258 units were intended for black residents, and that there would be no new public housing.[7]

The United Committee for Emergency Housing

Black civic leaders, organizing themselves into the United Committee for Emergency Housing (UCEH), protested the NHA's inadequate provision of housing. They communicated their displeasure in a series of meetings with William K. Divers and John Blandford, respectively the agency's regional and national directors.[8] A number of prominent black leaders participated in the initial meeting, including Harry J. Walker, executive secretary of the local NAACP; Frayser T. Lane and Earl Dickerson of the Chicago Urban League; Robert C. Travis of the CIO Cook County Council, and Horace R. Cayton of South Parkway Community Center. Walker and Cayton led this group and penned a blistering memorandum to Blandford and Divers outlining the committee's grievances. The memorandum was an extensive catalogue of complaints that reflected black civic elites' criticism of war housing policy. While the UCEH commented on the NHA's woeful performance in accommodating wartime black housing needs, the main purpose of the memorandum was to evaluate the NHA's plans to address those extensive needs. After noting that most of the planned housing had not even been constructed by January 1944, the UCEH memorandum concluded provocatively that "in a city where there is probably the greatest housing problem for Negroes in the country, this is not an impressive record of achievement."[9]

The UCEH memorandum stressed the fact that although migrant black workers were meeting the needs of the nation's defense program, their government continued to ignore their housing needs. The black civic committee argued that the NHA's failure was not accidental, but rather indicated "their deference to the principle of residential segregation." In line with the war's democratic rhetoric, the committee argued that the government should not discriminate against its own citizens, especially during war.[10] These black civic leaders asserted that residential segregation and housing discrimination diminished the government's capacity to fight and win the war. The committee referred to two decisions that reflected the NHA's discriminatory policy. The decision to locate the war housing center outside the black community made it inaccessible to black workers. When blacks did utilize the war housing center, they were not referred to available housing in or near white neighborhoods. The second was the decision by the NHA to accept the Home Owners Loan Corporation (HOLC) policy not to convert property for black occupancy if it was covered by restrictive covenants. This decision was critical since the number of private units available for conversion in the black community was inadequate. In general, the committee members found it inconsistent for the government to combat employment discrimination through the president's Fair Employment Practices Committee (FEPC) while enforcing residential segregation.[11]

The UCEH also contested what appeared to be race-neutral rules that put black workers at a disadvantage. Employees of the primary sectors (steel, rubber, and automobiles) in which whites were concentrated were given preference for defense housing over those employees in the secondary sector (services, communication, and transportation), which included most blacks. They found the categorization of "primary" and "secondary" sectors of defense work "at best artificial and unreal." The committee also argued that the distinction between migrant and nonmigrant black workers was arbitrary. Due to the overall shortage of housing units, they recommended that other black war workers, not just migrants, be eligible for government housing. They argued that the government should abolish the migrant-based eligibility for housing since Chicago represented "a special case" due to racial tensions and potential for violence.[12] The UCEH bluntly concluded that the government's racial policy "produced the special problem which now demands special treatment."[13]

The force with which black civic leaders criticized the federal government reflected their low expectations of private industry providing any housing to black workers. They pointed out that Princeton Park, with 926 units, offered the only example of privately financed housing for black occupancy constructed in the city during the war.[14] The committee had little hope that "conversions" would contribute units, since few unoccupied structures were available to blacks. They therefore wanted the federal government to finance new construction of permanent housing, especially for migrant war workers. They expressed fear that if the government followed its stated policy of only building temporary structures, this housing would eventually become slums.[15] The black civic committee argued that without permanent housing, "it would set back the struggle of the Negro to create a decent well-organized communal life to a large extent."[16] Permanent housing was needed because, contrary to federal policymakers' wishful thinking, black migrants would not be returning to the South after the war.

During World War II, when democratic rhetoric set the stage for highlighting racial disparities, it was not surprising that black civic elites would focus on the discriminatory impact of NHA's war housing policies. In 1944, UCEH's memorandum, both in analysis and in prescriptions, followed the work initiated by the Dickerson report and Horace Cayton's important articles on black housing made on the eve of the global war. Cayton's coauthorship of the memorandum ensured some continuity between the earlier and later analyses. Both political efforts spoke on behalf of wage-earning blacks' housing needs, with the UCEH focusing on the especially deserving black war production workers. Both sets of documents, before and toward the end of the war, stressed the negative moral and health impact of substandard housing on black workers.

The UCEH, in the face of discriminatory government policy, emphasized the racial causes of the overcrowding that the earlier documents had pinpointed. In addition to blaming racially restrictive covenants, which represented judicial sanction of private discrimination, the UCEH criticized bureaucracy-sanctioned discrimination against black war workers. While the reports and articles of 1940 requested more public and private housing, the UCEH memorandum sought government-provided permanent housing for black war workers, both new migrants and prewar settlers. The CHA heeded these black civic elites' call, however, by planning to build permanent homes for black war workers on the city's Far South Side. The only problem for these elites was the potential site. The CHA proposed to locate the housing project near the most affluent black enclave, not only in Chicago, but also in the country at the time.

West Chesterfield

In December 1943, the NHA commissioned the Federal Public Housing Authority (FPHA) and the CHA to build additional housing for black war workers. This authorization coincided with black civic elites' initial meeting with NHA regional administrator Divers. In response, the CHA proposed in February 1944 to build 250 single-family housing units for low-income defense workers employed in the South Chicago area. The project was originally slated as temporary housing, but the CHA commissioners, anticipating postwar housing needs and incorporating black civic leaders' concerns, convinced the NHA to authorize the building of permanent housing that would be sold to people after the war (which did occur in 1949).[17] Notwithstanding the obvious need for these homes, their proposed location was met with opposition from a group of affluent black homeowners who felt that their enclave of exclusive residences was threatened.[18] This rare public conflict challenged the assumption of homogeneous black housing interests. It further exposed the tension between the social and racial democratic commitments of black civic elites employed to analyze and advocate for wartime housing policy.

The Project

West Chesterfield was a neighborhood stretching from State Street to South Parkway and from Ninetieth to Ninety-Fifth Streets on the city's Far South Side. This area was adjacent to Lilydale, which by 1944 had been a working-class black enclave for thirty-three years.[19] West Chesterfield was founded when a group of affluent black professionals built homes (some valued at as much as $50,000) next to Lilydale, with the intention of remaining separate from that community. They took the name of a white community east of Cottage Grove, Chesterfield, calling their neighborhood West Chesterfield.

The war housing project was proposed for the area bounded by Ninety-First and Ninety-Third Streets, between Indiana (Burnside) and State Streets.[20] It was to cost $1.5 million and would be constructed with federal funds authorized by the Lanham Act. The net construction costs of each dwelling were estimated to be $4,000, but that included neither the cost of land, landscaping, sidewalks, grading, or curbs nor the installation of refrigerators, gas stoves, and so forth.[21] The dwellings would comprise 125 duplexes, each with 5 or 6 rooms and 2 bedrooms, and would create living space for 250 families. The public housing was unique in that the CHA had not previously developed single-family homes to be turned over to the private market.[22]

The CHA assured opponents of the project that these would be high-quality dwellings that would blend in architecturally with the surrounding neighborhood. In addition, recreational facilities for various age groups would be built in the project. The architects of the highly regarded Ida B. Wells project considered the new project superior to the Wells housing in design and materials. Moreover, since this project was to be built like a private development, it would provide more privacy and space than was typical of public housing.

The CHA determined that the site for the development was acceptable for a public housing project because it was zoned for fifty industrial lots. Since the land was low-lying and too costly to elevate for industrial plants, it had not attracted private investment and had remained vacant. In addition, along its northern border, the B&G Railroad tracks ran parallel to the site. Despite these features, the CHA assured black citizens that this area was suitable for residential development. The location of the housing was considered desirable for its proximity to the South Chicago industrial area that employed many black defense workers.

The Opposition

The Citizens Committee of West Chesterfield, whose membership consisted of affluent homeowners and professionals headed by Dr. William J. Walker, a prominent black dentist, led opposition to the building of the "war homes." Wage-earning blacks made up the client base of these upper-class black professionals and business owners. Their material base had not changed since World War I, when the group's prosperity became dependent on black patronage. The exceptional nature of this enclave was expressed by the *Chicago Bee*, which described West Chesterfield as "the nation's only exclusive residential community of wealthy Negro home owners."[23]

The arguments made by the Citizens Committee are familiar because they are typical of opposition to the siting of public or low-income housing in or near affluent neighborhoods. Citizens Committee members feared that CHA housing would eventually turn into a "slum project" and threaten their property values. In addition, they worried about general "deterioration of the community." Particularly, they argued that "lowered cultural and social standards . . . would result if there were no attempt made to restrict residents." One homeowner, referring to a slum area in the city, responded to a *Bee* reporter, "How would you like to live in a neighborhood like 24th Street?"[24] The affluent homeowners made detailed inquiries to the CHA about the cost of the dwellings, noting that the area had been rezoned for single-family dwellings costing no less than $8,000. They also sought protection of their property values through CHA guarantees from the Federal Housing Administration (FHA).

Despite the similarities between their objections to public housing and those of white homeowners, the circumstances of black professionals and white homeowners were different. The affluent black homeowners felt aggrieved by the housing authority's plan to build public housing near their homes. More than likely, they had confronted many barriers, such as racially restrictive covenants, in securing quality homes. Now, after having found a location and housing they thought suitable for their class, they felt threatened by the close proximity of public housing, even if it was intended for black war workers. It looked to them as if the white-run housing authority was using their own people—black workers—to undermine their hard-earned realization of the American Dream.

Critics of the Opposition

Apparently not all the homeowners of West Chesterfield felt threatened by the construction of the war homes. A majority in West Chesterfield, 119 homeowners, and also the people of adjacent Lilydale, supported their construction. Reverend E. W. White led the supporters' organization, the Community Council of West Chesterfield and Lilydale. More important, support came from a variety of citywide black civic leaders. Organizationally, support came from black labor leaders of the Douglass-Washington Institute, including its president, Wesley Thompson, international representative of United Auto Workers, and Willard Townsend, international president of the United Transport Services Union Employees and a member of Mayor Edward J. Kelly's Council on Race Relations. Support also came from the Chicago Council of the National Negro Congress , led by a black Communist, Ishmael P. Flory, which held a mass forum on the controversy in September 1944.

The main thrust of the criticisms against the Citizens Committee concerned the threat to the fight for racial equality that was posed by the affluent homeowners' efforts at class exclusion. Some civic leaders characterized the Citizens Committee's opposition as class discrimination, but most focused on the irony of its position in view of participants' proximity to racially restrictive areas. These critics were particularly concerned with how this stance subverted the moral high ground taken by African Americans in opposing race covenants. For example, an editorial in the *Chicago Bee* warned that if the opposition to the war homes were successful, "the whole race would lose. We would lose the moral weight of our total race argument for equality."[25]

A related argument emphasized the need for intraracial unity in the overall fight for racial democracy, based on the reasoning that since all blacks faced discrimination from whites, blacks should not treat each other differently. In fact, affluent blacks needed to help wage-earning blacks so that African Americans could present a united front in the fight against racial discrimination. Anthony Overton, prominent business owner and publisher of the *Chicago Bee*, observed that the race could not effectively fight for integration "until all of us are willing to accept and help those of us who are less fortunate."[26] In addition, an editorial in the *Bee* warned that if the Citizens Committee continued to fight against the war homes, "unfortunate disunities" would "weaken" African Americans' united force necessary to secure the "entire race's stake in a democratic future."[27] These examples demonstrate the rationale for condemning class bias; it undermined racial unity. Racial uplift and interclass unity were necessary for the fight for racial democracy.

Some critics carried the argument still further by pointing out the added irony of these elite professionals discriminating against the very group that provided them with their livelihood. This criticism stemmed from both a sense of social injustice and a sense of racial obligation. Oscar C. Brown Sr., manager of the Ida B. Wells and Altgeld Gardens public housing developments, pointed out that these affluent homeowners "made their money by serving the unfortunate group that they are now trying to keep out."[28] More pointedly, Mrs. E. C. Crawford, a resident, remarked bitterly, "If you are not good enough to live on the same street with him or two blocks away from him, you are too damn good to be his patient or customer." The economic vulnerability of the black upper class was reflected in her remarks that most West Chesterfield residents did not have independent wealth and were dependent on their salaries and FHA aid to buy their homes.[29] Since their status was fragile, Crawford reasoned that they ought to be more amenable to sharing their privilege with working-class blacks. Of course, the insecurity of this class caused it to seek greater spatial (and thus social) distance from the lower classes rather than pursue solidarity with them.

Many black civic leaders explicitly condemned the affluent homeowners for practicing class discrimination in their opposition to the war homes.[30] They challenged the assumptions about moral character that underlay the opposition's stance. Black labor leader Wesley Thompson remarked that the Citizen Committee's opposition reflected the fact that the "so-called better classes of Negroes" are not interested in "the welfare of the mass," whom they regard as "less prosperous and less intelligent."[31] Sidney A. Jones Jr., a prominent black lawyer, concurred; in a letter printed in the *Chicago Bee*, he argued that the opposition to the war homes "clearly raised the issue of the classes against the masses."[32] Some black elites more directly challenged the underlying assumptions of the opposition. Oscar Brown pointed out that "the desirability of a people" should not be dependent on the size of their income.[33] A *Chicago Bee* editorialist added, "Wealth is no index to character. Carver and Lincoln proved that the poor are worthy too."[34]

The position that "wealth is no index to character" is intriguing because it is an assumption consistent with social democracy, but one that the black upper class embraced in the context of racial disparities. Because of racism, affluent blacks could not obtain the same economic security as their white upper-class counterparts. They therefore claimed that character was a more accurate measure of membership in the "better classes" than wealth or income. In a truncated class structure with fewer distinctions of wealth and income than among whites, character was magnified as an indicator of black social status. Nonetheless, this claim carried an ambivalent message about the black popular classes. On one hand, the upper class included those whom Drake and Cayton identified as the "frugal and fortunate." On the other hand, some affluent homeowners of West Chesterfield clearly drew the inference that less income within the race did indeed indicate low character. This assumption of the faulty character of black defense workers displayed the homeowners' class bias and rationalized their protection of their exclusive dwellings. Ironically, the democratic sentiment of separating character from wealth was reformulated by an insecure black upper class to legitimize their own social status and rationalize their opposition to the close residential proximity of black war workers.

Not all black civic elites, however, criticized the Citizens Committee for demonstrating class bias and undermining racial unity. Some civic leaders and organizations either agreed with some of the West Chesterfield homeowners' assumptions or remained silent during the controversy, indicating the tenuousness of social democratic commitments in black civic ideology during World War II. Some black elites expressed concern about the character of the future residents of the war homes. A. L. Foster, executive director of the local Urban League, commented that there were no grounds for exclusion unless potential tenants "will be of the type that will run down the community."[35] Of course, Foster was not necessarily disparaging the defense workers, but he clearly refers to a "type" responsible for neighborhood deterioration.

More pointed were the comments of Reverend White and Carter Wilson, the latter an assistant secretary of the Community Council who also supported the war homes development. These supporters instead sought reassurance from the CHA, expressing concern about the neighbors they would get and exhorting the CHA to carefully screen the tenants.[36] Their remarks betray an anxiety about the suitability of the residents who would be selected from the mass of defense workers applying for wartime housing. White's and Wilson's concerns appear to be perfectly reasonable, yet if this had been a private development of black professionals, would they have expressed such anxiety?

Tellingly, the South Side branch of the NAACP did not take a stand on the controversy. It was unusual for such a prominent civic organization to remain silent on an issue unless there was severe conflict within the organization. The *Bee* reported that even though the majority attending a special meeting supported the war homes, those opposing the construction were able to get the organization to adopt a "hands off" posture.[37] This report suggested that affluent homeowners had sufficient influence within the organization to prevent it from taking a position.

Some other black elites recognized class bias in the affluent homeowners' opposition to the war homes but dismissed it with an interpretation of democracy that countenanced class inequality, demonstrating how contested was the idea of democracy in wartime black political discourse. A *Chicago Bee* editorial that ultimately criticized the Citizens Committee claimed that "there are democratic justifications on both sides." The editorial continued, "No one blames one for bettering himself in a democracy."[38] This last claim had the potential of rationalizing class privilege as earned "self-improvement," which was permissible in a liberal democracy. These divergent positions were significant because the social democratic position of class equality is in competition with the view that class status results from individual achievement and upward mobility—both are defensible with democratic norms. Such a defense of individual achievement can mask internal class privilege (and inequality, as it could in general society). The liberal interpretation makes eliminating racial obstacles the real work of democracy, arguing that deserving blacks ought to have unfettered access to higher social status. Of course, in practice, increased mobility for black elites did not eliminate all barriers for working-class blacks.

The shifting position taken by the opposition reflected their sensitivity to evoking crass social class terms in their criticism. Moreover, the affluent homeowners' opposition risked appearing antipatriotic since their opposition to the construction of the war homes could be construed as slowing down the nation's overall defense effort. In public meetings, Dr. Walker of the Citizens Committee backed off the statement that war workers were "undesirables" and instead expressed support for home ownership, explaining that his group was only encouraging the construction of "better homes," similar to those erected by the CHA in white residential communities. In other words, the Citizens Committee presented themselves as seeking only racial group parity. In this manner, Dr. Walker deftly buried the issue of black class prejudice by invoking the norm of home ownership. Walker also shrewdly deflected the charge of class bias by accusing the CHA of racism.

This subtle shift was enough to placate black labor leader Willard Townsend, who had earlier denounced the Citizens Committee. He found that West Chesterfield residents had changed their position, adding that he, too, wanted "better houses for members of my race."[39] Townsend later claimed that he had not retreated from his original position. Whether or not Townsend was looking for a reason to soften his earlier criticism of the affluent homeowners, it is striking how class discrimination could be reformulated as a concern for racial improvement. These claims suggest that even forthright stands on social democracy were riddled with conventional assumptions about class, private property, and morality that remained undisturbed in a racial approach to democracy.

That the opposition of affluent homeowners to the building of the wartime homes did not stop their construction indicates the powerlessness of this group to secure their own class privilege. Their failure contrasts with the success of white working- and middle-class homeowners in barring public housing from their neighborhoods after the war. White homeowners were successful in confining public housing to black neighborhoods because of the city government's leniency toward their violent resistance to housing black veterans and the city council's control over the siting of public housing developments.

Nonetheless, the West Chesterfield controversy indicates that social democracy was an important orientation that competed with more traditional racial democratic orientations during the war. The growth of indigenous social democratic sentiments during the Depression created some concern for class equality among black civic elites, but racial democracy remained dominant. Some critics condemned class prejudice outright. Most either apologized for class bias or criticized that bias because it subverted a racial obligation that supported racial unity and weakened the real fight for racial equality. Black civic elites were all too aware of their need to maintain the political loyalty of wage-earning blacks to their agenda of racial-group progress through civil rights and economic growth. The West Chesterfield conflict illustrates how social democratic concerns were absorbed, deflected, or reinterpreted to bolster the claim of racial democracy on black civic ideology during the war. This claim would only strengthen its hold during the turbulent postwar period.

Black Policy Elites Fight for Public Housing

Postwar Black Housing Crisis and the Housing Act of 1949

The economic circumstances of early post–World War II Chicago and other cities did not substantially alter black policy and civic elites' view of the world. In fact, blacks' relative stability of employment and income in the immediate postwar years served to reinforce their commitment to the idea of racial-group progress. The fact that blacks remained largely working class, however, meant that black elites' housing policies could potentially speak to both social and racial democratic concerns.

After the war, black civic leaders were confronted with a worsening housing situation. Because private housing was largely unavailable due to restrictive covenants and almost no new construction targeted them, black Americans were more dependent on public housing than other groups. In 1947, 5,000 of Chicago's African American families lived in public housing. They occupied 45 percent of the 4,000 low-rent housing units built before World War II. The 3,500 dwellings for black war workers that had been provided by the CHA returned to low-rent status after the war. Overall, 2,200 dwellings were added to the public housing inventory from developments designated as war housing. For instance, Wentworth Gardens, completed and fully occupied in June 1947, added its 422 units to the total occupied by black Americans. While one-third of all public housing residents had moved into private homes in the first ten years of the CHA, blacks stayed in public housing longer than others because they had fewer options.[40]

Chicago's inventory of public housing was due to increase with the passage of the Housing Act of 1949. Black policy elites from national civil rights organizations joined white housing advocates to lobby the Congress to pass new housing legislation. After the 1937 Housing Act, public housing had stalled after a concerted counterattack from real estate capital. As evidence, from 1939 to 1948, Congress, led by a coalition of conservative Republicans and Southern Democrats, refused to vote for any additional appropriations for public housing.[41] Both white and black housers realized that the Wagner-Taft-Ellender bill was a conservative one, since most of the federal subsidies supported the slum clearance and urban-development program, not public housing. However, they accepted the probusiness bias. Given the real estate lobby's political influence, they felt this might be the best way to restart public housing production. This proved to be a fatal embrace: public housing soon became an appendage to the slum clearance program, which wreaked its own havoc on inner-city black communities.[42]

Black Factions and the Struggle over Chicago Public Housing Sites

At the time, not knowing the disaster that the slum clearance policy would become, black civic leaders in Chicago were happy with the prospect of gaining more public housing units authorized by the 1949 Housing Act. It was now up to them to make sure that citizens of African descent got their share. In addition, in every city the question of where to locate public housing units available to blacks was given new urgency. After World War II, black policy and civic elites saw an opportunity to locate public housing sites outside the main concentrations of black residence in Chicago. The motivation for this policy came from two sources: one principled and the other practical.

In principle, black elites believed that as American citizens, blacks should have access to all the rights and responsibilities conferred to all citizens regardless of race. They felt it was an affront to African Americans' civil status as well as their humanity to be denied access to any goods and services in U.S. society, including decent housing in a neighborhood of their choice and means. Although black policy elites were aware of and fought against the federal government's policies and practices of racial discrimination (especially by the Federal Housing Administration), they also felt they had more legal and political recourse than private individuals or businesses to counteract government discrimination. Thus, they sought to influence the federal Public Housing Administration (PHA) to accept only those local applications for public housing units that planned to build mostly on vacant sites outside black ghettos and allow black tenants nondiscriminatory access. Robert Weaver and other black policy elites saw public housing as an opportunity to show the real estate industry and a skeptical white public that blacks and whites could live harmoniously in modern housing located in decent neighborhoods.

From a practical standpoint, the fact that there was little vacant land in the congested Black Belt meant blacks needed access to public housing outside the black community in order to improve their housing conditions. Black housing policy specialists saw increasing the quantity and quality of housing available to African Americans as the core of their policy and political agenda. In their eyes, dismantling the walls of the black ghetto was the only way to accomplish that agenda. In addition to addressing poor blacks' housing needs and experimenting with interracial living, public housing on vacant sites would be necessary to relocate those residents, mostly black, who would be displaced by the federal slum clearance program authorized by the 1949 Housing Act. As far as black policy elites and their white counterparts were concerned, it was rational planning to first build public housing on vacant sites outside the congested black community and relocate former slum residents into these projects before clearing and redeveloping inner-city land for new private and public housing developments. However rational this policy formulation seemed, ambitious white politicians and insecure white homeowners resisted both blacks and public housing as the two became increasingly linked.

A complicating factor in this racial politics was the opposition of black politicians, ministers, and businesspeople to the siting of public housing outside the black community. They feared that residential integration would spur a dispersal of their voters, parishioners, and customers. So the fight over public housing sites was not only an example of racial power politics whereby African Americans would be outgunned by more powerful whites; it also served as a terrain for competing agendas for racial democracy. While black civic leaders sought immediate democratization of housing policies and markets as the best means to improve blacks' housing choices, a rival faction of professional politicians and allied elites preferred to consolidate their power within a segregated black community in order to broker concessions from a white government and business elite in Chicago. Robert Taylor and William Harvey would advance the positions of the respective black factions. Taylor was the main CHA negotiator in the controversy over the site-selection struggle for public housing in Chicago; Harvey, the alderman from the Second Ward, the heart of Bronzeville, represented the base of Congressman Dawson's political organization.

The struggle over public housing sites in Chicago has been well covered by past scholarship, which has paid particular attention to the power of white politicians fueled by implacable white homeowner opposition to public housing in their neighborhoods.[43] These accounts show how their power overwhelmed the racially liberal CHA and the black civic community, both of which considered access to public housing on vacant sites in or near white neighborhoods a civil rights issue. My purpose is to use this controversy to delineate the policy differences between factions of black elites and to highlight how class interests informed the respective racial democratic vision of each faction.

There had been a number of contentious meetings between the CHA and the city council and the mayor over respective plans for locating new federal public housing. Since 1941 Illinois state legislation had given Chicago's city council the right to approve all public housing sites within its jurisdiction.[44] The conflict between Robert Taylor's and William Harvey's positions became manifest when Taylor and the CHA staff formally presented the package of sites to the city council in late November 1949. They stressed the need for the aldermen to make a decision on the sites to submit to Federal Public Housing Administration before August 1950, when their federal commitment would expire. At this meeting, the CHA confronted a wild card they had not expected. Some aldermen, including William Harvey, opposed the CHA sites during the meeting. Although Harvey had earlier assured the CHA staff privately that he would support the program with modifications, he was reported to have angrily said "that the people of his ward had no confidence in CHA and that he would not rubber-stamp CHA's plans."[45] Later, when questioned in the *Chicago Sun-Times* about his stand, Harvey explained that he opposed having a site in his ward because it was not a slum and too many "good houses" would be torn down.[46]

Harvey's argument contained a mixture of references that suggested various possible motivations for his position. The statement that the CHA "forces people on people" was probably a sop to white aldermen who opposed the "forced integration" that the CHA had planned for their neighborhoods on the grounds that the CHA was risking racial conflict and "bloodshed." In addition, he implied that white people would be victims of discrimination if the CHA forced black people to live in their neighborhoods. While these comments suggest Harvey was simply bowing to the pressure of white power in the name of the Cook County Democratic Party machine, competing motivations for Harvey's opposition may exist. One interpretation, suggested by the traditional "vested interests" argument, is that, as a black politician, Harvey simply wanted to keep his black electoral base intact, which would mean rejecting any vacant sites. This motivation is suggested by the comment that "too many Negroes would have to be displaced." This position caused Vernon Jarrett, a black reporter for the black-owned Associated Negro Press (ANP), to call Harvey one of the "confused Negroes" who joined with "spokesmen for white supremacy" in rejecting the CHA plan.

However, Harvey's concern about displacement might have had another cause. Harvey mentions his opposition to a new public housing site in his ward, which would have increased the number of African Americans in his ward after the initial displacement. The fact that he also challenged the designation of his ward as a "slum" suggests that he felt the housing in his ward was worth saving and should not be replaced by public housing. While there were clearly deteriorated houses in his ward, Harvey also referred to the "good houses" there. This was a point with which the civil rights faction could agree. Jarrett concurred, arguing that the targeted houses in the worst shape "should be cleared first."[47] These comments suggest that Harvey was defending the black property owners of his constituency. Furthermore, Harvey's comments reflect his siding with the growing opposition of black homeowners to the city's state-authorized slum clearance and public housing program within their neighborhoods. There had been opposition to the clearance of black neighborhoods for the Dearborn Homes in 1948, and there was opposition to the impending urban redevelopment project that would displace many black homes and businesses.[48] Harvey's comment that "forcing people out of their homes . . . is unconstitutional" suggests that he felt the rights of black property owners would be violated.[49] Both references suggest that the reasons for his opposition—the loss of middle-class housing and property-owning constituents—related partly to his wish to keep his black electoral base intact.

The Douglass community within the Second Ward already included a substantial amount of public housing compared to most other communities. Most of the 1,659 units in the still well-regarded Ida B. Wells project were located there, as was the 800-unit Dearborn Homes.[50] On balance, Harvey's position reflected the opposition of middle-class homeowners in his ward to being displaced by more public housing. Therefore, when the liberal *Sun-Times* told Harvey that "they couldn't believe that his constituents would not be willing to trade their slum hovels for modern, clean, safe apartments," they clearly had not realized which constituents counted for Harvey. His opposition to public housing in his ward meant he was listening to his property-owning constituents, probably the most politically active ones, not those who lived in slum housing.[51] By rejecting the CHA plan, Harvey rejected public housing in his ward as well as public housing on outlying vacant sites to retain his middle-class political base.[52]

Black Opposition to Public Housing

Black opposition to public housing did emerge as Taylor negotiated with city council leaders on behalf of the CHA. Alderman John Duffy, a white city council leader, sought responses from his black constituents to the CHA plan, which proposed building public housing in his Nineteenth Ward. All these constituents, living in a substantial black enclave in the Morgan Park community, sided against the siting of public housing near their community, as did the Morgan Park Association, representing affluent African American homeowners. The association's leaders resided in an affluent black enclave with houses priced at $25,000 or more. The political scientists Martin Meyerson and Edward Banfield note that affluent blacks' unsurprising opposition was further fueled by a potential loss of status since they were less able than whites to find comparable housing should they choose to relocate.[53] Given the sentiments expressed by middle-class blacks, Duffy and other city council leaders felt safe in rejecting vacant land sites and proposing only slum sites.[54]

In a clumsy attempt to persuade Taylor to reject the city hall's plan opposing vacant sites, the Public Housing Association invited thirty African American leaders to meet with him. Although only a few came to the meeting, all those who attended claimed to be strongly opposed to the city's compromise plan. One of these leaders, Nelson M. Willis, president of the local branch of the NAACP, later wrote CHA commissioners that two basic principles favored by black policy elites should not be yielded by the CHA— that all the potential sites should be on vacant land and large enough to build developments to resist surrounding blight. While Willis's position resonated with Taylor's fellow black civic leaders, it is unclear whether any of them other than Willis tried to influence Taylor to reject the city's plan or whether they felt he should try to get the best deal he could get at that point.[55] For his part, Taylor recalled that the only pressure he received was from those

African Americans, most likely his upper-class associates, who opposed the housing program, and unlike those who favored the CHA plan, he claimed, "there were plenty of these."[56]

At the city council housing committee's hearings on the compromise package in July 1950, white public housing opponents packed the room. Apparently blacks represented both supporters and opponents of public housing. Black tenants from Altgeld Gardens testified in favor of the proposed extension to their present project. The representatives were members of the tenants' council that included a college graduate and a minister. The minister trumpeted the tenants' values such as self-reliance, independence, and thrift, using these values associated with private homeowners to defend the need for public housing. He discussed improvements that the tenants had made to the project to make it livable. The speakers, clearly appealing to a hostile crowd, nonetheless betrayed their own ambivalence about the right of low-income citizens to decent housing.[57]

Other black Chicagoans opposed the public housing package at the hearings. One black property owner, opposed to the site at Lake Park Avenue and Oakwood Boulevard on the city's South Side near Lake Michigan, explained that this site could be used for "middle-income" housing. He saw this proposal as "the beginning of the destruction of yet another neighborhood where Negroes have bought property," intimating that black neighborhoods were considered slums for "sociological reasons," not because physical conditions warranted the designation. He defended the typical black small property owner who rented out a unit in the building where he lived. Despite the property owner operating within the law, he was considered "a criminal, a scoundrel, a public enemy number one." This speaker felt black small property owners were under attack, while white large property owners, he feared, were busy buying up the South Side, where blacks resided. Apparently, he complained, it was acceptable for big real estate companies to make money but not for small property owners to do so. He favored public housing only when it replaced "bad housing," was not built on expensive land and did not destroy small property owners.

Another black opponent was a minister who discussed the investment in the church and the homes in the community. Though he was not against public housing per se, he did not want it in his community because it would displace too many people who supported the church, their aldermen, and "the city in making it a better place in which to live." He argued that if housing were to be built, it should be "for the middle-class, who are going to pay taxes . . . and not [be] on relief." Other blacks who opposed the compromise plan did so because it would increase density in their communities while creating little additional housing. These black small property owners, like the minister, did not oppose public housing in principle, only its location in their neighborhoods. These opponents, however, did not argue that building public housing on slum sites would entrench racial and class segregation; rather, their opposition stemmed from a fear of lower property values and the loss of middle-income housing. Racial democracy for this petite bourgeoisie meant having an equal opportunity to own land and profit from it without being muscled out by large white real estate capital or undermined by liberal public housing supporters.[58]

Black Federal Housing Officials and the Chicago Program

As an example of the black housing policy network in operation, black federal housing officials attempted to support the civil rights faction of black elites in Chicago by lobbying their agency to reject the city's plan to build public housing almost exclusively on slum sites. There were strenuous protests by black officials inside the federal Housing and Home Finance Agency (HHFA) in Washington, D.C., in late summer and fall in 1950. Closely monitoring the fight over site selection for Chicago's public housing, Frank S. Horne, head of the HHFA Racial Relations Office, told Raymond M. Foley, HHFA administrator, that his office objected to the city plan recently approved by the city council. He argued, like Taylor before him, that the plan to build 10,000 units of public housing in "congested Negro neighborhoods" would result in the displacement of 8,000 or more black families, two-thirds of whom were not eligible for the proposed public housing. Horne pointed to his office's biweekly reports, which showed that Chicago's site selection was "politically inspired and motivated by the most reprehensible form of racism." He emphasized that the racial relations advisers in the Chicago field office, in the FPHA, and in his office were "all unalterably opposed to this program." The Chicago-based FPHA racial relations field adviser opposed the plan because it would cause too much hardship to the black community without providing adequate relocation housing. The Lake Meadows redevelopment plan, which was also being considered as part of the "Chicago

Development Program" at the same time in Washington, was purportedly going to displace an additional 4,600 persons.[59]

Horne expressed his office's opposition directly to Foley since he was concerned that the FPHA's newly decentralized procedure, whereby the Chicago field office submitted the CHA's application directly to Washington without review by regional racial relations advisers, cut them out of the decision-making process. Horne appealed to Foley to exercise his right of final review as the HHFA's chief administrator when the application came into the FPHA before the program was approved. He reminded Foley that he had earlier assured some liberal senators that a nonsegregation clause was not necessary in housing legislation because federal policy and administration under his direction would provide enough protection against expanding government-supported residential segregation in the North. Horne concluded by requesting Foley's "personal intervention to insist that the Chicago program be thoroughly revised to meet decent standards of planning, housing and racial relations or be rejected."[60]

Frank Horne succeeded in persuading his boss, Raymond Foley, to write Mayor Kennelly and tell him that he would accept the present plan if the city promised to include vacant sites over the six years remaining in the public housing and urban redevelopment portions of Chicago Development Program.[61] After lengthy negotiations over the course of a year that produced only vague promises from Chicago to facilitate the construction of private housing accessible to blacks, Foley made up his mind. On November 5, 1951, the HHFA issued a news release stating that administrator Foley had given approval to the four additional low-rent public housing projects that he had initially rejected and the Lake Meadows housing project, and promised more attention to relocation, especially to finding housing for displaced blacks who were ineligible for public housing. However, there would be little follow-up on the problems of relocation by federal housing agencies. The Chicago political regime had won, forcing Washington to accept their plan and defeating racial liberal forces that included national and local black civic elites. Chicago's political regime had made sure that any future attempts to find vacant sites and to desegregate public housing would meet the same fate.[62]

The Defeat of Public Housing in Chicago

So effective was the opposition to public housing that until the machine put pressure on the aldermen, there were not enough votes for the public housing program to pass; once that occurred, it passed easily by a vote of thirty-five to twelve in August 1950. A month later, Robert Taylor resigned from the CHA's Board of Commissioners. Although his reported reason for leaving was to attend to his "private affairs," many of his friends thought that white intransigence regarding the CHA's nondiscriminatory policy and site selection had caused him to step down. While he did not address issues of racial politics, Taylor did convey his enduring belief in the purpose of public housing. He lamented the "bitter fights and the terrific struggles" over building low-rent public housing but claimed that experience was overshadowed by "the deep satisfaction [he] derived out of witnessing thousands of families moving out of filth, slime, and slums into decent, sanitary homes in communities and environment[s] conducive to normal family life and good citizenship."[63] Commenting on Taylor's resignation, the Associated Negro Press argued that the power of the opposition made it "almost impossible" for the city to locate public housing in nonblack communities.[64] For many, Taylor's resignation was symbolic of the defeat suffered by black civic leaders and their liberal allies in their quest for racially democratic public housing policy in Chicago.

The *Chicago Defender*, representing the civil rights position, commented that unnamed powerful black political leaders "have remained mute and silent on this housing tragedy." It was also clear to the paper that some middle- and upper-class African Americans were actively opposed to public housing. Black civic leaders could not overcome the opposition of black machine politicians and affluent black homeowners to public housing. While it appeared that black property owners opposed public housing in the Second Ward on the *racial* grounds that it entrenched racial segregation, their opposition in fact was based on matters of *class:* public housing would deprive them of their property rights, lower property values, and risk elevating incidences of social disorganization in the neighborhood.[65] When William Harvey articulated his early opposition to the public housing program, he represented both large and small property owners in his district. He decried the displacement of "good homes" of the sort owned by doctors, post office clerks, and skilled workers. Harvey's (and William Dawson's) initial opposition to public housing makes clear that their "vested interest" was not only to keep a mass black electorate intact but also to be responsive to a critical constituency, the active black middle and upper strata who opposed it.

Conclusion

African American policy elites' support for public housing exhibited their commitment to racial *and* social democracy, more so than other housing policies. Attempting to secure adequate and affordable housing for the poorest members of their racial group satisfied both social and racial democratic standards. Social democracy was minimally met by seeking modern housing for wage-earning blacks who made up the majority of the race. Racial democracy, according to its adherents, was advanced by public housing that provided both material improvement and social rehabilitation to the stratum within the race most in need of modernizing. When the social democratic tendency came under attack in the West Chesterfield fight, some black civic elites found war housing more acceptable under racial democratic rationales. What started out as a charge of class bigotry and discrimination was reinterpreted as concern for racial fairness and expanded home ownership among upwardly mobile blacks. Black civic elites overcame the opposition of affluent black homeowners (and their own ambivalence about working-class blacks' ability to modernize on their own) by trumpeting racial democracy while deflecting or negating the idea of class equality endemic to the social democratic tendency within black civic ideology.

These same elites were less successful in the postwar era when opposition to public housing expanded to include black machine politicians and white homeowners. While Chicago's city leaders wanted public housing, the battle was over where to locate it. White redevelopment interests wanted public housing on nonprime property, where it could accommodate those displaced by the federal bulldozer. White machine politicians who did not want to antagonize their white or black home-owning constituents advocated for predominantly black slum sites. Many black property owners and politicians opposed public housing for their own reasons. Black politicians opposed the CHA public housing program because it threatened their property-owning constituents with property loss or devaluation. They opposed black civic elites' advocacy for the construction of public housing on vacant land sites, fearing it would lead to residential deconcentration.

Black politicians' preferred path to racial democracy was through the consolidation of black votes and dollars in order to break down institutional barriers to racial-group progress. This inclination collided with black policy elites' preference for using individual upward mobility as the lever to democratize employment and housing. Without critical support from a skeptical, if not hostile black middle class, the black civic elite could not marshal enough racial consensus in favor of dispersed public housing sites. The political weakness of black civic and policy elites was mirrored at the citywide and national levels by that of liberal housing reformers as a limited public housing policy went down in defeat. National and local black elites would revisit their argument with black politicians over the appropriate path to racial democracy when the debate shifted to a fight over the controversial slum clearance program.

4

Fighting "Negro Clearance"

Black Elites and Urban Redevelopment Policy

In their influential book *Black Metropolis*, St. Clair Drake and Horace Cayton comment on the ambivalence that black Chicagoans felt toward residential segregation. On the one hand, they took pride in Bronzeville, which represented territory that had been won through urban trench warfare with hostile whites since the turn of the twentieth century. On the other hand, all black Americans resented being told where they could live and considered the freedom of residential choice a civil right.[1] While some courageous and ambitious blacks, mainly middle class, breached the ghetto's walls into white enclaves in search of better housing and neighborhoods, equal or greater numbers of blacks, also middle class, valued the security and comfort of living in a predominantly black environment.[2] All would agree that housing and neighborhood conditions needed improvement, but some who felt these conditions would never improve enough within the black community sought better alternatives outside of it. This ambivalence made the drive for residential integration less potent than related campaigns for equal employment and public accommodations.[3]

This popular ambivalence was given political expression by different factions of black elites who sought modern housing for the race. These conflicting political positions informed a debate over what to do about slum conditions in the heart of the Black Metropolis. Three different positions were staked out in this debate. Black institutional elites—including black politicians, ministers, business and property owners, and black policy elites—who worked either for national civil rights organizations or in federal housing agencies took the extreme positions. Black institutional elites in Chicago publicly supported the principle of residential desegregation but privately feared the loss of voters, clients, congregants, and property owners. They opposed the city's slum clearance and urban redevelopment program as an assault on blacks' property rights. Black policy elites living in New York or Washington, D.C., saw urban redevelopment as a potential vehicle, though indirect, for residential desegregation. While they recognized the possibility that blacks could be displaced from valuable inner-city land, they felt that unless the walls of the ghetto were torn down, African Americans would never get more and improved housing. Therefore, they initially supported Chicago's slum clearance and urban redevelopment program even though they were not naive about its dangers. In fact, since Chicago's program was authorized by Illinois state legislation, these black housing experts saw it as a test case for whether the programs would in fact lead to residential desegregation.

Black civic elites, who headed the local branches of the Urban League and the NAACP or worked for other civic and municipal agencies in the city, represented the third position. These leaders had divided loyalties. As directors of local branches of civil rights organizations, they believed in and fought for residential integration, but their social base, especially that of the Urban League, consisted of the small property- and homeowners who were threatened by land clearance. While they strongly favored residential desegregation, they did not want to sacrifice good housing in the ghetto to achieve it. Either they thought that having a strong territorial base was important for pursuing that desegregation, like institutional elites, or, pragmatically, they did not want to give up good housing in the black community until they could secure decent housing in white neighborhoods.

These positions did *not* represent a conflict between affluent and working-class blacks; instead, they represented a conflict between factions of black elites who represented upwardly mobile strata. Neither took a social democratic approach to urban redevelopment, which would have targeted any improved housing to black working-class residents whose previous dwellings had been demolished. Instead, their conflict was between two versions of racial democracy. Black institutional elites' vision of racial democracy was racial parity. In other words, racial democratization of housing markets would come about by first preserving black middle-class housing in desirable locations within the community. Through housing rehabilitation and new construction, preferably by black developers, different black strata would be able to find decent housing according to their incomes and tastes *within* a black community. The social base of this faction was made up of professionals, managers, and white-collar employees of segregated institutions like schools, churches, stores, libraries, and recreational and community centers as well as large and small property owners.

Black policy elites envisioned achieving racial democratization more directly by pressuring government to institute antidiscriminatory policies that would lift the barriers against housing mobility for those blacks who had the income, culture, and motivation to locate and settle outside of the ghetto. This was a battle that primarily spoke to different groups of black property- and homeowners, not to the vast majority of black residents living in kitchenettes, rooming houses, and tenements who would be displaced and then compelled to look in vain for affordable and adequate housing within a slowly expanding ghetto.

Absent any overt class conflict between black housing interests in the slum clearance debate, competing racial agendas predominated. While the housing interests of working-class black tenants were not completely ignored, they did not occupy a central place in the debate. Aiding this result was the racialist framework adopted by all three positions. All black factions, to different degrees, feared "Negro clearance," the displacement of all blacks from their homes and businesses regardless of whether or not they owned property. They all proposed racial democratic remedies to what they diagnosed as a racial threat. This policy framework privileged a racial democratic viewpoint and inadequately accounted for the differential impact that slum clearance would have on different black housing strata.

In this chapter, I explore the urban redevelopment policy debate between national black housing analysts and black civic leaders and then show how this policy debate informed the responses of the three black elite factions to Chicago's redevelopment program. That response included a persistent opposition to the city's program by black middle-class women activists and their institutional elite allies. I articulate the critique of that opposition by national black policy elites and examine their case for supporting slum clearance, paying particular attention to how the plight of most displaced blacks, who were working class, was conceptualized within the racial democratic frameworks that each faction brought to the problem.

The Debate over Negro Clearance

The Fear of Negro Clearance

Although the rumors of black displacement from the Mid-South Side had circulated since the Great Migration, Horace Cayton, sociologist and director of the Parkway Community Center, articulated this community's fear in his writings in the late Depression years. Between 1937 and 1940, in important articles that appeared in the journals *Opportunity* and *Social Action*, Cayton analyzed black housing conditions and advocated policies that informed the housing debate between black elite factions in the postwar period.[4] Cayton warned that the recent demolition of buildings, initiated by downtown business interests, presaged the eventual displacement of blacks from the desirable location of the Mid-South Side. Cayton reported that real estate interests wanted to remove all blacks "from the lake front and west of South Parkway" and replace them with middle-class residential developments that would house whites who worked in the Loop. According to Cayton, many African Americans believed this scenario since white real estate interests refused to sell to blacks who wanted to purchase white-owned houses on South Parkway. These same real estate interests also wanted "desirable areas" such as Hyde Park and West Woodlawn, where affluent blacks lived or hoped to live, to be reserved for whites.[5] Cayton concluded that both the motivation and the impact of land clearance were racial—both affluent and poor blacks would be displaced.

In the postwar period, Sidney Williams, executive secretary of the Chicago Urban League (CUL), was able to see more clearly than Cayton the decentralizing trends that prompted progrowth elites to create redevelopment schemes. He argued that downtown elites planned to clear and redevelop blighted areas to resettle middle-class whites, who could either walk or take public transportation to downtown.[6] Though Williams characterized the motivation as "cold hard economic considerations," he, too, concluded that blacks would be pushed to the urban periphery "unless we do something to consolidate our position near the heart of American cities."[7]

Like Cayton, Williams did not single out wage-earning, non-property-owning blacks as being particularly vulnerable to this threat; *all* blacks were in danger. His advice to "consolidate our position" recognized the desirable location of the South Side ghetto, but it also conveyed a determination to defend the institutions and property that black Chicagoans had accrued over the years. Williams used a military metaphor, characterizing collective black actions in the previous thirty years as a form of urban trench warfare against white real estate interests. Instead of following the lead of the national black policy faction who supported slum clearance and urban development while seeking safeguards for blacks' displacement—a course of action that might have been expected for an Urban League executive—Williams articulated the thinking of black opponents to slum clearance that emerged during this period.

Williams saw downtown elites as seeking to *replace* the central-city neighborhoods and their residents with white newcomers instead of sharing the new redeveloped housing with blacks. Understandably, he interpreted the threat as primarily racial. If downtown elites used only economic criteria, such as high cost of the redeveloped housing, as the basis for access, however, most blacks would be displaced from the Mid-South Side, with only affluent blacks able to afford the new housing. In fact, the Chicago Plan Commission in 1942 proposed that the redeveloped housing be for affluent blacks. In the view of Williams and other black elites, the plan would most likely result in all blacks losing.[8]

Though all African Americans would be affected by such an assault, black property owners would have more recourse than would poor blacks, who, devoid of property rights, depended on substandard rental housing for their shelter. Though understandable, the fact that the fear of black displacement was expressed in exclusively racial terms by these black civic leaders obscured which black strata would bear the brunt of the costs, or which one was better able to survive the hardships that would result from the white real estate industry's plans. Without a clear analysis of those differential costs, appropriate housing policy solutions could not be advanced.

Preventing Negro Clearance

During the war, the National Urban League (NUL) proposed safeguards to minimize the threat of slum clearance, attempting to account for redevelopment's differential impact on African Americans. While the important NUL report on black housing conditions and policies condemned the slums, it was careful to point out that African Americans should not be shortchanged as a result of slum removal. The report articulated a set of policies the NUL hoped would protect black housing interests in the wake of postwar urban redevelopment. Ideally, emerging public–private partnerships would replace "slum hovels" with affordable, privately produced modern housing. The NUL declared, however, that "past experiences" had shown blacks they should not "believe that postwar housing redevelopment plans automatically protect their interests."

The NUL expressed alarm at trends of unregulated "private control of postwar building" even when public subsidies were involved. One example of this trend was Stuyvesant Town in New York City, where urban redevelopment policy made an inauspicious debut. Although the Metropolitan Life Insurance Company was given substantial public subsidies in the form of direct aid and tax exemption in the purchase of land and construction of the rental housing, black New Yorkers were excluded from the $50 million housing development. Partially in response to this exclusion, New York City passed an ordinance on July 5, 1944, that stipulated that the development's tax-exempt status could be removed if evidence of discrimination were found.[9] While the NUL applauded the nondiscrimination city ordinance, it also raised the possibility that "private control" without government protection could lead to black displacement and rebuilding for whites only.

Anticipating that postwar urban redevelopment would augment residential segregation, the NUL outlined a five-point program to protect racial minorities: (1) It wanted government to maintain "public ownership" of any land acquired under eminent domain; (2) this land should not have any restrictive covenants; (3) residents who were displaced by demolition should have preferred tenancy status if "economically eligible"; (4) relocation housing in "equivalent land area and equivalent residential units" with similar building standards should be required "to accommodate groups similar, economically, and *racially*, to the displaced site occupants who cannot qualify for tenancy" in the new redeveloped housing (original emphasis); and (5) the equivalent land provided should be at least as desirable in its "proximity to employment" and amenities as the new redeveloped area.

These five points reflected the NUL's concern that most blacks would be displaced from desirable locations and deemed not "eligible" for the new housing, mainly due to their racial identity as well as their inability to pay the expected higher rents. Although the NUL was primarily focused on racial exclusion, it tried to respond to the housing needs of all black strata (including those whose income was too high for public housing, but not high enough for the new redeveloped housing) through its demand for equivalent land, housing units, and desirable location. The NUL was concerned that left to their own efforts, displaced blacks would be forced to move to contiguous overcrowded, deteriorating areas.[10]

The NUL wanted the federal government to use its subsidies to real estate capital interests as leverage to prevent them from practicing racial exclusion. In order to avoid black displacement, the NUL included a role for itself and other black civic agencies by recommending that all planning boards have adequate minority representation in order "to ensure proper coordination of their housing needs" with city plans "and also to interpret social welfare standards to engineers, architects, etc. when necessary."[11] While the NUL did not oppose slum clearance and urban redevelopment, it sought racial protection in exchange for its support. Yet in doing so, the NUL made a key concession by accepting that the new housing could be priced beyond what the vast majority of black former residents could afford. It was clear that their demand for "public ownership" was made to avoid racial discrimination, not to ensure that moderate- and low-income black citizens would get access to the new housing in the same location

Black Self-Help Rehabilitation

Beyond the NUL response, there was robust debate among black policy and civic elites about how best to respond to the threat of Negro clearance. Sidney Williams presented his self-help rehabilitation plan in the Chicago Urban League's annual report in 1947, the same year he became the affiliate's new executive secretary. While it might have seemed presumptuous for Williams to present such a plan so early in his tenure, he was not unfamiliar with Chicago's housing conditions. He had been in the city before the war pursuing graduate study at the University of Chicago's School of Social Work. As a rising star in the Urban League movement, he had held management positions in St. Louis and Cleveland before taking the top position in Chicago, a prized, if troubled local affiliate.[12]

Williams presented his plan for self-help rehabilitation to address housing, which he considered "Chicago's most urgent immediate problem," and to avoid the prospect of wholesale slum clearance as a necessary antecedent to rebuilding the Mid-South Side. Under his plan, rather than suffering the effects of widespread demolition, black property owners would get government assistance to rehabilitate their buildings and houses in a piecemeal improvement of housing conditions. Williams proposed to test his plan as a pilot project, relying on longtime CUL professional Frayser Lane to identify suitable neighborhoods on the city's South and West Sides. Once a building had been selected for rehabilitation, the occupants would find temporary housing within their neighborhoods until the reconstruction was completed.

After the successful rehabilitation, Williams would enlist the mayor and the Health and Building departments to support his scheme. He hoped that city council members who represented predominantly black districts would elicit city funds "to subsidize the cleaning up of the buildings and alleys in these pilot areas." Key to Williams's plan was to get black "householders completely sold on the idea" so that they constituted "a political force of first magnitude." Williams argued that the main task for this "political force" was to secure an ordinance to ban any demolition that did not clear land for new housing to accommodate a greater number of people than before.[13] Williams was shrewd enough to solicit black homeowners whose potential support for his plan could, in turn, put pressure on black and white aldermen to pass an ordinance as well as commit public funds to hasten neighborhood conservation. Black property owners, he determined, would have the stake as well as the potential leverage to make such a scheme successful.

Williams highlighted the many advantages of his plan. One advantage was that blacks skilled in the construction trades could find work for the near future and could use these work opportunities, especially for youth and veterans, as a means to get access to the "building trades."[14] Perhaps the main advantage of the self-help plan to rebuild the South Side, according to Williams, however, was "to offset the opinion that we Negro people run down neighborhoods." He reasoned that an effort in this direction would strengthen the NAACP's fight against restrictive covenants, facilitating black residents' ability to live outside of the ghetto. After the league's conservation program was instituted, he argued, whites "would no longer associate uncleanliness, dirty streets, etc., with Negro neighborhoods."[15]

In the short term, Williams emphasized, blacks would live in "healthier and more inspiring surroundings," anticipating "the day when forced racial ghettoes are a thing of the past in Chicago." He made it clear that the CUL would both aid "the unobstructed infiltration" of black residents into white neighborhoods as well as "interpret to the mass of Negro people the standards of behavior and patterns of living that will make them more desirable neighbors."[16] Sidney Williams's belief in eventual racial dispersal distinguished black civic elites' position on slum clearance from that of black institutional elites, who favored prolonged racial consolidation.

Williams was aware that his plan appeared contradictory. While he supported residential integration, he wanted to hold onto and improve present black landholdings. Nonetheless, Williams saw the "ghetto-perpetuation issue" as a nonissue; he felt that the walls of the black ghetto would break down due to the "natural pressure" emanating from black home seekers through sheer housing need and motivation. Williams tried to use "natural pressure" to finesse the apparent contradiction between racial consolidation as a tactic and residential integration as a policy goal. However, he was mistaken that blacks' housing needs and desire to disperse alone would help to eliminate the ghetto rather than just expand it. Rejecting self-segregation, Williams also endorsed the idea of whites living with blacks in rehabilitated areas. So if "consolidating our position" does not suggest racial consolidation, it is not clear what Williams intended. On this point, he is less forthcoming. Since he feared that all blacks would be displaced through slum clearance, piecemeal rehabilitation, instead, would ensure that a critical mass of blacks remained in the area to maintain community institutions and own property. Williams, like black institutional elites, was interested in preserving, if not enhancing, blacks' political and residential hold on the center of the city.[17]

Critique of Self-Help Rehabilitation

Despite Sidney Williams's effort to finesse the issue, his plan could not escape the impression that it perpetuated the ghetto, even in the short term. This was Robert Weaver's main criticism in his response to Williams's proposal. Weaver, the foremost national expert on black housing, was based in Chicago at the time, working as the director of community services for the American Council on Race Relations. Williams's plan "greatly" disturbed Weaver. Weaver acknowledged "certain virtues" in Williams's scheme but quickly added that the "dangers far outweigh its potential benefits." He argued that the CUL director's plan, unfortunately, did not solve the major housing problems facing African Americans in Chicago such as "excessive densities, too little land space, impediments to normal expansion, overcrowding, unhealthy environment, inadequate community facilities and excessive rents for bad housing."[18]

Weaver's criticism of Williams's plan to rehabilitate current buildings and suspend demolition rested on three related grounds. First, he felt Williams's piecemeal approach would not reduce the "already alarmingly high densities in most of the South Side." He pointed out that rehabilitation without a reduction in density would undermine the objective of showing "that Negroes do not depress property values and are not undesirable occupants." Second, Weaver feared that Williams's plan would give "aid and comfort" to the forces that wanted to reinforce the ghetto's boundaries. Finally, Weaver approved of the plan to "clean up and make sanitary" slum properties, but he reminded Williams that "a slum area is more than a group of substandard and unsanitary houses." He thought Williams was confusing "slum areas" with "blighted areas," arguing that while the latter could benefit from rehabilitation, slum areas were so "disorganized and disintegrated" that they necessitated "a community approach" that entailed comprehensive elimination and rebuilding. Weaver cited a CHA study that asserted slum demolition was "more practical" than slum rehabilitation. Weaver worried that "strong forces" would interpret any attempt to rehabilitate slum properties as a "justification for no action on the basic problems of slum clearance and urban rehabilitation."[19]

The policy debate between Williams and Weaver in 1947 presaged the political conflict between local black institutional elites and middle-class homeowners and national black policy elites that would begin a few years later. It was clear that despite shared assumptions about, for instance, slum-induced social disorganization and the value of residential desegregation, there were significant differences in emphasis, priorities, and timing. Williams argued that he could rescue black housing from the evil slums through rehabilitation within the Black Belt, setting the conditions for eventual racial desegregation. Weaver countered that only successful experiments of inter-racial living outside the ghetto could change blacks' reputation for inducing housing decline and depressing property values.

Williams was more willing to trust that the end of restrictive covenants coupled with the pressure from upwardly mobile black households would hasten residential desegregation. Weaver, on the other hand, counted on federal housing policy to attack residential segregation and promote managed interracial living outside of black enclaves. He believed that black citizens' nondiscriminatory access to all housing markets was the first step to deconstructing the ghetto. Williams's priority was to consolidate blacks' presence on the Mid-South Side and, apparently, use it as a base for subsequent black "incursions" into different sections of the city. Though Weaver recognized that blacks resided in a "desirable location," he had no interest in even short-term racial consolidation, thinking blacks would not be able to get enough improved housing unless the housing market was open to all citizens regardless of racial identity.

The differences between Williams and Weaver were informed, in part, by their different geographical location and commitments. Weaver was in Chicago on a temporary basis. He had left the federal government during the war to head Mayor Edward Kelly's Committee on Race Relations. The American Council of Race Relations, where he worked after the war, though based in Chicago, had a national constituency. Williams, on the other hand, as CUL executive secretary, had a Chicago constituency. Williams felt accountable to black stakeholders in Bronzeville. Weaver was committed to establishing an optimal environment for interracial living, almost at all costs. Because both Williams and Weaver believed in democratizing housing markets along racial lines, they both adhered to tenets of racial democracy. However, different tendencies were present within this ideology: the "defensive" position of protecting and consolidating the black community versus the "offensive" strategy of advocating the dispersal of African Americans throughout the city through slum clearance, redevelopment, and integrated public and private housing.[20]

A Threat or an Opportunity?

Despite his opposition to Sidney Williams's plan, Robert Weaver was not unmindful of the dangers of Negro clearance in the nation's central cities, like Chicago, targeted for reconstruction. He presented his hopes and fears about urban redevelopment policy in his classic study *The Negro Ghetto*, published a year after his exchange with Williams. According to the former federal housing official, urban redevelopment represented a "triple threat" to black housing interests.[21] Federal and municipal officials could use urban redevelopment policy "as a guise" to displace blacks from desirable areas, to break up "established racially democratic neighborhoods," and to reduce blacks' limited living space even further.[22]

Weaver argued that acquiring more living space for black Americans was simply a matter of "justice." If whites displaced blacks in order to get access to redeveloped housing in central cities, then it was only fair, he reasoned, that new areas of outlying housing should be opened to blacks. Weaver criticized the real estate industry and local governments for creating the chief obstacles to blacks gaining more living space. The first obstacle was the lack of vacant land sites for housing developments that accepted black occupancy due to institutionalized residential segregation endorsed by "the better people and business interests." The second obstacle was "the disinclination of private enterprise to build for Negro occupancy." However, Weaver was encouraged that the "discovery of the Negro market" had occurred during World War II with the "earmarking of priorities" for wartime housing construction.[23] Weaver admitted that while there were a "few developers and financial institutions" who would develop housing only for middle-income blacks, "the [real] problem is one of encouraging them to include whites in an area where some or many Negroes will live."[24]

Although the government was capable of initiating and supporting residential segregation, Weaver placed the primary blame for the lack of residential integration at the doorsteps of private capital. He argued that those in the private housing industry were "the most consistent and effective foes of racially democratic housing." If government did not regulate finance capital in regard to the racial occupancy of publicly subsidized redevelopment, Weaver asserted, not only would they block integrated living but they would exclude black occupancy altogether. The result would be that displaced racial minorities would not have access to the new redeveloped housing.[25]

With private capital unwilling to build racially mixed housing developments, Weaver looked for the government to step in. Ideally, he wanted the government to use its aid and authority to establish interracial housing developments. If that was not possible, then he wanted to prevent local governments or private capital from using federal housing aid such as Federal Housing Administration (FHA) mortgage loans or public housing subsidies to create or augment residential segregation. It was inconceivable to Weaver that public subsidies for land acquisition intended to house Americans should be used to exclude any group "solely on the basis of color." He argued that black citizens would get little housing unless government required "private builders and sources of finance to include minorities in programs which receive Federal assistance."[26] These reasonable, if insufficient, standards would be the measure by which black policy elites evaluated the fairness of federal housing policy in the postwar era.

As much as he hoped the federal government would take this bold step, Weaver counted on more indirect factors to achieve integrated housing developments. He contended that the problem of relocation would be the reason the federal government and private capital, against their better wishes, could end up advancing residential integration by pursuing urban redevelopment. Here was the "opportunity" that redevelopment presented. Weaver reasoned that redeveloping the central areas could not be achieved unless relocation housing was first built for those who were going to be displaced. Since there was little vacant land inside the nation's Black Belts, he thought, for good reason, that relocation housing would *have* to be built in outlying vacant sites. If demolition was held up due to problems of relocation, the process of urban redevelopment would slow down significantly, if not stop.

At a minimum, Weaver counted on public and private officials wanting to avoid that possibility by making sure blacks were adequately rehoused. He also relied on the idea that federal and municipal officials wanted to avoid racial conflict caused by unmanaged black displacement by building relocation housing in "desirable areas" located nearby and on outlying vacant sites. Weaver warned city planners and private developers alike that unless urban redevelopment policy abandoned residential segregation, it would be "delayed and ultimately defeated."[27] These expectations allowed Weaver, and the black policy community he spoke for, to take a calculated risk in supporting slum clearance, seeing it as an indirect means to residential desegregation, and in turn, improved housing for blacks.

In Weaver's conception, all blacks could benefit from the process of displacement and resettlement. In order for that to happen, he had to confront two problems: income restrictions and density. Although he argued that those who lived in the area, mainly blacks, should have the ability to resettle into new housing, he realized that income restrictions would eliminate those who either made too much for public housing or made too little for redeveloped housing. Moreover, if one goal of redevelopment was to reduce density, something Weaver thought Williams had neglected, then it had to be accepted that not *every* former resident could be rehoused in the same area. Of course, this is why there had to be an outlet. If relocation housing outside the ghetto was built first, then it was possible that some blacks would want to stay in the new location rather than go back to their former, now improved, neighborhoods. According to Weaver, such a relocation plan would make redevelopment racially equitable. He foresaw that African Americans of all classes would benefit from redevelopment. Ideally, low-income citizens would get access to public housing, moderate-income people could move into relocation housing inside and outside the Black Belt, and upper-income folks could move into the new redeveloped housing designed for affluent renters. This scenario would not only reduce densities in the Black Belt, but Weaver thought it would also present the best conditions for "interracial living."[28]

Weaver outlined the optimal conditions needed for the success of the interracial living experiment. It had to be in an area where whites would not fear that the appearance of a few blacks meant an imminent black "invasion." Implicit in Weaver's plan was a limit on black occupancy in any particular development to avoid surpassing whites' "tipping point." He explained that any new housing development had to be large enough to create its own neighborhood, with its own patterns of interracial living and interaction in order to protect it from outside influences. He believed that the existence of multiple integrated developments would divert black housing needs else-where and avoid black pent-up demand overwhelming any particular white neighborhood.

Once blacks were adequately housed in new integrated housing develop-ments throughout the city, the central areas could be redeveloped, attracting whites with modern facilities and proximity to downtown employment and cultural activities. Weaver foresaw the simultaneous movement of black fam-ilies joining whites in new outside areas and of white families joining blacks in the redeveloped inner-city sites. While he knew that residential segrega-tion had been "institutionalized" in many cities including Chicago, Weaver pointed out that more integrated neighborhoods existed than planners and builders usually acknowledged. He was convinced that "racially democratic" or interracial living was possible in redeveloped central areas as well as out-lying neighborhoods of the city.[29]

Weaver articulated the black policy elite stance toward urban redevel-opment. Though he did not discount the fear of Negro clearance, he had a well-articulated plan to use the relocation process to organically integrate African Americans into new and existing housing throughout metropolitan areas. He accepted class-stratified housing as a given and saw nothing wrong with affluent blacks getting access to the redeveloped upscale housing since other black strata would be accommodated in suitable housing both inside and outside the inner city.

Chicago Redevelopment and the Problem of Relocation

Chicago's Redevelopment Plan

Chicago's redevelopment plan was the brainchild of business elites—real estate developers, bankers, downtown property owners—who were part of a progrowth coalition that included planners, architects, hospital and uni-versity administrators, public administrators, and elected officials.[30] The plan was conceived to tackle the problem of decentralization caused by commer-cial blight and encroaching slums. The coalition favored a modern, clean, orderly environment over what they perceived as the chaotic disorder of the slums. Civic reformers believed that private enterprise should take the lead on the city's redevelopment program, including building homes for those who could afford the price they set in order to make profits, while govern-ment provided housing for those who could not meet that price.

Government's role went beyond just providing public housing, however. In order for Chicago's inner city to be rebuilt, government must make it "easy and attractive for private capital to provide the necessary housing."[31] One private planner commented that it was "unrealistic and unfair" to expect housing investors to shoulder "the whole burden of slum clearance."[32] The federal government had to acquire and clear "blighted" inner-city land for private capital in order for central city rebuilding to be successful.[33] In particular, to combat the high cost of central-city land, the government would pay or "write-down" the difference between the land's assessed value and its current market value. Earlier efforts at redevelopment had been hampered by an inability to acquire enough contiguous properties to redevelop a large site. Chicago's downtown elites addressed this problem by inserting in subsequent legislation a mandate for the State Housing Board to assign eminent domain powers to a private corporation if the latter had already acquired 61 percent of the land on the designated site. Private capital needed government authority in order to take land from private owners, and government aid was crucial for reselling this land to a private development corporation at a significant discount.[34]

Plans for redeveloping the Mid-South Side began during World War II. In 1942, the Chicago Plan Commission had determined that Chicago had twenty-three square miles of blighted and near-blighted land that would need demolition and rebuilding.[35] After the war, the Metropolitan Housing and Planning Council (MHPC), which advocated a regional approach to planning and housing informed by downtown capital's prerogatives, took the lead in postwar planning.[36] In 1947, the MHPC joined with five other civic organizations, private institutions, and public agencies to form a public–private partnership that created a plan for the rebuilding of Mid-South Side neighborhoods.[37] The area designated for clearance and redevelopment was three square miles between Twenty-Second and Thirty-Ninth Streets, the Pennsylvania Railroad, and Lake Michigan.

Most of the homes in the area had been built in the late nineteenth century, which contributed to the fact that one in three was substandard, either unfit for habitation or needing major repairs. Many formerly large and opulent homes had been divided into kitchenettes with shared toilets and baths. The northern sections of the area had suffered from the encroachment of commercial and industrial enterprises. Due to heavy traffic, the area suffered from noise, dirt, and traffic hazards.[38] Chicago's elites saw "poverty, disorder, dirt and human misery of what was once the city's finest residential areas—now degenerated to a slum." The partnership's proposal claimed that within the seven-square-mile district "between 12th Street and 47th Street, lies the largest contiguous slum area in any American city."[39]

The designated site had a number of advantages including a desirable location near downtown and the lake; public transportation; and private and public institutions such as universities, hospitals, and the Ida B. Wells public housing project, all of which, the proposal claimed, acted as "stabilizing elements." The partnership determined that the "best use" of Near South Side land was for "residential purposes." They accepted the "densities" as "logical for this area." High-rise buildings were necessary in order to maximize open and recreational space. This kind of "site planning" as well as building design would facilitate "the light, air, and sense of freedom usually available only in suburban districts," they reasoned. They expected that private capital would be attracted to building new commercial properties as well as residential buildings if the government assisted with land acquisition.[40] The partnership argued that the huge public expenditures that redevelopment entailed would be offset by "increased tax revenue" from the new private investment.[41]

Throughout the 1947 proposal, it was clear that the new residential structures were meant to attract "Loop workers." The argument was presented that both white and black people working and living in adjacent districts south, west, and north of the Loop would "find the location advantageous." The coalition planned to house single or childless downtown workers in the high-rise apartment buildings, while providing two- or three-story walk-up houses and apartments to accommodate families with children. It sought to cut down on through traffic by rerouting thoroughfares around the planned developments. The report expressed confidence that downtown workers and nearby high-income families would fill the thirty thousand planned dwellings.[42] According to this plan, the residential area would not be exclusively affluent. The proposal argued that the area was "superior . . . to outlying districts as a location for low-rent projects." However, the coalition assured real estate capital that this subsidized housing would not compete with their private projects nor would it be concentrated in any specific area.[43] This report served as the basis for the subsequent New York Life project, later called Lake Meadows, in what would be designated Redevelopment Project Area No. 1.[44]

The proposal was incorporated in the report developed by the Mayor Kennelly–appointed Chicago Committee for Housing Action, which presented it to the mayor on July 11, 1947; it was adopted subsequently by the city council. The appointment of the Office of the Housing and Redevelopment

Coordinator and the Land Clearance Commission followed shortly after the committee presented its findings. The city's electorate passed two city bond issues in November 1947. Now municipal funds matched state funds authorized by the Illinois Redevelopment and Relocation Act of 1947. Including the CHA's federal money brought the total to an estimated $50 million.

It was hoped that this money would attract $125 million in private investment in redevelopment. The public funds were used to underwrite land assembly and write-off and to construct relocation housing.[45] The nine sites for 2,000 units of relocation housing were approved by the city council on August 27, 1948, combined with the 800-unit Dearborn Homes project. This vote was controversial because it selected mainly slum sites and very few vacant land sites, risking substantial delays in the rebuilding program as well as opposition from prominent black policy elites.[46] Eventually, a $2.5 million subsidy was given to the New York Life Insurance Co. to build a 1,800-unit private development between Thirty-First and Thirty-Third Streets, and South Parkway to the lake. New York Life offered $500,000 for constructing the project, but the cost to the taxpayers for demolition and land acquisition would be $3 million.[47]

The Problem of Black Relocation

The public-private partnership was aware that in 1940 approximately 66 percent of the site's 85,000 people had been African American and that the proportion of blacks had increased to 85 percent after wartime employment attracted them to migrate from the South. The majority of black people were low-income unskilled or semiskilled industrial workers, domestic servants, Pullman porters, or dining car stewards. The proposal recognized that restrictive covenants placed tight restrictions on land space available to blacks, whose housing needs had swelled during the war. As a result, black-occupied buildings were always overcrowded. While it was generally acknowledged that the deterioration of the buildings preceded blacks' arrival to this area, the 1947 proposal contended that blacks had contributed to the area's decline.

The public–private actors acknowledged that subsidized housing had to be constructed before area families could be relocated. They reasoned that the need to clear occupied buildings in combination with the housing shortage meant that relocation would necessitate "a planned, concerted attack." The partnership explained that where to rehouse displaced residents was "a matter of primary concern" for everyone committed to redevelopment. They calculated that 11,000 families that could not afford the new housing and that were ineligible for public housing needed to be rehoused. The MHPC-led partnership claimed that current developing projects in metropolitan Chicago could accommodate the housing needs of the different income groups that needed to be relocated. They thought, somewhat optimistically, that after this natural dispersal only 5,000 families would need relocation housing.

These policy elites were sure that planning "a definite re-housing program" would reduce the hardship that land clearance would create for current families and institutions. The partnership emphasized that slum clearance could not proceed until all displaced families were rehoused, adding that urban redevelopment was "frequently deadlocked by the inability of families living on sites to move away."[48] Due to the disproportionate number of "low-income families" in the black community, one urban planner argued, special consideration should be given to their housing needs since they had the potential to upset large-scale redevelopment plans.[49] Another planner concluded that it was not possible to relocate so many low-income families "in a humane fashion without public intervention."[50] Just as Robert Weaver had predicted, white business and civic leaders wanted to avoid unleashing "slum dwellers" on unsuspecting white communities through demolition and displacement. Accordingly, they endorsed the idea of building relocation housing on vacant land sites before beginning demolition. Though there was no mention of whether new housing developments would be integrated, it was reasonable for Robert Weaver and other black policy elites to see that the MHPC-led partnership was in agreement with them over building relocation housing to accommodate all black income groups.

Elizabeth Wood, CHA executive secretary, anticipated the political problems of displacing blacks from the redevelopment area. Moreover, she feared black middle-class stakeholders more than low-income citizens. She predicted the black middle-class opposition that the city's slum clearance program would face in a few years. The slums, she reminded her colleagues, contained enduring "sentimental ties to church or institutions" by ethnic and racial groups. She warned that such a population could not be displaced "without paying high costs, and without the kind of resentment and opposition which expresses itself in a long drawn-out haggling over prices, organized resistance (and even vandalism), nuisance suits brought against the developer, and obstacles put up by various pressure groups—all calculated to delay or block the process." Wood added that "home ownership ties" also solidified the residents' identification with and investment in the neighborhood.[51]

Given the delicate political situation, Wood made suggestions regarding the kinds of arguments that should be made to persuade black and other citizens that slum clearance and redevelopment was in their interest. She advised her colleagues to avoid evoking rationales such as "restoring purchasing power to the central business districts" or increasing municipal income as the stated purposes of redevelopment. Instead, they were to emphasize that redevelopment meant rebuilding attractive residential neighborhoods that compared favorably to suburbs.[52] Wood pointed out that the slum clearance program should include "building both public and private low and moderate rental housing on vacant land—in the outskirts of a town if this is necessary." Redevelopment officials were responsible for rehousing displaced families, preferably on peripheral vacant sites, and the costs should be included in the total cost of the program. A private planner agreed with Wood that relocation should be a public responsibility. However, he was leery about "professional do-gooders" who wanted to use redevelopment as a tool to dismantle residential segregation. Many white elites feared that this "racial policy" could jeopardize successful redevelopment in Chicago.[53]

Black Factions and Negro Clearance

The widespread fear of Negro clearance in Bronzeville translated into a persistent but ineffective opposition to the city's slum clearance and redevelopment plans. The worst fears of the city's progrowth elite, as predicted by Elizabeth Wood, were realized in 1947. While the opposition, which consisted of black politicians, ministers, and business and property owners, did not really endanger the program, it did delay the process and threatened to taint the city's housing program as racially biased. In national black policy circles based in New York and Washington, D.C., this *black* opposition was characterized as parochial, self-interested, and self-defeating. These national black elites, though aware of imminent black displacement, considered the city's redevelopment program to be a viable medium for African Americans to receive more land and better housing through residential desegregation. Their argument was best characterized by Robert Weaver's opinion that urban redevelopment, despite the perceived "threat" it posed, would represent an "opportunity" for realizing their goal of racial integration.

The city's black civic leadership, typified by Sidney Williams, was caught in the middle. While they subscribed to the same values of residential integration as their national counterparts, the fact that their black middle-class social base was threatened, coupled with their distrust of city officials, led to their request for "assurances" of adequate compensation and comparable or improved housing for displaced blacks *before* supporting the city's program. Though black civic elites often competed with black politicians for leadership of the black community, they, like their adversaries, had "vested interests" that led them, in this instance, to "defend the ghetto" or at least not lend consistent public support to the city's redevelopment plan.

Chicago's redevelopment and slum clearance program generated a political conflict among African Americans between those who wanted to "defend" as opposed to those who wanted to "break up" the black ghetto. Both positions were race based; the debate was largely between black elite factions. Class interests were derivative of their competing "racial ends."[54] In the slum clearance debate, the class element was represented by the fact that the majority of blacks who would be displaced were wage earners and renters who could not afford the redeveloped housing.[55] When the NUL and Weaver analyzed postwar plans for urban redevelopment, they spoke explicitly about the threat to blacks who could not afford to occupy the new housing. Conceding that lower-income blacks would not be able to resettle in the redeveloped housing, both advocated instead for adequate relocation housing.

Among the groups opposed to slum clearance, only the neighborhood group known as the Champions consistently spoke on behalf of the working-class black tenants, though they failed to organize them. The absence of an organized working-class black opposition allowed the debate to remain between competing racial versions of housing improvement. Ultimately, the "ghetto defense" position emerged triumphant as the only legitimate black position, eclipsing the position held by black policy elites. In either case, a primary racial analysis was unable to account for differential benefits and costs experienced by different black strata on the Mid-South Side. In particular, each racial position either ignored or accepted that the redeveloped housing would be for upper-income blacks.[56] An example of this partial response was the failed Carey Ordinance calling for nondiscriminatory access to publicly aided housing.[57] Although such a measure was necessary to combat racial discrimination, even if it had been approved, it would not have protected the majority of wage-earning blacks who were economically ineligible for the new housing. In a sense, for black elite factions, race became a proxy for class since most blacks were working class. The problem with this approach is that it cannot account for class injuries within the race.

Protesting Negro Clearance

The first hint of black resistance to black residential dispersion surfaced after Mayor Edward Kelly asserted the right of all Chicagoans to live where they could afford in the city, in reaction to the racial violence directed at black veterans in Airport Homes in 1946. Kelly's statement endorsed open occupancy, which earned him whites' enmity and most blacks' admiration. At the time, however, there were "rumors" that "certain Negro 'advisers'" to Mayor Kelly had "cautioned him that Negroes themselves were not anxious to go as far as he had gone with his declaration."[58]

The next indication of growing black opposition came during a public hearing in April 1947 on the city's bond issues to finance the "proposed Chicago housing program" and had a chilling effect on black civic elites' potential support. Despite endorsements by black leadership that appeared in the *Chicago Defender* and the local edition of the *Pittsburgh Courier* supporting the bond issues, representatives from the black civic community gave the city's program of slum clearance and urban redevelopment only lukewarm support. The general position, however, as expressed in a *Chicago Defender* editorial, was to accept the program while vigilantly monitoring its implementation.

Despite this formal support from black civic leadership, one observer detected "rumblings of strong dissatisfaction" among their ranks. Much to Robert Weaver's dismay, some unnamed black leaders attempted to have included in the state redevelopment legislation a provision that would restrict displaced blacks to housing on or near the redevelopment site. Before the vote on the state redevelopment program, fliers were distributed at the 1947 hearing exhorting black property owners to "Reclaim Our Old Time Chicago South Side! Protect Your Rights! Don't Be Fooled, Bluffed or Cheated Out of Your Community by Housing and Slum Clearance Propaganda! Household, Home and Property Owners Meeting." An observer reported that several black women at that meeting shouted "This is not slum clearance. It's Negro Clearance."[59] Such rhetoric was typical of the Champions, a neighborhood group led by black women that spearheaded opposition to the city's redevelopment plan in 1948 and 1949.[60] There was widespread sentiment that "a well-kept Negro area where the bulk of the property [was] resident owned, its taxes paid, and its maintenance above par" was targeted for demolition while real slum areas were being spared.[61]

As the date for the city council's hearings on the relocation sites in August 1948 approached, protest activity accelerated. Claiming to represent the "voice of the common people," more than 1,800 people gathered at Pilgrim Baptist Church in late February to protest city officials' plans to displace "residents of habitable houses."[62] The Champions were part of a meeting in late July 1948 "to protest slum clearance" in general and the "New York Life project specifically." The reasons cited for opposition included that "good housing" would be torn down through wholesale demolition; that rents for the redeveloped housing would be out of reach for many of the current black inhabitants; and that all blacks would be displaced.[63] The leaders in attendance included Oscar Brown Sr., head of the Negro Chamber of Commerce; Congressman William Dawson; Alderman William Harvey; State Representative Corneal Davis; and Alice Browning, head of the Champions.[64]

In early August, one hundred black property owners and business, civic, and religious representatives invaded Mayor Kennelly's office to protest the New York Life plan. This group was followed by a second delegation of fifty who marched into the mayor's office with the same message. In that delegation was a representative of the Park Lake Council of Neighborhood Clubs' planning committee, which the preceding March had submitted to Mayor Kennelly their "business-like plans for redevelopment of blighted parts of the neighborhood, incorporating parcels now vacant." The Park Lake Council's goal was to preserve "Negro property ownership in their neighborhoods." As part of the protesting delegation, the organization, while waiting to hear the mayor's response to their plans, pleaded "that they be allowed to say something about the future of their homes and property."[65] The council joined with the Champions to oppose the relocation of displaced families to outlying sites. They wanted relocation housing to be built in the same or nearby neighborhoods.[66] This stand revealed a clear conflict between those who wanted the majority of blacks to return to their neighborhoods and black policy elites who wanted a less dense and more integrated neighborhood after redevelopment.

As evidence of the effectiveness of the "ghetto defense" faction in determining the black position, the main advocate for building relocation housing on vacant land at the city council public hearing on August 23, 1948 was the white head of the Chicago Council against Racial and Religious

Discrimination. He proposed releasing new space for blacks who could live in "open or non-racial occupancy patterns." The city council rejected this position and forced the CHA to submit sites primarily located in the ghetto. One black federal housing official was appalled that the Urban League and Alderman Archibald Carey "constituted the sole Negro opposition to ghetto preservation and extension." He commented on the "conspicuous absence" of any black civic organizations other than the Urban League, an absence that contrasted with the support of the city's program a year earlier and suggested their opposition to slum clearance.[67] He reported that spokespersons for the Vigilantes, a little-known neighborhood group, and the Park Lake Council testified in support of "maintenance of community lines." This keen observer was surprised by the political strength of the "property elements" in an "economically depressed Negro slum area" and by the difficulty of breaking the internal support for the ghetto.[68]

Alice C. Browning and the Champions

The most visible black opponent of the city's redevelopment plan was a short-lived group called the Champions led by Alice C. Browning, a resident of the neighborhood who founded and edited *Negro Story*, the nation's first black short-story magazine.[69] Middle-class black women, offering a decided contrast to the mostly male-dominated black-run civic agencies engaged with housing policy locally and nationally, constituted the neighborhood group.[70] "Consultants and Advisors" to the protest organization included Ira Latimer, white head of the Chicago Civil Liberties Union, and five black ministers including Rev. J. C. Austin, pastor of the Pilgrim Baptist Church. The Champions served as a public face for many of the black groups that had a stake in racial consolidation but could not afford to fight in public. The neighborhood group admitted that they had a number of "silent partners" who were "big leaders" but whose jobs did not permit them to fight openly.

The Champions made an effort to distinguish between individual black elites and their affiliations with the "housing people." For instance, the organization claimed that it was not "personally" fighting Irene McCoy Gaines, head of the Chicago Council of Negro Organizations and a member of the South Side Planning Board (SSPB) who supported redevelopment, but rather "fighting the forces Mrs. Gaines and others happen to be representing."[71] However, the Champions were not entirely happy with being the public face for an amorphous black opposition. They complained that many unnamed black leaders were "afraid to fight for their race openly." The neighborhood group singled out black businessmen who "should reclaim the South Side now." The Champions' efforts to both recruit other vested groups as well as spare some "big leaders" direct criticism showed their commitment to racial unity even in the face of black divisions.[72]

The Champions mainly interpreted the threat of slum clearance in racial terms. Their message was largely directed to black property owners in the neighborhood, whom they implored not to sell their "valuable South Side property," adding that if they have to sell, "sell to another Negro." Their message was clear: "Hold the South Side for Negroes." The Champions' interest in preserving the neighborhood as a black stronghold was unmistakable, yet the organization did not contest the "integrationist" goals of the black policy elites who supported Chicago's redevelopment program. Pointedly, the organization, agreeing with Robert Weaver and Sidney Williams, stressed the need to have "integration both ways—out and in."[73] They said new homes should be built "for everyone on the vacant lands," finally declaring, "we want to be Loop workers too."[74]

While the Champions embraced residential desegregation, they were skeptical that the city shared the same goal after the city council's refusal to endorse vacant sites for relocation housing. Since they were not Loop workers, it was difficult for them to see how they could have access to the redeveloped housing.[75] They criticized the SSPB, wondering if "housing folk" would keep their promise to adequately compensate and rehouse people. They also targeted the Southside Housing Action Conference, which they considered a "tool" of SSPB.[76] In language reminiscent of Sidney Williams a year earlier, the Champions exclaimed, "Wake up Negro America!!!! Do you want to find yourself *moved off the Southside* without even knowing what is happening?" They explained that the SSPB planned to reclaim Thirty-First to Forty-Seventh Streets for Loop workers and warned that neighborhoods between Forty-Seventh and Sixty-Seventh Streets would be next. They lamented being pushed farther west and south, "away from the cool lake breezes and the best part of the city." The Champions commented that black homeowners had invested their lifetime earnings in their properties, and since the city was unlikely to compensate them fairly, they would not be able to afford the cost of replacing these properties. They encouraged their members "to fight for [their] rights, intelligently."[77]

In addition to protest, the Champions attempted to organize black property owners to defend their homes against the city's onslaught. They advocated the redesignation of their neighborhood not as a slum, but as a "conservation" area, which would avoid the approach of wholesale clearance and rebuilding, substituting in its stead the rehabilitation of their good housing stock. They asked the city pointedly, "Will the Negro property owners be allowed to retain and improve their houses?" They reminded their supporters to "Hold on to your property!"[78]

The neighborhood organization had very specific advice for black property owners. They instructed them to refuse to sell and not to let themselves be "bluffed" into selling their land; to get the block organized and work with adjacent organized blocks for "greater protection"; to be prepared to go to court for a "fair price" if property owners did decide to sell; and finally, not to allow their "above-standard housing be condemned as slums." They asked for donations of $100 each for potential legal fees. In addition, they implored black property owners to realize their political strength, send telegrams of protest to the mayor and city council, and send committees to lobby their city council and state representatives.[79]

The Champions attempted to organize residents to attend meetings on slum clearance. The group advised them to consider the motives of the speakers, and to question their facts. Residents were instructed to ask whether the speaker owned property on the South Side or was "thinking of the Negro first." They were to consider whether the program supporter was "paid to propagandize" and to check the statistics supporting arguments in favor of land clearance. They went as far as to instruct their members to break up meetings whose purpose was to propagandize. The Champions assured their supporters and detractors alike that "we all want better housing and a *beautiful community*, but we want to know definitively what will happen to the Negro *before* it is started."[80] This statement illustrates that the Champions did not contest the assumptions that supported urban redevelopment. What they wanted were guarantees that blacks would not end up bearing all the costs and gaining none of the benefits of the proposed reconstruction of the central city.

While the Champions were most attuned to the racial implications of the redevelopment program, they also realized that most blacks could be excluded for class reasons. As a grassroots organization claiming to represent the "masses," the Champions saw themselves as speaking not only for property owners but also for neighborhood tenants. They accurately analyzed the class implications of redevelopment policy, dismissing assurances that there would be no restrictive covenants. They pointed out that "high rents" would exclude the black masses and asked how much public housing would be included in the designated site. The members of the organization also wondered whether black tenants would receive priority to return to the "reclaimed district." They surmised that displacement would create "a worse congested ghetto in Woodlawn and other districts."[81] An observer at the March 1949 hearings on the New York project reported that Alice Browning had argued that homeowners' concerns were not the most important and that it was "poor tenants who should be considered." She claimed that no more than 2 percent of the population could afford to live in the New York Life project.[82]

While the Champions attempted to represent both homeowners and tenants, tension developed between the interests of the two groups. This became clear when the organization told homeowners to ignore "recent newcomers" who supported the city's housing program. The organization, asking what these newcomers had to lose, dismissed them as not being "tenants of long-standing" and argued that their jobs were dependent on their support for slum clearance.[83] In addition, on at least one occasion, people attending their meetings criticized the dominance of property owners in the organization. The officers of the Champions interpreted these actions as an attempt "to separate tenants and property owners." Despite these fissures, the organization sought interclass racial unity and saw its role as representing the "masses" against the "housing people."

The Champions and the Chicago Urban League

Black women's prominence in neighborhood opposition reflected the organizational work of the women's club movement as well as the neighborhood block associations organized by and affiliated with the CUL. The Champions encouraged support for the Urban League's block clubs as a means to conserve and protect property in order to prevent slum conditions. In these efforts, they praised Frayser T. Lane and Lovelyn Evans and singled out the Joanna Snowden Council of block associations located between Thirty-Ninth and Forty-Third Streets and South Parkway to Cottage Grove Avenues, a neighborhood just south of the designated redevelopment area.[84] The fact that these block associations represented part of the Urban League's social base helps to explain the league's defense of black property ownership in the land-clearance fight. Both the league and the Champions encouraged South Side residents to participate in the Block Beautiful Campaign. The Champions also attended a meeting on slum clearance at Sidney Williams's office, which included other slum clearance opponents such as Alderman William Harvey, and representatives from the Park-Lake Council and Property Conservation Commission as well as the CUL board's housing committee members William Hill and Dr. Arthur Falls.[85]

The Snowdenville Community Council, which had folded opposition to slum clearance into the Block Beautiful Campaign, requested that Lane speak to the Champions. Their relationship to the CUL's block-club program afforded Frayser Lane the opportunity to pose an alternative to their protest tactics in the struggle against slum clearance. While opposed to slum clearance, Lane offered a black-run redevelopment alternative to the city's efforts. He was contemptuous of the Champions' protest style and suspicious of their racialist rhetoric. Lane admonished that "appeals based on prejudice" would not be productive. He argued that "prayers and petitions" were not going to stop the "big money" behind the slum clearance and redevelopment program.[86] If people wanted to retain the Mid-South Side, then an organization needed to raise sufficient funds to hire a lawyer and technical advisers in order to purchase enough property to control thirty-two acres. He assured the Champions that if the organization met these conditions, it could negotiate a sizable loan for redevelopment of the area that would be consistent with the plans of the Chicago Plan Commission. In addition, Lane encouraged them to start a vigorous conservation campaign in nonslum areas. He advised that neighborhood residents could collectively "control their environment" by owning and controlling the land and the buildings in their neighborhoods. As far as Lane was concerned, this was a logical next step for Urban League block clubs.

With neighborhood residents' scarcity of capital in mind, Lane mentioned that "mutual ownership of large properties is possible and profitable." He argued that this approach "should be used to rebuild the slums by the people who need Housing most." He knew that there were "strenuous objections" to resettling blacks on vacant lands near whites. He concluded that since low-income blacks could not leave the slums, affordable housing should be built on vacant land within slums.[87] Lane countered the Champions' militant protest with a scheme that sought to put control of redevelopment in black residents' hands. His advice was to counter "big money" with a consolidation of property through private or "mutual ownership" by black residents. He felt it was inevitable that the neighborhood would be demolished and rebuilt; however, if blacks would act proactively, he advised, they could control the terms of the redevelopment. Despite his criticism of the Champions' racialism, Lane's plan to place redevelopment in black hands was no less racial.

Black Factions Opposing Slum Clearance

While the Champions were the most visible black opponent of slum clearance, other black opponents included institutional elites as well as property owners. Each group had a vested interest in maintaining a monopoly on black consumers, voters, renters, and congregants. These black strata emerged after the Great Migration, only to be augmented by a second wartime migration into a burgeoning segregated metropolis. Their livelihoods depended on the votes and money of the black men and women who labored in the stockyards, steel mills, and white people's homes.[88] They feared white capital would restrict their opportunities by retaking "the best market centers and the choice residential areas on the Central South Side." While the local black press was perhaps less dependent on geographic consolidation, it, nonetheless, was "very sensitive to group fears."[89]

Property owners represented the most diverse source of opposition to land clearance. This group included not only large and small property owners but also a smaller number of homeowners.[90] One observer pointed out that most black property owners gained "income" from "rooming houses, multifamily structures, or makeshift kitchenettes."[91] A smaller subset of property owners owned single-family homes or small apartment buildings. This group was the chief constituency of neighborhood groups like the Champions and made up the membership of organized block associations affiliated with the CUL.

While the Champions represented a militant neighborhood group, the Property Conservation Commission represented black property owners who gained income from their properties. William Thornton, an architect and building contractor, was president of the Property Conservation Commission, which was formed to provide legal protection and defense to black property owners threatened by slum clearance. At the New York Life hearings in March 1949, Thornton repeated many of the same themes of losing and protecting property rights articulated by the Champions without expressing that group's concern for black tenants.[92] For instance, Thornton calculated that the market value of targeted properties was between $9 and $10 million but doubted that area homeowners would get "fair market value" for their property.

It appeared that the concerns of black homeowners and their attorneys dominated the black opposition at the hearings. Richard Westbrooks, attorney for the Park-Lake Council of black homeowners, challenged the redevelopment statute's definition of a "blighted area." He argued that area homeowners paid their taxes, kept up their homes, and were "not responsible if run-down conditions exist around them." Not without reason, black homeowners placed the blame for poor conditions on "large investors" who had been exploiting the community, and insisted the area would improve once these absentee owners left. They testified that they did not want to live anywhere else because they liked "their homes, friends, neighbors, [and] churches" and enjoyed their "pleasant and convenient location—near beach[es], good transportation, and the loop."[93]

Black Policy Elites and Slum Clearance

So successful was the institutional elite faction in defining opposition to Negro clearance as the *only* legitimate position for the race that few black interest groups in the city advocated for slum clearance.[94] Still, a few black civic leaders identified with the supporters of land clearance. Perhaps the most visible was Truman Gibson Jr. of the Chicago Land Clearance Commission, who spearheaded the clearance and redevelopment effort. In addition, four black-owned insurance companies in the city planned to construct middle-class housing within the site adjacent to the Lake Meadows apartment complex.[95] In addition, a number of black civic elites sat on the South Side Planning Board (SSPB).[96] Organized in 1946, this organization represented progrowth interests in Chicago.[97] Black civic elites who joined or worked for the SSPB agreed with their white counterparts on the need to clear the slums; they saw themselves as protecting blacks' housing interests, however defined.[98]

Since black civic elites were largely invisible or unreliable in Chicago, black policy elites stepped into the breach. Black federal housing officials were disappointed that they could not get a major black civic leader to support the redevelopment program. In late spring of 1948, Frank Horne, head of HHFA racial relations service, characterized Sidney Williams's remarks against slum clearance as reflecting "the temper among Negro leadership in Chicago." Horne, who felt that the Urban League could be relied on for "progressive and thoughtful guidance," was disappointed.[99] In contrast, he affirmed the "positive and constructive approach" of the South Side

Housing Action Conference with whom George Nesbitt was cooperating. He remarked that it was "significant" that Nesbitt, a regional federal housing official based in Chicago, had to address "the vested interest of 'ghetto' dwellers" because he could not find any other spokesperson.[100] Nonetheless, Nesbitt chose to emphasize his local ties and spoke as a self-described "Southsider" for the South Side Housing Action Conference in favor of the city's program.[101] Nesbitt, representing black policy circles, was the most prominent black spokesperson against the opposition as he tried to persuade blacks that urban redevelopment would facilitate residential desegregation and improved housing.

Breaking Up the Black Ghetto

George Nesbitt spoke in favor of slum clearance during the spring of 1948 and published a provocative essay in the *Crisis* criticizing black slum clearance opponents a month before the public hearings commenced on the New York Life project in 1949.[102] While Nesbitt recognized the "threat" that slum clearance posed to black housing interests, he chose, following Robert Weaver, to focus on the "opportunity" presented by urban redevelopment to rid black Americans of the dreaded slum conditions and provide them with modern housing. In the vision of the black policy elites, the ghetto needed to be broken up, and it would take urban planning and government intervention using public housing and publicly aided redevelopment to promote residential integration. Because the Chicago program was authorized by state legislation in 1947, two years in advance of national legislation, it became an important test case to see if redevelopment policy would fulfill their version of racial democracy. They did not want black opposition to render the program stillborn and thwart a potential opportunity for housing improvement in favor of leaving the ghetto intact.

Nesbitt and fellow black federal housing official William Hill explained the "vested interests" of what they called the "ghetto defense" faction. They explained black business owners' and professionals' opposition to redevelopment as reflecting their fear of economic competition. Nesbitt and Hill welcomed this competition, arguing that black consumers would benefit by receiving "a better product, at a lower price, in a cleaner establishment, and with more courteous, efficient service." Nesbitt addressed concerns about the loss of black political strength through residential dispersion, arguing that black votes beyond a simple majority to elect black representatives were wasted. In an analysis that anticipated future criticism of minority–majority legislative districts, Nesbitt explained that it would be better to redistribute "surplus" black votes to those "districts whose elected officials now have no direct responsibility to Negro voters whatsoever." Hill criticized the local black press for being "passive and neutral with regard to these programs."[103]

Both black housing experts, however, were most sympathetic to the plight of black homeowners. They pointed out that "these residences, hard-won and purchased at excessive prices, have an almost irreplaceable value to their owners—who are not free to repurchase elsewhere." Because of their special circumstance, Nesbitt argued that these homeowners not only should be fairly compensated for their demolished structures but also should be in a position to sponsor rebuilding projects when practicable. If their properties were in sound condition, perhaps they could be saved and included in the redevelopment project.[104]

While they were mostly concerned with the organized opposition, they realized that the apparent support given by the large mass of blacks made it difficult to contest the institutional elite faction. Nesbitt described this group as "a large but loose element [that] provides an indirect but effective support in defense of an intact black ghetto."[105] He identified this "element" as the "lower-income and tenant masses" that had joined in opposition with those who had a stake in maintaining black concentration. Hill pointed out that these folks were "acutely aware" that their housing needs would not be accommodated by any planned housing. While they were encouraged by the building of low-rent public housing, many were ineligible because of their incomes or the composition of their households. Hill argued that what tied the tenant masses to the property owners was "an over-weaning fear" that land space for homes, churches, businesses, schools, and parks would "be reduced further and thus compress the already over-crowded sections of their community." Both black property owners and tenants agreed that their land space should be increased, not reduced further.[106]

Nesbitt explained that this sentiment buttressed opposition to urban redevelopment. He insightfully surmised that the "racial differential in opportunity is easily communicated to and gets a sympathetic response from all of the inhabitants of the clearance area," including working-class tenants. Nesbitt explained that "the Negro businessmen, professionals, and property owners having made 'good,' despite racial barriers, symbolized racial advancement." Any threat to their individual success would be considered "anti-racial." He pointed out that political gains from racial concentration were jealously guarded because "civil rights" had been won and defended politically. Working-class tenants were not organized, according to Nesbitt, but their subtle support for "ghettoism" came across "by carefully saying nothing in the midst of the tempest."[107] Nesbitt concluded that "this easy cloaking of selfish interests behind the group objectives of social advancement and political strength effectively buttress the major fear of space loss."[108] Black working-class tenants' quiet support allowed, he contended, "busy women and spellbinding politicians and preachers [to] deride and dismiss the valiant few anti-ghettoists as 'Uncle Toms' and 'tools of the whites.'"[109] Despite these difficulties, Nesbitt, speaking for black national policy elites, argued that the interests of ministers, merchants, politicians, and homeowners "ought not be permitted to stand in the way of progress and public purpose."[110]

Taking this opposition seriously, Nesbitt attempted to allay the historic fears of black Chicagoans about the designs to remove them wholesale from the desirable location of the Central South Side. Nesbitt felt the current fear of Negro clearance was stoked by two factors. One was a "latent counter-racialism" that had been produced by the very existence of a "racially produced, unbroken solidity of a huge, hemmed-in mass of Negroes." The other factor he described as one of natural defense: "The South Siders, then, who fought as Negroes to gain living space, fight back, as Negroes, to hold it."[111] Nesbitt described a defensive racialization of space by African Americans. He argued that these factors were in evidence in early private and public efforts by blacks to derail the slum clearance program.

The debate between black defenders and opponents of Chicago's redevelopment plan represented a contest over which racial position would define black housing policy direction. Nesbitt emphasized that the housing problem affected all blacks. Despite wartime employment gains, Nesbitt acknowledged that blacks did not live in good homes and decent neighborhoods. He argued the housing problem encompassed "all of us, the high and mighty, and the lowest and latest-to-come." He continued that blacks were "hemmed [in] by jim-crow, and *most* of us bogged down in the slums." By emphasizing the racial impact of housing problems, Nesbitt agreed with his opponents.

Nesbitt presciently warned the black middle class that their improved housing in racially transitioned neighborhoods was temporary since the ghetto would reengulf them in a few years if overall patterns of residential segregation were not disrupted. Writing in early 1949, Nesbitt downplayed the role of the recent Supreme Court decision that outlawed the legal enforcement of racially restrictive covenants as a mechanism for residential dispersion. Only "naïve" blacks or "Negrophobic" whites, he offered, would assume that "the walls of the black ghettos" would come "tumbling down" after the decision.[112] He predicted dourly that migration would "heap" another four hundred thousand blacks in the next twenty years "on the man heaps we call 'our neighborhoods.'" Speaking as a "Southsider," Nesbitt said, "our Chicago situation" offered "conclusive proof that racial restrictions prevent sufficient space for decent living by racial minorities." Nesbitt believed the black community's congestion and slum conditions would never be adequately addressed without first confronting residential segregation.[113]

Making the Case for Slum Clearance

Nesbitt tried to convince black Chicagoans they should support the city's slum clearance and redevelopment program. In one approach, he argued unconvincingly that the city recognized that racial restrictions on land space were the main cause of blacks' poor housing conditions.[114] In another approach, Nesbitt reminded black Chicagoans of their de facto support for urban redevelopment through the actions of their leadership and rank and file. He stressed that black representatives had participated in the formulation of the policy throughout the process as members of the Mayor's Action Committee, the city council, the state legislature, and, finally, as voters. Prominent evidence of their support, he argued, was their role in the successful vote for the city's $60 million slum clearance and urban redevelopment program. Nesbitt contended that the issue of black citizens needing more space had been "kept alive" by black participation "every step of the way," and as a result, state legislation prohibited racial restrictions on publicly subsidized land for redevelopment.

However, Nesbitt commented that the 1947 state legislation had almost "contain[ed] a dangerous provision" that would have specified that those displaced be housed on or near the redevelopment site. Nesbitt charged that this aborted provision would have "kept us bottled-up in the Black Belt." He was concerned that, if adopted, this provision would have meant that displaced blacks would not have access to relocation housing outside of the ghetto.[115] At the end of the day, according to Nesbitt, blacks could not realistically say that white government officials and business leaders had imposed this policy on them.[116]

After linking the city's redevelopment program to residential desegregation, the regional housing official attempted to make the case that the initiative would lead to more land and housing for African Americans. Black Chicagoans' housing supply would be expanded by the city's redevelopment program, according to Nesbitt, adding "potentially thousands of units of public low-rent, non-profit corporation or middle-income, and privately developed housing." He argued that housing was being produced mainly for working-class black tenants but also "appreciably" for the middle class. He pointed out that in order to get this new housing, the old, dilapidated structures they currently inhabited would have to be cleared away. In addition, there was no vacant land inside the ghetto for new housing, but there were twenty square miles of open land in white communities that could accommodate some blacks.[117]

Nesbitt did not understand why, after achieving these "concessions," fellow black Chicagoans were not now embracing the program. He lamented, "We who first made the point, have forgotten it." According to Nesbitt, blacks did not want any "part of it" and had mounted "head-on resistance to slum clearance and redevelopment." Perplexed by evidence of public hostility, Nesbitt continued, "We complain of over-crowding but now that some relief is in the offing, [we] begin to shout: 'The South Side is ours! Only ours! We are not leaving.'" He complained scornfully that blacks had deserted their allies in the fight against slums and made "bedfellows with those who keep us, all of us, in our 'precious' slums. *We are confused*," he emphasized. Nesbitt acknowledged that the twenty-year fear of black displacement from the lake might have once had a factual basis, but now it was only a "wild phantasy." The threat was minimal, he argued, since the money for slum clearance would only finance the clearance and development of a small area of the slums on the South Side.[118]

The redevelopment program was novel, according to Nesbitt, and admittedly, some problems might remain, especially around relocation and rehousing of families. Yet, he argued, those who suffered the most from the slums and housing shortage should be the chief defenders of the slum clearance program. He then subtly shifted his argument from blacks' investment in the policy and its potential benefits to the fact that their opposition at this stage was all but moot. He candidly pointed out that since powerful forces such as city officials and private developers were behind its creation, the program was a foregone conclusion. He asked, "Can so much be turned back?" and then answered that it could and should not, "despite our questions and reservations." He contended, tellingly, that the city must rebuild in order to "live," suggesting that he agreed with business elites and housing reformers alike that redevelopment was crucial for the fiscal and social health of central cities.

Nesbitt sidestepped the power question and argued unpersuasively that the urban redevelopment program could still be modified to meet black housing interests; it could still be shaped, he said, by those who were "alert and active. Not those who sit by in fear and idle complaint." He complained that while blacks were protesting, the opportunity to influence the direction of the program was fading, and warned, "If we continue to do nothing but fuss and fume among ourselves, the South Side will lose out, by default!"[119]

Nesbitt believed the program could address African Americans' greatest needs and goals. He declared, "Our greatest need is space and our historic goal has been integration." Nesbitt told Mid-South Side residents, "If we are to have integration, we must accept the movement of other people into the South Side." He then reassured his audience about the ability of the black community to get their elected and appointed representatives to pursue the black community's interest in these "public programs." In addition, he said, "we have savings in our own institutions which should be responsive to our needs," referring to black-owned savings and loans and insurance companies. Nesbitt concluded, "Negroes ought to help usher out the black ghettos in which they suffer and not be beguiled by the few who wax fat on its drippings."[120]

Conclusion

The slum clearance fight was over before it began. Not only was the pro-growth elite who created and implemented Chicago's program of slum clearance and redevelopment more powerful but black opponents wrestled with internal conflicts that weakened their political opposition. While divisions among black political forces and the lack of full commitment from William Dawson to fight the city's plan were factors, a limited ideological framework and inadequate political tools shared by all black factions made it impossible for black opponents to give themselves a fighting chance. Both black opponents and supporters of the city's program agreed with its architects' claims that the slums were a menace to the health and morals of working-class blacks, albeit for slightly different reasons. Though the National Urban League had argued during the war for public ownership of land taken by eminent domain, black elites no longer advocated this after the war. Instead of questioning private control, most blacks on both sides of the slum clearance issue felt that black-led, publicly subsidized, but privately controlled, rehabilitation and redevelopment could lead to improved black housing and neighborhoods (see chapter 6).

In addition to these shared assumptions, the most important obstacle was the racial characterization of the impact of slum clearance—that is, Negro clearance. While there were white voices calling for mass displacement of blacks from the Mid-South Side, official pronouncements dating back to the Chicago Plan Commission in 1942 proposed that affluent blacks would occupy the new housing that would replace the "slum hovels" then in place. This proposal made clear that different classes in the black community would not share the costs and benefits of slum clearance evenly. Black policy elites and middle-class activists were not unaware of this potential intraracial disparity. Most addressed the problem by adopting Frayser Lane's concern that all blacks be rehoused in his redevelopment plan. Few followed the Champions, who consistently advocated for the tenants. Unfortunately, any concern for wage-earning tenants was minimized in their collective racial definition of the assault and its solutions.

For those black elites who opposed "counter-racialism," their trust that a race-neutral market and government policy would serve this group was as ill founded as their gamble that slum clearance would lead to residential integration. Arguably, the racial framework was apt because the overwhelming majority of blacks were tenants; however, its adherents believed that racial access would automatically mean that low-income blacks would be accommodated. The problem with this line of thought is that race-based solutions held differential benefits for different strata within the black community. The class content of "race" is often unspecified in these solutions; therefore accommodating only affluent blacks could constitute *racial* access. Furthermore, it is doubtful that any of the multiple proposals for black-led redevelopment would result in adequate housing for most poor blacks (see chapter 6). Since the core of the black opposition was petit bourgeois property and business owners, the political terrain was largely limited to privatist and legalistic tactics that were likely to fail against the more powerful progrowth elite. Even if the Carey Ordinance had succeeded, wage-earning blacks would have lacked access to Lake Meadows because they could not afford the rent. Though racial unity in the face of the city's onslaught might have been desirable, it was unobtainable given different factional interests, and if obtainable, likely ineffective. Neither race-based nor race-neutral solutions adequately addressed the housing preferences and needs of black working-class tenants.

5

From Negro Clearance to Negro Containment

Black civic elites and neighborhood activists correctly predicted the massive displacement of blacks resulting from slum clearance on the Mid-South Side. The impact of displacement on African Americans, however, was uneven across social classes. While public housing would accommodate some low-income blacks, the majority of blacks earned incomes too high to qualify for public housing and therefore needed the most attention during the implementation of the city's redevelopment program.[1] The black defenders of slum clearance counted on the fact that city officials, wanting to prevent relocation obstacles from slowing down redevelopment, would initiate plans to house displaced blacks in integrated public housing developments near white areas. They also hoped that these same city officials would pressure Federal Housing Administration (FHA) officials to provide mortgage guarantees to private developers who planned to build apartment complexes or single-family homes both outside and inside the ghetto. They were sadly mistaken. They did not count on callous or indifferent Chicago Land Clearance Commission (CLCC) officials being "successful" at relocating displaced blacks within the confines of a racial dual housing market. Soon the defenders of slum clearance—George Nesbitt, Frank Horne, and Robert Weaver—joined the critics in contesting Chicago's slum clearance policy, particularly its failure to adequately relocate African Americans displaced by the city's first redevelopment project.

While the two black political factions debated their respective positions on the city's slum clearance and urban redevelopment program in 1948–49, the pending federal housing legislation promised to add additional resources to the city's program. The nation's slum clearance and urban redevelopment program was authorized by Title I of the Housing Act of 1949.[2] Once the Housing Act had been signed by President Harry S. Truman, Chicago's redevelopment officials immediately sought federal aid for their slum clearance and redevelopment program, authorized by 1947 state legislation, as well as for new public housing units that would mainly serve to rehouse people displaced from the redevelopment site. Because Chicago's slum clearance and urban redevelopment program predated the federal program, black national housing officials could observe the problems with the relocation of the displaced there before the same problems appeared in other localities. For these officials, Chicago was a testing ground for whether a relocation policy could be manipulated for the purpose of integrating the housing market, or whether it would, in fact, usher in a "second ghetto."

Despite ominous signs, black policy analysts clung to the idea that city officials would not undermine their own interests by allowing a failed relocation policy to sabotage their plans to reconstruct the central city. After the city council rejected both the vacant land sites for relocation housing in August 1948 and the Carey Ordinance for nondiscrimination in publicly aided housing seven months later, black local and national elites grew concerned that Chicago's political regime would use federal aid to displace African Americans without compensatory housing and residential space. If these troubling actions were not evidence enough, the city council's adoption of predominantly slum sites for new public housing in August 1950 convinced black policy elites in Chicago and Washington, D.C., that the city wanted its new housing program to achieve "Negro containment."

Soon after this decision, black policy elites realized that African Americans were facing mass displacement and relocation due to simultaneous land-clearance assaults necessitated by redevelopment, public housing, and highway construction programs. While they were always aware that redevelopment policy could be used to initiate or reinforce racial segregation, they overestimated the extent to which the city or federal government would ensure that relocation occur in a racially equitable fashion, let alone promote residential desegregation. They had hoped to convince the head of the Housing and Home Finance Agency (HHFA) to withhold federal approval by rejecting Chicago's application for federal aid on the grounds of a flawed site selection and relocation policy. Other than wishful thinking, the only card they held, in their calculation, was that the Truman administration sought to avoid the poor racial and public relations that could result from appearing to endorse racial segregation while giving symbolic support for civil rights. Even at mid-twentieth century, however, this was a thin reed on which to grab.

In this chapter, I examine the extent to which blacks were displaced by land clearance and the flawed relocation practices of the Chicago Land

Clearance Commission. I explore the protests of black civic elites such as the professionals who worked for the Chicago NAACP as well as those of black policy elites who worked for national civil rights organizations and federal housing agencies. The Chicago NAACP sought redress for those blacks victimized by the haphazard, and in some cases exploitative, relocation process. The national black policy elites sought to pressure municipal and federal housing officials to reverse what they thought was federal endorsement of Chicago's goal of containing African Americans in an expanding ghetto.

Displacement, Relocation, and Land Clearance

Black Displacement

Chicago's South Side became the site for massive displacement of its black residents due to the city's slum clearance and public housing programs. After the 1949 Housing Act, public housing was relegated to rehousing those who had been displaced by the slum clearance and urban redevelopment program. Of course, since public housing was meant, in part, to replace slum housing with modern buildings, it, too, generated its own displacement problems. George Nesbitt, racial relations adviser for the Public Housing Administration (PHA), argued that the Chicago Housing Authority's (CHA) rehousing of its own displacees, coupled with off-site demand for low-rent housing, would "jeopardize its ability" to absorb those displaced from the CLCC projects that would follow the New York Life Insurance redevelopment project. Nesbitt concluded that the city's commitment to relocation housing on former slum sites "may severely affect the future of Title I in Chicago."[3]

The number of displaced black families ineligible for public housing illustrated Nesbitt's concerns. In order to build half of the authorized 21,000 federally subsidized units on city council approved sites, 11,126 families, of which 80 percent, or 9,042, were black, would have to be relocated. Only 30 percent of these families, however, were eligible for public housing. The ineligible families numbered 7,800—6,000 of which were black.[4] The 101-acre redevelopment area was predominantly residential and home to roughly 3,600 black families. Of that number, only 900 families were eligible for public housing; the remaining 2,700 families were not.[5] A survey on the redevelopment site in Chicago found 42 percent of reporting families had annual incomes of more than $2,500, which exceeded the maximum income limit for public housing eligibility. Moreover, 60 percent of the reporting families were either single or childless couples, which also rendered them ineligible for public housing.[6] Robert Weaver estimated that, of the 12,200 black households being displaced by Title I and Title III programs, 8,000 families were not eligible for public housing.[7]

According to the CLCC, those eligible for public housing would be accommodated by a combination of turnover in the current public housing available to blacks (4,560 units); planned state-aided relocation housing (750 units scheduled for completion in 1952); and 10,535 units of federal public housing in the design and land purchase stage. Relocating the 2,700 black families ineligible for public housing from the redevelopment site was more daunting.

As for land clearance for new public housing, a racial relations official, in an evaluation of the "Chicago Relocation Plan" in May 1951, argued that while the CHA had a "feasible method" for housing site displacees eligible for public housing, this was not the case for those whose incomes made them ineligible. This black federal housing official disputed the assumptions and methods used by the economists of the PHA Chicago Field Office. He cited evidence to show that the current Chicago housing market could not absorb those displaced in the clearing of slum sites.[8] A March 1951 CHA report determined that there was a shortage of 292,000 homes in the city, half of which were needed by black Chicagoans. A month earlier, the CHA had reported that 90,000 families lived "doubled-up" while 180,000 families lived in "substandard dwellings which are fully occupied because *there is no place else to live*" (original emphasis).[9]

The Challenges of Black Relocation

Black policy elites contended that Chicago's housing officials faced a variety of factors that would increase the difficulty of relocating black residents from the land clearance sites into affordable and adequate homes. A number of these factors were related to changing demographic, physical, and social conditions in the South Side black community. George Nesbitt, who was based in Chicago as a regional federal housing official until 1950, was an acute observer of the black community. Nesbitt began working for the Public Housing Administration (PHA) in 1942. In 1946, he was race relations advisor for the PHA at the Chicago regional office of the National Housing Agency. Four years later, Nesbitt was reassigned to the national office in the Division of Slum Clearance and Urban Redevelopment.[10] Nesbitt noted the following aspects of the "changing pattern of Negro residence in Chicago" that he thought made relocation more difficult: (1) less vacant land in the black slum areas than before the war, (2) a large increase in black population due to migration, (3) increased socioeconomic differentiation among blacks, and (4) political factors that militated against dismantling residential segregation.

Contributing to the disappearance of vacancies was the continued migration of blacks to Chicago during and after the war. Between 1940 and 1947, almost two million African Americans migrated from the South to the North and West, increasing Chicago's minority population by 35.9 percent. In 1950, Nesbitt estimated that between 120,000 and 140,000 blacks had migrated to Chicago since 1940.[11] Some sources reported that 2,000 black families were arriving per month and suggested that this would "saturate the limited supply of dwellings available to Negroes in Chicago."[12] The slum areas, due to the availability of relatively cheap housing and greater social acceptance, absorbed most of the newcomers.

Nesbitt also noted that although they were still lagging behind whites in the city, blacks made employment and income gains from unionized industrial work during and after the war. Despite these gains, African Americans, regardless of income, remained largely restricted to the slum areas. The many middle-class and few upper-class black families that were now looking for housing had "housing ability and tastes not easily met in the racially restricted market." These families had the income to rent apartments in "better neighborhoods" and savings to own homes like the ones they saw featured in magazines.[13]

All these physical, demographic, and socioeconomic factors were complicated by political concerns. By 1950, the city had proven that it was committed to maintaining residential segregation. Nesbitt claimed that both city and black institutional elites' investment in residential segregation hindered the relocation effort. Earlier black South Siders had been willing to endure land clearance if it meant more public housing. But the prospect of losing one's home or business because the city wanted to build either a commercial project or new housing that was inaccessible due to either income or race meant there was going to be less public support for land clearance. Nesbitt found that the fear of displacement had persisted, especially since no public policy or controls were in place to prevent it.[14]

Nesbitt noted that the increase in black property ownership since 1940 did not bring with it increased housing for blacks. The ownership of multifamily housing where many blacks resided in the ghetto simply shifted from whites to blacks. During the war, blacks did gain additional housing through structural conversion, but this was difficult to come by after the war. Moreover, those conversions represented by kitchenettes and basements, according to Nesbitt, were only a "passing social virtue" soon to "become ghetto vice" after the war. Illegal conversions produced more housing for a desperate black population, but the overcrowding and substandard housing that followed contributed to the slum conditions in Bronzeville.[15]

The difficulties black South Siders faced in finding adequate housing were exacerbated by the lack of housing production and continued housing discrimination in Chicago. In general, the construction of multifamily housing had slowed. In addition, few private housing developments in Chicago were open to blacks. Only the "excavation of the long-delayed Parkway Gardens," a mutual ownership-trust development with 694 apartments located at Sixty-Third and South Parkway, had begun. A few units were also being built in the West Chesterfield area.[16] Two years later in 1952, the CLCC reported that only 35 rental and 35 owner-occupied units of newly constructed housing were available to African Americans.[17]

Nesbitt pointed out that, nationally, blacks relied more on public housing for rehousing than whites, who more readily found private alternatives. In fact, a third of minority families depended on public housing compared to only an eighth of whites. Moreover, of the displaced families moving into public housing, nine out of ten were minorities. However, since land clearance for public housing had exacerbated blacks' displacement, at least in the short term, many of those eligible for public housing could not readily find accommodations. Nesbitt pointed out that it was likely that eligible minority families not absorbed by public housing were "almost certain to be rehoused under conditions of excessive occupancy or in substandard housing or both."[18]

In terms of purchased housing, Nesbitt reported there were more minority families with the income and desire to purchase housing than there were available units. He commented that these families seemed to prefer home ownership to renting, but that most of the opportunity for purchasing housing was in racial transition areas. Nesbitt complained that "the relocation plan for rehousing" over-income blacks targeted these bordering neighborhoods. The unlikelihood that this housing would be adequate for all displaced families was underscored by the fact that these families competed with other black families who sought to upgrade their housing through racial succession after the *Shelley v. Kraemer* decision in 1948.[19]

Racial Transition Neighborhoods

With the lack of new housing construction available to displaced blacks, the main outlet for new housing was in contiguous white neighborhoods, which quickly gave way to the pressure of housing needs emanating from the ghetto. Since 1940, black Chicagoans' increased incomes, ongoing migration, and slum clearance made it possible to expand the black ghetto by annexing contiguous neighborhoods through rapid racial transition. Leading this process were middle-class blacks, who felt "compelled to push out from the ghettos" into white neighborhoods. This increased racial tensions in the transitioning neighborhoods and quickly led to overcrowding and subsequent housing deterioration. Black geographic expansion was so rapid in the early 1950s that black families occupied a previously all-white block every ten days.[20] As a result, in 1950, Nesbitt noted, twelve thousand to fifteen thousand black families had rented apartments or bought and occupied housing in formerly all-white neighborhoods.[21] Two years later, and four years after the 1948 Supreme Court decision declaring restrictive racial covenants unenforceable, that number increased to twenty-one thousand black families.[22]

Though this process of racial transition gained more housing for blacks, especially the middle class, it was fraught with problems. Nesbitt reported that black occupancy only occurred once either blacks or white investors had purchased "Negro properties." He was concerned, however, that the racial transition trends might "crystallize a pattern of Negro upper-income equity investment in makeshift-kitchenettes and pseudo hotels."[23] These multifamily properties, including "rooming house operations," all rented for excessive amounts despite postwar rent controls. Nesbitt complained that, in terms of housing standards in black-occupied rental areas, "anything goes" so long as it benefited the landlord, whether black or white.[24]

Blacks realized that they could gain private housing through the expansion of the ghetto, Nesbitt reported, and they therefore "unhesitantly fought against racial bars against [such] expansion."[25] Nesbitt pointed out that part of Chicago's "distinctiveness," in addition to "the thoroughgoingness of residential segregation," was the predominance of large multifamily buildings among the housing available for occupancy, reflecting the relative absence of "normal single family owner-occupancy, [and] retention of original use and incentive for good maintenance, as Negroes moved into new neighborhoods." These were factors, according to Nesbitt, that put Chicago blacks at a greater disadvantage in rehousing than their counterparts in other cities such as Detroit, St. Louis, and Washington, D.C.[26]

The Chicago Land Clearance Commission admitted that most of the black families displaced by slum clearance were rehoused in "racial transition" areas of owner-occupied and rental housing between 1949 and 1952. During this time, 4,535 units were purchased for prices ranging from $4,999 to more than $17,500. There were 17,218 rental units available with monthly rents between $29.99 and $75.00. For nonwhites, the median value of owner-occupied housing was $9,619 in 1950, and the median rent was $41.05.[27] Nesbitt called the tendency of cities, including Chicago, to rehouse black families in racial transition areas "extremely tenuous" and was contemptuous of the CLCC's plan to take advantage of these areas as "major resources for rehousing displaced Negro families who are ineligible for public housing."[28] By 1956, Nesbitt determined that Chicago had rehoused only 3,802 minority families and had referred 1,230 to private rental units. He concluded that housing minorities in areas of racial transition did not appreciably increase the number of standard rental housing available to them and that displaced families competed with other families for that small number.[29]

Nesbitt opposed rehousing black families in racial transition areas for a number of reasons. First, it was an admission that blacks would mainly or exclusively gain standard housing only through racial succession, not through new construction, especially on outlying vacant land. Second, this de facto policy exposed black citizens to racial harassment and violence. Black citizens forced to look for decent housing were confronted by hostile whites who resisted blacks' entrance into their neighborhoods. Nesbitt even charged the city with cynically tolerating intermittent racial violence and tension in racial transition areas so that it could avoid dealing with the full-blown race riots that might occur if blacks attempted to integrate outlying white neighborhoods. Last, the practice left black home seekers open to exploitation by white and black realtors engaged in "blockbusting," the practice of realtors purchasing whites' homes below market value only to resell them to black home buyers high above the market price for huge profits that would not ordinarily have been earned from the development of interracial housing in outlying neighborhoods.[30]

Black Elites Fight Negro Containment

Black Civic Leaders and the Problem of Displacement

George Nesbitt began his investigation of housing in Chicago, ironically, on the same day, July 24, 1950, that the city council's housing committee voted to approve predominantly slum sites for new public housing.[31] The purpose of Nesbitt's Chicago "field trip" was to report to federal housing officials on the "Negro community attitudes toward urban redevelopment" a year after the public hearing on the New York Life project. Chicago's black civic leadership had been calling periodically for the assistance of black federal housing officials throughout the slum clearance battle.[32] For instance, the Chicago Urban League (CUL) had requested a visit from the HHFA's "racial relations service" because of "disturbing features of both the Title III and Title I programs."[33] The federal housing official met with the city's housing and redevelopment officials; public and civic agencies directors; and a number of black civic and political leaders including Alderman Archibald Carey, Sidney Williams of the CUL, and Nelson Willis, president of the Chicago branch of the NAACP.[34]

During Nesbitt's field trip, black civic leaders shared with him their criticism of the city's housing program, condemnation of the CLCC relocation practices, and persistent fears of displacement. Some black informants severely criticized the city's decision to choose mainly slum sites for black-occupied public housing because it would make redevelopment more costly and "slow-moving" and would create large racial and economic "public housing ghettos."[35] Nesbitt referred to a statement by the Chicago NAACP as representing the "Negro community viewpoint" on this matter. The Chicago NAACP considered the "compromise" site selection a cynical attempt to defeat public housing "while seeming to accept it." In other words, the city council treated the public housing program as if it were "a special favor for Negro wards rather than a necessity for persons of low income regardless of race." The Chicago NAACP concluded that the city's "recommendations attempt to move the Mason-Dixon line to Howard Street."[36]

Nesbitt reported that many people he consulted on the trip expressed concern about relocation due to demolition for both the New York Life project and the construction of public housing on slum sites. The informants were sharply critical of the CLCC relocation practices, charging that black families ineligible for public housing had to resort to living in kitchenettes in Lawndale, on the West Side, and in South Side Oakland-Kenwood, which had adopted a "conservation program" partly to prevent "Negro inundation." Nesbitt's city contacts were concerned that "the haphazard movement of Negro families into areas of increasing Negro residence will help frustrate both the conservation and the anti-inundation aims."[37] The representatives from the Chicago Commission on Human Relations (CCHR) reported to Nesbitt that the CLCC did not consider the relocation of slum residents as their official responsibility but undertook it for "humanitarian" reasons. The CCHR charged that the CLCC sought to place displaced black families only in adjacent black neighborhoods, not in white ones. If their policy contributed to the overcrowding in nearby black neighborhoods, according to the city's race relations agency, the CLCC did not consider this to be their problem.[38]

Nesbitt was dismayed that blacks still characterized the New York Life project as "Negro clearance" even though affluent African Americans would occupy Lake Meadows. He reported that many black property owners were still contesting condemnation and that black ministers were raising funds for litigation challenging the constitutionality of urban redevelopment.[39] Nesbitt was disappointed that the four black-owned insurance companies, which were expected to build middle-class housing on the redevelopment site, were reported to be "disturbingly apathetic" and had shown no interest in developing commercial property.[40]

To characterize black Chicagoans' "mistrust" of urban redevelopment, Nesbitt quoted an editorial in Chicago-based *Ebony* magazine, then the largest black-owned magazine in the country. The editorial charged whites with wanting "integration" only when they stood to benefit, for example, from moving into desirable, former predominantly black areas but blocking blacks' efforts to move into white communities. To blacks, according to the magazine, redevelopment looked more like a land grab by the city than a commitment to improving black housing conditions. If blacks were unable to move into white communities, *Ebony*'s editor asked, what other choice did they have? He advised that blacks should not "surrender a . . . whit" of land but should "push ever outward from the ghetto" against the efforts by politicians and real estate capital to circumscribe their living space even further.[41]

Nesbitt was careful to note that not all black citizens took this uncompromising position. He mentioned that "persons of responsibility" would support redevelopment if it only included "protections against blacks getting worse housing in newly created slum areas." Nesbitt lamented that the city's political regime had repeatedly rejected those protections, causing black Chicagoans to conclude that the city's program was less dependent on "sound housing and city planning" and more a "product of *racial* politics" (original emphasis). The city's racist recalcitrance had soured Nesbitt's earlier cautious optimism in support of urban redevelopment. The negative changes he observed had placed redevelopment squarely in the business of supporting residential segregation, not creating the "opportunities" for interracial living that he and other black policy elites had hoped the policy would advance.[42]

Chicago NAACP and Black Displacement Cases

Six months after Nesbitt's assessment of Chicago's housing situation, the Chicago branch of the NAACP registered complaints with the federal government about the CLCC's record of rehousing black site occupants. In a January 8, 1951, letter, Nelson Willis, president of the Chicago branch, charged the CLCC with mishandling the rehousing of blacks who had been displaced by the site preparation for the New York Life project. Willis knew the city had sought federal aid to supplement the New York Life project's state and municipal funds. He could not believe that the HHFA would consider giving the City of Chicago federal assistance for relocation when the CLCC's "relocation activities are not being conducted according to Federal standards." These principles required that "every displaced family is rehoused in a decent, safe and sanitary home" accessible to a family's workplace and within their income to rent. Willis announced that unfortunately relocation had not been carried out this way in Chicago for families ineligible for public housing. He claimed that displaced black families were "being sent to any kind of housing no matter how bad its location, its condition, or how crowded it is."

Willis further claimed that these families were being pressured to leave their homes through unscrupulous deals. In too many cases, the rents for the new housing exceeded the ceilings set by the federal rent control agency. In some cases, the families thought they were renting an apartment only to find out they were committed to purchase it. Indignant, Willis remarked that the Chicago NAACP was "appalled" by the fact that the HHFA, in an effort to "help" a city, would "force from their homes the very families who are the most helpless in the city." He urged an "appropriate inquiry" in order to determine whether the CLCC met federal standards. Willis threatened that if the city's redevelopment agency did not undertake "corrective actions," the Chicago NAACP would "be compelled to take other steps to stop illegal displacement of Negro families by the Land Clearance Commission."[43]

The Chicago NAACP did not just speak in generalities. They provided HHFA officials with documentation that showed the hardships suffered by displaced black homeowners and tenants. As predicted by several black housing analysts, displaced black homeowners could not find comparable housing at affordable prices in other locations. For example, Henry Baker, a black homeowner located at 3126 S. Rhodes Avenue, did not want to sell his home for $7,000 when he felt that a comparable house in another location would cost him between $14,000 and $17,000. And Baker found that other recommended housing often was too far away, in places such as suburban Harvey, twenty-three miles from his current location.[44]

In a couple of cases, black tenant families had to move because their building had been sold to the CLCC by the landlord. In at least one case, the CLCC used the building to house families on public assistance. Displaced black tenants either were not getting help from the CLCC or were referred to apartments they could not afford. Mr. and Mrs. Robert Grant, who both worked unskilled jobs, declared that the apartments they were shown were "not as nice" and "more expensive" than their current place. In another instance, the CLCC referred black tenants to a rental service that required the exorbitant fee of $50. If some black tenants found affordable and desirable apartments, it was not because they had received help from the CLCC; instead, according to the NAACP report, many black tenants claimed they had received only harassment and intimidation.[45]

The NAACP charged that the CLCC often referred site occupants to unscrupulous real estate agencies. While many of those agencies were white owned, at least one was owned by black realtors, Mr. and Mrs. Journee White. The Chicago NAACP report documented abuses committed by Journee White against relocating black working-class families. In one case, the Breakfield family had been referred to White but refused to deal with him because many of their friends had paid White more than $1,000 and had not received any accommodations in return. In the another case, the Brownlee family went from paying $30 a month for six rooms with heat, water, and utilities included to paying $80 for a five-room apartment—that is, until an Office of Price Administration (OPA) ruling reduced the rent to $32.50. Not only was the apartment in poor condition and in need of repairs but the Whites demanded the Brownlees pay $260 for two months' advance rent plus a security deposit.[46]

In other cases, Mr. and Mrs. Journee White refused to make repairs in their apartments, telling the new tenants that they were "buying into the building," not renting. For instance, Journee White told the Weatherspoon family "that their security payment could be considered a down payment." Mr. Weatherspoon refused to sign the papers and went to the OPA to report on the Whites' irregular real estate practices. He also contacted the CLCC and asked them why they had not told his family that when they contracted for housing with the Whites they were investing in cooperative ownership rather than rental housing. The CLCC responded candidly that Mrs. White had informed the agency of her intentions, but the agency needed to clear the property as soon as possible. According to Weatherspoon, a CLCC official had pressured them to take this place, pointing out that if they did not they would have to accept whatever the agency offered or find housing without the agency's assistance.[47]

Another black family, the Jacksons, who lived with the Weatherspoons, found out that white tenants were paying only $30 a month in their new building while they were required to pay $70 for four rooms. When they reported this to the OPA, their rent was reduced to $30 a month. Like the other families, the Jacksons had paid $240 in advance. When they attempted to contact the CLCC, they were told, "After you left this area, we have no further responsibility for you."[48] These and other stories of hardships faced by displaced blacks offer evidence that Chicago's relocation practices were seriously flawed, if not criminal. Yet these cases were not exceptional. They were representative of the overall problems of black displacement and relocation experienced as the Lake Meadows project proceeded.

Black Policy Elites and the "Chicago Situation"

George Nesbitt captured black policy elites' thinking on this matter best when he determined that if slum clearance and redevelopment were going to take place, then "the undoing of residential segregation" needed to begin with "the relocation effort."[49] Even though they lost the early battle to get Chicago's officials to endorse vacant land sites for displaced black families, they did not entirely give up their position. While black civic and national elites were at odds during the slum clearance debate, two years later they would join forces to condemn the City of Chicago and appeal to Washington,

D.C., to intervene by withholding crucial federal aid. These collective efforts would emerge from a national black housing policy network that sought to form and implement a racially democratic housing agenda in the post-war period. Unable to reverse the adverse political trend in Chicago, black civic and policy elites sought the intervention of federal housing agencies to accomplish *their* vision of urban redevelopment. Black policy elites affiliated with the nation's housing agencies or in national civil rights organizations argued that what happened in Chicago could determine the future of urban redevelopment policy, particularly whether it could be used to achieve their goal of residential integration.

The "Chicago Situation"

The "Chicago Situation" faced by these housing experts was how to contend with the commitment of the city's political regime to maintaining a racial dual housing market. Like their local colleagues, they concentrated on two decisions made by Chicago officials. One was the adoption of slum sites for public housing, while the other was the relocation policies of the CLCC. They sought to zero in on the relocation policies not only of the city but also of the HHFA constituent agencies, the Public Housing Administration (PHA) and the Division of Slum Clearance and Urban Redevelopment (DSCUR). Having given up on the city government by 1950, black policy elites concentrated on putting pressure on the head administrators of those agencies as well as on Raymond Foley, administrator of the HHFA, the umbrella housing agency encompassing all the constituent agencies. Black policy elites felt they had leverage since the city sought federal approval and aid under Titles I and III of the 1949 Housing Act for both public housing and redevelopment. In other words, they attempted to persuade the federal government to join their side in their battle with the Chicago officials intent on using federal aid for slum clearance, urban redevelopment, and public housing in order to reinforce, instead of dismantle, the black ghetto.

Black policy elites agreed with black civic leaders' critique of Chicago's adoption of predominantly slum sites for public housing. Black federal housing policy analysts found predominant slum sites problematic for three reasons: (1) The majority of black residents displaced would be ineligible for public housing, (2) it was more costly to build on slum land than on open land because inner-city property was more expensive and had to be cleared,[50] and (3) it created a relocation problem that would either delay construction of new public housing or stop it altogether.[51] They concluded that Chicago's program represented a lack of planning, irrational land use, and bad race and public relations.[52]

Title I aid for Chicago was already under federal scrutiny due to the CLCC's flawed relocation practices. In fact, at the end of 1950, Frank Horne stated that the HHFA racial relations office had been monitoring the housing program in Chicago "for several years." Black federal housing officials were certainly aware of the charges leveled by the Chicago NAACP and the Chicago Urban League of the CLCC's callous disregard for black tenants and homeowners.[53] Based on his own observations during his fact-finding trip to Chicago, Nesbitt advised that particular attention be paid to the CLCC's "apparent limited conception" of Title I relocation standards, which had led to the local agency treating rehousing as a temporary rather than a permanent responsibility.[54]

Horne advised DSCUR head Nathaniel Keith that the agency should "disassociate itself" from Chicago's "relocation process" because it failed to meet the standards outlined in Section 105 of Title I. Furthermore, the CLCC would not get federal assistance under Title I unless it immediately stopped displacing families until a relocation plan had been approved. He added that the DSCUR should not engage in any contracts for demolition "with Chicago until we have satisfactory evidence that the families displaced have been relocated in decent, safe and sanitary accommodations."[55]

Two years later, Keith defended the CLCC's flawed relocation policies. Since the CLCC had initiated the city's first redevelopment project through state legislation enacted before the 1949 Housing Act, he reasoned, its relocation efforts were not governed by Title I standards. Keith admitted that trying to impose federal standards on an "existing operation . . . helps in part to explain some of the difficulties encountered." Keith described how "inmigration" was responsible for the large increase in population in the targeted areas and the overcrowding of available housing. Since the DSCUR ruled out "high density dwellings" for rehousing, the CLCC made the case that it was acceptable for displaced blacks to resettle in racial transition areas, which had housing that met federal standards. Although many of the dwellings were purchased as single-family homes, many of these were also "large enough to permit legal conversions" into rental housing.

Though concerned about overcrowding in new transition areas, the DSCUR was reassured by the city that its inspection system and law enforcement would prevent illegal conversions and overcrowding. In regard to the

Chicago NAACP's indictment of the CLCC's inadequate relocation policy, Keith accepted the city's explanation that problems resulted from relocating families' "misunderstanding" of the process brought about by the inadequate explanations of the CLCC staff. The city reassured the federal officials that "these practices were corrected." Keith had the CLCC adopt other measures to prevent displaced families from accepting inadequate new housing for fear of eviction.[56]

Reconciling Federal Site Selection and Relocation Standards

The problem of rehousing those who were ineligible for public housing called the PHA agency rules and regulations into question. Upon review of these rules, both black housing officials and civil rights analysts like Weaver found a number of inconsistencies and omissions. For the purpose of consistency and coordination, they wanted the PHA and the DSCUR to adopt standardized site-selection and relocation policies based on Title I.

While black policy elites severely criticized Chicago's officials for their preference for slum sites, they also held the PHA responsible for approving this decision. Horne identified the agency's "most fundamental problem" as its inability to establish a sound policy for site selection.[57] A "sound policy," Horne implied, would entail the PHA instructing local housing authorities to select sufficient vacant sites for public housing and rejecting those local applications that proposed mainly slum sites. Both Robert Weaver and racial relations officers interpreted Chicago's and the PHA's "current insistence upon slums sites [as] generally associated with projects planned to effect racial containment." According to Weaver, "Negro containment" could be avoided with "a more realistic site selection policy for Title III programs."[58]

Not only was the lack of a site selection policy a problem but black policy elites found the PHA's relocation policy equally problematic. They wanted PHA relocation standards to conform to Title I's Section 105c rehousing requirements, which required a plan for relocating displacees in decent, safe, and sanitary housing.[59] Weaver considered the PHA relocation standard of placing families in areas "no worse than those on site" unacceptable and a "rejection of Title I relocation standards," which also represented an "abrogation of responsibilities implicit in the federal Housing Act of 1949."[60] Horne and racial relations officials thought that if the PHA adopted the Title I relocation policy, it would be more likely to provide more land areas to racial minorities.[61] To facilitate this outcome, Nesbitt emphasized that the city could use "public-acquired" land to address the "space needs" of blacks concentrated in slum clearance areas.[62]

Reforming relocation standards would discourage the use of public housing to restrict racial minorities to "high-density occupancy" and to "predetermine racial occupancy patterns." In addition, they expected that the policy change would be spur local action to find decent housing for displaced black families who constitute a part of the "private enterprise market."[63] To this end, Weaver wanted relocatees to have preference in FHA agreements to increase the supply of private housing. Weaver insisted that the site-selection process for relocation housing should not reinforce racial containment, should minimize dislocation for overincome minority families, and should ensure there was no net loss of housing units available to displaced minority families.[64]

Horne agreed with Weaver but added, reflecting an earlier NUL position, that all racial groups should have access to new redeveloped housing. Horne argued that slum sites were acceptable if there was no evidence the sites had been selected for the purpose of restricting land areas available to minorities.[65] All these positions were consistently held throughout the fight over relocation policy; however, Horne hedged on the position on slum sites. Rather than requiring a certain proportion of vacant sites, he gave an out to localities that could "prove" their selection of slum sites was not based on a policy of racial containment.

In order to coordinate multiple site-selection and relocation practices, Weaver recommended reviewing together all the projects in a city's development program rather than have the site and relocation criteria reviewed project by project. Nesbitt made a specific recommendation that a city's development program be given "joint agency attention," rather than, for instance, only the PHA evaluating CHA proposals within the overall program.[66] Weaver suggested that a local central relocation agency should be required for all relocation programs arising out of federally financed housing, with power to recommend HHFA priorities in demolition.

Black policy professionals both in the federal bureaucracy and working in the nongovernmental realm agreed that top federal housing officials should insist that "the principle of racial equity" become a required criterion in site review. This was just one of the "new standards safeguarding the equal treatment of minorities affected by federally assisted housing programs."[67] Black policy professionals attempted to combat bureaucratic decentralization and fragmentation, thinking that black housing interests would be better met with a more centralized approach.

Combating Negro Containment

It was one thing to make policy recommendations, but quite another to persuade federal housing policymakers to implement them. Black policy elites in Washington, D.C., New York, and Chicago focused their lobbying efforts on the HHFA and its constituent agencies, the PHA and the DSCUR, in order to confront the "Chicago Situation." After George Nesbitt's important field trip to Chicago in the summer of 1950, which led to his report on widespread black dissatisfaction with Chicago's site-selection and relocation policies, Frank Horne began to express his concerns to administrator Foley. Everything came to a head a week before Christmas of 1950. The city was in the process of applying for federal funds to supplement its state-aided redevelopment program when the city council formally adopted predominantly slum sites for public housing.

Horne had strongly advised the DSCUR director, Nathaniel Keith, to disapprove Chicago's application for redevelopment aid until the city adopted Title I relocation standards. When news arrived that Chicago had not adopted those standards, he proclaimed defiantly, "It is time we washed our hands of this entire dirty business. As long as Chicago shuts its official eyes while its most disadvantaged people are pushed around, herded into fire-traps and overtly exploited, it should be allowed to proceed until it reaps its own whirlwind." Horne added, uncompromisingly, "Certainly, Federal funds or sanctions should be completely withheld."[68] Horne assured Foley and Keith that Chicago had enough city and state funds to complete the New York Life project without federal assistance and recommended "a clean slate as far as Federal involvement is concerned." Horne warned presciently that if the agency allowed Chicago to continue because of the "prior commitment" to receive public housing units, the city would present them with "a fait accompli relocation plan" whose effectiveness would be difficult to determine. He then predicted waiting until that point would subject the agency to "persuasive political pressures." He argued that the time had come to extricate themselves from the situation.[69]

Horne's strong language was soon backed up by protests and appeals from both the national and Chicago branches of the NAACP and Robert Weaver, the executive director of the newly founded National Committee Against Discrimination in Housing (NCDH) and a member of the DSCUR advisory committee. The similarity in purpose and perspective between black federal housing officials and black housing experts in civil rights organizations reflected not only their similar social backgrounds but also the work of a national housing policy network that had its roots in the New Deal but that had emerged in earnest in the postwar period.

The new year had hardly begun when the Chicago NAACP branch struck first, presenting its hardship cases of relocated blacks to Foley. By the end of January, Walter White, executive secretary of the NAACP, took his protests to the White House, where he conveyed to President Truman and administrator Foley the statement of the NAACP board of directors "calling upon the government to cease and desist from aiding in the development of housing on a racially discriminatory basis." They found that federal housing agencies, through "making direct grants, loans, subsidies, and mortgage commitments—public funds and credits," were giving federal sanction to locally directed discrimination and segregation. The NAACP said that the nation's "most aggrieved and least advantaged citizens" should not have to seek legal relief "from acts of its national government." The civil rights organization adopted the militant stand taken by Horne, advocating the withholding of federal authority and funds from local areas that followed a policy of racial segregation in tenant and site selection. Reflecting their legalistic approach, they called upon the U.S. attorney general and the Department of Justice to make sure federal housing agencies' policies reflected Supreme Court decisions "regarding racial restrictive covenants and segregation in dining cars and state universities."[70] The NAACP promised to instruct its local affiliates to look for any evidence that any publicly aided housing was exclusionary.[71]

The federal housing officials took immediate notice of the NAACP board resolution. Foley solicited a response to the NAACP's charges from PHA commissioner John Taylor Egan since the charges, in part, implicated PHA site selection and relocation policies. Egan bluntly informed Foley that "the prohibition of segregation on account of race is not one of the conditions to entering into such contracts nor one of the provisions required to be included in such contracts" with local public agencies. He reminded Foley that Congress had refused to require such a condition in the Housing Act of 1949 and that no U.S. court had required that principle in PHA contracts with local public housing agencies. Egan concluded that, given the lack of legislative or judicial authority, his agency could not require in their contracts with local public agencies "any prohibition of segregation on account of race," adding, "I believe the above points reflect the only position that this agency could take in replying to this communication."[72] Egan's statement to Foley goes a long way in explaining federal housing agencies' accommodation to racial segregation. Ultimately, Foley, backed by the Truman White House, accepted a decentralist view of federalism and deferred to local government.[73]

After receiving Foley's unsatisfactory response, White zeroed in on the point that Foley had evaded. Local authorities had used federal funds to develop racially segregated housing, and federal agencies had failed to "halt this practice." White recounted for Foley the myriad uses of federal funds to bolster segregation in many communities. The NAACP had told Foley that these local actions were "in conflict with the spirit of your announced policies." White did not back off, continuing that the NAACP board of directors felt "that only vigorous action by the federal agencies will stop discrimination and segregation in the federally aided housing." They urged that this "ultimate step"—"the withholding of federal funds"—be taken in communities that use "federal funds to maintain the anti-democratic and outmoded pattern of residential segregation."[74] The NAACP had formally endorsed a position that Horne had advocated internally in regard to Chicago's desire for Title I funds.[75]

In May 1951, the HHFA racial relations office wanted Foley to approve only three of the seven slum sites proposed by the city. The office used the CHA's estimation that it would take five to six years to construct public housing on slum sites to support its recommendation that PHA approve only the current three sites and delay action on the remainder. They recommended that the PHA commissioner indicate to CHA that three slum sites should be the maximum number of slum sites approved until more housing on vacant land should become available for displaced families. They argued that a viable public housing program required a balance of vacant and slum sites. They claimed that Chicago had as many as sixty vacant sites available for housing development.[76]

The following month, Foley told Weaver that his agency had made officials in Chicago more aware of the "relocation difficulties involved in the extensive slum clearance operations." After careful review, Foley, apparently following the advice of racial relations officials, told Weaver he would approve eight of the twelve projects proposed by the CHA.[77] Of the eight sites, five were on vacant sites and three on slum sites with "considerable vacant land."[78] He argued that he thought displacement would be minimal in selecting these sites, noting that "the development of the eight projects will contribute substantially to the living space and housing accommodations available to minority group families."

As for the CLCC's relocation plan, Foley did not approve it because it did not meet Title I rehousing requirements. He assured Weaver that the DSCUR would "not enter a loan and grant contract" until the CLCC satisfied these requirements. Foley added that the FHA district office in Chicago, in recognition of the need to produce "new private housing for Negro families," had discussed "land acquisition" with the CLCC and "developmental and financial problems" with white and black builders and lenders.[79]

Early in the fall of 1951, Weaver endorsed Foley's decision to withhold his "approval of the Title I program and of four of the slum sites proposed for public housing." On a recent trip to Chicago, Weaver had learned that although there were numerous meetings between the FHA and the local real estate industry, no "financial support has been gained" for private housing open to blacks. Weaver interpreted this failure as a result of the real estate industry being more interested in maintaining racial segregation than "in profitability [by] satisfying the unprecedented demand for private housing among Negro families." Weaver also criticized the actions of city officials that reinforced "the racial exclusion policy of real estate and financial interests." Noting that the fears he had expressed three years earlier in his book had proven accurate, Weaver observed that all-white redevelopment projects had replaced either all-black or integrated neighborhoods.[80] If the HHFA was interested in stopping the spread of blight and reaching federal housing standards, he explained, it "cannot afford to accept plans designed to perpetuate Negro containment."[81]

Yet all the protests and appeals both within and outside the HHFA came to naught. On November 5, 1951, Raymond Foley approved the four remaining public housing sites and Redevelopment Project Area No. 1 for Chicago's program. He also announced the employment of "coordinated Federal Housing aids to assist local communities in solving difficult relocation problems, especially where substantial numbers of minority group families are involved." The Chicago program of public housing and urban redevelopment was a key piece of the Truman administration's housing program. Foley was not going to oppose the city and derail such an important initiative over some concerns about reinforcing racial segregation.

Unable to stop the approval of Chicago's program, the NAACP reminded Foley that "much remains to be done in attaining full democracy."[82] However, at the end of the day, black citizens in Chicago did not receive more land or better housing, and publicly aided developments of integrated private developments outside the ghetto were not achieved. Black policy elites' quest for racial democratic housing had failed through the federal government's acquiescence to the city's racial intransigence.

The Aftermath of Defeat

After administrator Foley had approved Chicago's housing program, the DSCUR found many promising signs that relocation would go more smoothly and equitably after they had worked with the CLCC.[83] Keith's optimistic assessment of the changes made by the CLCC's relocation policy was seconded by Mayor Kennelly in the city's application for urban renewal funds under the new Housing Act of 1954.[84] In its application, the city commented on the "considerable emphasis [that] has been placed upon the development of an adequate relocation program." The new proposal reassured federal officials that the CLCC had accepted the responsibility to relocate displaced families and to add "the cost of relocation services" to the overall project cost. In addition, the city was studying "the possibility of consolidating the relocation activities of all public agencies operating with the City." Finally, the proposal admitted that "special efforts" were necessary to combat "the typical housing problems" faced by minority families.[85]

Despite this misleading rhetoric, Chicago still refused to provide "open land for new construction open to Negroes."[86] Black federal housing officials argued that Chicago's relocation housing needs were more critical than those of other cities because there was no open land project planned, even though the HHFA had insisted that Chicago undertake such projects.[87] According to black federal officials, "thousands of acres of partially vacant and vacant land fit for residential use are to be found in the city." They complained that blacks did not have access to a project located on forty acres of predominantly open land located at Seventy-Ninth Street and Western Avenue. Frank Horne reported that nothing had changed in this regard in Chicago. He reported that the Urban Renewal Administration (formerly the DSCUR) had funded a redeveloper with plans to build new housing only for whites, complaining "that displacement affected mainly Negro families."[88]

As for the displacement of black families after redevelopment, Chicago was representative of a dismal national picture. As of September 1955, racial minorities were involved in every one of the fifty-four redevelopment projects across the country. George Nesbitt reported that "nonwhite families" comprised two-thirds of the 39,169 families who had been displaced by slum clearance and redevelopment activity nationally.[89] A 1958 Chicago Urban League report on the impact of urban renewal on blacks in the city reported that between 1948 and 1956, an estimated "86,000 persons were displaced by various urban renewal projects." Approximately 67 percent of those displaced were African American. The report calculated that "over 11 per cent of the Chicago black population of 1950 was forced to relocate in an eight-year period."[90]

Conclusion

The black policy elites who had favored the city's program before 1950 calculated that redevelopment could not proceed unless those displaced from the Lake Meadows project were properly rehoused, preferably in new private integrated housing on open lands outside the ghetto. Feeling that "relocation" was the Achilles heel of the redevelopment policy, they sought, not unreasonably, to use this feature as a lever to expand land space for African Americans and to pursue open occupancy. National black housing officials continued to push this policy position in their criticism of both federal and municipal relocation policy. Initially, these black policy elites sought to show Chicago officials the error of their ways. Considering the political nature of such adverse decisions as the rejection of predominantly vacant public housing sites, black policy elites sought to reverse the decisions by appealing to city officials' self-interest. When that failed, they turned to HHFA administrator Foley, who subsequently refused to withhold federal aid to Chicago's housing program. Despite persistent efforts, black civic and policy elites failed to influence Chicago government officials, either directly or indirectly through federal influence, to offer and subsidize private housing for blacks or to permit "open" occupancy on vacant lands outside the Black Belt. Instead, a *de facto* policy was instituted of rehousing those displaced from black slums either in adjacent slum neighborhoods or, if they could afford it, in racial transition areas. Black settlement in these white neighborhoods bordering the ghetto, in turn, ignited racial tensions and antiblack violence.

The massive displacement and unsuccessful rehousing that followed slum clearance probably exceeded the predictions of the black petit bourgeois stratum of politicians and business and property owners. Before and after the struggle against the downtown elite's program, they had sought other means to forestall additional slum clearance by choosing conservation and rehabilitation. They rejected wholesale clearance because it eliminated "good housing" along with substandard dwellings. That their standard housing had been designated as "blighted" indicated to these black elites that city officials wanted their neighborhood for its desirable location. In recognition of deteriorating conditions in their neighborhoods, this group of black elites embraced and promoted self-help rehabilitation and redevelopment. In other words, the rehabilitation of housing and conservation of neighborhoods would be directed and controlled by the black property owners of the Mid-South Side.

In some ways, both the relocation protests and the black-led redevelopment plans were logical extensions of the diverging lines of debate within black elite circles that had emerged in earlier stages of the slum clearance debacle (see chapter 4). One side hoped that if they could correct the city's relocation policy, redirecting it toward providing integrated housing to blacks, it would lessen the ghetto's density and weaken its walls. The other side, less concerned with density and immediate desegregation, sought to control the territory that their forbears had carved out from battling hostile whites. The division of opinion was perfectly clear, but this was a matter of one elite confronting another. Each spoke for middle-class blacks, who would likely be first either to relocate outside Bronzeville or, as property owners, to fight for self-help rehabilitation within it.

6

Black Redevelopment and Negro Conservation

While black civic and policy elites concentrated their efforts on getting government to protect the interests of displaced black homeowners and tenants by relocating them to housing that suited their tastes and their pocketbooks, other influential blacks organized their own resources to better defend their homes and neighborhoods. Though protests and self-help rehabilitation efforts could not prevent a neighborhood from being replaced by the upscale Lake Meadows apartment buildings, affluent black residents felt it was still possible to rescue their nearby neighborhoods that were threatened by a continued land-clearance offensive. At the height of the slum clearance debate within black political and social circles, a number of self-help rehabilitation plans circulated, including those by Sidney Williams, Oscar Brown Sr., Frayser T. Lane, and William Thornton (see chapter 4). Yet since the fear of Negro clearance predated the building of Lake Meadows and persisted afterward, black institutional elites and affluent property owners continued to make ambitious plans that often came to naught. What these plans had in common was that, whether or not they sought help from white capital or from government, redevelopment efforts would be black led and property would be black owned. What they also had in common was that they ran into the same immovable obstacle that had always stymied black elite-controlled private development—the scarcity of capital. No plan epitomized this problem more than the aborted attempt by four black-owned insurance companies to build middle-class homes within Chicago's first redevelopment site.

Predating, accompanying, and succeeding neighborhood protests, black self-help redevelopment became the most favored, though flawed, strategy employed by black institutional elites in their attempt to control the Black Metropolis.[1] This strategy—a natural choice for black elites given their class, professions, and civic ideology—set the terms of the conflict in particular ways. Since the protagonists and antagonists in the slum clearance drama were white and black elites, the conflict was fought on racial terms. The fact that black small property owners and middle-class homeowners were pushed off their land by more powerful white business, real estate, and political elites gave traction to the charge of racial injustice. The racial character of the conflict was underscored by the fact that both sides agreed on so much, including a hatred of slums and the concomitant belief that private-led, publicly aided redevelopment would best eradicate them. The fight between these two forces was not over the approach to black slum clearance, but over which racial elite would dictate the process. Given the disproportionate power of white elites, however, the outcome seemed predetermined.

Yet the racial nature of the conflict also depended on other factors. Since the struggle was over real estate, which is governed by the U.S. legal system, which in turn confers standing, rights, and redress, the actors were limited to those who could claim property rights. In other words, black property owners were enfranchised actors with rights, at least formally, with which to defend themselves through conventional means. The large majority of working-class black tenants lacked these rights and thus were either relegated to bit parts in the land-clearance drama or moved offstage altogether. Yet the exclusion of black tenants, with few exceptions, was also the result of the class nature of black elites' *racial* representation of the conflict. In other words, black institutional leaders and property owners interpreted their conflict in racial terms because, as leading members of the race, they felt they represented the housing interests of all African Americans, even in instances such as this when they did not. In this drama of competing land interests, black tenants were mere props, largely mute and occasionally ushered into the spotlight to highlight racial suffering.

The proliferation and persistence of black self-help redevelopment plans spoke to the potency of a competing current within racial democratic ideology at mid-twentieth century. The main political action involved black policy elites utilizing their policy network to advocate for their version of black housing interests, which featured eliminating residential segregation and planning interracial housing. Black politicians, ministers, and business and property owners—the same faction that defended the ghetto—interpreted black housing interests as tolerating de facto residential segregation in order to use racial–geographical consolidation as a potential power base of property and institutions to win more permanent gains in the U.S. political economy through profitable investment and electoral strength. The historian Andrew Wiese aptly characterizes this position as "territorial nationalism."[2]

Since its politics was "race based" and invested in democratic or equal access to housing capital, markets, and government aid, it still circulated within the ideological orbit of racial democracy.

In this chapter, I explore black institutional and civic elites' persistent efforts to grab the reins of redevelopment in Bronzeville, and I chronicle their struggles to accumulate enough capital to fund their redevelopment dreams. I also show their interest in using new federal, state, and municipal laws to direct conservation efforts in their neighborhoods. This chapter shows that whether black elites wanted to control redevelopment on the Mid-South Side or to safeguard their affluent enclaves in Hyde Park and Kenwood, their housing interests trumped those of working-class blacks.

Black Capital and Urban Redevelopment

The most prominent attempt at black-led redevelopment during this period was the decision by the largest black businesses in Chicago to join with the city in redeveloping the Mid-South Side.[3] In late December 1948, Supreme Liberty, Victory Mutual, and Unity Mutual life insurance companies, along with Metropolitan Mutual Assurance Company, announced their intention to join together "to construct new homes in one of Chicago's worst blighted districts," according to an Associated Negro Press release. Truman K. Gibson Sr., president of Supreme Liberty, announced that the plan, approved by the Chicago Land Clearance Commission (CLCC), was to begin with the construction of fifty homes in a two-square-block area that would eventually expand into a six-block development. The project financed by black firms would be located just south of the Lake Meadows project, between Thirty-Third and Thirty-Fourth Places, from Rhodes Avenue to Cottage Grove Avenue.

According to the plan, the black insurance companies would make an initial investment of $650,000 and would set the price of the single-family homes between $12,000 and $15,000. Gibson intimated that the homes would be for "property owners" displaced by the New York Life project. He said that the project provided "an excellent opportunity of assisting our policyholders through not only taking care of persons displaced by other projects, but also contributing to the economic life of this district by helping get rid of the slums." Chicago's city officials praised the plan as an endorsement by "Negro capital" of "the city's slum clearance and redevelopment program." Black capital's participation legitimized the principle of "private enterprise," taking the lead in "cleaning up the slums." According to black insurance executives, the area proposed, within Redevelopment Project Area No. 1, was once "the best Negro residential district in the city," but as blacks "moved southward the community was allowed to deteriorate." Deterioration resulted from the age of the residential structures compounded by their absentee owners' neglect. Here was a chance for indigenous capital to restore a black elite enclave to its former stature.[4]

A significant portion of Supreme Liberty Life Insurance Company's capital derived from mortgage financing.[5] This opportunity to join the city's redevelopment program seemed to finally address the call that Claude Barnett, owner of the Associated Negro Press and member of the company's board of directors, had made five years earlier to the company's agents:

> There is more money around the streets going to waste, crying for some one with the force and vision to put it to good use than ever before in our racial history. If we could double our intake we would be performing the greatest possible service to the men and women and their families whom we insured that it would be possible to perform. Let's get our people in the habit of piling up real money for the future, building estates, saving, putting their money to work. Let's get them to WANTING homes and help them to finance them; let's make them HUNGER to have their children educated and show them how to save toward that goal. Let's build a pool of money here so big that this desperate housing condition which exists here and in the other cities where we operate can have big dents made in it because [of] the fund of money which Supreme Liberty has. (original emphasis)

Barnett's appeal was an explicit call for black capital accumulation, which both signified and facilitated racial progress. He further explained that government subsidies would be available for any private company that wanted to rebuild housing. Supreme Liberty Life's directors, all members of Chicago's black upper class, saw their capitalist enterprise as the answer to the race's housing problem.[6]

Nevertheless, the black capitalist dream came to naught. In June 1951, the Associated Negro Press announced that the black insurance firms led by Supreme Liberty Life were pulling out of the project. The two reasons cited were opposition from neighborhood black property owners and the risk of the investment. The press release explained that most of the property owners were African American, with a large number "making rental profits from their holdings." They resisted the city's plans because they "considered the selling of their land a loss of a profitable venture." H. G. Hall, general manager of Metropolitan Mutual Assurance Company, said ministers, local leaders, and residents had criticized the insurance companies' "investment" as joining with the city "to push them out." Hall explained that their project was meant to help blacks own property in the area, thereby ensuring "the Negro interest" and long-term presence in this desirable location. For these businessmen, gaining a foothold did not mean renting an upscale apartment but rather owning property in the rebuilt area.

The black insurance executives had to respect the views of the people who constituted their market, so they withdrew from the project. Earl B. Dickerson, civic leader and counsel for Supreme Liberty Life Insurance Company, commented with resignation, "The whole idea got to be unpopular among colored people. I feel like this was unjust criticism, but it was there."[7] Because black insurance executives articulated their motivation in racial terms, their venture was susceptible to the racial critique that they were collaborating with white capital to victimize black property owners. The sting of the criticism was testimony to the power of one black stratum—small black property owners—donning the mantle of *race* and effectively wielding it against competing class interests within the race. Black insurance executives were dismayed that what would normally be considered a progressive "race-conscious" action—building homes for black middle-class ownership—was portrayed as legitimating a land grab by powerful whites. Two-and-a-half years after their announcement, the black executives found themselves in opposition to black property owners, their erstwhile supporters.

Opposition from black property owners was not the only reason for the withdrawal. The high costs of building the duplexes (houses with two residential units) would have required the firms "to charge more than potential buyers would be willing to pay." Apparently, the black insurance executives' market study had revealed that only an upscale apartment building similar to Lake Meadows could be profitable in that area. Yet the black insurance firms did not like the idea of tying up their investment in one building and thought that selling individual units would give them an immediate return. Dickerson asserted that the firms could not sell duplex homes for any less than $15,000 and that "families with this money would prefer to build on the outskirts of the city." Truman K. Gibson Sr. expressed disappointment at the prospect of not being able to carry out the original plans. The Associated

Negro Press reported that the New York Life Insurance Company would build on the land instead.[8]

A look at the housing market in the Douglass community where the redevelopment site was located seems to corroborate the concerns of the black insurance executives. In 1950, the median value of nonwhite owner-occupied units in this community was $8,960. Only 14.3 percent of households in the neighborhood owned homes valued at more than $15,000 compared to 28.5 percent of all nonwhite households citywide. In contrast, 62.4 percent of all nonwhite owner-occupied homes in Roseland, located on the Far South Side, were valued at more than $15,000. In addition, the median value of all nonwhite owner-occupied units was $11,130 in Roseland.[9] Affluent black homeowners' preference for the periphery, like that of their white counterparts, not only undermined black insurance capital's investment plans but also threatened some black elites' dreams of rebuilding affluent black neighborhoods in the heart of Bronzeville.

Claude A. Barnett and Black Capital Redevelopment

While black insurance capital found itself on the wrong side of this internal conflict, in previous and subsequent self-help plans the insurance firms worked in concert with other black business and property owners in their attempt to rehabilitate and redevelop the neighborhoods adjacent to Redevelopment Area No. 1 located at Thirty-First to Thirty-Fifth Streets, South Parkway to the Illinois Central Railroad. These neighborhoods had some of the highest percentages of black home ownership in Chicago.[10]

The area had once been an upscale white district but had begun to deteriorate before the Great Migration, when African Americans first entered the area east of Michigan Avenue and took over large homes on Grand Boulevard, later known as South Parkway Avenue. The usual combination of heavy migration and restrictive covenants caused overcrowding; the conversion of apartments into kitchenettes and the added neglect of city sanitary and building standards accelerated physical deterioration. Middle-class blacks attempted to resist the deterioration of the neighborhood that seemed to accompany the arrival of migrant blacks in nearby blocks. Claude A. Barnett, the wealthy owner of the Associated Negro Press, the first black news service in the country, was one of the elites who lived in the neighborhood. A graduate of Tuskegee Institute, Barnett spent his early years working for the *Chicago Defender*. He spent the interwar years building up his publishing and cosmetics businesses.[11] Although the record is incomplete, Barnett had engaged since at least 1940 in a number of schemes, all short-lived and under-capitalized, to "save" his formerly affluent neighborhood through black-led rehabilitation and redevelopment.[12]

All the efforts were broadly concentrated in the area between Thirty-Fifth to Thirty-Seventh Streets and from South Parkway Avenue to Lake Michigan, just south of the city's first redevelopment area. A number of black elites' homes and important black institutions were located in this area. Barnett lived at 3531 South Parkway, and the Associated Negro Press office was on the second floor of the Supreme Liberty Life building located at 3501 South Parkway. A. L. Foster, the former executive secretary of the CUL and secretary of the Chamber of Negro Commerce, had an office located at 3647 South Parkway. West and slightly north of this area was the Chicago Urban League office, located at 3032 South Wabash. On the western side of South Parkway was the *Chicago Bee* newspaper, located at 3653 South State Street, the *Chicago Defender* at 3435 Indiana Avenue, and the Wabash Avenue YMCA at 3763 Wabash Avenue.

Because of the concentration of black institutional power in this location, black elites felt their "land-base" needed to be protected and preserved. All Barnett's efforts expressed the belief that self-help redevelopment could improve the neighborhood to a "real standard" that would serve as an example for rehabilitating the South Side.[13] Barnett and other black elites' material and social investment in the area reflected the nexus between racial pride and property ownership that informed their class outlook. Also, they felt that a black elite–led redevelopment would serve as a model for other black neighborhood rehabilitation efforts on the South Side.[14]

Barnett traced neighborhood improvement efforts back to his aunt, who had started a club "which inculcated a certain sense of pride among the older residents."[15] During World War II, Barnett and other black elites attempted to enlist the Chicago Housing Authority (CHA) and the Mayor's Commission on Race Relations to support their plans for neighborhood redevelopment. As early as 1940, Barnett and other elites discussed the need for neighborhood improvement in the smaller area of Thirty-Fifth to Thirty-Seventh Streets and Vernon to Rhodes Avenues. In considering the development of this area, blacks expressed some initial anxiety about the impact of the proposed Ida B. Wells public housing project on nearby property values.[16] Four years later, Barnett, when referring to the area for investment, commented that the Ida B. Wells housing project had proved an asset "despite fears to the contrary," noting that it had added to the appreciation of surrounding property "by virtue of its excellent management."[17]

In 1944, Barnett, Earl Dickerson, and Robert Taylor discussed planning a "development of reclamation and modernization in that very area, 35th to 37th—South Parkway—East" that they had discussed before. Taylor had the CHA set aside $20,000 for the planning. Barnett told Truman Gibson Sr. that "private capital and home owners" within the black community would have to finance the work. Dickerson suggested that "the answer" might be for South Side leaders to develop "a private corporation."[18] A month or so later, Barnett made the case to Milton Shufro, assistant executive secretary of the CHA, that the area lent "itself admirably to a remodeling or rehabilitation effort." The fact that Thirty-Sixth Street was not a through street meant the site was fairly self-contained. Barnett assured the CHA official that the two blocks held "considerable ownership." He admitted, however, that not much property maintenance had occurred due to some residents' "economic condition" and the prevalence of absentee landlords who "have permitted their properties to run down totally and have shown no interest in the neighborhood at all."[19]

Barnett told the officers of Supreme Liberty Life Insurance Company that since their office was a block from the area, it was in their interest to look for possibilities for reinvestment. He intimated to Shufro that the insurance company had agreed to "lend money to any reasonable risk who wishes to purchase or remodel within that area if such a plan goes through." Even Barnett had expressed interest in "buying some of the property, remodeling it and offering it for sale to desirable tenants who might fit into such a program." Barnett made the final pitch to the Housing Authority that if they planned a "vigorous program" for the area, it would represent "an example which would invite capital to other sections of the South Side which have been permitted to deteriorate."[20] A year later in 1945, the CHA conducted a rehabilitation survey of buildings in the same two square blocks between Thirty-Fifth and Thirty-Seventh Streets and Vernon and Rhodes Avenues.[21] As an example of distressed housing conditions in the area, the survey reported that one single-family house had been converted to seven residential units plus a barbershop and beauty salon. The study also noted that the redevelopment and relocations acts of 1947 were then pending, which would "facilitate slum rehabilitation under private auspices."[22]

In the same year, Barnett sought to interest Edwin Embree, chairman of the Mayor's Commission on Race Relations, in rehabilitating the area. He asked Embree to support an effort to organize black business and property owners to "initiate a corporation to reclaim some of the blighted area on the South Side." He thought area residents and businesses would initiate the investment but expected "downtown capital would be interested in helping it though not on a charity basis but just as good business." Barnett sought the aid of the mayor's committee staff to get the organization started. Proposing an alliance between black property owners and downtown capital, he implied that in exchange for capital to rehabilitate their area they would provide a black middle-class buffer between the slums and the borders of the University of Chicago.[23] His appeal to quasi-public corporations and agencies, the CHA and the Mayor's Committee, offers evidence that he was having trouble getting his self-help effort off the ground without an initial public investment or at least endorsement. Alas, nothing seemed to come of these private-led, publicly aided collaborative or "self-help" efforts at rehabilitation and conservation.

Barnett and his associates redoubled their efforts after the city's land-clearance program had replaced the neighborhood north of their own with the Lake Meadows project. Communicating a profound sense of loss, Barnett mourned the fact that the neighborhood cleared to build Lake Meadows "was a neighborhood just like ours and . . . was part of ours." Now its former residents "were scattered all over the city." He reported that few could buy comparable buildings to those that had been demolished, many of which "were in excellent condition," and noted that some of the former residents were still searching for "a stable place in which to live." Barnett and his fellow residents did not want to suffer the same fate; they liked their neighborhood and did not want to move.[24] While they had opposed the clearing of their land, many later welcomed the Lake Meadows project because it was a "high-class accommodation" not usually offered for "colored occupancy." However, the residents regretted "the loss of the professional and economically secure classes" who had fled to Hyde Park in anticipation of land clearance. They argued that this black stratum would have been "natural tenants for the Lake Meadows project."[25]

After 1953, Barnett, battle-weary from repeated redevelopment failures and land conflicts, founded a series of fledgling groups in order to redevelop the area east of South Parkway between Thirty-Fifth and Thirty-Seventh Streets. Barnett helped to form the Neighborhood Protection Association and later the East Central Douglass Redevelopment Corporation with the aim of using new legislative tools to aid his effort to redevelop the same area

he had been targeting for fourteen years.[26] These legislative aids were produced by the Urban Community Conservation Act of 1953, a revision (also
in 1953) of the 1947 Neighborhood Redevelopment Corporation law, and the
federal Urban Renewal Act of 1954.[27] Barnett realized that, under the revised
Neighborhood Redevelopment Corporation law, Supreme Liberty Life, the
largest property owner in the neighborhood, could "qualify as the agency
handling rehabilitation loans."[28] In addition, other insurance companies as
well as black building and loan associations could also be eligible for low-
interest funds for conservation and redevelopment purposes. Black property
owners could get access to the loan money from these agencies to improve
and modernize their property. These were indeed new tools to aid the conservation work of private citizens that had not been available in the earlier
years of Barnett's dogged efforts.

Through the Neighborhood Protection Association, Barnett focused on
two tasks. The first and more important task was to establish a redevelopment corporation that could receive federal and state funds. The second was
to encourage self-help rehabilitation among his neighbors, especially those
who did not keep up their property. He did this by telling them that the city
would take their land if they did not improve it.[29] The neighborhood had not
changed much since the early attempts at redevelopment in the late 1940s.
It still had a high rate of black homeownership (over 75 percent), and it still
suffered from "deterioration, over crowding and neglect."[30] According to
Barnett, this neighborhood had been overlooked, condemned as slums, and
subject to "poor and indifferent" city services. Though there was not as much
absentee ownership as in other areas on the South Side, Barnett planned to
recruit these absentee owners into the organization. While some absentee
owners had already joined the effort, Barnett, in particular, took "steps to
get a couple of absentee owners in who are renting to undesirables" into
the organization.[31] The Neighborhood Protection Association wanted the
"worst buildings" demolished but hoped the Chicago Dwellings Association,
a quasi-public agency formed to build middle-class housing, would build
homes selling for $12,000 to $15,000 on the vacant lots. It appeared that the
organization wanted to remove poor residents from the kitchenette buildings and replace them with middle-class black homeowners.[32]

By 1955, it appeared that Barnett had met his objective. The Neighborhood
Protective Association became the East Central Douglass Neighborhood
Redevelopment Corporation. The redevelopment corporation had the same
purposes as its predecessors. It asked each property owner to contribute $100

per property to raise the funds for the 25 percent down payment needed to incorporate. The corporation had $4,000 subscribed but wanted to raise $10,000 in total, with 25 percent of the monies collected before they went before the Redevelopment Commission downtown. Keeping in mind the advice from the city's neighborhood redevelopment commission to raise sufficient capital, Barnett complained to his colleagues at Supreme Liberty Life that their efforts at attracting subscribers to the corporation in the neighborhood were lacking. He grumbled, in classic black self-help language, "It is difficult to make people understand that here is something for their own development." He criticized the fatalism in their belief that no matter what they did, "the government and white people are determined to take this area back." He reported that 27 out of 125 property owners had subscribed but asserted that they could get the majority in a week or ten days if they had "two or three real salesmen to cover these people." In addition, Barnett asked Supreme Liberty Life to buy shares. He appealed to Supreme Liberty Life to demonstrate its capacity to save people's property and create a trend that would be emulated across the black South Side.[33]

Despite these elaborate plans, the area was not developed due to the lack of insufficient capital from black businesses and property owners. Ten years earlier, Barnett had sought an alliance with the city's progrowth elite. After black property owners' opposition to slum clearance in 1948 and 1949 had led black insurance companies to withdraw from the city's urban redevelopment site, there was antagonism between powerful private–public coalition partners and black institutional elites seeking autonomy in what they considered to be their racial sphere of influence. The antagonism stemmed from black business and civic elites' sense of downtown capital and public officials' neglect or lack of interest in conserving their neighborhood. But it also was based on the fear that if these "outside interests" did get involved, black property owners would lose control of the redevelopment process and become displaced like their neighbors.

Barnett and his associates concluded that large capital would get involved only on their own terms, which they feared would result in their further displacement. Despite the mistrust, these black elites realized they needed both the private capital and the government aid that the potential white coalition partners could provide. Despite their self-help instincts, black elites determined they could not do it alone, nor did they think they should since large white corporations were getting massive public subsidies. In addition, underlying their self-help approach, black elites shared the same privatist bias inherent in progrowth ideology. They hoped that their own plans, with outside aid, would lead to simultaneously securing their class housing interests and achieving racial-group progress. It was clear that they wanted to preserve the area's elite enclaves (and therefore the community's stratified housing patterns) and hoped their redeveloped area would become a model for other black home-owning neighborhoods throughout the South Side. However, their embrace of self-help redevelopment made them ideologically susceptible to the underlying principles of the city's slum clearance and urban redevelopment program. This fact, coupled with their dependence on external aid, made it difficult for them to compete with more powerful white capital in trying to control their land base.

Black Conservation in Bronzeville

The Urban Community Conservation Act

Not only did Claude Barnett want to save his once affluent neighborhood, he also had larger ambitions for the South Side. He treated plans to redevelop the neighborhoods contiguous with the city's first redevelopment site as pilot projects. He would take the lessons learned and apply them to the entire black South Side. With this larger focus, black elites like Barnett planned to utilize the programmatic tools available from the Urban Community Conservation Act and revisions of the law that covered neighborhood redevelopment corporations, both passed in 1953. The impetus for developing these two new legislative tools was the length of time that it took to develop Lake Meadows. It had taken three years to break ground after the city council approved the project in 1949.[34] In addition, the long process of condemnation, compensation, and relocation gave the opposition time to organize and to delay subsequent clearance and rebuilding.[35] After a while, it was clear that Lake Meadows "as a model for future treatment of slums, has been slow, exasperating, and unencouraging" to the progrowth elites.[36]

In three years, less than two square miles had been redeveloped at a cost of $150 million per square mile. At this rate, Chicago's business elites discovered, the slums were growing twice as fast as the city could eliminate them. When the Chicago Plan Commission had determined that the city had twenty-three square miles of blighted or near-blighted areas, it had also identified fifty-six square miles of "conservation areas" in the path of fast-spreading blight. Business elites realized they needed to check the progression of blight, or it would "damage the living environment of great numbers of people, destroy tax values, and rapidly reach the slum stage."[37] In fact, half of all families in Chicago resided in these fifty-six square miles, making the stakes of slum prevention quite high. Chicago's civic leaders feared that the all-too-familiar causes of blight such as overcrowding, neglected maintenance, illegal conversions, and inadequate municipal services now threatened conservation areas.

Moreover, slum prevention, like slum clearance, would necessitate engagement with the black community. Since 1950, city leaders felt the "overcrowding and deterioration had worsened in black slum areas, threatening surrounding conservation areas." An estimated 575,000 black people lived in Chicago in 1953. Since poor wage earners constituted a large majority of the black population, "providing them with decently maintained standard housing" was even more challenging. For instance, their desperate housing demand had led to 50,000 illegal conversions since 1943. For city planners, these were "the danger signs that point up incipient blight and forecast the trend toward decay."[38]

The Urban Community Conservation Act authorized any Illinois municipality to set up a conservation board with the purpose of instituting slum-prevention strategies. A conservation area was defined as "an area of not less than 160 acres in which the structures in 50 percent or more of the area are residential having an average age of thirty-five years or more."[39] These areas, though they might have had blighted square blocks within them, by and large were not yet blighted at that stage but would be without improvements. The act allowed property owners under an approved conservation plan to force other property owners to maintain minimum standards through legal enforcement. Unlike slum clearance legislation, the property did not have to be deteriorated or substandard. The board could condemn any property if it was "necessary or appropriate for the implementation of a conservation plan for a Conservation Area." The acquired property could be resold to private owners as long as it conformed to the approved conservation plan. These wide-ranging powers were granted because conservation for the purpose of slum prevention was considered a "public purpose." The Illinois State Supreme Court upheld the constitutionality of both the Urban Community Conservation Act and the revised Neighborhood Redevelopment Corporation law, giving "Chicago the most powerful weapons that any city has ever had to stop the spread of blight."[40]

Mid-South Chicago Council

With these new state laws on the books, black civic leaders did not want the initiative to "conserve" black neighborhoods to remain in the hands of the city. After 1953, they began to organize in order to create their own conservation plans like the one crafted by the Barnett-led East Central Douglass Neighborhood Redevelopment Corporation in 1955. Oscar C. Brown Sr., representing the Mid-South Chicago Council, initiated a meeting on April 27, 1954, "to discuss the possibilities of arranging for coordinated conservation effort in the Negro Southside area (about 33rd to 63rd; State to Cottage)." At this meeting, which included the city's housing and redevelopment coordinator, the Mid-South Chicago Council was selected to coordinate conservation efforts on the "Negro Southside area." However, the sordid legacy of the slum clearance fight persisted. One meeting participant observed that there was a fear and a "lack of confidence in major community improvement" in some districts of the black community where people confused conservation with slum clearance. The new organization was tasked with clearing up this confusion and restoring confidence in the new proposals. At this meeting, it was decided that the Mid-South Chicago Council, which was sponsored by the Negro Chamber of Commerce, should work with both the Urban League, which utilized its block clubs to conserve black neighborhoods in order to prevent more land clearance, and the South Side Planning Board.[41]

Mid-South Chicago Council membership was restricted to a person "who lives, works or otherwise is identified with real estate, business, educational, religious and community interest in the area of operation" and agrees with the council's purposes. The council employed a multipronged approach to arresting blight. It proposed to conserve good property, rehabilitate those houses and buildings that were sound, and have any redevelopment controlled by the people who live or work in the area.[42] The rejection of wholesale clearance and support for local control of redevelopment reflected the approach of black institutional elites and property owners to redevelopment. The council was intended to act as a coordinating organization, supporting groups active in conservation, rehabilitation, and redevelopment efforts.[43]

The political scientist James Q. Wilson reports that the Mid-South Chicago Council was short-lived due to internal conflicts that emerged around its conservation activities. Apparently, "the vigorous prosecution of laws, building codes, and city cleaning programs" proved a double-edged sword. It could benefit some black property owners through "enhanced property values" but could also expose violations by other black property owners. Once the council got serious with its "clean-up campaign" that sought building code enforcement, a council member reported to Wilson, "one or two guys in the Council started to stink." Apparently, those council members in violation told the leadership that they had "to keep this thing under control." Presumably, according to Wilson's source, the disgruntled members did not make their appeal from a position of self-interest, insisting instead that they spoke on the behalf of poor small black property owners who could not afford the mandated improvements. The potential for enforcing code violations against some black property owners was not the only conflict, according to Wilson. Opposition to the housing rehabilitation entailed in black conservation plans also threatened some black and white commercial interests that benefited from high black population densities.

These cumulative conflicts led to the demise of the Mid-South Chicago Council after two or three years. Wilson explained that eventually black business owners, real estate brokers, and property owners "grew cool to the idea of area conservation when they realized that building code enforcement would mean a reduction in population density and hence a shrinkage in their market." They feared that neighborhood rehabilitation would introduce "competition from new white businesses brought into a redeveloped area or population losses or both."[44] So the faction that opposed slum clearance split within itself when it came to slum prevention. Black civic leaders and middle-class homeowners who favored rehabilitation and conservation now opposed business owners, real estate brokers, and owners of rental property who tolerated or facilitated overcrowding and substandard housing conditions associated with blight.[45]

"Negro Clearance" Revisited: Urban Renewal in Hyde Park

African Americans had a tortured history in Hyde Park during the first half of the twentieth century. The resistance to integration had been so effective in that neighborhood since the violent 1920s that by 1940, Hyde Park, the home of the University of Chicago, was largely white and affluent, with blacks constituting less than 4 percent of the population.[46] Black population had only increased to 6 percent by 1950. In 1940, however, the black presence had spread to within a mile of Hyde Park. During the following decade, for the first time, blacks got closer to crossing Cottage Grove Avenue, which represented a racial border separating Hyde Park from black communities that lay to the west. Observers noted that by 1950, "the areas to the north and west of Kenwood were rapidly being consolidated as Negro neighborhoods and Hyde Park-Kenwood itself was in the process of being entered."[47] By 1956, the black population in Hyde Park had increased to 36 percent. Between 1950 and 1956, it was estimated that twenty thousand whites were replaced by twenty-three thousand racial minorities. Black migration to Hyde Park-Kenwood followed what was becoming a familiar pattern of racial succession, with blacks filling up "solid blocks" before moving into new areas. As a result, blacks were not evenly distributed throughout the community. Unsurprisingly, they were concentrated in those areas that bordered the ghetto.[48]

Upper-middle-class blacks were the first to puncture racial barriers in North West Hyde Park, which experienced more black migration than other parts of the Hyde Park-Kenwood community.[49] These African Americans had moved into the community between 1948 and 1953 after "the lifting of the restrictive covenants" and the land clearance in the Douglas neighborhood. They were among the earliest arrivals of the "nonwhite migrants" and were considered stable residents. These early black arrivals were mostly educated business owners and professionals including journalists, teachers, social workers, realtors, and others. They either purchased and renovated the better maintained two-flat buildings or rented upscale apartments, mostly in Drexel Square, an expensive apartment complex on the western edge of Hyde Park.[50]

Usually, skilled and stably employed workers who were able to afford the higher purchase prices or rents in the new area followed middle-class blacks.[51] Next in the housing queue were unskilled workers who could only afford the rents in illegally converted or already deteriorating multifamily buildings. In anticipation of the latter group, real estate speculators cut up three-family houses into kitchenettes in order to pile more blacks into the buildings, causing overcrowding and such consequences as deteriorating physical structures, diminishing municipal services, and crime.[52]

To many observers, liberal white residents of Hyde Park, many of whom were associated with the university, seemed less disturbed by a different racial presence than by a different class presence and the accompanying "blight." In the areas to which blacks moved, west of the Illinois Central railroad, the buildings were as old and dilapidated as those in the black ghetto. The sections south and east of the community between the university and

Lake Michigan were more white and affluent. Whatever the cause, it was apparent to those liberal white residents that by 1950, Hyde Park-Kenwood had lost its reputation as a "high-status area."[53]

Two factors made neighborhood conservation unique in Hyde Park. First, white residents were more accepting of black middle-class neighbors than in other areas in the city. Second, the presence of the university meant that many citizens utilized their professional expertise in the service of neighborhood conservation. The sociologists Peter Rossi and Robert Dentler pointed out that professional expertise in law, real estate, and race and public relations was more available than in the average middle-class urban neighborhood.[54] However, Hyde Park white citizens' racial liberalism had its limits; they were still committed to keeping the area predominantly white. The fact that racial minorities neared 40 percent meant to remaining white residents that something had to be done to stop a white exodus. Aware of the association of urban renewal with "Negro removal," many white citizens assured detractors that they only wanted "a safe, clean, well-serviced community." Nonetheless, it did not matter whether or not they specifically targeted blacks for removal; the fact that blacks and working-class whites were predominantly concentrated in the most dilapidated structures in the community meant they would suffer disproportionately from any clearance activity.

In Rossi and Dentler's estimation, it was clear that "neighborhood conservation and renewal meant the preservation of Hyde Park-Kenwood as a primarily *white* middle-class residential neighborhood" (original emphasis). Their study determined that Hyde Park's citizens had decided that "economic homogeneity will take precedence over racial integration." The University of Chicago not only agreed with white residents that the area should remain predominantly white and be upgraded economically, but it had the power to achieve its objectives.[55] At the end of the day, Hyde Park was to become an "interracial middle-class neighborhood." However, only African Americans who already lived in good housing or could afford to buy or rent the new housing would be accepted as neighborhood residents. Rossi and Dentler contended that the Hyde Park-Kenwood community confronted the problem of racial integration more than other communities in the country, but in doing so decided "that integration cannot succeed unless the class level and customs of the two groups are approximately equal."[56]

The process by which Hyde Park-Kenwood practiced urban renewal has been well studied.[57] My account focuses less on whites' agency and more on the participation of black elites, activists, and residents in the process, paying close attention to the conflict between different segments of the black community. In particular, this section explains the crosscurrents of race and class in blacks' ineffectual opposition to the Hyde Park urban renewal plan. The historian Arnold Hirsch makes a compelling case that the main force behind Hyde Park's urban renewal plan was the largest landowner in the community, the University of Chicago, and its instrument, the South East Chicago Commission (SECC).[58] Hirsch shows how first the university's real estate office, then the commission, prevented illegal conversions that helped to manage black entrance into the community.[59] An interracial homeowners group, Hyde Park-Kenwood Community Conference (HPKCC), played a complementary role legitimating the urban renewal plan with other residents.[60]

Hyde Park's blight was not conducive to the wholesale clearance program of the 1949 federal Housing Act or the 1947 Illinois redevelopment law. It was more suited for the conservation and redevelopment approaches that were eventually incorporated in the Urban Conservation Act and the revised Neighborhood Development Corporation laws.[61] In fact, forces associated with the University of Chicago and Hyde Park, according to Hirsch, helped to shape this legislation for the purposes of arresting blight and managing racial succession in Hyde Park-Kenwood.[62] In particular, the university wanted the neighborhood development corporation to have eminent domain powers if it received the *consent* of 60 percent of the property owners in the redevelopment site, since the prior requirement that the corporation *own* 60 percent of the designated site property itself had proven unworkable.[63]

Urban Renewal in Hyde Park

South West Hyde Park's renewal was governed by the university-sponsored redevelopment corporation, which acquired the power of eminent domain to clear "blight" on the western edge of the campus. The university and the SECC had the most direct control over renewal of this area, which represented, in Hirsch's judgment, "the most visible attempt to regulate the university's racial environment."[64] Located just behind North West Hyde Park, this area experienced more migration of blacks than any other area from 1945 to 1956.[65] Jack Meltzer, SECC planning director, warned decision makers that the areas north of Fifty-Fifth Street and west of Ellis Avenue from Fifty-Fifth to Fifty-Eighth Streets were "becoming 100% Negro." The problem was clearly conceptualized in "racial terms."[66]

While most of the redevelopment site was designed for rehabilitation, the university through its corporation wanted to clear and acquire property on a 14.5-acre segment between Fifty-Fifth and Fifty-Sixth Streets, from Cottage Grove to Ellis Avenues. The population of the acquisition site was overwhelmingly black, 80 percent, compared to 54 percent in the overall redevelopment area.[67] Fifty-one percent of the acquisition site's "local residents" worked as domestic servants, manual laborers, or industrial workers.[68] In June 1956, the university-sponsored South West Hyde Park Redevelopment Corporation proposed to acquire and clear the area for an estimated $2.5 million. The university wanted to construct five, of a planned seven, five-story buildings for married student housing. When completed, the new development would replace the existing 660 dwelling units with 394. The university expected to invest $4.3 million for "acquisition, demolition, and construction with the four square-block site." The corporation planned to conserve the remaining forty acres of the surrounding area through modernization and rehabilitation of existing structures. It "proposed to write covenants into property deeds requiring future owners to maintain building standards, and proposed rezoning of the area to allow only multiple dwellings."[69]

The HPKCC endorsed the corporation's plan in July 1956. The previous April, a black property owners association, the South West Hyde Park Neighborhood Association, had informed the conference that it wanted to participate in the planning process in the interest of protecting owners from wholesale clearance and displacement from the neighborhood. The association, formed under the leadership of St. Clair Drake, wished "to work with but not through the Conference." Drake, who had received his doctorate from the University of Chicago and was coauthor of *Black Metropolis*, was at the time a professor of sociology at Roosevelt University; he had just purchased a home in the 5600 block of Maryland Avenue, one block south of the acquisition site.[70] Upon his return in 1955 after a two-year absence, he tried to purchase housing east of the university near the University Lab School, which his children attended. Due to racial discrimination, Drake was not able to purchase a place in spite of the numerous vacancies that existed. The university, wanting to keep South East Hyde Park all white, was instrumental in preventing Drake from buying a home in that neighborhood.[71]

Drake's personal experiences contributed to his skeptical attitude toward the university's intentions and actions once he became president of the association. In a letter to friends and neighbors in July 1956, he commented that he and other "Negro property owners . . . west of Ellis" were unsure of whether the university-sponsored redevelopment corporation wanted "integration" or, instead, wanted to move blacks back across Cottage Grove Avenue. He complained that no one from the university, commission, or corporation had communicated to them "just where they stand in this contemplated process of 'urban renewal.'" Therefore, Drake refused to join the 60 percent of residents needed to give their consent so that the corporation gained the power of eminent domain. Nonetheless, the South West Hyde Park Neighborhood Association agreed in large part with the agenda of the HPKCC, including the principle of "planning for conservation," and agreed to work together with them to achieve a "clean, safe, orderly, attractive community." They also accepted the university's need for space. However, their memo declared, "We feel the rights of resident owners in this area are every whit as important as the rights of the institutions."

The South West Hyde Park Neighborhood Association did not feel adequately consulted and felt the university's redevelopment corporation had not considered any locations for university housing other than the four square blocks slated for clearance. The association leadership claimed the area could be improved through "spot clearance and rehabilitation." However, Julian Levi and Jack Meltzer, who doubled as SECC planning unit director and head of the South West Hyde Park Neighborhood Corporation, said rehabilitation was not economical and that modern housing was needed to attract married students to the university. Drake's organization also wanted a commitment from the university, the SECC, and the realtors to take "a clear stand for 'open occupancy' east of Ellis Avenue." Drake explicitly stated that he would not consent to the university's housing plan unless housing east of Ellis and south of Fifty-Fifth Streets was open to "Negro occupancy."[72]

There were two hearings before the city's Neighborhood Redevelopment Commission. Levi presented the necessary consent of more than 60 percent of the owners in the designated conservation area. He also gave assurances that the Mayors' Housing Coordinator and the Chicago Housing Authority would provide relocation services. The head of the HPKCC provided testimony about the acquisition site resident owners' lack of interest in coming to meetings hosted by the conference.[73] Drake countered that residents were disinclined to come to a meeting to discuss their "extinction." He also pointed out that lack of attendance at the meetings did not indicate lack of interest in improving their property. Moreover, Drake attacked the methodology of the housing surveys gathered by the redevelopment corporation. He claimed the surveys identified some properties as dilapidated when in fact they needed only minor improvements. Drake proposed that some demo-lition of buildings should occur, but that spot clearance and rehabilitation could conserve the rest of the area. He felt the university could buy buildings on the open market to use for married student housing.

After Drake's criticism, a chagrined HPKCC found, in subsequent sur-veys, that homeowners in a two-block area had done more to improve their property than the organization had indicated in their testimony. The con-ference's real estate director also discovered eight buildings designated as "dilapidated" in the proposal to be in "excellent condition." In addition, the conference talked to fifteen of twenty-five property owners in the redevel-opment area who signed the consents and found support was weaker than they supposed. Ten of the fifteen who had described the acquisition area as deteriorating were affluent white homeowners, including five university employees, who lived outside the acquisition area. The others were African Americans, including three who thought the neighborhood was deteriorat-ing and revealed their plans to move anyway. They figured that "if we played ball with the University we'd get a better deal."[74]

Drake and the redevelopment corporation sparred over what constituted a dilapidated building. Several black homeowners talked about the improve-ments they had made in their property. Yet these improvements were deemed irrelevant since the redevelopment corporation lawyer was able to establish that most properties had been "converted through usage." In other words, by exceeding the number of persons per room, these dwellings were labeled "overcrowded" and therefore susceptible to blight. Given the chronic hous-ing shortage, many black families lived doubled up in the buildings, with six or seven families in a three-flat building. Rossi and Dentler commented on the conflict of "housing values between Negroes recently moved from the 'ghetto' and upper-middle-class whites who establish housing standards." They reported that "the [black] witnesses were indignant that their proper-ties, into which they had poured so much energy and scarce capital, were designated as dilapidated."

Furthermore, using the context of a severely overcrowded Black Belt that they had just escaped, "they felt that two couples related through blood or marriage and their children could occupy a four-room apartment without necessarily being overcrowded." They found their present quarters "luxuri-ous" compared to their former housing.[75] Nevertheless, the redevelopment corporation did not budge from its position that the area was headed toward blight. They enlisted Philip Hauser, chairman of the Department of

Sociology at the University of Chicago, to affirm their position that "over-crowding" threatened the area with blight. Hauser and other professional housing and census specialists used the housing standards of affluent whites, according to Rossi and Dentler, to discredit those of black "resident owners" in the acquisition area.[76]

The South West Hyde Park Neighborhood Association summed up their opposition to the proposal in the fourth hearing. Their attorney, Michael Hagiwara, concluded that the university had not proven that its plan served a public purpose, which was required by the legislation, and that it had in fact caused undue hardship to the area residents. He called upon a black block leader to testify, who asked plaintively, "Must we always be on the move? . . . Must we always be afraid to invest in anything except expensive cars? Must we be told in an undertone that we are not needed?" Hagiwara concluded, "It is our belief . . . that the basic purpose of this plan . . . is to allow the University of Chicago to set up a buffer against the presence of Negro residents in large numbers." The HPKCC, perceiving itself as an interracial organization and leery about being seen as the university's tool, chafed under the charge that the plan was racially biased. Nonetheless, because they believed that institutions were the key to neighborhood stability, an assumption that also underlay earlier redevelopment plans, the HPKCC endorsed the plan while expressing some concerns about relocation, fair compensation, and nondiscrimination. Alderman Leon Depres of the Fifth Ward, despite questioning the plan's "public purpose" and citing the university's participation in racially restrictive covenants before 1948, also ended up endorsing the plan.[77]

The new HPKCC chairman, James Cunningham, arranged a meeting between university chancellor Lawrence Kimpton and Louis Martin, editor and publisher of the *Chicago Defender*, to head off any black criticism of the urban renewal plan. Martin asserted that the university intended only to prevent blight, but the black newsweekly also published a commentary by St. Clair Drake, who charged, "The issue is whether a law designed to conserve a neighborhood should be used to reduce the proportion of Negroes in the area." According to Rossi and Dentler, Drake's comments set the tone for the *Defender* to criticize the university's motives throughout 1957 and 1958, culminating in the newspaper's opposition to the final renewal plan.[78] Nonetheless, the city's Neighborhood Redevelopment Commission, by a vote of two to one, approved the proposed plan of the South West Hyde Park Corporation on November 26, 1956. The lone black member cast the dissenting vote, arguing that the corporation had failed to convince him that the area was deteriorating fast enough to warrant demolition. The South West Hyde Park Neighborhood Association fought the decision through the courts until the U.S. Supreme Court refused to hear the case in 1958. In effect, the court "upheld the right of the neighborhood redevelopment corporation to use condemnation procedures in blighted areas." In the intervening two years, attorney Hagiwara died, and Drake left Hyde Park for Africa.[79]

In a letter to the *Hyde Park Herald* written before he left for Africa, Drake gave his assessment of the fight. He was critical of the HPKCC's role in legitimizing the university's and the SECC's plans. In addition, he wrote, "every Hyde Park Negro leader is almost driven schizophrenic trying to decide whether to act as a 'Race Man' or in terms of his social class position." In a letter to Alderman Depres, Drake wrote perceptively that current race relations were more fluid, making "the issues in some places matters of class and proportions of Negroes rather than the presence of Negroes per se. . . . And this *is* involved . . . in Hyde Park's renewal effort."[80] The Neighborhood Association was able to delay action for two years. More importantly, their opposition, according to Rossi and Dentler, cast a pall on the use of private redevelopment corporations to clear and redevelop neighborhoods in the name of conservation.[81]

Final Urban Renewal Plan

There was widespread opposition to the university's final urban renewal plan, much of it union led. The United Packinghouse Workers of America, which had earlier endorsed a statement of support for urban renewal drawn up by the HPKCC, now joined with other "left wing militant unions in the Chicago area" to form the Hyde Park Tenants and Home Owners Association.[82] They opposed the urban renewal plan because it "did not meet the housing needs of the lower-income segment of the community" and because the organization's "social base came from householders whose homes were being demolished and those who lived around the borders of Hyde Park" redevelopment sites. According to Rossi and Dentler, the opposition both advised targeted residents of their relocation rights and helped them secure those rights.[83]

On May 22, 1958, the *Chicago Defender* published an editorial titled "Urban Renewal for Whom?" that asked, "Would not this plan benefit most of those people least in need of federal assistance?" Without any revision of the plan, the *Defender* asserted, that is exactly what it would do. The editorial also asked whether the plan neglected "lower class and Negro housing needs."[84] The Hyde Park Tenants and Home Owners Association asserted accurately in a paid advertisement in the *Hyde Park Herald* that "the real purpose of the renewal plan is to create an upper income community." Opposition soon spread to include the Chicago Urban League, the NAACP, along with the policy unit of the CIO Packinghouse Workers Union.[85] All these groups called for more public *and* middle-income housing.[86] Alderman William Harvey, who had opposed the city's first slum clearance project, consistently supported black property rights. He said that he "could not approve of owner-occupied housing being torn down for institutional expansion, as was the case in the present plan." Rossi and Dentler mentioned that Harvey "was most critical of the Urban Renewal Plan, or expressed the greatest doubts."[87] The Communist Party of Illinois and the CIO Cook County Industrial Union Council joined the Chicago Urban League, the NAACP, and the United Packinghouse Workers Union in opposition to the plan.[88]

By all accounts, black opposition to Hyde Park's urban renewal plan was ineffectual. The fact that the Archdiocese of Chicago presented the most "sustained and unequivocal" opposition to antiblack elements of the plan was testimony to the weakness of the black opposition.[89] What was the basis for their weakness this time? In the earlier land-clearance fight, a cleavage had emerged between black elite groups, one focused on "breaking up the ghetto" and the other seeking to protect black-owned property and institutions within it.[90] What was at stake was the race-based vision of two different segments of black elites not intraracial class conflict. During the first land-clearance battle, the issue of class had been muted. The competing black elite groups based their appeal on a different version of what was supposed to be a unitary racial interest, either collective black property ownership or integrated housing. The "ghetto-defense" group was more successful at defining the race's collective interest even to the point of forcing black insurance companies to abandon their plans to redevelop a portion of the land-clearance site for black middle-class housing. The term "Negro clearance" alluded to the fact that blacks of all housing classes would suffer from wholesale demolition. However, what neither the term nor its implied analytical framework could capture due to its racial lens was the fact that Lake Meadows' spacious and upmarket apartments would be largely occupied by black professionals and white-collar clerks. In other words, the costs and benefits of the city's slum clearance program were not evenly borne by all black strata.

This time around, the issue of class, so insightfully posed by St. Clair Drake, was raised publicly, but it could not gain traction as the basis for a broad-based black opposition to the Hyde Park plan. In ten years, what had changed? Though all blacks were largely confined to an expanding ghetto, after 1948, the pioneering black middle class found housing commensurate with their status on the outskirts of that geographic expansion.[91] Both income growth and employment stability for black white-collar and skilled blue-collar workers increased the demand for nearby brick bungalows or two- and three-flat buildings. The targets of the city's redevelopment strategy and accompanying legislative tools had also changed. In the case of Lake Meadows, its one hundred–acre site was cleared, targeting both large and small property owners and defenseless tenants. With the focus on spot clearance and rehabilitation in Hyde Park, only pockets of black residence, mainly working-class sections, were under attack. This programmatic change led to the greatest difference between the two conflicts.

In the first land clearance fight, all black property owners were victimized in some fashion. In the Hyde Park battle, not only were affluent blacks who could afford standard housing spared but they joined the erstwhile enemy. Thus upper- and middle-class blacks who lived in upscale homes and apartments in Kenwood and North West Hyde Park and who feared being engulfed by the ghetto approved the urban renewal plan. In other words, they joined their white counterparts to support the University of Chicago's clearance of deteriorated housing largely owned by small black property owners that accommodated working-class tenants. The sentiment of this class was best expressed by the black civic leader Earl Dickerson at a meeting in Hyde Park in 1949: "Every one of the Negroes in this room moved here, as I did, to get away from a slum. We've spent thousands of dollars on our properties, and they look a lot better today than when we bought them from the white people who left. We have an even greater stake than white neighbors in keeping the area from deteriorating."[92]

Some black elites knew who to blame for the deteriorating conditions Dickerson described. One such leader said outright, "Negroes right now are a real threat in housing. They can cause a neighborhood to go down. Look at Hyde Park; it went down when Negroes moved in. . . . People convert to multifamily units and kitchenettes, and the behavior patterns of the Negroes that move in are bad."[93] Other black civic leaders and residents were candid in their preference for class homogeneity in their respective neighborhoods. One "prominent Negro" who lived in the area informed the political scientist

James Q. Wilson, "When you get people living together whose actions and culture are far apart, then you are bound to have dissatisfactions arise, race notwithstanding." He added, "It is better to have in one neighborhood people of like thinking and tastes." A black civic leader who also lived in the area agreed: "You can't create a homogeneous community out of heterogeneous elements. . . . You have to have a homogeneous community, education- ally and economically, if it is to be a stable community."[94] Affluent blacks, tired of keeping one step ahead of the ghetto, saw it in their *interest* to align themselves with the forces that would keep those conditions at bay—the university and an interracial homeowners association—who accepted *their* presence and participation in the process. Whether that meant preventing absentee landlords (white and black) from illegally converting large houses or apartment buildings into kitchenettes or displacing the black "resident- owner" who struggled to keep up his property on a modest income did not matter. None could not be spared, and this prosperous black stratum sup- ported these actions.[95]

Therefore, it was no surprise that subsequent scholars found the efforts of the CUL and the Chicago NAACP in this fight "half-hearted."[96] The stratum that served as board members, professional staff, financial donors, or the "attentive public" of these black civic organizations made sure the organiza- tion's opposition was pro forma.[97] The fact that they could not enlist their organizations on behalf of their class interests in public support of the Hyde Park urban renewal plan spoke to the residual power of racial unity to blunt public expressions of such bare class interests by black groups.[98] James Q. Wilson concluded, perceptively, that "race values resist the normal operation of the processes of social stratification in the Negro community."[99]

The appeal of racial unity, however, was a double-edged sword. On the one hand, it could be wielded on behalf of the large working-class black majority who, as tenants or struggling property owners, were victimized by land clearance by ensuring that the racial appeal was defined by *their* class interests. On the other hand, by not specifying a class calculation of costs and benefits, the politics of racial unity more than likely allows elite interests to pose uncontested as representing those of the race.[100] It is the shifting class content of racial appeals that makes it slippery when it comes to determin- ing who wins and who loses in any housing policy proposal. At least for an anonymous black civic leader, the nature of the urban renewal conflict was not complicated. He explained his opposition to public housing in the Hyde Park plan, declaring, "I think [we] would take the same position as a white man of similar class and status would. It's a class question, really."[101] Some black civic elites recognized that the Hyde Park plan did not practice "overt racial discrimination," but there was disagreement over how to characterize the disadvantage experienced by displaced black residents. For some, the fact that, in Wilson's terms, the "impersonal effect of the market mechanism" excluded many blacks meant "income" no less than "race" was an "insufficient or immoral reason [for] excluding Negroes from the area."[102] For others, of course, the fact that only *racial* exclusion mattered meant the ability to pay should determine who lives in Hyde Park and other affluent neighborhoods in Chicago.

While Wilson focuses on black civic leadership's response to housing policies like the Hyde Park urban renewal plan, Hirsch interprets the motivations of the white architects of the urban renewal plan. Though he admits that class was a factor in the Hyde Park case, Hirsch argues the primary motivation was racial—managing black movement into the community so that it would not detract from its predominantly white and economically upgraded character. Hirsch accurately portrays the university's use of class as a device to prevent "racial succession," which it witnessed spreading to surrounding white neighborhoods. For these powerful white elites, class was used to distinguish between "desirable" and "undesirable" blacks. As an apparently race-neutral tool, it minimized the number of blacks who qualified, in terms of income and cultural standards, for Hyde Park residence. Hirsch argues against those who claim that class substituted for race as the "crucial variable" in this land-clearance battle. He dismisses their contention that working-class whites suffered equally. For instance, he points out that more whites than blacks were relocated to other parts of Hyde Park.[103]

In addition, Hirsch also sees through the ruse of substituting "cultural" for unacceptable "racial" grounds for Hyde Park exclusion. He cites a number of university officials and supporting scholars who identified the cultural deficiency of Southern-born black migrants who were unadjusted to "urban living" as the reason to exclude the majority of blacks. Hirsch shows that most blacks victimized by the University of Chicago's plan did not fit the social description proffered by social analysts.[104] What he doesn't account for is the resonance that such race-neutral but class-based cultural arguments had for affluent black residents and civic leaders in justifying their support for the university's urban renewal plan. The belief of the black upper stratum that poor blacks suffered from social disorganization provided them with an acceptable *class* reason for exclusion when they needed one to cover their complicity. Upper- and middle-class blacks may not have felt comfortable citing lack of income as a basis for exclusion, but they were decidedly more comfortable referring to excluded blacks' lack of urban acculturation. Wilson's black informants confirmed the importance of middle-class culture in their preference for class homogeneity and indictment of black working-class residential behavior. It is telling that the University of Chicago's chancellor, Lawrence Kimpton, tried to make the case for working-class black exclusion based on their "habits of life" to members of the black fraternity Kappa Alpha Psi. While there is no record of the response of the black middle-class audience to the chancellor's remarks, however, it is not unreasonable to assume that they accepted, if not welcomed his remarks. Indeed, the fact that black attorney William Ming had provided the "base of the speech" that Julian Levi and Kimpton subsequently revised suggests that the reaction of the audience was very likely positive.[105] Hyde Park's affluent black residents accepted these explanations as legitimate reasons to oppose the housing interests of those who shared their racial identity but not their class.

For an influential minority within Chicago's black population, the critical question was not why the "black opposition" was ineffective since the race's most privileged strata clearly did not intend it to be effective.[106] From the point of view of black agency, the critical question was how the most advantaged segment of that population, under the guise of confronting a "racial problem," was able to satisfy their class interests at the expense of those of the lower strata. The whole episode illustrates that this upper- and middle-class black public and their civic leadership valued class stratification in housing (though quietly at the time) and worked to make it compatible with a racial democratic housing agenda. The class appeals and social democratic sentiments expressed by a predominantly black labor leadership did not gain traction precisely because they opposed the class interests of a more influential black elite segment that drove a black civic agenda for housing reform in Hyde Park as well as in the rest of the city.

Conclusion

For the black institutional elite faction, controlling redevelopment on the Mid-South Side was the main objective. Both black institutional and civic elites had advocated self-help rehabilitation since the city began to wrestle with the problems of blight and slums. Over time, legislation was introduced or revised to make rehabilitation easier and conservation more successful.

Yet black institutional elites failed to wrest control of their "territory" from the city's progrowth interests, although this was not for want of trying. Their narrow focus on conserving black property and their lack of capital doomed their fragmented and sporadic efforts, which fell far short of the black homeowner power bloc imagined by the militant Sidney Williams or the "force and vision" of black capital-led redevelopment articulated by the bourgeois Claude A. Barnett. Black elites' lack of capital and political clout meant they were unable to take advantage of the new legislative tools to launch their own redevelopment and conservation schemes. Ironically, black civic leaders' failure to reconstruct their communities was brought into sharp relief by the University of Chicago's successful exploitation of these same tools to redevelop the Hyde Park-Kenwood area.

Haunted by the Lake Meadows land clearance drama, Barnett and other black institutional elites promoted self-help rehabilitation schemes in order to avoid the demolition of another black neighborhood where middle-class blacks owned homes and rental property. In the Lake Meadows struggle, black middle-class homeowners had taken the lead in fighting the city's efforts to displace them. In Hyde Park-Kenwood, affluent black residents played a significant role by *promoting* urban renewal (and with it housing stratification), and what had previously been a conflict between competing racial programs was effectively redrawn along class lines.

Unable to alter the plans of the city's progrowth elite for controlling redevelopment on the Mid-South Side or Hyde Park, black institutional and civic elites were confronted with a crisis as "black pioneers" came face-to-face with white hostility and violence when they attempted to escape the ghetto. Unlike the hidden struggles of black families that had been displaced from the Douglas and Hyde Park neighborhoods, these incidents of white racial violence were quite public and called for an effective response by black civic leaders. Black elite factions put aside their differences over urban redevelopment to face a common problem of mob violence that targeted blacks. They would find that success in this arena was as elusive as it had been in the land clearance drama.

7

Racial Violence and the Crisis of Black Elite Leadership

Racial violence in postwar Chicago united black elites more than the issues surrounding slum clearance and public housing had. This issue generated no split between national and local elites of the sort evident in the debate on the city's redevelopment program. Nothing represented a greater threat to all African Americans, regardless of class, geography, or affiliation, than violence targeted at a person or persons because of their race. Nothing better dramatized the restrictions that blacks experienced seeking improved housing than the harassment, intimidation, and violence committed by whites to keep blacks in the ghetto. Despite the ambivalence African Americans felt about living in integrated neighborhoods, they were united in the belief that as citizens of the United States they had the right to live wherever they chose. Chicago's history of housing-based racial violence demonstrated to them throughout the postwar period that they would have a difficult time exercising that right.

Since racial violence demonstrated that African Americans were victimized solely because they were black, it is not surprising that black elites analyzed the situation exclusively in racial terms. Black civic and labor organizations argued that the root cause of the violence was African Americans' lack of nondiscriminatory access to Chicago's metropolitan housing markets. They used the occasion of racial violence to articulate their critique of federal and municipal housing policies, whether it was urban redevelopment or public or FHA housing. While they held individual whites accountable for racist acts, they nonetheless saw the exclusionary practices of white realtors and developers as the underlying cause of housing-based violence. Yet they did not directly target the diffused real estate industry. Instead, they set their sights on city government either because the bulk of the violence was located at government housing developments or because black elites surmised that it was government's responsibility to protect black victims. They targeted municipal governmental institutions such as the mayor's office, the Chicago

Housing Authority (CHA), and the police department for their failure to guarantee nondiscriminatory access to public and private housing, or at least to physically protect black citizens in exercising their right to live anywhere in the city.

Housing-based racial violence occurred either in neighborhoods experiencing or under the threat of racial transition or in formerly all-white public housing projects. It dramatized and reinforced for black elites the primacy of strictly racial exclusion since the residence of both middle-class and working-class African Americans was resisted. The point was driven home further because often the victims represented "model African American families." Many of the men were World War II veterans, well educated and/or employed as white-collar workers. The women were either well-educated homemakers or also white-collar workers. If whites did not accept *these people*, the black public must have wondered, what would be the fate of a less ideal, in societal terms, black family?

Of course, the failure of black civic and political leaders to influence city government to stop the racial violence or implement nondiscriminatory housing policy did not invalidate their efforts to do so. It only reinforced for them the need for racial democracy. When black civic and labor leaders referred to democracy in confronting racial violence, they meant its racial version. In other words, a "full democracy" was one without racial disparities and violence. The lack of democratic rights meant that a particular race, not the American people, lacked those rights. If racial democracy was achieved, black elites argued, then racial violence and its underlying cause, housing segregation, would disappear.

Despite the consensus that racial violence represented a lack of racial democracy, black organizations approached the goal of ending racial violence in different ways. During the postwar era of racial violence, the Chicago Urban League, the Chicago NAACP, and the local United Packinghouse Workers of America (UPWA) union adopted a more aggressive and militant political style. Despite the shared goal of racial integration, these organizations rejected the paternalism of white-led race relations agencies and the moderation of national black organizations. Instead, they protested the treatment of black families that sought better housing by making militant demands on public authorities. Black civic and labor organizations emphasized the need for black elites to lead effective efforts to quell racial violence. Disillusioned with the white-led race relations agencies' moderate, insider strategy of responding to violence by conducting private negotiations, these organizations increasingly attempted to mobilize the black masses to protest and bring political pressure on city government to implement policy changes. Since antiblack violence persisted throughout the period, it is hard to argue that militant protest was more effective than insider politics in quelling it. Nevertheless, it appeared that "black assertiveness" in the face of white intransigence might have worked to increase racial consciousness, thus solidifying the primacy of race in black civic elites' estimation of African Americans' oppression.

The fight against racial violence constituted black labor leaders' principal engagement with housing issues in the postwar era. Their entrance into racial housing conflicts bolstered the shift to militant protest among black civic leaders. The UPWA, a national biracial labor organization with several black-led locals in Chicago, sought to influence and mobilize a white rank and file against the violence committed by other whites against blacks. As member-based organizations, black-led unions at least threatened the possibility of mobilizing black and white workers in an effort to stop the violence. Yet this class-based approach proved no more effective than racial protest. By the 1950s, the patterns of racial segregation based on white racial entitlement that spawned neighborhood violence had become too entrenched. If it had proved impossible to institute a social democratic policy of more government control of housing provision immediately after the Second World War, a class-based approach now would surely fail in the one area where the lines of racial division were most stark. Thus, the predominant response to antiblack violence would be shaped by the civic ideology of racial democracy. The shift in leadership styles did not change the basic commitment to racial democratic goals. Access to more land and better housing in a stratified market for African Americans was still the goal. When it came to "political style," racial democracy was flexible; it could accommodate either a moderate or a militant style. In fact, it was the consensus about racial democratic goals that made differences in political style notable. Housing-based racial violence, which coexisted with and reinforced the city's slum clearance and public housing policy decisions, would give further credence to the view of black elites that a racial lens was the only legitimate one for analyzing and evaluating housing policy in the city and that racial democracy was the only legitimate political goal.

In this chapter, I explore the growth of the militant approach taken by Sidney Williams, UPWA activists, and the Conference to End Mob Violence (CEMV) to quell racial violence. I draw comparisons with the more moderate approaches of white-led race relations agencies and the cautious leaders of the National Urban League who opposed the more militant approach. Even among the black civic and labor organizations with a more militant protest style, tensions developed over the legal approach of the Chicago NAACP and the popular front politics of the Packinghouse Workers militants. This chapter delineates the limits of a militant, sometimes biracial, approach to white violence that remained trapped within the bounds of racial democratic ideology.

Housing-Based Racial Tensions and Racial Violence

Before racial violence began in postwar Chicago, black and white reformers during World War II predicted its occurrence. Increased black in-migration to work in the defense industry and real and artificial shortages of housing for blacks caused them to seek dwellings in areas bordering all-white neighborhoods, resulting in flare-ups of racial tension. Black and white civic elites recognized that racial violence would emerge largely around housing issues. It was, after all, conflict over space and racial boundaries that had ignited the 1919 racial conflagration. The memory of the 1919 riot weighed heavily on the minds of the city's leaders when they contemplated what could unfold in Chicago during and after the war. In June 1943, the race riot in Detroit presented a more recent reminder of what could happen in the Windy City if racial and housing reforms were not implemented.[1] While black and white elites largely agreed about the causes of housing-based racial violence, they differed in their recommendations for reform.

During the war, a number of civic organizations or committees warned the city that racial violence was imminent if the housing problem were not addressed. These organizations included the Metropolitan Housing and Planning Council (MHPC); the Mayor's Committee on Race Relations (MCRR); and, at the national level, the National Urban League (NUL). In January 1943, the MHPC issued a joint report with the Defense Housing Committee of the Office of Civilian Defense on wartime black housing conditions. The work of the Mayor's Committee on Race Relations, created a month after the Detroit race riot, was discussed by the first director, Robert C. Weaver, in another report.[2] The national report, generated by the NUL, frequently described Chicago's "racial problems in housing" as being typical of those of the nation at large.[3]

All the reports agreed that racial violence would likely be housing based. In other words, housing congestion, created in part by residential segregation, created the underlying conditions for racial tension, conflict, and violence. These reports were all attuned to the shifting character of racial violence evidenced by the wartime Detroit and Harlem riots.[4] Though aware of the potential for antiblack violence, the sponsoring organizations focused more on the potential for black-led violence fomented by the frustration and anger blacks felt about their inability to get decent housing. While the reports also agreed that the in-migration of black war workers contributed to a housing demand that exceeded supply, they disagreed about what to do about it. There was consensus on affirming African Americans' right to decent housing. During the war, white civic organizations used both patriotism and a market-defined Americanism to legitimize black claims for more and better housing. While these reform organizations understood the causes of housing-based racial tensions, black civic leaders opposed some of their recommendations for not directly confronting residential segregation, advocating temporary instead of permanent housing and seeking to control black in-migration.[5]

It would not be long before black and white elites' prediction of housing-based racial violence would be realized in the postwar period, though the elites were wrong about its character. It would turn out to be the more familiar antiblack aggression that plagued Chicago throughout the twentieth century rather than the feared black-led violence. Airport Homes and Fernwood Park Homes in 1946 and 1947, respectively, became the sites of the first major racial confrontations since the horrendous 1919 race riot in Chicago.[6] In both cases, white neighborhood residents rioted when black veterans and their families attempted to move into the temporary housing projects. Housing-based racial violence would become a constant feature of race relations throughout Chicago's postwar history. According to one government source, Chicago had the most violent incidents in the country at the time.[7]

These two violent incidents, notwithstanding some differences, would set a pattern of responses by the city's administration and black and white civic leadership that would be replayed in subsequent race riots from the late 1940s through the 1950s. The pattern was set as such: After the initial incident of racial violence, black and white civic leadership sought official condemnation from the mayor. In pursuit of this goal, a delegation of civic, labor, racial, and religious organizations visited the mayor in every case. Prominent in the leadership of these delegations, along with black elites, were the white leaders of the Mayor's Commission on Human Relations (CHR) and the Council Against Discrimination (CAD).[8] Next, both black and white civic leaders called for a strong police presence to protect home-seeking blacks while firmly denouncing the white perpetrators. They demanded that once arrested, white rioters should not be treated lightly by the court system. They were disappointed on both scores. Black elites consistently criticized police officials for treating black victims as if they were responsible for the violence meted out to them, while coddling white perpetrators. The black civic leaders were no less critical of the city courts' lenient sentencing of white rioters.

Black elite leadership, in particular, never felt the rioting was spontaneous. Not only did they think that the racial violence was "organized," but they also suspected that white real estate interests were involved in fomenting the trouble or at least setting the stage for it through their opposition to government housing and/or black residents. National civil rights leaders usually appeared on the scene to condemn the racial violence and connect its existence to the city's thoroughgoing residential segregation bolstered by its slum clearance and public housing policies. They usually took the lead in trying to involve the federal government in the form of a Justice Department investigation and calling on the Housing and Home Finance Agency (HHFA) to punish the city by withholding aid from its housing programs.[9]

While the early patterns of black elite response to housing-based racial violence did not change very much when Sidney Williams and black labor leaders entered the scene after the Peoria Street riots in 1949, militant public demands did begin to replace insider lobbying. While the underlying assumptions remained race based, both Williams and black labor leaders replayed the militant political style of the leftist Popular Front during the late 1930s. They were more likely to think that publicizing race riots could arouse a black mass-based organization in coalition with left-wing white labor leaders. The Conference to End Mob Violence became that organizational vehicle for a militant opposition to housing-based racial violence.

Sidney Williams and the Conference to End Mob Violence

Sidney Williams was a pivotal figure in black housing politics in postwar Chicago. Though he shared the goal of racial integration with national civil rights leaders, he also responded to his constituency of black middle-class homeowners and property owners. Balancing these two forces meant he took a variety of positions. He favored building public housing in white areas, but opposed slum clearance. More important, Williams's militancy combined with his commitment to racial democracy illustrated how a primary focus on race could accommodate many different political styles. Williams's militant race politics highlighted the struggle of the Urban League to keep up with changing expectations of upwardly mobile blacks in the postwar era. It also showed black civic elites' impatience with liberal whites' racial paternalism. The struggle with white-led human relations agencies points to black elites' expectation that "race relations" was *their* industry. Their expectation of dominating the burgeoning race relations industry was an example of the conflation of political and career interests by black civic elites.

Park Manor and the Peoria Street Riots

The Conference to End Mob Violence was formed after an outbreak of racial violence in the Park Manor and Englewood neighborhoods in 1949. The first incident involved a black family who bought a two-flat building at 7153 St. Lawrence Avenue on the city's South Side. By buying a building at this location, Roscoe and Ethel Johnson had crossed the southern boundary that whites marked to resist black incursions into their all-white strongholds. On July 25, 1949, an estimated two thousand whites attacked the Johnsons' newly purchased home with missiles and Molotov cocktails thrown from across the street. The police failed to disperse the mob but cordoned off the area to prevent further violence.[10]

In the second case, white residents in Englewood, on the city's Southwest Side, targeted the home of two Jewish labor unionists who had invited black labor officials to their home for a meeting. On November 8, 1949, a crowd of white people gathered across the street from 5643 Peoria Street, where Aaron Bindman and William Sennett and their families shared ownership and residence. Three nights later, the situation escalated when Bindman's friends and supporters were harassed and arrested by the police and beaten by a mob of ten thousand whites, both in front of his house and outside the police station. Racist, anti-Semitic, and anti-Communist insults were hurled at Bindman's friends, who were from liberal and left-wing groups like the Progressive Party, the Civil Rights Congress, the NAACP, and various labor unions.[11]

Both the Park Manor and Englewood communities were threatened by the black "invasion" of their all-white enclaves after 1945. After the 1948 Supreme Court decision outlawing the legal enforcement of restrictive covenants, Park Manor along with other communities received their first black residents. Typically, the first purchase by blacks in previously all-white neighborhoods was made with their own funds or through black financial institutions. Usually once a block had "turned," white banks and savings and loans facilitated racial succession by making financing available to blacks.[12] The all-white enclave in Englewood was already surrounded on three sides by black communities. Community institutions such as the Southtown Planning Association and the Southtown Land and Building Corporation attempted to prevent blacks' entry into Englewood through a variety of means including buying property from blacks when they first purchased homes in the neighborhood. Despite these efforts, Englewood was no more successful in remaining all-white than Park Manor had been.[13]

The nature of the racial violence in the Englewood community confirmed black civic leaders' suspicions that white neighborhood resistance was organized and supported by such institutions as the Catholic Church and the local real estate industry. For instance, it appeared that a local Catholic church had organized the Garfield Boulevard Improvement Association with the expressed purpose of keeping "undesirables out of the neighborhood." Apparently, the Chicago City Bank and Trust Co. expressed interest in purchasing Bindman and Sennett's house for a "substantial profit." After they refused to sell, the Colonial Loan and Savings Co. threatened to cancel the labor leaders' home mortgage and insurance, saying they would not have given them the mortgage if they had known the labor unionists intended to have black guests.

Another significant factor in the Peoria Street riot is that since two white labor officials from a left-wing union had been attacked, organized labor and the political Left were brought more squarely into the cause of racial violence. Bindman appealed for help to Michael Mann of the CIO Industrial Council, of which his union was a member. Mann told him he knew about the situation, and his advice for Bindman was not to invite his "Progressive Party friends" to visit him at home. When Bindman replied that these people had come to protect him from mob violence, Mann "advised him that the position of the CIO was to keep the Progressive Party people out of there."[14] Mann's hostility reflected the fact that Bindman and "his friends" had Communist Party membership or affiliation through apparent front organizations such as the Civil Rights Congress and the South Side Negro Labor Council.[15] Mann was part of the anti-Communist faction of the CIO, which included conservatives, liberals, and social democrats, and they considered the Progressive Party rife with Communist Party activists.[16] Mann's CIO Industrial Council was dominated by conservative labor unions with close ties to the Cook County Democratic Party machine and the Catholic Church.[17]

Conference to End Mob Violence in Chicago

The Peoria Street riot brought forth an immediate response from black civic and labor leaders in the formation of the Conference to End Mob Violence (CEMV).[18] Sidney Williams, the force behind the creation of the CEMV, had inserted himself centrally in the housing policy debates within black civic elite circles as well as in the city at large almost as soon as he arrived in the city.[19] Within the first year of his arrival, he crafted a self-help rehabilitation plan that was spurned by national black policy elites, and he sat on the coroner's jury investigating the tragic West Ohio Street fire in which ten black women and children had died.[20] In 1948, Williams was embroiled in the city's land-clearance battle, exhorting his fellow black Chicagoans to defend their land, much to the disappointment of black federal housing officials who expected him to defend a slum clearance policy they hoped would lead to residential integration. The CEMV was designed to be a militant pressure group directed at the intransigence of Chicago's political regime. It was not the kind of organization usually headed by an Urban League official, but Sidney Williams represented a new generation of leaders within the national organization. Williams along with other young executive secretaries of League affiliates were considered "Young Turks" because they advocated an aggressive approach to civil rights. This group advocated for a shift in the NUL's political approach, arguing that unless the organization engaged in aggressive pursuit of black interests, it would lose legitimacy with the African American public in the postwar period.[21] However, it appears that such an approach was politically risky, especially in a city wracked by repeated neighborhood race riots.

The CEMV was advertised to be a temporary organization to fight racial violence, with representatives from civic, religious, race relations, and labor organizations. As a pressure group, the conference was without the bureaucratic infrastructure that normally characterized its members' home organizations. It was a council of representatives from municipal interest groups designed to come together for the one specific purpose of pressuring the city's political and administrative establishment to protect African Americans and their white allies when they were subject to intimidation, harassment, and attack from racist whites.

The impetus for the CEMV's founding was Williams's disagreement with the CHR's response to the Park Manor and earlier racial disturbances. In particular, he criticized CHR's policy not to publicize racial disorders in the city press, and he wanted black policemen included in the details assigned to sites of racial violence. The CHR had persuaded the city's newspapers to either ignore or downplay acts of racial violence for fear of drawing in more troublemakers from other parts of the city. Williams criticized this "hush hush" policy as a "colossal failure" because it "kept thousands of democratic-minded people ignorant of Chicago's danger." He further argued that rumors were more dangerous than facts in fanning the flames of racial violence. Moreover, he charged, the "conspiracy of silence" would allow the "real culprits" to go unpunished while the only people who suffered would be "innocent Negro families seeking a way out of their miserable housing conditions, and . . . white friends who dare to have Negro guests."[22] After the Park Manor racial incidents, Williams advocated for black police officers to be included in "mixed-details" at the riot scene. While this was perhaps Williams's most provocative suggestion, it was understandable given the hostility or indifference that white police officers showed to black victims and the leniency with which they treated white rioters.[23]

After the groundwork had been laid for an organization like the CEMV, all it took was a dramatic racial incident such as the Peoria Street riot to launch it. The call went out ten days after the last disturbance of the Peoria Street riot in November 1949. The initial call for the founding of the conference came from Sidney Williams and Russell Lasley, international vice president of the UPWA. Williams and Lasley did not cite the Peoria Street riot specifically but referred to "the rising number of outrageous acts of mob violence against Negro citizens exercising their right to buy and rent homes outside the ghetto." The steering committee, with Williams as chairman and Lasley as vice chairman, represented a broad selection of Chicago's black civic leadership, including well-known leaders such as Irene McCoy Gaines, president of the Council of Negro Organizations, and Reverend Joseph M. Evans, pastor of Metropolitan Community Church. The conference's steering committee included both left-leaning labor leaders such as Lasley and Willoughby Abner of the UAW and Chicago NAACP as well as moderate business leaders such as John Sengstacke, publisher of the *Chicago Defender*.[24] They called for an all-day conference on November 26 at the Parkway Community Center. A press release announcing a meeting in December boasted that the conference had rallied representatives from "more than 200 civic, labor, business, veteran, religious, and community organizations in less than a month of its existence."[25] After the first meeting, Lasley claimed with élan that this was "biggest thing of its kind on the South Side."[26]

The CEMV's first order of business was to get city officials to support the right of any citizens, "especially Negro citizens," "to buy or rent, or to visit in houses anywhere in Chicago without being molested or harmed in any manner." The conference planned to inform "the general public on the Negro community's position on these illegal acts."[27] The overall purpose of the conference, however, was to "map out a program to take vigorous action against the recent outrages," around which it would "organiz[e] the Negro community and its allies." Williams argued that black people would continue to seek adequate space and housing because this was "the only way our housing dollars can bring us the same value as the housing dollars of our fellow white citizens." Ultimately, Williams and the CEMV sought market equality for blacks.[28]

In addition to increasing pressure on the mayor and police commissioner for more effective police and legal action, the coalition had ambitions of representing the black community in Chicago on housing and other racial issues. While the conference focused on the immediate task of safeguarding blacks moving into racially transitional or outlying areas, it had in mind long-range policy solutions to the black housing crisis as well as other violations of their civil rights.[29] Taking on the role of a black housing interest group, the CEMV's "long-range solution" to black housing needs was to facilitate the construction of public and private housing that would be available to black families. These ambitions as well as the conference's uncompromising stand on open occupancy would come back to haunt Sidney Williams and the Chicago Urban League.

With the Park Manor riot still fresh in their minds, CEMV members focused on the most visible organized group associated with white resistance to desegregation. The White Circle League had been created after the Park Manor race riot in July 1949. Led by Joseph Beauharnais, its stated purpose was to keep blacks out of white neighborhoods. Although White Circle League leaders hoped to organize all of white Chicago, they remained largely limited to Park Manor, and even there they ultimately proved ineffective.[30] CEMV coalition members differed on how to respond to the White Circle League. The debate emerged between Sam Parks of the UPWA with other labor and leftist activists and Frayser T. Lane of the CUL. Parks represented the approach of his union to racial violence—aggressive militance with an emphasis on publicity of the sort they hoped would mobilize the grass roots to put pressure on elected officials. Parks, endorsing the method of mass mailings to reach union members, added that not enough people knew about the purpose and work of the conference. He recommended informing them by passing leaflets "to churches and other organizations that will help when you get ready to hold your mass meeting." Frayser T. Lane of the CUL said that as a "social welfare worker" he felt that too many leaflets would be counterproductive. He feared that publicizing attacks by a racist organization would intimidate many blacks, 80 percent of whom, he claimed, had lived in the South. In typical Urban League fashion, he thought the information should be directed to city hall and the business community, arguing, "I think we ought to keep this in a leadership capacity" as opposed to engaging in mass publicity. In contrast, John Gray, a black left-wing activist, wanted to make sure "we get some material to the man in the street immediately."[31]

The UPWA, perhaps the backbone of the CEMV, took the lead in rallying left-wing labor unions with significant black leadership and membership to support the work of CEMV. On December 1, 1949, a labor rally against mob violence attended by three hundred people was held at the Packinghouse Workers Labor Center at 4859 South Wabash Avenue. The rally brought together members from three unions: Packinghouse Workers Local 208, Warehousemen's and Distribution Workers Union (a branch of the International Longshoremen's Union), and United Auto Workers Local 453.[32] Members of these unions had been victimized in the Peoria Street attacks. The featured speaker was Saul D. Alinsky, organizer of the Back of the Yards Neighborhood Council and a CEMV member. Harold E. Nielsen, Chicago director of the UPWA and rally chairman, said before the meeting that its purpose was to "call upon all active unionists in the city to take action against the recent mob attacks on Negroes in Chicago." The goal of the rally was "to take action to get a law enacted to prevent future riots." In fact, at the rally workers adopted a resolution condemning the poor performance of the mayor and police.[33]

Critics of the Conference to End Mob Violence

A major feature of the CEMV's brief existence was its contentious relationship with mainstream race relations agencies like the Chicago Commission on Human Relations (CHR) and the Council Against Discrimination (CAD). The CHR and the CAD were concerned that the CEMV would become an unwelcome rival to them in managing civic agencies' response to the city's racial violence. These critics also rejected the CEMV for being black-led and/or for allowing left-wing CIO union members, suspected of having

Communist Party ties, to join the coalition. There was also a clash of methods. These critics preferred the private, insider, though aggressive, lobbying role that the CHR and the CAD had taken rather than the militant public approach preferred by the CEMV and its labor allies.[34]

Sidney Williams gave mixed signals about CEMV intentions. On the one hand, he emphasized the temporary nature of the CEMV, focusing solely on the issue of fighting mob violence. He tried to reassure his critics, unconvincingly, that the CEMV was not a rival to the CHR in the general race relations field. On the other hand, he defended the right of a black-led organization to represent black citizens in their efforts to gain protection from white violence. Yet he claimed a black-led effort would only complement the work of the city's race relations agencies. Williams emphasized that the CEMV "is primarily and predominantly a product and an organization of the Negro community," boasting that "no other organization has [been able] to mobilize a grass roots movement in the Negro community to combat mob violence."[35] Williams's assurances notwithstanding, the organizations' differences and the CEMV's interest in influencing city policy made them competitors.[36]

Homer Jack, former CAD director, attacked Williams primarily for his political ambitions and for allowing Communists to participate in the CEMV. He doubted whether the coalition was truly "responsible" since it was organized by "people whose ideology is suspect from the beginning." Jack argued that some of the CEMV leaders "are not out to stop mob violence as much as to push their particular political product." For instance, Jack claimed, they sought a new nondiscrimination ordinance, certain of defeat, to only "then raise a huge cry and no doubt more funds for its fight." He lamented, "Peoria Street has given the Communists and their willing and innocent dupes a field day in Chicago." While he acknowledged that the mainstream race relations agencies had made some mistakes, Jack concluded, "only disillusion and confusion can result from cooperating with the Conference to End Mob Violence."[37]

Williams detected racial paternalism in the Communist front charges and in the tone of his white critics. Specifically, he bristled at the presumption that the CHR or the CAD could better represent black citizens in designing an effective response to racial violence or that he needed their permission to create a group like the CEMV. He asserted that African Americans could speak for themselves, pick their own leaders, devise their own strategy, and "direct the attack" with white assistance. He added, "From our own ranks we pick our generals. And we decide the hows and wheres and the terms and circumstances of our battles for freedom."[38] Pointedly, he declared, "We are handicapped, yes, but not to the degree that we are incapable of doing our own thinking." He then added emphatically that blacks would not subordinate themselves to the CHR or the CAD "in matters where the welfare of Negro citizens is at stake." Williams emphasized the indigenous knowledge of black civic activists versus the outsider status of white liberal professionals. He claimed Jack was "totally unaware of what's going on down here on the Southside," wondering if "the information that filtered through to you in Evanston was both selected and distorted."[39]

Williams and Lasley had ambitions for the CEMV to represent black housing interests more broadly than simply protecting the right of black citizens to move unfettered into white communities. Along with this challenging task, they expressed interest in getting more public and private housing for blacks, a goal that most black civic, business, and real estate leaders would endorse. Some black leaders, however, would not have liked the CEMV's militant approach or its left-wing reputation. Williams and the CEMV had become a "lightning rod" for those who wanted either to stop racial succession or to manage it without large-scale conflict and violence. Williams's audacity and visibility as a militant protest leader did not fit the image of an Urban League executive cultivated by the Lester Granger–led NUL. Soon Williams's enemies would move against him in Chicago with assistance from the League's national office.[40]

The Backlash at Sidney Williams

The criticism of Williams and the short-lived CEMV was not just rhetorical; it had a political and financial impact on the Chicago Urban League. Catholic board members of the CUL resigned due to their perception of an anti-Catholic bias, though they blamed Williams's association with "communist groups" or "left-wing elements."[41] Two gatekeepers for funding nonprofit organizations—the Community Fund and the Chicago Association of Commerce and Industry (Chicago's version of the Chamber of Commerce) also responded negatively to the CUL's political associations. The Community Fund determined whether nonprofit social welfare organizations would be eligible to receive funds from the contributions they collected. The Association of Commerce and Industry endorsed the same organizations for receiving funds from private businesses. In February 1950, the Community Fund and the Association of Commerce and Industry threatened to drop the

CUL from its list of endorsed organizations. The Community Fund, particularly, said it was losing donations because the League had become tainted by Williams's politics. Essentially, the CUL board and staff had to fight a two-front war to ensure the organization's survival.

Williams posed the threat of black labor and white civic opposition to convince the gatekeepers not to withdraw funding from the CUL. At the same time, he relied upon strategic CUL board members, some of whom were also members of the fund or the association, to lobby on behalf of the League.[42] He tried to deflect the gatekeepers' criticism by suggesting that their opposition to the CEMV resulted from their reluctance to confront racial violence. Williams felt "the League was being penalized" because he had confronted a "critical situation." At various points in the organizations' review of the CUL budget request, Williams threatened that the UPWA, in particular, would drop its support for the Community Fund if the agency severed its ties with the CUL. In fact, Williams told NUL executive secretary Lester Granger that black labor and liberal organizations were just waiting for the "go" sign from him to mount their opposition to the fund.[43] Anti-Communist CIO factions' opposition to his politics complicated Williams's evocation of the black labor threat. Not only did opposition include the conservative CIO Industrial Council but Williams also had also a tortuous relationship with the top black CIO official in Chicago, if not the nation, Willard Townsend. Townsend, an anti-Communist social democrat, was probably wary of the UPWA, the union that had the most "Negro CIO officials."[44]

Williams and CUL board members had successfully negotiated compromises with both the fund and the association to get funding for 1950. The League had to agree to implement recommendations made in the McMillen report that the organization improve its board and administrative functions. This report, authored by Wayne McMillen in 1946, entailed recommendations made after the Chicago Urban League was last reorganized. It was this reorganization that brought Sidney Williams in a year later.[45] It appears that the CUL had successfully dodged one bullet, only to get worse news the following month. In March 1950, the CUL board learned that officials from the two largest meat companies, Armour and Swift, had decided to suspend their respective annual gifts of $1,500. Since Swift was the largest corporation in the meatpacking industry, the ramifications of this action would undoubtedly spread. When a CUL board member visited Swift to learn what was behind their action, the board member found great antipathy toward Williams. He reported that the company considered Williams's politics "suspect" and "had compile[d] a voluminous file" on him.[46] Only four months after the founding of the CEMV, the white business community had joined with conservative labor officials and rival human relations professionals in registering their opposition to Williams's politics.

The threats from the Community Fund and the Chicago Association of Commerce and Industry to curtail their contributions to CUL in 1950 got the attention of the national office. Maurice Moss, associate executive director of the NUL, was sent to Chicago on a fact-finding mission sometime before early February 1950 in the midst of the controversy.[47] Moss had made it known to Williams that the national office was disappointed that Williams had not kept them informed about the CEMV development. Williams later explained to Granger the nature of the opposition to the CEMV. He thought the focus of the criticism was on the group's "open door policy," which admitted member organizations without screening for Communists. Williams told Granger he advised all member groups, without singling out the Communists, to "check their political badges with their wraps." Undaunted, he defended the CEMV, saying, "It is common opinion that the Conference achieved outstanding results."[48]

Sidney Williams's Dismissal

In 1954, four years after the dissolution of the CEMV, the Chicago Urban League was still plagued by real estate and white neighborhood organizations charging that it sponsored and subsidized "the moving of Negro families into white areas."[49] This "wide-spread rumor" had a significant impact on the CUL's budget. The persistence of the rumor, however, may have depended as much on Earl Dickerson's affiliation with Supreme Liberty Life, which funded blacks moving into white neighborhoods, as on Sidney Williams's involvement with CEMV four years earlier.[50] Not only were contributions to the League suffering but the Community Fund was still being hurt by their sponsorship of the organization.[51] The League and other organizations blamed racial prejudice. Others, including some conservative CUL board members, thought it was the organization's leadership.[52] While the League denied it had anything to do with settling blacks in all-white neighborhoods, they categorically endorsed the principle of residential desegregation.[53]

It appeared that no explanation to the Community Fund or to the national office could stop the political or financial crisis. In its October 28, 1954, meeting, the CUL board members voted "to accept recommendation of the Community Fund's Committee on the Urban League that a study be made of the philosophy, purpose and function of the Chicago Urban League." According to the historian Arvarh Strickland, the Community Fund forced the League to accept the study because their budget would not be approved without this agreement, and then decided the NUL should conduct the study.[54]

In 1955, Nelson C. Jackson, director of community services for the NUL, and three national staff members conducted the study.[55] The report argued that it was Williams's visible role as chairman of CEMV that was "a source for widespread rumors and critical public relations for the Chicago Urban League." Some CUL members "questioned the advisability of the Executive accepting the Chairmanship without consulting his Board." These same members were dismayed, according to the report, when despite the board's reaction Williams remained as chairman. So persistent was the impression of the CUL's militant defense of blacks' rights to open occupancy that the investigators were told by fellow civic organizations that they had used the threat that the Urban League would be brought in if they did not receive any cooperation from white neighborhood organizations.

Although the report blamed the rumors on a racial climate particular to Chicago, the investigators questioned Williams's judgment in getting himself and the League involved in housing conflicts. They were concerned about the fact that the "public spotlight ha[d] made [Williams] a natural target for drawing rumor charges at him and the Chicago Urban League"; and the impression that the league under Williams tended "to work alone, rather than utilize the organization resources of the community." Perhaps more distressing to the authors was their realization that "the Executive Director has also become a leader and hero to those who are not fully aware of the program responsibility of an Urban League executive, and believe the agency should be a source for crusading and a mass pressure approach to racial amity." Here was the rub, a basic philosophical difference between Williams's militant approach and the staid tactics of the old-line Urban Leaguers that was costing the League local financial support.[56] The report concluded the CUL had lost funds and prestige due to "malicious rumors." For an organization dependent on public support for "effecting a constructive program," persistent rumors would cause "irreparable damage." The report recommended that, in order to restore the prestige of the organization, the board locate the source of these persistent rumors and follow the recommendations in other sections.[57]

White and black conservatives on the Urban League's board took advantage of the local nonprofit and business community's faltering support for the organization to remove Sidney Williams from office.[58] Nelson Jackson asked Williams to resign before the study was complete. Williams initially refused and allegedly intimated that if he were fired, he would take his case to the public. The historian Arvarh Strickland commented that because "Williams' militant activities had attracted a considerable following, especially among Negroes . . . although he could not have won, a conflict over ideology would have greatly disrupted the reorganization." Whenever Williams was confronted by an attack, his impulse was to make it public and mobilize his allies primarily in black CIO circles, especially the Packinghouse Workers. Evidence existed that these groups were very concerned about Williams's dismissal. In a memo, Richard Durham, national program coordinator of the UPWA, wrote, "I think labor would lose a friend if Sidney Williams were bounced from the Urban League." He suggested that Charles Hayes help Williams with "some CIO support." Williams had been a strong supporter of the Packinghouse Workers. According to Durham, right after Williams was hired in 1947, he "chaired the South Side Committee to Support Packinghouse Strikers and coordinated assistance from black churches and fraternal organizations." It was probably this action as well as the subsequent CEMV involvement that earned Williams the enmity of the meatpacking corporations.[59]

Despite his inclinations, there is no evidence that Williams went public, nor did any massive protest arise in response to his termination. If Williams thought his allies would be able to mobilize the black masses or would be strong enough to confront the alliance of white nonprofit funders, human relations agencies, and business groups, as well as black and white conservatives on the Urban League board, he was mistaken. Williams made some miscalculations, including misjudging the strength of black CIO leaders, especially the United Packinghouse Workers (UPWA) and their ability to mobilize mass protest around his ouster. Yet to his detractors, Williams's biggest crime was his politics. The operations of the Chicago Urban League ceased on July 15, 1955, and Sidney Williams and his staff were dismissed. The purge was complete.

The removal of Sidney Williams spoke to the potency of race-based housing issues in postwar Chicago. The policy of racial succession was an unofficial one, adopted by the CLCC and its allies in the real estate development community. They did not need someone inflaming white neighborhood activists who were already on guard due to the expected racial dispersal from the city's land clearance program. The fact that the "rumors" about CUL aiding racial integration persisted five years after the CEMV's demise spoke more to whites' fears than to the capability of black civic and business elites to orchestrate such a campaign. The city's white elites preferred quiet acceptance of neighborhood racial succession to a militant and public defense of black Chicagoans' right to live where they pleased. Williams's advocacy for the Fair Employment Practices Committee (FEPC) and his alliance with left-wing black labor added to his notoriety for business elites. Many whites associated a militant racial politics with the Communist Party and other left-wing groups. Of all the black civic leaders on the scene, Williams, due to his popularity, appeared to both white and black elites as the most likely to mobilize a frustrated black community on the issue of racial violence, perhaps including black retaliation, leading to a citywide race riot. Moreover, if he developed a following with the help of the UPWA, it could spill over into other housing issues, which was the CEMV's ambition. Subsequent black responses to racial violence would belie this possibility, but it might not have seemed so far-fetched at the time. Since the UPWA expressed interest in mobilizing white union members, which it attempted during the Trumbull Park racial disorders, the potential for developing a biracial following for social democratic housing policies was apparent. Though the possibility of mobilizing black workers and their white allies to stop racial violence was unlikely, the threat was palpable, and Williams had to go.

The Cicero Riot

A year after Williams was forced to abandon the short-lived Conference to End Mob Violence project, racial violence struck in Cicero, an inner-ring suburb just west of Chicago. Like its predecessors, the July 10, 1951, Cicero riot was touched off by the attempt of a black family, the Clarks, to move into a rented home in an all-white community. However, the response of the public to the racial violence in Cicero deviated from previous patterns in postwar Chicago. George Nesbitt, racial relations adviser for the Public Housing Administration, cited four reasons why the Cicero riot generated more attention than earlier race riots: (1) The National Guard rather than local police was used to quell racial violence; (2) Cicero was known as a hangout for organized crime;[60] (3) Cicero's public officials were directly involved in preventing black residence;[61] and (4) the victims represented a model African American family composed of a father who was a university-educated

public employee and a World War II veteran, "an attractive and well educated mother," and two small children.

By far the biggest factor in the public response to the Cicero riot was
its exposure in the news: it was the first incident of racial violence to be
broadcast on local television.[62] The additional attention came not only from
the local and national news but also from the international media, which
meant the riot would be interpreted through the lens of cold-war politics.
Black policy elites were very much aware of how racial violence played in
the propaganda war between the United States and the Soviet Union. Antiblack violence in Cicero, according to Nesbitt, was "the clear reflection of
democratic weakness for world-wide consumption in the midst of the democratic struggle with Communism."[63] Walter White, executive secretary of
the NAACP, commented that Cicero was "the most valuable assist to Pravda
because the news won't have to be distorted."[64] While there was much to distinguish events in Cicero from earlier racial violence, Nesbitt asserted that
beneath all the housing-based racial violence lay the "simple reality that a
Negro family was seeking more living space." He explained that moving into
all-white neighborhoods was the only option available to "thousands and
thousands of Negro families in the city of Chicago."[65]

Within black elite circles, the inability to get the city to protect home-
seeking African American families caused consternation about their
ineffectiveness. Claude Barnett, the wealthy owner of the Associated Negro
Press, expressed disappointment in Chicago black civic, professional, and
business leaders' response to the racial violence in Cicero, saying it represented failed leadership. The fact that "Walter White flew out and took
command" irked Barnett, who wrote, "It was as though no local Negroes had
either the ability, the civic pride or the confidence of the people sufficient
to rally them behind a program." There was a mass meeting sponsored by
the NAACP, but according to Barnett, only "a dozen so-called prominent
Negroes [were] in attendance or not many more." He was outraged that "they
raised peanuts insofar as money was concerned," prompting him to ask,
"What are they doing now?" Barnett proceeded to question the commitment
of ministers, lawyers, political leaders, and businessmen.[66] Apparently some
black insurance executives agreed with Barnett, complaining that business
and professional men, by failing to lead blacks in raising "a huge fund" to
fight racial violence, "did not realize their obligation to the community."[67]

Barnett's ire did not spare his own industry, the black press. He asked,
"What leadership have newspapers given? Why do newspapers not call on

Negro leaders to come to the front[?]" Barnett criticized the black newspapers' propensity for focusing on sensational news, asking, "Have we played up the cheap chiselers and racketeers to such extent that no one believes in the leaders we set up[?] Have we lent ourselves to promotion and exploitation to such a degree that we no longer can command a following?" This soul searching could be seen as questioning not only his fellow black editors and publishers but also the legitimacy of the black elite leadership.[68]

Of all the black elites, Barnett was most impressed with the "executive of the Chicago Urban League." Referring to, but not naming, Sidney Williams, he reported that Williams had "proposed a plan which most people howled down." He said Williams had recommended that black women in white dresses, and black men in white shirts and black pants march through the Loop with "muffled drums and heads bowed just to show how the Negro population felt." Barnett felt, this plan notwithstanding, that "the Urban League man" was not vocal enough, due to his organization not wanting him to take a leadership role against racial violence. Furthermore, Barnett was disappointed that Williams did not advocate strongly enough for the League's "best program"—neighborhood improvement—to get the city behind them.[69]

Though Barnett's criticism was directed at the inadequate response to the Cicero riots, it was clear that such ineffectiveness was not an isolated incident but rather a generalized problem.[70] While the Cicero riot reflected official leaders' failure to protect blacks' right to an unfettered housing market, conversely the riots posed as a highly visible moment that put on display black elites' failure to influence housing policy. The fact that the conservative Barnett touted the militant Sidney Williams, predictably endorsing the CUL neighborhood improvement program but even affirming the derivative "silent protest" idea, spoke to their shared commitment to a unitary black polity led by a black elite. Barnett bemoaned the leadership vacuum left in the wake of Williams's evisceration and before the disposal of the body four years later.

The Racial Siege of Trumbull Park Homes

Trumbull Park Homes Disorders

Black civic elites and their white allies in the city's race relations industry suffered a number of defeats during the 1950s. Their inability to get the city's political regime to respond effectively to racial violence not only exacerbated the other political failures but also highlighted black civic leadership's ineffectiveness in an admittedly tough political environment. No incident of racial violence illustrated their impotence more than the racial siege at Trumbull Park Homes. Most acts of racial violence, while serious, dissipated after a few or several days. Yet at Trumbull Park Homes, acts of violence and intimidation against the project's black tenants continued for several years. This long-standing saga spoke volumes about the entrenched nature of residential segregation in Chicago.

Trumbull Park was one of the first public housing developments built under the Public Works Administration (PWA) program in the city, and it was designated for white occupancy. Because of the duration of the conflict, the neighborhood-based racial violence captured national attention, including special reports in *Time* magazine and on CBS news. Eventually, Trumbull Park became a symbol of "racial containment" or represented "little Mississippi" in the North, mirroring Southern whites' desperate efforts to preserve Jim Crow. The conflict's longevity also reflected poorly on black elites as they tried old and new tactics to break the racial impasse. The battle represented another defeat for racial democracy, which favored residential desegregation through a nondiscriminatory policy of tenant selection for public housing projects. Nonetheless, it highlighted not only black civic elites' commitment to public housing integration but also the convictions and courage of ordinary black citizens who, in seeking modern housing facilities, found themselves on the front line of a race war.

Federal housing agencies in both the Truman and Eisenhower administrations were committed to providing proportionate units of public housing to African Americans that would have comparable features and amenities to those provided to whites. However, both administrations allowed local communities to determine the racial occupancy of federal public housing projects. With federal permission, local housing authorities could specify which projects would be segregated or integrated. Chicago's public housing was either all-white or predominantly black, with few biracial projects.

In early 1953, the local branch of the NAACP challenged the CHA on its all-white projects, which included Lathrop Homes, Bridgeport Homes, Lawndale Gardens, and Trumbull Park Homes.[71] However, the actual effort to integrate Trumbull Park Homes took authorities by surprise. Because the project was located in an outlying neighborhood in the southeastern corner of the city, it handled its own applications for occupancy rather than processing them in the customary fashion through the CHA's central office. When a woman named Betty Howard applied for a vacant apartment at Trumbull

Park Homes in July 1953, she was approved at the housing project's office under the mistaken assumption that she was white. Not until the housing manager saw her husband, Donald, a twenty-four-year-old veteran and postal worker, and the couple's two small children did they realize the family was African American. By August 5, word of the family's racial identity had spread in the surrounding white working-class neighborhood, and crowds gathered to protest their occupancy in Trumbull Park Homes. As people began to throw bricks and stones, the police were called in. By August 9, a few thousand people had gathered again, shouting insults and throwing bricks at the Howards' apartment. During this time, black motorists in the vicinity were also attacked. Police arrested rioters but could not quell the racial violence.[72]

Over the several years of the siege, violence was intermittent, but intimidation and harassment were ongoing.[73] The CHA introduced new black tenants only to have them harassed by local residents and roughly treated, if protected at all, by the police detailed to the site.[74] In 1957, the number of black families had decreased to twenty-five from a high of thirty-one in 1955. In subsequent years, the number of new families moving in decreased from twenty-four in 1954 to nine in 1955 and only six in 1956. It was clear that the constant racial strife had taken its toll on black families in Trumbull Park.[75]

The response to the racial siege in Trumbull Park fell to the network of black housing policy analysts and activists that had been forming in the postwar period. There was collaboration between the African American racial relations officers in federal housing agencies, who monitored the situation and tried to put pressure on federal policymakers, and the Chicago NAACP and the United Packinghouse Workers union, who pressured city authorities and aided the black tenants. For instance, while the Chicago NAACP took aim at the CHA tenant selection policy, William Hill, a PHA racial relations adviser located at Chicago's field office and a long-term member of the CUL board, attempted to change the PHA policy that supported segregated projects.[76] Nevertheless, neither the black federal housing officials nor local black civic and labor activists broke new ground in terms of analysis, strategies, methods, or reforms when it came to Trumbull Park. Strategies that had been pursued in earlier instances of neighborhood-based racial violence and that had failed were attempted again in the mid-1950s, without much success.

Trumbull Park, like Cicero, was testimony to the increased limitations on black responses to racial violence after the CEMV debacle. While Sidney

Williams had been effectively eliminated from playing an active role in resistance, his erstwhile black labor allies, UPWA leaders, and Willoughby Abner with the UAW and the Chicago NAACP continued the fight. Unfortunately, they ran into the same obstacle that the CEMV had met three years earlier: the local political regime's unwillingness to institute the kinds of policy reforms that would protect black citizens' right to occupy housing of their own choosing. While the same CEMV script was often followed, the UPWA took advantage of its biracial leadership and membership to try to mobilize white union leaders and rank-and-file workers to oppose antiblack violence. They were not successful because, at that point, Chicago's residential segregation had become too entrenched. Moreover, a policy against housing-based racial violence, unless it was part of a broader agenda of social democratic policies that attacked racial and class deficits in gaining adequate and affordable housing, was useless.

The Chicago NAACP

The all-white Trumbull Park called into question the CHA occupancy policy. By the mid-1950s and due to persistent poverty, blacks were clamoring to gain access to public housing. By this time, more blacks than whites were applying to enter public housing. In many cases, whites' income was too high to qualify, or they pursued private housing options, which were more accessible to them than to blacks. Additional blacks were entering public housing because they had been displaced by slum clearance and other public housing construction. Prior to Trumbull Park's racial disorders, the CHA had admitted that a number of all-white public housing projects existed. Former chair Robert Taylor claimed that the CHA had followed a nondiscrimination and nonsegregation policy adopted on January 6, 1950.

According to William Hill, a black regional PHA official, it was assumed that the latter policy would pertain only to future public housing, leaving undisturbed current all-white housing projects. He added that CHA officials had thought, mistakenly, that by accepting all-white projects they would gain the city's cooperation in getting vacant sites for new public housing. Taylor explained that when the CHA had inherited the PWA-constructed Trumbull Park, it had also inherited its segregation policy. He stated emphatically, however, that there had been no agreement with the aldermen about keeping Trumbull Park all white. Whether an agreement had existed or not, by August 1953, Trumbull Park was all white. On August 18, 1953, the

Chicago NAACP filed suit, seeking to integrate all of Chicago's public housing. A week later, the CHA reaffirmed its policy of nondiscrimination and nonsegregation.[77]

Neither the Chicago NAACP letters to federal officials nor a subsequent meeting with Mayor Kennelly produced any results. Shortly after the NAACP meeting with the mayor, two rallies were organized—one sponsored by the Chicago NAACP and the other by the Negro Chamber of Commerce—to keep up the pressure on the mayor.[78] The Chicago NAACP appealed to the national office, arguing that ending northern segregation was necessary to eliminate Jim Crow in the South. They had hoped to redirect the national office's preoccupation with the legal dismantling of de jure segregation. The Chicago branch requested that the national office assign a full-time staff person "to work in Chicago with the Chicago Branch on a full scale mobilization and a fund raising campaign around the Trumbull case." Chicago was also seeking aid from the NAACP National Defense Fund and sought national publicity on the Trumbull case.[79] It was unlikely that the national office would devote staff or funds to a case of racial violence and de facto segregation with no imminent resolution in sight. Besides, the civil rights organization had won the historic *Brown v. Board of Education in Topeka, Kansas*, Supreme Court case just a few months before the appeal from Chicago.

NAACP national officials were not persuaded by the local chapter's appeals. As far as they were concerned, Northern black civic activists could learn from the Southern-based struggle. In May, Thurgood Marshall, in Chicago to accept the eighth annual Robert S. Abbott Memorial Award from John Sengstacke, told an audience of seven hundred at the Grand Ballroom of the Sheraton Hotel that African Americans and city officials needed to take a strong stand against mob violence in response to efforts at housing integration. In his remarks, Marshall complained, "In Chicago a poor Negro can't live in a housing project without being afraid of getting his head shot off." When he compared the situation of African Americans in the North to the South, he exhorted Northern blacks to show the courage their Southern brethren displayed if they indeed wanted to defeat racism.[80]

Undaunted, in September 1954, the Chicago NAACP registered a formal complaint against the CHA commissioners for their failure to implement their policy of nonsegregation in public housing occupancy. The NAACP counted four times that the CHA had passed or affirmed a resolution on nondiscrimination and nonsegregation but had failed to fully implement it. They cited the recently fired Elizabeth Wood, who said, "the Authority has paid lip-service to policies publicly proclaimed while privately issuing instructions thwarting those policies." The NAACP charged not only that blacks were excluded from all-white projects but also that the CHA had used quotas to limit the number of black Americans admitted to public housing. The problem they had with quotas was that black applicants who had "legal priority for public housing are by-passed in favor of white applicants with less or no priority." In other words, in order to boost the numbers of white occupants in public housing projects, whites were selected ahead of blacks with higher priorities. The NAACP told the State Housing Board that it had presented their concerns to the commissioners before, but to no avail.[81]

United Packinghouse Workers Action

The United Packinghouse Workers matched the activity of the Chicago NAACP in the Trumbull Park disorders but took a different approach than did black civic organizations. The black union officials played a prominent role in supporting the besieged tenants as well as organizing protests. In addition, the black left-wing union leadership reached out to white labor officials and rank-and-file workers to join in protests. While there was an overlap with the Chicago NAACP in terms of militancy, protest tactics, and membership, the UPWA saw itself as utilizing different methods and engaging different constituencies than did the civil rights organization. Black UPWA officials saw the local NAACP as a black interest-group organization with a black constituency. Instead, they favored public outreach to black and white union members to protect the right of black families to live in Trumbull Park Homes. These labor leaders felt that labor unity was the answer to stopping racial violence. Yet this unity, at both the union leadership and the rank-and-file levels, would be difficult to achieve even in the best of circumstances, which certainly did not include a city wracked by housing-based racial conflict.

The difficulty of the labor unity approach lay in enlisting the help of white CIO rank-and-file members who supported or tolerated racial amity at the workplace, but participated in or supported the racial resistance in communities such as South Deering, where Trumbull Park was located.[82] Given the lack of worker unity, it is unsurprising that UPWA's campaign proved no more successful than the persistent efforts of the Chicago NAACP in ending the racial siege. Black UPWA officials underestimated white workers' commitment to racially homogeneous neighborhoods, which was linked to the fear that they would lose their life's savings through falling property values. Their efforts could not match the effects of years of residential segregation institutionalized by the real estate industry and federal government, whereby racial homogeneity was equated with the stable property values crucial for the economic security of white working-class homeowners.[83]

The UPWA had a number of high-ranking black officials and majority black locals in the Chicago area. Earlier on in the Trumbull Park battle, black UPWA officials stressed the importance of unity between black and white workers. Oscar Brown Jr., program coordinator for UPWA District #1 and son of the head of the Negro Chamber of Commerce, organized a picket line of black and white packinghouse workers around the CHA office, "demanding that the authority stand firm in defense of the rights of this Negro family to occupy the project." He intimated that it was the union's pressure, including picket lines around the CHA and city hall, that influenced the CHA to come out in support of the Howard family. Brown added that the union's actions received a lot of publicity from major newspapers, enthusing that "it was action that brought our Union into the front line of struggle in a case of major proportions, with white and Negro members fighting side by side in defense of full democracy." Apparently other CIO unions found the Packinghouse Workers' action "unilateral," but Brown argued that the union's action "shed light upon our relationships with CIO and [emphasized] our determination to influence all sections of labor to pursue the kind of vigorous Anti-Discrimination program that UPWA has adopted."[84]

In June 1954, about the same time that the Chicago NAACP appealed to the national office for help, the Packinghouse Workers set up their structure and strategy to deal with the Trumbull Park situation. Richard Durham, national program coordinator of the UPWA, instructed Oscar Brown Jr. and Charles Hayes, the first African American director of District #1 and future congressman in Chicago, on how he thought the union should approach Trumbull Park.[85] Durham asserted that "while the big operation on Trumbull Park is being worked out on top," the union could work with the families "down below." In Durham's plans, black and white workers would work together, even in activities intended to support black tenants. He recommended that Trumbull Park committees composed of both black and white members be set up in each local and have as their primary activity the support of black families inside the project. Major locals should "adopt" one or more families for protection and support, and these families should be brought to speak at the locals. He recommended that District #1's Women's

Activities Committee should support the Trumbull mothers and children as their main project. He also wanted at least one field representative to become "intimately acquainted with at least one of the families in the project." He suggested that the supported families be asked to send letters to the union welcoming the union's support and stating their agreement with "the joint objectives for better housing, jobs and security in common with UPWA." Durham recommended that these letters be distributed in "the Yards." He advised that all these initiatives should be at minimum publicized by the black press.[86]

In early June, Brown wrote to Durham declaring that "the key to the anti-discrimination work in the Chicago community is for us, as it should be for all of labor—Trumbull Park." He reported that the union had developed a close working relationship with "the NAACP and other groups." The District #1 program department printed a piece on Trumbull Park to be distributed to the "Back of the Yards Community" near the stockyards. Brown sought funding from the International and hoped the Amalgamated AFL's contribution would be sizeable. Within two weeks, on June 18, 1954, contact had been made with the Trumbull Park black families. Brown reported at the end of June that the Women's Action Committee had made contact with the mothers and children.

As part of the outreach effort, Trumbull tenant Frank Brown helped organize a June 20 dinner at the Parkway Dining Room, 420 East Forty-Fifth Street in Bronzeville, which was attended by six families from the project.[87] Six women and children met with the Women's Action Committee and plans were made "for the UPWA sisters to give assistance to the Trumbull women with their shopping." Committee chair Lydia Durham and Oscar Brown Jr. set up a picnic for the July 4 holiday for the families.[88] Activities were funded by $5,000 that had been raised to support their activities and to send tenant Frank Brown to the national NAACP convention to report on the racial disturbances.[89] Oscar Brown Jr. pointed out that he had "established a very close personal relationship with tenant Frank Brown making it possible for us to maintain an almost day to day picture of developments in the project."[90]

At the June 20 dinner, Charles Hayes welcomed the black families from Trumbull Park, proclaiming, "If organized labor got itself together, something might be done." He felt the Steelworkers Union alone "could disburse the mobs." He feared that if a race riot broke out, "unity between Negro and white workers in our union will be shot to the devil." In other words, the biracial stability within the union would be undermined by racial violence.

At the dinner, another official said the union was engaged in the Trumbull Park situation because it believed in fighting "for the rights of the Negro People," even though their adherence to this belief meant the union was considered "communistic." Addie Wyatt, UPWA official, assured the families that the "victory" against racial violence was possible given the relationship of the unions with the tenant families.

Director Hayes announced that the union had collected $4,000 (the Amalgamated Meat Cutters Union had contributed $2,500) and that they would "launch a terrific publicity campaign." Oscar Brown Jr. told the tenants that they and union members were "all pretty much the same kinds of folks. If you are hurt, we are hurt." The tenants at the dinner thanked the union officials for their support in the midst of violence and intimidation. They related that a few white tenants had offered friendship, but their main concern was the toll the conflict was having on their own children. Clarence Young said, "Come to my house and see the agony on all sides. It tears your heart out as a man." Contradicting Brown's sentiment, he chided the black union officials, "You people don't have any idea of what Chicago is doing to the families out in Trumbull Park." He continued defiantly, "You can believe one thing—I will be there as long as there is a Trumbull Park, as long as somebody is out there to take the rent."[91]

In August 1954, the UPWA joined the AFL Amalgamated Meat Cutters union to wage a publicity campaign against Mayor Kennelly's reluctance to protect black families in the Trumbull Park disturbances. On August 25, a meeting between the UPWA and the Amalgamated Butchers Union took place to decide on the contents of the advertisement. During their negotiations on the message of the publicity campaign, differences cropped up between the two unions. The first disagreement concerned the content of the publicity campaign. Hayes complained that the Amalgamated Butchers Union president Earl W. Jimerson had sat on the advertisement draft for a month, only recently indicating his uneasiness with its demand that Mayor Kennelly resign. One Amalgamated union official said, "The trouble is in the hearts of the people, not in Mayor Kennelly."[92] The Butchers Union officials said that the hostile actions of white people in the neighborhood actions resulted from "economic fear . . . propagated by the real estate lobby," adding, "we are interested in the white people learning to live with the other people." They discussed bringing on board the South Chicago Trades and Labor Council, which included the more conservative carpenters, steelworkers, teamsters, and butchers. Sam Parks agreed that they needed the labor council as a counterweight to South Deering alderman Emil Pacini's stand against public housing. Parks, a black UPWA official who had been a member of the CEMV four years earlier, reiterated the power of newspapers to influence people, and in particular, white people.

The second argument was over their different relationships with the Chicago NAACP. The AFL union wanted to send the publicity campaign money to the NAACP because Trumbull Park had depleted the NAACP's treasury due to various legal actions it had initiated. Charles Hayes felt that "the NAACP's battle around Trumbull Park is primarily a legal one." He disagreed with the idea of giving union money earmarked for "trying to influence the public" to the NAACP, who "should have [enough] money" for their legal strategy. Moreover, he said, "Other unions can contribute to their legal battles." He added that the UPWA had previously contributed to the NAACP legal department.[93] Parks also disagreed with sending the money to the NAACP. He pointed out that the "NAACP is a Negro organization and white people must be reached." He felt that Willoughby Abner, a UAW official and member of the Chicago NAACP board, could get the UAW to donate more to the NAACP. He did not think it was the union's "business to underwrite the NAACP." Parks stated that he felt the NAACP attempted to address racial problems by "maneuvering" and that they did "not have a labor unity point of view."[94] Harkening back to 1932, when interracial labor unity existed, Parks hoped that same interracial labor unity would confront racial violence in Trumbull Park. He advised the AFL union officials to separately donate money to the NAACP, just not their share of the advertisement money. Parks concluded evenly, "If we sit here and think this is a Negro problem let's refer it to the NAACP. That approach doesn't reach the white workers." Hayes added that Russell Lasley, both a UPWA vice president and a NAACP board member, had earlier met with Jimerson and discussed the "NAACP approach." Indirectly dismissing that approach, Parks concluded that "Trumbull Park could not exist for a year and 2 months if organized labor would move."[95]

At the end of the day, UPWA's "publicity campaign" was no more imaginative or effective than the Chicago NAACP's legal suits and mass rallies. In fact, Russell Lasley perhaps captured the limitations of his union and black civic forces best when he stated, "We must let the 'bigots' know that the Negroes in the city of Chicago don't intend to be pushed around."[96] In other words, the UPWA and the Chicago NAACP acted as witnesses to injustice meted out by Chicago's neighborhood improvement associations backed by the political establishment. Not to minimize the support that they gave to black tenants, none of the black civic or labor organizations' methods, tactics, or strategies changed policy or altered the situation. In fact, they would lose two allies during the Trumbull Park disorder, Sidney Williams and Elizabeth Wood.[97] At least the UPWA attempted to blaze a new trail by trying, unsuccessfully, to enlist white union leaders and rank-and-file members to support public housing integration in Chicago. Yet their valiant efforts to end the racial siege came to naught. The Chicago NAACP would regroup and try the same tactics with a new mayor in office after the 1955 election. Nevertheless, they were no more effective with Richard J. Daley than they had been with Martin Kennelly.[98]

At the end of the 1950s, the NAACP assessed the state of housing desegregation and outlined the work needed for the next ten years. They determined that they would focus on placing black homeowners and renters into "white sections of the city and suburbs" as well as attempting to prevent "transition areas" from resegregating. In other words, they would institute one version of a racial democratic housing agenda. There was still attention to placing blacks in the "four white projects"—Bridgeport, Lathrop, Lawndale, and Trumbull.[99] No definitive end came to the racial violence and intimidation in Trumbull Park. In March 1957, almost four years after the initial attacks, aerial bombs were still being exploded there almost nightly. The number of new black families admitted to Trumbull Park dwindled over time. Twenty-four black families had moved into the project in 1954, but only nine did so in 1955, and six in 1956.[100]

So the racial siege continued. The white neighborhood activists and politicians of South Deering had successfully neutralized the city officials' ability to disperse the mobs and quell the violence and intimidation. Black federal housing officials, civic elites, and labor leaders had failed to pressure either Mayor Kennelly or Mayor Daley, both of whom were concerned about angering white voters, to be more aggressive in law enforcement. Nonetheless, no black or race relations organization was powerful enough to force the end of the racial disturbances at Trumbull Park, which handed a ringing defeat to racial democratic housing policy in Chicago in the 1950s.

Conclusion

The entrenchment of racial segregation in postwar Chicago was most dramatically expressed by persistent episodes of racial violence. Whether blacks sought housing in temporary veterans housing, public housing, housing in racially transitional areas like Park Manor, or in inner-ring suburbs, they were met with hostility, harassment, intimidation, physical harm, and property damage. Despite black elites' persistent efforts, they and their allies failed to influence or pressure the City of Chicago to abandon racial segregation or federal housing officials to punish the city for adhering to racial exclusion. However, opposition to housing-based racial violence brought all the factions of black elites together to fight for a genuine nonsegregation policy.

Most black elites viewed the fact that black homeowners and renters could not freely buy or rent housing as a failure of democracy. When these elites made reference to the fact that blacks did not have "full democracy" or lacked "democratic rights," they meant that blacks did not have equal access to the housing market or housing aid because of their race. While they may have thought "democracy" was not complete in other ways, it was evident from their analyses and actions that they thought the biggest or most pressing deficit of American democracy was racial. Thus their focus on getting the city to adopt a nondiscrimination and nonsegregation policy represented an effort to attain racial democracy. Given the context of racial exclusion, and the racial violence that was deployed to maintain that exclusion, it is not surprising that the racial deficits of democracy would become more urgent to black elites. In fact, it seemed that the very intransigence of white resistance to black residence reinforced the already strong tendency for black elites to view the problem exclusively through a racial lens. Even the United Packinghouse Workers of America, whose constituency included both black and white workers, employed a racial democratic framework when analyzing the causes of the racial violence. Their attempt to remedy that situation with interracial worker unity crashed against the shoals of an institutionalized racial homogeneity–property values nexus that had informed federal housing policy since 1934. To succeed, their approach would have had to have been bolstered by a social democratic policy of public provision of moderate- and low-income housing emerging from the New Deal and World War II; instead, they fought against the increasingly entrenched economic interests of white homeowners, which had become racialized.

The strength of racial democracy as the predominant ideological source of policy reforms for black elites was also augmented by its flexibility. When black elites did conflict, it was over methods, strategies, and styles, not policy goals. The conflict that the Sidney Williams–led CEMV, the UPWA, and the Chicago NAACP had with more conservative black elites was over the former groups' militant and aggressive approach to race-based goals. Racial democratic policy advocacy could be advanced using conventional "insider" means, or it could be militantly expressed through protests and demonstrations. Perhaps the most important ideological glue was a shared understanding by all black civic and labor organizations that all blacks constituted a unitary racial group that they expected to lead and represent. The militant Sidney Williams and CEMV were the most ambitious in this regard, but Barnett's profession of a black leadership crisis betrayed the same assumptions. Underlying the assumption of a unitary black subjectivity is one that leadership claims were based on racial authenticity. This idea was evident in the postwar cohort of black elites challenging white-led race relations agencies for leadership in the anti-racial violence fight. UPWA's biracial approach had the potential to challenge this assumption but was not able to develop in the polarizing environment of a racial siege.

Increasingly, black elites sought for black citizens a nondiscriminatory use of conventional housing policies. In a sense, what they sought was housing market equality: to have their incomes, high or low, offer the same purchasing power as that of a white person. As the postwar period became more conservative, the tendencies of black elites to embrace racial democracy were reinforced by pragmatic considerations and a sense of more limited possibilities. Yet what appeared initially to be a temporary accommodation to a capitalist political economy after the war would become naturalized over time by black elites as the only legitimate framework within which to analyze and redress housing inequalities.

8

Class and Racial Democracy

While their responses to racial violence proved ineffective, black policy elites met with some success in attacking federal housing discrimination in racially restrictive covenants. While such covenants were private agreements among white property owners not to sell or lease their property to racial and religious minorities, the courts' enforcement of these practices gave them legal sanction and formal status. In the *sub rosa* world of discriminatory and segregative housing practices, the government's sanction of racially restrictive covenants offered the most visible target. It was also the discriminatory practice most insulting to black elites who claimed first-class citizenship and class status recognition. Thus, among the black bourgeoisie, the issue became a cause célèbre.

While restrictive covenants were common in many cities nationwide, Chicago proved an important battleground in the fight against them. The fight against restrictive covenants began with the *Hansberry v. Lee* decision in 1940 and moved through a series of court cases until the *Shelley v. Kraemer* decision in 1948, when the U.S. Supreme Court ruled that the legal enforcement of private restrictive covenants was unconstitutional. The battle against restrictive covenants illuminates a number of important aspects of the black civic and policy elites' approach to housing reform. Black elites, who led the campaign, claimed that all blacks would benefit. However, affluent blacks stood to gain more readily than working class blacks, thus revealing the differential class outcomes of racial reform. In fact, the legal fight against restrictive covenants for those blacks in the real estate industry best expressed the confluence of personal, professional, class, and racial interests in the expected outcome—entrance into a desirable neighborhood where all blacks had once been forbidden to live.

Because the exclusion of blacks from covenanted neighborhoods was racial, the reform that would make them eligible to live in those neighborhoods also was racial. Thus the reform of racially restrictive covenants offers a perfect example of how black elites and their middle-class public could simultaneously attain racial progress and advance their class housing interests. Yet the issue of class was not as hidden in restrictive covenants as it was in other housing policies. In order to isolate and counter the *racial* aspects of restrictive covenants in one reform strategy, black policy elites advocated occupancy restrictions that limited new housing to blacks with economic and cultural capital. In other words, black elites used class exclusion as a tool to democratize housing along racial lines.

Whereas the failure to quell racial violence reinforced a racial analysis on the part of black policy elites, ironically the elites' success in stripping restrictive covenants of their legal sanction accomplished the same thing. The formal nature of the restrictive covenants allowed them to be successfully opposed, reinforcing the notion that democratization meant black people would now have legal access to previously all-white neighborhoods. In other words, the fight against racial covenants not only highlighted the racial deficits in an otherwise complete democracy, implying that *racial* democracy was the most legitimate reform, but it also promised to produce more and better housing for most blacks, the goal of black policy elites' housing agenda. Black outward mobility to contiguous white neighborhoods, always a steady trickle, became a flood after the 1948 Supreme Court decision.

In this chapter, I delineate how black elites achieved all their interests in the reform of restrictive covenants and how their class positioned them to direct the reform efforts. Though latent all along in each housing policy they had supported, class interests became more explicit when the reform was criticized for not focusing on poor housing conditions within the ghetto. Black civic elites defended the anticovenant campaign against this charge by pointing out the benefits that the reform would bring to working-class blacks. In the second half of the chapter, the debate over class and racial reform takes a different turn with Robert Weaver's proposal to replace racially restrictive covenants with race-neutral occupancy standards. Weaver argued that pragmatic racial reform should take precedence against social democratic commitments. The chapter concludes by exploring the use of occupancy standards in the Oakland neighborhood and other class controls in Kenwood. This chapter, perhaps more than others, makes explicit black civic and policy elites' embrace of class stratification in housing as a means of achieving racial democracy.

The Fight against Restrictive Covenants

Rather than provide a narrative account of the fight against restrictive covenants in Chicago, I focus in this section on the ways in which this campaign represented aspects of racial reform, highlighting the role of class interests. The historian Wendy Plotkin, in her authoritative history of the fight against restrictive covenants, "Deeds of Mistrust," discusses how black elites were able to merge their personal, professional, racial, and class interests in their opposition to residential segregation.[1] There is evidence that black civic elites were aware of the class nature of the racial reform reflected in the antirestrictive covenant campaign. Nevertheless, they defended their investment in this campaign as benefiting all blacks, not just those privileged enough to move into white neighborhoods once the racial barriers had been lowered. Because this fight attacked a legal racial barrier and necessitated substantial financial and legal resources, the campaign also represented quintessential middle-class reform. Moreover, since it targeted racial barriers alone, the logical end goal of the campaign was equality within the income-sensitive marketplace. In other words, the objective was for African Americans to have access to the best housing they could afford and properly maintain.

The 1940 Hansberry v. Lee Case

The year 1940 was pivotal in the field of Negro housing in Chicago.[2] Black housing reformers such as Robert Taylor, Horace Cayton, and Robert Weaver who dramatized blacks' housing woes in the late 1930s finally found some success. In 1940, contruction began on the black community's first federal public housing project, Ida B. Wells, after the three-year delay caused by white opposition to the site.[3] That same year, the Supreme Court decided in favor of Carl Hansberry, an affluent black businessman who had moved into an apartment building that had a racially restrictive covenant proscribing his occupancy.[4] Due to a legal technicality, Hansberry, father of the playwright Lorraine Hansberry, and his family were allowed to stay. In addition, following successful litigation led by Earl B. Dickerson, the former Washington Park subdivision became available to five hundred additional black households due to faulty covenants and dwindling white resolve. What linked the two situations was the opposition to black residential expansion by white real estate interests.[5] On the eve of World War II, black civic elites had reason to be optimistic about the progress of their efforts to secure more adequate housing for their race.

The successful *Hansberry v. Lee* case represented the best victory, at the time, in a long fight against racially restrictive covenants. Restrictive covenants were agreements entered into by white homeowners and real estate developers and agents, usually written into the deed of the property that forbade the owners to sell, lease, or rent to racial or religious minorities for a specified period of time unless all signers agreed with the transaction.[6] This contract could be made at the time the housing was built or later, when white homeowners decided to enter into agreements in their neighborhoods.[7] This discriminatory device had come into existence in 1917, when the Supreme Court struck down racially exclusionary zoning in Louisville. White middle-class neighborhood improvement associations and the real estate industry seized upon this legal alternative to physical violence to stall the post–World War I migration of blacks into "white" neighborhoods.[8] Although restrictive covenants were used against Jews, Asian Americans, and Latinos, African Americans were the main target, especially in Chicago.

Though restrictive covenants in Chicago first appeared in 1927, twenty years later, they reportedly covered the principal settlement of black Americans on the city's South Side.[9] To the east, the racial boundary was Lake Michigan and Cottage Grove Avenue, between Thirty-Sixth and Seventy-First Streets; to the west, the boundaries were railroad lines and deteriorated housing that extended to Sixty-Third Street along Wentworth Avenue; and covenants covered as far south as Seventy-First Street. Historically, the Black Belt had expanded in a southern direction, with the boundary moving frequently during this period because the nearby restricted areas were not as solid as they were on the east and west boundaries.[10] So well established were the covenants that the FHA not only insured property that carried them but when the agency was created it promoted a "model covenant" that property owners could adopt.[11] With renewed black migration during and after World War II, the land area covered by restrictive covenants reputedly spread to 80 percent of Chicago's residential property.[12] Although many other northern, western, and southern cities relied upon these compacts, Chicago's national significance on this issue derived from its status as the home of the national real estate industry, which created and institutionalized restrictive covenants.[13] With *Hansberry v. Lee*, Chicago would also become the city where black civic forces converged to fight restrictive covenants.

Carl Hansberry was one of the two principal black actors in the *Hansberry v. Lee* case.[14] Like many in his 1930s cohort, Hansberry had professional parents, had migrated from the South, and combined an entrepreneurial career with civic activism, especially with the Chicago branch of the NAACP.[15] He migrated to Chicago in 1915 and graduated two years later from Chicago Technical College. As a young business owner, Hansberry benefited, like many of his class, from the election of William Hale Thompson as mayor in 1927. He held a series of political appointments when he began to acquire real estate property.[16] By 1941, he owned residential real estate valued at more than $250,000 and that provided accommodation to more than four hundred families. He took advantage of the depressed real estate market in Chicago in the 1930s to acquire many foreclosed properties. Many of these properties were older declining buildings that he converted into kitchenettes, in so doing overcrowding the structures. According to his daughter Mamie, he was, in fact, "the founder of the kitchenettes."[17]

During the time when Hansberry was amassing his real estate fortune, he was also active in Chicago's civic affairs.[18] He and his wife, Nannie, established the Hansberry Foundation with a $10,000 endowment to support legal remedies to racial discrimination. Throughout the 1930s, he served as secretary or treasurer on the executive committee of the Chicago NAACP. In 1937, Hansberry filed suit against restrictive covenants, thus activating a black elite network associated with the local NAACP. Hansberry, like many fellow black businessmen, was committed to residential integration and black institution building. The black institutions, such as real estate, law, and insurance firms, were in the forefront of the struggle for civil rights, a fight that gave them a "progressive" cast beyond their profit motive.[19]

The Hansberry case went to trial in March 1938. Hansberry was the defendant in the case because he was accused by the white plaintiffs of being in violation of the restrictive covenant on the property. The plaintiffs wanted the restrictive covenant enforced and Hansberry removed from the property he had bought. The defense raised the issue of whether the restrictive covenant had ever taken effect due to "changed conditions," meaning that the racial composition of the neighborhood had changed so much that the covenant was unenforceable. This defense had been the basis for overturning restrictive covenant cases on technical grounds in other parts of the United States. In addition, Hansberry's attorneys included in their briefs claims that restrictive covenants violated state and federal constitutions and "public policy."[20] They mainly argued on technical rather than constitutional grounds, however, focusing on the failure of covenant organizers to secure enough signatures or challenging the legitimacy of the signatures collected.

In his ruling, Judge Bristow rejected the argument that restrictive covenants were unconstitutional or violated public policy. Even though he acknowledged that the covenant did not have enough legitimate signatures, he used a prior case that had endorsed restrictive covenants as a precedent to rule against Hansberry's claim.[21] In early 1939, Hansberry's lawyers appealed the decision to the Illinois Supreme Court, which upheld the circuit court decision. Hansberry then appealed to the U.S. Supreme Court, which agreed in October 1939 to hear the case. Earl Dickerson argued the case at the Supreme Court a year later.[22]

In *Hansberry v. Lee*, the U.S. Supreme Court ruled in Hansberry's favor in November 1940. The Associated Negro Press reported that Judge Harlan Stone, who wrote for the Court, said, "the covenant was invalid because the required number of property owners had not signed it."[23] Carl Hansberry regained his home in December 1940 but was disappointed that the ruling did not find restrictive covenants unconstitutional. However, Hansberry felt the decision projected "a ray of hope for the ultimate survival and maintenance of the democratic ideals."[24] Despite this optimistic sentiment, Lorraine recollects that her father experienced deep disillusionment after the ruling. She claimed that the cost of the victory "in emotional turmoil, time and money . . . led to my father's early death."[25] Not long after the decision, Carl Hansberry moved his family to a suburb of Mexico City. He was there in March 1946 when he suffered a cerebral hemorrhage and died at the age of fifty-two.[26]

The *Chicago Defender* and the Chicago NAACP declared victory at the Supreme Court ruling. An ANP headline, "Hailed as Biggest Social Victory in Years," illustrated the black press's estimation of the ruling's importance.[27] The article stressed the significance of the "decision as a social victory in contrast with other decisions of an educational nature or giving Negroes the right to a fair trial or personal safety." The stress on "social victory" suggested that the ruling would have a larger impact on black citizens' access to social goods like housing. The fact that the judicial decision was expected to open up five hundred new homes for black South Siders meant it would go beyond an individual or symbolic victory.[28] Another ANP article quoted Attorney Truman Gibson Jr.'s comment that the decision was the first case ruling against restrictive covenants. Gibson interpreted the decision as society recognizing "Negroes in their fight for full measure of citizenship" as well as attaining "social rights."[29] The *Chicago Defender* concurred that the decision reflected "a recognition by the court of the right of Negroes as citizens to live" where they chose.[30] A black realtor accurately predicted "in all probability the restrictive covenant will now die a natural death." Robert Taylor emphasized that the Supreme Court did not decide whether an American citizen could be restricted from purchasing or renting real estate "by reason of race, color or religion." He cautioned that until this question is answered, African Americans would still suffer disadvantages due to "their inability to rent or purchase adequate housing facilities at normal competitive prices."

Quintessential Middle-Class Reform

Racially restrictive covenants provided a popular target for black civic opposition because of their explicit, legal exclusion of any African Americans from neighborhoods regardless of their ability to pay or maintain property. Black elites found restrictive covenants easier to address than the more surreptitious forms of housing discrimination that occurred in a white realtor's or banker's office. Since these covenants thwarted liberal democratic values of individual choice and mobility, these black civic leaders felt they could appeal to the rights of the individual enshrined in the U.S. Constitution. Also, since covenant holders needed the legal system to enforce their prejudices, black elites felt the same system could be used to attack the agreements, which were based on legally unsound bigotry.[31]

The opposition to restrictive covenants represented quintessential middle-class reform. The individual household decision represented an act of upward mobility affirming the possibilities of class ascendancy in a capitalist political economy. It signified that society would reward an individual's work ethic, thrift, self-reliance, and self-improvement with a steady and rising income sufficient to buy a single-family home in an outlying setting or rent a spacious apartment with all modern appliances in the central city's best locations. This "American Dream" was subsidized by the federal government through Veteran Administration (VA)– and FHA-insured mortgage loans requiring a low down payment and offering lower interest rates. The existence of the racial covenant, among other discriminatory practices, prevented African Americans from realizing the American Dream. It blocked their means of class mobility, which denied them full membership in a socially stratified society.[32]

Wendy Plotkin has astutely pointed out that the *Hansberry v. Lee* restrictive covenant case provided a window into a network of upper-class African Americans who had found a target whose elimination satisfied their personal, professional, class, and racial interests.[33] This network of black realtors, lawyers, and insurance executives sought to broaden access to desirable neighborhoods while challenging the barrier that prevented them, as well as other blacks, with means from residing or doing business in these neighborhoods. The professional motivation for Hansberry and other blacks in the real estate business was a wish to profit from their access to an expanded market. Hansberry's personal motivations, similar to those of other affluent or upwardly mobile blacks, included seeking better schools for his children in new neighborhoods.[34] The Hansberry case is instructive because it seamlessly combines all levels of interests—racial, class, professional, and personal—within the civic ideology of racial democracy.

This confluence of interests was possible in this case because blacks' individual agency also was bound to a collective strategy. Most decisions to move outside the ghetto were not made in order to challenge restrictive covenants. Often a black family did not immediately realize that the property they sought to buy carried a dormant restrictive covenant. However, when Carl Hansberry and other upper-class blacks chose to move to racially covenanted Woodlawn in the late 1930s, they moved there as an act of class mobility and racial defiance. They chose individually to challenge the strength of racial covenants knowing they could rely on their own economic resources and legal expertise, as well as that of other black elites, to take that challenge into the judicial system.[35]

For instance, affluent blacks, such as the upper-class Gibson family, sometimes bought a rare noncovenanted building in a covenanted area in order to challenge the restrictive contracts. Truman K. Gibson Sr., an executive of the Supreme Liberty Life Insurance Company, bought such a building in 1932 in a strategic effort to get a toehold in a restricted area in Woodlawn.[36] If a restricted area became predominantly black, then lawyers could argue that it was moot to evoke a dormant covenant. Some white property owners, wanting to keep their options open, chose to let racial covenants lie dormant, which allowed them to sell to blacks if their neighborhood fell in the path of ghetto expansion. This was the scenario when the real estate market bottomed out during the Depression and white home buyers alone could not sustain housing demand. Affluent blacks, desperate to escape the ghetto and willing to pay a premium price to do so, were a ready market for these white property owners. As of 1947, more than 3,000 black families lived in covenanted areas. Over half, 1,850 of these families, lived in the predominantly black Douglass and Grand Boulevard communities, as well as the predominantly white Oakland community, where, in 1940, only a third of the population had been black.

The institutional foundation of the black elite network was formed by black financial institutions, especially Supreme Liberty Life Insurance. Supreme Liberty Life was the most prominent black-owned life insurance company in Chicago, and one of the most profitable in the country. Founded in 1929 through a merger of three companies, Supreme Liberty Life, like other insurance companies, derived a significant portion of its profits from real estate investments. The company was prominent in the black community not only because it was "a source of internal investment and employment" but also because it financed "the assault on residential racial boundaries."[37] The testament to Supreme Liberty Life's financial strength was its ability to survive the Depression when so many other black-owned enterprises did not. Between 1937 and 1943, the company's mortgage portfolio grew from 14 percent to 36 percent of total assets—by comparison, other black insurance companies ran about 18 percent to 23 percent. Wendy Plotkin observes that "this renewed attention to real estate financing proved profitable with mortgages becoming the most remunerative investment made by African-American life insurance companies."[38]

Supreme Liberty Life would prove to be a major player in the fight against restrictive covenants since it had both racial and economic interests in their elimination.[39] When African Americans breached racially covenanted South Oakland in 1944, the black insurance company had financed a number of the purchases by blacks. In that year, a black police officer became the first to buy a home in the neighborhood between Cottage Grove and Drexel Avenues; he was followed by other black purchasers over the next three years. Since white property owners rarely sold their houses directly to blacks, a white intermediary was often used to purchase the property on the black buyer's behalf. In fact, white intermediaries who bought property in South Oakland had their mortgages financed by Supreme Liberty Life.[40] In one case, a white intermediary sold a property to another white, who then sold it to a black citizen. Another sold the house to a black home buyer financed by an exploitative "land contract" whereby the black buyer paid monthly installments while the white seller retained the title until the entire contract had been paid.[41] Blacks bought thirty-four houses over the three-year period, most with a higher assessed value than comparable dwellings acquired by whites. Black-owned companies financed half of blacks' purchases in South Oakland between 1944 and 1947. Black home buyers benefited from the legal and financial expertise of these companies, who by this time had gained considerable experience in real estate transactions. In addition, their status conveyed confidence to white financial institutions in the purchasing process.[42] The financial role played by Supreme Liberty Life and other black-owned insurance companies assisting individual black households to move into covenanted areas provided institutional support for individual agency.

Class and the Campaign against Restrictive Covenants

Those most directly affected by these restrictions were black citizens with the income to purchase a single-family home or multifamily apartment building in a white neighborhood outside the ghetto. Due to wartime and postwar job opportunities and higher earnings, this group included even clerical and skilled blue-collar workers in addition to black businesspeople and professionals. Nevertheless, those in the forefront were middle class.[43] Their reasons for leaving the ghetto reflected the normative class behavior of many Americans. Due to the housing shortage, many black households had to double up with kin. Often moving out of the ghetto was an attempt by some to establish a household of their own. Upwardly mobile blacks wanted to flee both the dilapidated housing and the poor residents in Chicago's South Side ghetto. While there were basic material reasons for moving, these home seekers also clearly sought housing and neighborhoods that reflected the class status they had either attained or that they aspired to attain. Increasingly, in the postwar United States, one's home and neighborhood reflected better than almost anything else the social status of the individual family, a fact not lost on either blacks or whites.[44]

While working-class blacks valued the maintenance of the ghetto, according to Drake and Cayton, as "a gain in political strength and group solidarity," "they resent[ed] being compelled to live in a Black Belt."[45] Clearly, the average black person wanted the *choice* of whether to stay in an all-black setting or move into an integrated neighborhood. For many, the best option was an expanding black ghetto that incorporated better housing and neighborhoods. While there was broad agreement in principle against racial containment, the ambivalence and likelihood that reform would not bring better housing for low-income blacks dampened blacks' enthusiasm for struggling for fair housing. In addition, the nature of the anticovenant issue shaped the political response of blacks toward it: opposition through individual market transactions and legal challenges determined the middle-class character of this response.

Black elites realized that invalidating restrictive covenants could be construed as mainly benefiting privileged blacks. Horace Cayton, who had urged black civic organizations to mobilize their resources to fight against well-funded and well-organized white neighborhood associations, explained the elite view of how the elimination of restrictive covenants would help all blacks' housing interests.[46] Cayton's argument became clear when he responded to some controversial remarks by the editor of a University of Chicago student magazine in 1939. The significance of this controversy was that it illuminated not only black real estate elites' economic interest in eliminating racial covenants but also black civic leaders' interest in downplaying those interests, preferring instead to emphasize the benefit that the defeat of racial covenants afforded all blacks.

In commenting on the *Hansberry* case, the student magazine editor had made disparaging remarks about "Negro Landlords," claiming that they were the only group who would benefit from the elimination of restrictive covenants. The editor explained that black landlords would profit from purchasing fleeing whites' property at a discount while charging fellow blacks "exorbitant rentals." A perturbed Cayton claimed the editor's charges were "an over simplification, if not [a] distortion of the truth." Cayton claimed that after blacks purchased unrestricted property, they still would own less than 10 percent of the property in Woodlawn. He described the fact that "a few Negroes . . . would benefit along with the multitude of white real estate owners" as "an interesting, but unimportant detail."[47]

Cayton argued that the entire black community would benefit from the expansion in blacks' living area. The resulting increase in the supply of housing would potentially lower rent and relax overall overcrowded conditions, allowing more black "families to live under more healthy and sanitary conditions."[48] On the question of "Negro Landlords," we have no reason to doubt Cayton's estimation that a limited number of black landlords would benefit compared to a "multitude" of whites. Despite the overwhelming number of white landlords, both Carl Hansberry and Supreme Liberty Life, and undoubtedly others, had profited or become wealthy through real estate investment in racially transitional neighborhoods. Though it undoubtedly was not their sole, or main, reason for fighting restrictive covenants, Cayton's dismissal ignores the fact that upper-strata blacks would derive greater benefit from this racial reform than would those with less income and status in the black community.[49]

This very issue was brought to the forefront by a letter to the editor of the *Chicago Defender* complaining that the newspaper had devoted inordinate attention to restrictive covenants, which the writer considered to be the housing problems of affluent blacks, rather than to the overcrowded and poor housing conditions experienced by lower-income blacks.[50] Apparently, "grumblings" during the anticovenant campaign had echoed the same sentiment.[51] It was probably not lost on the letter writer or others that some of these affluent blacks profited from the overcrowded and substandard housing of working-class blacks. It was clear, at least to some, that the victory over restrictive covenants would mainly benefit the affluent blacks who invested in rental property as well as their own homes in the newly opened areas. At least for this letter writer, this *racial reform* did not promise to spread its benefits widely across the race.[52]

Black Social Scientists and The Campaign against Restrictive Covenants

After the *Hansberry* decision in 1940, Chicago remained a center of action against restrictive covenants. The Chicago NAACP, at its 1944 annual meeting, announced "an all-out attack against restrictive housing covenants." Its legal strategy, closely coordinated with that of the national organization, was twofold: It aimed to prevent the eviction of African Americans who resided on covenanted land and to establish the unconstitutionality of restrictive covenants.[53] The fact that the conference at which the national strategy was crafted in July 1945 was held in Chicago aided the coordination between the national and local NAACP. William H. Hastie, governor of the Virgin Islands and NAACP litigator, presided over the meeting, which was attended by numerous lawyers who had been fighting restrictive covenant cases in other cities.[54] The purpose of the conference, explained by NAACP special counsel Thurgood Marshall, was to develop cases for the Supreme Court in order to test "the constitutionality of enforcement."[55] Unsurprisingly, black Chicago elites, including attorneys Irvin Mollison and Loring B. Moore and housing expert Robert Weaver, were prominent at the conference.[56] At the end of the meeting, Marshall committed the NAACP to giving more attention and resources to restrictive covenant cases and urged that this network keep in touch by meeting regularly.[57] But despite the efforts of the NAACP and black attorneys, prospects did not look good for Chicago's test case. A superior court judge in Chicago upheld the legality of the restrictive covenants in *Tovey v. Levy*, ruling against the argument of attorneys Mollison and Moore.[58]

Not only did black opponents of restrictive covenants utilize legal principles and methods, but they also brought in social science analysis to substantiate their arguments in the litigation against restrictive covenants in Chicago and other cities that preceded the landmark 1948 Supreme Court decision. Black social scientists employed arguments that not only helped the legal attack on restrictive covenants but also shaped the opposition to other housing segregative practices. Furthermore, they pinpointed the precise significance of restrictive covenants in the overall opposition to housing discrimination and segregation.

The most prominent social scientist to oppose restrictive covenants was Robert Weaver, the leading voice in the national black housing policy community. Considered an expert on housing, including restrictive covenants, due to his academic credentials and governmental experience, Weaver—still in Chicago working as the community services director of the American Council on Race Relations, along with Horace Cayton—testified on behalf of the defendants in the *Tovey v. Levy* case in Chicago's Superior Court.[59] Levy's attorney, Loring Moore, pointedly incorporated the sociological and economic impact of restrictive covenants.[60] While he was in the American Council position, Weaver wrote *Hemmed In: ABC's of Race Restrictive Housing Covenants*, an influential pamphlet that delineated the history and current status of racially restrictive covenants.[61] In it, Weaver argued, "of all the instruments which effect this residential segregation, race restrictive covenants are the most dangerous" because these agreements gave "legal sanction . . . and the appearance of respectability to residential segregation" for middle- and upper-income whites. Fellow black social scientists Herman Long and Charles Johnson, in their study of restrictive agreements, agreed that the presumed legal and constitutional endorsement of race restrictive covenants "provides a rationalization for all the other types of restrictive practices, and forms the basis for efforts to extend them."[62]

These black social scientists analyzed the economic, social, and political impact of racial restrictive covenants on blacks and other Americans. Economically, the scholars focused on how restrictive covenants disrupted the "normal" supply and demand of the market. By restricting the supply of housing for blacks, racial covenants worked to artificially inflate the demand for available scarce housing, raising rents and sale prices. According to Long and Johnson, the discrimination did not occur only at lower rent levels: "The more rent the Negro family pays, the less housing value it receives, in comparison with a white family."[63] Weaver argued that "slum property owners and race restrictive covenant manipulators are two sides of the same coin," with both invested in maintaining the Black Belt. "One reaps large returns by encouraging a limited supply of housing for minorities; the other sells a false sense of protection to white occupants of surrounding neighborhoods."[64]

According to Weaver, if blacks had access to an "open market," they could settle wherever their purchasing power and tastes took them, presumably all over the city. Since the housing market was not open to blacks, they had to go to formerly white areas adjacent to the ghetto for more and better housing. Because new housing was available only in these border areas, all classes of African Americans eventually flocked to them. Weaver pointed out that in these neighborhoods, the "dwellings involved are usually ill adapted to the family needs and rent-paying abilities of low-income families [which] leads inevitably to doubling-up and physical deterioration." Weaver argued that this misallocation of housing stock to housing classes accelerated deterioration and in the process bolstered residential racial exclusion in "areas into which low-income families would normally move."[65] In other words, it would repeat the familiar process of segregation, racial transition, resegregation, and ghettoization.

To Weaver, it was obvious that the only way to lessen the demand for housing in neighborhoods adjacent to ghettos would be to open more areas to black residence. For working-class blacks, he sought to increase the availability of low-rent housing and remove barriers to their movement into existing low-rent areas. For their higher-income counterparts, Weaver sought access to "established neighborhoods designed for families of their economic level."[66] Weaver believed that the racially unfettered operation of the housing market would sort black consumers according to income and tastes, thus reducing the conditions that led whites to fear black residence. Of course, purging the housing market of artificial racial fetters (while sustaining class controls by price and standards) had the added benefit to black middle-class homeowners of excluding low-income black renters, who were usually accommodated in transitional neighborhoods in kitchenettes or rooming houses.[67]

Socially, black social scientists applied to restrictive covenants the causal sequence that began with residential segregation and ended with blight and slums. Restrictive covenants caused overcrowding, which in turn caused stressed and deteriorated housing conditions and congestion with its social consequences.[68] Long and Johnson wrote that "the disease, the crime, and the family disorganization note[d] in such areas take their toll on the whole community, not only in the dollars and cents cost of police, fire, and health protection, but in the waste of human resources and the disfigurement of personalities."[69] They also pointed to the effect of "isolation that breeds misunderstanding and antagonism which at times have flared into destructive violence" in segregated areas. These arguments echo those of the National Urban League warning against blacks developing a "slum psychology" by which frustration from stunted class aspirations could lead to violence.[70]

Politically, residential segregation had an impact that went beyond creating poor housing conditions. It also facilitated de facto segregation in schools and recreational facilities where legal segregation was outlawed.[71] Weaver emphasized that "unless we develop non-segregated housing, we cannot make real progress in establishing democratic schools, recreation and other public facilities."[72] Furthermore, he expressed concern that restrictive covenants and residential segregation racialized geography, arguing that over time a particular place would become associated with a particular racial group. If that place were considered "undesirable," then so would be the people associated with it. The association of blacks with slums reinforced for whites the presumed links between race and crime, disorder, and declining property values. With whites' racial prejudices confirmed, they engaged in racial exclusion, which facilitated exploitation. Weaver warned that blacks would resent this attempt to contain them, arguing that "these mutual fears, so often fanned by housing situations, are a terrible cost for any democratic community to pay."[73] Because of the cold-war political environment, Weaver advocated some urgency in addressing restrictive covenants and residential segregation, warning, "The Negro ghetto weakens us internally, while it embarrasses us internationally."[74]

In addition to gauging the economic, social, and political impact of restrictive covenants, black social scientists analyzed their effectiveness and proposed remedial action against them. Weaver spoke directly to the ineffectiveness of the restrictive covenants to contain blacks when he emphasized, "*As a matter of fact, race restrictive covenants have not prevented and cannot prevent the expansion of living space for mounting Negro populations*" (original emphasis). All that restrictive covenants did in these contested areas, according to Weaver, was "delay this movement" and bolster whites' resolve to exclude blacks until "the final break-through becomes almost a rout." This haphazard process offended both Weaver's technocratic and his democratic sensibilities.[75] His solution was to engage in a three-pronged attack that included eliminating restrictive covenants, developing "neighborhood controls," and making more housing and land available to minorities. Weaver argued that the legal strategy was more promising than a legislative one, even though the advocacy for state legislation generated public discussion and increased awareness of the social costs and moral dimension of the problem.[76] While expanded access to more land might take a while, Weaver pointed out, the institution of "neighborhood controls" could happen immediately. He then created an innovative policy tool—occupancy standards—to operationalize those controls. Occupancy standards, which I discuss at length later, were residential property-use restrictions that were not based on race.

Shelley v. Kraemer *and Its Aftermath*

In 1948, black housing reformers, lawyers, and civic leaders and their white allies reached their goal of eliminating the legal sanction of racial restrictive covenants. In May that year, the U.S. Supreme Court ruled in *Shelley v. Kraemer* that while it was not unconstitutional for private citizens to enter freely into a contract that bars residency to nonwhites, it was a violation of the Fourteenth Amendment for the government to enforce these agreements.[77] The NAACP had amassed an array of legal talent under the direction of future Supreme Court justice Thurgood Marshall. They had labored since the 1945 conference in Chicago to find the right restrictive covenant cases to bring to the Supreme Court to challenge the constitutionality of their enforcement. It was in these cases that Marshall, William Hastie, Charles Houston, Loren Miller, Loring Moore, and others marshaled the sociological data to document the social consequences of racial inequality. Robert Weaver, under the auspices of the American Council of Racial Relations, directed the production of the social science memorandum utilized by the NAACP lawyers.[78]

Black national and civic elites knew that the elimination of restrictive covenants was only the first step in fighting housing discrimination and residential segregation. As early as 1945, Robert C. Weaver said, "It is important not to imply that doing away with race restrictive covenants is going to secure adequate living space for Negroes. It will be an important contributing factor, but will not accomplish the result in itself. But it must be done first."[79] This was still true after the ruling. Black federal housing official

George Nesbitt remarked almost a year after the decision, "the rulings, of course, will neither end residential segregation nor readily open up existing housing supplies to additional Negro residence."[80] In fact, the growth of the housing supply that resulted from whites abandoning their homes in favor of new housing in suburbia proved to be more beneficial than the *Shelley* ruling.[81] In the wake of the ruling, white neighborhood improvement associations responded either through more entrenched opposition or by working with new black middle-class households to institute building restrictions to prevent the illegal conversions that often made rental housing affordable for poor working-class blacks. Little reduction in residential segregation in Chicago resulted from the *Shelley v. Kraemer* decision.[82]

Although the legal strategy was crucial, it represented only part of the means used to eliminate restrictive covenants. Perhaps what was most effective, according to Plotkin, was that African Americans "continued to move into covenanted neighborhoods" throughout the 1940s.[83] After the 1948 decision, this movement, led by the middle class, became much more rapid, with bordering white neighborhoods seeming to turn black overnight. Just as the legal and legislative strategies required an infrastructure of black professional and civic organizations, so did the efforts of individual black homeowners. Although an individual would need initiative and courage to become one of the first persons of color to move into an often hostile white neighborhood, they usually needed a black financial institution to provide financing or a black realtor to facilitate the right place and time to upgrade their housing. The "black real estate industry," minimal as it was, provided crucial support for blacks' efforts to buy homes. This in turn facilitated the black upward mobility that advanced blacks' class as well as racial interests.

Managing Racial Transition by Occupancy Standards

Black elites recognized that the chief effect of the Supreme Court decision in 1948 was to accelerate the expansion of the black South Side ghetto that had slowly evolved throughout the twentieth century. While the decision had some material effects in formally relaxing the racial borders surrounding the ghetto, it was a largely symbolic victory against housing discrimination and its formidable offspring, residential segregation. As black migrants continued to settle in the inner-city communities of the Near South Side, Douglass, Grand Boulevard, and Washington Park, more upwardly mobile blacks joined new communities such as Hyde Park, Oakland, Kenwood, Woodlawn,

Englewood, and Park Manor. Some of these communities already had enclaves of middle-class blacks before 1948.[84] Black elites, including Robert Weaver, worried that it was the influx of working-class blacks into kitchenettes and rooming houses that had caused overcrowding and congestion. The link that whites made between black residence and property devaluation could be minimized, Weaver reasoned, if their contact was with those blacks who had the income and class culture to uphold neighborhood standards of property maintenance and behavior. Therefore, Weaver determined that low-income black renters' residency in formerly all-white middle-class neighborhoods needed to be controlled or managed. To achieve this, he created "occupancy standards" as race-neutral property rules that anyone with the requisite income and "training" could uphold.

A Tool of Democratic Housing

Occupancy standards included rules and norms that pertained to the configuration, use, and maintenance of a housing unit or parcel of property. For example, the standards might limit the number of people or families per dwelling or the number of people per room. Sometimes the size of the lot was specified, along with the modifications to the property that were permitted.[85] Occupancy standards, according to Weaver, could succeed if they required "property owners not to sell or lease except to single families, barring excessive roomers, and otherwise dealing with the type of occupancy, [and] properties would be better protected during both white and Negro occupancy."[86] These standards were included in agreements signed, for instance, by members of a neighborhood improvement association. In explaining the benefits of adopting universal standards, Weaver noted that it would become possible for a black family "with the means and the urge to live in a desirable neighborhood." In addition, he asserted, the neighborhood's "integrity" would be protected, making it less likely that all whites would flee "upon the entrance of a *few* Negroes," which, he added emphatically, "*is what depresses property values*" (original emphasis).[87]

Weaver expressed confidence that new neighborhoods would not resegregate if they were "well planned and desirably located," and if neighborhood standards were given "adequate protection."[88] He endorsed occupancy standards as a response to what he saw as a legitimate concern underlying the adoption of racially restrictive covenants: white fears that blacks entering "their neighborhoods" would not, due to low incomes or improper habits, maintain the property standards of current residents. Yet as the preceding quote makes clear, these race-neutral devices also protected affluent racial minorities from "resegregation" into the mixed-income, all-black communities that they had fled.

Occupancy standards, he reasoned, would supplant the need for racial restrictions. While agreements based on these standards would not explicitly forbid occupancy by specific races, they had both racial and class implications because compliance required the resources and socialization to maintain property in ways that met the approval of one's neighbors. Weaver called occupancy standards "a tool for democratic housing." However, since a homeowner needed economic and cultural capital to order to meet occupancy standards, Weaver's critics accused him of substituting class restrictions for racial ones.

Stabilizing Racial Transition

Weaver believed that occupancy standards would stabilize racial transition by allowing only those blacks who could meet prevailing standards into bordering white neighborhoods, while excluding those blacks who could not.[89] He argued that whites associated black residents with declining property values because they had witnessed the decline of former high-rent neighborhoods contiguous to the Black Belt after numerous (including low-income) blacks moved in. The deterioration associated with working-class blacks stemmed largely from the fact that absentee landlords charged exploitative rents and neglected necessary repairs in their buildings. Weaver also saw unscrupulous real estate speculators, both white and black, take former luxury apartment buildings and subdivide each apartment into kitchenettes, thereby contributing to overcrowding and blight.[90]

Weaver thought whites made an "emotional" association between race and neighborhood deterioration. If they understood the situation rationally, he averred, they would recognize that segregation only worsened the situation by causing overcrowding and deterioration and putting pressure on blacks to escape poor conditions by moving to "their neighborhoods." However, Weaver did take whites' fears seriously.[91] He argued that if whites feared the impact of blacks moving into the neighborhood, it did not "do much good" to explain that "the possible result is due to social and economic rather than racial factors."[92]

He also conceded, however, that there were "certain circumstances associated with the entrance of colored minorities in new areas which those
interested in abolishing the ghetto cannot ignore." He advocated the use of
occupancy standards to avoid the "circumstances" that identified all blacks
with ghetto conditions, since whites did not usually distinguish between
affluent and poor blacks. The adoption of occupancy standards, Weaver
argued, would cause "race restrictive housing covenants [to] appear in their
true light—not as instruments to protect neighborhood standards but as
devices to discriminate against racial groups and as impediments to sound
city planning."[93]

Weaver maintained that black and white residents had "a common interest in maintaining community standards."[94] In sum, he thought, occupancy
standards would promote a "normal expansion of space open to minorities";
act as a basis for cooperation between the races; arrest blight that resulted
from unmanaged racial turnover; and, with the addition of low-rent housing
available to blacks, open up "interracial living on the fringes of the Negro
ghetto."[95] For Weaver, occupancy standards could be a critical tool for achieving racial democracy in housing.

Occupancy Standards, Not Class Restrictions

Weaver's retelling of how he got the idea of using occupancy standards
to undermine racial covenants illustrates that he was aware he would be
charged with promoting class restrictions. He related the story of a colleague
in the race relations field who lived, according to Weaver, in "one of the few
racially democratic neighborhoods in America" at the time. Racial integration went smoothly when only "a small number of colored families" moved
in, his friend observed. Older white residents feared a "black invasion," but
this did not occur immediately. The new black homeowners "conformed
to and often exceeded existing standards of conduct and property maintenance."[96] Trouble began, however, when "a rooming house for colored people
was opened." Before long, "all Negroes in the community and those possibly or remotely interested in moving to it suddenly became symbols of a
threat to property values." Soon "the race restrictive covenant boys started
to work. Interracial housing was endangered."[97] Weaver concluded that his
friend knew "how to encourage continuing acceptance of colored people in
the area" but did not want to raise this issue for fear of being accused of "proposing a class approach to housing." As a social technician, however, Weaver

had no reservations about urging the adoption of occupancy standards in response to what he thought was an untenable situation. In fact, he stood ready to face the charge of class bias head on.

An editorial in the *Chicago Defender* criticized Weaver and the American Council of Race Relations for advocating occupancy standards, which they argued substituted class considerations for racial ones in restricting access to housing. Weaver defended himself and the organization by first declaring his opposition to what he saw as a trend toward exclusive "single-class" living spaces, which he termed a "danger" to American democracy.[98] He then asserted that occupancy standards did not "*introduce*" class into housing policy, but that class was already a determining factor in the distribution of housing opportunities in the United States (original emphasis). In other words, in U.S. housing markets, people acquired the quality, size, and location of housing that their financial resources permitted. While Weaver found this outcome distasteful, he considered it a normal function of the market. When it came to racially exclusive areas, however, he argued that the market failed to behave according to its own impartial principles.[99]

Weaver insisted that occupancy standards were class neutral, pointing out to reformers that rejecting occupancy standards would not get them any closer to their goal of multi-income housing. In fact, he thought that not isolating racial factors from the economic factors that caused blight delayed the opportunity for "planning truly democratic housing."[100] He reminded reformers that "the unplanned entrance of low-income families into high-rent neighborhoods does not create stable areas of multi-income group living."[101] Weaver also said that reformers were not doing low-income folks any favors by defending their right to housing that would become an economic burden to them. Occupancy standards, Weaver claimed, transcended race and class. He insisted that even in a classless society, "there still would be need for occupancy standards in order to assure desirable use and maintenance of facilities."[102] It is clear that Weaver favored mixed-race, multi-income housing developments, and unsurprisingly given his New Deal background, he argued that these new projects must be large scale and planned. He thought that "truly democratic neighborhoods" had to be planned "with facilities designed to meet the needs and rentpaying abilities of a crosssection of the income groups in our society and when such neighborhoods are open to all ethnic groups."[103]

Yet Weaver's response to the charge of class bias remains misleading. He correctly observed that occupancy standards did not create class exclusiveness in housing, but he failed to acknowledge that such standards reinforced class segregation when people of lower incomes could not afford to live in certain neighborhoods because of them. For example, occupancy standards often limited the number of people or families per dwelling or people per room within the dwelling, directly affecting poorer blacks. Many working-class blacks could not afford adequate housing unless it was broken up into smaller units or unless they rented rooms to nonfamily members, which usually violated occupancy standards. Weaver's attempt to rationalize his use of occupancy standards suggests that racial democracy governed his approach. Clearly he was not without social democratic commitments, but he was foremost a racial pragmatist. He appeared to be saying that, since reformers were powerless to change the overall structure of housing opportunities, they should at least minimize race as a factor by relying instead on income (and behavior) for integrating neighborhoods. He claimed that "it is more desirable to make a success of achieving *racial democracy* than acquiring more shelter for a limited number of colored people at the cost of undesirable property use, interracial conflict, strengthening segregation elsewhere in the city (and the nation), and further characterizing Negro occupancy with blight" (emphasis added).[104]

For those blacks desperate for housing, Weaver's rationale would seem callous. Yet Weaver deemed such a sacrifice necessary to break the nexus between race and lower property values that served as the chief obstacle to the racial democratization of housing markets. Racial democracy meant to Weaver that some blacks would gain nondiscriminatory access to good neighborhoods based on their ability to pay and conduct themselves properly. In other words, his policy advocated the use of class privilege to facilitate racial reform. Perhaps it was a Faustian bargain with a class-stratifying housing market, but to him the alternative was worse. Not to use occupancy standards guaranteed the status quo of unmanaged racial succession, blight, and rigid barriers to blacks acquiring decent housing. "Covenants based on occupancy standards," he argued, "would permit areas open to minority group occupancy to expand more normally." More space "would lessen the pressure upon other neighborhoods (ill adapted from the economic point of view), [and] *permit selective infiltration of minorities into such areas*" (emphasis added).[105]

Weaver's rejection of the class-bias criticism and his advocacy of theoretical multi-income housing reveal his latent social democratic sentiments. His pragmatism, governed by his ideological convictions, led him to promote racial democracy as a necessary move in a technocratic project. This for-mer federal housing official counted on whites' class prejudices outweighing their racial bigotry. He accepted racial parity in class-exclusive housing, at least momentarily. The implication is that upward mobility for a qualified few would prove more palatable than the planned mixed-race and mixed-income housing delineated in his social democratic vision. Despite all his emphasis on "planning," Weaver's advocacy of occupancy standards, agreed upon by private homeowner associations, called into question who or what would guarantee public accountability. There is a real tension between the market and state planning in Weaver's thinking here. Occupancy standards appear to be a very market-friendly tool for eliminating the racial distortion in what Weaver accepted as a fundamentally self-regulating market. Only a very narrow reading of democracy would claim occupancy standards as a "tool for democratic housing." Weaver's pragmatism meant social democ-racy would have to wait for the success of his racial democratic experiment.

Racial Transition and Occupancy Standards in Oakland

It would not be long before Weaver's occupancy standards would be put to the test of managing "racial transition." As discussed earlier in this chapter, Oakland was a battleground for contesting racial covenants. The Oakland community experienced rapid racial transition when the black population grew from less than one-quarter of the community's residents in 1940 to more than three-quarters in 1950. Oakland was located north of Kenwood and Hyde Park. Hyde Park was under the firm grip of the University of Chi-cago, which kept tight control over black working-class residency at the time (see chapter 6). Kenwood, which had experienced significantly less black in-migration than its neighbor Oakland, provided a buffer for Hyde Park. Woodlawn, directly south of Hyde Park, also experienced more black resi-dential mobility than either Kenwood or Hyde Park.[106] Kenwood and Hyde Park had some of the neighborhood improvement associations most active in enforcing restrictive covenants before 1948. Both communities, along with Oakland, had neighborhood organizations that experimented with occu-pancy standards.

The Oakland-Kenwood Property Owners' Association had experimented with occupancy standards in the early postwar period. However, they real-ized that these agreements were ineffective with absentee owners. According to Plotkin, they were more successful "in the sections of the neighborhood dominated by single family residences still in excellent shape."[107] It was not surprising, given the ineffectiveness of restrictive covenants in the northern section of its service area, that an organization that had been one of the most successful in restricting blacks was now advocating occupancy standards. Even before *Shelley*, many members of the property owners' organization perceived the inadequacy of restrictive covenants and began to see signs of impending black residence. They witnessed neighboring areas becoming all black despite racial covenants. After World War II, with the expansion of housing opportunities in surrounding suburbs for whites, the association members realized that more vacancies combined with the "higher purchasing power in the Negro community" would result in black entry into Oakland. As Weaver noted, the willingness of blacks to pay more than whites for the same dwelling appealed to "speculators and operators [who] would acquire property in the area and convert it to Negro use with high densities." Given the potential for high profits, white residents knew that racial covenants would not be sufficient to prevent building conversions and poor black tenants.[108]

Convinced that black residence was inevitable, the Oakland-Kenwood Property Owners' Association, in the summer of 1947, took the initiative to call "a conference with the community agencies concerned with better housing and race relations in order to discuss the possibilities of developing occupancy standards in the area." The association apparently sought "a new type of organization—a community association which would include all ethnic groups." In January 1948, five months before *Shelley*, the property owners' association announced that it would not enforce restrictive covenants in seven blocks of the northern section (north of Thirty-Ninth Street) of the organization's service area. At the same time, the association adopted a "Community Conservation Agreement establishing occupancy standards in the designated area." Once the standards garnered public acceptance, they reasoned, the association would explore similar agreements in other sections of the community.[109]

In November 1947, before the Oakland-Kenwood Property Owners' Association had adopted occupancy standards, Frank Horne, director of the Racial Relations Office in the HHFA, became aware of the association's interest in experimenting with occupancy standards. Thomas Wright, Commission on Human Relations (CHR) director, alerted Horne to this development on the eve of the Supreme Court decision. The Oakland-Kenwood association and the CHR advised Horne that they planned to submit a joint "housing plan" that included not only occupancy standards but also a rehabilitation plan. While they could have gone to any federal housing official, they approached Horne because of the racial implications of the occupancy standards experiment. Horne responded positively, asking Wright for details of the plan. Since he planned to be in Chicago to attend the American Council of Race Relations conference, he suggested that Wright contact George Nesbitt, regional racial relations officer for the Public Housing Administration, based in Chicago, and arrange for the both of them "to visit the site and neighborhood in question."[110]

While Horne was in the city, he evaluated the Oakland-Kenwood Property Owners' Association's rehabilitation proposal. After describing the coverage area of the plan as South Oakland and Kenwood, he noted, "the 'infiltration' of Negroes, Orientals and other minorities has already begun, especially in the blocks just south of Oakwood Boulevard and east of Cottage Grove." Horne added that this neighborhood was largely white and "constitutes first class owner-occupied and rental properties." He reported on white residents' concerns about "the relentless and unchanneled pressure of non-white groups seeking necessary expansion out of the Black Belt." Furthermore, he wrote, "white and Negro operators" have acquired a few properties in the area and were subdividing them "into 'kitchenettes' apartments with resultant high profits." Moreover, the neighborhood association "realize[d] that this process of over-use will inevitably spread and blight the entire area."[111]

After his visit, Horne explained that white residents had shifted strategies for "preserving the standards of the neighborhood" because they had observed "several instances where Negro property owners, of economic and cultural status similar to whites already in the area, have acquired properties, rehabilitated and maintained them in full accord with the maintenance standards of the neighborhood." Horne added that white residents also anticipated that the Supreme Court would rule against the constitutionality of enforcing racially restrictive covenants. While reading the judicial handwriting on the wall, whites saw an opportunity to preserve at least the class character of their neighborhood by accepting upper- and middle-class blacks and restricting working-class blacks and whites.[112]

The Oakland-Kenwood association wanted to construct a class and racial buffer on Oakwood Boulevard, which divided North and South Oakland.[113] The neighborhood association had bought up vacant lots and proposed populating them with "large rental developments with cooperative apartments to sell at $8,000 to $10,000 per unit." Horne was pleased to announce that the association planned "to open these units to occupancy on the basis of objective occupancy standards rather than purely racial restrictions." He reported that the association's members felt the adoption of these standards with "the concurrence of responsible Negro leadership will limit the degree of minority occupancy to those whose proved economic and cultural levels will maintain and utilize the properties in accord with the standards of the Association." Apparently, the Oakland-Kenwood association, in conjunction with the Mayor's Committee, was "drafting the Occupancy Standards Agreement to cover the rehabilitation projects proposed for the five or six blocks immediately to the south of Oakwood Boulevard." Horne emphasized that the "final agreements will cover *all* properties in the *entire* area" (original emphasis).[114]

Horne explained the potential national impact of this "highly significant proposal," which offered "the first instance" of a white property owners' association "abandoning the outmoded device of racial covenants and substituting controlled occupancy by non-racial and objective occupancy standards."[115] Horne added approvingly that the University of Chicago and its surrogate "Hyde Park Association" were monitoring the impact of the Oakland-Kenwood plan.[116] He thought the Oakland-Kenwood association would pursue private financing for their "rehabilitation plan" whether the FHA supported it or not. Horne advised Raymond Foley that if the FHA supported the project, "it would redound to the prestige of the Agency and utilize federal credit in the interest of many segments of the population groups represented in Chicago." In addition to suggesting that Foley consult with FHA commissioner Franklin Richards, racial relations advisers, and the field office, Horne recommended he dispatch "DeHart Hubbard, FHA Racial Relations Adviser for that zone, into Chicago as soon as possible to work with the Chicago Office in getting up the full story and advice on the minority group aspects of this proposal."[117]

Weaver's "tool for democratic housing" represented an intervention into the racial transition of a neighborhood in Chicago. The Oakland-Kenwood association's adoption of occupancy standards was a test to see if it would lead to a stable, racially integrated neighborhood. It also reaffirmed the importance of Chicago as a place for innovation in race relations and housing policy. More importantly, however, it represented black elite cooperation, both nongovernmental and governmental, with a white middle-class homeowners' association in developing measures that excluded working-class blacks from desirable neighborhoods in order to achieve racially democratic policy goals. Black policy elites countered whites' racism with race-neutral occupancy standards and acceptable black homeowners who had attained similar, if not superior, "economic and cultural levels." These actions were heavily supported by the race relations industry, including the CHR. For instance, the Chicago Council Against Discrimination called occupancy standards a "democratic kind of restrictive covenant."[118] That Weaver, Horne, the *Chicago Defender*, and "responsible Negro leadership" all embraced "objective occupancy standards" demonstrated a black elite consensus that class exclusion was a price they were willing to pay for racial democracy. It appears that the adoption of occupancy standards failed to hold back the tide of blacks seeking homes in Oakland. By 1950, it was predominantly black. Kenwood, on the other hand, was more successful in retaining its white population; blacks constituted less than 10 percent of that community's population.[119]

Racial Democracy in Kenwood

Unlike Oakland, where racial transition had already advanced significantly, Kenwood adopted the same strategy as neighboring Hyde Park, using high purchase and rental prices to limit black occupancy (see chapter 6). During the early 1950s, Kenwood residents fought "blockbusters" who wanted to profit from an increased number of black working-class residents paying premium rents for rooming houses and kitchenettes. Blockbusting referred to the tactics used by realtors to get whites to sell their homes by warning them of an imminent black "invasion" and the ill effects it would have on their property values and neighborhood life. Fearful that blacks moving in would mean lower property values, whites would sell under market value so as not lose even more money by waiting longer to sell. Unscrupulous realtors would then sell homes above market value to housing-starved blacks and garner huge profits in the process. Even rooming houses carved out of illegally converted mansions represented a step up for many working-class blacks.[120]

An article in *Harper's* magazine about Kenwood in 1963 touted it as "the only established American community with a large proportion of Negroes where white residency has increased without controls." Most African American residents were described as "upper-income (several are millionaires)

while its whites are mainly middle- and upper-middle-income professionals." The author, Elinor Richey, added, "If poor families had not been
removed from Hyde Park, the half-mile or so between Kenwood and the
University campus would probably have become a Negro slum and Kenwood would have found it all but impossible not to follow suit."[121] After Dr.
Maurice Gleason and "his Ph.D.-holding wife" became the neighborhood's
first black residents, only eleven black families followed over the next three
years, widely dispersed over central Kenwood. These new black residents
included Lloyd Hall, a nationally renowned chemist; Judge Edith Sampson;
Roi Ottley, a writer; Earl Dickerson; and Jewel Rogers, an attorney who nom-
inated Richard Nixon at the 1960 Republican convention.[122] Since the Great
Migration, black upper-class residence in Kenwood and Hyde Park represented the greatest success of the black bourgeoisie fleeing the ghetto and its
inhabitants.[123]

In this context, Richey described the efforts of white women to fight
blockbusting and maintain an interracial, middle-class neighborhood; she
profiled the experiences of upper-class blacks who applauded and joined
their efforts. She reported the irony noted by new black residents "that the
whites who criticize Negro living patterns still push them into congested,
rat-infested ghettos where decent homes are impossible." When "middle-
and upper-income Negroes had sought to form high-standard Negro or
interracial neighborhoods," Richey wrote, they were thwarted by real estate
brokers who did not uphold "standard-of-living homogeneity" as they did
in white neighborhoods. In other words, once the black middle class had
successfully integrated a previously all-white neighborhood, "agents delib-
erately introduce Negroes from a much lower economic level to frighten
whites away." The result, Richey sympathetically concluded, was that "Negro
professionals and businessmen are thus deprived of the kind of environments they want."[124]

Richey quoted Hyde Park alderman Leon Despres, commenting on
blacks' lack of class privilege and summarizing the message the city of Chicago was sending to its black citizens by its actions: "No matter how urbane
you may be, no matter how educated, no matter how good your reputation
or high your honor, you must stay in the ghetto."[125] Also included in the
article were the comments of a black woman who was a Howard University
graduate and the wife of a doctor: "We had more at stake in fighting neighborhood deterioration than did our white neighbors. When white people are
forced out by slums, they have a choice of places to go. We don't. We can

only keep moving just ahead of the slum—an awful prospect."[126] Ironically, because upper-class blacks had fewer options for their housing dollars, they were more equipped than middle-class whites to outbid the blockbusters.[127]

As the *Harper's* story suggested, upper- and middle-class African Americans fought residential segregation partly because it denied them their class privilege of living in a "high-standards" neighborhood, a motivation that had played a part in the battle against restrictive covenants some fifteen years earlier. According to Richey, black residents attempted to buy themselves into an upscale, integrated neighborhood, but if they did not buy multifamily buildings in Kenwood and other new neighborhoods, they would be confronted with the fact that "luxury apartments [would be] converted into 'studios' by installing a Negro family and a hot plate in every room." Eventually, "service broke down, and mounting garbage drew flies, rats, and stray dogs." Residents explained, "Landlords got away with it because conditions in Chicago's 'Black Belt' are so bad that almost any change is an improvement."[128]

The cases of Oakland and Kenwood suggest that neither black policy analysts nor black upper-class homeowners hesitated to use class controls— either occupancy standards or purchasing power—to stop the conversions of large homes and multifamily buildings into kitchenettes accommodating working-class blacks. Kitchenette buildings were harbingers of the ghetto and slum, and black elites wanted to live in neither. In their use of class tools to accomplish middle-class and integrated living, they saw themselves as serving a racial democratic ideal. Their actions demonstrated that class exclusion in housing was essential for a limited idea of racial progress in the increasingly conservative postwar period.

Conclusion

Black policy elites' approach to attacking racially restrictive covenants was governed by their racial democratic ideology. Their opposition to racially restrictive contracts involved legal activism and technocratic policy innovations such as occupancy standards. While the symbolic consequences of restrictive covenants concerned all African Americans, the benefits of their undoing redounded more to the black middle class eager to take advantage of the new housing opportunities for residence and income property. Black policy elites, after investing a lot of attention and resources, came away victorious in 1940 and 1948. Yet they failed to change the federal government's support of housing discrimination and segregation. By advocating the use of "occupancy standards," a supposedly "color-blind" policy tool, black elites reaffirmed the primacy of race; they also demonstrated their confidence that an open housing market would serve most black housing needs by eliminating race as an allocational principle. Nonetheless, black policy elites' willingness to substitute class restrictions for racial ones marked the death of social democracy in their politics and, in its absence, the dominance of racial democracy.

9

Selling the Negro Housing Market

The track record of the private housing industry in producing housing for racial minorities was woeful. Between 1940 and 1950, only 100,000 of the 9 million new private housing units produced nationally went to nonwhites.[1] Since 1940, black policy elites had recognized the importance of fighting this severe racial disparity. While they accepted the role of private enterprise in producing housing for African Americans in Chicago and other U.S. cities, they decided to confront its racially discriminatory practices. Every facet of the industry—construction, development, and finance—had long discriminated against African Americans, producing residential segregation. Black housing officials in Washington, representatives of national civil rights organizations in New York, and black civic activists in Chicago worked together to pressure the federal government to correct its own discriminatory practices and to use its authority to stop racial discrimination and exclusion by real estate developers, home builders, mortgage lenders, and realtors.

Black housing policy elites knew they needed an ally in their efforts to get the real estate industry to serve the emerging Negro housing market. They calculated that public institutions might be more amenable than private industry to appeals for racial fairness and equality. Even though the federal government had been instrumental in institutionalizing residential segregation when it formed its housing agencies during the early 1930s, black elites were encouraged by President Truman's executive orders and civil rights commission, as well as the Supreme Court's decisions outlawing restrictive covenants and school segregation in 1948 and 1954. Black civic and national elites, although they were aware that these gains from the executive and judicial branches would not easily translate to a nondiscriminatory housing policy, nonetheless sought to exploit inconsistencies and contradictions within the federal government. Initially they used civil rights gains to pressure the Housing and Home Finance Agency (HHFA) to end discrimination in the implementation of housing and redevelopment policies. Beyond this, black housing officials and activists tried to pressure federal housing agencies to use housing subsidies as leverage to get real estate interests to serve black home buyers and renters in housing markets in Chicago and other cities. In other words, they wanted federal housing officials to influence, cajole or pressure private developers, builders, financiers, and realtors to serve black citizens and to sanction those that did not.

During the Truman administration, black policy elites attempted to use federal agencies to pressure the real estate industry into ensuring that African Americans received their fair share of public and private housing units, especially after being displaced by urban redevelopment and slum clearance policies. In 1950, following the outbreak of the Korean War, Congress reduced the modest number of public housing units promised by the Housing Act of 1949. The fallout from "Negro clearance" made private provision of black-occupied housing all the more urgent since many displaced blacks were ineligible even for the limited number of public housing units available.

On the eve of the Eisenhower administration, the selling of the Negro housing market was primed to proceed in earnest. Along with a Republican administration came more emphasis on the private housing industry's fitness to serve the American public with only supplemental participation of the federal government. Sensing a more conservative environment, black policy elites called on both the federal government and the real estate industry to honor their collective claim that the housing market was in fact "free" and "open." They pressed government officials and housing industry leaders to reject timeworn beliefs about blacks' behavior in the housing market and to recognize both the economic and political benefits of serving this market. Economically, upper- and middle-income black Americans represented a virgin market to be exploited by real estate professionals who could see beyond stereotypes. Politically, the more evidence that both government and industry could point to regarding the largest minority group's opportunities for acquiring modern homes and apartments, the more they could trumpet the power of private enterprise to rid America of a visible inequality without direct government intervention.

Organized capital was successful in putting liberal reform forces on the defensive after World War II by arguing that private enterprise could produce more and better social goods at an affordable price without jeopardizing the private freedom of ordinary citizens. Capital's political success meant the state shied away from asserting public control of the economy, including direct production of social goods such as housing. Instead, the government subsidized the costs of private housing production while property developers, home builders, realtors, and mortgage lenders reaped the profits. Since black policy elites seldom made pronouncements about the political economy separate from their racial advocacy work, it is difficult to ascertain their position on the respective roles of government and private enterprise in housing provision. Because so much of their animus toward business was about its racial practices, their position on private enterprise's general role in housing since the war was not as explicit. It was clear that on racial grounds alone, black housing policy elites had more confidence in government than private industry when it came to achieving their racial democratic housing agenda.

Yet, in the 1950s, black policy elites noticeably shifted to embrace private enterprise, which perhaps was to be expected with a resurgent business class and an increasingly cowed state. But these black elites had their own reasons for embracing the free market beyond simply an inhospitable political environment. Their support was based on a growing confidence that an increasing number of upwardly mobile black professionals, clerks, and skilled workers would secure housing in a racially democratic housing market. As black policy elites sought the racial democratization of housing markets in Chicago and other cities, they found a receptive audience, especially in the real estate industry. In 1954, the year of the historic Supreme Court decision *Brown v. the Board of Education of Topeka, Kansas*, which outlawed the constitutional validity of "separate but equal," the national housing industry suddenly discovered the Negro housing market in Chicago as well as other major cities throughout the United States, but it did so at a cost. As the political climate became more accepting of formal racial equality, the class-stratifying principles of housing markets remained unchallenged. Because of their predominant focus on racial democracy, black policy elites affirmed the leading role of private enterprise in housing provision, thereby contributing to legitimizing the capitalist political economy of housing in the postwar period.

In this chapter, I examine the positions that black housing officials took on the role of private enterprise in housing professional and wage-earning blacks. Through their reports, memoranda, and market studies, black policy elites, along with white Federal Housing Administration (FHA) analysts, presented national housing industry leaders with the case for serving the black housing market. Both black policy elites and white market analysts faced an audience skeptical about the financial ability and inclination of

African Americans to buy and maintain property. Advocates responded with evidence of middle-class blacks' worthiness, arguing that it was blacks' previous lack of income and class culture, not their racial behavior, that stood in the way of their meeting acceptable housing market standards.

I then look at home builders' interests in the black housing market in Chicago, along with black civic elites' response. Though most new housing for blacks came as a result of white flight, black policy elites appeared to be successful in engaging the real estate industry's interest in making home loans and selling and building houses for black Chicagoans in the 1950s. Black civic leaders steered white builders to the black middle-class market, fearing that the economic insecurity of wage-earning blacks during a recession in 1954 would undermine the broader project of selling the Negro housing market.

Last, I trace the campaign that black federal housing officials mounted to get the national real estate trade organizations to serve black housing markets. This campaign shows the consensus among black policy elites over the role of private enterprise in pursuing racially democratic housing and the tension they experienced over open occupancy. I highlight, in the housing policy proposals of some black government officials, an explicit discussion of the relationship between state and capital. At this time, the ideology of racial democracy shifted to accommodate private enterprise and open occupancy, the accomplishment of which was dependent on selling the idea of a housing market consisting of confident and competent black middle-class citizens.

The Negro Housing Market

Black housing professionals in Chicago and Washington, D.C., paid close attention to the growing number of black citizens who could afford to buy a house or rent a modern apartment in the postwar period. Home ownership among blacks was definitely on the rise. In 1940, there were 5,717 "nonwhite owners" in Chicago, occupying 7 percent of all minority-occupied housing units. Ten years later, that number almost tripled to 15,928. The percentage of nonwhite owner-occupied units had increased to 12 percent of all nonwhite housing units in 1950. By 1960, the number of nonwhite owner-occupied units had more than doubled to 36,667, which constituted 15 percent of all nonwhite housing units (see Table 9.1). Despite having to shop in a racially restricted housing market, black Chicagoans were making steady progress toward becoming homeowners.

TABLE 9.1.

Black Home Ownership in Chicago, 1940–60

POPULATION	1940	%TTL	1950	%TTL	1960	%TTL
Negro population	277,731		526,058		837,656*	
Nonwhite housing units	76,265		131,416		233,494	
Nonwhite owner units	5,717	7	15,928	12	36,667	16
Nonwhite renter units	70,548	93	115,488	88	196,827	84

Sources: Table 1. "Summary of Selected Characteristics: 1950, 1940, 1930," *Local Community Fact Book for Chicago, 1950*, ed. Philip M. Hauser and Evelyn M. Kitagawa (Chicago, Ill.: Chicago Community Inventory, University of Chicago, 1953), 6.

*Nonwhite population. Note: "In the Chicago Consolidated Area in 1960, 97 percent of the nonwhites were Negroes," xix. Table IV-4. "Characteristics of the Nonwhite Population. For Community Areas with 400 or More Such Persons: Chicago, 1960," p. 269. Table IV-6. "Occupancy and Structural Characteristics of Housing Units, by Community Areas: City of Chicago, 1960," p. 273. *Local Community Fact Book, Chicago Metropolitan Area, 1960*, ed. Evelyn M. Kitagawa and Karl E. Taeuber (1963; Chicago: Chicago Community Inventory, University of Chicago, 1967).

An examination of black housing elites' analyses and policy positions reveals that when they referred to the private housing market for blacks, they had various markets in mind. Sometimes the reference denoted all blacks who were ineligible for public housing because of income or family size. Most of the time, however, for a variety of reasons, the term "Negro housing market" referred only to the upper or middle class. Most likely this was because black elites felt the black middle class was more *ready* to take advantage of housing opportunities—either new construction or existing housing—than were wage-earning blacks. The implication was that once working-class blacks became upwardly mobile through an expected expansive (and racially fair) postwar economy, they, too, would be ready for new housing opportunities.

For some black policy elites, it was also a question of what kind of housing was becoming available in the neighborhoods undergoing racial transition, or of what class of consumers the housing industry was most likely to serve. While one sector of the building industry was mass-producing housing for the newly upwardly mobile whites in the suburbs, another was planning sleek high-rise apartment buildings in the central city to attract mobile corporate managers and professionals of the new postindustrial urban economy. In other words, in constructing mass-produced suburban housing for the middle and working classes, the real estate industry shifted from its preoccupation with building mainly for the affluent market—although only partially and temporarily—in response to the unprecedented union-based wages and benefits that flowed after World War II and bolstered working-class purchasing power. Since most suburban housing markets were off-limits to African Americans, they were under the sway of the housing industry sector that built high and moderately priced homes in central cities.

When black housing policy analysts lamented that upscale housing formerly occupied by whites was being illegally converted to kitchenette buildings or rooming houses for lower-income blacks, it is not always clear precisely to what they objected. Following Robert Weaver, they advocated policies that would distribute different black classes to the appropriate housing and neighborhoods based on their respective incomes and the extent to which they had been socialized to appreciate the link between maintenance and property values. A strictly pragmatic reading of black elites' housing policy preferences suggests that they were only responding to the class bias of the housing industry. I would argue, in addition, that black policy elites were responding to a racist real estate industry by putting forward the "best" representatives of the race to undermine racial stereotypes, in the hope that this strategy would eventually open housing markets to all blacks, though along class-stratified lines. This led them to advance the cause of the class that they believed had both the economic and cultural capital to prove African Americans were deserving of modern housing and therefore full citizenship in the postwar United States. Of course, this approach meant, at the time, that housing for the black upper and middle classes was sought most assiduously and secured first, while wage-earning blacks who could not afford the asking prices for shelter were forced to take advantage of what was left over in the ghetto or to occupy new kitchenette buildings in formerly white neighborhoods.

In other words, the racial *and* class bias of the private housing industry led black policy elites to favor upwardly mobile blacks. Yet while black elites made *choices* about which class's attainment of housing would represent racial progress, they were not simply responding to a more powerful institution. What these elites considered politically possible was also determined by their reform ideology. They brought to their understanding of racial-group progress the idea that middle-class blacks, either individually or as a class, would best pursue racial democratic access to American institutions. This idea was not explicitly advocated in black political institutions, nor did it need to be, since it was broadly assumed by black and white policy elites in postwar America. The further politics traveled from the class-conscious struggles of the Depression, the easier it became for African American elites to ignore, marginalize, or eclipse social democratic ideas within their own housing agenda. Racial democracy or democratization of racial access privileged the black middle class and accommodated, sometimes encouraged, an enduring class bias that could provide only a partial solution to "the Negro housing crisis."

In the following section, I examine a number of studies produced by both black policy elites and white policy analysts employed by the FHA between 1948 and 1954. These studies explicitly identified African Americans as a potential private housing market, both in Chicago and nationally. Black and white analysts made the case to investors of the desirability of a private housing market of black consumers; describing it in order to ascertain and communicate both the existence and the readiness of this market to be served by the real estate industry. While promoting the black housing market, the officials and activists engaged in a debate about the locational preferences of black home seekers. They discussed whether blacks were more comfortable inside or near the Black Metropolis, or whether they would be interested in potential housing developments distant from family and friends. If blacks admitted to their ambivalence about residential integration, it might sap the drive by black interest-group elites and governmental officials for racial democratization of housing markets and policy. Reluctant white government officials and recalcitrant real estate elites might use blacks' preference for black communities as a reason to promote "voluntary" segregated housing. The black policy elites feared that the subtle position of embracing open occupancy in principle, but personally preferring the familiarity of a critical mass of black residents would be lost on white elites.

Making the Case for the Negro Housing Market

Both black and white housing analysts encouraged the real estate industry to pay attention to the African American housing market. Aware of blacks' reputation as either having too little income or being too irresponsible to properly maintain property, housing analysts tried to disabuse their audience of these notions. They highlighted African Americans' new purchasing power, pointing to examples of blacks improving previously run-down properties. They also pointed investors in the direction of the Negro housing market, highlighting blacks' ability to purchase or rent upscale housing.

Housing Aspirations

Black and white policy analysts attempted to convey African Americans' desire for good housing and their ability to maintain, if not improve, property. They provided evidence of blacks' housing aspirations and economic competence by showing how blacks had improved formerly upscale housing that had begun to deteriorate and documented the consumption habits of blacks. In addition, they commented that middle-class blacks' ability to become homeowners in the face of many obstacles and few opportunities proved their worthiness as a viable housing market.

Frayser T. Lane of the Chicago Urban League (CUL) prepared two studies of the black housing market in Chicago for private housing planners: the first in 1948 and the second some time after 1950.[2] First, he focused on the valuable property that affluent blacks had held within the ghetto for long periods. Lane touted blacks' ownership of residential property on desirable boulevards, some of the best real estate on the South and West Sides, including South Parkway, Michigan, Oakwood, Marquette, Washington, Warren, Garfield, Douglas and, increasingly, on Drexel.[3] The homes in these areas had originally been built for a "higher-income group" but had begun to deteriorate long before blacks moved in. Lane touted their present condition, which proved the new black residents had "an appreciation for better standards." For confirmation, Lane reported that an employee of the University of Chicago regularly brought his friends to Woodlawn to show "how the Negroes had enhanced the value of the property." Lane also pointed to black enclaves on the Far South Side including Lilydale and Morgan Park, miles distant from the Mid-South Side ghetto. African Americans, avoiding the congested parts of the city, had carved out these enclaves in the early twentieth century when they bought lots and built humble homes. According to Lane, over time affluent blacks moved to these southern enclaves and built beautiful homes overshadowing those of the original settlers.[4] West Chesterfield, the most affluent black enclave prior to World War II, had homes costing from $8,000 to $25,000, handsome sums at that time.[5]

After demonstrating middle-class blacks' desire for modern housing, market analysts commented on blacks' ability to make the most of the few housing opportunities available to them. FHA analyst Margaret Kane discussed African Americans' limited access to the housing supply, especially the "inadequate" amount of new housing specifically built for them. She explained that much of black demand for public housing was the result of private enterprise failing to take advantage of blacks as a viable housing market. According to her, blacks and other racial minorities suffered from inadequate housing because they were disproportionately poor as a group and the private housing industry did not generally build for that class. She pointed out that after 1940, there was a major discrepancy, with the nonwhite population increasing by 11.6 percent, while their housing only increased by 6.9 percent, compared to whites' housing, which increased by 12.5 percent even though their population increased by only 7.5 percent. Allan Thornton, another FHA market analyst, added that this discrepancy left blacks actually facing more overcrowded housing conditions in 1950 than they had ten years earlier.[6]

In this vein, Lane pointed out the irony that while blacks desired and could afford "good housing," very little of it was available to them. In 1948, Lane lamented the fact that since the construction of Michigan Boulevard Gardens twenty years previously, not one other private housing project had been built for blacks.[7] Lane mentioned that one-third of the Gardens' tenants had the means to pay for "expensive private homes, but prefer the protection and social aspects of the Gardens." He surmised that racial discrimination and the shortage of housing combined to force black families to pay higher prices for lower-quality housing. Black families routinely paid more than 20 percent of their income for shelter, a significant proportion at the time. After 1950, Lane observed that while there was increased home ownership, most African Americans were forced "to buy old multiple family dwellings in traditional 'Negro' neighborhoods," rather than newly constructed or available single-family homes.[8]

James Geer, a regional FHA market analyst based in Chicago, showed that black home ownership increased under less than optimal circumstances, indicating for him their "definite interest."[9] Geer pointed out that the growth in home ownership was larger among blacks than for city residents as a whole.[10] He cited data from a large black savings and loan association in Chicago to show that the increase came almost solely through blacks taking over formerly white-owned property. Citing the same source, he noted that in recent years, two thousand owner-occupied units had been added annually to the black housing supply through racial transfers. Black access to home ownership depended on whites' willingness to "abandon" their homes, something they had been less willing to do in the "tight housing situation" immediately after the war than in later years, when subdivisions were multiplying on the suburban periphery.[11]

Margaret Kane argued that the difficulty that blacks experienced in get-ting good housing only "enhance[d] their appreciation of and pride in good homes." It had been her experience that African Americans "who feel that they are getting good value for their money tend to keep their properties in good condition and to pay the cost even at great sacrifice."[12] Furthermore, black federal housing officials George B. Nesbitt and Booker T. McGraw determined that a large number of blacks who rented, especially those with "better income levels," would buy houses if they were available. They argued that black homeowners demonstrated this desire by consistently purchasing homes even though they were subject to "hard financing terms" and neigh-borhood resistance, including violence. They explained, insightfully, that racial minorities not only "view[ed] homeownership as an index of social status" but also saw it "as a welcome opportunity to escape from the harsh exploitation of a circumscribed rental market."[13] All the housing analysts, black and white, acknowledged African Americans' housing aspirations by arguing that they strove to attain conventional standards even when they had to overcome racial and economic obstacles to do so.[14]

Economic Competence

Even if the real estate industry was convinced that African Americans *desired* improved housing, it was another thing to demonstrate their ability to pay for and maintain it at the high end of the market. In the past, the real estate industry had argued that the reason it did not serve blacks was not because of their race, but because of their employment instability as a group, which caused them to represent an investment risk.[15] Due to the industry's skepti-cism, market studies on black housing consumers needed to establish their economic stability. Lane's phrase "economic competence of the group" spoke to blacks' ability to purchase and maintain property. Black and white analysts made their case by citing income and employment data as well as comment-ing on blacks' class consumption habits.

The market analysts reported on African Americans' income gains in the postwar period. In 1946, the national median income for nonwhite families was $1,800 compared to $3,100 for whites. Margaret Kane calculated that roughly 16 percent of nonwhite families made incomes of $3,000 or more.[16] By 1948, Lane reported, blacks' average income in Chicago had grown, largely due to many black families having multiple incomes because black women were more likely than white women to work outside the home.[17] For example, he explained that most of the black female schoolteachers and clerical workers were married to black professionals and businessmen, or sometimes two or three of them would share an apartment.[18] After 1950, African Americans' average income, determined by Chicago Community Inventory reports, was $2,900.[19] While still only 45 percent to 55 percent of white income, the figure did indicate to Lane that many blacks had good incomes and were employed in more diverse sectors in Chicago than in other comparable cities.[20] In a "sample census tract," Lane counted 225 household heads with annual incomes of $5,000 to $10,000.[21]

In response to the industry's concerns about employment instability, Lane commented on the employment gains in major industries that black Chicagoans had made during and after World War II. For instance, Lane observed that blacks constituted one-fifth of the total work force in food, chemicals, wood and wood products, and service. Blacks had also moved into commerce, transportation, and human resources. The FHA's Allen Thornton predicted future economic mobility for African Americans since they had proven themselves when their jobs were "upgraded," adding that they had not yet enjoyed the full utilization of their skills in the postwar economy.[22] In addition to expanding industrial employment opportunities, which Lane credited to the CIO, the war brought "a new group of businesses and small tradesmen." The Negro Chamber of Commerce, according to Lane, reported that two thousand black retail establishments and fifty small manufacturing concerns had been created after World War II.[23] As additional evidence of blacks' "new financial position" in Chicago, Lane pointed out that four church congregations constructed new buildings and that most of the "well organized" churches had paid off their mortgages.[24] The upward economic trends had continued after the war with the emergence of "grocers, cosmetic and hair goods dealers, manufactur[ers] and distributors, owners of kitchenette apartments and many similar instances of the new class of 'well to do' people."[25] One grocer on Thirty-First Street was making between $2,500 and $4,000 a month in cash sales, according to Lane. He stated that this petit bourgeois stratum, while "not regarded in the professional group," nonetheless had "social desires and demands" best met by residence in a "high class and controlled HOUSING development" (original emphasis).[26]

The "accumulation of war bonds" and "the benefits of price controls and the discipline of rationing" had fueled postwar consumption. The black "upper set" was busy acquiring deep freezers, air-conditioning, and venetian blinds, as well as putting in modern kitchens, "rumpus rooms," and portable bars. According to Lane, this consumer activity showed housing planners that, just like other Americans, blacks "want good housing and good housing equipment."[27] He also observed the large number of new cars owned by blacks, including Cadillacs and Buicks, pointing out that the owners of these luxury cars could be persuaded to buy homes. Lane also reported that not only were more African Americans taking vacations, including traveling to the South to visit relatives, but they were also buying farms in outlying rural areas. He added that a sizeable number of black beauticians were accustomed to spending more than $1,000 on vacations in Europe. Lane declared that these women would make "good prospects as home buyers."[28] With market studies demonstrating African Americans' employment and income stability in the postwar period, the real estate industry could no longer use their lack of buying power as an excuse to ignore the black housing market.

Description of the Black Housing Market

All the housing studies on blacks outlined the composition and size of this potential market. Some described the potential of most blacks to constitute a private housing market, but most studies focused exclusively on affluent blacks. Not only were the potential consumers identified, but also the market studies described the volume of sales and rental housing that would be attractive and affordable to this market segment.

The focus on a black middle-class housing market was explained by HHFA race relations advisers Nesbitt and McGraw, who pointed to the difficulties that other strata would have constituting themselves as a viable housing market. They referred to the special problems that the "immigrant population" posed for addressing racial-group housing needs and interests. They observed that the housing demand of "abnormal" families, whose numbers had become "excessive" due to "immigration and other factors," had become "significant" in the postwar period. They attributed such unconventional family structures as female-headed households to migration, and characterized migrant households as larger and with younger members than long-term resident households. Nesbitt and McGraw resisted passing moral judgment on these families, but instead pointed to the challenges of accommodating them through private housing production, thus underscoring black policy elites' emphasis on middle-class blacks as the prime target for real estate developers.[29]

Based on demographic, economic, and cultural profiles of black middle-class consumers, black housing market studies predicted the volume and price of sales and rental housing that could be absorbed. James M. Geer, regional FHA market analyst, provided the most thorough studies of Chicago's black sales and rental housing markets.[30] In both studies, Geer attempted to measure the demand for higher-priced housing among African Americans. In his 1951 study of the black sales market, Geer estimated conservatively that in the next twelve months, "the Negro market has the capacity to absorb from 5,000 to 7,000 additional homes for sale." He further calculated that "1,900 to 2,600 of these units would be at or near the $12,000 price level, about the minimum price for new single family dwellings in this area." Geer concluded that more black families were interested in and capable of buying housing than the housing industry had previously believed.[31]

Geer's second study tried to gauge how many housing units renting at $100 or more a month could be absorbed by Chicago's black rental market. He estimated that eighteen thousand black families, representing 13 percent of the total number of black families in the Chicago area, earned at least $5,000 a year in 1950, the household income necessary to afford $100 or more in monthly rent.[32] Within this relatively small group, about half rented or preferred to rent. He found that the demand among blacks for rental apartments at that level was "very small," an estimated 425 to 450 units, constituting less than one-half of 1 percent of the metropolitan area's total black-occupied rental units.

However, he identified two types of households that could afford that rent. The first type consisted of professionals and businesspeople, and the second type included households containing multiple wage earners, whether related or not. He observed that both types lived in the elite Michigan Boulevard Gardens, which featured "moderate rents and high quality living accommodations."[33] Geer asserted that members of the first group, professionals, were "more stable economically" because they had greater financial resources and exercised more responsibility than the average black citizen. Despite the potential desirability of such accommodations to professional households, Geer believed that housing developments that charged $100 or more for monthly rent would still have a hard time attracting black tenants.[34]

Geer's analysis also covered the supply of rental units available to African Americans as it stood in 1951. He believed that after a long period of scarcity, an unprecedented number of units available to black Chicagoans was about to appear on the city's housing market. The city's first redevelopment project, Lake Meadows, would supply 1,400 high-rise and garden-style apartments, from efficiencies to three-bedroom units, renting at $20 to $26 per room. In addition, Parkway Gardens would contribute 694 larger apartments, renting at $92 to $110 per month. Geer determined that Lake Meadows and Parkway Gardens, with a combined total of nearly 2,100 rental units, would dampen demand for high-priced two-bedroom apartments unless they were located "in a most desired neighborhood and [feature] luxury type living quarters." The additional advantage of Parkway Gardens' large apartments, Geer explained, was the possibility of including "lodgers" to help pay the rent. In 1949, lodgers still made up almost 12 percent of all blacks living in households.

Contributing to the lack of demand for high-end rental property was what middle-class blacks acquired through racial succession. Geer reported that there was "rental housing of very good quality gradually becoming available to Negroes in fine residential areas of Hyde Park, Kenwood and Woodlawn." The attraction of these neighborhoods was the size of their apartments as well as their close proximity to other neighborhoods experiencing residential succession. Clearly, "racial transfers" had changed the rental market for blacks from one of "extreme shortage of units" in the immediate postwar years to a larger supply in later years. Considering all these factors, Geer concluded, "relatively few families are willing and able to pay over $100 in rent."[35]

By 1954, the housing picture for blacks in Chicago had not changed much. Another FHA market analyst at the time observed that while good-quality housing owned by blacks was well maintained, the housing rented by blacks had experienced deterioration, usually as a result of overcrowding. The sales housing available to blacks was located in "small developments and in scattered individual house construction."[36] If more housing was not made available, the steady demand but limited supply would threaten the gains blacks made in recent years.

The Debate over Black Housing Preferences

While black and white analysts of the Negro housing market agreed that the real estate industry should serve it, they disagreed on how. The crux of the disagreement concerned the housing preferences of African Americans, primarily regarding location. At issue was whether blacks favored occupying new housing in close proximity to the ghetto or at some distance from it. The former position suggested self-segregation, which made black policy elites uneasy. In the context of Chicago's volatile political mix of race and real estate, they feared that any hint of preference for voluntary segregation would give aid and comfort to white segregationists while disrupting a key component of their racial democratic agenda—open occupancy.

James Geer contended in his two studies that financially able black families "have been noticeably reluctant to invest in homes located away from established Negro areas." Geer suggested to developers of black housing that "less risk is involved in building for sale in or on the fringe of these already established areas, either on vacant land or through area redevelopment." He warned that the "marketability" of new housing developments for black occupancy was in jeopardy if they were located "in districts new to Negroes . . . unless volume is sufficiently large to create an entire new community." Geer added that most black families preferred small private homes in the city.[37]

The controversy over black housing preferences within federal housing circles was touched off by Geer's comments, which were welcomed and distributed by George Bremer, FHA zone commissioner for the Midwest in 1951, who had requested this study. After receiving Geer's report, Bremer endorsed its findings on black housing preferences to Roland M. Sawyer, minority group housing adviser for the FHA. Bremer discovered from Geer's study that there were opportunities for "prudent builders and investors" to construct and finance several thousand housing units for black occupancy a year in "scattered fringe areas." Bremer felt that if Geer's findings were correct, this scenario represented "the greatest possibility of real achievement in the construction and sale of new homes to Negroes."[38] Roland Sawyer delicately commended Bremer for his "keen interest" in the "Chicago Situation," at a time when HHFA administrator Raymond Foley was encouraging FHA involvement in subsidizing new construction to accommodate black families displaced by Lake Meadows.[39] Nevertheless, his lack of comment on Geer's "findings" despite Bremer's enthusiasm reflected Sawyer's concern that self-contained communities in areas bordering the Black Belt would not be racially integrated.[40]

The topic of black locational preferences reappeared within the federal housing agencies in 1954. George Nesbitt and Booker McGraw contested the idea that blacks did not want to live "too far out." They emphasized that potential black home buyers held no set positions on this question. Some blacks, they argued, would "see the values, real or fancied, in living 'way out' as well as in living 'close in.'" However, the different interpretations of black locational preferences did not break down strictly along racial lines.[41] White FHA analyst Allan Thornton added, "new housing on carefully selected sites outside of the central city would be marketable" to black home buyers.[42] They all argued that dissatisfaction with outlying sites had been due to black residents' isolation from adequate transportation and labor markets.[43] Essentially Nesbitt and McGraw stressed that blacks' housing preferences, like those of whites, varied. Though they attempted to normalize blacks' locational preferences, the black housing officials acknowledged that segregation could affect black and white home buyers' housing choices in different ways.

The Impact of Segregation on Housing Preferences

Nesbitt and McGraw weighed in on the debate over black locational preferences because of what they saw at stake—changing FHA policy so that it insured housing developments that included black residency. Location mattered to them because housing developments far from the ghetto, they felt, were more likely to have mixed residency than those near the ghetto. Apart from the disagreements about blacks' locational preferences, which caused some black housing officials to question other interpretations of black housing behavior made by white FHA market analysts, there was much agreement between black and white policy analysts. As we have seen, white analysts Kane, Geer, and Thornton helped make the case that the black housing market needed more attention from FHA underwriters, home builders, realtors, and lenders.[44] They all agreed with the conventional wisdom in the housing policy community that the chief obstacles to providing private housing to blacks were finding suitable sites and adequate financing. They disagreed, however, on whether the FHA added to those conventional obstacles with its own racial practices.[45]

In 1954, two months before the *Brown* decision, Nesbitt and McGraw reflected the trend within the black housing policy community to replace racial equity with "open occupancy" as the standard for whether a housing market was considered racially democratic or not.[46] As a result, Nesbitt and McGraw were insistent about judging FHA market studies solely on the basis of whether they facilitated or endorsed "racially open occupancy" in housing developments. When it came to comparing black *and* white housing behavior, Nesbitt and McGraw weighed the impact of segregated housing on the assumptions and expectations that both black and white consumers brought to the housing market. They were particularly concerned that because both racial groups were unfamiliar with racially mixed housing, their housing preferences could not be taken at face value.[47]

Nesbitt and McGraw argued that pervasive segregation might be responsible for skewing both white analysts' observations about blacks' housing behavior as well as blacks' *own* understanding of their housing preferences. White analysts can make "fallacious assumptions" about black consumer preferences, they observed, by interpreting their residential "use patterns" and housing conditions without appreciating the underlying forces that produced these patterns and conditions.[48] In addition, they cautioned, white analysts should not assume that racial minorities would be willing to pay for housing solely because it would be nonsegregated. They argued that the analysts should gather and carefully interpret additional data, which "should be useful in facilitating racially open occupancy."[49] Pertinent data included information on prospective black home buyers' occupations, education, war record, union and church membership, "and related cultural indicia." These data were useful not only for advertising blacks' worthiness as neighbors but also for providing blacks with information they wanted about potential white residents. Whites' class status also mattered, they contended, since black middle-class home buyers were not eager to share their neighborhood with "poor whites."[50]

Nesbitt and McGraw explained the difficulty of accurately judging black residential behavior in restricted communities. They argued that "long habituation to old and ill-adapted shelter may have tended to narrow and suppress the new housing *expectations* and *perspectives*" of segregated black consumers (original emphasis). Nesbitt and McGraw explained that black "consumer[s] themselves have been previously accorded so *little choice* in the matter of housing that they may lack settled attitudes or not freely relate them" (original emphasis). Yet according to these race relations advisers, class neutralized the negative effects of segregated living, making it less likely that "such a depressed outlook" would exist among blacks with a "higher income and cultural level." Nesbitt and McGraw concluded that in removing racial barriers to the housing market, this "outlook may disappear altogether."[51]

Nesbitt and McGraw encouraged FHA housing analysts to connect locally with "citizens housing associations, residential building industry leaders, university research people and students," who could provide "valuable *first-hand* information" about the black housing market (original emphasis).[52] They advised housing analysts to carefully use data collected from potential housing consumers through interviews and questionnaires. They were concerned that whites' responses would reflect their unfamiliarity with integrated housing and its possible benefits and might therefore contain racial stereotypes regarding blacks' residential behavior. According to these black housing officials, residential segregation had a way of perverting both black and white considerations of "racially open occupancy." Nesbitt and McGraw realized the fragility of open occupancy and wanted to make sure that neither uneducated blacks nor naive white analysts would discredit its appeal.[53]

Serving the Negro Housing Market in Chicago

Black civic elites in Chicago had recognized African Americans' need for private housing for some time. The need that resulted initially from both segregation and a housing shortage became particularly acute after 1950, when slum clearance policy displaced many black families who were ineligible for public housing. Black housing reformers promoted the "Negro housing market" to convey not only the desperate need for housing to both local and federal officials but also the new buying power of the black middle class.[54]

Of all the black civic organizations engaged in housing policy in the city, the Chicago Urban League became the best known for promoting a private housing market for blacks. Frayser T. Lane aggressively provided information on Chicago's black housing market to private planners. However, the promotion of open occupancy got the League in trouble in some circles because threatened whites thought the black civic agency was financing black home buyers engaged in "blockbusting" white neighborhoods.[55] Though the League was not promoting racial succession, it was clearly invested in securing more and better housing for African Americans, however it was acquired.[56]

By the mid-1950s, white home builders were interested in getting a better feel for Chicago's black housing market and often contacted the CUL. Two themes emerged from the CUL response to their inquiries. One revisited the question of black locational preferences. The academic discussion by Nesbitt and McGraw was put to the test when white builders asked black civic leaders if they would buy houses built far from "established Negro areas." The second theme concerned the question of disaggregating black housing demand.[57] FHA analysts and race relations advisers had focused on serving a black upper- and middle-class market. The scant evidence available suggested that builders and developers seemed more interested in building housing for a black moderate- or low-income market in Chicago. Despite this interest, black civic elites were cautious about recommending building for this market segment due to the economic tenuousness of the lower strata. In 1954, at the time of the inquiries, the nation was experiencing a recession that had hit the black community hard in terms of unemployment and purchasing power. Therefore, CUL officials tended to discourage building for wage-earning blacks and to steer prospective builders to a safer market made up of black professionals and managers.

Sidney Williams, executive secretary of the CUL, received a number of inquiries from white builders and investors regarding the city's black housing market.[58] In 1954, Williams heard from at least three builders in Chicago as well as a marketing firm in New York that represented home builders, each interested in building moderately priced housing for black Chicagoans. One Chicago builder, Fred Rubenstein, informed Williams that his company had land on the South Side and was looking to build "reasonably priced homes for the average or lower income Negro family." His company planned to construct "a 2 or 3 bedroom house selling for approximately $10,000 to $12,000 with a down payment ranging from $500 to $1,000." Clarence L. Holte wrote from a New York City advertising agency to say that his firm represented a client who "manufactures one-family, frame houses which are erected at a cost ranging from $9,000 to $14,000."[59] It appeared that both companies were seeking to build for the same housing market. Three years before, FHA analyst Geer had used $12,000 or more as a minimum price for single-family homes on the South Side available to African Americans. It could be that the upper-income black housing market, still small despite income and employment growth, was not large enough for these builders. Instead, they sought a wider income range, including home buyers who might be upwardly mobile clerical and skilled workers able to save enough to afford the down payment and rely on multiple household incomes to pay the monthly mortgage payments.

Williams, sensitive about persistent rumors that the CUL supported blockbusting, was not particularly encouraging to either inquirer.[60] Factors that might have influenced Williams's lack of enthusiasm were the nationwide recession that may have affected the targeted market's employment and income stability and the fact that some recently built homes for blacks remained empty. Williams reported that two builders who had constructed homes selling for $16,000 in a "new area" had made only three sales since the housing had come on the market the previous winter.[61] The "new area" was Eighty-Ninth and Indiana, a location with some vacant land but near neighborhoods going through racial transition.[62] He then cited a counter-example that cast doubt on whether the recession alone had caused the lack of sales. The homes that Arthur Rubloff & Co. had constructed at Forty-Ninth and Drexel, he wrote, were "already over-subscribed," supporting his impression that "location is undoubtedly a fact here."[63] After receiving Williams's reply, Rubenstein countered that the homes he proposed to build were the "type of house and price range [that] would appeal to many families with average incomes who could not perhaps afford the other homes about which you wrote."[64]

The New York advertising agency's inquiry was more in-depth than Rubenstein's. Clarence Holte asked a series of questions about the makeup of the black housing market in Chicago, wondering if there had been many changes since the 1950 census. Holte wanted to know about blacks' mobility within the city, their reception by white neighbors, their access to mortgage financing (conventional and FHA), and the best way to advertise new homes to potential home buyers. Regarding the new areas to which they had moved, Holte wanted to know how many families had relocated and whether they had bought or rented and, if houses were bought, whether they were new or existing homes and in what price range. He also wanted Williams's opinion about the possible expansion of housing construction in these new areas.[65]

Williams wrote a detailed reply to Holte, reporting that blacks had moved to new areas to the west, east, and south of traditional black ghettos. He pointed out that the movement had been increased by displacement from slum clearance, public housing, and highway construction. Some blacks who had moved to Lawndale on the West Side, he said, lived largely in multi-family housing, though there were "a few exceptions when some of the old mansions were purchased by well-to-do Negroes."[66] The blacks who moved into single-family homes were the ones who had moved about a mile south of the previous Black Belt boundary. Williams reported that "many Negroes purchased homes in all of these areas and became landlords with income property." Still, he reminded Holte, "the largest percentage remained tenants." The two- and three-flat buildings that blacks bought were generally between thirty-five and sixty years old, ranging in price from $20,000 to $35,000. Single-family homes in the racially transitional neighborhoods in the southern areas cost between $15,000 and $25,000, obviously more expensive than the houses that Holte's client planned to build.

As far as the mortgage-financing situation was concerned, Williams reported candidly that it was currently "poor," though improving with new FHA attention.[67] He credited black savings and loan (S&L) associations and insurance companies with being "an important resource in the field." In terms of reaching potential black home buyers, Williams suggested that Holte place advertisements in the *Chicago Defender* and daily papers, hire "distributors to put colorful cards in the vestibules of the Negro community," and sponsor a luncheon for potential clients and "representative people from the community" to present their product. Williams told Holte that blacks had more freedom of choice "in the central section than they do in the suburbs." He reported that while white homeowners very much resented blacks moving in or near their neighborhoods, blacks got new and better homes because of white flight to the suburbs. He said that working-class whites dominated the older suburbs of South Chicago, Chicago Heights, and Harvey, and that in other suburbs "like Western Springs and Oak Park Negroes with money and social prestige have been rejected."[68]

Some conclusions can be drawn from these exchanges between Williams and the building industry on the appropriate black housing market to serve. Williams discouraged builders for the "average income" market because at the time a recession had reduced working-class blacks' buying power, making them unable to comfortably afford even moderately priced single-family homes.[69] Aware that each success and failure in black home buying would be scrutinized and add to or detract from the reputation of the race, Williams steered potential developers to the more stable, though better-served, middle-class market. Williams's advice was based more on working-class blacks' lack of income than on their housing needs. No segment of the Negro housing market had been saturated at this point.[70] In the mid-1950s, building for black occupancy still was considered experimental, and black policy elites were careful to ensure successful results.[71]

It appears that there was good reason for all the attention Chicago builders paid to the Negro housing market in 1954. The following year, a newspaper article reported on black home buyers benefiting from a building boom in the city. James Downs, who headed the Real Estate Research Corporation and doubled as Chicago's housing and redevelopment coordinator, estimated that one-third of the fifteen thousand new houses constructed in the first five months of 1955, at a cost of $210 million, "were sparked directly by this mass home-buying drive among Negroes." Downs attributed the construction activity to blacks' good wages from the "industrial boom"; the pressure to expand land space from unabated in-migration; and last and most disingenuous, the redevelopment programs that had spurred blacks to spread out farther from the center of the city.[72]

According to a Chicago Title & Trust Co. survey, buyers on the South Side (not all of them black) led the city in the purchase of existing homes, with 31.5 percent of the city's total in the first three months of 1955. A number of black-owned financial companies also reported increased home purchasing by black consumers. The Illinois Federal Savings and Loan Association reported that it "made mortgage loans totaling $1,000,000 in the first five months of 1955." Robert Taylor, Illinois Federal's spokesperson, reported that this figure was 25 percent higher than in the first five months of 1954. According to the story, black real estate firms "agree[d] that this is the greatest year of non white home buying here."[73] Moreover, black real estate men reported that due to the "Negro housing boom," African Americans were seeking to build new homes in suburbs such as Evanston, Maywood, Harvey, and Waukegan, Illinois, and Gary, Indiana.[74]

By 1959, of the almost 270,000 housing units occupied by nonwhites, 124,047 were gained from racial succession, while new construction provided only 17,188 units.[75] While it is hard to tell which class of blacks was able to buy homes during this "boom," Williams's earlier pessimism seems to have been unwarranted. Nonetheless, since "the black real estate industry's" boosterism was naturally inclined to optimistic readings, it is difficult to know how far this "boom" went toward satisfying the housing needs of a broad spectrum of black Chicagoans. Whether Williams's skepticism or black real estate elites' optimism was warranted, confidence in black middle-class home buying was a key component of black policy elites' embrace of the free market and its correlate, open occupancy.

Real Estate Capital and the Black Housing Market

By 1954, all the major real estate trade organizations were focused on the black housing market.[76] Not all were convinced that the market was profitable to service, but through the promotion by black federal housing officials, they at least gave some attention to its investment potential. Two basic issues faced white builders and lenders. Should they serve blacks at all? And if they did, should it be in integrated or segregated housing? While many in the real estate industry had decided, by the mid-1950s, that they would serve blacks, they were not at all convinced it should be in integrated housing. So black housing officials not only pushed for the real estate industry's attention but they also advocated for new housing developments to be open to black citizens just as they were to whites.

In promoting the black housing market, black housing officials emphasized a preference for private enterprise and the goal of open occupancy, revealing a more privatist turn in their racial democratic ideology. This helped to bolster the postwar trend of the federal government playing a supplemental role to capital in the production and distribution of housing. Even government's role in correcting racial imbalances in the housing market was called into question by some black housing officials who expressed faith that an unshackled private enterprise would bring about open occupancy to the benefit of those blacks who were ready to take advantage of new housing opportunities. The continued dearth of low-income public or private housing, however, meant this approach would not adequately address the shelter needs of wage-earning blacks.[77]

The National Association of Home Builders

The National Association of Home Builders (NAHB), based in Washington, D.C., like its partners in the real estate industry, began to pay serious attention to the black housing market in 1954.[78] In late 1953, Joseph Ray was invited by the NAHB to participate in a panel discussion titled "Housing for Minorities" at its convention to be held in Chicago in January 1954. Since the NAHB was "anxious to develop housing for minority groups," the program literature explained, "the conference will be an exploratory effort to outline the field, identify the problems and suggest ways of producing this type of housing." Ray was to share the panel with well-known figures associated with the black housing field such as his colleague Frank Horne; Reginald A. Johnson, director of NUL Housing and Field Services; and George S. Harris, president of the National Association of Real Estate Brokers, an organization of black realtists based in Chicago.[79]

The panel discussion was to follow a round-table format intended to permit "an informal discussion" of minority housing provision. The NAHB expected panel discussion participants to "come prepared to outline case histories of successful operations of this type." Ensuring that this would be a "working," not an academic, conference, the NAHB advised panelists that it was "urgent that the discussion concentrate on practicality and avoid theorizing."[80] They emphasized that "the fundamental purpose of the conference will be to determine ways and means by which builders can produce this kind of housing on a businesslike, practical basis." Ray was instructed to make an advance copy of his talk and other materials available to the press since "over 400 newspaper, trade press and magazine editors and reporters" were expected to attend the convention.[81]

Ray's talk, titled "The Negro Market in Housing," offered a basic exposition of the makeup and contours of the market and, as such, gave NAHB members baseline information. Ray's main task, however, was to convince his audience that this was a housing market they needed to exploit. He tried to do this by "establish[ing] four basic facts about the Negro market," including that the market existed and that it was open and undeveloped, socially variable, and economically sound. More than "sound," Ray said, this market was lucrative. Ray calculated that blacks nationally needed one million additional units, which he thought would be worth $5 billion to the construction industry alone. He added that amount "could *well be more* than double . . . , if we capitalize on the full potential of this market" (original emphasis). To further buttress his contention, Ray discussed the increased buying power of African Americans and the growing recognition of their credit-worthiness.

The collaboration between the NAHB and the Racial Relations Service of HHFA on minority housing continued for a time after the conference.[82] The NAHB's minority group housing committee took the lead in enlisting black housing officials to make the case for a minority housing program to the NAHB executive committee. The committee's remaining recommendations mainly involved educational work within the real estate industry, especially at the local level. They reminded their members "to plan suitable housing for minority families in the middle and higher income brackets as well as adequate living units of lower cost housing." Apparently, many white builders still believed that all blacks had low incomes, which helps to explain, in part, why black policy elites emphasized the existence of an upper- and middle-income black housing market.

In their deliberations, the NAHB minority housing committee focused on two problems. The first, internal to the housing industry, was how to find adequate mortgage financing and suitable sites for building.[83] The other problem was whether the housing available to blacks would be provided on an "open occupancy" or on a segregated basis. On the former issue, the minority housing committee advised the national office to publicize blacks' record of regular payments and rare foreclosures in "colored developments" in order to attract mortgage investors.[84] They recommended that the Voluntary Mortgage Credit Extension Committee established by the Housing Act of 1954 link mortgage lenders to qualified minority and underserved rural applicants of any race, and "give special attention to Home Financing for Minorities."[85] The committee was confident that the NAHB would meet its production goal of 10 percent of housing production for minority home buyers through the national voluntary mortgage credit committee and "a strong concentrated effort at the local level." On the second issue, the NAHB board was concerned that "the segregation problem" in light of "Supreme Court rulings and pending legal actions alleging discrimination in housing" would discourage builders from serving the minority market.[86] Apparently, the average white builder either was personally opposed to integrated housing or thought it was a risky investment, seeing that whites would not buy houses in interracial developments. The NAHB may have feared that if its members could not build for blacks on a segregated basis, they might not build for them at all, scuttling any plans to move into the Negro housing market.

The Mortgage Bankers Association

Shortly after black federal housing officials began working with the NAHB to build for the black housing market, these housing professionals began a relationship with the Mortgage Bankers Association (MBA) in order to tackle the problems of housing finance for African Americans. The MBA convention in Chicago, September 27–30, 1954, gave federal housing officials an unprecedented opportunity to exercise what HHFA administrator Albert Cole argued was his agency's primary role of informing the private lending industry about the problem of minority housing finance and correcting misconceptions about black home buyers. It was the first time that any of the racial relations officers had been invited to make presentations to the mortgage bankers.[87]

George Snowden, the FHA's minority group housing advisor who was invited to speak, felt his participation in the convention represented "a real challenge and opportunity to present the case for nonwhite housing to one of the most important industry groups in America."[88] Though it made sense that George Snowden would address the MBA convention because he worked for the FHA, he undoubtedly was the best man to sell the black housing market to an audience of skeptical mortgage bankers. Snowden's faith in the "free market" probably exceeded that of anyone else in the HHFA Racial Relations Service. While some black federal housing officials may have accepted the idea of the "free" market only because it offered an obvious contrast to blacks' restricted mobility, or they may have compromised their social democratic commitments in order to make limited racial-group gains in a probusiness political environment, Snowden's support was unambiguous. In addition to his main task—to promote black consumers as responsible borrowers and property owners—Snowden's real political task was to assure mortgage lenders that the problem of minority home finance could be solved safely within the confines of the conventional political economy. While the relationship between state and capital was often murky in the politics of most black policy elites, Snowden was clear about what the appropriate relationship should be and how black housing interests could be achieved in that context. As the black housing policy community increasingly came around to the "free and open market" view, Snowden's elaborated position illuminated the stakes and compromises black elites would make by embracing this position.

There were three themes in Snowden's speech at the MBA convention. One was a racial critique, which decried financial discrimination and promoted African Americans as exemplary housing consumers with sufficient income, savings, and creditworthiness. Next, Snowden used the ideas of open occupancy, the free market, and, ironically, the *Brown* decision to delegitimize any "special programs" to correct racial disparities in housing finance. The last theme rejected any direct role for government in the mortgage finance business, with Snowden again professing that a freer market would apply nonracial criteria to black home buyers, thereby assuring that they would get their share of home finance dollars.

Snowden's racial critique consisted of telling mortgage bankers that housing acquisition through racial transfers was inadequate because blacks could not get access to modern design and amenities. Therefore, he argued, blacks needed more mortgage finance for new construction.[89] Snowden's racial critique, however, did not entail a racial solution. He disagreed with the federal government's effort to treat minority home buyers separately through "special gimmicks" like the "special market surveys of the housing needs and requirements among nonwhites." This approach, he argued, had fed the real estate industry's misconceptions about black housing behavior. In addition, Snowden rejected "special programs" for minority home buyers, in part because they were vulnerable to a "potential challenge on civil rights grounds." More importantly, these programs undermined "the optimum and economical application of our full energies and resources." He emphasized that the FHA had learned "that the so-called peculiarities" of the minority market "tend to disappear" in an open housing market characterized by the nondiscriminatory treatment of qualified minorities. Snowden argued that "the record of sound business and experience dictates a uniform single-standard, lending policy," assessing creditworthiness on a case-by-case basis and allowing for the fact that minority households might have more than one income earner.[90]

Snowden's optimism about minority housing finance caused him not only to reject "special programs" but also to discard any direct governmental role in mortgage finance. He considered *Shelley* a pivotal moment, after which "any willing buyer and seller can get together" and create a scenario where blacks could live anywhere in the city. Snowden promoted the new Voluntary Home Mortgage Credit Extension Program in order to contest the "notion fairly widespread" that minority group housing needed direct financing from the government.[91] Snowden thought this voluntarist program had more potential than government financing to be productive because the job of providing minority housing would be placed "in the hands of those who have the 'know-how'—the lenders, the builders, and the responsible civic leaders." He was emphatic that "do-gooders" should be avoided. He confidently told MBA members that "[you] will do this job in the right way and in the only way you know how to do it and that is in the free and open competitive enterprise way."

Snowden's rejection of a more direct government role reflected his faith in both the private enterprise system and the notion that racial discrimination would soon be outdated. Snowden observed that the "isolation and segregation of groups" was declining just when "free open competitive housing market[s]" were expanding. He argued that these trends were "inevitable since the only way American private industry knows how to operate is in a free competitive open market." Snowden was convinced that a self-regulating housing market would rid itself of any obstacle to free competition and profit maximization, which meant that open occupancy was inevitable since it best facilitated a rational utilization of economic resources.[92]

While there was broad agreement over the role of private enterprise, there was some tension among the racial relations officers over the direction of housing policy for African Americans, particularly regarding the role of government. George Snowden rejected any hint of direct government intervention while exhibiting an almost religious faith in a market that had to be *fair* because it was *free*. He believed racial impediments would disappear with the liberating effect of market forces. Open occupancy would work because if the market operated impartially, without any racial considerations, it would adjust itself to serve those according to their tastes and means.

Snowden's colleague Joseph R. Ray, a former realtor and a Republican from Louisville, Kentucky, disagreed. Although he had no less faith in free enterprise, his Southern experience told him that open occupancy might take some time to become the norm.[93] At a speech in Memphis, Tennessee, in September 1955, Ray outlined two prevalent approaches to the problem of minority housing. The first he characterized as a kind of "sit down strike," with the ultimate goal of full integration. The problem with this approach was that blacks could not purchase new modern homes that were presently available only in segregated neighborhoods. Clearly, he favored the second approach, which involved building homes for blacks, even on a segregated basis, "while the fight goes on to permit all Americans to exercise the right of choice in selecting their place of abode." For Ray, the two approaches to integrated housing simply reflected "differences of opinion" among fellow proponents. If both approaches were not accommodated, it could delay serving "the great needs of thousands of families" who lived doubled up or in "undesirable homes." Ray argued that the future held the promise of a more open housing market once lenders and builders learned "the facts" about a viable black housing market. Meanwhile, modern, segregated housing should not be sacrificed for the far-reaching goal of "total integration."[94]

The United States Savings and Loan League

In 1955, the United States Savings and Loan League (USSLL), with its national headquarters in Chicago's financial district and representing the $31 billion savings and loan industry, issued a series of three news releases to discuss the relationship between "the home financing practices of savings and loan associations and Negro families."[95] The purpose of the news releases, which went to local savings and loans associations throughout the country, was to resurrect the reputation of "minority group mortgagors [who] make good borrowers." The news releases related the successful experiences of individual savings and loan associations with black consumers, revealing the industry's effort to alert its members to a potentially lucrative market. The USSLL joined the MBA and the NAHB in focusing on the Negro housing market in the second half of the 1950s.

Edwin W. Zwergel, assistant treasurer of East Brooklyn Savings and Loan, reported that, based on its record with "Negro mortgagors," his institution would welcome them as "future mortgagors" as part of its commitment to "provide home ownership facilities to ALL American families." Zwergel reported, in the USSLL news release, that black loan recipients had received 39 percent of East Brooklyn Savings' mortgage loans in the six-year period between 1946 and 1951. There were no major differences between blacks and whites in handling conventional loans, according to Zwergel. In fact, more than 50 percent of the loans paid ahead of either their fifteen-year or thirty-year term were held by minority mortgagors.

In the same news release, Walter H. Dreier, USSLL vice president and president of the Union Federal Savings and Loan Association in Evansville, Indiana, confirmed Zwergel's experience. He commended black home buyers for being "sensible, honest and eager to pay off [their] housing debt," commenting that "in 36 years of making home loans to minority families, his institution had not had to foreclose on a single Negro loan" and that delinquencies were "practically nil."[96]

Because black borrowers were still considered a special market segment, Dreier outlined the "characteristics" of the black consumers his savings and loan company had served. In his experience, black home buyers paid a "sizable down-payment" and took "out as small a mortgage as possible, one commensurate with their monthly income." He found that black families took "special pains to keep from over-extending themselves," choosing to pay the mortgage in ten to fifteen years, a significantly shorter period than that chosen by white families. In general, black families preferred "older, existing homes with more and larger rooms, and in a neighborhood where other colored families reside," according to Dreier.[97] He found that black home buyers invested a great deal of time and money in improving their new homes, including "remodeling the kitchen and bath, repainting, and performing a host of other tasks to get the property in top condition."

Dreier, consistent with observations by FHA market analysts, stressed that "the Negro family values title to the property as it would its life, making every effort to pay off the mortgage—even at the sacrifice of other necessities." In other words, black families valued thrift, solvency, property ownership, and exhibited financial responsibility beyond reproach. Ironically, it was black families' experience with the scarcity of capital that engendered behavior that made them excellent credit risks, contrary to popular perceptions, especially with enterprising, less-capitalized financial institutions such as savings and loans. Dreier argued that if other financial institutions took on black borrowers, they would gain valuable customers who would give them a good and steady return on their investment. He explained that the rise of black home ownership was driven not only by postwar economic gains but also by "a more favorable social climate." He advocated "giving responsible minority families all the help they need in acquiring a home of their own."

Dreier commented on the credit American capitalism would gain from extending to blacks the opportunity to become homeowners. Savings and loan manager Zwergel, too, explained that the more home ownership was facilitated, the less people would need to rely on government-financed housing projects. He contended, like Margaret Kane before him, that blacks' demand for public housing was due to the failure of private enterprise to provide them adequate housing.[98] Dreier was quoted as saying, "We believe that the Negro who has tasted of the fruits of home ownership—who owns a plot of ground and a house in the country in which he lives—is a much better citizen than the one who has grown up in a tenement or in a federally subsidized housing project."[99]

In addition to encouraging more of their members to lend to African Americans, the USSLL used these news releases to encourage the recruitment of black customers as depositors in local savings and loan associations. The release asserted that these institutions provided blacks with more home loans than all other financial institutions combined, reporting that S&Ls had invested more than $230 million in black home mortgages, thus constituting 56 percent of all the mortgage loans made to blacks in the country.

The USLL advised that if minority families made weekly deposits with an S&L, they were more likely to be granted a mortgage loan from the same institution since having a savings account was regarded as evidence of a family's financial stability. Not only would the individual minority family help itself by opening an S&L savings account, it would also be helpful to other borrowers since it took, on average, "eight savers to provide one home loan." The trade organization argued that more savings expressed communal solidarity, proposing that the more money a community could save, the more money would be available for home loans to community members. The trade organization asserted that if a "minority family of good character" saved in an S&L, they would "experience little or no difficulty getting a loan from that institution." Through their promotional campaign, the USSLL joined with other industry groups and government officials in a campaign to "normalize" black consumers' market behavior as a way both to open new markets and to bolster the ideological case for the primacy of private property.[100]

Conclusion

The national real estate industry's recognition that African Americans constituted a viable and profitable housing market resulted from the tireless efforts of black housing officials and civic reformers. After 1948, black civic activists, black housing officials, and white housing market analysts made the case for serving a black private housing market in reports, memoranda, speeches, and government publications. They set out to convince the housing industry's trade organizations that many black home seekers had the incomes and values to ensure that mortgage lenders' investment not only was secure but would grow. These studies attempted to pinpoint the level of housing, price, size, and accommodation that could be absorbed by this neglected market. Armed with the positive findings of these market studies, black federal housing officials began proselytizing at the Mortgage Bankers Association and National Association of Home Builders annual conventions in 1954. In Chicago, local builders sought to serve the "average" income black housing market, but were steered by black civic leaders to the more economically secure and culturally competent black middle class.

In order to sell the black housing market, black policy elites decided to promote the upper- and middle-income segments of that market. They were confident that elite and middle-class blacks not only displayed conventional housing market behavior but would make exemplary loan recipients and desirable neighbors who would maintain their property well. If the real estate industry chose to neglect such an obviously meritorious group, racial discrimination would seem the only explanation.

As a strategy, promoting affluent blacks' housing interests had other benefits. It was consistent with the housing industry's preference for building and selling more expensive housing. Additionally, it addressed the needs of the most vocal and active public within the black community. Elite and middle-class blacks were precisely the people most likely to join black civic and national organizations, to complain to black political and civic leaders about discrimination (and about the behavior of lower-income blacks), to own rental property, and to have ties to black professionals in the real estate business. This cohort, whose income and cultural capital gave them both the impetus and the means to seek appropriate housing in formerly white, affluent neighborhoods, became the black policy elites' main political constituency.

After black policy elites sought to racially democratize federal and municipal housing policy in the 1940s, they took aim at private housing markets in the following decade. Their agenda dovetailed with that of federal government officials who wanted to rid the United States polity of formal racial inequality. The concern that government and business leaders had for protecting the reputation of American democracy abroad meant that the Negro housing market would be a terrain for battles over the appropriate relationship between state and capital taking shape in the postwar period. While presidents and chief housing administrators rhetorically objected to official or government-sanctioned racial discrimination and segregation, they only embraced policy tools that featured the primacy of private enterprise, thus ensuring that substantive racial inequality remained untouched.

George Snowden and Joseph Ray of the HHFA Racial Relations Service also preferred to let the "free and open market" work its magic on behalf of jilted black home seekers. While Ray and especially Snowden were more rhapsodic about the virtues of private enterprise, even those to the left of them—Frank Horne, Booker McGraw, George Nesbitt, and Reginald Johnson of the NUL—embraced the free market as the guarantor of improved housing conditions for black citizens. As the consensus among black policy elites to endorse the primacy of private enterprise emerged by the mid-1950s, the only subject for internal debate was how quickly to pursue open occupancy and "total integration," whose achievement would confirm that the private market was really free. Ray favored a "sequential approach" that tolerated segregation if it meant blacks would receive the immediate benefits of more and better housing. Snowden, along with Horne and Johnson, rejected any toleration of "separate but equal," pursuing residential integration through open occupancy at all costs.

It was clear that in the debate among black policy elites in that pivotal year of 1954, social democracy was no longer considered a viable approach. Rather, the triumph of private enterprise's role in their policy prescriptions meant that the only matter for discussion was *how* to accomplish racial democratic goals, sequentially or immediately, through "racially open occupancy." Black civic elites' pursuit of racially democratic housing policy, including fair mortgage lending, dovetailed with and helped to legitimate the federal government's and private housing industry's ideological mission to limit the postwar role of government in the provision of adequate housing and other social goods to citizens.

10

Self-Help and the Black Real Estate Industry

In early 1941, black real estate professionals Elmore Baker, based in Chicago, and William Occomy published a clarion call titled "A Real Estate Program for Negroes" in the pages of *Opportunity*, the National Urban League's journal. When the authors asked its black readership, "Just what can we do for ourselves?" it was clear that the new program was formulated in a black self-help idiom. Baker and Occomy called for a national trade organization to organize thousands of black real estate professionals and provide leadership to black property owners in the areas of property acquisition and mortgage financing. Their call, at the end of the New Deal, presented a proposal that would inaugurate the black real estate industry and give renewed prominence to black self-help ideology, which dovetailed with the more privatist orientation of the Eisenhower administration in the 1950s.[1]

In the postwar period, the black real estate industry was made up of national trade organizations and local affiliates run by African Americans. National black trade organizations included the National Association of Real Estate Brokers (NAREB), the National Home Builders Association, the National Negro Insurance Association (NNIA), and the American Savings and Loan League (ASLL). These organizations represented black-owned and -operated real estate and financial institutions. The American Savings and Loan League defined itself as "A Non-Profit Membership Organization of Home Financing Institutions." The National Home Builders Association was described by one of its founders as "the oldest organization of builders in the country" whose members "include[d] a number of contractors, architects and engineers as well as teachers of these subjects in Land Grant Colleges."[2] The National Negro Insurance Association represented fifty-eight black-owned insurance companies, and the National Association of Real Estate Brokers represented more than one thousand black brokers nationally by 1955.[3] These organizations came into existence, like many black institutions, because black professionals were excluded from mainstream organizations such as the National Association of Real Estate Boards, the National Association of Home Builders, the Mortgage Bankers Association, and the United States Savings and Loan League. The growth of real estate professions and businesses resulted from servicing burgeoning black populations that were annually replenished by new migrants in segregated communities.

The idea that black realtists, builders, and financiers constituted an "industry" is a relatively novel idea.[4] More often acknowledged is the fact that white realtors, builders, and financiers did constitute an industry because their respective professions were nationally organized into segregated trade organizations that cooperated with each other to represent their individual and collective interests in Washington, D.C., as well as in state capitals.[5] They were committed to keeping business decisions—such as where and what to build, how much to invest, which builders to finance, which consumers should receive credit, to which customers to sell housing—in private hands. While they were ideologically opposed to government intervention in general, they welcomed the role of the federal government in absorbing risk by insuring and subsidizing the financing, building, buying, and selling of housing. They gained advantages such as access to prime inner-city land at heavily discounted prices because the federal government, after the 1949 Housing Act, took possession of thousands of acres of central-city real estate and resold it to developers at a fraction of its market value. The government also subsidized the demolition of old structures. In other words, the private housing industry was happy to have its costs subsidized by the nation's taxpayers while its members alone reaped the profits. For the nation's taxpayers, the payoff was supposedly good and affordable housing. For cities, it promised enhanced revenues from taxable improved property.

There is no reason to believe that the black real estate industry was not equally satisfied with this arrangement of socialized costs and private profits. What they were not happy with, though, was the fact that they could not fully participate in the government-subsidized, private housing market in the way that white firms could. As both producers *and* consumers of housing, they suffered in a restricted housing market controlled by white firms. The fact that the housing industry was government subsidized meant their exclusion was even more an insult to them, and a glaring contradiction to the nation's professed ideal of democracy. As a result, black realtists, builders, and financiers could not get enough business or gain sufficient capital to adequately serve an emerging black housing market. Despite being hampered by discrimination and segregation, however, black firms did constitute a fledgling segment of the private housing industry. This industry, like all black enterprise, accumulated only a fraction of the capital of the white housing industry. Nonetheless, it is not their accumulation of capital, however limited, that warrants the designation "industry" as much as their interest and efforts to establish the institutional arrangements and public policies to facilitate that accumulation. In this chapter, I detail how the positions of black real estate and financial firms on housing policy after 1940, both in Chicago and nationally, facilitated their participation in the real estate business, and examine whether this participation was guided by racial democratic goals.

This chapter explores the makeup of the black real estate industry as well as its political agenda, a key part of which was to garner from the federal government standing and benefits equal to that of the white real estate industry. The focus on government recognition also privileged the role of black housing officials in an emerging black housing policy network, which included black civil rights leaders and black real estate elites. I detail the operation of this network and the self-help orientation that undergirded its actions. The tension between self-help and antidiscrimination as two strains of racial democracy simmers just beneath the surface of many of the situations described.

The Black Real Estate Industry

Chicago realtist Baker and coauthor Occomy outlined the agenda of the black real estate industry in their call for a national organization in 1941. The authors argued that such an organization was long overdue. Since other black professionals had organized nationally, they asked, "Why not our real estate men?" Moreover, they noted, black property owners as well as those "directly or indirectly, connected with the real estate business" constituted the natural constituency for a "permanent organization." They asserted that a national organization was necessary because black realtists faced a competitive disadvantage with organized white brokers controlling the all-important listing of available real estate property.

Baker and Occomy credited national civil rights organizations for their housing activism, but argued that those who knew real estate best were in a better position to find "a complete solution" to the "Negro housing crisis." The organization Baker and Occomy proposed would have a number of responsibilities including acting as a repository for complaints against FHA discriminatory practices, educating potential home buyers about what represented a good investment and optimal available financing terms, and creating a national mortgage corporation to address the problem of inadequate home financing for blacks. The call for a national black real estate organization and program set the parameters of black real estate elites' participation in housing policy debates in the 1950s. During this period, these parameters conclusively embraced the goal of racial democracy.

While black real estate trade organizations joined with national black civil rights officials in fighting both public and private discrimination, they focused increasingly on self-help ventures such as developing black-owned mortgage corporations and savings and loans companies to solve the problem of home finance that plagued them and their customers. Ironically, this self-help approach depended on persuading, with government's help, larger white firms to invest in black-owned companies. Black civil rights elites, though supportive of black real estate institutions, gave greater priority than these professionals to the use of direct government action to break down racial barriers.

Black federal housing officials supported both antidiscrimination and self-help approaches to racial democracy. In some cases, black housing administrators prompted black financial institutions to organize self-help mortgage-financing schemes. Local black civic leaders' social and professional ties with black real estate entrepreneurs and their commitment to, and occasional participation in, black business development translated into steadfast support for black real estate firms. Black real estate elites and their governmental allies felt that their self-help orientation furthered the goal of racial democracy since their fuller participation in housing markets would democratize them racially. This support under the flexible rubric of racial democracy, in turn, reinforced black policy elites' endorsement of the primary role of private enterprise in solving the nation's housing problems.

Perhaps the key institutional arrangement adopted by national trade organizations representing black realtists, financiers, and builders was to help to construct and participate in a black housing policy network that included black federal housing officials, black civic leaders, and black policy elites. This network was strengthened by the fact that some important black civic elites in Chicago and other cities who participated in local housing policy debates and advocacy depended on some segment of the real estate business for their livelihood.[6] Robert R. Taylor was perhaps the civic leader most involved in the private housing industry of Chicago. Apart from chairing the Chicago Housing Authority's board of commissioners until 1950, he was the manager of the prestigious Michigan Boulevard Gardens apartment building throughout his long and distinguished career. He was also secretary of the black-owned Illinois Federal Savings and Loan Company. Nationally, Taylor served as vice president of the American Savings and Loan League in 1950.[7] Mortgage financing for blacks, especially those benefiting from blockbusting, came, at least initially, from either black-owned insurance companies or savings and loan companies. The few black-owned banks in Chicago were not the primary institutions financing housing and property acquisition by blacks.

Earl Dickerson, a civic leader on housing issues since at least the days he chaired the Subcommittee on Negro Housing as a Second Ward alderman, worked for an insurance company that issued mortgages to many black pioneers settling in formerly all-white neighborhoods. He worked for the Supreme Liberty Life Insurance Company for more than fifty years, serving as general counsel until 1955, when he became chief executive officer. Dickerson, considered a "Communist sympathizer" by the FBI due to his social democratic sentiments, did not find any contradiction between racial democratic reform and building a profitable race enterprise serving black property owners and policyholders.[8] Other black civic leaders who were also part of the black real estate industry included Claude Barnett, founder and owner of Associated Negro Press, who served on the board of directors of Supreme Liberty Life; and Oscar Brown Sr., lawyer and real estate broker, who was a former manager of the Ida B. Wells and Altgeld public housing projects and head of the Negro Chamber of Commerce. While Horace Cayton, Sidney Williams, and Robert Weaver did not work in the for-profit realm, their nonprofit work defended the right of black real estate professionals to practice their profession and profit like their white counterparts in the housing field.

Black real estate professionals from Chicago also played prominent roles in national and local black trade associations. For example, many of them belonged to the National Association of Real Estate Brokers (NAREB). NAREB, which was founded in 1947, was modeled after Baker and Occomy's proposal and was the most important national black trade organization in the postwar period.[9] George S. Harris and Elmore Baker served as presidents of the NAREB at different times. Harris's expertise in real estate developed from his directing the Real Estate and Investment Department of Chicago Metropolitan Mutual Assurance Company.[10] Baker, who cowrote the 1941 call, founded and was the first president of the Dearborn Real Estate Board in Chicago the same year, and was an elected member of NAREB's executive board in 1949.[11] His firm, E. Baker & Company, located on the southern edge of the Black Belt on Sixty-Third Street, managed mortgage loans and insurance. Bolin V. Bland served as president of the Dearborn Real Estate Board and as NAREB's regional vice president for the Midwest in 1949. He headed the DuSable Realty Company, which was located in the Loop, and handled mortgages, sales, insurance, and property management. The president of the Dearborn Real Estate Board in 1958 and 1959, Dempsey J. Travis, doubled as vice president of NAREB.[12] Marion S. McDowell, the only black woman to own a real estate firm, was named to the NAREB's board of directors. McDowell Realty Company, also located on Sixty-Third Street not far from Baker's company, specialized in property management, sales, insurance, and mortgage loans. There were other black firms from Chicago that participated in NAREB, including King S. Range Realty located at 3650 S. Michigan Avenue, J. Goodsell Jacobs & Company located in the Loop, and Landrum Realty Company, Incorporated.[13] Many of these firms were multipurpose, not only selling housing and real estate, but also securing financing for their sales and even managing rental properties. The prominence of black realtists in Chicago was augmented by the fact that the city was often a site for NAREB national and regional meetings. These black real estate professionals, as esteemed members of the city's black business and professional elite, could be seen alongside black civic leaders at important social events in Bronzeville.[14]

Government Recognition and Benefits

At the top of the agenda for black real estate trade organizations was to gain recognition by the federal government as representing the black professionals in the real estate field and as experts in the field of "Negro housing."[15] The goal was to be treated on equal terms with the white organizations that excluded them. There was an expectation that along with and following this recognition, their members would benefit from federal government aid in the building, selling, and financing of housing to black customers.[16] Federal government recognition came in a variety of ways: appearances by top housing officials at black trade organizations' annual conventions; appointments on committees whose purpose was to work with government officials in dispensing federal aid or exercising authority in housing programs such as the FHA's Economy Housing program in 1949 and the Voluntary Home Mortgage Credit Program (VHMCP) in 1954.[17] The federal government was most solicitous of the black real estate industry when it came to the issue of fair mortgage lending. Black real estate elites considered recognition and inclusion in a public–private housing partnership a significant achievement for their professional and business interests as well as a step forward for the black community's access to housing.

In order to gain government recognition and legitimacy, black real estate elites engaged in protest actions that resembled those of black civil rights organizations. While they protested on behalf of all black citizens, their protests against their exclusion as professionals and business owners related directly to their business profits, which was not necessarily true for black professionals working solely in government or in the civic realm. National black real estate organizations more closely resembled "special interests" than organizations like the NAACP or the NUL that promoted "civil rights" and incorporated black interests.[18] However, highlighting the racism of the white real estate industry and so furthering the cause of fair housing gave cover to the more narrowly defined self-interests of the black trade organizations.

The NAREB fulfilled one of the objectives of the 1941 national real estate program by joining with civil rights organizations to protest the FHA's refusal to approve loans for black housing in the redlined Black Belt and for "mixed" housing located elsewhere. In 1949, at the NAREB's regional meeting in Chicago, its members criticized the policies, operations, and employment practices of most FHA field offices. Their main criticism was that most state and district FHA directors and their staff typically failed to include minority housing needs in the agency's "normal operations," thus depriving minorities of its "normal benefits." Members argued that these regional offices preferred to ghettoize these concerns by making them the exclusive purview of FHA race relations advisers.[19] They also criticized the fact that the regional offices neither hired qualified black professionals nor placed them on their advisory committees, where blacks would be in a position to challenge the way in which the housing agency went about its business.[20]

Amid all its members' complaints, the NAREB devoted most of its energy to the problem of representation in its encounters with FHA regional offices. President Truman's Housing and Home Finance Agency (HHFA) administrator Raymond M. Foley invited NAREB members to participate in the advisory committees appointed to oversee the FHA Economy Housing Program in different regions.[21] However, some FHA regional offices were better about appointing minorities than others.[22] For instance, prominent black realtist Lenerte Roberts of Philadelphia challenged FHA regional director

Leo Kirk on why he had not appointed black realtists to the Economy Housing advisory committee. Kirk responded that builders were appointed to the committee because they could do something about the cost of constructing housing, adding that he saw no need for minority representation at the time. Kirk's response was typical of the more recalcitrant FHA field office directors, who usually had close ties to the white real estate industry.[23]

The issue of the NAREB's representation on government committees resurfaced during the Eisenhower administration. The NAREB's protest of federal housing policy was closely related to its claims for more representation on government program committees. This connection was highlighted by the 1941 program that linked realtist activism regarding discrimination against black citizens with their exclusion from white trade organizations and government program committees. In August 1954, the NAREB, under the leadership of Chicagoan George S. Harris, protested to the Eisenhower administration about its discriminatory housing policies. Harris insisted, joining the NUL and the NAACP, that housing agencies needed to revise their policies so that federally assisted housing would be open to all citizens regardless of "race, creed, or color." He simply wanted housing policy to reflect Eisenhower's own pronouncement that "where federal funds and authority are involved, there should be no discrimination based upon any reason that was not recognized by our Constitution."[24] Moreover, the NAREB argued that black citizens would not be served properly if they did not participate on government advisory committees.

The NAREB felt snubbed from the very beginning of the Voluntary Home Mortgage Credit Program (VHMCP) in 1954. The VHMCP was created by the Housing Act of 1954, which authorized the formation of a national committee and sixteen regional credit extension committees whose purpose was to recruit lenders to provide private funds for FHA-approved or VA-guaranteed loans to minority home buyers and residents of small communities and remote areas. This group was often unable to obtain residential mortgage loans under fair terms and conditions.[25] The sixteen regional committees acted as a "clearing house" matching "eligible borrowers with willing, private lenders" in their localities. President Eisenhower's HHFA administrator Albert Cole, nominal head of the National Voluntary Mortgage Credit Extension Committee, invited the NAREB, along with other black real estate trade organizations, to make recommendations for membership in the regional committees.[26]

The black realtists, of course, felt they should have representation on both the national and regional committees. The legislation called for a national committee consisting of fourteen members, including representatives from real estate boards, insurance companies, mortgage companies, commercial and mutual savings banks, and savings and loan associations. The fact that the white-only National Association of Real Estate Boards filled the only two designated positions on the national committee looked to black real estate brokers like double exclusion. Their exclusion from the national realtor organization meant that they also were excluded from the national committee.[27]

In a letter accepting his appointment to join a regional committee, George Harris took the opportunity to protest the black real estate industry's lack of representation on the national committee.[28] Apparently FHA commissioner Norman Mason had solicited names from the FHA Minority Housing Group advisor George Snowden, who recommended Asa Spaulding of Durham, North Carolina, or A. Maceo Walker from Memphis for the national committee. Both men were on boards of directors of black-owned insurance companies and savings banks in their respective cities.[29] It is not clear why no appointment was made at the time the national committee was constituted unless it was due to opposition within HHFA and/or from white real estate trade organizations.

In October 1956, two years later, the controversy resurfaced. Seemingly taking the color-blind principle to the extreme, Harris recommended to Cole that the minority designation for regional committee representation be dropped in favor of trade organization representation only. The national committee of the VHMCP endorsed Harris's idea.[30] He felt that black trade organizations were hamstrung by the minority designation and thought that representation on the basis of industry or association could potentially gain them more slots, including a coveted position on the national committee, than could the minority designation, which allotted one position per regional committee. A miffed Harris reminded Cole that the NAREB had submitted recommendations as "a national real estate board," not as a minority trade organization. Harris argued strenuously that the NAREB should be the sole representative of all real estate boards on the national and regional committees.[31] Cole agreed with Harris's recommendation to drop minority designation. However, after citing both the intent of Congress and the fact that NAREB members were already well represented on the regional committees, he refused to commit to selecting a NAREB member as the sole real estate board representative on the national committee. At the time, black representatives on the VHMCP's regional committees included four real estate brokers, two savings and loan officials, five insurance executives, one builder, and two commercial bankers.[32]

Weighing in on this controversy, Joseph Ray, assistant to Cole and head of Racial Relations Service (RRS), disagreed with Harris, probably assuming that the NAREB president's long-standing dispute with the white realtors' organization was clouding his judgment. He argued, "While [a minority designation] is not so worded in the VHMCP Title VI of the 1954 Housing Act, it is very definitely spelled out in the policy under which the program has operated from the beginning." Ray wanted both the minority and individual trade organization designations to remain intact. It made sense that a program meant to benefit minorities would have mandated minority membership of its committees, according to Ray. He warned that dropping the minority designation "minimizes the importance of the place that minorities really occupy in the program and also provides a gap for probable circumvention and, perhaps, ultimate extermination."[33] Though the minority designation was not dropped, Harris's pressure proved effective, since Asa T. Spaulding of North Carolina Mutual Life Insurance Company was named to the VHMCP national committee at the end of 1956.[34]

Black representation on the VHMCP's national committee represented official recognition of the black real estate industry. In addition, in 1956, President Eisenhower added further recognition by sending a message to the NAREB's ninth annual convention in Los Angeles. This message, drafted by Cole, recognized the organization's leadership in the black housing field and its cooperation with HHFA's programs. The NAREB became officially incorporated into the public–private partnership sponsored by the federal housing agency when the president commented, "I believe that through the partnership of government and private enterprise we are moving with ever-increasing speed toward [equal opportunity in housing's] realization, and I am confident that the principles to which your Association is dedicated will prove to be a substantial contribution to this end."[35]

The Black Policy Elite Network

In earlier chapters, I mention the growth of a dense network of black elites engaged in housing policy in different institutional settings including the government and the civic arena. This network had both local and national nodes. Black civic elites in Chicago regularly communicated, collaborated, and sometimes conflicted with representatives of black national civil rights organizations located in New York and Washington, D.C. Both local and national sets of black interest-group elites worked closely with black federal housing officials in Chicago and Washington. Throughout the postwar period, the representatives of the black real estate industry actively participated in this network, seeking information as well as support for their policy and business proposals. While relations with the NUL and the NAACP were important to black real estate elites, the latter channeled their energy toward black housing officials who were in a better position to look after their interests. Black housing officials were in either the HHFA Office of the Administrator or one of the constituent agencies or divisions of that office, or in a regional office. What linked these black officials to each other was their participation in the Racial Relations Service and, more generally, their personal, professional, and ideological ties with black elites in the nonprofit and for-profit realms.[36]

Joseph Ray stated that the purpose of the Racial Relations Service was "to provide expert guidance to industry and local communities in [finding] constructive, realistic solutions to the housing problems of minority families."[37] As Ray's description implies, black housing officials could provide black real estate elites with expertise as well as help them get access to federal resources. When they needed information or data, they asked these housing officials. When the officials had already obtained the data, they shared it with these black businesspeople, usually at the annual conventions of black trade organizations that black housing officials regularly attended. There they conveyed information about government programs and benefits and at the same time made proposals or planted new ideas that promised to grow black real estate businesses and, hopefully, increase the supply of good housing for black citizens. While the heads of black trade organizations lobbied the president and top housing officials, they expected black housing officials, within limits, to lobby internally for the same objectives, which they did. The boundaries between black elites in different institutional arenas—government, civic, and business—were porous. Some black elites spent time in more than one institutional arena over a career, sometimes serially and sometimes simultaneously. No matter in which arena network members found themselves, their politics was governed by racial democratic goals.

Black government officials pursued self-help schemes, akin to the "racial equity" approach in its race-based orientation and tolerance for segregation, to empower black real estate organizations to serve the immediate housing needs of black citizens. While self-help constituted a minority approach compared to antidiscrimination protest, it resurfaced periodically throughout the postwar period, especially in the mid-1950s with government retrenchment in the housing field.[38] Sometimes there was tension between these two paths to racial democracy, but it did not deter their respective proponents from working in concert for their shared political goal.

Black federal housing officials did not just receive complaints and defend a sometimes indefensible housing agency record. They also served as experts willing to share their knowledge about the housing industry. The importance of this role came up in 1954 when the American Savings and Loan League (ASLL) requested Booker McGraw to attend its annual convention. How the request was negotiated revealed some of the relationships that animated the black housing policy network. By this time, McGraw was considered the most knowledgeable of all black housing officials on the issue of mortgage financing. William Hudgins, president of the ASLL, regarded him as their organization's "expert," noting that McGraw had been of "immense value" to the ASLL since its founding and had made "excellent contributions" to the annual conventions he had attended in the past four years. Hudgins alerted Joseph Ray, McGraw's immediate boss, that he was going to ask Albert Cole to invite McGraw to participate in their annual conference. Anticipating that Cole would decline his request, citing budgetary reasons, he solicited Ray's "help in the matter."

Hudgins's expectation that Ray would lobby Cole on the ASLL's behalf was based on a set of shared objectives and an operating principle of *quid pro quo* that animates any political network. He told Ray, "It is our conviction that what you do for the common cause can be influenced a great deal by the support we are able to give you. We shall do our part."[39] When Cole, through Ray, denied Hudgins's request, the ASLL president reassured Ray that "I have no doubt that you supported the request." As Hudgins anticipated, the agency's denial was based on the fact that "budget requirements [would] hardly justify" McGraw traveling to Los Angeles for the ASLL convention after recent trips to conferences in New York, Chicago, and Philadelphia.[40] Hudgins complained to Ray about the "incongruity" of the HHFA sending two, three, or four staff professionals to other national and regional trade organizations' annual meetings "but pleading economy when we request a single expert once a year." He remarked that if the Federal Home Loan Bank Board, which regulated savings and loan associations, had someone like McGraw on its staff, he would have directed his request there.[41] Hudgins wondered if Cole regarded their problems as "serious" even though he had told ASLL, "minority housing is the [administration's] 'No. 1 domestic problem.'"[42] Apparently, Hudgins's appeal was successful. McGraw attended the convention in Los Angeles in mid-November 1954.[43]

Race relations advisers such as Booker McGraw possessed expert knowledge of the savings and loan industry, in particular, as well as problems around mortgage financing for minorities in general, which made them especially valuable to different sectors of the black real estate industry. What McGraw was to mortgage financing, George Nesbitt was to urban redevelopment issues. Nesbitt, a longtime housing official, had moved around in the different constituent housing agencies, gathering much experience and expertise. Between 1948 and 1952, he served as a racial relations adviser for the Public Housing Administration based in Chicago and later with the national office during the slum clearance controversy.[44] Afterward he became the special assistant for racial relations to the director of the Division of Slum Clearance and Urban Redevelopment (DSCUR) in Washington. The NAREB drew upon Nesbitt's expertise after urban redevelopment became "urban renewal" following the Housing Act of 1954.

Nesbitt was responsible for organizing a panel on urban renewal at NAREB's annual convention in Philadelphia in October 1954. The theme for the conference was "Democracy in Housing." This event illustrates how black housing officials' "interpretation" of federal rules and regulations to NAREB members helped them identify potential business opportunities. Nesbitt sensed that the brokers wanted the panel to figure out "how to make a buck or two." Nesbitt's willingness to frame the discussion in this way was both a recognition and an acceptance of the fact that business was the primary interest of black real estate brokers. Given this orientation, Nesbitt sought black realtists for the panel who had taken advantage of opportunities that emerged from slum clearance and urban redevelopment in various cities. He wanted "four or five persons telling how they got the work; the problems encountered and overcome; and how they made it 'pay.'"[45]

Nesbitt wanted the panel to outline every aspect of slum clearance and redevelopment in order to identify specific opportunities in developing the proposal, acquiring the land, negotiating over condemned properties, dealing with displaced property owners, seeking new rental housing including legally converted structures, managing new housing, and conducting home modernization and repair work. These opportunities represented work for black architects, community planners, engineers, draftsmen, appraisers, real estate brokers, housing managers, and developers. Nesbitt pointed out that since black families were disproportionately displaced by slum clearance, rehousing them represented a special opportunity for "realtists" to act as "consultants" in the process. Since assessing "minority demand for private housing" is particularly difficult, Nesbitt was dismayed that black professionals had not been hired as consultants to wrestle with this "knotty problem."[46] For Nesbitt, it was high time that black realtists got in on the action.[47]

Nesbitt seemed untroubled by the fact he was advising black realtists to take advantage of a situation that had caused great distress to other African Americans, especially those with limited resources for relocating. While he never wavered from the position that slum clearance and urban redevelopment were in the long-term interests of African Americans seeking improved housing conditions and residential integration, he later became critical of Chicago's failure to properly relocate displaced families. His aim was to correct the racial disparities that had occurred in the process, such as the relocation of black families or the exclusion of black entrepreneurs in urban redevelopment. The purpose of the NAREB panel was to address the latter. In doing so, Nesbitt provides early evidence of black elites' independent interest in making sure a progrowth policy was achieved. The role he played for black realtists was a microcosm of the larger facilitative relationship between government and business in the postwar period.[48] Lenerte Roberts said it best when he commented on the role of black federal housing officials at the convention to NAREB members: "These officials interpreted the new administration's housing policy, which in my opinion is very important to all of our fellow Realtist[s], inasmuch as the future success of your business depends on your knowledge of these new laws."[49]

Black Capital and Mortgage Financing

Black interest-group elites and government officials pursued fair mortgage lending by pressuring federal housing agencies to clean up their act and put pressure on the banking industry to attend to a neglected market. Black real estate trade organizations had a different response to the problem of minority housing financing, namely, the creation of black-owned and -operated mortgage lending institutions. Rather than depend on obstructionist FHA officials or reluctant lenders, black real estate trade leaders asked what they could do for themselves. Knowing the answer to their own question, they embraced a self-help approach that defined black real estate activism throughout the postwar period. Black self-help, legitimized by appeals to racial independence, vied with other policy tools like fair lending when black elites confronted the problem of inadequate mortgage capital. Their self-help proposals took one of two forms: the organization of a black-owned national or regional mortgage corporation that would lend to blacks or the creation of more black-owned savings and loans to do the same at the local level. While the savings and loans companies required less start-up capital, they faced the same roadblock that prevented any of the mortgage corporation proposals from coming to fruition, the shortage of capital. Because of this major obstacle, it was clear to its proponents that black self-help, ironically, needed white capital to succeed.

Black Mortgage Corporations

The need to amass capital in black hands was a prominent feature of the 1941 program. The authors, Baker and Occomy, proposed "a mortgage company which would grant long-time loans at standard rates on properties where losses will be at a reasonable minimum." Anyone familiar with property acquisition by blacks knew about the difficulty of getting a mortgage loan under any terms. As the two realtists explained, for black applicants, mortgage companies "increase the interest rate either by raising the fees charged or by making the loans for a shorter period than is allowed on other realty." These companies, they argued, apply "far more rigid and exacting" standards "when it comes to granting long-term loans on property owned by Negroes than on property owned by white persons." The 1941 program authors implied that only through black-controlled mortgage capital would black home buyers secure home financing under fair terms.

Following the lead of the 1941 call, proposals for self-help mortgage financing nationwide and in Chicago surfaced periodically throughout the postwar period. Proponents argued that mortgage corporations could be organized on a national or regional basis. These proposals were initiated not only by black trade professionals but also by black housing officials who prompted the black real estate industry to pool resources to effectuate self-help financing schemes. All the proposals had to address the question of finding and sustaining sources of capital since none of them believed the money could come solely from within the still cash-strapped black community. Although black incomes had tripled since World War II, there had not been enough time to amass the capital sufficient to launch such an enterprise. Nor did any proponents suggest that all black home buyers could be serviced by black-owned mortgage capital.

Nonetheless, white federal administrators closely scrutinized the performance of black financial institutions, and expected them to cover for the lack of white-controlled capital available to blacks seeking loans. Most proposals limited black finance capital to the role of breaking up minority financing "bottlenecks" or priming the pump for large-scale white lenders who were expected to eventually service the black housing market. All the proposals delineated the uneasy and multifaceted relationship between black and white capital. In all their schemes, black self-help represented a kind of ideological hybrid asserting racial independence and institution building with the ultimate objective of residential integration.[50] However, what might have looked like a hybrid in racial debates had the look of petty capitalism when it came to questions of political economy. The problem of inadequate mortgage financing and its prospective solutions illustrate that black self-help in the 1950s was strictly contained by racial democratic policy goals.

One of the early proposals for black mortgage capital was initiated by black officials working in the Truman administration's housing agencies. In a twist in the relationship between black trade professionals and black housing officials, the latter prompted the former to consider ways of organizing black capital to serve the desperate needs of African Americans seeking to acquire property. In 1948, Frank S. Horne, head of the RRS at the time, and Booker McGraw, his deputy, took the lead on this mortgage-financing initiative. They saw that the problem of inadequate mortgage financing affected two parties: the individual black consumer who sought a way to finance the mortgage taken on a house; and the housing developer, white or black, who was interested in building subdivisions open to black residence. Even if a "responsible developer or sponsor" could resolve the equally difficult problem of acquiring a suitable site, their plans were frustrated by the shortage of capital available to them.[51] Commercial banks or mortgage companies refused to finance these developers, fearing lower property valuations in black or mixed residential neighborhoods or worried that whites would not buy housing if the development were not racially and socially homogeneous.

In response, Horne, McGraw, and other colleagues discussed the possibility of black-owned insurance and savings and loans companies "pooling part of their investment funds to underwrite FHA-insured mortgages on developments to accommodate Negroes and other minorities." McGraw approached

Asa Spaulding of the North Carolina Mutual Insurance Company, who was the convention program chairman of the National Negro Insurance Association meeting, June 22–25, 1948, in New Orleans. Spaulding came out of the black business community in Durham, a city E. Franklin Frazier once called the capital of the black bourgeoisie.[52] Horne and McGraw approached the black insurance trade association because it represented the largest source of home loans to African Americans among black financial institutions. McGraw argued to Spaulding that the "advantages of fuller participation of Negro controlled capital, particularly our insurance companies, in financing of housing to accommodate minorities, with or without FHA-insured loans, would be cumulative to the lender, the builder, the homeowner, the renter, as well as the general public."[53]

McGraw and his racial relations colleagues did not see black capital serving all the needs of black homeowners and renters, however. More likely, McGraw explained, the role of "self-help efforts among Negroes" would be to break up "the two major bottlenecks—sites and financing—to alleviating the most acute housing conditions of minorities." Afterward, McGraw expected that financing would become available for developers seeking to accommodate minority home buyers. Despite their different institutional settings, black housing officials' interest in stimulating black capital to organize its own efforts to finance black-occupied housing illustrates the broad acceptance of self-help within the African American housing policy community.[54]

Unlike Baker and Occomy's proposal, black housing officials did not explicitly call for a national mortgage corporation owned and operated by African Americans. Yet, while their proposal did not go that far, the implication was that its form could very well approximate a mortgage corporation with a national scope. Walter "Chief" Aiken made an explicit proposal for a black-owned corporation in early 1950, roughly two years after McGraw's proposal. Aiken, based in Atlanta, was president of the National Home Builders Association at the time and considered the largest black builder in the country.[55] As a builder who had received FHA-approved financing for the subdivisions he built for blacks in suburban Atlanta, Aiken inquired whether the FHA would approve "as a lending institution a mortgage company with $1,000,000 capital, incorporated and chartered for the purpose of purchasing and selling insured mortgages on a nationwide basis." Warren Lockwood, assistant commissioner for FHA Field Operations, conveyed his agency's openness to such a proposal, but cautioned Aiken to have all the "intents and purposes" of the organization spelled out in its charter. If such an institution were approved, Lockwood explained, it would be authorized to originate, purchase, and sell loans nationwide, as long as they were serviced by "qualified lending institutions." He warned that the FHA would need to be assured that the mortgage corporation had "establish[ed] substantial lines of credit" in order to get its approval. Lockwood added that the national mortgage company needed to be directed by "experienced mortgage men."[56] Aiken's inquiry received a detailed and encouraging response from the FHA, but like other proposals for a black-owned national mortgage corporation made during the Truman administration, it never reached fruition.

With each proposal or inquiry, we understand more about what was needed to put this idea into action. The biggest stumbling block was amassing the initial capital to launch such a venture. There needed to be enough capital to finance mortgages at rates that would allow such a corporation to sustain itself. The next time that a proposal for a mortgage corporation appeared was during President Eisenhower's second term, and the coverage area was regional instead of national. This proposal was more developed than the previous ideas and inquiries had been. In addition to providing a more complete picture of what it would take to launch and sustain such an endeavor, it made evident how the black policy elite network would provide the ballast. In 1958, Bolin V. Bland, former president of the Dearborn Real Estate Board in Chicago and then vice president of the NAREB, was part of "a group of local Negro businessmen" who founded the DuSable Mortgage and Investment Company. They created the company to originate and purchase mortgage loans in the Midwest. The company was incorporated with $250,000 as its capital base, a quarter of what Aiken had sought for a national corporation eight years earlier. Bland mentioned that most of the capital would be used for new construction for which there was high demand in the region. He was interested in large-scale production, seeing a division of labor with DuSable Builders constructing new buildings and the mortgage and investment company providing construction loans.

Bland contacted Joseph Ray about the problem of getting the mortgage corporation on sound financial footing. Apparently Bland's company had enough capital to originate first mortgages but needed to sell these loans on the secondary market in order to be able to originate more loans. Bland claimed that having "secondary purchasers" of first mortgages was necessary "in order to be effective in the minority housing field," explaining that since the company was ready "to originate first mortgages not only in Chicago but elsewhere . . . it would greatly assist us if we can get commitments for our first

mortgage paper after we have completed the original first mortgage transaction." He gave an example of a mortgage they were trying to finance. A
black realtist in Columbus, Ohio, had a buyer for a home selling for $18,000.
The buyer had $10,000 toward the asking price and needed financing only
for the remaining $8,000. Bland added that he was considering making the
first mortgage if the realtor could identify "a secondary purchaser for the
mortgage after I make it." He advertised, "This is the type of cooperation
we can give to other real estate brokers through the DuSable Mortgage and
Investment Company." Without a black-owned mortgage company, Bland
explained, black realtists were at a disadvantage because a discriminatory
financial industry did not finance their clients, especially if they were trying
to purchase in an all-white area.[57]

Bland enlisted Ray's help in identifying contacts who knew of "secondary
purchasers," adding that he sought capital from insurance and other financial
companies. Ray suggested Fred B. Morrison, vice president of Metropolitan
Life Insurance Company in New York City, for contacts with mortgage loan
purchasers in the secondary market. Morrison had formerly worked in the
federal housing agencies and had served on the VHMCP national committee.
Now he was "an important factor in the upper echelon of mortgage financing,"
according to Ray, and "in a position" to give Bland "information and even
suggest contacts necessary to make the Du Sable a sound and useful enterprise."[58] To Morrison, in turn, Ray vouched for Bland, whom he described as
"a staunch supporter of our housing program" and as instrumental in encouraging other blacks to add "self-help" to the government's efforts to serve
families neglected by mortgage companies. Ray concluded by telling Morrison that he and his colleagues would "be pleased and indebted to you for
any assistance given this Organization in this early stage of its development."[59]

Feeling a sense of urgency, Bland contacted Morrison right away. He
introduced himself as someone who had been buying and selling property
in the minority housing market for twenty years and claimed some success
in securing mortgage financing for his clients. Although home financing
was available from "quite a few liberal financing institutions" in the city, he
nonetheless found it inadequate. Bland revealed that only 20 percent of the
$250,000 capital was "subscribed and paid for up to the present time." In
addition, "when our corporation reaches $100,000 in assets, we expect to
become an approved F.H.A. mortgagee." Bland explained that until that time
they needed a secondary market for their mortgages of either "new construction" or buildings less than twenty years old. He implied, following George

Nesbitt, that the success of DuSable was even more necessary because of a demand for financing the rehousing needs of nearly two hundred thousand people, mostly black, displaced by "Chicago's tremendous urban renewal program."[60] To emphasize the urgency of their project, Bland mentioned that "plans for new construction for minority groups" in other communities "are awaiting the arrangement of proper financing." Bland assured Morrison that more capital would allow them to serve "displaced" and new homeowners.[61]

It is not clear how Morrison responded to Bland's appeal. What is clear is that Bland needed Ray's help to find larger sources of capital for his enterprise, highlighting the utility of the political network they shared. Bland's appeal also revealed the limited capital that black entrepreneurs could get their hands on even during a period of rising incomes for African Americans. Despite this economic progress, rising wages and salaries did not translate into the capital needed to fund the construction of housing for blacks.

Black Savings and Loan Associations

Proposals for mortgage corporations were not the only way that African Americans sought to burst through the "bottleneck" that blocked their access to mortgage capital. There were also concomitant efforts to create more black-owned savings and loan associations. Black civic and business elites advocated for more attention to black-owned savings and loans to remedy the problem of minority housing finance. One of the most prominent spokesmen for this was Robert Taylor. As secretary of Illinois Federal Savings and Loan Association, he wrote about the business in the industry's organ, *Savings and Loans News*, in 1949, announcing that Illinois Federal had "loaned millions of dollars predominantly to Negro home owners" since 1934, the year it was founded. During that time, he wrote, it did not have "to take over a single piece of property through foreclosure." He further reported that Illinois Federal "paid consecutive semi-annual dividends at the rate of 3% for 13 years and has developed and maintained satisfactory reserves."[62]

Based on this experience of black-owned savings and loans, at least two efforts were made to expand their number. In both cases, a black businessperson sought information and advice from black housing officials regarding how to set up a black-owned savings and loan company. The first was a proposal by Loring B. Moore, a key black litigator against restrictive covenants, who sought to start up another black-owned savings and loan association in Chicago. The other was "Chief" Aiken, who sought information and advice about the development of black-owned federal savings and loan associations in selected cities that might be eligible for the government's home financing aids. Moore got into contact with George Nesbitt, who in turn sought advice from Booker McGraw. McGraw saw the need for more than one black-owned savings and loan in Chicago, and he outlined for Moore and Aiken all the advantages of a federal savings and loan association, including a federal charter, which brought federal supervision and federal insurance for deposited funds. In addition, its federal status not only would make the savings and loan eligible to borrow additional funds from the regional Home Loan Board but also would qualify it for becoming an approved FHA mortgagee, which made receiving "FHA mortgage insurance aids" possible.[63] Since Aiken sought to start up black savings and loans in numerous cities, McGraw sent him information about the location and jurisdiction of "FHA Zone Racial Relations Advisers," thinking they could assist the efforts of local groups to organize federal savings and loan associations. He advised Aiken to take the same steps in organizing a federal savings and loan in different locations that he had relayed to Loring Moore for Chicago.[64]

Black Financial Institutions' Role and Performance

All the proposals to create or sustain black-owned mortgage corporations and federal savings and loans emerged in a climate where the general housing policy community paid increasing attention to racial disparities in private housing provision. The attention by housing reformers, government officials, and real estate businesses to serving the African American housing market through increased construction and financing crested in the mid-1950s. This attention also brought unprecedented interest in the performance of black real estate brokers, builders, savings and loan officers, and insurance executives in covering the racial gap. Suddenly, black and white housing officials wanted to know how well the black real estate industry served black citizens. During this period, a government report concentrated on the contribution of the black real estate industry to serving the black housing market, and on the relationship between black and white real estate capital. It put an emphasis on the American South, where the black real estate industry had more opportunities to build, lend, and sell to black home buyers, albeit in segregated subdivisions. Throughout the report, the FHA came in for praise for its assistance to black builders and lenders. The report credited these builders and lenders with achieving historical racial progress by developing assets worth millions of dollars, employing thousands, and most importantly, making decent housing affordable.[65]

The government report credited the black real estate industry not only for discovering the black housing market but also for learning how to serve it in a discriminatory financial environment. The report did not fault black financial institutions for inadequate minority financing given that they had done all they could to fix "one of the most nettlesome embarrassments in the housing situation facing minorities." It explained that while black capital had been invaluable, no one could reasonably expect it to serve this market all on its own since "the housing problem and market among Negroes are much larger than can be adequately met by Negro businessmen alone." Instead, in language similar to that of McGraw (its likely author), the report said that the role of black financial institutions was to "establish the validity of loans to non-white families and to loosen up other lending resources by initiating action in strategic locations." Once black real estate capital showed that the black housing market was "sound . . . and profitable," the report predicted that "more and more lenders and builders should be attracted to it." The government report concluded that while the entire private housing industry had to serve the black housing market, the most we could expect from black builders and lenders was to "prime the pump" for the larger industry to finally serve this neglected market.[66]

The report gave the perhaps misleading impression that the promise outlined in the 1941 program had been met by 1953. While black real estate entrepreneurs were probably relieved that they were not expected to solve the whole mortgage-financing problem for minorities, they were probably less happy with a role that limited them to priming the pump or loosening up bottlenecks for larger white capital to swoop in and scoop up the profits in what these black entrepreneurs considered their own backyard. Black government officials, not their own trade representatives, assigned this catalytic role to them. This report and earlier government analyses were to define the role of black capital as a stalking horse for large white capital in the black housing market.

Black Self-Help and Fair Mortgage Lending

Not everyone agreed that the black real estate industry was doing enough to serve black housing markets. In fact, criticism came from a source to which black real estate entrepreneurs had to pay attention: Albert Cole, head of the HHFA. Cole encouraged black self-help in mortgage financing for two reasons. It gave him some lead time to get white housing industry leaders on board to serve black citizens, and it lessened the pressure on the federal government to provide a direct solution to the minority housing finance problem. Cole selected Joseph Ray to replace Frank Horne as the HHFA's Racial Relations Service (RSS) director in 1953. Horne advocated more aggressive public action, whereas Ray embraced a self-help philosophy, which made Ray an ideal choice for assistant to the administrator and head of the RRS.[67]

Cole held a "Short Sleeve" conference on minority housing in Washington on May 31, 1955, inviting representatives from sixteen black lending agencies from across the country including George S. Harris from Metropolitan Mutual Assurance Company and Earl B. Dickerson and Truman K. Gibson Sr. of Supreme Liberty Life Company from Chicago. Cole's purpose in calling the meeting was to persuade black lenders to make more FHA-approved loans available to minority borrowers. In a HHFA news release reporting on the meeting, Cole congratulated "minority owned lending agencies" for their support, but charged that "most of them are not assuming their responsibility toward minority borrowers." Moreover, Cole pointed out that comparable white and black firms did not offer the same loan terms and conditions to blacks that they offered to whites. Cole warned the black financiers that they could not "afford to have a finger pointed at them as exploiters of prospective Negro home buyers."[68] He cited data to support his point that black lenders were not doing enough, stating of sixteen black-owned insurance companies, only six had invested between 21.6 percent and 38.6 percent of their mortgage investments in FHA-subsidized properties. Another six invested less, from 2.2 percent to 14.3 percent. Based on this data, Cole determined that black firms could accomplish more "in this field," although he did acknowledge that white firms needed to do more, noting that he had been pushing them in that direction. Cole concluded that he hoped black and white companies "would invest in liberal-term government insured or guaranteed mortgage loans to Negro borrowers" so that they could "purchase homes under equal financial conditions." Cole's implication was clear. Black leaders could not fault white lenders or the government for not doing more when they were not doing their fair share and, on top of that, were exploiting their own people.[69]

Cole's criticisms did not go unanswered. At the conference, and in subsequent correspondence provoked by HHFA press releases, proud and accomplished African American lenders responded to what they felt were

Cole's unfair criticisms. At the conference, black lenders based their defense on the small size of their firms and their limited capital base. When that was taken into account, they claimed, their performance was not any worse than that of similarly sized white firms. Other explanations rested on the "peculiar" characteristics of the black clients themselves. According to one black lender, blacks' high mortality rate justified their higher premiums. Others contended that "the Negro public ha[d] not been conditioned to FHA insured loans," which were available at more liberal financing terms. Because they were small firms, they argued, they could not afford to offer the same rates as large insurance companies or get "into the FHA mortgage business on a large scale." Some black lenders argued they needed to charge higher rates in order to accumulate enough capital to survive. Others declared it was "simply good business."[70]

Following a HHFA press release on the controversy, C. L. Townes Jr., president of the NNIA, who did not attend the conference, objected to Cole's "allegation" that black lending firms were "not assuming their responsibility toward minority borrowers." Townes countered with data he felt demonstrated significant lending to black borrowers by NNIA members. He reported that of the total assets of forty-three reporting companies, which amounted to roughly $180 million, 25.8 percent was "invested in mortgage loans on real estate of which much of it was FHA loans." He contended that the share of FHA-subsidized loans in their investment portfolio was only 3.5 percent below the national average of all U.S. financial institutions. Though special challenges faced black-owned lending agencies, Townes argued that their performance was commendable given "that the total insurance minority people carry in their own companies represents only a pittance of the vast amount they carry in white companies." He assured Cole that if black firms could win over from white firms even half the insurance policies that blacks carried, they would have no problem reaching, and possibly exceeding, the national average of 29.7 percent of the investment portfolio devoted to mortgage lending. In repeating this characteristic lament of black businesses, Townes went a step further than his colleagues in blaming black citizens for black firms' limited capital reserves. He then denied Cole's accusation that "our lending institutions" exploit black clients by requiring "excessive interest rates and other charges," assuring Cole that NNIA's members' charged the same interest rates and fees as "comparable white lending agencies in the same communities." According to Townes, black insurance companies did not condone these practices, making sure their interest rates are within the "legal limitations of their respective states." Townes said he found no "evidences of exploitation" by his member organizations and called upon Cole to publicly withdraw his charges.[71]

Before and after Cole's remarks, the HHFA produced two reports on the performance of black financial institutions in issuing FHA-approved mortgage loans. These reports shed some light on his allegations.[72] The first report examined FHA-insured mortgage investments by black-owned and black-operated life insurance companies, banking institutions, and savings and loan associations. The report showed that those life insurance companies that actively held FHA-approved mortgages were significantly better capitalized at $123 million than non-FHA-approved and active companies at $11 million. This report supported black lenders' contention that the more capital they accrued, the better able they were to extend FHA-approved mortgages and consequently to ensure better interest rates for their customers, but that the cost of this was a lower profit returned on their investments unless they could significantly increase volume.[73]

The second report was compiled in October 1955, four months after the White House conference. It measured the growth of black institutions' investment in FHA-approved mortgages from 1951 to 1954 compared to those of similarly sized white lending institutions. It determined that the black-owned firms' growth during this period was "impressive," showing that they had "more than easily doubled their FHA-insured mortgage portfolio." Black-owned firms saw a two-and-one-third increase in their FHA-insured mortgage holdings, nearly equal to those of all comparable white lending institutions. Between 1951 and 1954, black insurance companies saw their FHA-approved mortgage investments increase by over one-third, allowing them to catch up and surpass "by a small margin" the combined FHA-mortgage portfolios of comparable white life insurance companies. The report concluded that black life insurance companies increased the amount of FHA-insured mortgages to their overall portfolio from 1951 to 1954, thus supporting Townes's contention and refuting Cole's allegations.[74]

None of the black lenders who responded to Cole's criticism denied that they charged their black clients higher interest rates. Rather, the focus of their defense was that they had no choice in the matter if they wanted to "survive" in a competitive real estate market. They argued that similarly sized white institutions behaved in the same manner. Their argument is reasonable if we assume that market-determined interest rates were fair, and if not, that the survival of their businesses was more important than avoiding the exploitation of black home buyers. Of course, they would not be the first racial or ethnic business elite to have accumulated capital on the backs of their own racial or ethnic group members. While the 1941 call for a national real estate organization and program for blacks promised that a black-owned mortgage company could be held to a higher standard,[75] the Baker-Occomy proposal noted that "the existing type of mortgage company has only profit in view; a mortgage company owned and operated by Negro realtors would have a dual purpose—the making of a profit and the extension of colored ownership and possession of real property." The program's "dual purpose" implied that black property owners' investments and well-being were of equal concern to a black-owned mortgage corporation. "Colored citizens all over the country are badly in need of sound leadership to lift them out of the morass of burdensome, pyramidal mortgage financing, inadequate municipal services, and inflated sales prices and rents." Baker and Occomy asserted that African Americans "are entitled to the same opportunities in purchasing homes, and financing them, as persons of other racial groups."[76]

Given the standards outlined in the 1941 program, the practices of black financial institutions appeared to be disappointing. Or were they? Even the 1941 program distinguished between high interest rates that were legitimate if a borrower had a poor credit record or lacked adequate security, and those that were levied solely because of an applicant's racial identity. Both the authors of the early program and black lenders who defended their practices to Cole affirmed the need for differential terms based on market criteria. While black-owned firms did not explicitly treat black clients differently due to their race, indirectly they did. The secondary effects that emanate from racial inequality such as high mortality rates or lower valuations of inner-city property put black clients at a disadvantage even when they are subject to apparently race-neutral market standards.

In the end, black lenders, too, victimized black mortgage loan applicants, especially the poorer ones. Yet from their racialist point of view, as long as they charged the same rates as similar-sized white firms and stayed within the "legal requirements," they were not exploiting black clients or treating them unfairly. Black lenders must have felt that these secondary effects and associated market requirements were out of their control. They were presented with a dilemma: apply dual market criteria to black clients in the same way white firms did or reduce their profits and possibly go out of business. Were these businesspeople in effect saying to other blacks: We will only need to exploit you until we earn enough capital to treat the next generation more fairly? Black firms not only felt they were justified in gaining profits in this manner, but with their "dual purpose" ethos, they also believed they were providing a "community service" to potential black home buyers and advancing the race by facilitating collective property acquisition. Black real estate capital must have felt that the proposed benefits that accrued to black citizens represented the invisible hand behind the veil.[77]

Not all black responses to Cole's criticism were negative. He received a supportive letter from a black lender who attended the minority lending conference. A. L. Robinson, secretary of the Quincy Savings and Loan Company in Cleveland and a member of the ASLL's executive committee, wrote that he agreed with Cole that black firms should do more, highlighting some of the internal tension that black financiers felt about the self-help approach. Robinson told Cole that he had disagreed with many of the participants at the meeting, but had chosen not to voice his opinions since they were "out of tune with the thinking of many of those in attendance."

In his letter, Robinson quoted from an earlier speech he had made that reflected his black self-help philosophy. He intimated that the discriminatory practices of white financial institutions were similar to "challenges" that other groups who had built "this country of ours" had accepted. These other groups "did not shirk responsibilities or throw their burdens on others," as he implied blacks did. To Robinson, protesting discrimination rather than accepting it as one of the inevitable hardships along the way toward development was shirking responsibility and blaming someone else. Suggesting that black protesters sought racial paternalism, he wrote, "No race can expect to advance when its problems are placed in the hands of another race to be solved." To seek government intervention was the same to him as asking white people to solve black people's problems. In Robinson's worldview, black people's character would be irreparably harmed if they looked toward government for a solution to housing finance problems. All the problems blacks faced, he continued, could "be solved when we face the realities of life" and adopt the approach of other groups to these same problems. Robinson added passionately, "We must develop within ourselves a will to achieve, a will to free ourselves from economic and social serfdom, or no amount of legislation, presidential executive orders or supreme court decisions can possibly make us first-class citizens. Our freedom must spring from within our own souls."[78]

In classic bootstrap rhetoric, Robinson minimized the impact of discrimination, likening it to other "challenges," and rejected any political solution to racial subordination. In his opinion, blacks who sought government action

lacked the values of self-reliance necessary to achieve "freedom." He concluded unself-consciously by asking for capital investment by whites to fuel
black self-help. Robinson asked Cole, without any hint of irony, to use his
influence to assist in achieving this goal: "The only recommendation that I
would like to make is this . . . that if you can use your good offices to encourage some of the large (white) life insurance companies doing business with
minority groups to invest some of their monies in savings accounts and cer-
tificates of deposit with savings and loan associations and banks owned and
operated by minority groups, I believe that will be of some assistance in solving the problem in the matter of housing which this nation faces."[79]

Robinson was asking Cole, in a sense, to "help us help ourselves." While
it was ineffectual, and perhaps inappropriate, for government to initiate
antidiscriminatory public policy, according to Robinson's logic, it *was* appropriate for government to "encourage" white capital to invest in black financial
institutions like Robinson's savings and loan company. White capital did
not have to lend to minority borrowers directly, according to Robinson; all
they needed to do to acquit their responsibility was to invest some of their
abundant capital in black financial institutions, which would then lend to,
and profit from, black borrowers. So dependence on white government was
inconsistent with escaping "economic and social serfdom," in this perspective, but receiving funds from white capital would facilitate liberation. This
position was increasingly articulated by the black real estate industry in the
fifteen years after World War II. Although Townes and Robinson had different responses to Cole's criticism and its implications regarding government
action, they agreed on the need for more capital for black firms from either
an increase in black clients or more investment by large white firms.[80]

Black Self-Help and White Voluntarism

Albert Cole's criticism of black lending institutions coupled with his efforts
to persuade white capital to help serve blacks' housing needs put a premium
on private as opposed to public action when it came to the problem of inadequate minority housing finance. He and other Eisenhower administration
officials resisted any direct government intervention into the marketplace to
reduce the "bottlenecks" on minority home financing. The signature housing
program for the Eisenhower administration was the Voluntary Home Mortgage Credit Program (VHMCP), which consisted of committees of private
lenders and government officials who recruited mortgage lenders willing to

lend to minorities or residents of underserved areas. Government's role was limited to recruiting, persuading, and coordinating reluctant lenders; there were no disincentives or penalties for nonparticipation. Under Eisenhower's housing policies, black self-help and white voluntarism were different sides of the same privatist coin.

Black self-help, usually associated with the accommodation of segregation, was not a dominant orientation among black elites, including even real estate entrepreneurs in the postwar period. The position was a historical reflex for black businesspeople who presumed that support for their black business would automatically advance the race. In its postwar form, it did not threaten either the importance of government action or integration. It did, however, dictate what *role* government action should take. Pure self-help, like a "free market," was a fiction. Both black and white capital relied on government action, but in different ways. The significance of black self-help proposals was that they registered how black business leaders and government officials envisioned the role of government as facilitating black capital accumulation either by striking down racial barriers in the marketplace or, in the last instance, by making government money available to black firms. In these self-help proposals, they saw no contradiction in accepting aid from either the federal government or from white-owned corporations.

The Voluntary Home Mortgage Credit Program

It is difficult to determine how successful the VHMCP was in serving African American borrowers, but clearly it was in the interest of the Cole-run HHFA to emphasize its successes. Some black policy elites and trade leaders, however, were skeptical. Overall, the black government officials Joseph Ray and Booker McGraw defended the program and attempted to encourage more black participation when the early returns did not look good. A HHFA release in 1955 on the first black family to get a mortgage through the VHMCP was a model of how its architects thought it should work. The husband directed "a vocational and academic school for veterans," the wife taught at a high school in Washington, D.C., and the couple had a ten-year-old son. With the help of a realtor, they found a house and drew up a contract for purchase. The real estate agent mentioned that all he needed was financing. The home buyer, a World War II veteran, sought a VA loan. After being turned down at the bank where he had a savings account, he applied for a loan from another bank, only to be turned down again. He reported that in neither case had they "raised a question about the size of the loan . . . or about [his] credit." When he read about the VHMCP program, he contacted the region IV office since he met the program's requirement of having been rejected by two lending agencies. After putting in his application, he contacted several other lending agencies, only to be turned down in every case. Finally, the VHMCP office "found a large insurance company willing to make . . . a VA-guaranteed loan of $17,950, with a mortgage term of 25 years." The home buyer claimed he would not have found a mortgage loan without the program.[81]

However, it was not long before some federal housing officials became concerned about the lack of black applicants for VHMCP assistance. After the statistical reports came out in early July 1955, Ray termed the results "disappointing" and labeled as "regrettable" the lack of interest demonstrated by the program's targeted group. To remedy the situation, Ray offered the services of the race relations staff, especially Booker McGraw, to Arthur Viner, executive secretary of the national VHMCP program. According to Ray, McGraw's job was twofold: to keep "the minority members of the regional committees enthused and encouraged" and to dispense information about the program's benefits to "minority groups through . . . public relations and other means." McGraw's overall role was to examine "VHMCP operations" and "spearhead effective steps to increase the flow of eligible applications to VHMCP in behalf of minorities." Eventually, McGraw confirmed that there were a "very small number of applications" from minorities. McGraw's complaint to Ray that he had a difficult time getting participation from the minority members of the VHMCP committees mirrored the lack of enthusiasm for the program from "the Negro public."[82]

Despite the program's disappointing or, at best, uneven results, HHFA trumpeted its progress. An October 1955 HHFA press release announced that VHMCP regional committees were getting more applications from minorities and developers providing housing open to minorities. The press release also attempted to explain the heretofore poor track record, attributing the low rate of black participation, like McGraw, to a lack of awareness of the program by minority borrowers and "many brokers in the Minority field." It reported that the VHMCP had been particularly helpful to local housing and redevelopment agencies trying to place black families who had been displaced by urban renewal. Because the VHMCP facilitated access to "mortgage financing at FHA and VA interest rates and amortization periods," the program reportedly helped minority families find housing at prices "within the financial means of the families displaced."[83]

Not all black policy elites criticized the VHMCP. In late 1955, at the NAREB's "Institute on Minority Housing" in South Bend, Indiana, both the FHA's George Snowden, who was a featured speaker, and George Harris, the NAREB president, spoke about the virtues of the VHMCP. Snowden credited its regional committees with the fact that "a large amount of good new housing has been placed on the market in the last two years for purchase by Negroes and other minorities. This housing is priced from $6,500 to $20,000 or more." He also credited the regional committees for the fact that blacks were able to buy good housing on affordable terms within white communities. Harris also endorsed the primary role of "free enterprise" in obtaining financing for minority group housing. The NAREB president added that the VHMCP's efforts had benefited racial minorities "who previously had been unable to get adequate financing." He emphasized that "trade organizations in the housing industry should do the job themselves, not depend on the government." Snowden concurred that "the real problem lies in action by private enterprise, not the government, to provide such facilities through an agency like the Voluntary Home Mortgage Credit Committee." Harris concluded the white housing industry needed to do a better job of "voluntarily" serving the black housing market.[84]

The Detroit Case

In 1956, two years into the program, disturbing complaints about the VHMCP began to emerge from the Detroit area. In one instance, a large builder who was constructing a 180-unit development that was open to blacks received only two responses to his application for financing from the VHMCP, and found the proposed terms unsatisfactory. In another instance, a group of black brokers had a "highly unfavorable" general reaction to the VHMCP program, according to the regional race relations adviser, DeHart Hubbard.[85] The complaints of Detroit-area black brokers reached Albert Cole via letters from Michigan senators Pat McNamara and Charles Potter. The senators' inquiries moved Cole to send Ray to investigate. As part of his investigation, Ray convened "an impartial jury of five Negro brokers" on the effectiveness of the program in Detroit. The charges were that of the eighty-six applications submitted since October 1955, only six had been successfully processed, amounting to only $171,000 in loan disbursements. Apparently, white real estate companies sold more than that amount to blacks in the form of land contracts, and averaged $37 million each month on mortgage loans to "non-Negro buyers." Of the eighty-six applications, forty-eight had come from one broker, John S. Humphrey, an ex-labor organizer turned real estate salesman. Ray determined that "Humphrey's grounds for complaint seem more or less personal" since only a few of his clients received loan commitments. On May 29, after weighing the facts, the jury "upheld the charges and found them to be justified." While Ray agreed with the jury, the main issue he reported to Cole was that the complaints were personal and thus had "no organizational" backing from the NAREB affiliate.[86]

Ray's and Cole's defense of the VHMCP in this case underscored the limitations of a government program that relied solely on the private sector to remedy a housing problem. Cole defended the program, citing Humphrey's past and continuing use of it, despite his complaints, as evidence of its relevance. He also cited the participation of private lending agencies in Detroit, including five major insurance companies. Cole argued that "VHMCP effectiveness in Detroit is easily equal, or better than, the national average." Yet the defense of its deficiencies centered on the fact that VHMCP was a reflection of the general mortgage market. Ray thought Humphrey and other black realtists were "confused" in thinking the VHMCP program could do more than the general market allowed, and he observed that "the over-all mortgage market is rather tight in and around Detroit at present." In his response to Michigan's senators who prompted the investigation Cole agreed that "Since the VHMCP relies entirely on private lending institutions, it cannot help but reflect the general condition of the mortgage market."[87] Cole assured the senators that the program did bring the best available terms to the program applicants, attributing the lack of loan commitment to the fact that "mortgage lending is intrinsically a time consuming business," which was not the VHMCP's fault.

In response to a request for direct government lending, Cole concluded that given significant lender participation and the success of the program to date, he did not see "any present need for the Government to intervene with direct loans through the Federal National Mortgage Association." He added that depending on private lenders' resources through the VHMCP was "the only realistic solution to the problem." He was reluctant to try "an alternative which would prove unworkable."[88] Cole's reluctance to directly intervene in the mortgage market reflected, in part, the white real estate industry's complaints about government-subsidized housing programs, which surfaced during the renewal of VHMCP.

Finally, the HHFA had some data to back up its assertions that the VHMCP was a success at extending home financing to black citizens. In February 1957, Cole reported on the results of twenty-one months of VHMCP activity. To date, he said, "VHMCP has placed with private lenders nearly 26,000 home loans underwritten by FHA and VA for a total of $230 million." According to Cole, more than 4,000 loans had been made to minority applicants, amounting to $38,585,000 from March 1955 to the end of 1956. Such figures, Cole remarked, demonstrated private lenders' ability to meet the demand without government participation in mortgage lending.[89]

However, Cole's statistics were misleading. A closer analysis suggests that the bulk of loans were going to whites from underserved areas rather than to minority applicants.[90] George Harris chimed in that the NAREB had done "a rather extensive study" of VHMCP activities and had arrived at a different conclusion from Cole. While his organization did not think the VHMCP had been "a complete failure so far as service to minority home seekers" was concerned, he declared that there was reason to believe that a "satisfactory program" was possible if "links" between minority applicants and willing lenders could be strengthened. Harris intimated that VHMCP committees lacked the "grass roots information regarding minority home seekers" that black realtists could provide.[91]

Ray's support for the program was not dampened by the NAREB's misgivings. He claimed that the program had "made notable strides towards eliminating one of the greatest obstacles to adequate housing for Negroes and members of other minority groups." Apparently, minority borrowers represented 20 percent of all borrowers in the VHMCP and secured 17.6 percent of the money spent. At this time, he said, "over 6,000 individual members of minority groups had obtained mortgage financing amounting to nearly $53 million." The program helped a total of 31,000 families to secure almost $300 million in FHA-insured and VA-guaranteed loans. Ray concluded that the VHMCP mainly served "families of modest means who buy low-priced homes," adding, "Persons having incomes of between $3,000 and $6,000 have obtained 63% of the home mortgage loans made through VHMCP." A subsequent July 1958 news release pointed out that "three out of every five minority members who sought assistance in obtaining a housing loan through the VHMCP were successful. The report explained that applicants were turned down only when they had "insufficient income or unacceptable property."[92]

The FHA and the VA served the black housing market better in the second half of the 1950s. Nationally, racial minorities acquired 300,000 FHA-insured housing units between 1945 and 1960.[93] It is difficult to determine what proportion of these units was acquired through the VHMCP, not to mention how well these new units met black housing demand. It was not in the political interests of the HHFA to place the outcomes of the VHMCP in the context of national black housing demand. The HHFA even admitted that, despite renewed efforts led by race relations staff members, it had not fully tapped into the potential black home-buying market. Intermittent criticism from black real estate professionals about the program also pointed to its overall ineffectiveness.

The Price of Black Self-Help

In 1957, three years after George Snowden's inaugural address, the NAREB held a series of unprecedented meetings with the Mortgage Bankers Association (MBA). The purpose of these meetings was to establish a cooperative working relationship between representatives of black and white real estate trade organizations in the area of minority financing. The trade organizations decided to exchange membership lists in order to facilitate "a liaison arrangement" between the two organizations' members "in various regions throughout the country." Each organization agreed to share its unique services with the other and "cooperate closely . . . for future activities." Chicagoan Bolin Bland took the lead in initiating these meetings, and William A. Clark of Philadelphia was his main contact from the MBA. Clark, a "loan correspondent" for Metropolitan Insurance Company, was a former president of the MBA and current member of the national VHMCP committee.

In the ensuing discussion, differences of opinions emerged between the NAREB, which favored open occupancy, and the MBA, which still believed loans in "all Negro" neighborhoods were more "stable" than "loans in mixed neighborhoods or changing neighborhoods." In the past five years, however, there had been progress in challenging the "gentlemen's agreement" that lenders would not lend to blacks attempting to integrate white neighborhoods. In general, the NAREB offered their practical knowledge to the MBA so that their "experiments in financing minority housing succeed."[94]

There appeared to be easier agreement when it came to urban renewal. The MBA liked the fact that "older sections of larger cities" could be redeveloped and that MBA members would finance the new housing. Clark suggested that the NAREB make, and submit to the MBA, a survey study of new housing opportunities in urban renewal areas. Another bone of contention, however, was mortgage lenders' opinion that African Americans did not get their share of new construction because of their aversion to living in suburbs, where the majority of new housing was located. The two observations seemed to suggest that the MBA was willing to lend to blacks in the redeveloped inner city but not in the suburbs, given their self-serving rationalization that blacks did not want to live there.[95]

Predictably, the VHMCP was one of the topics of discussion between the two groups. The MBA had very specific criticisms of the program and wanted to see some changes before it would support its renewal. The mortgage bankers indicated that their support for the program would not continue unless the terms of direct and indirect government loans programs did "not put the private investor at a competitive disadvantage." In other words, "Private enterprise cannot compete with a government subsidized program." The MBA explained that in order to attract mortgage investment into underdeveloped areas, "the return from mortgage investment must be competitive with similar forms of investment," thus "the return must be responsive to changing market conditions."

Between 1957 and 1958, the United States went through its worst recession since 1938.[96] MBA representatives were clear about what they wanted from the NAREB in exchange for their "cooperation": they wanted the NAREB to assign two or three members to support their "resolution" in testimony before the subcommittee of the House Banking and Currency Committee. The ensuing discussion between the two trade organizations brought to the fore the mortgage lenders' desire for "interest rates [to] be more flexible; and that these rates conform with the rise and fall of supply and demand in the mortgage market; and that legislation vest in the Housing and Home Finance Agency and Veterans Administration the power to fix interest rates in conformity with the current market."[97] So in the tight mortgage credit market of the day, the MBA wanted government agencies to raise their subsidized interest rates so that private lenders' conventional rates would remain competitive.

In exchange for their support of the MBA's advocacy of legislative changes on VHMCP, the NAREB's only "demands" were that the MBA help in getting a NAREB representative on the VHMCP national committee as a "statutory requirement" and that it aid in setting up "liaison meetings" between the USSLL and the ASLL. While the NAREB was looking for recognition and legitimacy, the more powerful MBA wanted legislative changes in the VHMCP that would restore profitability during a period of tight mortgage credit. They needed a black imprimatur for their policy changes because VHMCP was perceived as a "minority housing program."

It would appear that the NAREB's endorsement of these changes went against the interests of its members in securing lower interest rates on behalf of their clients. That this was a case of a more powerful white institution compelling a weaker black organization to act against its material interests in favor of symbolic gains is obvious at first glance. But was raising government-subsidized interest rates not actually in the black real estate industry's interest? This may be where the industry's welfare and that of its clients' diverged, and where the 1941 program's two purposes, profits and fairness, were really at odds with each other. Earlier black lenders had complained that they could not devote too much of their business to FHA-approved mortgages because as small firms they needed a higher return on their investment to build their small capital base, unless they could increase their volume. While the FHA-approved mortgage holdings of black financial institutions had increased, their investments in conventional mortgage holdings had grown even faster. So while the MBA's changes in the VHMCP were likely to hurt moderate-income black home buyers, black lending institutions, like other institutions specializing in housing finance, stood to benefit from them.[98]

The NAREB followed through on its part of the bargain with the MBA. George Harris sent a telegram to the Subcommittee on Housing of the Committee on Banking and Currency in both the Senate and the House of Representatives. The "night letter" to Congress recommended the continuation of VHMCP "with the following provisions in order to operate at a maximum effectiveness": "(1) The government lending program both direct and indirect must be on a competitive basis with the mortgage market as a whole. The returns from mortgage investments in government insured loans must be competitive with similar forms of investment and returns must be responsive to changing market conditions. (2) A member of the National Association of Real Estate Brokers should be appointed to the National Committee and a member on each regional sub-committee."

Despite the fact that black insurance executive Asa Spaulding was named to the national committee, Harris specifically wanted a NAREB member as a trade representative on that committee (his original request to Cole) as a statutory requirement.[99] NAREB was willing to sacrifice the affordability of government-insured loans, which working-class blacks desperately needed, for government recognition and a more substantial capital base.

The Black Real Estate Industry and the Role of Government

Antidiscrimination and Self-Help

The black real estate industry had a complex relationship with the federal government. It has been assumed that African Americans invariably coveted government intervention to protect their rights and distribute social benefits more equally. On the other hand, it has also been assumed that large capital was against any government intervention. A deeper look at the U.S. postwar political economy presents a more contextualized view of capital's stance toward government action. Private capital wanted government intervention, but only on its own terms. Since the Great Depression, big business has been interested in government action that socializes its costs, while disdaining any actions that attempt to take investment decisions and profits out of private hands. Black real estate firms, as black and small capital, sought to influence government policy to offset the disadvantages that resulted from racial exclusion and discrimination, as well as boost their modest capital reserves.

Black real estate trade leaders expressed a continuum of racial ideologies from a race-conscious self-help stance to a color-blind open-occupancy position that resulted in a variety of positions on government action. They wanted more government regulation of the private housing industry to police discriminatory behavior that disadvantaged black lenders and builders. They favored implementation of antidiscrimination policies to ensure "democracy in housing." They also wanted government to encourage, persuade, or cajole large white capital to invest in black firms, who would use that investment to service the black housing market. What these "positions" had in common was the joining of race and private enterprise. They were intended to use the state to counteract the intertwined racial and capital disadvantages of the competitive black real estate industry. Regardless of the position taken on government action, business interests always came first.

An instance of a black trade organization seeking more government regulation is illustrated by the opposition of the American Savings and Loan League to the privatization of the Federal National Mortgage Bank (FNMB, aka "Fannie Mae") in January 1954. ASLL president William Hudgins argued that replacing the FNMB "with a new federally chartered but privately operated central mortgage bank was a threat to 'Negro or interracial home building.'" President Eisenhower's Advisory Commission on Housing recommended, according to Hudgins, "that Congress enact legislation enabling the federal government to charter a new mortgage marketing corporation, invest up to $180,000,000 to get it started, but to hand over direction of the new corporation to private interests."

The ASLL opposed this recommendation because of the private housing industry's long track record of refusing to finance black or interracial housing, and because the FNMB had "at least given evidence that it will accept mortgage[s] on this class of construction." The ASLL executive committee feared that without "specific guarantees and safeguards," the new federally financed but privately run mortgage bank would mirror the discriminatory behavior characteristic of the housing industry. Hudgins quoted the testimony of Elmer Henderson, black executive director of the American Council on Human Rights, before the Senate Banking and Currency Committee, in which he argued that Fannie Mae's existence offered "the only ray of hope" for "new large-scale housing for minorities" in a "dismal . . . climate" of private mortgage lending discrimination. At a time when the private housing industry's racism was steadfast, it was in ASLL's *business* interest to endorse more government regulation.[100]

The theme of NAREB's annual convention held in Philadelphia in 1954, "democracy in housing," provides another instance of how greater governmental regulation was in their interest. The "Resolution on Housing and Home Finance" that was passed at the convention on October 14 resembled similar resolutions by national civil rights organizations asserting that all federal housing aid should be conditional on the nondiscriminatory status of federally subsidized housing. The NAREB also wanted no consideration of race "in underwriting, property valuation, and credit rating determinations and results." In his presidential message, George S. Harris explained that open occupancy would be the means to achieve a color-blind "democracy in housing." He intimated that black realtists upheld their profession by "practicing the democratic principles of our country" and ensuring that race did not bar citizens from being "properly housed according to their economic and moral status." Harris's message conveniently identified democracy with the freedom to buy and sell housing and property. Emphasizing "economic and moral status" as qualifications eliminated "race" as a legitimate standard while reaffirming class criteria as appropriate distributive mechanisms. Harris's and the NAREB's interpretation of democracy focused on the absence of race in the determination of housing distribution. The elimination of racial criteria in favor of a focus instead on economic and moral qualifications meant that black realtists, perhaps unsurprisingly, affirmed a racial definition of democracy.[101]

Uneasily joined to open occupancy within the racial democratic ideology was black self-help. In 1955, Joseph Ray articulated his self-help position to his former NAREB colleagues. Ray delineated the role of the RRS in the public–private partnership that governed federal housing policy, specifically its relationship with minority housing groups. He assured his audience that RRS would not be "an office of special pleading for special interests." He was focused on "promoting constructive efforts by private industry and local leadership in obtaining equal—not preferential—benefits for minority families in the free American economy." Ray added that RRS could assist NAREB members in expanding "the market opportunities of minorities" in their area.[102] Ray indicated his desire for private and local action to take the place of federal government intervention that might punish discriminatory white firms by withholding federal aid from them.

Ray amplified and operationalized black self-help in his talk at the NAREB's ninth annual midwinter meeting in Louisville, Kentucky, in February 1957. In this talk, titled "Housing Outlook Facing Minorities in 1957," he tried to allay "undue alarm" at the "present tight mortgage market," noting that home building in Louisville continued despite the fact that "mortgage money is still in short supply compared to the demand for homes." He assured his audience of black realtists that "the government is giving special attention to the needs of minority, and particularly lower income families." So as not to confuse "special attention" with government-backed preferential treatment, he added that "real estate brokers understand these special instruments since they can be effective for minority families only as they are used and applied by private enterprise." He promoted the VHMCP as an important vehicle for black families getting previously unavailable mortgage credit. Ray emphasized the importance of these "special interests" during this mortgage credit crunch. He reassured his former colleagues that the U.S. economy was "highly prosperous," and that the "greatly increased incomes" of minority families "put them into the private market for good homes." He reminded them, "It is your responsibility as well as ours to help minority families to enjoy a continuing improvement in their housing opportunities and a fuller and freer participation in the housing market."[103]

At the Louisville meeting, Ray introduced his plan for the NAREB and black mortgage lending institutions. The plan specified that during the next two years, black lending institutions would set aside $50 million for minority housing finance, and through "salesmanship[,] invitation[,] and persuasion" get "similar White institutions to match their $50,000,000 five-to-one." He pointed out that this plan would make available $300 million to the "minority market." Ray explained how this "self-help" plan was different from the "special pleading" that he had denounced more than a year ago. It differed because in the past whites had designed and led the plan. In his scheme, black organizations and institutions would take the lead on "a plan of their own," with whites playing a cooperative but supplemental role. Ray commented to Cole in a follow-up memo that he wanted to use Louisville, his hometown, as a test case for his black-led self-help minority financing plan.[104] Ray's concept of self-help, no less dependent on white capital than earlier schemes, nonetheless saw black real estate elites taking the leadership role promised by the 1941 program. While both Harris and Ray supported private enterprise, government's role for them alternated from getting white capital to ignore race in its real estate transactions to correcting racial disparities by bankrolling black capital. Racial democracy accommodated racial positions that ranged from race-conscious self-help to color-blind open occupancy.

Direct Government Intervention in the Mortgage Market

Ray's idea of a limited role for government was soon put to the test. The black real estate industry was not shy about calling for government intervention to protect its members by removing racial barriers to their full market and government participation. In the Housing Act of 1954, there was a provision for a special fund to be set aside by the FNMA for direct mortgage loans. George Harris, reversing his earlier position in the midst of a tight mortgage market in 1957, appealed to Albert Cole to use the $82 million fund to make "direct loans" to identified minority borrowers who would be selected by VHMCP regional committees, rather than match them with private mortgage lenders. Ray endorsed Harris's proposal, recommending to Albert Cole "that a Special Assistance program be established for minority housing."[105]

Cole, after rejecting a similar request from Michigan senators a year earlier, pointed to the creation and success of the VHMCP in its three-year existence. He endorsed what the FNMA had concluded: "that a special assistance program for minority housing is not justified at this time." He continued that the FNMA "believe[d] it is the intent of Congress that Special Assistance funds, which are Government funds, should not be used for any program for which private financing is now available." Cole said he "quite agree[d] with this philosophy," adding he "would be quite reluctant to recommend further Government expenditures for any need which can be met privately." He stated emphatically, "I think the record of the VHMCP clearly indicates that private financing can be provided for minority housing." He concluded by suggesting to Ray that he find more creative ways to use the underutilized "VHMCP for the financing of minority housing."[106]

Despite Ray's earlier concern about "special pleading," his willingness to back a "special assistance fund" was trumped by Cole's resistance to direct government intervention in mortgage markets. Well aware of the tight market, Cole chose to ignore the scarcity of capital, pointing instead to black consumers' lack of knowledge or apathy as a justification for his refusal to use government funds on their behalf. While direct financing undoubtedly would have benefited minority home buyers, it would also have provided a stimulus to the black real estate industry, which was suffering from the tight credit market.

The black real estate industry's concept of the role of government was consistent with that of any business seeking protection from its competition. In the case of black business, it needed "extra" protection due to the racist practices of its more powerful competition. When the industry tested the limits of what government would do, it found that it would not get the protection it needed. Instead voluntarism and privatism would be trotted out by federal housing officials to legitimate their refusal to correct a market failure. It appears that when the black real estate industry and the black policy elite network agreed, for their own reasons, to affirm the primary role of private enterprise, they endorsed a political economy that would not reciprocate by providing the limited amount of help that they requested when they needed that help the most.

Conclusion

The Eisenhower administration's VHMCP was representative of the approach the federal government took to providing mortgage financing to black home buyers and those developers who planned to build homes for the

"Negro housing market." The federal government could not compel banks, mortgage companies, insurance companies, and savings and loans to lend to black citizens, but it sought to coax these institutions into doing so. The "voluntary" efforts on the part of white real estate capital were mirrored by the self-help efforts of black real estate capital, which HHFA administrator Albert Cole promoted. Throughout this period, black government and business elites devised plans to support "self-help" financing of black home mortgages that featured prominent roles for large capital and the national government. None of these plans came to fruition. But what was important was how their plans favored a privatist response that not only would have given them more capital to develop their businesses but would also have had the additional benefit of bolstering black real estate professionals' leadership in serving black housing interests. Both white capital's voluntarism and black capital's self-help endorsed a privatist solution to serving black housing interests, with the federal government playing an indirect rather than a direct role. This approach was consonant with the resurgence of organized business power after World War II, which discouraged the state from directly producing housing but encouraged the granting of subsidies to private builders, developers, and financiers serving the housing market, including its Negro segment.

Black real estate and government elites embraced racial democracy in their efforts to get white capital to serve the Negro housing market either directly or through investing in start-up black mortgage companies. Their embrace of racial democracy implicitly accepted the absence of government in housing production and the increasing privatist response. Of course, black real estate, policy, and civic elites could not have stemmed this privatist tide on their own if they had wanted. Nonetheless, they had their own reasons for embracing private enterprise as the solution to black housing problems, and accordingly, sought to protect their auxiliary position with the emergent business welfare state. By doing so, not only did they accept that the housing needs of the majority of blacks would not be addressed but also legitimized an approach that would leave working-class blacks and other economically insecure Americans to face the vagaries of a unforgiving housing market for the remainder of the twentieth century.

Conclusion

Many observers of the late twentieth and early twenty-first centuries have commented on the existence of a class divide within the nation's African American population. While this class inequality reflects the recent widening of the divide within the larger American political economy, both the mechanisms and indicators of class division in the black community were evident as early as the 1950s. The mechanisms were particularly marked in a housing system that rewarded those with the income and culture of the middle class, whether black or white, with quality housing and good neighborhoods, but punished those who lacked either by denying them decent and affordable housing. While all blacks suffered from persistent residential segregation, affluent blacks suffered less due to the class stratification of housing both within and outside of the black community.

Black civic leaders and policy elites focused on challenging racial inequality in both the housing market and the government's housing programs. This necessary and important fight was successful in achieving some good housing, which otherwise would not have been available to many African Americans. Nonetheless, the terms of that fight—as determined both by the larger political economy and by the political needs of the black civic elites—dictated that these elites did not challenge the class stratification that characterized the allocation of housing. The decision to pursue racial democracy rather than to challenge class inequality in housing allocation after World War II meant at best accepting as a *fait accompli* that most wage-earning blacks would continue to be denied adequate and affordable housing in the United States.

Though black civic elites in Chicago and across the nation brought both racial and social democratic commitments to their housing advocacy during the 1930s, the latter were pushed aside during the more conservative 1940s and 1950s. The combination of a resurgent business class and a compliant state rendered difficult the pursuit of social democracy, which held the promise of better housing for most African Americans. Achieving the narrower aims of racial democracy also proved difficult given the opposition of the real estate industry and the state. Nonetheless, during this period the political benefits of having at least a privileged segment of the black population realize a slice of the American Dream resulted in concessions to a limited racial democracy in the housing market.

When black civic elites focused on public housing, it was easier for them to marshal a class and racial critique of the real estate industry. Since most blacks were working class, their lack of adequate housing could be traced to both their lack of income and their racial identity. Although black civic elites supported public housing for social democratic reasons, they found a more compelling basis for their support in the racial democratic notion that public housing could be used as a tool to counteract the social disorganization of poor blacks. The emergence of slum clearance and urban redevelopment policy after the Housing Act of 1949 meant that black civic elites, like white housing reformers, did not challenge the prerogative of the real estate industry to reserve valuable land for the higher classes. Their racial democratic commitment and their lack of a class critique worked together to obscure the reality that some affluent blacks in Lake Meadows and Hyde Park stood to benefit from adopting the real estate principle of "the highest and best use of land" and the implications of that reality for the notion that their political agendas unproblematically represented the needs of a broader black community. Enterprising blacks also sought to use the same redevelopment tools as the city to wrest control of their neighborhoods from the city's land-clearance assault. When the housing policy terrain shifted to private housing markets, black civic and policy elites who believed in social democratic housing schemes nonetheless used class controls in order to manage racial succession and ensure racial democracy. They promoted the agency of black middle-class homeowners to counteract negative stereotypes of black residential behavior. While their class critique previously had been aimed directly at the powerful white real estate industry, it faltered when confronted with the practices of upper-class blacks who invested in kitchenettes and charged poor blacks exorbitant rents for substandard housing. At the end of the day, whether through advocacy or quiet acceptance, black civic and policy elites pursued racial democracy at the expense of broader social democratic commitments.

It is true that black civic and policy elites' embrace of social democracy would not have changed the structure of housing markets and policies without the crucial aid of organized labor and liberals, who made their own Faustian bargains with cold-war capitalism. Nonetheless, their commitment to racial democracy, whether in its self-help or antidiscrimination strain, and the concomitant underdevelopment of a social democratic housing policy, established black housing politics on a class-skewed foundation that has prevented subsequent generations of black housing activists from articulating, crafting, and pursuing policies that would have benefitted the vast majority of African Americans who currently lack access to adequate and affordable housing.

The class dynamics within African American politics that I examine throughout the book have not typically appeared in scholarly literature. This is true for the two most important texts on black housing politics in postwar Chicago: James Q. Wilson, *Negro Politics: The Search for Leadership* (1960), and Arnold R. Hirsch, *Making the Second Ghetto: Race and Housing, 1940– 1960* (1983). Wilson's study includes explicit references to class bigotry and class interests on the part of black civic elites in Chicago in the arena of land-use politics in 1950s. He goes so far as to point out how racism obscured the "normal" stratification of a capitalist political economy in the black community. Wilson implies that in the absence of racism, the class structure among blacks would have taken the shape of that among whites, and class interests would have supplanted racial goals.

Since racial disparities were evident in the Jim Crow-North, Wilson proceeds to build his analytical framework around what he calls "race ends," which consist of "welfare" and "status" goals.[1] According to his typology, those black political leaders who favored welfare goals accommodated or found "vested interests" in racial segregation. Those who pursued status goals favored strategies that would lead to racial integration even if doing so entailed the sacrifice of short-term gains in improved housing. This dichotomy may be useful in explaining the conflict between black policy and institutional elites in siting public housing projects, and in supporting slum clearance and urban redevelopment. However, Wilson's analysis fails to point out that these goals were pursued within a circumscribed arena that accepted the prerogative of private capital to remake central cities.

Wilson's intraracial framework builds on other dichotomies (such as accommodation versus protest, and nationalism versus integration) that have informed the study of black politics in the postwar era. Like its analytical antecedents, Wilson's framework assumes that blacks represent a unitary racial subject.[2] In other words, the differential interests of black strata are

overridden by an assumed consensus over fighting racial group disparities. In this way, Wilson's framework interprets black politics to be only, or
mainly, the conflict between different black elite cohorts over racial goals.
Not only are the common class interests of black elites obscured in his analysis of black housing politics, but working-class blacks do not even enter the
picture. For example, the interests of working-class black tenants are largely
unrepresented in the conflict between black policy and institutional elites
in the slum clearance drama. Through his narrow focus Wilson reflects and
reinforces a longstanding black elite reflex to reduce both the interpretation
and the practice of black politics to their custodial role in speaking for and
acting on the behalf of the whole black population.

While Hirsch does not focus on black political elites like Wilson, he does
borrow Wilson's typology when he briefly explains black political behavior. Hirsch's concern is the lack of racial unity among black political elites
in the fight for integrated public housing and against black displacement.
He portrays black civic elites such as Archibald Carey and Robert Taylor as
committed to civil rights but thwarted by white political and economic elites.
He blames William Dawson and his black submachine for not taking the
lead in opposing the city's policies, thus fracturing the common racial front
against white power. Like Wilson, he charges Dawson with a lack of commitment to civil rights or "status" goals, in favor of the more tangible "welfare"
goals that accommodated forced racial segregation. Though Hirsch doubts
that this racial unity would have made *the* difference, he thinks it was the
best possibility for blacks to prevent racial containment.

Much has been written about Hirsch's lack of attention to "black agency"
in his book.[3] In response, Hirsch points out that his primary focus on white
elites at the expense of black political agents was deliberate; black elites could
only react to the actions of the dominant white elites, who had the power and
thus bore the responsibility for the creation of the black ghetto.[4] One response
to Hirsch's one-sided focus is a new spate of scholarship inaugurated by Tom
Sugrue's *The Origins of the Urban Crisis* which gives equal treatment to black
resistance and white power.[5] The benefit of this approach is that it permits
an examination, in Sugrue's case for example, not only of what happened to
black Detroit, but also of how black civic and labor organizations sought to
prevent the use of postwar federal housing programs to reinforce segregation. However, a shortcoming of this more "integrated" approach to urban
political history is its lack of depth in examining black policy debates and
political conflicts over postwar housing programs.

This new scholarship does not give sufficient attention to the cleavages that divided black civic, policy, and institutional elites. More importantly, it does not examine their shared assumption that the political and economic gains of all blacks depended on a custodial black elite and a muted black rank and file. Moreover, this scholarship assumes that there is a corporate racial subject, in other words, that the black population acts collectively in pursuit of a common goal: ending racial disparities.[6] Even when this scholarship acknowledges class cleavages among blacks, it treats these cleavages as discrete episodes of class conflict rather than a systematic class politics that informs black elites' *racial* positions on housing policy. The assumption of a unitary black subjectivity elides a politics informed by class interests, and it obscures the class-skewed foundation of black politics in postwar Chicago. In reproducing a perspective on black politics that reduces it to the effort to eliminate racial disparity, this scholarship legitimates the practice of elite-dominated black politics.

Racial Democracy and the Black Metropolis shows cleavages among black elites as well as their common commitment to a custodial racial politics. I have also shown how different elite cohorts competed to have their policy positions represent the assumed singular position of the race. Neither the antidiscrimination nor the self-help strain of racial democracy departed from the idea that black elites should lead the race, and that all blacks had a common interest that supersedes the particular interests of any stratum. It is clear from my argument in this book that whether the issue was public housing or urban redevelopment, working-class blacks were not consulted and thus did not help to shape the positions that represented "sound racial policy." I am sure that the black civic and policy elites at the time did not see the need to consult ordinary blacks because the path seemed obvious to them. Their decision to pursue racial democracy was neither naïve nor shortsighted. Their racial politics were informed and limited by an unspoken acceptance of a class-stratified social order that ensured that their racial and class politics would be one and the same.

Acknowledgments

In the process of working on a long-term project such as this one, a lot of debts are accrued along the way. While researching and writing this book, I have been a member of the Politics department and African American and African Studies program at Mount Holyoke College. I have been supported intellectually and personally by my wonderful colleagues at the college. Grace Caligtan and Aimee Eubanks were two of the many students who contributed their enthusiasm and research skills to the project. I would especially like to thank Giorgia Scribellito who contributed the most, poring over endless microfilms of the *Chicago Defender*. I would also like to thank Mary Elizabeth Murphy, who assisted me once she graduated from Mount Holyoke and joined the doctoral program in history at the University of Maryland. Mary Elizabeth's scholarly instincts and conscientious research skills were invaluable in tracking down many elusive sources. I want to acknowledge my editor Pieter Martin, who inherited the project, and believed in it enough to provide timely support for it at the University of Minnesota Press. The Ford Foundation provided financial support during the early stages of research for this project. This project would not have been possible without research support from the Dean of Faculty at the college, Donal O'Shea, who also provided encouragement throughout.

I have had many expert and patient guides in my search for material in the archives, special collections, and libraries in Chicago and Washington, D.C. My research was made much more productive by the staff at the Chicago Historical Society, especially the late Archibald Motley, who introduced me to the rich Claude A. Barnett papers and much more, and also the staff at the University of Illinois at Chicago Special Collections, the National Archives, and the Library of Congress. I would also like to acknowledge Michael Flug at the Vivian Harsh Collection at the Carter Woodson Branch at the Chicago Public Library, who introduced me to the Horace Cayton papers. Last, I would like to thank the library staff at Mount Holyoke, who endured many interlibrary loan requests and multiple renewals for library holdings. My research efforts would have been less fruitful without the knowledgeable and dedicated people who staff these libraries.

Of course, those who are knowledgeable about sources are not found only in libraries. I also found many other well-informed sources outside the libraries. I benefitted a great deal early in my research from Timuel Black, who was a rich source of information and wisdom about black political history in Chicago. I also had the opportunity to learn from the late Vernon Jarrett, Addie Wyatt, Dempsey Travis, the late Congressman Charles Hayes, the late Oscar Brown Jr., and Truman Gibson Jr. An intellectual and personal companion on more than one research trip to Chicago was Roger House. We share a love for the rich culture and complex politics of the Black Metropolis.

I have benefitted from many people reading and commenting on the manuscript. Rogers Smith read an early draft of the manuscript when it was much too long and gave me salient comments about the content as well as guidance for editing it. He should be given the academic equivalent of a Purple Heart for his efforts. I also like to thank the anonymous reader for the University of Minnesota Press who gave me concrete and fruitful suggestions for streamlining the argument. Once I rounded the manuscript into shape, I benefitted from the comments of Dan Czitrom, Dennis Judd, Michael Ford, Adolph Reed Jr., Toure Reed, and especially Larry Bennett. I want to thank Jan Whitaker, whose incisive pen helped me turn a manuscript into a book. In addition, Susan Murray helped me to polish the manuscript draft before I delivered the final product to the press. Lastly, I would like to thank Adolph Reed Jr. for the many years of conversations about African American politics that helped me create the analytical framework by which I interpreted the thoughts, actions, and interests of black policy elites in Chicago. He has been a constant source of encouragement, constructive criticism, and comradeship throughout the years.

This project would not have happened if it wasn't for the support that I have received from my friends and family. My many research trips would not have been possible without my family welcoming me into their homes in Chicago and Washington, D.C. My uncle Joseph McBurnett Smith and his wife Linda were my home base in Chicago. Over the years, I have benefitted from the many debates about black politics in the city in the home of my late aunt and uncle, Edna and Gaylord Thomas. My guide to black Chicago since high school has been my cousin Gaylord Thomas Jr. Research in Washington, D.C., would not have been possible without my cousin Dr.

Raymond Patterson and his wife Deborah welcoming and supporting me on many trips over the years. Many friends, including Dean Robinson, Barry Magnus, Harry Kokkinos, Jen Cannon, Paul Collins, Rochelle Calhoun, Joan Cocks, Lucas Wilson, Patricia Romney, Paul Fleischmann, Agustin Lao, and the Amherst Family have lived with me and "the book" for many years. Other family members I want to thank are Teena Johnson-Smith, the late Mary Elaine Johnson, the late Ernest R. Graham who asked me periodically when he would hear me on the NPR (maybe now Uncle Robert!), my sisters Kathryn and Kimberly and their families, and my brother Edward. I want to thank my children Eris and Kendall, who have lived with this project from adolescence to young adulthood, for their love, patience, and belief that Dad would finish his book. They inspire me with their spirit, passion, and dedication to educating young people of color about the world and themselves. Without the guidance, love, encouragement, and intellectual curiosity of my parents, the late Preston H. Smith Sr. and Mariam Graham Smith, I would not have been able to stay the course and complete the manuscript. Through them the South Side of Chicago lived with us in California, Michigan, and Massachusetts.

I have saved my greatest thanks to my wife and partner Lynda Pickbourn. Though she came into my life later in the process, she came at a critical time. She was there when I had to make sense of a massive amount of archival research and try to put it into some narrative and connected form. No one has been more important to my ability to complete the manuscript than Lynda. Not only has she read and commented on every chapter, she is my intellectual, social, and political companion, and my source of inspiration, encouragement, wisdom, and loving support, whether we are visiting family and friends in Accra and Tamale, writing together at the Book Mill, or taking a walk around the Lower Lake.

Notes

Introduction

1. Everett C. Hughes, introduction to the Torchbook Edition of *Black Metropolis: A Study of Negro Life in a Northern City*, by St. Clair Drake and Horace R. Cayton (New York, N.Y.: Harper & Row, 1962), xxxix.

2. St. Clair Drake, "The Social and Economic Status of the Negro in the United States," in *The Negro American,* ed. Talcott Parsons and Kenneth B. Clark (Boston, Mass.: Beacon Press, 1966), 9.

3. Hughes, introduction, xxxix. Drake, "The Social and Economic Status of the Negro," 9. See also Harold M Baron and Bennett Hymer, "The Negro Worker in the Chicago Labor Market: A Case Study of De Facto Segregation," in *The Negro and the American Labor Movement*, ed. Julius Jacobsen (Garden City, N.Y.: Anchor Books, 1968), 233.

4. St. Clair Drake and Horace R. Cayton, *Black Metropolis*; Bill V. Mullen, *Popular Fronts: Chicago and African-American Cultural Politics, 1935–1946* (Urbana, Ill.: University of Illinois Press, 1999); Jonathan Scott Holloway, *Confronting the Veil: Abram Harris Jr., E. Franklin Frazier, and Ralph Bunche, 1919–1941* (Chapel Hill, N.C.: University of North Carolina Press, 2002); John B. Kirby, *Black Americans in the Roosevelt Era: Liberalism and Race* (Knoxville, Tenn.: University of Tennessee Press, 1980).

5. Michael E. Stone, "Housing, Mortgage Lending, and the Contradictions of Capitalism," in *Marxism and the Metropolis: New Perspectives in Urban Political Economy*, ed. William K. Tabb and Larry Sawers (Oxford: Oxford University Press, 1978): 180–81. National Association of Housing Officials, *A Housing Program For the United States* (Chicago, Ill.: National Association of Housing Officials, [November] 1934), 6.

6. People are shelter poor when they have to spend so much of their incomes for housing that it does not allow them to afford other nonshelter needs such as food, clothing, and transportation; see Michael E. Stone, *Shelter Poverty: New Ideas on Housing Affordability* (Philadelphia, Pa.: Temple University Press, 1993), 6, 104, 105, 108, 91.

7. Another work argues that what was considered "civil rights" narrowed during the 1950s. See Risa L. Goluboff, *The Lost Promise of Civil Rights* (Cambridge, Mass.: Harvard University Press, 2007).

8. For a trenchant critique of open occupancy as housing policy see Beryl Satter, *Family Properties: Race, Real Estate, and the Exploitation of Urban America* (New York, N.Y.: Metropolitan Books, 2009).

9. Arnold R. Hirsch, *Making a Second Ghetto: Race and Housing, 1940–1960* (Cambridge: Cambridge University Press, 1983).

10. Andrew Wiese, *Places of Their Own: African American Suburbanization in the Twentieth Century* (Chicago, Ill.: University of Chicago Press Press, 2005).

11. Mary L. Dudziak, *Cold War Civil Rights: Race and the Image of American Democracy* (Princeton, N.J.: Princeton University Press, 2000).

12. Dona Cooper Hamilton and Charles V. Hamilton, *The Dual Agenda: Race and Social Welfare Policies of Civil Rights Organizations* (New York, N.Y.: Columbia University Press, 1997). The Hamiltons argue that while black elites favored both racial and social democracy, their white liberal allies betrayed them by refusing to endorse civil rights protections in order to garner southern Democrats' votes for social legislation.

13. The political scientist James Q. Wilson was one of the early scholars to recognize diverging class interests in black Chicago, though class still was not a salient category in his analysis of black politics (Wilson, *Negro Politics: The Search for Leadership* [New York: Free Press, 1960], 105–6). For scholarship that does employ class as an analytic category in examining black politics see Adolph Reed Jr., *W. E. B. Du Bois and American Political Thought: Fabianism and the Color Line* (New York, N.Y.: Oxford University Press, 1997) and *Stirrings in the Jug: Black Politics in the Post-Segregation Era* (Minneapolis, Minn.: University of Minnesota Press, 1999); Dean E. Robinson, *Black Nationalism in American Politics and Thought* (Cambridge: Cambridge University Press, 2001); Cedric Johnson, *Revolutionaries to Race Leaders: Black Power and the Making of African American Politics* (Minneapolis, Minn.: University of Minnesota Press, 2007); Michelle R. Boyd, *Jim Crow Nostalgia: Reconstructing Race in Bronzeville* (Minneapolis, Minn.: University of Minnesota Press, 2008); and Toure F. Reed, *Not Alms but Opportunity: The Urban League & The Politics of Racial Uplift, 1910–1950* (Chapel Hill, N.C.: University of North Carolina Press, 2008).

14. Dean E. Robinson, "Black Power Nationalism as Ethnic Pluralism: Postwar Liberalism's Ethnic Paradigm in Black Radicalism," 184–214 in *Renewing Black Intellectual History: The Ideological and Material Foundations of African American Thought* (Boulder, Colo.: Paradigm Publishers, 2010). Also, his *Black Nationalism in American Politics and Thought* (Cambridge: Cambridge University Press, 2001). Reed, *Stirrings in the Jug,* 55–78.

15. See Kevin Boyle, *The UAW and the Heyday of American Liberalism, 1945–1968* (Ithaca, N.Y.: Cornell University Press, 1995); Nelson Lichtenstein, *Walter Reuther: The Most Dangerous Man in Detroit* (Urbana, Ill.: University of Illinois Press, 1995); Nelson Lichtenstein, "From Corporatism to Collective Bargaining: Organized Labor and the Eclipse of Social Democracy in the Postwar Era," 122–52; and Ira Katznelson, "Was the Great Society a Lost Opportunity?" 186–92, both in *The Rise and Fall of the New Deal Order, 1930–1980,* ed. Steve Fraser and Gary Gerstle (Princeton, N.J.: Princeton University Press, 1989).

1. Black Civic Ideology and Political Economy in Postwar Chicago

1. "One Toilet for 24 on South Side," *Daily Record*, July 17, 1939, Chicago Historical Society (CHS), Earl Dickerson Papers.

2. Roy Wilkins, "The Negro Wants Full Equality," in *What the Negro Wants*, ed. Rayford W. Logan (Chapel Hill, N.C.: University of North Carolina Press, 1944), 128.

3. Preston H. Smith II, "The Chicago School of Human Ecology and Ideology of Black Civic Elites," in *Renewing Black Intellectual History: The Ideological and Material Foundations of Black American Thought* (Boulder, Colo.: Paradigm Press, 2009), 129–30, 137–39.

4. Ibid., 141–47.

5. Dean E. Robinson, "Black Power Nationalism as Ethnic Pluralism: Postwar Liberalism's Ethnic Paradigm in Black Radicalism," in *Renewing Black Intellectual History: The Ideological and Material Foundations of African American Thought* (Boulder, Colo.: Paradigm Publishers, 2010), 191.

6. See Robert A. Dahl, *Who Governs?: Democracy and Power in an American City*, 2nd ed. (1961; New Haven, Conn.: Yale University Press, 2005), and David B. Truman, *The Governmental Process: Political Interests and Public Opinion*, 2nd ed. (1951; Berkeley, Calif.: University of California Press, 1993).

7. Dianne M. Pinderhughes, *Race and Ethnicity in Chicago Politics: A Reexamination of Pluralist Theory* (Urbana, Ill.: University of Illinois Press, 1987).

8. David E. Apter, *The Politics of Modernization* (Chicago, Ill.: University of Chicago Press Press, 1965).

9. Perhaps the scholar who applied his work on the modernization of African states to black Americans was Martin Kilson, "Political Change in the Negro Ghetto," in *Key Issues in the Afro-American Experience*, vol. 1, ed. Nathan Huggins, Martin Kilson, and Daniel Fox (New York, N.Y.: Harcourt Brace Jovanovich, 1971). See also Kilson's *Political Change in a West African State: A Study of Modernization of Sierra Leone* (Cambridge, Mass.: Center for International Affairs, Harvard University, 1966). For another application to black politics see Stokely Carmichael and Charles Hamilton, *Black Power: The Politics of Liberation in America* (New York, N.Y.: Random House, 1967).

10. Frederick D. Patterson, "The Negro Wants Full Participation in the American Democracy," 277; Rayford Logan, "The Negro Wants First-Class Citizenship," 14; Gordon B. Hancock, "Race Relations in the United States: A Summary," 230, all in *What the Negro Wants*, ed. Rayford W. Logan (Chapel Hill, N.C.: University of North Carolina Press, 1944).

11. Logan, "The Negro Wants First-Class Citizenship," 13.

12. Ibid., 30.

13. Mary L. Dudziak, *Cold War Civil Rights: Race and the Image of American Democracy* (Princeton, N.J.: Princeton University Press, 2000), 49. Lee Finkle points

out the conservative nature of the Double-V campaign, which restrained rather than challenged militant sentiment from the restive black rank and file (Finkle, "The Conservative Aims of Militant Rhetoric: Black Protest during World War II," *Journal of American History* 60, no. 3 [December 1973]: 692–713). See also Philip A. Klinkner with Rogers M. Smith, *The Unsteady March: The Rise and Decline of Racial Equality in America* (Chicago, Ill.: University of Chicago Press Press, 1999).

14. Charles H. Wesley, "The Negro Has Always Wanted the Four Freedoms," in *What the Negro Wants*, ed. Logan, 110, 112. Andrew Wiese, following Thomas Sugrue's idea about the contradictory racial interpretations of the New Deal, argues that there were black and white "brands" of racial democracy. White racial democracy interpreted the New Deal to support the racial claims of whites to government benefits and justified their privileges by arguing that they fulfilled their civic duties and responsibilities better than racial minorities (Wiese, *Places of Their Own: African American Suburbanization in the Twentieth Century* [Chicago, Ill.: University of Chicago Press Press, 2005], 131, 162). See also Thomas J. Sugrue, *The Origins of the Urban Crisis: Race and Inequality in Postwar Detroit* (Princeton, N.J.: Princeton University Press, 1996). My use of the term refers exclusively to African Americans' primary focus on race in the democratization of U.S. institutions (see my "The Quest for Racial Democracy: Black Civic Ideology and Housing Interests in Postwar Chicago," *Journal of Urban History* 26 [January 2000]: 131–57).

15. Dona Cooper Hamilton and Charles V. Hamilton, *The Dual Agenda: Race and Social Welfare Policies of Civil Rights Organizations* (New York, N.Y.: Columbia University Press, 1997), 20.

16. Gordon B. Hancock, "Race Relations in the United States: A Summary," 234; Patterson, "The Negro Wants Full Participation in the American Democracy," in *What the Negro Wants*, ed. Rayford W. Logan (Chapel Hill, N.C.: University of North Carolina Press, 1944), 274. Wiese, *Places of Their Own*, 164–208.

17. The historian Jonathan Holloway argues that the class-based politics of Abram Harris Jr., E. Franklin Frazier, and Ralph Bunche during the 1930s was constantly challenged by the racialist thinking on the part of blacks and whites as well as by how racism circumscribed their careers and political choices. For various personal and political reasons, these black intellectuals either adopted a race-based focus or turned to the right after 1940 (Holloway, *Confronting the Veil: Abram Harris Jr., E. Franklin Frazier, and Ralph Bunche, 1919–1941* [Chapel Hill: University of North Carolina Press, 2002]). For an exploration of social democracy in the United States, see Ira Katznelson, "Was the Great Society a Lost Opportunity?" in *The Rise and Fall of the New Deal Order, 1930–1980*, ed. Steve Fraser and Gary Gerstle (Princeton, N.J.: Princeton University Press, 1989), 186–92.

18. A. Philip Randolph, "March on Washington Movement Presents Program for the Negro," 137, 141; Wesley "The Negro Has Always Wanted the Four Freedoms," 106; Bethune, "Certain Unalienable Rights," 255; Patterson, "The Negro Wants Full

Participation in the American Democracy," 266–68, all in *What the Negro Wants*, ed. Rayford W. Logan (Chapel Hill, N.C.: University of North Carolina Press, 1944).

19. A. Philip Randolph, "March on Washington Movement Presents Program for the Negro," 135–36; Elizabeth A. Fones-Wolf, *Selling Free Enterprise: The Business Assault on Labor and Liberalism, 1945–1960* (Urbana, Ill.: University of Illinois Press, 1994); Brian Waddell, *The War against the New Deal: World War II and American Democracy* (DeKalb, Ill.: Northern Illinois University Press, 2001); Kim McQuaid, *Uneasy Partners: Big Business in American Politics, 1945–1990* (Baltimore, Md.: Johns Hopkins University Press, 1994); Michael K. Brown, *Race, Money, and the American Welfare State* (Ithaca, N.Y.: Cornell University Press, 1999).

20. Logan, "The Negro Wants First-Class Citizenship," 22. For organized labor, see Nelson Lichtenstein, "From Corporatism to Collective Bargaining: Organized Labor and the Eclipse of Social Democracy in the Postwar Era," in *The Rise and Fall of the New Deal Order, 1930–1980*, ed. Steve Fraser and Gary Gerstle (Princeton, N.J.: Princeton University Press, 1989), 122–52.

21. A. Philip Randolph, though he clearly supported social democracy, still advocated for the primacy of racial democracy through the March on Washington Movement ("March on Washington Movement Presents Program for the Negro," 136). Only Willard Townsend challenged the "primacy of race" in his contribution to the *What the Negro Wants* volume (see his "One American Problem and a Possible Solution," 174, 165–66, 181).

22. Gunnar Myrdal, *An American Dilemma: The Negro Problem & Modern Democracy*, vols. 1 & 2 (1944; New York, N.Y.: Pantheon Books, 1962).

23. Wesley, "The Negro Has Always Wanted the Four Freedoms," in *What the Negro Wants*, ed. Rayford W. Logan (Chapel Hill, N.C.: University of North Carolina Press, 1944), 95–96.

24. Of course, this recognition did not immediately change policy, but it did provide an ideological context for treating civil rights as a normative enterprise among liberal elites who were influential in government and business circles (President's Committee on Civil Rights, *To Secure These Rights* [Washington, D.C.: U.S. Government Printing Office, 1947]). See Klinkner, *Unsteady March*, 215; Charles V. Hamilton, *Adam Clayton Powell Jr.: The Political Biography of an American Dilemma* (1991; New York, N.Y.: Cooper Square Press, 2002).

25. Drake and Cayton put it another way when discussing the racial and class impact of working-class blacks entering white neighborhoods: "Race prejudice becomes aggravated by class antagonisms, and class-feeling is often expressed in racial terms" (Drake and Cayton, *Black Metropolis*, 114).

26. W. E. B. Du Bois, "My Evolving Program for Negro Freedom," in *What the Negro Wants*, ed. Rayford W. Logan (Chapel Hill, N.C.: University of North Carolina Press, 1944), 67. Adolph Reed Jr. "The Study of Black Politics and the Practice of Black Politics: Their Historical Relation and Evolution" in *Problems and Methods in*

the Study of Politics, ed. Ian Shapiro, Rogers A. Smith, and Tarek E. Masoud (Cambridge: Cambridge University Press, 2004), 111. Wiese, *Places of Their Own*, 159.

27. Dudziak, *Cold War Civil Rights*, 52.

28. Drake and Cayton, *Black Metropolis*, 393, 710, 714.

29. E. Franklin Frazier, "The Negro Middle-Class and Desegregation" (1957) in *E. Franklin Frazier on Race Relations*, ed. G. Franklin Edwards (Chicago, Ill.: University of Chicago Press, 1968), 306–7; E. Franklin Frazier, *The Negro Family in the United States* (Chicago, Ill.: University of Chicago Press Press, 1939), 453; James Q. Wilson, *Negro Politics: The Search for Leadership* (New York, N.Y.: Free Press, 1960), 120.

30. Frazier would revise much of his own thinking by the early 1950s, indicting the black middle class for not fulfilling their class responsibility in leading the race toward progress. Frazier had first published *Black Bourgeoisie* in France in 1952 (see E. Franklin Frazier, *Black Bourgeoisie* [Glencoe, Ill.: Free Press and Falcon's Wing Press, 1957]).

31. E. Franklin Frazier, *Negro in the United States*, rev. ed. (1949; New York, N.Y.: Macmillan, 1957), 302, 298; Frazier, *Negro Family in the United States*, 436.

32. Drake and Cayton, *Black Metropolis*, 389. See also Wilson, *Negro Politics*, 174.

33. Drake and Cayton, *Black Metropolis*, 710, 714, 393; Roy Wilkins, "The Negro Wants Full Equality," 126.

34. Drake and Cayton, *Black Metropolis*, 393; Frazier, *Negro Family in the United States*, 436.

35. See Preston H. Smith II, "The Limitations of Racial Democracy: The Politics of Chicago Urban League, 1916–40" (PhD diss., University of Massachusetts, Amherst, 1990). Toure F. Reed, *Not Alms but Opportunity: The Urban League & the Politics of Racial Uplift, 1910–1950* (Chapel Hill, N.C.: University of North Carolina Press, 2008).

36. Rayford Logan, "The Negro Wants First-Class Citizenship," 13; Leslie Pinckney Hill, "What the Negro Wants and How to Get It," 81, 84; Mary McLeod Bethune, "Certain Unalienable Rights," 256, all in *What the Negro Wants*, ed. Rayford W. Logan (Chapel Hill, N.C.: University of North Carolina Press, 1944).

37. The very title of the influential book *What the Negro Wants* expresses the assumption of unitary agency and the expectation that a group of black academics, educators, labor and interest-group leaders can speak for the "race." Reflecting a reality of black social and political differentiation, there were also pleas that black leaders, in particular, needed to unify in a collective, unitary racial effort.

38. Randolph, "March on Washington Movement Presents Program for the Negro," in *What the Negro Wants*, ed. Rayford W. Logan (Chapel Hill, N.C.: University of North Carolina Press, 1944), 145. See also Leslie Pinckney Hill, "What the Negro Wants and How to Get It: The Inward Power of the Masses, 73; and Charles H. Wesley, "The Negro Has Always Wanted the Four Freedoms," 98, both in *What the Negro Wants*, ed. Rayford W. Logan (Chapel Hill, N.C.: University of North Carolina Press, 1944).

39. The emphasis on "unity" and the primacy of race makes this politics akin to black nationalism. Despite the oppositional stance of black nationalism toward "integration," it has a lot in common with mainstream American politics. After World War II, black nationalism as "black power" argued for a unified black agent or "nation" to extract concessions from an institutionally racist polity (Dean E. Robinson, "Black Power Nationalism as Ethnic Pluralism: Postwar Liberalism's Ethnic Paradigm in Black Radicalism," in *Renewing Black Intellectual History: The Ideological and Material Foundations of African American Thought* [Boulder, Colo.: Paradigm Publishers, 2010], 184–214; Dean E. Robinson, *Black Nationalism in American Politics and Thought* [Cambridge: Cambridge University Press, 2001]). Andrew Wiese sees similar links between the self-help ideology of Booker T. Washington, racial and business practices of black real estate brokers, and current black suburban elites constituting a "territorial nationalism" (Wiese, *Places of Our Own*, 277).

40. For Rayford Logan, the "surprising unanimity" on the goal of racial equality by all the African American contributors to the *What the Negro Wants* volume despite their radical, moderate, and conservative politics was impressive. For me, it speaks to a conscious suppression of those differences for constructing a strategic unity around the goal of racial democracy (editor's preface in Logan, ed., *What the Negro Wants*).

41. A few black analysts were aware of class conflict within the race (A. Philip Randolph, "March on Washington Movement Presents Program for the Negro," in *What the Negro Wants*, ed. Rayford W. Logan [Chapel Hill: University of North Carolina Press, 1944], 153).

42. Drake and Cayton, *Black Metropolis*, 88.

43. The historian Lizabeth Cohen counts five hundred black members in Chicago (Cohen, *Making a New Deal: Industrial Workers in Chicago, 1919–1939* [Cambridge: Cambridge University Press, 1990], 262). According to Drake and Cayton, "hundreds" of blacks voted for Foster (Drake and Cayton, *Black Metropolis*, 736).

44. Drake and Cayton, *Black Metropolis*, 88.

45. St. Clair Drake, "Profiles: Chicago," *Journal of Educational Sociology* 17, no. 5 (January 1944): 269.

46. Drake and Cayton, *Black Metropolis*, 737–38.

47. Wilson, *Negro Politics*, 176.

48. Drake and Cayton, *Black Metropolis*, 737–38.

49. Ibid., 654; Frazier, *Negro Family in the United States*, 474–75, 453.

50. Wilson, *Negro Politics*, 112–17.

51. Ibid., 114–15, 221–22, 224. Some African American civic leaders also held elected or appointed political office. Archibald J. Carey Jr., a minister and lawyer, was a long-standing Republican alderman of the Third Ward. Earl B. Dickerson, whose civic credentials were unparalleled in Chicago and nationally, sought and briefly held the city council seat in the predominantly black Second Ward. Dickerson's electoral

ambitions were cut short by William Dawson, who sought to control the Second Ward at the center of the Black Metropolis. Mayor Edward Kelly appointed Robert R. Taylor, a housing manager, lender, and policy expert with training in architecture, to the Chicago Housing Authority (CHA) Board of Commissioners, serving as its chairperson from 1938 to 1950 (Roger Biles, *Big City Boss in Depression and War: Mayor Edward J. Kelly of Chicago* [DeKalb: Northern Illinois University Press, 1984], 98–100; Drake and Cayton, *Black Metropolis*, 356; Dempsey Travis, *An Autobiography of Black Politics* [Chicago: Urban Research Press, 1987], 151–56). For more on Archibald J. Carey Jr. see Dennis C. Dickerson, *African American Preachers and Politicians: The Careys of Chicago* (Jackson, Miss.: University Press of Mississippi, 2010).

52. According to some commentators, black machine leaders did not even receive in patronage what they delivered in votes (St. Clair Drake, "The Social and Economic Status of the Negro in the United States," in *The Negro American*, ed. Talcott Parsons and Kenneth B. Clark [Boston: Beacon Press, 1966], 8; Harold M Baron and Bennett Hymer, "The Negro Worker in the Chicago Labor Market: A Case Study of De Facto Segregation," in *The Negro and the American Labor Movement*, ed. Julius Jacobson [Garden City, N.Y.: Anchor Books, 1968], 277).

53. Wiese, *Places of Their Own*, 124.

54. Baron and Hymer, "The Negro Worker in the Chicago Labor Market," 242.

55. Ibid.

56. While black women fared better, at 10 percent, during the same period, this larger proportion was mainly explained by their occupying low-status professions such as teaching, nursing, and social work (Figs. 15 and 16, in Drake and Cayton, *Black Metropolis*, 226–27; Table 9, in *Local Community Fact Book for Chicago, 1950*, ed. Philip M. Hauser and Evelyn M. Kitagawa [Chicago: Chicago Community Inventory, University of Chicago, 1953], 8; Table IV-4, in *Local Community Fact Book, Chicago Metropolitan Area, 1960*, ed. Evelyn M. Kitagawa and Karl E. Taeuber [Chicago: Chicago Community Inventory, University of Chicago, 1963], 269). Note: For 1930 and 1940, the population is classed as "Negro," but for 1950 and 1960, it is termed "Nonwhite." "Clerical" refers to clerical and sales workers in 1950 and 1960. "Service" refers to service and private household workers combined for 1950 and 1960.

57. Baron and Hymer, "The Negro Worker in the Chicago Labor Market," 254. As clerical work became more female dominated, it lost status. Women were paid less in these positions, and the ladder to management that existed for men disappeared when women took over these jobs. C. Wright Mills discusses the gender hierarchy within white-collar occupations in his *White Collar: The American Middle Classes* (1951; New York, N.Y.: Oxford University Press, 1956), 74–75. Nationally, the white-collar sector among blacks increased from 8 percent to 13 percent from 1940 to 1960. Skilled blue-collar occupations among black men increased to 10 percent during the same time (Wiese, *Places of Their Own*, 124).

58. When it came to middle-class occupations in 1960, whites and blacks changed places, with 44.1 percent of all whites and 13.4 percent of all blacks (see note 68 for sources).

59. Skilled blacks experienced less discrimination in government employment than in the private sector. This led to an estimated 60 percent of black professionals working in the public sector compared to only 22 percent for whites in 1968. The largest employer of black professionals was the Chicago Board of Education (Baron and Hymer, "The Negro Worker in the Chicago Labor Market," 264–65).

60. U.S. Bureau of Labor Statistics, "Employment and Economic Status of Negroes in the United States" (Washington, D.C.: U.S. Government Printing Office, 1952), 7.

61. Karl E. Taeuber and Alma F. Taeuber, *Negroes in Cities: Residential Segregation and Neighborhood Change* (New York, N.Y.: Atheneum, 1969), 66.

62. A 1941 survey reported that two-thirds of 358 Chicago defense plants refused to hire African Americans (Kerstein, *Race, Jobs, and the War*, 25–26, 43). For a specific example of discrimination in Chicago's aircraft industry, see Dempsey Travis, *An Autobiography of Black Chicago*, 87–89; and Logan, "The Negro Wants First-Class Citizenship," 8. Willard Townsend, black labor leader, reported in 1944, "the vast majority entered war work during the latter half of 1942 and the first quarter of 1943" ("Full Employment and the Negro Worker," *Journal of Negro Education* 14, no. 1 [Winter 1945]: 6). Wendell E. Pritchett, *Robert Clifton Weaver and the American City: The Life and Times of an Urban Reformer* (Chicago, Ill.: University of Chicago Press Press, 2008), 88–115.

63. Commission on Human Relations, *Information on New Migration* (Chicago, Commission on Human Relations, 1952). On blacks' industrial participation in Chicago, see Dorothy M. Powell, "The Negro Worker in Chicago Industry," *Journal of Business of the University of Chicago* 20, no. 1 (January 1947): 24.

64. Weaver, *Negro Labor*, 79, 81. For the limited gains in industrial employment made by black women, see Karen Tucker Anderson, "Last Hired, First Fired: Black Women Workers during World War II," *Journal of American History* 69, no. 1 (June 1982): 82–97.

65. Drake and Cayton, *Black Metropolis*, 288. On skilled positions nationally, see Weaver, *Negro Labor*, 124, 126.

66. Mayor's Commission on Race Relations, *Appendix of the Annual Report of the Mayor's Commission for 1945*, 1945, Box 29, CHS, Chicago Commons Papers. See also Powell, "The Negro Worker in Chicago Industry," 22.

67. Randolph, "March on Washington Movement Presents Program for the Negro," in *What the Negro Wants*, ed. Rayford W. Logan (Chapel Hill, N.C.: University of North Carolina Press, 1944), 133–62.

68. Ibid., 142, 144–45; Drake and Cayton, *Black Metropolis*, 90; William L. O'Neill, *A Democracy at War: America's Fight at Home & Abroad in World War II* (Cambridge, Mass.: Harvard University Press), 238–39. For sources that discuss the significance as

seen by black leaders at the time, see Klinkner, *The Unsteady March*, 151–60; and Andrew Edmund Kerstein, *Race, Jobs, and the War: The FEPC in the Midwest, 1941–1946* (Urbana, Ill.: University of Illinois Press, 2000), 14–18. For an account of Randolph's threat that questioned the benefits gained, see Richard Dalfiume, *Desegregation of the U.S. Armed Forces*, 118–22.

69. Political groups included the local chapters of NAACP, the National Negro Congress, and the March-on-Washington Movement (Drake, "Profiles: Chicago," 267). The National Negro Congress, which held its first meeting in Chicago with 817 delegates from 585 organizations, was organized in 1936. "The Congress grew out of the need for union among the several organizations and has been urging the creation of a United Front in action. Its work goes forward for the full participation of the Negro in the privileges of American democracy" (Charles H. Wesley, "The Negro Has Always Wanted the Four Freedoms," in *What the Negro Wants*, ed. Rayford W. Logan [Chapel Hill: University of North Carolina Press, 1944], 103).

70. CIO unions played an important role in easing workplace integration in Chicago during the war (Powell, "The Negro Worker in Chicago Industry," 31–32).

71. Kerstein, *Race, Jobs, and the War*, 54.

72. Drake, "Profiles: Chicago," 267. There is some disagreement on when blacks were fully employed in Chicago's defense industry. Drake and Cayton asserted that blacks were hired in 1939 (*Black Metropolis*, 289, 288, 297). Most observers pinpoint 1942 as the turning point when blacks were hired by the defense industry (Powell, "The Negro Worker in Chicago Industry," 21, 25–26, 32; Robert Weaver, "Racial Tensions in Chicago," 1943, p. 2, Box 750, Folder Chicago IL, I, RG 207, NAII). The historian Andrew Kerstein argues that discrimination was present in Chicago throughout the war period. Despite persistent labor shortages, he finds employment discrimination in Chicago and other Midwestern cities (Kerstein, *Race, Jobs, and the War*, 43, 44, 48, 52).

73. Drake and Cayton, *Black Metropolis*, 300.

74. Ibid.

75. Blacks had been protesting against their exclusion from municipal transportation jobs since 1931. However, a mass protest campaign in 1943 coordinated by the local branches of the NAACP, the Civil Liberties Committee, the Urban League, and the National Negro Congress and supported by the regional FEPC culminated in the hiring of blacks as platform men, trainmen, and bus drivers (Weaver, *Negro Labor*, 181–86).

76. Kerstein, *Race, Jobs, and the War*, 59.

77. "Nonetheless, World War II still represented a significant upsurge in black political activism, especially in contrast with World War I. Traditional civil rights groups such as the NAACP became more militant. . . . Most importantly, ordinary blacks increasingly became part of the NAACP struggle" (Klinkner, *Unsteady March*, 165–66).

78. Chicago Plan Commission, *Industrial and Commercial Background for Planning Chicago*, 1942, 33, 52.

79. Gregory Squires et al., *Chicago: Race, Class, and the Response to Urban Decline* (Philadelphia, Pa.: Temple University, 1987), 26–27. Evelyn Kitagawa and Donald Bogue argue that the "suburbanization" of manufacturing did not occur until after the industrial expansion of World War II from 1939 to 1947 (see their *Suburbanization of Manufacturing Activity within Standard Metropolitan Areas* [Oxford, Ohio: Scripps Foundation for Research Population Problems, Miami University; and Population Research and Training Center, University of Chicago, 1955], 22).

80. According to Baron and Hymer, the Black Metropolis lost 93,000 jobs between 1957 and 1963. Over the same period, the suburbs gained 72,000 jobs. Moreover, they estimated that African Americans lost 30,000 jobs due to housing segregation. They argue that 117,000 unskilled black workers could have taken jobs in suburban workplaces, if they had not been racially segregated. Although some blacks relocated to the suburbs, they were still racially segregated and excluded from the northwestern suburbs, which experienced the most job growth (Baron and Hymer, "The Negro Worker in the Chicago Labor Market," 275, 284). For a broader discussion of black suburban growth in the Chicago metropolitan area, see Wiese, *Places of Their Own*, 114, 116; on Chicago, see 118–23.

81. John H. Mollenkopf, *The Contested City* (Princeton, N.J.: Princeton University Press, 1983): 20–29; Joel Rast, *Remaking Chicago: The Political Origins of Urban Industrial Change* (DeKalb, Ill.: Northern Illinois University Press, 1999), 4.

82. Jon C. Teaford, *The Rough Road to Renaissance: Urban Revitalization in America, 1940–1985* (Baltimore, Md.: Johns Hopkins University Press, 1990), 11.

83. Milton C. Mumford, "A Review of the Parking Problem with Particular Reference to Chicago," *Urban Land* 6 (June 1947): 3 in Teaford, *Rough Road to Renaissance*, 19. Mumford, who worked for the Marshall Field Company, was one of the architects of redevelopment in Chicago, according to the historian Arnold Hirsch (see Hirsch, *Making a Second Ghetto: Race and Housing, 1940–1960* [Cambridge: Cambridge University Press, 1983]).

84. Teaford, *Rough Road to Renaissance*, 26–29.

85. Ibid., 26.

86. Mollenkopf, *Contested City*, 3, 4.

87. Hirsch, *Making the Second Ghetto*.

2. Racial Democracy and the Case for Public Housing

1. The housing reformer Catherine Bauer and the Labor Housing Conference (LHC) that she led in the mid-1930s rejected means-tested public housing as well as slum clearance and urban redevelopment policies. The LHC considered slum clearance as a scheme for government to subsidize private redevelopment for the narrow interests of real estate capital. The LHC sought government financing for nonprofit, large-scale

housing developments planned with groups of workers and consumers. They advocated for government-provided housing to the broad swath of low- and moderate-income Americans (Resolution by John A. Phillips, President of the Pennsylvania Federation of Labor, *Report of the Proceedings of the Fifty-Fourth Annual Convention of the American Federation of Labor* [Washington, D.C.: Judd and Detweiler, 1934], 580, quoted in Gail Radford, *Modern Housing for America: Policy Struggles in the New Deal Era* [Chicago, Ill.: University of Chicago Press Press, 1996], 180–81). For the evolution of Catherine Bauer's thought about public housing and urban redevelopment see D. Bradford Hunt, *Blueprint for Disaster: The Unraveling of Chicago Public Housing* (Chicago, Ill.: University of Chicago Press Press, 2009), and H. Peter Oberlander and Eva Newbrun, *Houser: The Life and Work of Catherine Bauer* (Vancouver: UBC Press, 1999).

2. Any room occupied by more than 1.5 persons was considered overcrowded (Wayne McMillen, "Public Housing in Chicago, 1946," *Social Service Review* 20, no. 2 [June 1946]: 150).

3. Metropolitan Council, January 1943, 2, Chicago Commons Papers, Box 29, University of Illinois, Chicago (UIC) Library.

4. The formal name for Dickerson's subcommittee report was "the Report of the Subcommittee to Investigate Housing Among Colored People, which was submitted to the city council's Committee on Housing on April 10, 1941." Robert J. Blakely with Marcus Shepard, *Earl B. Dickerson: A Voice For Freedom and Equality* (Evanston, Ill.: Northwestern University Press, 2006), 76, 77.

5. "Our Deplorable Housing Situation," *Chicago Defender*, July 15, 1939; "Demand More Homes for War Plant Workers," *Chicago Defender*, January 15, 1944, 1, 4; Horace R. Cayton, "Negro Housing in Chicago," *Social Action* 6, no. 4 (April 15, 1940): 19.

6. "Demand More Homes for War Plant Workers," 1, 4.

7. "Our Deplorable Housing Situation"; "South Side Housing Ills Laid to Gov't," *Chicago Defender,* December 18, 1943, 1, 2.

8. Horace R. Cayton, "Negroes Live in Chicago: A Short Statement of the Housing Problem in the Black Belt of Chicago," *Opportunity: Journal of Negro Life* 15, no. 12 (December 1937): 366–69; Horace R. Cayton, "No Friendly Voice," *Opportunity: Journal of Negro Life* 16, no. 1 (January 1938): 12–14; Horace R. Cayton, "Negro Housing in Chicago," 4–40; Horace R. Cayton to Claude A. Barnett, October 21, 1937, in Claude A. Barnett (CAB) Papers, Box 346, Folder 3, Chicago Historical Society (CHS).

9. Harold Lawrence, "Negro Rents Higher Than Gold Coast: Housing Expert Tells Council Subcommittee of Exorbitant Rents on South Side," *Daily Record*, July 7, 1939, CHS, Earl Dickerson Papers, Scrapbooks; Robert C. Weaver, "Racial Policy in Public Housing," *Phylon* 1, no. 2 (2nd Quarter 1940): 149–56, 161.

10. Harold Preece, "Dickerson Spurs Drive on Firetraps: Demands South Side Cleanup: New Deal Alderman Pushes Building Inspection, Housing after Tragedy of 7 Killed in Rooming House Blaze," *Daily Record,* April 14, 1939, CHS, Earl Dickerson

Papers, Scrapbooks. At the same time he chaired the city council subcommittee on Negro housing, he also chaired the Chicago Conference on Race Relations' probe on housing ("Chicago Conference on Race Relations Will Take Up the Housing Situation," *News Ledger*, July 22, 1939, CHS, Earl Dickerson Papers, Scrapbooks).

11. "One Toilet for 24 on South Side," *Daily Record*, July 17, 1939, CHS, Earl Dickerson Papers. See also "Bitten by Rats in Slums," *Daily Record*, July 14, 1939, CHS, Earl Dickerson Papers. See Horace R. Cayton, "Negro Housing in Chicago," *Social Action* 6, no. 4 (April 15, 1940): 21–22. On kitchenettes, see "The Chicago Housing Authority: Manager and Builder of Low-Rent Communities, 1938, 1939, 1940," 9, Chicago Housing Authority Library, Chicago.

12. "Our Deplorable Housing Situation," *Chicago Defender*, July 15, 1939.

13. Taylor orchestrated a campaign to create a race relations position within the USHA with the expectation that Robert Weaver would be hired to fill it (see letters from Robert R. Taylor to Robert C. Weaver, September 27 and October 30, 1937, Robert C. Weaver Papers, R-2 microfilm, Schomburg Library Collection, New York Public Library). Wendell Pritchett argues that Taylor was just one of a few black elites who supported Weaver getting the office (*Robert Clifton Weaver and the American City: The Life and Times of an Urban Reformer* [Chicago, Ill.: University of Chicago Press Press, 2008], 79).

14. Devereux Bowly Jr., *The Poorhouse: Subsidized Housing in Chicago, 1895–1976* (Carbondale: Southern Illinois University Press, 1978), 27–29; "Chicago Whites Renew Fight against WPA Negro Housing Project," Associated Negro Press (ANP), July 8, 1936, in CAB Papers, Box 317, Folder 2. See also correspondence between Claude A. Barnett and the Federal Emergency Administration of Public Works, Housing Division, in Washington and the district office in Chicago for the status of "South Park Gardens, Project H-1402" (Barnett to C. A. Inman, District Manager, Housing Division, WPA, Chicago, August 30, 1937; Inman to Barnett, September 1, 1937; and Barnett to H. A. Gray, Director of Housing, Federal Emergency Administration of Public Works, Washington, September 16, 1937, CAB Papers, Box 346, Folder 3); and Cayton, "Negro Housing in Chicago," 32. In 1943, the Ida B. Wells projects represented 41 percent of all the public housing units occupied by blacks in Chicago ("Negroes Will Have 41% of Chicago's Low Cost Housing," ANP, 1943, CAB Papers, Box 351, Folder 2). For other reasons causing the delay see Hunt, *Blueprint for Disaster*, 39–40, and Toure Reed, *Not Alms but Opportunity: The Urban League & The Politics of Racial Uplift, 1910–1950* (Chapel Hill, N.C.: University of North Carolina, 2008), 177–178.

15. "Taylor Studies Defense Housing for 22 Additional Cities," ANP, no date, CAB Papers, Box 351, Folder 2, Chicago Historical Society (CHS). Taylor was a graduate of the Tuskegee Institute and studied architectural engineering at Howard University. He also earned a degree from the University of Illinois and did graduate work at Northwestern University ("Taylor Named on Chicago City Planning Board," ANP, 1942, CAB Papers, Box 351, Folder 2, CHS). During the war, Robert R. Taylor was

transferred from the Division of Defense Housing Coordination to the Office of the Administrator of the National Housing Agency. Not long after the switch to the NHA, Taylor returned to Chicago to chair the Chicago Housing Authority in 1943 (Public Housing Administration [PHA], "The Dream and the Substance: A Short History of Public Housing for Negroes," unpublished report [Washington, D.C.: Public Housing Administration, 1954], 53).

16. PHA, "The Dream and the Substance," 16. This section draws heavily on this unpublished history of African American participation in the public housing program. This history was probably written by the Office of Racial Relations under the auspices of the Public Housing Administration constituent agency of the Housing and Home Finance Agency in 1954. Pritchett, *Robert Clifton Weaver*, 78–80.

17. Ibid., 16, 40, 49.

18. As federal housing agencies evolved, this office was also called the Racial Relations Service, and the advisers were referred to as "racial relations officers." At the time, only African Americans were racial relations advisers, and all black federal housing officials were employed as racial relations advisers. For more on racial relations advisers, see Arnold R. Hirsch, "Containment on the Home Front: Race and Federal Housing Policy from the New Deal to the Cold War," *Journal of Urban History* 26 (January 2000): 158–90; and Arnold R. Hirsch, "Searching for a 'Sound Negro Policy': A Racial Agenda for the Housing Acts of 1949 and 1954," *Housing Policy Debate* 11, no. 2 (2000): 393–441.

19. PHA, "The Dream and the Substance," 16.

20. Ibid., 17.

21. If black workers were not employed in the proportion they constituted in occupations in the local labor market, it was considered prima facie evidence of discrimination.

22. Weaver, "Racial Policy in Public Housing," 152.

23. Ibid., 154. For black labor participation in public housing construction in Chicago, see PHA, "The Dream and the Substance," 20–21, 22. Pritchett, *Robert Clifton Weaver*, 59–60.

24. In 1941, when Frank Horne took over as special assistant, three more regional advisers were appointed including William E. Hill in Region III, which was the Midwest. Hill was based in Chicago (PHA, "The Dream and the Substance," 53). On Frank Horne see Gail Lumet Buckley, *The Hornes: An American Family* (New York, N.Y.: Knopf, 1986).

25. Ibid., 25, 26, 43, 44.

26. Ibid., 27–28.

27. Ibid., 44–45.

28. Subcommittee on Negro Housing report (1940), p. 16, CHS, Earl Dickerson Papers; "Alderman to Attend Parley on Housing Tenancy Rules," *Chicago Daily News,*

July 21, 1939, CHS, Earl Dickerson Papers, Scrapbooks; Cayton, "Negro Housing in Chicago," 36.

29. Subcommittee on Negro Housing report, p. 16; "Alderman to Attend Parley on Housing Tenancy Rules," *Chicago Daily News,* July 21, 1939, CHS, Earl Dickerson Papers, Scrapbooks; Robert Taylor, "Low Rent Housing in America," *Crisis* (1935): 86.

30. Robert C. Weaver, "The Negro in a Program of Public Housing," *Opportunity,* July 1938, 198–203; Weaver, "Racial Policy in Public Housing," 149–56, 161; Robert C. Weaver, *The Negro Ghetto,* 75. See also PHA, "The Dream and the Substance," 18.

31. Robert C. Weaver, "The Relative Status of the Housing of Negroes in the United States," *Journal of Negro Education* 22, no. 3 (Summer, 1953): 343–54. For Weaver's support of public housing throughout his career see Pritchett, *Robert Clifton Weaver.*

32. See chapter 1. See also Preston H. Smith II, "The Chicago School of Human Ecology and Ideology of Black Civic Elites," in *Renewing Black Intellectual History: the Ideological and Material Foundations of Black American Thought* (Boulder, Colo.: Paradigm Press, 2009), 141–47.

33. Horace Cayton typified the thinking of black social scientists who linked slum conditions and social disorganization. For Cayton and others, direct causal connection was not necessary; correlation would do (Cayton, "Negro Housing in Chicago," 25).

34. Taylor, "Low-Rent Housing," 76.

35. Ibid. On spatial determinism, see Smith, "Human Ecology and Black Civic Ideology," 137–38.

36. Subcommittee on Negro Housing report, 8.

37. Ibid., 9–10. Cayton cited a Cook County woman probation officer who reported that in the cases of seventy-two of one hundred black female delinquents charged with "sex offenses," the "kitchenette" was the scene of the delinquent act ("Negro Housing in Chicago," 25).

38. Richard Wright, *Native Son* (1940), quoted in Cayton, "Negro Housing in Chicago," 14. Cayton thought highly of Wright's novel (see Horace R. Cayton, *Long Old Road* [Seattle: University of Washington Press, 1963]).

39. Subcommittee on Negro Housing report, 10.

40. National Urban League, *Racial Problems in Housing,* Interracial Planning for Community Organization, Bulletin No. 2, Fall (New York, N.Y.: National Urban League, 1944), 26.

41. Subcommittee on Negro Housing report, 10.

42. Horace Cayton, "Filthy Black Belts: Nazi Inhumanity to Minorities Has Counterpart in the United States," *Pittsburgh Courier,* January 11, 1947; Subcommittee on Negro Housing report, 10.

43. Weaver, "The Negro in a Program of Public Housing," 200.

44. Reginald A. Johnson, NUL, 1945, 4.

45. Weaver, "The Negro in a Program of Public Housing," 200. Pritchett, *Robert Clifton Weaver*, 80.

46. They both believed that rehabilitating a few row houses in slum neighborhoods or developing small isolated public housing projects was ill advised (Robert Taylor to Robert Weaver, May 31, 1939; Robert Weaver to Robert Taylor, June 2, 1939, both in Robert C. Weaver Papers, R-2 microfilm, Schomburg Library Collection). In 1934, Taylor studied housing in a number of European countries including England, France, Holland, Belgium, Germany, and others ("Taylor Named on Chicago City Planning Board," Associated Negro Press [ANP], 1942, CAB Papers, Box 351, Folder 2, CHS).

47. Subcommittee on Negro Housing report.

48. Ibid.

49. Claude A. Barnett to Miss Elizabeth Wood, April 2, 1940, attached to Wood to Barnett, April 5, 1940, CAB Papers, Box 346, Folder 4, CHS. See also Claude A. Barnett to Dr. F. D. Patterson, Tuskegee Institute, Alabama, February 2, 1949, CAB Papers, Box 346, Folder 5, CHS. To get a sense of the career trajectory and civic bonds of a black public housing manager, see "Chicago's Ida B. Wells Homes Get New Manager," ANP, November 1944, CAB Papers, Box 351, Folder 2, CHS.

50. Leslie Perry memorandum to NAACP branches, November 4, 1949, RG 207, Box 751, NAACP.

51. Al Thompson, "Getting Tenants to Maintain Property," Racial Relations Officers Annual Conference, Washington, D.C., September 12–18, 1953, RG 207, Box 745, FHA—Racial Relations, National Archives (hereafter NAII).

52. Robert C. Weaver, *The Negro Ghetto* (New York, N.Y.: Harcourt, Brace, 1948), 75. "Once a growing number of nonwhite families were exposed to decent, sanitary and desirable dwellings in good neighborhoods, their desire for home ownership increased at a much more rapid rate than the supply" (Robert Weaver's statement on October 28, 1953, RG 207, Box 745, AC-Pres.). Pritchett, *Robert Clifton Weaver*, 85.

53. William E. Hill to Harold A. Odom Sr., Racial Relations Officer, October 6, 1954.

3. Black Factions Contesting Public Housing

1. Racial unity would not have been enough to defeat white opposition to desegregated public housing in Chicago. I stress racial unity here because of the assumptions of a racial democratic ideology that racial unity is necessary for effective political action and to point out that perhaps real racial unity could not have been achieved without adopting an explicit class critique of black public housing opponents.

2. In 1940, Congress passed the Lanham Act, which provided for direct federal funding for war housing. All defense housing activity was placed under the Division of Defense Housing Coordination under the USHA. Two years later, all government housing operations were reorganized under the National Housing Agency (NHA),

at which time the USHA became the Federal Public Housing Authority (FPHA). Government housing was converted from low-rent use to sheltering defense workers during the war (Public Housing Administration [PHA], "The Dream and the Substance: A Short History of Public Housing for Negroes," unpublished report [Washington, D.C.: Public Housing Administration, 1954, 53, RG 196, PHA, Records of Intergroup Relations Branch, 1936–1963, Box 1; John F. Bauman, *Public Housing, Race and Renewal: Urban Planning in Philadelphia, 1920–1974* [Philadelphia: Temple University Press, 1987], 59; Gwendolyn Wright, *Building the Dream: A Social History of Housing in America* [Cambridge, Mass.: The MIT Press, 1981], 242).

3. Devereux Bowly Jr., *The Poorhouse: Subsidized Housing in Chicago, 1895–1976* (Carbondale: Southern Illinois University Press, 1978), 42, 45.

4. Bauman, *Public Housing*, 58. See also chap. 1.

5. PHA, "Dream and Substance," 51.

6. "Call Hearing on Drastic U.S. Housing Curb," *Chicago Defender*, December 11, 1943, 1.

7. Altgeld Gardens (1,500 units) and Brooks Homes (834 units) went to black war workers, not to low-income blacks working in the civilian economy ("Call Hearing," 1).

8. A *Chicago Defender* article reporting on the group referred to them as the "United Committee of War Housing" (Frank A. Young, "Blandford, NHA, Flayed for Housing Shortage," *Chicago Defender*, January 22, 1944, 1, 2). In addition to the initial meeting, an interracial group of civic leaders met with Divers to urge him to push for another public housing project on the South Side ("Citizens Group Urges So. Side Housing Project," *Chicago Defender*, December 18, 1943, 13).

9. Memorandum to Mr. Blandford and Mr. Divers, National Housing Agency, "The Problem of Negro Housing and the Program of the National Housing Agency," January 14, 1944, prepared by Horace R. Cayton and Harry J. Walker, Box 750, Folder Chicago IL, I, RG 207, NAII; "Demand More Homes for War Plant Workers," *Chicago Defender*, January 15, 1944, 1, 4.

10. Cayton and Walker, "Problem of Negro Housing."

11. Ibid.

12. Ibid. The concern about racial violence was widely shared (see Metropolitan Housing Council, January 1943, 3–4, Chicago Commons Papers, Box 29, UIC Library; and PHA, "Dream and Substance," 51).

13. Cayton and Walker, "Problem of Negro Housing."

14. Ibid. The *Defender* reported about the structures that the NHA was converting in the black community for housing ("U.S. Housing Agencies Fighting Slums Here," *Chicago Defender*, November 19, 1944, 2).

15. Cayton and Walker, "Problem of Negro Housing."

16. Ibid.; Arnold R. Hirsch, *Making the Second Ghetto: Race and Housing in Chicago, 1940–1960* (Cambridge: Cambridge University Press, 1983), 13.

17. Bowly, *Poorhouse*, 46; Elizabeth Wood, *The Beautiful Beginnings, The Failure to Learn: Fifty Years of Public Housing in America* (Washington, D.C.: National Center for Housing Management, 1982), 17; Cayton and Walker, "Problem of Negro Housing."

18. Hirsch, *Making the Second Ghetto*, 64.

19. On Lilydale, see Thomas Philpott, *The Slum and the Ghetto: Neighborhood Deterioration and Middle-Class Reform, Chicago, 1880–1930* (New York, N.Y.: Oxford University Press, 1978), 182. What Philpott describes represented many black working-class enclaves outside the city limits that Andrew Wiese documents in his study on black suburbanization (Wiese, *Places of Their Own: African American Suburbanization in the Twentieth Century* [Chicago, Ill.: University of Chicago Press Press, 2005]).

20. *Chicago Bee*, February 27, 1944; March 19, 1944.

21. Ibid., March 5, 1944.

22. "Inventory of Events in the Housing Field of Significance for Human Relations in Chicago, 1945–1948," p. 3, 1948, Box 750, Folder, Chicago IL, I, RG 207, NA II. An observer commented that thirty years later the homes were still "in very good condition . . . , including handsome landscaping . . . [and the] houses fit well in their community, and in fact are larger and of better construction than many of the newer, privately developed houses in the area" (Bowly, *Poorhouse*, 47). At the end of the war, Congress changed its mind about selling the units to the tenants. But "the well-to-do neighbors joined with the occupants in protest. The battle was ultimately won by the occupants, and all but five of the 250 families bought their homes" (Wood, *Beautiful Beginnings*, 17).

23. The *Chicago Bee* was a citywide black weekly published by Anthony Overton, a prominent South Side black business owner.

24. "The West Chesterfield Tempest," *Chicago Bee*, March 12, 1944.

25. *Chicago Bee*, March 19, 1944.

26. Ibid., February 27, 1944.

27. "West Chesterfield Tempest."

28. *Chicago Bee*, February 27, 1944. An attorney by training, Oscar Brown Sr. was named manager of Ida B. Wells from its inception in 1941. He had taken on the additional job of managing Altgeld Gardens at the time his comment appeared in the *Chicago Bee* ("Chicago's Ida B. Wells Homes Get New Manager," Claude A. Barnett [CAB] Papers, Box 351, Folder 2, CHS).

29. Reported in a meeting on March 2, 1944. See *Chicago Bee*, March 19, 1944.

30. Four years later, Robert Weaver referred to the situation as an instance of black class discrimination in his study (Weaver, *The Negro Ghetto* [New York: Harcourt, Brace, 1948], 347).

31. *Chicago Bee*, April 2, 1944.

32. Ibid., September 3, 1944.

33. Ibid., February 27, 1944.

34. "West Chesterfield Tempest."

35. *Chicago Bee*, February 2, 1944.

36. Ibid., April 23, 1944.

37. Ibid., April 9, 1944.

38. Ibid.

39. Ibid.

40. Chicago Housing Authority, "The Tenth Year of the Chicago Housing Author-ity" (Chicago, Ill.: Chicago Housing Authority, 1947), 14, 38, CHA Library. See also Chicago Housing Authority, "The Chicago Housing Authority Reports for 1948" (Chicago, Ill.: Chicago Housing Authority, 1948), 10, CHA Library.

41. "Fewer than 100,000 housing units were built by USHA by the time the U.S. entered WWII" (Mark I. Gelfand, *A Nation of Cities: The Federal Government and Urban America, 1933–1945* [New York: Oxford University Press, 1975], 122).

42. See Marc A. Weiss, "The Origins and Legacy of Urban Renewal," in *Urban and Regional Planning in an Age of Austerity,* ed. Pierre Clavel, John Forrester, and William W. Goldsmith (New York, N.Y.: Pergamon Press, 1980), 53–79; and Charles Abrams, *The City Is the Frontier* (New York, N.Y.: Harper Colophon Books, 1967), 84, 85. See also A. Scott Henderson, *Housing and the Democratic Ideal: The Life and Thought of Charles Abrams* (New York, N.Y.: Columbia University Press, 2000), 201.

43. Martin Meyerson and Edward C. Banfield, *Politics, Planning and the Public Interest: The Case of Public Housing in Chicago* (Glencoe, Ill.: Free Press, 1955); Hirsch, *Making the Second Ghetto*; D. Bradford Hunt, *Blueprint for Disaster: The Unraveling of Chicago Public Housing* (Chicago, Ill.: University of Chicago Press Press, 2009), 84–91.

44. Hunt, *Blueprint for Disaster*, 84.

45. Meyerson and Banfield, *Politics,* 175.

46. *Chicago Sun-Times*, December 27, 1949, quoted in Meyerson and Banfield, *Politics, Planning and the Public Interest*, 178–79.

47. Ibid.

48. On the opposition to the land clearance for the Dearborn project, see Hunt, *Blueprint for Disaster*, 79. Hunt comments that the income of the majority of those displaced exceeded $2,150, the income ceiling for public housing. He was surprised to find that over 30 percent made more than $3,000. On the opposition to the Lake Meadows redevelopment project, see chap. 4.

49. *Chicago Sun-Times*, December 27, 1949, quoted in Meyerson and Banfield, *Politics*, 178–79.

50. On the Douglass community, which was also the future site of the Lake Meadows project, see Louis Wirth and Eleanor H. Bernert, eds., *Local Community Fact Book of Chicago* (Chicago, Ill.: University of Chicago Press Press, 1949); Philip M. Hauser and Evelyn M. Kitagawa, eds., *Local Community Fact Book for Chicago 1950* (Chicago, Ill.:

Chicago Community Inventory, 1953), 146–49; and Evelyn M. Kitagawa and Karl E. Taeuber, eds., *Local Community Fact Book: Chicago Metropolitan Area, 1960* (Chicago, Ill.: Chicago Community Inventory, University of Chicago, 1963), 84–85.

51. Black middle-class activists would wage a losing fight against slum clearance, which preceded but was linked to the public housing program in the Second Ward. Harvey was opposed to slum clearance (see chap. 4), but like many black civic elites and middle-class home owners, he favored black-led redevelopment and conservation that featured slum rehabilitation (see chap. 6).

52. Meyerson and Banfield, *Politics, Planning and the Public Interest*, 175; *Chicago Sun-Times*, December 27, 1949, quoted in Meyerson and Banfield, *Politics, Planning and the Public Interest*, 178–79. For William Harvey's subsequent support for slum sites see Hunt, *Blueprint for Disaster*, 93–93, 110, 112.

53. These arguments reflected some of the opposition to government-provided war housing by many affluent black West Chesterfield home owners (see earlier) (Meyerson and Banfield, *Politics*, 198). FHA housing for blacks was constructed in Morgan Park (Weaver, *Negro Ghetto*, 96). See also Hirsch, *Making the Second Ghetto*, 3, 4; and Hauser and Kitagawa, eds., *Local Community Fact Book for Chicago 1950*, 306. Kitagawa and Taeuber, eds., *Local Community Fact Book*, 164–65.

54. Meyerson and Banfield, *Politics*, 196–98; Hirsch, *Making the Second Ghetto*, 226.

55. Hirsch cited opposition from Robert C. Weaver, the Urban League, and the *Chicago Defender* to the city's plan (see Robert C. Weaver to Wayne McMillen, December 12, 1950, Louis Wirth Papers, UC Archives; Chicago Urban League, "League's Position on Proposed Compromise Housing Sites," n.d., Chicago Urban League Papers; and *Chicago Defender*, April 29, May 6, 1950, all quoted in Hirsch, *Making the Second Ghetto*, 226–27, 339n38.

56. Meyerson and Banfield, *Politics*, 199–200, 205.

57. Ibid., 229–30.

58. Ibid., 233–34, 221, 175.

59. Memorandum from Frank S. Horne, Racial Relations Service, to Raymond M. Foley, Administrator, "Proposed Public Housing Program in Chicago," August 14, 1950, attached to Neal J. Hardy, Operations Analysis to Frank S. Horne, Assistant to the Administrator, Racial Relations Service, "Low-Rent Housing Sites, Chicago, Illinois," November 16, 1950 in NA, HHFA Papers, RG 207, Box 41.

60. Ibid.

61. Meyerson and Banfield, *Politics*, 238, 242–46.

62. Horne to Foley, "Letter and Memorandum to the Mayor of Chicago, October 18, 1951, NA, RG 207, Box 53, Racial Relations Folder; Meyerson and Banfield, *Politics*, 246.

63. "Taylor Resigns as Head of Chicago Housing Authority," Associated Negro Press (ANP), September 27, 1950. Frank Horne expressed his concern about the

"implications of the recent resignation of the Chairman of the Chicago Housing Authority," an ally (Frank S. Horne to Raymond M. Foley, "Proposed Public Housing Program in Chicago," October 16, 1950, attached to Hardy to Horne, November 16, 1950). Horne sent copies of the August 14 and October 16, 1950, memos to Franklin Thorne, Racial Relations Branch, PHA, on October 16 (Frank S. Horne to Franklin Thorne, October 16, 1950).

64. "Taylor Resigns." James Q. Wilson wrote that Taylor was "successful in business and sought after by whites both as a private adviser and a public servant." Furthermore, "no one is in the position of having almost all civic issues affecting housing of Negroes referred to him for advice or direction—as Taylor did. Today no single Negro is preeminent in this field and a number of Negroes, none with Taylor's qualifications, now serve in this representative capacity." Taylor died seven years later (Wilson, *Negro Politics: The Search for Leadership* [Glencoe, Ill.: Free Press, 1960], 267).

65. Wilson, *Negro Politics*, 105, 185–88, 197.

4. Fighting "Negro Clearance"

1. St. Clair Drake and Horace R. Cayton, *Black Metropolis: A Study of Negro Life in a Northern City* (New York, N.Y.: Harcourt, Brace, 1945), 114–15.

2. For the divided opinion regarding those privileged blacks who elected to leave the ghetto, see James Q. Wilson, *Negro Politics: The Search for Leadership* (New York, N.Y.: Free Press, 1960), 198. The historian Andrew Wiese captures this diversity of opinion on the question of black suburbanization well in his *Places of Their Own: African American Suburbanization in the Twentieth Century* (Chicago, Ill.: University of Chicago Press Press, 2005), 129–32, 157–59.

3. Drake and Cayton, *Black Metropolis*, 113–14, 196.

4. Horace R. Cayton, "Negroes Live in Chicago: A Short Statement of the Housing Problem in the Black Belt of Chicago," *Opportunity: Journal of Negro Life* 15, no. 12 (December 1937): 366–69; Horace R. Cayton, "No Friendly Voice," *Opportunity: Journal of Negro Life* 16, no. 1 (January 1938): 12–14; Horace R. Cayton, "Negro Housing in Chicago," *Social Action* 6, no. 4 (April 15, 1940): 4–40; Horace R. Cayton to Claude A. Barnett, October 21, 1937, in Claude A. Barnett (CAB) Papers, Box 346, Folder 3, Chicago Historical Society (CHS).

5. Cayton, "No Friendly Voice," 13; Cayton, "Negro Housing in Chicago," 31.

6. "The Chicago Urban League Prospectus 1947," National Urban League (NUL) Papers, Administration Department, Affiliates File, Box 84, Folder 2, "1948, Chicago, Illinois, Chicago Urban League."

7. Sidney Williams to Oscar C. Brown, March 10, 1947, Chicago Urban League (CUL) Papers, Folder 703, University of Illinois at Chicago (UIC); "The Chicago Urban League Prospectus 1947."

8. "Community Council Told Housing Plan: Commission Head Fails to Explain Possibility of 'Restriction,'" *Chicago Defender*, February 7, 1942. See also "Kincaid to Discuss Southside Redevelopment," *Chicago Defender*, January 24, 1942.

9. National Urban League, *Racial Problems in Housing*, Interracial Planning for Community Organization, Bulletin No. 2, Fall (New York, N.Y.: National Urban League, 1944), 23. See also Wilson, *Negro Politics*, 152–53.

10. National Urban League, *Racial Problems in Housing*, 24.

11. Ibid.

12. Avarah Strickland, *History of Chicago Urban League* (Urbana, Ill.: University of Illinois Press, 1966).

13. "The Chicago Urban League Prospectus 1947."

14. In 1950, the construction sector in Chicago employed 5,600 nonwhites, only 2.9 percent of all employed nonwhites, compared to 66,146 whites, or 4.1 percent of all employed whites (Table 9, in *Local Community Fact Book for Chicago, 1950*, 8).

15. "The Chicago Urban League Prospectus 1947," Sidney Williams to Oscar C. Brown, March 10, 1947.

16. Ibid. The role of dual interpretation—combating racial discrimination while confronting social disorganization among black migrants—has long been a feature of the Urban League's traditional race relations work (see Preston H. Smith II, "The Limitations of Racial Democracy: The Politics of Chicago Urban League, 1916–40" [PhD diss., University of Massachusetts, Amherst, 1990]).

17. "The Chicago Urban League Prospectus 1947," Sidney Williams to Oscar C. Brown, March 10, 1947.

18. Robert C. Weaver to Sidney R. Williams, April 3, 1947, CUL Papers, Folder 703, University of Illinois at Chicago (UIC), University Library, Department of Special Collections.

19. Weaver to Williams, April 3, 1947. The historian Mark Gelfand explains the distinction between the economic concept of "blight" and the social concept of "slums." A blighted neighborhood could have standard housing, but still not be profitable due to an inability to sell or rent at a profit; slums, on the other hand, contain substandard housing, which could be profitable through exploitation (Gelfand, *A Nation of Cities: The Federal Government and Urban America, 1933–1945* [New York: Oxford University Press, 1975], 109).

20. A year after his exchange with Williams, Weaver affirmed a similar plan presented by Oscar Brown. The chief difference for Weaver between the two plans was that Williams's plan seemed piecemeal. In Brown's plan, the city would clear the slums, and only the redeveloped housing would be designed, owned, and occupied by the current residents, almost all black Americans. Of course, the major drawback in Brown's plan and subsequent plans for black-led redevelopment was the lack of

capital that I discuss in chapter 6 (Robert C. Weaver, *The Negro Ghetto* [New York: Harcourt, Brace, 1948], 335).

21. Ibid., 312. Wendell Pritchett, *Robert Clifton Weaver and the American City: The Life and Times of an Urban Reformer* (Chicago, Ill.: University of Chicago Press Press, 2008), 145–46.

22. Ibid., 324. Of all the black national and civic elites, only Robert Weaver used the term "racial democratic," which he used to describe racially integrated neighborhoods and housing. I have broadened Weaver's use of the term to define an ideological position that African Americans' democratic or equal access to public goods and private opportunities should not be hindered, but it could be helped, by their race.

23. Earlier, before the war began, Cayton had also commented on the lack of interest on the part of private capital in building for all blacks, especially upper-income blacks (Cayton, "Negro Housing in Chicago," 36).

24. Weaver, *Negro Ghetto*, 312, 324, 330, 316–17, 312, 338–39.

25. Ibid., 319.

26. Ibid., 312.

27. Ibid., 323, 312, 318–19.

28. Ibid., 312, 326–27.

29. Ibid., 333, 328, 331, 334, 335, 330.

30. Arnold R. Hirsch, *Making the Second Ghetto: Race and Housing in Chicago, 1940–1960* (Cambridge: Cambridge University Press, 1983), chapter 4.

31. Reginald R. Issacs, Planning Director, Michael Reese Hospital, "Urban Development," second draft of an address to Citizens' Governmental Research Bureau of Milwaukee, December 10, 1948, pp. 2, 3, 4, 6, MHPC Papers, Acc. 75–104, Box 13, Folder 7, UIC.

32. Ibid.

33. MHPC, "Interim Report on Post War Planning and Housing."

34. Philip M. Klutznick, "Urban Redevelopment," address to United States Conference of Mayors, January 20, 1947, p. 4, MHPC Papers, Acc. 75–104, Box 13, Folder 7, UIC; Hirsch, *Making the Second Ghetto*, 102–4.

35. Chicago Plan Commission, *Master Plan of Residential Land Use of Chicago*, Chicago, 1943, 74, cited in Jack M. Siegel, "Slum Prevention—A Public Purpose," MHPC Papers, Acc. 74–20, Box 23, Folder 1, UIC.

36. The Metropolitan Housing [and Planning] Council was formed in 1934. It added "planning" to its title in 1949 (Hirsch, *Making the Second Ghetto*, 103, 278). See also Grace E. Morris, "Why Slums?" January 1941, MHPC Papers, Acc. 75–104, Box 14, Folder 2, UIC; "An Opportunity for Private and Public Investment in Rebuilding Chicago" 1947, 58, MHPC Papers, Acc. 74–20, Box 21, Folder 240, UIC.

37. These organizations include Illinois Institute of Technology, Michael Reese Hospital, South Side Planning Board, Metropolitan Housing [and Planning] Council,

Pace Associates, Architects, and Chicago Housing Authority ("An Opportunity for private and public investment in rebuilding Chicago" 1947, 14, MHPC Papers, Acc. 74–20, Box 21, Folder 240, UIC; Hirsch, *Making the Second Ghetto*, 117).

38. "An Opportunity for Private and Public Investment in Rebuilding Chicago."

39. Ibid.; Hirsch, *Making the Second Ghetto*, 117.

40. An important concession won by progrowth elites was the latitude regarding the ways in which redeveloped land could be used, including for commercial purposes. Housing reformers had insisted that slum clearance was legitimate only when it was used to produce modern housing (Gelfand, *Nation of Cities*, 144).

41. "An Opportunity for Private and Public Investment in Rebuilding Chicago," 1–12.

42. Ibid., 25, 32, 33.

43. Ibid., 40.

44. The groundbreaking ceremony for Lake Meadows took place on February 18, 1952, and was attended by Congressman William Dawson; Truman K. Gibson Sr.; Robert Merriam, chairman of the city council Housing Committee; and Nathaniel S. Keith, director of the federal Division of Slum Clearance and Urban Redevelopment agency of HHFA. The 101-acre site extended from Thirty-First to Thirty-Fifth Streets, South Parkway to Illinois Central Railroad. The residential buildings were to cover 15 percent of the site while the rest would be devoted to recreation. The Chicago Land Clearance Commission condemned and acquired the land. Acquisition costs were estimated at $14.1 million, of which $4.7 million came from city and state funds, leaving the remaining $9.4 million to be reimbursed by the federal government. The first parcel was sold to New York Life Insurance Company for almost $49,000; the company was to pay $28 million in construction costs (Chicago Land Clearance Commission press release, February 11, 1952, CAB Papers, Box 351, Folder 2; Chicago Land Clearance Commission press releases, February 13 and 18, 1952, CAB Papers, Box 351, Folder 1).

45. Issacs, "Urban Development." MHPC, "Interim Evaluation of Chicago's Housing and Redevelopment Program."

46. See chapter 3.

47. "Oppose Subsidy for Private Homes Project," *Chicago Defender*, September 4, 1948, 1, 2.

48. "An Opportunity for Private and Public Investment in Rebuilding Chicago," 48–50, 56.

49. Herbert A. Simon, "What Is Urban Redevelopment?" reprint from *Illinois Tech Engineer*, December 1946, MHPC Papers, Acc. 75–104, Box 13, Folder 7, UIC.

50. Klutznick, "Urban Redevelopment."

51. Elizabeth Wood, "Realities of Urban Redevelopment," *Journal of Housing* (January 1946), MHPC Papers, Acc. 75–104, Box 13, Folder 7, UIC.

52. Ibid.

53. Ibid.; Reginald R. Issacs, "Panel on Criteria for the Selection of Initial Redevelopment Areas," draft (undated), 4, MHPC Papers, Acc. 75–104, Box 13, Folder 7, UIC.

54. Wilson, *Negro Politics*, 185.

55. Of course, this is after conceding the progrowth urban redevelopment program in the first place. A social democratic program would have asserted more public control rather than simply providing a public subsidy, perhaps making sure that moderate- and low-income blacks (and whites), and not just the poorest of the poor, would have new housing and community facilities. Note the Labor Housing Conference's opposition to slum clearance and redevelopment in the 1937 housing act (Gail Radford, *Modern Housing for America: Policy Struggles in the New Deal Era* [Chicago, Ill.: University of Chicago Press Press, 1996]; Alexander von Hoffman, "A Study in Contradictions: The Origins and Legacy of the Housing Act of 1949," *Housing Policy Debate* 11, no. 2 [2000]: 301); D. Bradford Hunt, *Blueprint for Disaster: The Unraveling of Chicago Public Housing* (Chicago, Ill.: University of Chicago Press Press, 2009), 24.

56. The idea that redeveloped housing would be for middle-class blacks, not white downtown workers was first broached by H. E. Kincaid of the Chicago Plan Commission in 1942 ("Community Council Told Housing Plan: Commission Head Fails to Explain Possibility of 'Restriction,'" *Chicago Defender*, February 7, 1942). See also "Kincaid to Discuss Southside Redevelopment," *Chicago Defender*, January 24, 1942. Kincaid's pronouncement came five years *before* the Miles Colean study, which asserted that redeveloped housing for affluent black occupancy, like an affluent white project, would "remove slums, 'anchor' the Loop, and provide new infusions of money into the central city" (Hirsch, *Making the Second Ghetto*, 106).

57. Preston H. Smith II, "The Quest for Racial Democracy: Black Civic Ideology and Housing Interests in Postwar Chicago," *Journal of Urban History* 26, no. 2 (January 2000): 131–57.

58. George Nesbitt interpreted this ambiguous "advice" as black politicians' interest in maintaining segregation (Nesbitt, "Break up the Black Ghetto?" *Crisis*, February 1949, 49–50).

59. Ibid., 49–50. The same placards were in evidence at a meeting sponsored by Chicago Council of Negro Organizations. The meeting was planned for Metropolitan Community Church, Thursday, October 30, 1947, 8:00 p.m. ("Hear the Truth by Speakers with a Message," MHPC Papers, Box 17, Folder 2, UIC). The MHPC, which was in favor of the redevelopment program, tracked opposition in the black community.

60. "'Negro Clearance' Foes Praise Defender's Forum on Housing," *Chicago Defender* (national edition), April 17, 1948, 20.

61. Quoted from Notes on the Annual Dinner of the Chicago Council of Negro Organizations, June 26, 1950, Irene McCoy Gaines Papers, CHS, in Hirsch, *Making the Second Ghetto*, 125.

62. "Citizen's Group Act in Housing Crisis," *Chicago Defender*, March 7, 1948.

63. The protest that good housing was being targeted while slum housing ignored revealed, as Milton Mumford and other architects of Chicago's program had feared, that a primary aim of demolition was to clear the view of the lake (Hirsch, *Making the Second Ghetto*, 125).

64. "Informa. on New York Protest," MHPC Papers, Box 17, Folder 2, UIC, Dept. of Special Collections. On black politicians' position on slum clearance, see Hirsch, *Making the Second Ghetto*, 129–30.

65. "100 Negroes Protest at Being Moved from Homes," *Southeast Economist*, August 9, 1948, news clipping in MHPC Papers, Acc. 74–20, Box 23, Folder 2, UIC.

66. Nesbitt, "Break up the Black Ghetto?" 50.

67. Ibid.

68. Nesbitt reported on private sentiment of black leaders against residential dispersion (ibid., 50).

69. Alice C. Browning was the daughter of a minister. She was educated in Chicago's public schools including Englewood High School. She graduated from the University of Chicago in 1931. Browning, as founder and editor of the *Negro Story*, a magazine for short stories by and about African Americans, was captured in a photo in the November 1946 issue of *Ebony* magazine. The caption read: "Two editors talk business at the lawn party. They are Alice Browning of *Negro Story* and Frank Marshall Davis of the Associated Negro Press" (Bill V. Mullen, *Popular Fronts: Chicago and African-American Cultural Politics, 1935–1946* [Urbana: University of Illinois Press, 1999], 106–7. I would like to thank Bill for sharing his materials on Alice Browning with me).

70. There are a few surviving primary documents about the black neighborhood opposition that might give us some insight into these groups. Most of the documents referred to or were produced by an apparently short-lived group called "the Champions." George Nesbitt named two groups of black women called the Champions and the Vigilantes in his "Break up the Ghetto?" 50. A handbill of a mass protest meeting at city hall probably in March 1948 included a number of neighborhood groups (Hirsch, *Making the Second Ghetto*, 126). Mullen highlights Browning's middle-class background and commitments when depicting her involvement in the *Negro Story* with more radical black colleagues (see *Popular Fronts*, 109).

71. Irene McCoy Gaines appeared to be the only African American professional woman who was a member of the SSPB. This was not an anomaly during this period. Very few black women were publicly involved in housing policy work in Chicago. This fact reflects the sexism of the era when it came to deciding which individuals would play visible roles in housing analysis and advocacy within the black community.

72. "Break up the Black Ghetto?" 50.

73. Apparently this was not a unanimous position. Nesbitt reported that one of the Champions dismissed the idea of whites moving into congested areas and remarked that "Negroes are not going to risk their lives for integration." This view could be interpreted as less a rebuke of integration as a goal than a pragmatic response to whites' violent resistance to integration (Nesbitt, "Break up the Black Ghetto?" 50).

74. Ibid.

75. As property owners this stratum was actually in the best position to afford the rents at Lake Meadows. Milton Mumford found black opposition's response reflective of a "natural fear," which, according to him, was "unfounded" (Hirsch, *Making the Second Ghetto*, 125).

76. The South Side Housing Action Conference had a conference for more than fifty directors of community organizations on March 6, 1948, at the Metropolitan Community Church. The organization planned to take up the question of relocation at this meeting. George Nesbitt, regional housing official based in Chicago, presented a pro-slum clearance viewpoint at the meeting (*Chicago Defender* [national edition], March 7, 1948, 12; George B. Nesbitt, "A Southsider Looks at the Slum Clearance-Redevelopment Program," address presented to the South Side Housing Action Conference, March 6, 1948, RG 207, Box 750, Chicago, Illinois, I, National Archives; Nesbitt, "Break up the Ghetto?" 50; *Champions' Weekly News*, in Folder 193, "The Champions," CUL Papers, UIC).

77. Alice C. Browning's notes and handwritten Bulletin #1, February 1948, in Folder 193, "The Champions," CUL Papers, UIC.

78. Browning's notes and handwritten Bulletin #1, February 1948.

79. Ibid.

80. Ibid.

81. Browning's notes and handwritten Bulletin 1, February 1948. Alice C. Browning, "Plan for Slum Clearance and Reclaming the South Side's Blighted Areas" in Folder 193, "The Champions," CUL Papers, UIC. At the time, Woodlawn included a stable black middle-class enclave. In 1950, African Americans comprised over 98 percent of the population in census tracts 623, 624, and 625 between South Parkway and Cottage Grove avenues, between Sixtieth and Sixty-Seventh Streets. The percentage of professional and technical workers was 7 to 8 percent, mirroring the citywide average. However, owner-occupied housing ranged from 11 percent to 25 percent, way above the citywide average for nonwhites. Some of these figures reflect the fact that these areas probably absorbed more working-class blacks displaced by slum clearance (*Local Community Fact Book for Chicago, 1950*, 175). The only other evidence of concern for black tenants who would be ineligible for economic reasons was an apparently fringe left-wing group that called itself the Negro Protection Association (see Helen Sharples, "The New York City Housing Predicament," *Protector*

[The Negro Protective Association], Newsletter 2, vol. 1 [January 15, 1949], Folder 193, "The Champions," CUL papers, UIC).

82. If the 2 percent figure is correct, it suggests that a sizable section of the black middle class was excluded; it would also explain their activism (Phil Klutznick of the Illinois State Housing Board on "Memo on public hearing on the opposition to the N.Y. Life Site—3/22/49," MHPC Papers).

83. *Champions' Weekly News*, Folder 193, "The Champions," CUL Papers, UIC.

84. This happened at a mass protest meeting in March 1948 that was sponsored by, in addition to the Park Lake Council and the Champions, the South Side Property Owners Association, the Neighborhood Civic Improvement Club, Englewood Citizens Protective Association, Property Owners Associations, 43rd Civic Block Organization, Youth Champions, R. A. Crulley Block Club, Joanna Snowden Council, Southside Housing Committee (handbill from CUL Papers, Manuscript Collection, UIC Library, in Hirsch, *Making the Second Ghetto*, 126). On the neighborhood, see Table 5, 159.

85. William Hill's presence at this meeting suggests that he was there to learn about the opposition's position. As the SSPB director of community relations, he both educated his white colleagues about the neighborhood's opposition as well as sought "assurances" about black home owners' compensation and the relocation of black tenants from the businessmen and planners who dominated the planning board. The meeting took place in late March after Hill wrote his memo to SSPB executive council earlier in the month (Hill, "An Effective Community Relations Program for the South Side Planning Board").

86. Lane's paternalistic attitude toward the Champions' black female leadership was probably representative of the black male housing analysts that they encountered around housing policy issues.

87. Statement made to the meetings of the Champions—March 25, 1948 by F. T. Lane, Folder 193, "The Champions," CUL Papers, UIC. Lane was sympathetic to the CUL executive secretary's self-help rehabilitation plan in 1947. His plan, however, sounds more like Oscar Brown's plans related by Robert Weaver. In both of their schemes, redevelopment was black led and black owned (Weaver, *Negro Ghetto*, 335).

88. Hill "An Effective Community Relations Program for the South Side Planning Board"; Nesbitt, "A Southsider Looks at the Slum Clearance-Redevelopment Program"; Nesbitt, "Break up the Black Ghetto?" 50.

89. See also Wilson, *Negro Politics*, 120.

90. Hill explained that only one of twenty black families owned their own homes. In the designated site for slum clearance, 6.2 percent of the housing units were owner occupied in 1940, a little more than one in twenty. In 1950, the percentage had grown to 8.1 percent of all nonwhite housing units (Tables A, G, and D, in *Local Community Fact Book of Chicago*; Tables 1, 9, and 10, in *Local Community Fact Book for Chicago, 1950*).

91. Nesbitt cited a report of a public meeting where a "heckler" who said he owned the largest kitchenette building in the area claimed he would defend his property with "shotguns." Although the "heckler's" race was not specified, given the fact that Nesbitt was analyzing black opposition, it is safe to assume he was black. Nesbitt's commentary helps to document those African Americans who made or supplemented their living by renting property (Nesbitt, "Break up the Black Ghetto?" 50, 52; Nesbitt, "A Southside Looks at the Slum Clearance-Redevelopment Program").

92. Thornton's constituency was narrower than that of the Champions, and his legalistic approach differed from their protest style, but they sought to achieve the same goals (William F. Thornton, president of the Property Conservation Commission, to "All Property Owners from 31st to 35th Streets, and from South Parkway to the Lake," "Plans for Legal Defense for Protection of All Property Owners Subject to Slum Clearance," November 9, 1948, in Carey Papers, Chicago Historical Society). Almost exactly two years later, Thornton and his group were still fighting. They opposed closing of Cottage Grove Avenue from Twenty-Sixth to Thirty-Fifth Streets in order "that no street will pass through the Housing Project contemplated by the New York Life Insurance Company" (William F. Thornton to Sidney Williams, November 8, 1950, CUL Papers, UIC, Department of Special Collections).

93. Phil Klutznick of the Illinois State Housing Board on "Memo on public hearing on the opposition to the N.Y. Life Site—3/22/49," MHPC Papers, UIC. Not all lost out in the aftermath of slum clearance, according to Wilson. He reports that a black minister was able to save his church by appealing to the city officials. Wilson comments that "other aspects of the plan, which touched Negroes but not Negro members of his church, did not concern him" (Wilson, *Negro Politics*, 130). Ultimately, black property owners' bid to render Illinois redevelopment law unconstitutional failed when the U.S. Supreme Court failed to consider the case in October 1952 ("Chicago Property Owners Lose High Court Fight to Block Slum Clearance," *Chicago Defender* [national edition], October 25, 1952, 5).

94. Wilson discusses how the value of racial unity often compels a single racial interest that does not tolerate other interpretations (*Negro Politics*, 174, 181).

95. See chapter 6.

96. The black leaders who were members of the SSPB represented communitywide organizations and businesses such as Supreme Liberty Life (largest black-owned business in the northern United States), local chapters of the Urban League and NAACP, the Woodlawn AME Church, the Negro Chamber of Commerce, and the Council of Negro Organizations. The SSPB also had black representation on staff. The first two directors of community relations were African American. Harry J. Walker, who had coauthored a report with Horace Cayton for the United Committee on Emergency Housing in 1944, was the first SSPB community relations director. He was succeeded by William E. Hill in February 1948. It was not a coincidence that the directors of

community relations were both African American and housing experts. It was clear that part of their job was to interpret black concerns about the city's program to their colleagues, but at the end of the day their task was to sell that program to black home owners and tenants who were going to be displaced by the city's bulldozers (South Side Planning Board, "Prospectus," 9, 10, MHPC Papers, Acc. 75–104, Box 26, Folder 8). There is more evidence about the role black civic elites played in selling Chicago's urban redevelopment program to black "publics" in the Mid-South Side community (Wilford Winholtz to Raymond M. Foley, July 7, 1948, attached to B. T. Fitzpatrick to Wilford Winholtz, July 15, 1948, National Archives, RG 207, HHFA Subject Files, Box 18, Racial Relations, Jun.–Dec. 1948; Hill, "An Effective Community Relations Program for the South Side Planning Board").

97. Its power notwithstanding, the SSPB board gave evidence that broad support existed for the city's redevelopment program in business circles. Its membership consisted of mainly businessmen who considered civic responsibility to be good for business (South Side Planning Board, "Prospectus," 9, 10, MHPC Papers, Acc. 75–104, Box 26, Folder 8).

98. The SSPB was the public face of redevelopment, according to Hirsch, and the forces behind Chicago's redevelopment program were downtown financial and retail elites (Hirsch, *Making the Second Ghetto*, 117, 101).

99. While Horne does not identify Sidney Williams by name, the language he quotes reflected the CUL's executive secretary in language that prefaced his self-help rehabilitation plan (Frank S. Horne to Earl Von Storch, director, Urban Studies Staff, May 14, 1948, RG 207, HHFA, Box 18, Race Relations 1947). The summer brought more mass protests including delegations besieging Mayor Kennelly's office. The SSPB director, Wilfred Winholtz, with the support of the CUL, requested that Frank Horne and fellow HHFA racial relations adviser Booker McGraw come to Chicago to help address the "confusion" that the black community must be suffering since they failed to realize that slum clearance and redevelopment were in their interest (Wilford Winholtz to Raymond M. Foley, July 7, 1948, attached to B. T. Fitzpatrick to Wilford Winholtz, July 15, 1948, National Archives, RG 207, HHFA Subject Files, Box 18, Racial Relations, Jun.–Dec. 1948).

100. Frank S. Horne to Earl Von Storch, Director, Urban Studies Staff, May 14, 1948, RG 207, HHFA, Box 18, Race Relations, 1947.

101. Nesbitt, "A Southsider Looks at the Slum Clearance-Redevelopment Program."

102. George B. Nesbitt was from Champaign, Illinois, where he graduated from the University of Illinois. He began working for the Public Housing Administration (PHA) in 1942. In 1946, he was race relations advisor for the PHA at the Chicago regional office of the National Housing Agency. In February 1950, Nesbitt was reassigned to the national office. He was replaced by William Hill, who during the slum clearance conference was community relations officer for the SSPB and on the housing committee of the Chicago Urban League. In 1955, Nesbitt transferred to the Urban

Renewal Division of the Housing and Home Finance Agency as a race relations adviser to the division's commissioner. The following year he won the Littauer Fellowship for a year of graduate study in public administration at Harvard University. Nesbitt was a member of the American Society of Planning Officials, the National Association of Housing and Redevelopment Officials, and the National Association of Intergroup Relations Officials ("Discrimination Key Factor in Bogged Down Housing Program," *Chicago Defender* [national edition], September 21, 1946, 7; "Up and at 'Em," *Chicago Defender* [national edition], November 12, 1949, 6; "Deadline for Discrimination," *Chicago Defender* [national edition], February 25, 1950, 6; "In and out the Window," *Chicago Defender* [national edition], November 5, 1955, 2; "George Nesbitt Wins Graduate Study Grant," *Chicago Defender* [national edition], August 18, 1956, 10).

103. Hill, "An Effective Community Relations Program for the South Side Planning Board"; Nesbitt, "A Southsider Looks at the Slum Clearance-Redevelopment Program." See Nesbitt, "Break up the Black Ghetto?" 50.

104. Nesbitt, "A Southsider Looks at the Slum Clearance-Redevelopment Program." In another context, Nesbitt described the typical individual in these groups as a man who made his gains "in a most rugged fashion since he overcame the added racial barriers to attain his status. He appreciates what he has and is" ("Break up the Black Ghetto?" 50).

105. Nesbitt, "Break up the Black Ghetto?" 50.

106. Hill "An Effective Community Relations Program for the South Side Planning Board."

107. George B. Nesbitt, "Relocating Negroes from Urban Slum Clearance Sites," *Land Economics* 25 (August 1949): 284–86; Nesbitt, "Break up the Black Ghetto?" 50.

108. Nesbitt, "Relocating Negroes from Urban Slum Clearance Sites," 284–86. In an earlier analysis, Nesbitt had ignored low-income tenants, while William Hill commented on their unorganized state. In this article, Nesbitt pointed to the broad appeal of racial injustice for wage-earning blacks, which does not allow them to see that it was institutional black elites' class interests all along that were driving the racial-group interests under attack.

109. Nesbitt, "Break up the Black Ghetto?" 50. Nesbitt makes an obvious and disparaging reference to the Champions and the Vigilantes' black female leadership. While he was sympathetic to black home owners' plight, he nonetheless dismissed the militant black middle-class female activists.

110. Nesbitt, "A Southsider Looks at the Slum Clearance-Redevelopment Program." The national black elite faction saw itself broadly aligned with cosmopolitan white elites, with both attacking "selfish interests" in their respective communities. Among white elites, it was the slum landlords who profited from the overcrowded and decrepit conditions targeted by slum clearance. The SSPB prospectus saw the organization's outlook as different from "short-sighted, selfish interests which usually can never see far enough ahead to realize how they can share in the profits of the

total community" (South Side Planning Board, "Prospectus," 9, 10, Acc. 75–104, Box 26, Folder 8, MHPC Papers, UIC).

111. Nesbitt, "Break up the Black Ghetto?" 50.

112. Ibid., 48–49.

113. Nesbitt, "A Southsider Looks at the Slum Clearance-Redevelopment Program"; Nesbitt, "Break up the Black Ghetto?" 48–49.

114. Nesbitt, "Break up the Black Ghetto?" 48–49. Other black elites shared Nesbitt's optimism (Earnest R. Rather, "What the Community Expects of the South Side Planning Board," address at SSPB annual meeting, June 15, 1949, MHPC papers, 75-104, Box 26, Folder 8, UIC; Nesbitt, "Break up the Black Ghetto?" 49–50).

115. This provision is a good example of the complexity of translating nondiscrimination into legislation. The provision, at least partially, was crafted to protect displaced blacks' ability to obtain improved housing within communities that were desirably located and where they had social ties. This was a position that coincided with those who had an interest in racial consolidation. However, this provision was interpreted by Nesbitt and others as an attempt to reinforce segregation by not allowing the siting of relocation housing for black displacees outside of the ghetto. To them it did not protect blacks' ability to live anywhere they could afford, so it was struck.

116. Nesbitt, "A Southsider Looks at the Slum Clearance-Redevelopment Program."

117. Nesbitt, "Break up the Black Ghetto?" 48–49.

118. After this last reassurance, a black resident might have asked Nesbitt if the program was so small, what real impact would it have on getting more and better housing for blacks? (Nesbitt, "A Southsider Looks at the Slum Clearance-Redevelopment Program"). See also Nesbitt, "Break up the Black Ghetto?" 50. The strange bedfellow comment probably refers to the whites who feared clearance would push blacks onto their communities. Some went as far as to help finance black property owners' court fight against condemnation proceedings (see David Wallace, "Residential Concentration of Negroes in Chicago" [PhD diss., Harvard University, 1953], 258–61, cited in Wilson, *Negro Politics*, 326).

119. Nesbitt, "A Southside Looks at the Slum Clearance-Redevelopment Program."

120. Nesbitt, "Break up the Black Ghetto?," 48, 52.

5. From Negro Clearance to Negro Containment

1. This does not mean all or most low-income black citizens could get public housing. If they were single or childless, they were ineligible regardless of income. Also, there were not enough units. Many poor blacks ended up in kitchenettes and other substandard housing in slums contiguous to Redevelopment Area No. 1.

2. *Slum Clearance under the Housing Act of 1949: A Preliminary Explanatory Statement to American Cities*, Housing and Home Finance Agency (August 1949), 2; Title I under Housing Act of 1949 was titled "Slum Clearance and Community

Development and Redevelopment" (81st Cong., 1st sess., Chapter 338, July 15, 1949, *Congressional Record*, p. 414).

3. George B. Nesbitt, field representative, to C. L. Farris, Chief, Field Operations Branch, Chicago, Illinois Field Trip—July 24 through 28, 1950, August 3, 1950, 14–17, Box 749, Folder 3, RG 207, NAII.

4. Nesbitt to Farris, Chicago Field Trip, August 3, 1950, 2–5.

5. Part II. "Summary of Racial Aspects of Relocation Planning in Five Localities," in a report compiled by N. S. Keith, director, Division of Slum Clearance and Urban Redevelopment, for Raymond M. Foley, administrator, on April 17, 1952, RG 207, Box 751, National Council of Negro Women, National Archives (NA). In 1947, there were 12,134 blacks living on the 100-acre redevelopment site, which was a 33 percent increase from the 9,079 living there in 1940 (George B. Nesbitt, "Relocating Negroes from Urban Slum Clearance Sites," *Land Economics* 25 [August 1949]: 284–86).

6. Nesbitt, Relocating Negroes, 275–79.

7. A total of 19,000 families and single persons being displaced altogether (Robert C. Weaver to Raymond M. Foley, February 6, 1951, Robert Weaver Papers, Microfilm R-1, Robert Weaver Correspondence). If that were not enough, 8,000 families still needed to be rehoused due to demolition for the Congress Street Expressway (Warren R. Cochrane, Racial Relations Branch, memorandum to Commissioner, PHA, re: "Review of Chicago Relocation Plan," May 7, 1951, RG 207, Box 750, "Chicago, Illinois"). Sidney Williams estimated that 17,000 black families would be displaced by all three phenomena (Sidney Williams to Raymond M. Foley, March 16, 1951, Chicago Urban League [CUL] Papers, UIC).

8. Even though the Chicago Field Office economists admitted that they could not determine whether the vacancies available would be accessible to black public housing ineligibles, he inexplicably "recommended, at this time, that the Chicago Housing Authority be allowed to proceed with *several of the slum clearance sites*" (Cochrane, "Review of Chicago Relocation Plan" [original emphasis]).

9. Cochrane, "Review of Chicago Relocation Plan."

10. "Discrimination Key Factor in Bogged Down Housing Program," *Chicago Defender* (national edition), September 21, 1946, 7; "Up and at 'Em," *Chicago Defender* (national edition), November 12, 1949, 6; "Deadline for Discrimination," *Chicago Defender* (national edition), February 25, 1950, 6; "In and Out the Window," *Chicago Defender* (national edition), November 5, 1955, 2; "George Nesbitt Wins Graduate Study Grant," *Chicago Defender* (national edition), August 18, 1956, 10.

11. The black population in Chicago had increased by 214,534 from 1940 to 1950 (Philip M. Hauser and Evelyn M. Kitagawa, eds., *Local Community Fact Book for Chicago, 1950* [Chicago, Ill.: University of Chicago Press, 1953], 2).

12. Part III, "Summary of Evidence of Five Selected Cities in Rehousing Racial Minority Families Displaced from Title I Project Areas"; Nathaniel S. Keith to

Raymond M. Foley, April 17, 1952, Box 274, Race Relations Folder, Urban Renewal Administration General Subject Files, RG 207, NAII.

13. Nesbitt to Farris, Chicago Field Trip July 24 through 28, 1950, August 3, 1950.

14. Nesbitt, "Relocating Negroes from Urban Slum Clearance Sites," 284–86. See chapter 4.

15. Nesbitt to Farris, Chicago Field Trip, August 3, 1950, 11–16; Nesbitt, "Relocating Negroes from Urban Slum Clearance Sites," 284–86.

16. Nesbitt to Farris, Chicago Field Trip, August 3, 1950, 7–9.

17. Part II, "Summary of Racial Aspects of Relocation Planning in Five Localities," in a report compiled by N. S. Keith, director, Division of Slum Clearance and Urban Redevelopment, for Raymond M. Foley, administrator, on April 17, 1952, RG 207, Box 751, National Council of Negro Women, NA.

18. "Notes in Review of 'Relocation of Families, through September 1955', HHFA-URA," attached to George B. Nesbitt to J. W. Follin, "Review of 'Relocation of Families,' through September 1955," July 25, 1956, RG 207, Racial Relations, Box 749, Reports to URA; Nesbitt to Farris, Chicago Field Trip, August 3, 1950, 7–9.

19. George Nesbitt, "Relocation of Families," July 1956.

20. Jack M. Siegel, "Slum Prevention—A Public Purpose," 1–3, MHPC Papers, Acc. 74–20, Box 23, Folder 1.

21. The areas of black infiltration included Park Manor, Oakland-Kenwood, Hyde Park, Woodlawn, Near North Side, Lawndale, and areas surrounding the Chicago Commons House on the West Side (Nesbitt to Farris, Chicago Field Trip, August 3, 1950, 7–9).

22. Richard Kluger, *Simple Justice: The History of Brown v. Board of Education and Black America's Struggle for Equality, Volume I* (New York, N.Y.: Knopf, 1975), 319. See also Otis D. Duncan and Beverly Duncan, *The Negro Population of Chicago* (Chicago, Ill.: University of Chicago Press Press, 1957); and Karl E. Taeuber and Alma F. Taeuber, *Negroes in Cities: Residential Segregation and Neighborhood Change* (New York, N.Y.: Atheneum, 1969).

23. Nesbitt to Farris, Chicago Field Trip, August 3, 1950, 7–9.

24. Nesbitt, "Relocating Negroes from Urban Slum Clearance Sites," 279–81.

25. Nesbitt to Farris, Chicago Field Trip, August 3, 1950, 11–16.

26. Ibid.

27. It appears that house prices in racial transition areas were around the median level of house prices elsewhere. Yet Chicago NAACP displacement cases reported more exorbitant prices compared to what black residents had paid at the redevelopment site (Part II, "Summary of Racial Aspects of Relocation Planning in Five Localities," in a report compiled by N. S. Keith, director, Division of Slum Clearance and Urban Redevelopment, for Raymond M. Foley, administrator, on April 17, 1952, RG 207, Box 751, National Council of Negro Women, National Archives; *Local*

Community Fact Book of 1950, 8; Nelson M. Willis to Raymond M. Foley, January 8, 1951, copy attached to Frank S. Horne, RG 207, Box 750, Chicago).

28. George Nesbitt, special assistant (Racial Relations) to J. W. Follin, director, DSCUR, "Racial Relations Activities—Bi-Weekly Report—Period Ending December 11, 1953," Dec. 15, 1953, HHFA, RG 207, RR, Box 749, Reports to Urban Renewal Administration (URA). While Nesbitt was critical of the CLCC for relying on housing in racial transition areas, he recognized the limited options available to black home seekers. He explained that moving into all-white neighborhoods was the only option available to "thousands and thousands of Negro families in the city of Chicago" ([George Nesbitt], "Housing Implications of Anti-Negro Violence in Cicero, Illinois," July 1951, Claude A. Barnett [CAB] Papers, Box 305, Folder 7, CHS).

29. "Notes in Review of 'Relocation of Families, through September 1955', HHFA-URA," attached to George B. Nesbitt to J. W. Follin, "Review of 'Relocation of Families', through September 1955," July 25, 1956, RG 207, Racial Relations, Box 749, Reports to URA.

30. George Nesbitt, special assistant (Racial Relations) to J. W. Follin, director, DSCUR, "Racial Relations Activities—Bi-Weekly Report—Period Ending December 11, 1953," Dec. 15, 1953, HHFA, RG 207, RR, Box 749, Reports to Urban Renewal Administration (URA). James Q. Wilson reports on the negative opinion that some blacks had toward black real estate professionals who bought property in racial transition areas and contributed to "block-busting" (*Negro Politics: The Search for Leadership* [New York: Free Press, 1960], 107–8).

31. The city council rejected the CHA proposal for sites for a new 12,000-unit development program, choosing instead the city's program (see chapter 3). Only 2,100 of the 11,550 to 15,050 public housing units planned were to be built on vacant land. The full council would approve this plan on August 4, roughly a week after Nesbitt's visit.

32. Wilford Winholtz to Raymond M. Foley, July 7, 1948, attached to B. T. Fitzpatrick to Wilford Winholtz, July 15, 1948, National Archives, Record Group 207, HHFA Subject Files, Box 18, Racial Relations, Jun.–Dec. 1948.

33. Title III in the Housing Act of 1949 referred to federal public housing (Nesbitt to Farris "Field Trip," August 3, 1950, 2; Arnold Hirsch, "Searching for a 'Sound Negro Policy': A Racial Agenda for the Housing Acts of 1949 and 1954," *Housing Policy Debate* 11, no. 2 [2000]: 405).

34. Nesbitt also met with Theodore Robinson, secretary of the Chicago Industrial Union Housing Committee and chairman of the Illinois State NAACP Conference Housing Committee, and his successor, William E. Hill, racial relations officer, Chicago Field Office, Public Housing Administration (PHA) (Nesbitt to Farris "Field Trip," August 3, 1950, 2).

35. Nesbitt to Farris, Chicago Field Trip, August 3, 1950, 2–5.

36. Ibid.

37. Ibid.

38. Ibid., 6.

39. For more about the black minister who was able to save his church from being demolished, see Wilson, *Negro Politics*, 130.

40. This was an early sign that black insurance companies would have to pull out of the deal due to black community's opposition and economic reasons, which they did almost a year later (see chapter 6). Wilson reported on the ability of black politicians to stall the building of the Lake Meadows shopping center in the interest of protecting neighborhood businessmen from new competition (Wilson, *Negro Politics*, 62).

41. "The Plot to Kill Public Housing," *Ebony* photo-editorial, June 1950, 94; Nesbitt to Farris, Chicago Field Trip, August 3, 1950, 9–11.

42. Ibid.

43. Nelson M. Willis to Raymond M. Foley, January 8, 1951, copy attached to Frank S. Horne, RG 207, Box 750, Chicago. Copies of this letter were sent to Nathaniel S. Keith, head of HHFA's Division of Slum Clearance and Urban Redevelopment (DSCUR), Dr. Frank S. Horne, and George Nesbitt.

44. Interviews with Henry Baker, 3126 S. Rhodes Avenue, attached to Willis to Foley, January 8, 1951. Harvey was one of a number of suburbs on the southern boundary of the city that had long had black residents, and thus was an acceptable location during this period (see Andrew Wiese, *Places of Their Own: African American Suburbanization in the Twentieth Century* [Chicago, Ill.: University of Chicago Press Press, 2005], 118–23).

45. Interviews with Mr. and Mrs. Robert Grant, 4239 South Parkway, attached to Willis to Foley, January 8, 1951.

46. Interviews with Mr. and Mrs. Leonard Breakfield, 6341 Ingleside, and James and Dora Brownlee, 1021 E. 65th St., attached to Willis to Foley, January 8, 1951. Apparently, in 1942, Journee White was involved with Earl Dickerson, Theodore Jones, and Truman Gibson Jr., in developing the White City Homes Project. Robert J. Blakely with Marcus Shepard, *Earl B. Dickerson: A Voice for Freedom and Equality* (Evanston, Ill.: Northwestern University Press, 2006), 178.

47. Interview with Philip and Delores Weatherspoon, 1027 E. 65th Street, attached to Willis to Foley, January 8, 1951.

48. Interview with Ira and Arie Jackson, 1023 E. 65th Street, attached to Willis to Foley, January 8, 1951.

49. Nesbitt, "Relocating Negroes from Urban Slum Clearance Sites," 284–86.

50. Construction on vacant land cost $391 per housing unit versus $1,770 per housing unit on slum land (ibid.).

51. Nesbitt to Farris, Chicago Field Trip, August 3, 1950, 14–17; Frank S. Horne to Raymond M. Foley, "PHA Relocation Policy," January 11, 1951, RG 207, Box 53, Racial

Relations, National Archives; Robert C. Weaver to Raymond M. Foley, February 6, 1951, Robert Weaver Papers, Microfilm R-1, Robert Weaver Correspondence.

52. Nesbitt to Farris, Chicago Field Trip, August 3, 1950, 14–17; Robert C. Weaver to Raymond M. Foley, February 6, 1951, Robert Weaver Papers, Microfilm R-1, Robert Weaver Correspondence.

53. In addition to Chicago NAACP charges for the Chicago Urban League, see Sidney Williams to Raymond M. Foley, March 16, 1951, Chicago Urban League Papers, UIC.

54. See Section 105c of Title I of the Housing Act of 1949 states, 81st Cong., 1st sess., Chapter 338, July 15, 1949, *Congressional Record*, 417.

55. Frank S. Horne to Nathaniel S. Keith, Relocation in Chicago, December 19, 1950, Robert Weaver Papers, Microfilm R-1, Robert Weaver Correspondence; Frank S. Horne to Raymond M. Foley, Relocation in Chicago, December 20, 1950, Robert Weaver Papers, Microfilm R-1, Robert Weaver Correspondence; Hirsch, "Sound Negro Policy," 406.

56. Part III, "Summary of Evidence of Five Selected Cities in Rehousing Racial Minority Families Displaced from Title I Project Areas"; Nathaniel S. Keith to Raymond M. Foley, April 17, 1952, Box 274, Race Relations Folder, Urban Renewal Administration General Subject Files, RG 207, NAII; Hirsch, "Sound Negro Policy," 404.

57. Frank S. Horne to Raymond M. Foley, "PHA Relocation Policy," January 11, 1951, RG 207, Box 53, Racial Relations Folder, National Archives.

58. Ibid.; Robert C. Weaver to Raymond M. Foley, September 7, 1951, Robert Weaver Papers, Microfilm R-1, Robert Weaver Correspondence; Hirsch, "Sound Negro Policy," 405–6, 412; Arnold Hirsch, "Containment on the Home Front: Race and Federal Housing Policy from the New Deal to the Cold War," *Journal of Urban History* 26 (January 2000): 167.

59. In January 1951, there was discussion among the federal housing agencies about reconciling the relocation standards and procedures of Title I and Title III of the 1949 Housing Act (Frank S. Horne to Raymond M. Foley, "PHA Relocation Policy," January 11, 1951, RG 207, Box 53, Racial Relations, National Archives).

60. Robert C. Weaver to Raymond M. Foley. September 7, 1951, Robert Weaver Papers, Microfilm R-1, Robert Weaver Correspondence.

61. Frank S. Horne to Raymond M. Foley, "PHA Relocation Policy," January 11, 1951, RG 207, Box 53, Racial Relations, National Archives; Robert C. Weaver to Raymond M. Foley, September 7, 1951.

62. Nesbitt to Farris, Chicago Field Trip, August 3, 1950, 14–17.

63. Frank S. Horne to Raymond M. Foley, "PHA Relocation Policy," January 11, 1951, RG 207, Box 53, Racial Relations, NA.

64. Robert C. Weaver to Raymond M. Foley, September 7, 1951, Robert Weaver Papers, Microfilm R-1, Robert Weaver Correspondence. Agreeing with racial relations

advisers, the NCADH recommended "Standardization of Title I and Title III relocation requirements." Weaver pointed out that "PHA did not accept responsibility for rehousing site displacees who are ineligible for public housing" (Robert C. Weaver to Raymond M. Foley, February 6, 1951, Robert Weaver Papers, Microfilm R-1, Robert Weaver Correspondence; N. S. Keith to Robert C. Weaver, January 6, 1950, Robert Weaver Papers, Microfilm R-1, Robert Weaver Correspondence; Robert C. Weaver to Raymond M. Foley, February 6, 1951, Robert Weaver Papers, Microfilm R-1).

65. Frank S. Horne to the Administrator, "Letter from Dr. Robert C. Weaver, National Committee Against Discrimination in Housing, February 6, 1951," February 16, 1951. Reaction to letter of Robert C. Weaver to the Administrator, dated Feb. 6, 1951, February 16, 1951, attached to Robert C. Weaver to Raymond M. Foley, September 25, 1951, RG 207, Box 53, Racial Relations.

66. Nesbitt to Farris, Chicago Field Trip, August 3, 1950, 14–17.

67. Robert C. Weaver to Raymond M. Foley, February 6, 1951, Robert Weaver Papers, Microfilm R-1, Robert Weaver Correspondence; N. S. Keith to Robert C. Weaver, January 6, 1950, Robert Weaver Papers, Microfilm R-1, Robert Weaver Correspondence.

68. Frank S. Horne to Raymond M. Foley, Relocation in Chicago, December 20, 1950, Robert Weaver Papers, Microfilm R-1, Robert Weaver Correspondence.

69. Horne accurately predicted that city officials would convince Truman administration officials this was the only way public housing would be accepted in Chicago. Thereafter, the administration advised Foley to accept the program intact (Frank S. Horne to Raymond M. Foley, Racial Relations Items Requiring Early Decision, August 14, 1950, RG 207, HHFA, Box 41, National Archives; Frank S. Horne to Nathaniel S. Keith, Relocation in Chicago, December 19, 1950, Robert Weaver Correspondence, Microfilm R-1, Robert Weaver Papers). Horne followed up his blistering memo to Keith with a memo to Foley the next day. Horne expressed concern that no one in the federal agencies was monitoring "the mutual impacts and interrelation of planning and relocation features involved in Title I and Title III programs" in Detroit and Chicago that were seeking federal assistance. Horne suggested that representatives from the DSCUR, the PHA, and the Racial Relations Service meet and evaluate both the Title I and Title III proposals in order to "determine the principles to govern the approval of contracts in these two rather special cases" (Frank S. Horne to Raymond M. Foley, Relocation in Chicago, December 20, 1950, Robert Weaver Correspondence, Microfilm R-1, Robert Weaver Papers).

70. The case against segregation in dining cars on interstate trains was *Henderson v. United States*. The cases against segregation in state universities referred to their graduate and law schools, *McLaurin v. Oklahoma* and *Sweatt v. Texas*. In all three cases, Truman's Justice Department wrote an amicus brief against segregation. Klinkner and Smith point out the foreign policy concerns, such as the United States

needing to eliminate legal racial inequality in order to win the ideological battle with the Soviet Union, were prominent in each brief (Philip A. Klinkner with Rogers M. Smith, *The Unsteady March: The Rise and Decline of Racial Equality in America* [Chicago, Ill.: University of Chicago Press Press, 1999], 226, 234).

71. Resolution of the NAACP Board of Directors against Discrimination and Segregation in Federally-Aided Housing, Walter White to President Truman, January 30, 1951, Walter White to Raymond Foley, January 30, 1951, attached to Robert C. Weaver to Raymond M. Foley, September 25, 1951, RG 207, Box 53, Racial Relations. The Chicago branch of the NAACP was ahead of the game. Note that the Chicago branch of the NAACP protested to Foley in a letter on January 8, 1951, three weeks before White's letter. The Chicago NAACP had collected testimony from those displaced by slum clearance before the letter was sent (Nelson M. Willis to Raymond M. Foley, January 8, 1951, copy attached to FSH, RG 207, Box 750, Chicago, Illinois; Hirsch, "A Sound Negro Policy," 405–6; Hirsch, "Race and Federal Housing Policy," 168).

72. John Taylor Egan to Raymond M. Foley, "Letter of January 30, 1951, from Mr. Walter White, Executive Secretary of the NAACP, February 8, 1951, attached to Robert C. Weaver to Raymond M. Foley, September 25, 1951, RG 207, Box 53, Racial Relations; Hirsch, "A Sound Negro Policy," 406–7; Hirsch, "Race and Federal Housing Policy," 168.

73. Raymond M. Foley to Walter White, February 27, 1951, attached to Robert C. Weaver to Raymond M. Foley, September 25, 1951, RG 207, Box 53, Racial Relations. See also David K. Niles to Raymond M. Foley, February 20, 1951; Raymond M. Foley to David K. Niles, February 23, 1951; David K. Niles to Raymond M. Foley, February 26, 1951, attached to Robert C. Weaver to Raymond M. Foley, September 25, 1951, RG 207, Box 53, Racial Relations.

74. Walter White to Raymond Foley, March 14, 1951, attached to Robert C. Weaver to Raymond M. Foley, September 25, 1951, RG 207, Box 53, Racial Relations.

75. Robert C. Weaver to Raymond M. Foley, February 6, 1951, Robert Weaver Papers, Microfilm R-1, Robert Weaver Correspondence; Hirsch, "A Sound Negro Policy," 405–6; Hirsch, "Race and Federal Housing Policy," 168.

76. Cochrane to PHA Commissioner, May 7, 1951.

77. It was also Weaver's advice (Robert C. Weaver to Raymond M. Foley, February 6, 1951, Robert Weaver Papers, Microfilm R-1, Robert Weaver Correspondence; Hirsch, "A Sound Negro Policy," 408; Hirsch, "Race and Federal Housing Policy," 168).

78. Racial relations advisers had recommended three slum sites in Warren Cochrane's May 7, 1951, report on Chicago relocation policies (Cochrane to PHA commissioner, May 7, 1951).

79. Raymond M. Foley to Robert C. Weaver, June 5, 1951, attached to Robert C. Weaver to Raymond M. Foley, September 25, 1951, RG 207, Box 53, Racial Relations; Hirsch, "A Sound Negro Policy," 407.

80. Robert C. Weaver to Raymond M. Foley, September 7, 1951, Robert Weaver Papers, Microfilm R-1, Robert Weaver Correspondence.

81. Ibid.

82. Stephen Gill Spottswood, president, NAACP, to Raymond M. Foley, November 22, 1951, attached to B. T. Fitzpatrick, Acting Administrator to Rev. Stephen G. Spottswood, December 20, 1951, RG 207, Box 53, Racial Relations. Weaver continued to press for reforms, attempting to see segregation outlawed in all levels and phases of housing policy (Robert C. Weaver to Raymond M. Foley, November 20, 1951; B. J. Fitzpatrick to Robert C. Weaver, December 21, 1951, RG 207, HHFA, Subject Files, 1947–1960, Box 53, Racial Relations; Hirsch, "A Sound Negro Policy," 409).

83. Part III, "Summary of Evidence of Five Selected Cities in Rehousing Racial Minority Families Displaced from Title I Project Areas"; Nathaniel S. Keith to Raymond M. Foley, April 17, 1952, Box 274, Race Relations Folder, Urban Renewal Administration General Subject Files, RG 207, NAII.

84. Kennelly made reference to "a full statement on the Enforcement and Conservation Program of the City of Chicago to Mr. James Follin, Director, Division of Slum Clearance and Urban Redevelopment," on December 30, 1953. The Housing Act of 1954 shifted focus from slum clearance and urban redevelopment to "urban renewal." The emphasis also shifted from residential improvement to urban reconstruction. There was also more stress on rehabilitation and conservation than demolition. The legislation was so influenced by the Illinois Urban Conservation Act of 1953 that the historian Arnold Hirsch commented that the 1954 Housing Act was the Illinois legislation "writ large" (Hirsch, *Making the Second Ghetto*, 271–72).

85. "Summary of the Workable Program of the City of Chicago," Office of the Housing and Redevelopment Coordinator, November 12, 1954, attached to Kennelly to Cole, November 1, 1954, CAB Papers, Box 347, Folder 1, CHS.

86. "Racial Minority Families and Title I Predominantly Open and Open Land Projects," no author or date.

87. In contrast, in Cleveland and Washington, D.C., the principle that "new additions to the housing supply available to minorities are prerequisite to successful redevelopment" was recognized (Frank S. Horne, Minority Studies, to Albert M. Cole, administrator, "Current Racial Considerations in the Urban Renewal Program," February 15, 1955, RG 207, Box 748, Policy, Racial Relations).

88. Ibid. The new Urban Renewal Administration (URA) took the place of the Division of Slum Clearance and Urban Redevelopment after the Housing Act of 1954. In the Eisenhower housing bureaucracy, J. W. Follin took Nathaniel Keith's place as the director of the DSCUR and became urban renewal commissioner after the new housing law.

89. "Notes in Review of 'Relocation of Families, through September 1955,' HHFA-URA," attached to George B. Nesbitt to J. W. Follin, "Review of 'Relocation of Families,'

through September 1955," July 25, 1956, RG 207, Racial Relations, Box 749, Reports to URA. Frank Horne found that as of January 1952, 74 percent of the families displaced in Title III projects and 60 percent of those displaced in Title I projects were racial minorities. He found that in northern cities, one-half to three-quarters of displaced black families needed private housing (B. T. McGraw to Frank S. Horne, "Family Displacement by Slum Clearance Projects under Title I and III," March 18, 1953, RG 207, HHFA, Box 75).

90. *Urban Renewal and the Negro in Chicago*, report by the Chicago Urban League Community Services Department, approved by the Board of Directors, Chicago Urban League, June 18, 1958, 4–5. For national figures, see B. T. McGraw to Frank S. Horne, "Family Displacement by Slum Clearance Projects under Titles I and III," March 18, 1953.

6. Black Redevelopment and Negro Conservation

1. Unlike other ethnic groups, African Americans did not own most of the property or businesses in the communities they populated. This fact would be a constant reminder to black capitalists that they had not attained the status of a real bourgeoisie in what they considered to be their territory.

2. Andrew Wiese uses this term to characterize southern black elites in contradistinction to northern black elites, who pursued racial integration. Seeing the same policy orientation that Wiese observes in their southern counterparts, I assign this term to include the black institutional elites in northern black communities (Wiese, *Places of Their Own: African American Suburbanization in the Twentieth Century* [Chicago, Ill.: University of Chicago Press Press, 2004], 277).

3. "Supreme Liberty Life is a highly race-conscious organization, but it has prospered mainly because of a sound, conservative investment policy, shrewd management, and a stern emphasis on training and efficiency in the selection of personnel" ("Biggest Northern Business," *Ebony*, August 1946, 42–44). Supreme Liberty Life was a good example of how racial consciousness and the profit motive were not incompatible.

4. "Negro Insurance Firms Take Lead in Building New Homes in Chicago," December 29, 1948, Associated Negro Press, attached to "Negro Insurance Firms Give up Housing Project Plans in Chicago," June 20, 1951, in Claude A. Barnett (CAB) Papers, Box 267, Folder 3, Chicago Historical Society (CHS).

5. "Biggest Northern Business," *Ebony*, August 1946, 43, 44. The publisher of *Ebony*, John H. Johnson, worked for Supreme Liberty Life before founding the periodical (A. L. Foster to Managers of Branch Offices of Supreme Liberty Life, August 1952, CAB Papers, Box 266, Folder 6, CHS). Foster, former executive secretary of the Chicago Urban League, was advertising representative for *Ebony* magazine and on the board of directors for Supreme Liberty Life (Robert C. Puth, *Supreme Life: The*

History of a Negro Life Insurance Company [New York: Arno Press], 251–52; I would like to thank Wendy Plotkin for drawing my attention to this source).

6. Speech at 22nd annual Agency Conference, Supreme Liberty Life Ins., Co. Meeting at Chicago, Illinois, 1943, CAB Papers, Box 266, Folder 6, CHS.

7. "Negro Insurance Firms Give Up Housing Project Plans in Chicago," June 20, 1951, CAB Papers, Box 267, Folder 3, CHS. See also David Wallace, "Residential Concentration of Negroes in Chicago" (PhD diss., Harvard University, 1953), 261, cited in James Q. Wilson, *Negro Politics: The Search for Leadership* (New York, N.Y.: Free Press, 1960), 181. In August 1950, George Nesbitt, a black federal housing official, commented on the "apathy" of black insurance companies in terms of investment in the redevelopment site (George B. Nesbitt, field representative, to C. L. Farris, Chief, Field Operations Branch, Chicago, Illinois Field Trip—July 24 through 28, 1950, August 3, 1950, 11–16, Box 749, Folder 3, RG 207, NAII).

8. "Negro Insurance Firms Give Up Housing Project Plans in Chicago." At public hearings on the New York Life project site in March 1949, an area white businessman "warned of high cost of land due to the commercial properties which would have to be acquired in the section to be developed by the 3 Negro insurance companies" (Philip Klutznick, Illinois State Housing Board, "Memo on the opposition to the N.Y. Life Site—3/22/49," MHPC Papers).

9. Chicago Community Inventory, *Housing—Part I: Number of Dwelling Units, Rental, Value of Home and Persons Per Room, in the City of Chicago and the Chicago Metropolitan Area: 1949 and 1940;* Tables 2 and 8, CSS—No. 8, February 24, 1950, University of Chicago; Chicago Community Inventory, *Income of Families and Persons in the City of Chicago and the Chicago Metropolitan Area: 1948*, Table 3, CSS—No. 3, November 21, 1949, University of Chicago; Philip M. Hauser and Evelyn M. Kitagawa, eds., *Local Community Fact Book for Chicago*, 1950, Table 10, p. 149, and for Roseland, Community Area 49, pp. 205 and 203, Chicago Community Inventory, University of Chicago, 1953.

10. Barnett (no title, no date), CAB Papers, Box 347, Folder 1, CHS. For more on Claude Barnett see Adam Green, *Selling the Race: Culture, Community, and Black Chicago, 1940–1955* (Chicago, Ill.: University of Chicago Press Press, 2009), 93–127.

11. According to Bill Mullen, the ANP was "the second most important journalistic enterprise in Chicago" after the *Defender*. Moreover, "he had revolutionized the relationship between the black press and black capital" (Bill V. Mullen, *Popular Fronts: Chicago and African-American Cultural Politics, 1935–1946* [Urbana: University of Illinois Press, 1999], 49–50).

12. Sandy Trice and S. R. Cheevers to Claude Barnett, May 21, 1940, CAB Papers, Box 346, Folder 4, CHS; Oscar C. Brown and Wendell E. Green to Claude A. Barnett, September 4, 1945, CAB Papers, Box 346, Folder 4, CHS.

13. See statement presumably by Barnett (no author, no date) in CAB Papers, Box 347, Folder 1, CHS. Attached to this statement is another, no author or date, that

appears to be a press release announcing the formation of a organization to improve Thirty-Fifth to Thirty-Seventh Streets, Rhodes to South Parkway Avenues.

14. Many of these black institutions got their start in Chicago before or during the Great Migration. The historian Allan Spear spoke about this time period when an "institutional ghetto" was created (Spear, *Black Chicago: The Making of a Negro Ghetto, 1890–1920* [Chicago, Ill.: University of Chicago Press Press, 1967], especially chapter 5).

15. Claude A. Barnett to Chicago Housing Authority, Attention to Mr. Milton Shufro, Assistant Executive Secretary, April 28, 1944, CAB Papers, Box 346, Folder 4, CHS.

16. A note with no author, 1940, CAB Papers, Box 346, Folder 4, CHS.

17. Claude A. Barnett to Chicago Housing Authority, attention to Mr. Milton Shufro, Assistant Executive Secretary, April 28, 1944, CAB Papers, Box 346, Folder 4, CHS.

18. Claude A. Barnett to T. K. Gibson, March 9, 1944, CAB Papers, Box 266, Folder 6, CHS. In 1941, Dickerson, as Alderman for the Second Ward, argued that CHA and FHA should acquire slum properties for the purpose of rehabilitating them. D. Bradford Hunt, *Blueprint for Disaster: The Unraveling of Chicago Public Housing* (Chicago, Ill.: University of Chicago Press Press, 2009), 72.

19. Barnett to Shufro, April 28, 1944.

20. Ibid. The CHA had slum clearance responsibilities when it came to constructing public housing and redevelopment before the CLCC was given the responsibility by the state legislature in 1947 (Arnold R. Hirsch, *Making the Second Ghetto: Race and Housing in Chicago, 1940–1960* [Cambridge: Cambridge University Press, 1983], 109–10).

21. Barnett's targeted neighborhood was in census tract 557. The population almost doubled in ten years, going from 4,754 Negroes to 9,065 nonwhite persons. In 1950, the median schooling was 8.8 grades, and median income was $1,696. More than two-thirds of the dwellings had neither private bath nor running water and were dilapidated. (U.S. Bureau of the Census, 17th Census, 1950, United States Census of Population, vol. 3. Census Tract Statistics, Chicago, Bulletin, P-D10, Table 1, p. 38; Table 4, p. 280; Table 5, p. 288, Washington D.C.: U.S. Government Printing Office, 1952).

22. Ray Runnion, "Survey Bares Squalor in S. Side Area: Appalling Conditions Shown in Report by Housing Investigators," *Chicago Sun*, March 26, 1945, CAB Papers, Box 305, Folder 7.

23. Claude A. Barnett, "Memo for Mr. Embree: A Suggestion for a Concrete Step in Housing," March 27, 1945, CAB Papers, Box 346, Folder 4, CHS.

24. Statement of Purpose for Conservation Organization Being Developed in Rhodes—South Parkway—35th & 37th Streets Area by Claude A. Barnett, no date, CAB Papers, Box 347, Folder 1; notes (no author or date) attached, ibid.

25. Barnett (no title, no date), CAB Papers, Box 347, Folder 1, CHS. Given the content of the notice, it seems that it came after the height of the slum clearance debate between 1948 and 1949.

26. Memorandum for Mr. Robert Williams by C. A. Barnett, October 23, 1954, attached to Jack Bryan, HHFA to Barnett, September 30, 1954, CAB Papers, Box 347, Folder 1, CHS; some addresses from "The Sponsoring Committee," CAB Papers, Box 346, Folder 4.

27. The amendments to the Neighborhood Redevelopment Corporation law extended its applicability to conservation areas, which were defined as areas that were either "deteriorated" or "overcrowded" and therefore in a preblight stage. Neighborhood redevelopment corporations were responsible for smaller blighted areas, while "urban conservation" normally covered larger areas of salvageable housing with some blight. Under the Urban Conservation Act, the Conservation Board has the right of eminent domain, while under the Neighborhood Redevelopment Corporation law, the corporation, if it represented at least 60 percent of the property owners, could also condemn and take property. Barnett requested information from the Housing and Home Finance Agency about "major developments in housing activities, including urban renewal" (Jack H. Bryan, Director of Information, HHFA, to Claude A. Barnett, September 30, 1954). Attached to this letter is correspondence between Barnett and Robert Williams, who was in charge of getting the word out about the Neighborhood Protection Organization's meetings (memorandum for Mr. Robert Williams by C. A. Barnett, October 23, 1954, attached to HHFA letter, CAB Papers, Box 347, Folder 1, CHS; "How Court Helped Slum Fighters Here: Condemnation, Enforced Repair Laws Ready for Use Now," *Chicago Daily News*, September 23, 1954, news clipping, CAB Papers, Box 351, Folder 1, CHS).

28. A statement, no author or date, appears to be a press release announcing the formation of an organization to improve Thirty-Fifth to Thirty-Seventh Streets, Rhodes to South Parkway Avenues. Attached to another statement presumably by Barnett (no author, no date), in CAB Papers, Box 347, Folder 1, CHS.

29. Notes (no author or date) and Statement of Purpose for Conservation Organization.

30. Ibid.

31. Memorandum for Mr. Robert Williams by C. A. Barnett, October 23, 1954, attached to Jack Bryan, HHFA to Barnett, September 30, 1954, CAB Papers, Box 347, Folder 1, CHS.

32. Ibid.

33. Notes (August 9) attached to Statement of Purpose for Conservation Organization. Supreme Life may not have been able to provide the necessary assistance given its own economic trouble. Black insurance firms began to feel competition from white firms for the black market with the increase in black income and lower mortality rates after World War II. However, Supreme Liberty Life rebounded and experienced considerable growth after 1956 (Robert C. Puth, *Supreme Life: The History of a Negro Life Insurance Company* [New York: Arno Press, 1976], 266–67). Just

before this rapid growth, Barnett expressed alarm over the company's status to President Truman K. Gibson Sr.: "More and more it seems the opinion is getting around that all is not well with Supreme Liberty Life" (Claude A. Barnett to Truman K. Gibson Sr., March 26, 1955, CAB Papers, Box 266, Folder 7, CHS). It could be that at the very time Barnett sought assistance from Supreme Life, they were unable to give it. Barnett's experiences were not unique; some observers commented that "precisely in those areas of the community which needed the most extensive renewal private funds was least in evidence." For the difficulty of private neighborhood redevelopment corporations, see Peter H. Rossi and Robert A. Dentler, *The Politics of Urban Renewal: The Chicago Findings* (New York, N.Y.: Free Press of Glencoe, 1961), 60.

34. Chicago Land Clearance Commission press release, February 11, 1952, CAB Papers, Box 351, Folder 2; Chicago Land Clearance Commission press releases, February 13 and 18, 1952, CAB Papers, Box 351, Folder 1.

35. In addition to the New York Life project, Ferd Kramer, prominent real estate developer and civic leader, reported on "clearance in progress for two superhighways, two medical centers, several housing projects, a school, parks and a technology center" ("What It Takes to Make Redevelopment Workable," speech by Ferd Kramer, president of the Metropolitan Housing and Planning Council, to a one-day conference of Baltimore business leaders at 2:30 p.m., Friday, April 18, 1952, Emerson Hotel, Baltimore, Maryland, MHPC Papers, Acc. 77–29, Box 1, Folder 2). See also Hirsch, *Making the Second Ghetto*, 136.

36. "The Loop and the Slums: Chicago's Businesses Are Trying Some Strong Medicine to Save Themselves from Slums," Seligman (E. Smith), 1st draft, November 3, 1953, pp. 14–15, MHPC Papers, Acc. 74–20, Box 23, Folder 1.

37. "Preventing Tomorrow's Slums: A Citizens Action Program," RG 207, Box 750, Chicago, IL, I, National Archives.

38. Jack M. Siegel, "Slum Prevention—A Public Purpose," pp. 1–3. Jack M. Siegel was a former staff member of the city council Committee on Housing and now staff attorney of the Metropolitan Housing and Planning Council, MHPC Papers, Acc. 74–20, Box 23, Folder 1; "The Loop and the Slums: Chicago's Businesses Are Trying Some Strong Medicine to Save Themselves from Slums," pp. 10–13, 16.

39. Urban Community Conservation Act, Ill. Rev. Statute, 1953, Chapter 67 ½, par. 91.8–91.16, Section 3(d) quoted in Jack M. Siegel, "Slum Prevention—A Public Purpose," p. 9.

40. Jack M. Siegel, "Slum Prevention—A Public Purpose," pp. 9–13, 21; "The Loop and the Slums: Chicago's Businesses Are Trying Some Strong Medicine to Save Themselves from Slums"; "Court Upholds 2 Slum Laws: State Tribunal OKs City's Right to Name Conservation Board," *Chicago Daily News*, September 23, 1954; "The Urban Community Conservation Act: Its Background, Purposes and Utilization," August 7, 1953, pp. 6–10, MHPC Papers, Acc. 74–20, Box 6, Folder 66; "Summary

of the Urban Community Conservation Act By Sections," Office of the Housing and Redevelopment Coordinator, August 28, 1953, National Urban League Papers, III, C, Box 51, Chicago, 1944–1955, Library of Congress. "Preventing Tomorrow's Slums: A Citizens Action Program." RG 207, Box 750, Chicago, IL, I, National Archives.

41. Summary Notes on a meeting between Mid-South Chicago Council, the Calumet Conservation and Rehabilitation Association, the Southside Conservation Association, and Office of the Housing and Redevelopment Coordinator on April 27, 1954, at 4649 Cottage Grove Avenue by Tom Jenkins, community representative, Chicago Urban League Papers, UIC. See also Wilson, *Negro Politics*, 163–64.

42. Oscar C. Brown, president, pro-tem, of Mid-South Chicago Council, to Claude A. Barnett, August 23, 1954; "By-Laws of the Mid-South Chicago Council, Inc., July 25, 1954, pp. 1–2, CAB Papers, Box 347, Folder 1, CHS.

43. The organization was concerned with racial discrimination against black property owners in terms of financing, city services, equal accommodation, access to good relocation housing, and the effects of overcrowding on housing conditions and property values, Brown to Barnett, August 23, 1954.

44. Wilson, *Negro Politics*, 160, 201–2.

45. Black homeowners' interests in conservation were represented best by the Chicago Urban League's block club movement (see The Community Organization Department, Chicago Urban League, 1953 Annual Report, by A. B. Maxey, director, Community Organization Department, National Urban League Papers, Box 84, Folder 5, 1953, Chicago Urban League, Library of Congress).

46. Spear, *Black Chicago*, 210–13; Thomas L. Philpott, *The Slum and the Ghetto: Neighborhood Deterioration and Middle-Class Reform, Chicago, 1880–1930* (New York, N.Y.: Oxford University Press, 1978), 154–56; Hirsch, *Making the Second Ghetto*, 145.

47. Peter H. Rossi and Robert A. Dentler, *The Politics of Urban Renewal: The Chicago Findings* (New York, N.Y.: Free Press of Glencoe, 1961), 21, 19; *Local Community Fact Book for Chicago, 1950*, ed. Philip M. Hauser and Evelyn M. Kitagawa (Chicago Community Inventory, University of Chicago, 1953), 170; *Local Community Fact Book, Chicago Metropolitan Area, 1960*, ed. Evelyn M. Kitagawa and Karl E. Taeuber (Chicago, Ill.: Chicago Community Inventory, University of Chicago, 1963), 96.

48. Otis D. Duncan and Beverly Duncan, *The Negro Population of Chicago* (Chicago, Ill.: University of Chicago Press Press, 1957).

49. *Local Community Fact Book for Chicago, 1950*, 171. See also *Local Community Fact Book Chicago Metropolitan Area 1960*, 96.

50. Rossi and Dentler, *The Politics of Urban Renewal*, 192; Julia Abrahamson, *A Neighborhood Finds Itself* (New York, N.Y.: Harper and Brothers, 1959), 9; Hirsch, *Making the Second Ghetto*, 136.

51. The professional and technical occupations made up 8 percent of the nonwhite population in the community exceeding the 3.5 percent citywide average at the time (Rossi and Dentler, *Politics of Urban Renewal*, 28).

52. "Before the Negroes moved in, Hyde Park had experienced an increase in conversions; this was accelerated with the coming of this new group" (*Local Community Fact Book for Chicago, 1950*, 170).

53. Rossi and Dentler, *Politics of Urban Renewal*, 22, 24–27; Abrahamson, *Neighborhood Finds Itself*, 9.

54. Rossi and Dentler, *Politics of Urban Renewal*, 49–50.

55. Hirsch, *Making the Second Ghetto*, 157.

56. Rossi and Dentler, *Politics of Urban Renewal*, 51; Abrahamson, *Neighborhood Finds Itself*, 15, 300, 301.

57. Abrahamson, *Neighborhood Finds Itself*; Rossi and Dentler, *Politics of Urban Renewal*; Hirsch, *Making the Second Ghetto*, chapter 5.

58. Hirsch, *Making the Second Ghetto*, 148–49, 152. The South East Chicago Commission's board of directors was selected from "'power groups' in the community, including the hotel owners, the white and nonwhite real estate firms, the business and professional men's associations, and the several institutions" (Rossi and Dentler, *Politics of Urban Renewal*, 76).

59. Rossi and Dentler, *Politics of Urban Renewal*, 80–82; *Negro Politics*, 143–144.

60. The Hyde Park-Kenwood Community Conference was founded in 1949 in opposition to the racial segregation policies of the Hyde Park Planning Association. The association drew its members from the "large hotels east of the Illinois Central tracks, from realtors, and from the University of Chicago" (Rossi and Dentler, *Politics of Urban Renewal*, 71). Hirsch argued that previous scholars had given the HPKCC too much credit for the urban renewal program in Hyde Park. In fact, most of his account is dedicated to reinterpreting their role, which he characterized as, at best, supplementary to the university or, at worst, irrelevant (Hirsch, *Making the Second Ghetto*, 153, 157).

61. Rossi and Dentler, *Politics of Urban Renewal*, 76–77.

62. Hirsch, *Making the Second Ghetto*, 149–50.

63. Ibid., 151.

64. Ibid., 159.

65. Rossi and Dentler, *Politics of Urban Renewal*, 157.

66. Hirsch, *Making the Second Ghetto*, 159.

67. Ibid. Rossi and Dentler, *Politics of Urban Renewal*, 158–59; Abrahamson, *Neighborhood Finds Itself*, 236.

68. Rossi and Dentler, *Politics of Urban Renewal*, 177.

69. Ibid., 158–59; Abrahamson, *Neighborhood Finds Itself*, 236; Hirsch, *Making the Second Ghetto*, 159.

70. Rossi and Dentler, *Politics of Urban Renewal*, 165–66; Abrahamson, *Neighborhood Finds Itself*, 240.

71. Hirsch reports that Julian Levi, executive director of SECC, personally intervened to prevent Drake from buying the property because Levi claimed Drake did

not have enough money to maintain the property. When a white buyer, poorer than Drake, was permitted to purchase the house, Drake knew the university had discriminated against him. He was offered a house in the same area after he began leading the opposition to the university plans, but he refused, understanding the university wanted him to "sell out" his neighbors (St. Clair Drake to Leon Despres, November 27, 1956, Leon Despres Papers, CHS, cited in Hirsch, *Making the Second Ghetto*, 184).

72. Rossi and Dentler, *Politics of Urban Renewal*, 165–69; Abrahamson, *Neighborhood Finds Itself*, 240; Hirsch, *Making the Second Ghetto*, 153–54.

73. Hirsch points out that Levi approved of the conference's testimony and selected the HPKCC witnesses prior to Neighborhood Redevelopment Commission meeting (*Making the Second Ghetto*, 161).

74. Drake was the first chairman of the Community Survey Committee of HPKCC (Abrahamson, *Neighborhood Finds Itself*, 237; Rossi and Dentler, *Politics of Urban Renewal*, 171–74).

75. My mother's family, the Grahams, was representative of how black families occupied housing space against official housing standards. In summer of 1951, the Grahams, like many black families with means, took advantage of the 1948 Supreme Court decision not to enforce racially restrictive covenants, and moved to Park Manor. My mother's brother Ernest, the eldest child, had bought a two-flat building located at 7210 S. Indiana Avenue. Ernest, who was employed by Swift meatpacking company as an electrician, was the first African American to hold such a position. He and his wife, Margaret, plus my mother's sister Edna, her husband, Gaylord, and their son lived on the second floor. My mother, Mariam, the youngest, her sister Kathryn, her parents, and her maternal grandmother, Nana, lived on the first floor.

76. Rossi and Dentler, *Politics of Urban Renewal*, 175–77; Abrahamson, *Neighborhood Finds Itself*, 237. Hirsch reports that Hauser was the "leading academic advocate" of the view that "the rural southern background of the black migrants and their need to be acculturated to a 'completely industrialized civilization' before they could be accepted as urban neighbors" (*Making the Second Ghetto*, 183).

77. Rossi and Dentler, *Politics of Urban Renewal*, 177–78. The city council had to vote the final plan up or down, Aldermen were not able to offer amendments (Hirsch, *Making the Second Ghetto*, 164).

78. Hirsch, *Making the Second Ghetto*, 161.

79. Rossi and Dentler, *Politics of Urban Renewal*, 179–81.

80. St. Clair Drake to Leon Despres, November 27, 1956, Leon Despres Papers, CHS, cited in Hirsch, *Making the Second Ghetto*, 170.

81. Rossi and Dentler, *Politics of Urban Renewal*, 179–81, 194–95, 197.

82. Ibid., 141, 224–25.

83. Ibid.

84. Ibid., 254.

85. Ibid., 255, 260; on NAACP efforts to modify the plan, see 264–65. Theodore Jones's efforts "suggested to all concerned that one crucial segment of organized Negro leadership could be expected to consent to approval of the Urban Renewal Plan with only minor reservations," 265 (Rossi and Dentler, *Politics of Urban Renewal*, 264–65; Wilson, *Negro Politics*, 204).

86. For black labor leaders' advocacy of public housing in the urban renewal plan, see Wilson, *Negro Politics*, 202.

87. Alderman Harvey was consistent in his support of black homeowners and property owners from the battle over Lake Meadows (1949) and the public housing slum site struggle (1950) to supporting black-led conservation efforts (1953) and opposing Hyde Park's plan (1958). The "resident owners" formed a core group of constituents in his ward. Apparently, Dawson was privately opposed to the Hyde Park urban renewal plan as well (Wilson, *Negro Politics*, 86–87, 202).

88. Rossi and Dentler, *The Politics of Urban Renewal*, 268–69; Wilson, *Negro Politics*, 127. On black opposition to urban renewal from Lake Meadows to Hyde Park, see 253–54.

89. Wilson, *Negro Politics*, 151. Hirsch argued that the archdiocese provided the "most cogent critique of the Final plan" (*Making the Second Ghetto*, 164–66).

90. See chapter 4; and Hirsch, *Making the Second Ghetto*, 251–52.

91. In the four years after the 1948 Supreme Court decision declaring restrictive racial covenants as unenforceable, 21,000 black families purchased or rented housing in formerly all-white neighborhoods in Chicago (Richard Kluger, *Simple Justice: The History of Brown v. Board of Education and Black America's Struggle for Equality*, vol. 1 [New York: Knopf, 1975], 319).

92. According to Abrahamson, in addition to Dickerson other prominent blacks were new residents in Hyde Park at the time including Oscar C. Brown Sr.; Jerome E. Morgan, president of the Midway Television Institute; Dr. and Mrs. Walter S. Grant; Mrs. Sydney P. Brown; Mrs. E. W. Beasley; and Mrs. Albert Williams. Abrahamson identified "William Y. Browne, a well-known real estate man," as one of the "new Negro residents," adding, "At the same time, it was also clear that many Negroes were as concerned as whites about having neighbors of similar standards" (Abrahamson, *Neighborhood Finds Itself*, 16, 300, 14). The "area" Dickerson referred to was Hyde Park-Kenwood. Dickerson was a resident of Kenwood, which boasted it had defeated blockbusting in an effort to maintain an interracial community. The author of a congratulatory portrayal in a popular magazine credited Hyde Park with stopping the flow of poor blacks (Elinor Richey, "Kenwood Foils the Block-busters," *Harper's*, August 1963, 43, copy in CAB Papers, Box 351, Folder 3).

93. Wilson, *Negro Politics*, 249.

94. Ibid., 202–3.

95. Ibid., 183, 202–3.

96. Hirsch, *Making the Second Ghetto*, 250–51.

97. Wilson does note that the NAACP at the time was under "moderate or conservative leadership," which meant, for him, not taking "a race position on a given issue" (*Negro Politics*, 183). Later he explains the three positions taken on public housing by black civic leadership. Only black labor leaders called for extensive public housing in Hyde Park. Black civic leaders formally favored public housing but held no "strong convictions" for it. The last group, residents, "vigorously, but privately" opposed public housing (202). For an NAACP leader's ability to finesse the public housing issue to making no commitment for any units in the community, see ibid., 204.

98. Wilson describes this process where an issue defined as a "racial problem" drives "racial differences" around class "underground" (*Negro Politics*, 253–54).

99. Ibid., 203.

100. He reports one black informant who claimed "at cocktail parties, and over highballs" that "the NAACP people" opposed public housing in the Hyde Park urban renewal plan but could not say this publicly because of "their constituents." This suggests that their constituents could not have the organization publicly oppose a position that would be interpreted as counter to the interests of poor black tenants (*Negro Politics*, 183, see also 202).

101. For him it perhaps represented "racial progress" to take "the same position" as a comparable white man (Wilson, *Negro Politics*, 202–3).

102. Ibid., 193.

103. As far as working-class whites were concerned, Hirsch noted that they were tolerated until the reality that their "relatively cheap housing" would be entry points for working-class blacks meant they represented "gangrenous appendages that had to be sacrificed to preserve the health of the larger organism" (Hirsch, *Making the Second Ghetto*, 168–70, 185, 170).

104. Ibid., 182–85.

105. Hirsch clearly shows, by highlighting Ming's contribution, that he understood the motivation of Kimpton and Levi to utilize cultural arguments to appeal to a black audience. He reports Levi telling Kimpton that "there is a good deal to be gained by your making this statement." He even hints that the black audience would have found this explanation "acceptable" when he writes without reference to race, cultural arguments "had its primary value in the psychological comfort it provided its adherents rather than in its descriptive accuracy." But it is not clear whether Hirsch includes affluent blacks as among the "adherents." Since he does not focus on black agency, he does not explore the motivation for affluent blacks' agreement with the plan. We are left to wonder how they explained to themselves the exclusion of other blacks in order to reconcile the schizophrenic fate so well described by Drake. (Lawrence A. Kimpton, address delivered at a public forum of the forty-third grand chapter of Kappa Alpha Psi fraternity, December 27, 1953; and Julian to Larry, December 7,

1953, Lawrence A. Kimpton Papers, University of Chicago [UC] Archives, cited in Hirsch, *Making the Second Ghetto*, 182–183, 325 nn. 33 and 35, 185).

106. Hirsch relies on Wilson's welfare and status goals to explain divisions among black activists on every housing issue during the postwar period. He does not entertain the idea that class might have been a basis for those enervating divisions. For the purpose of his study to determine who influenced urban redevelopment and housing policy, Hirsch focused on white agency. Admittedly, the complicated motivations for black agency were not explored. He determined that race, not class, was the primary motivation of white elites. Though surely aware of blacks' class sentiments, he does not appreciate the role of such beliefs and interests in dividing blacks in response to Hyde Park's urban renewal plan (Hirsch, *Making the Second Ghetto*, 250–51). Even Wilson with his depictions of blacks' class bigotry and naked class interests goes further than Hirsch in suggesting class as the basis for such black divisions (Wilson, *Negro Politics*, 105–6, 159). Both authors recognize how black civic leaders' class interests, only expressed privately, sapped an expected strong racial conviction against working-class black displacement and in favor of public housing. Still class was not deployed analytically by either scholar as an important basis to explain intraracial conflict over Hyde Park's land-clearance struggle.

7. Racial Violence and the Crisis of Black Elite Leadership

1. Interestingly enough, during the war, there were not any major racial disturbances in Chicago. The first major racial conflicts came after the war with temporary veteran housing. On the lack of wartime racial conflict in Chicago, see Public Housing Administration (PHA), "The Dream and the Substance: A Short History of Public Housing for Negroes," unpublished report (Washington, D.C.: Public Housing Administration, 1954), 60, RG 196, PHA, Records of Intergroup Relations Branch, 1936–1963, Box 1.

2. MCRR was funded by the mayor and operated out of his office (Arnold Hirsch, *Making the Second Ghetto: Race and Housing in Chicago, 1940–1960* [Cambridge: Cambridge University Press, 1983], 44; Robert C. Weaver, "Racial Tensions in Chicago," pp. 1–8, 1943, Box 750, Folder Chicago IL, I, RG 207, NAII). Robert C. Weaver's appointment was controversial. Many of Chicago's black elites resented the fact that an outsider was appointed to what they considered a very prestigious and influential position ("Kelly Inter-Racial Board Flayed by Urban League," *Chicago Defender*, July 17, 1943, 1; "Weaver Heads Mayor Kelly's Race Committee," *Chicago Defender*, January 8, 1944, 1, 2). For Weaver's motivation for leaving the federal government, see Harry McAlpin, "Weaver Resigns, Sees Race Gains in Danger," *Chicago Defender*, January 15, 1944, 3. See also "Weaver to Leave WMC for Chicago," *Chicago Defender*,

January 22, 1944, 1; and "Weaver Resigns Post on Mayor's Race Committee," *Chicago Defender*, October 21, 1944, 1, 2. See also Wendell Pritchett, *Robert Clifton Weaver and the American City: The Life and Times of an Urban Reformer* (Chicago, Ill.: University of Chicago Press, 2008), 118–124.

3. Chicago-based black housing expert Horace Cayton and the city of Chicago were mentioned often and prominently in the text (National Urban League, *Interracial Planning for Community Organization: Racial Problems in Housing*, National Urban League Bulletin No. 2 [1944]: 1–29, Box 29, Chicago Historical Society [CHS], Chicago Common Papers).

4. Rather than the previous pattern of whites attacking blacks, in the Detroit and Harlem race riots blacks focused on destroying property, particularly white-owned stores.

5. MHPC, "Report on Negro Housing," 4. For disagreement on what do about black in-migration, see Citizens' Committee to Fight Slums, Housing Action Report of 1954: To Mayor Martin H. Kennelly, February 1954, p. 9, RG 207, Program Files, Racial Relations Program, 1946–1958, Box 750, Chicago, Illinois, Racial Relations Folder, Part I, National Archives (NA); George Nesbitt, special assistant (Racial Relations), to J. W. Follin, director, DSCUR, "Racial Relations Activities—Bi-Weekly Report—Period Ending February 19, 1954," Feb. 23, 1954, HHFA, RG 207, RR, Box 749, Reports to Urban Renewal Administration.

6. On Airport Homes, see "First Veteran's Family Moves in Airport Homes," *Chicago Defender*, November 16, 1946; Vernon Jarrett, "Gang Threatens Mixed Group with Violence," *Chicago Defender*, November 23, 1946; "Cops Fight Mob as Vets Occupy Homes," *Chicago Defender*, December 7, 1946; "File Suits as Clashes Subside at Vet Project," *Chicago Defender*, December 14, 1946; Mayor's Commission on Human Relations (CHR), "Memorandum on Airport Homes—60th and Karlov" (Chicago, Ill.: Mayor's Commission on Human Relations, 1946), NA, DHUDR, RG 207, Box 750, Chicago, IL, I Folder; Homer A. Jack, "The Racial Factor in the Veterans Airport Housing Project: Documented Memorandum VIII," 1946, NA, DHUDR, RG 207, Box 750. Chicago, IL, I Folder; Devereux Bowly Jr., *The Poorhouse: Subsidized Housing in Chicago, 1895–1976* (Carbondale: Southern Illinois University Press, 1978), 50. Some veterans' projects were successfully integrated (Chicago Housing Authority, "The Tenth Year of the Chicago Housing Authority" [Chicago: Chicago Housing Authority, 1947], pp. 22, 24, CHA Library). See also Martin Meyerson and Edward C. Banfield, *Politics, Planning and the Public Interest: The Case of Public Housing in Chicago* (Glencoe, Ill.: Free Press, 1955), 125–26. On Fernwood Homes, see Arnold Hirsch, *Making the Second Ghetto*, 54–55; and Bowly, *The Poorhouse*, 51. See also PHA, "The Dream and the Substance," 76–77.

7. PHA, "The Dream and the Substance," 76.

8. The Mayor's Commission on Race Relations had been renamed Human Relations during the war.

9. CHR, "Memorandum on Airport Homes"; "Cops Fight Mob As Vets Occupy Homes," *Chicago Defender*, December 7, 1946; "File Suits as Clashes Subside at Vet Project," *Chicago Defender*, December 14, 1946.

10. According to Hirsch, this attack was a culmination of racial violence that commenced in 1945. In July 1946, a black doctor was driven out of his home by 2,000 to 3,000 whites when they burned his garage and broke several windows with rocks. Hirsch describes a "virtual guerilla warfare" existing between Sixty-Seventh and Seventy-First Streets by the late 1940s. Whites' violent resistance, however, did not dissuade blacks from purchasing four pieces of property in 1947 and another thirty-five by August 1948 (Hirsch, *Making the Second Ghetto*, 58–59, 56).

11. A report by Max Strulovich and John Kelly, no date, United Packinghouse Workers of America (UPWA) Papers, Program Department, Correspondence, Subject Files, 1946–1951, Box 343, Folder 3; "Organized Character of Peoria Street Violence Revealed," *Crusader*, November 19, 1949, 7, UPWA Papers, Box 345, Folder 3; Hirsch, *Making the Second Ghetto*, 55.

12. Hirsch, *Making the Second Ghetto*, 5, 59

13. Ibid., 37, 216. Hirsch noted that Park Manor and Englewood represented more "well-to-do or middle class" communities than others that experienced severe racial violence, and they were the ones "that changed more rapidly" (ibid., 217).

14. Strulovich and Kelly's report, p. 4, UPWA Papers, Box 343, Folder 3. The CIO presence during the Airport Homes riots was very evident. White CIO officials were on hand to survey the scene as black veterans attempted to integrate Airport Homes. (Mayor's Commission on Human Relations [CHR], "Memorandum on Airport Homes—60th and Karlov" (Chicago, Ill.: Mayor's Commission on Human Relations, 1946), NA, DHUDR, RG 207, Box 750, Chicago, IL, I Folder; Homer A. Jack, "The Racial Factor in the Veterans Airport Housing Project: Documented Memorandum VIII," 1946, NA, DHUDR, RG 207, Box 750, Chicago, IL, I Folder; Bowly, *The Poorhouse*, 50.

15. Most white neighborhood activists were explicit about Bindman keeping the "colored" out. It was the Democratic Party officials who wanted to exclude left-wing unions and political groups who supported open occupancy (Strulovich and Kelly's report, p. 4, UPWA Papers, Box 343, Folder 3).

16. Nationally, the CIO was split over whether to support Henry Wallace's 1948 presidential campaign on the Progressive Party ticket. On the CIO and the Progressive Party, see Kevin Boyle, *The UAW and the Heyday of American Liberalism, 1945–1968* (Ithaca, N.Y.: Cornell University Press, 1995), 551–52; and Nelson Lichtenstein, *Walter Reuther: The Most Dangerous Man in Detroit* (Urbana, Ill.: University of Illinois Press, 1995), 269, 304–5.

17. The split over the Progressive Party was reflected in the split within the CIO between the steelworker unions, which were considered "conservative," versus the autoworker and meatpacking worker unions, which were considered "left-wing." However, within the "left-wing" faction, there were pro- and anti-Communist subfactions that took opposing stands on the Progressive Party. This national division within the CIO was reflected in Chicago (Wilson, *Negro Politics*, 123).

18. The conference's name undoubtedly derived from a similarly named national group, the National Emergency Committee Against Mob Violence, organized in August 1946. After a series of racial attacks on black veterans and race riots, a coalition of civil rights, labor, religious, and veterans group formed the national committee "to publicize violence against blacks" and pressure the federal government to investigate and prosecute the perpetrators (Klinkner with Smith, *The Unsteady March*, 205–6).

19. Sidney Williams was born in South Carolina. One of his ancestors had participated in Denmark Vesey's slave rebellion in 1836. Williams's grandfather and father amassed large landholdings in South Carolina. He received a B.A. at historically black South Carolina State College, studied at Fisk University, and did graduate work at the University of Chicago's School of Social Work. He started working for the Urban League movement in 1930 as industrial secretary in St. Louis. During World War II, he traveled to Europe as American Red Cross club director, the second African American director assigned abroad. He was initially assigned to London in 1942, then later to Morocco. After the war, he became executive secretary in Cleveland, only to leave for Chicago in 1947. It was after his experience in Morocco that he developed his concept of "domestic colonialism" (personal papers in possession of the author).

20. Report of the Commission on Human Relations, October 1947, in Chicago Commons Papers, Box 31, September—November 1947 Folder; Hirsch, *Making the Second Ghetto*, 36.

21. Guichard Parris and Lester Brooks, *Blacks in the City: A History of the National Urban League* (Boston, Mass.: Little, Brown, 1971), 387–88; Dennis C. Dickerson, *Militant Mediator: Whitney M. Young Jr.* (Lexington: University Press of Kentucky, 1998), 85; Jesse Thomas Moore Jr., *A Search for Equality: The National Urban League, 1910–1961* (University Park: Pennsylvania State University Press, 1981), 154–55, 152–54.

22. "Conference to End Mob Violence in Chicago" press release, November 26, 1949, UPWA Papers; Ruby Cooper, "Chicago Parley Maps Plan to Halt Attacks on Negroes," *New York Daily Worker*, November 29, 1949, National Urban League (NUL) Papers, Chicago Urban League 1950 file, Box 84, Folder 3.

23. Williams reasoned that the presence of black police officers would convey that, "we mean business" to the rioters. He added it would "tend to assure first-class, efficient and professional police performance," not to mention "inspire confidence in the police on the part of the Negro community and its friends" (Albert Towers, President, and Michael Mann, Secretary, Chicago Industrial Union Council, to Mr.

Sidney Williams, Executive Secretary, The Chicago Urban League, from CIO, December 1, 1949, in CUL Papers, UIC, Folder 73).

24. For the listed members of the steering committee, see "The Chicago Conference to End Mob Violence," Sidney Williams, Chairman, Steering Committee, and Russell Lasley, Chairman, Organizing Committee, letter to community leaders, November 22, 1949, UPWA Papers. However, the lack of meeting minutes except for one meeting, January 7, 1950, makes it difficult to know which of the listed leaders actually participated in the conference. "Conference to End Mob Violence in Chicago" press release, November 25, 1949, UPWA Papers; "Conference to End Mob Violence in Chicago" press release, November 26, 1949, UPWA Papers; "New Charges in Disorders," *Chicago Sun-Times*, December 13, 1949, UPWA Papers, Box 342, Folder 18.

25. "The Chicago Conference to End Mob Violence," Williams and Lasley to community leaders, December 7, 1949, UPWA Papers; press release from Chicago Conference to End Mob Violence, December 9, 1949, Chicago Urban League Papers, Folder 73.

26. Ruby Cooper, "Chicago Parley Maps Plan to Halt Attacks on Negroes," *New York Daily Worker*, November 29, 1949, NUL Papers, Chicago Urban League 1950 file, Box 84, Folder 3; "Conference to End Mob Violence in Chicago" press release, November 26, 1949, UPWA Papers; "New Charges in Disorders," *Chicago Sun-Times*, December 13, 1949, UPWA Papers, Box 342, Folder 18.

27. "The Chicago Conference to End Mob Violence," November 22, 1949, UPWA Papers; "Conference to End Mob Violence in Chicago" press release, November 25, 1949, UPWA Papers. While the CEMV welcomed any organization that wanted to eliminate mob violence, it was primarily organized to "unite all Negro organizations" (Ruby Cooper, "Chicago Parley Maps Plan to Halt Attacks on Negroes," *New York Daily Worker*, November 29, 1949, NUL Papers, Chicago Urban League 1950 file, Box 84, Folder 3).

28. "Agenda: Community Action Meeting," a reprint of the agenda of probably the CEMV November 26, 1949, meeting and reprint of *Chicago Daily News* editorial, November 16, 1949, UPWA Papers; Sidney Williams, Chairman, The Chicago Conference to End Mob Violence in Chicago, "To All Participating Organizations, Individuals, and Friends of the Conference," November 29, 1949, UPWA Papers, "Chicago Conference to End Mob Violence 1949," Box 324, Folder 18.

29. The CEMV went as far as advocating that all blacks "be served and accommodated without discrimination in *all* public places" (original emphasis). As further evidence of the CEMV's broader focus, one of its committees planned to persuade the public schools to institute "a vigorous program for improved inter-cultural education in the schools" so "that the children of Chicago are inoculated against the virus of racism." The agenda included committee reports on talks with Chicago Public Schools Superintendent Harold Hunt, and plans for "End Mob Violence" week

(reprint of the agenda of what is probably the CEMV November 26, 1949, meeting, no date or source, UPWA Papers).

30. Hirsch, *Making the Second Ghetto*, 59, 73, 216.

31. CEMV meeting, January 7, 1950, pp. 64–85. As part of the delegation that met the mayor on November 11, 1949, John Gray of the South Side Negro Labor Council told the mayor that he had lived in the city for twenty-six years, and that he had moved to Chicago from Vicksburg, Mississippi, after his grandfather had been lynched (Strulovich and Kelly's report, p. 4, UPWA Papers, Box 343, Folder 3).

32. All three unions were considered left-wing, if not "Communist-infiltrated." The International Longshoreman Union was one of the unions targeted by CIO leaders Walter Reuther, Philip Murray, and the anticommunist faction in "a two-year purge of the CIO left-wing unions beginning in 1949." Chicago Amalgamated Local 453 of the United Auto Workers leadership supported Henry Wallace's campaign against Reuther and UAW officers' wishes (Boyle, *The UAW*, 64, 247, 52). The UPWA was considered "Communist-infiltrated" but survived the CIO purge. In the late 1950s, a black civic leader "condemned Negro-led opposition to a civic proposal because the union that provided the leadership was 'Commie from top to bottom.'" More than likely, he was referring to the UPWA. Another "moderate" black leader considered the "NAACP run by reds" when the packinghouse workers worked with NAACP to lobby for a FEPC bill in Springfield (Wilson, *Negro Politics*, 124–25, 234, 161). In the early 1950s, a UAW officer declared the UPWA "free from communist domination or influence." Afterward, Ralph Helstein, UPWA international president, considered Reuther a reliable ally in organized labor leadership circles (Lichtenstein, *Walter Reuther*, 324). See also Boyle, *The UAW*, 157.

33. "Rally against Mob Violence," no source or date, UPWA Papers; "Labor Rally: Assail City Laxity on Mob Issue," *Chicago Daily News*, December 2, 1949.

34. The criticisms came from Homer Jack, former director of CAD, and Michael Mann and Albert Towers of the CIO Industrial Council and former board members of the CUL.

35. Hirsch, *Making the Second Ghetto*, 60–62.

36. Sidney Williams to Dr. Homer Jack, December 19, 1949, attached to a memo from Russell Lasley to UPWA officials, January 5, 1950, UPWA Papers, "Anti-Discrimination," File; Wilson, *Negro Politics*, 160–61; Hirsch, *Making the Second Ghetto*, 247.

37. Jack, "The Charge," December 17, 1949. Although Towers and Mann did not mention that known or suspected Communists were part of the CEMV, their knowledge of left-wing CIO unions', especially the UPWA's, participation in late 1949 during the beginning of CIO purge had to be one of the reasons for their opposition to the CEMV. Remember Mann's hostility to Bindman and his "Progressive Party" friends during the Peoria Street riots in July 1949 (Albert Towers, President, and Michael Mann, Secretary, Chicago Industrial Union Council, CIO, to Mr. Sidney

Williams, Executive Secretary, The Chicago Urban League, December 1, 1949, CUL Papers, Folder 73).

38. Sidney Williams to Towers and Mann, December 8, 1949, CUL Papers, UIC, Folder 73.

39. Sidney Williams to Homer Jack, December 19, 1949, UPWA Papers.

40. Sidney Williams to Lester Granger, February 24, 1947, NUL papers, Affiliates, Box 84, 1948, Chicago, CUL. For a discussion of moderate and militant political styles among black civic leaders in Chicago, see Wilson, *Negro Politics*, especially chapters 9 and 10.

41. The CEMV criticized the use of Catholic facilities by Peoria Street rioters and called for the impeachment of a Catholic mayor and police chief. On Catholics' resignation from the CUL board, see Hirsch, *Making the Second Ghetto*, 247, 85–86.

42. Elbridge Pierce, president of the CUL board at the time, was also a member of the Community Fund's budget review committee. Sidney Williams to E. B. Pierce, February 28, 1950, and Sidney Williams to E. B. Pierce, March 8, 1950, both in CUL Papers, Folder 74, UIC.

43. It appears that Williams used the external threat more with the Community Fund than with the association, which was not threatened by labor or liberal opposition (Sidney Williams, Executive Secretary of the Chicago Urban League, to Lester B. Granger, Executive Secretary of the National Urban League, February 21, 1950, NUL Papers, Box 84, File 3, 1950, Chicago Urban League; Sidney Williams to Maurice Moss, February 17, 1950, NUL Papers, Box 84, File 3, 1950, Chicago Urban League. He related to a CUL board member that "Saul Alinsky of Back of the Yards, the Packing House workers, many other unions and several agency executives are ready to go to battle. He quoted Earl Dickerson saying 'to hell with both of them [Community Fund and Association of Commerce and Industry]. Let's fight it out and in the open even if we have to cut staff down to three or four'" (Sidney Williams to Samuel Golan, February 17, 1950, NUL Papers, D, Box 84, Folder 3, "1950. Chicago Urban League").

44. For that relationship, see Williams to Granger, February 21, 1950; Sidney Williams to Lester Granger, August 25, 1948; Willard Townsend to Sidney Williams, August 21, 1948, copy attached to Williams to Granger, August 25, 1948, both in NUL Papers, Affiliates File, Box 84, Chicago Urban League, 1948. For earlier commentary on Townsend by Williams, see Williams to Granger, February 24, 1947. See also Willard Townsend, "One American Problem and a Possible Solution," in *What the Negro Wants*, ed. Rayford W. Logan (Chapel Hill, N.C.: University of North Carolina Press, 1944), 163–92; and Willard Townsend, "Full Employment and the Negro Worker," *Journal of Negro Education* 14, no.1 (Winter 1945): 6–10. On Willard Townsend see Eric Arnesen, "Willard Townsend: Black Workers, Civil Rights, and the Labor Movement," in *Portraits of African American Life Since 1965*, ed. Nina Mjagkig (Wilmington, Del.: Scholarly Resources, 2003), 147–64. Also, it is not clear who the "Negro

CIO Officials" were except for Russell Lasley, UPWA, and Willoughby Abner, UAW (see Williams to Towers and Mann, December 8, 1949; Williams to Granger, February 21, 1950; Williams to Moss, February 17, 1950; Minutes of the Board of Directors, February 23, 1950, copy appended to the Minutes of the Executive Committee, February 23, 1950; Minutes of the Board of Directors, April 14, 1950, and June 30, 1950; and interview, Chicago, July 19, 1961, in *History of the Chicago Urban League*, 175–76.

45. On February 8, 1950, a committee from the CUL board met with Wayne McMillen, the author of the report. Apparently, not much was settled (Nelson Jackson, "An Evaluation of the Chicago Urban League," 1955, p. 47; Minutes of the Board of Directors, February 23, 1950, cited in Arvarh E. Strickland, *History of the Chicago Urban League* (Urbana, Ill.: University of Illinois, 1966), 172–75.

46. Strickland, based on Minutes of the Board of Directors, April 14, 1950, and June 30, 1950; and interview, Chicago, July 19, 1961 in *History of Chicago Urban League*, 175–76; Hirsch, *Making the Second Ghetto*, 247. Williams began his letter to Golan in an almost paranoid style, claiming, "They're after us—Mike Mann, Tom Wright, Homer Jack, Willard Townsend, Chamber of Commerce, Mayor Kennelly and the Community Fund" (Sidney Williams to Samuel Golan, February 17, 1950, in NUL Papers, D, Box 84, Folder 3, "1950. Chicago Urban League"). Williams may not have been as paranoid as he sounds. Lester Granger, in a 1948 letter to Williams, referred to "organized real estate" collaborating with the Washington Board of Trade in a campaign to get the Washington Urban League removed from that city's Community Chest, writing: "Our various activities in the interests of better housing have won no love for us from realtors. . . . It looks now as if the effort will be successful. The National Office and the local Board are standing firm and yielding not a step. We are saying 'drop us and we will campaign on the basis of Chest action and raise our budget in spite of you.'" Granger's defiance seemed uncharacteristic. He seems to have given Williams different advice when he faced the same threat in Chicago (Lester Granger to Sidney Williams, March 15, 1948).

47. While the Chicago Urban League was an independent agency under the authority of its own board of directors, an affiliate rather than a subsidiary of the national office, it mostly followed the policies of the national office. "The Chicago Urban League is a part of but not controlled by the National Urban League." (Chicago Urban League report, January 1950, NUL Papers, D, Box 84, Folder 3, "1950. Chicago Urban League").

48. Sidney Williams, Executive Secretary of the Chicago Urban League, to Lester B. Granger, Executive Secretary of the National Urban League, February 21, 1950, NUL Papers, Box 84, File 3, 1950, Chicago Urban League. See also Sidney Williams to Maurice Moss, February 17, 1950, NUL Papers, Box 84, File 3, 1950, Chicago Urban League; Williams to Granger, February 21, 1950.

49. Sometimes the rumors made it into print. The *Daily News* ran an article that mentioned "that the League would serve as administrator of proposed defense fund

raised by Dearborn Real Estate Board, to be used by Negro families facing problems in new areas" (entry for September 26, 1951, in "Excerpts from Board Minutes, Reference to Housing 1950–1954," under the section "Housing Problem" in the draft of the evaluation of the Chicago Urban League, NUL Papers, Housing Activities Department, General Department File, "Chicago Report," "Miscellany").

50. Apparently, one of Williams's sources had told him of downtown capital's opposition to Earl Dickerson and Supreme Liberty Life aiding residential desegregation and making profits from real estate transactions (Sidney Williams to Lester Granger, August 20, 1954). In 1942, Dickerson became a vice president of Supreme Liberty Life Insurance Co., and in charge of the investments and mortgages department. See also Robert J. Blakely with Marcus Shepard, *Earl B. Dickerson: A Voice for Freedom and Equality* (Evanston, Ill: Northwestern University Press, 2006), 177, 153. Earl Dickerson was certainly aware of his reputation among the political and economic establishment. He had been president of the board off and on since 1939 and had wanted to step down after the 1947 reorganization that brought Sidney Williams to the directorship. At the time, he saw "himself as a 'caretaker' who would hold the office until a man 'untouched by past forces' could be found." The board turned to him in 1950 when it could not find a suitable candidate. He served until he resigned in 1953 (interview with Earl Dickerson, August 12, 1961, cited in Strickland, *History of Chicago Urban League*, 179–80).

51. Sidney Williams to Lester Granger, June 28, 1954, 1–2; Strickland, *History of Chicago Urban League*, 182.

52. Sidney Williams to Lester Granger, June 28, 1954, 3; Strickland, *History of Chicago Urban League*, 182.

53. "The Urban League is, of course, committed to the principle that every American citizen has the right to make his home wherever he chooses—and that any attempt to abridge this right is not only illegal but immoral." The CUL offered to open its books to the Community Fund to refute the allegations (Memorandum by the Board of the Chicago Urban League to the Community Fund's Special Committee, August 3, 1954, NUL Papers, Administration Department, Affiliates File, Chicago, Ill., 1954, Jan-Sept., Box 84, revised statement was dated August 6, 1954).

54. A confidential letter from Lester Granger to Herman Dunlap Smith, Community Fund executive director, suggested that the fund and the national office had had some conversations prior to the "agreement" by the league's board to accept the deal. The letter itself casts some suspicion on Granger's motives and possible collusion with the citywide funding agency in ushering Williams out of office (see "Minutes of Chicago Urban League Board of Directors' Meeting," Thursday, October 28, 1954, attached to Hill's October 28, 1954, memorandum; and Lester Granger to Hermon Dunlap Smith, Community Fund of Chicago, October 8, 1954). Granger was not above drastic reprisals toward local directors who opposed his policies. Memphis Urban League executive secretary, Benjamin Y. Bell Jr., had been removed from office

in 1944 when he refused to stop organizing black laundry workers who had their pay automatically docked for contributions to the local Community Chest. Before Sidney Williams took on the mantle of the leadership of CEMV in late 1949, he was already identified by Granger as a dissident to be either ignored or disciplined when he did not follow Granger's positions or approach to race relations work (Parris and Lester Brooks, *Blacks in the City: A History of the National Urban League*, 387–88; Dickerson, *Militant Mediator*, 85; Moore, *Struggle for Equality*, 154–55; 152–54). For an interpretation that places more blame on the Community Fund, see Linn Brandenburg, associate executive director of the Community Fund, quoted in Jackson, "An Evaluation of the Chicago Urban League," ii, cited by Strickland, *History of Chicago Urban League*, 183.

55. The study and reorganization was also sanctioned by the Welfare Council of Metropolitan Chicago in addition to the Community Fund and the NUL.

56. During Sidney Williams's tenure as CUL executive secretary, he clashed repeatedly with Lester Granger over tactics and approach (Lester Granger to Sidney Williams, March 31, 1948, NUL Papers, Affiliates File, Box 84, Chicago Urban League. 1948).

57. "Rumor" section of draft report of the evaluation of the Chicago Urban League by Nelson C. Jackson, NUL Papers, Housing Activities File, "Chicago report." Strickland argued, "The causes of the 1955 upheaval were apparent to all concerned; there was no need for a cover-up study" (*History of Chicago Urban League*, 188).

58. According to Strickland, the reorganization under the conservatives led by an African American physician, Nathaniel O. Calloway, had started as early as November 1954. He blamed the tumultuous years under Sidney Williams on the board of directors who were not invested in Urban League work (Strickland, *History of Chicago Urban League*, 185–88).

59. Ibid., 188–89. The *Chicago Defender* commented that "firings of staff members failed to raise as huge a ripple in community opinion as did the announcement that the league was closing down offices for six months to 'reorganize'" ("Sidney Williams Fired by Chicago Urban League," *Chicago Defender* [national edition], July 23, 1955; memorandum from Richard Durham to Charles Fischer, United Packinghouse Workers of America, March 16, 1955). No wonder the Swift officials were keeping a file on Sidney Williams. Rick Halpern, *Down on the Killing Floor: Black and White Workers in Chicago's Packinghouse, 1904–1954* (Urbana, Ill.: University of Illinois Press, 1997), 229. See 240–41 for Halpern's interpretation of Williams's dismissal. Another indication of Williams's support for Packinghouse Workers causes was evident in a memo from Russell R. Lasley to A. T. Stephens commenting that Williams and Whitney Young, then director of the Omaha Urban League, had pledged their support in a UPWA fight against an employer (October 2, 1953). See also Hirsch, *Making the Second Ghetto*, 247.

60. Nesbitt agreed with Abrams, who argued that Cicero's racial violence was not "a by-product of Al Capone's rule over Cicero" nor was it due to "'alien' Czechs and Poles [who were] unschooled in democratic ways" (Charles Abrams, "The Blame for Cicero: Behind the Riot Lies a National Problem of Providing for Negro Expansion," *New York Herald Tribune*, October 25, 1951, NUL Papers, Housing Activities, 1958–1962, Chicago, Illinois).

61. Walter White emphasized, "Never before, even in the South, have officers of the law been posted in a building to keep Negroes from moving in" (White to Foley, August 2, 1951).

62. Hirsch, *Making the Second Ghetto*, 62–63.

63. Nesbitt, "Housing Implications of Anti-Negro Violence in Cicero, Illinois," July 1951.

64. White to Foley, August 2, 1951. Klinkner with Smith comment on civil rights organizations taking "self-conscious advantage of America's new global rule" (*The Unsteady March*, 209–10). On Walter White, particularly, using the cold-war context to argue for racial democratic reforms as a way to bolster the United States' ability to win the propaganda war with the Soviet Union, especially with Third World nations, see Dudziak, *Cold War Civil Rights*, 83–84.

65. Nesbitt, "Housing Implications of Anti-Negro Violence in Cicero, Illinois," July 1951.

66. He suggested that someone should phone the South Side Business Men's Association and ask, "What do they think about the riot? What can be done about it? What did they do?" ([Barnett], "Cicero Riots," no date, Claude A. Barnett [CAB] Papers, Box 305, Folder 7).

67. Ibid.

68. Ibid.

69. A few years later, Williams reported that he had gotten "many requests to take leadership in the Cicero situation" but had refused to take a leadership position. He claimed that his only involvement in Cicero was to "commend the Governor for calling out the Militia" as well as keeping the national office informed of events as they unfolded. Despite his restraint, Williams mentioned there were rumors that the league had moved the Clarks into Cicero, precipitating the violence ("Housing Activities of the Board of Directors and the Executive Director," section of draft report of the evaluation of the Chicago Urban League by Nelson C. Jackson, NUL Papers, Housing Activities File, "Chicago report").

70. See chapter 6.

71. Hirsch reports that well into the 1960s these projects either remained all-white or accommodated token integration (*Making the Second Ghetto*, 239).

72. Bowly, *The Poorhouse*, 80; William E. Hill, Chicago Field Office, to Philip G. Sadler, Special Assistant to the Commissioner, "Mob Violence at Trumbull Park Homes in Chicago," September 11, 1953, HHFA Papers, RG 207, NAII.

73. Bowly, *The Poorhouse*, 80–81; William E. Hill, Chicago Field Office, to Philip G. Sadler, Special Assistant to the Commissioner, "Mob Violence at Trumbull Park Homes in Chicago," September 11, 1953, HHFA Papers, RG 207, NAII; "Report on Trumbull Park Issued by Chicago Branch NAACP," UPWA Papers, Box 353, Folder 11, Willoughby Abner, NAACP Trumbull Park Action Committee, May 24, 1954; Arnold R. Hirsch, "Massive Resistance in the Urban North: Trumbull Park, Chicago, 1953–1966," *Journal of American History* 82, no. 2 (1995): 522–50.

74. "Report on Trumbull Park Issued by Chicago Branch NAACP," UPWA Papers, Box 353, Folder 11, Willoughby Abner, NAACP Trumbull Park Action Committee, May 24, 1954.

75. Bowly, *The Poorhouse*, 82–83. Probably more important than blacks' reluctance to move into troubled Trumbull Park was the deal SDIA made with the city housing officials to limit the number of black families to roughly twenty-five (Hirsch, *Making the Second Ghetto*, 98–99, 237).

76. Hill to William E. Bergeron, Director, "Proposing a Recommendation on Racial Policy for Submission to the Commissioner, PHA," March 12, 1954; Hill, Chicago Field Office, PHA to Philip G. Sadler, Special Assistant to the Commissioner, "Chicago Field Office Disapproves Proposal to Revise PHA Racial Policy," April 16, 1954.

77. William E. Hill, Chicago Field Office, to Philip G. Sadler, Special Assistant to the Commissioner, "Mob Violence at Trumbull Park Homes in Chicago," September 11, 1953; "Statement by Robert R. Taylor, former Chairman of the Chicago Housing Authority Regarding Racial Policies at C.H.A.," attached to Corrienne R. Morrow, Acting Director of Racial Relations Branch, to Commissioner, PHA, "Situation in Chicago re Move-in of Negro Tenant, Trumbull Homes," August 13, 1953, NA, HHFA, RG 207, Box 750, Chicago, Illinois Folder.

78. "Calls Mayor Lax on Trumbull Riots," *Chicago Sun-Times*, March 8, 1954, clipping in UPWA Papers, Box 353, Folder 11; Chicago Commission on Human Relations, "The Trumbull Park Homes Disturbances: A Chronological Report, August 4, 1953 to June 30, 1955," pp. 35–37, NA, RG 207, Program Files, Racial Relations, Box 750, Chicago, IL Folder; *A Shame on Chicago!* Chicago Negro Chamber of Commerce flyer for Mass Mobilization, City Hall, March 19, 1954, UPWA Papers, Box 353, Folder 11.

79. "Report on Trumbull Park Issued by Chicago Branch NAACP," UPWA Papers, Box 353, Folder 11.

80. "Thurgood Marshall Denounces Mob Violence in Chicago, Receives Abbott Award," Associated Negro Press, May 10, 1954, CAB Papers, Box 395, Folder 1.

81. Cora Patton, President, Chicago Branch, NAACP, to Temple McFayden, Chairman, Illinois State Housing Board, September 18, 1954.

82. Most of the community's residents, who were of southern and eastern European background, worked in the local steel mills (Hirsch, *Making the Second Ghetto*,

79). When Albert Cole, head of HHFA, visited Chicago in October 1954, he called upon Reverend Bernard J. Sheil, Catholic auxiliary bishop of Chicago and CIO President Walter P. Reuther to work with Mayor Kennelly to restore peace, order, and "simple human decency" (Albert Cole to Mayor Kennelly, October 28, 1954, NA, RG 207, Box 750, Chicago, Illinois Folder; Carleton Kent, "End Trumbull Park Disorders, Cole Warns," October 30, 1954, news clipping in UPWA Papers, Box 353, Folder 11.

83. For a compelling argument of that institutionalization and its impact, see Kevin Fox Gotham, *Race, Real Estate, and Uneven Development: The Kansas City Experience, 1900–2000* (Albany: State University of New York Press, 2002), chapter 3. For an early history of working-class home ownership, white and black, see Margaret Garb, *City of American Dreams: A History of Home Ownership and Housing Reform in Chicago, 1871–1919* (Chicago, Ill.: University of Chicago Press Press, 2005).

84. "The First Year," A Progress Report on the Coordinator Program in District #1, UPWA-CIO submitted by Oscar Brown Jr., Program Coordinator, UPWA Papers, "Brown, Oscar Jr., Correspondence," 1954 Box 354, Folder 11, Oscar Brown Jr., as program coordinator, often personally directed much of the support activity. In October 1953, he requested aid from the CIO's Cook County Council for the Howard family, explaining that both parents were unemployed and needed food and clothing. He mentioned that his union had contributed quite a bit and thought the CIO could help out. He described the Howards' circumstances at Trumbull Park as "living practically besieged." Brown pointedly asked a council member if they could help Donald Howard find a job at any of the industrial plants where the CIO had bargaining rights. He thought the CIO had "considerable influence" with "responsible agencies," which would give "practical support to their efforts to maintain a beachhead for democracy in Trumbull Park" (Oscar Brown Jr., Program Coordinator, District #1, UPWA-CIO to Robert Levin, Cook County Council-CIO, October 8, 1953. UPWA Papers, Box 349, Folder 7).

85. Richard Durham to A. T. Stephens and Russell R. Lasley, memorandum, January 12, 1954, UPWA Papers, Box 357, Folder 20. It was reported that the "Chicago area has now established permanent committee for equal housing" ("Meeting—Sept. 4, 1954—Lasley, Stephens, Durham, Brosnan," UPWA Papers, Box 359, Folder 7).

86. Richard Durham to Charles Hayes and Oscar Brown Jr., memorandum, June 2, 1954, UPWA Papers, Box 359, Folder 1.

87. Union members experienced violence and intimidation firsthand as stones were thrown at them as they picked up the families for the dinner. The union put together a list of physicians who could treat the families if needed, and it arranged for Clarence Young, who had been assaulted with baseball bats, to see a specialist in internal medicine (Brown report to Durham, June 2, 1954, UPWA Papers, Box 354, Folder 11). "District One Program Report," June 29, 1954, Oscar Brown Jr., UPWA

Papers, Box 354, Folder 11; Richard Durham, "Program Report from Oscar Brown Jr.," July 10, 1954.

88. The union was expecting racial violence around the Fourth of July ("The Projects from July 1–15," Oscar Brown Jr., UPWA Papers, Box 362, Folder 11).

89. Frank Brown became Trumbull Park's most well-known black tenant after Donald Howard left in May 1954. Brown and his family had moved into Trumbull Park in January 1953, just six months after the disturbances began. He took on a leadership role after Donald Howard left. A veteran of World War II, Brown was born in Kansas City, Missouri, in 1927. Brown and his family appeared on a CBS news program on Trumbull Park on July 4, 1954. He received quite a bit of favorable mail and some celebrity status. He succeeded Oscar Brown Jr. as program coordinator for District #1 of UPWA ("Report of Program Coordinator: Frank Brown, District #1, UPWA," October, 1955, UPWA Papers, Box 362, Folder 11). He later wrote a novel entitled *Trumbull Park: A Novel by Frank London Brown* (Chicago, Ill.: Regnery, 1959).

90. Brown report to Durham, June 2, 1954, UPWA Papers, Box 354, Folder 11; "District One Program Report," June 29, 1954, Oscar Brown Jr., UPWA Papers, Box 354, Folder 11; Richard Durham, "Program Report from Oscar Brown Jr.," July 10, 1954, "Minutes of Meeting of District #1 Staff and Trumbull Park Families on Sunday, June 20, 1954," UPWA Papers, Box 353, Folder 12.

91. "Minutes of Meeting of District #1 Staff and Trumbull Park Families on Sunday, June 20, 1954," UPWA Papers, Box 353, Folder 12; Catherine Brosnan, Organization Department, to Officers and Office Staff, UPWA, June 30, 1954; "CIO Union Backs Negroes in Project," *Chicago Daily News*, June 22, 1954, news clipping, in UPWA Papers, Box 353, Folder 12.

92. An ad hoc committee of UPWA antidiscrimination department representatives constructed a program for their union members. "Out of these sessions a program of education for our membership was formulated, and a decision to help stimulate a community-wide organization to attack the basic housing problem in Chicago. The basic problem can be summarized as the need to break through the many restrictions that have been erected over the years to confine Negroes to certain neighborhoods" (CIO Civil Rights Committee Officer's Report, March 24, 1954, UPWA Papers, "Civil Rights, 1952–1954, Box 349, Folder 13).

93. "Notes on Joint AFL-CIO Trumbull Park Meeting, August 25, 1954," UPWA Papers, Box 353, Folder 12.

94. Parks expressed the chief differences he saw between a liberal black civic organization and a black-led, left-wing interracial labor union. Perhaps Parks's criticism of Abner also reflected Abner's anticommunist position. Abner aligned himself with the Reutherite anticommunist faction within the UAW and broader CIO, which

targeted Parks's union in a 1949 purge (Wilson, *Negro Politics*, 125). The labor historian Nelson Lichtenstein referred to Abner, a law school graduate, as "perhaps the union equivalent of a Rhodes scholar," describes him as a "Reuther loyalist in the 1940s and 1950s who had been politically educated by the anti-Stalinist left." Abner repeatedly clashed with the "Communist-oriented blacks in the Cook County Industrial Union Council and the Chicago branch of the NAACP, of which he had been president in for two terms in the early 1950s" (Lichtenstein, *Walter Reuther*, 377). See also Boyle, *The UAW*, 129.

95. "Notes on Joint AFL-CIO Trumbull Park Meeting, August 25, 1954," UPWA Papers, Box 353, Folder 12. Prior to the meeting, some dissatisfaction was expressed with the ad that the UPWA had drafted. The Amalgamated union officials felt the advertisement had "too much propaganda rather than the simple statement of fact" (Lasley to Ralph Helstein, G. R. Hathaway, A. T. Stephens, and Richard Durham, memorandum, August 23, 1954).

96. Russell R. Lasley, Vice President, UPWA—CIO, and Board Member, Chicago NAACP to N. B. Andrews, Secretary-Treasurer, Chicago Branch, NAACP, February 11, 1954; Lasley to Rev. E. H. Harris, Pastor and Members, Canaan Baptist Church, February 16, 1954, UPWA Papers, Box 352, Folder 6.

97. Bowly, *The Poorhouse*, 83–84; Hirsch, *Making the Second Ghetto*, 234–38. On activists' response, see "Miss Wood 'Goaded' by CHA: Carey: Ask City Council to Probe Ouster," *Chicago Daily News*, September 10, 1954, news clipping in UPWA Papers, Box 353, Folder 11. See also Linda Marvis, "3 Groups Ask Probe of CHA," *Chicago Defender*, September 10, 1954, UPWA Papers, Box 353, Folder 11; Cora M. Patton, President, Chicago Branch of NAACP, to Mayor Martin H. Kennelly, September 20, 1954; NAACP Chicago Branch to Honorable Martin H. Kennelly, no date, UPWA Papers, Box 353, Folder 11; M H to Richard Durham, November 18, 1954, UPWA Papers, Box 353, Folder 12.

98. Despite his comments supporting civil rights, Daley showed his hand when he appointed yet another commission to study the racial conflict at Trumbull Park. Adding insult to injury, he excluded the UPWA and the NAACP from the membership of this new commission (Russell Lasley to Mayor Daley, telegram, UPWA, Richard Durham, Correspondence, 1955, Box 366, Folder 4; Russell R. Lasley to Mayor Richard J. Daley, June 14, 1955, UPWA Papers, Box 370, Folder 1).

99. Chicago NAACP, "Housing Desegregation in 1959," AFSC Papers, Box 93, Folder 1.

100. In 1954, a deal was struck between the city and SDIA that limited black families to twenty (Hirsch, *Making the Second Ghetto*, 98–99; CIO Civil Rights Committee Officer's Report, March 24, 1954, UPWA Papers, "Civil Rights, 1952–1954, Box 349, Folder 13).

8. Class and Racial Democracy

1. Wendy Plotkin, "Deeds of Mistrust: Race, Housing, and Restrictive Covenants in Chicago, 1900–1953" (PhD diss., University of Illinois at Chicago, 1999).

2. "Chicagoans Voice Views on U.S. Decree," *Chicago Defender*, November 16, 1940, 6, cited in Plotkin, "Deeds of Mistrust," 160–75.

3. Robert Moore Fisher, *20 Years of Public Housing: Economic Aspects of the Federal Program* (New York, N.Y.: Harper and Brothers, 1959), 96; "Chicago Whites Renew Fight against WPA Negro Housing Project," ANP, July 8, 1936, in Claude A. Barnett (CAB) Papers, Box 317, Folder 2; Plotkin, "Deeds of Mistrust," 218.

4. Much of this section draws substantially from Plotkin's comprehensive treatment of racially restrictive covenants in Chicago (Plotkin, "Deeds of Mistrust," 97).

5. Plotkin, "Deeds of Mistrust," 97; Dempsey J. Travis, *An Autobiography of Black Politics* (Chicago, Ill.: Urban Research Press, 1987), 143–44.

6. Clement E. Vose, *Caucasians Only: The Supreme Court, the NAACP, and the Restrictive Covenant Cases* (Berkeley, Calif.: University of California Press, 1959), 7.

7. Robert C. Weaver, *Hemmed In: ABC's of Race Restrictive Housing Covenants*. American Council on Race Relations, 1945, 2; Illinois State Library, Springfield, Illinois; Charles Abrams, *Race Bias in Housing*. American Civil Liberties Union, National Association for the Advancement of Colored People, and American Council on Race Relations, July 1947, pp. 12–13, Chicago Commons Papers, Box 30, January-August 1947 File; Herman Long and Charles S. Johnson, *People v. Property: Race Restrictive Covenants in Housing* (Nashville, Tenn.: Fisk University Press, 1947), 86, 10–11.

8. The *Buchanan v. Warley* 245 U.S. 60 Supreme Court decision struck down the Louisville ordinance that forbade a black family to move into a white majority neighborhood (Abrams, *Race Bias*, 11; Weaver, *Hemmed In*, 2, 1; St. Clair Drake and Horace Cayton, *Black Metropolis: A Study of Negro Life in a Northern City* [New York: Harcourt, Brace, 1945], 182; Plotkin, "Deeds of Mistrust," 100; see 96 on the class character of covenanted neighborhoods). Weaver identified developers of subdivisions, "ably aided and supported by the FHA and financial institutions," as creators of racial restrictive covenants. The real estate developers initiated the covenants on their own or were pressured to do so by the financial backers (Robert C. Weaver, *The Negro Ghetto* [New York: Harcourt, Brace, 1948], 233, 249, 253). On the relationship between neighborhood improvement associations and real estate interests, see Long and Johnson, *People v. Property*, 38; and Vose, *Caucasians Only*, 66–67.

9. Apparently, there were 222 racial covenants in Chicago compared to 378 in St. Louis. "In the two years between 1927 and 1929, two-fifths of the covenants located on Chicago's Southside were enacted" (Long and Johnson, *People v. Property*, 12, see also 44).

10. Ibid., 27–29. The historian Arnold Hirsch, instead, argues that whites' communal resistance to blacks was stronger on the West Side, hence the need for devices like

restrictive covenants on the South Side (Hirsch, *Making the Second Ghetto: Race and Housing in Chicago, 1940–1960* [Cambridge: Cambridge University Press, 1983], 217).

11. Abrams, *Race Bias*, 19; Andrew Wiese, *Places of Their Own: African American Suburbanization in the Twentieth Century* (Chicago, Ill.: University of Chicago Press Press, 2004), 41; Kevin Fox Gotham, *Race, Real Estate and Uneven Development: The Kansas City Experience, 1900–2000* (Albany: State University of New York Press, 2002), 37–39.

12. Opponents to racial covenants disagreed over the proportion of land covered by racial covenants. Weaver contended that Chicago still had both residential and vacant land not covered by restrictive covenants. At another point in his study, Weaver declared that trying to determine what percentage of housing outside the ghetto is under racial covenant was "not very important. The significant thing is the pattern of the coverage of restrictive covenants in many cities" (Weaver, *The Negro Ghetto*, 235, 246, 247, 213, 255).

13. Chicago "had an active pro-covenant real estate industry whose national organization, the National Association of Real Estate Boards (NAREB), was located in the city" (Plotkin, "Deeds of Mistrust," 43, 45–46). See also Long and Johnson, *People v. Property*, 57–58, 66; Gotham, *Race, Real Estate, Uneven Development*, 34–35; and Wiese, *Places of Their Own*, 41). "We know, for example, that in Chicago the birthplace of widespread use of covenants against Negroes was in middle-income neighborhoods and their objectives seeped down to the lower-income areas" (*The Kit of Tools for Slum Clearance*, Chicago Housing Authority, 1947, quoted in Weaver, *The Negro Ghetto*, 232–33).

14. The other was Harry Pace, one of the founders of Supreme Liberty Life. Both were part of the black elite cohort that dominated prewar housing reform in the black community. They both died prematurely due to health problems. Pace died in 1943 at the age of fifty-nine, and Hansberry died three years later at the age of fifty-two (Plotkin, "Deeds of Mistrust").

15. Ibid., 140.

16. Weaver reported that "real estate was the traditional investment for the more prosperous members of the Black Belt, and it had acquired certain prestige value" (Weaver, *The Negro Ghetto*, 137).

17. Plotkin, "Deeds of Mistrust," 141, 178–79. Plotkin countered one source's charge that Carl Hansberry was a "slum landlord" with "his business in conversions was small in comparison to those of white owners and managers in the Black Belt. The extent to which he himself was guilty of encouraging over-crowding or the subject of these initiatives is unclear." While it is true that Hansberry's holdings did not compare to the larger white real estate companies, Hansberry did participate and profit from illegal conversions into "kitchenettes," the black tenants of which were overcrowded and overcharged. While many upper-class blacks did not derive their wealth from the exploitation of their working-class brothers, Hansberry did. There

was sporadic but persistent evidence that part of the black bourgeoisie's affluence stemmed from real estate. Black federal housing official George Nesbitt commented on an increase in black upper-class investments in kitchenettes and rooming houses on his trip to Chicago in 1950 (George B. Nesbitt, field representative, to C. L. Farris, Chief, Field Operations Branch, Chicago, Illinois Field Trip—July 24 through 28, 1950, August 3, 1950, 11–16). For an early history of black real estate developers in Chicago see Michelle R. Boyd, *Jim Crow Nostalgia: Reconstructing Race in Bronzeville* (Minneapolis, Minn.: University of Minnesota Press, 2008), 20–22.

18. Carl Hansberry, "wealthy Negro Chicago real estate owner," participated in an evening meeting on July 1, 1943, of the March on Washington Movement held at Metropolitan Community Church with six hundred people in attendance. According to the FBI informant, "Hansberry advised Negroes to take advantage of all legal means to secure freedom from racial discrimination" (*The FBI's RACON: Racial Conditions in the United States during World War II*, comp. and ed. Robert A. Hill [Boston: Northeastern University Press, 1995], 100). Carl's older brother, William Leo Hansberry, was an Africanist and taught African history at Howard University from 1922. He was in Chicago to work at the University of Chicago's Oriental Institute in 1935–1936. Carl Hansberry's home was frequented by black scholars, artists, and political activists including W. E. B. Du Bois, Langston Hughes, and Paul Robeson. Unsurprisingly, Hansberry, the conservative businessman, disapproved of Robeson's politics and questioned the value of his brother's academic life. Of course, this environment helped to shape the literary career of his daughter Lorraine (Plotkin, "Deeds of Mistrust," 142–46).

19. The lawyers who defended Carl Hansberry, Harry Pace, and Supreme Liberty Life came from the same black elite networks as their clients. Plotkin describes the Hansberry case lawyers as the "cream" of Chicago's black legal talent. They were sons of accomplished professionals who went on to graduate from the nation's elite law schools, including four from the University of Chicago Law School, and to establish national and local African American law associations. The prominent lawyers involved in the case include Earl Dickerson, Cornelius Francis Stradford, Loring B. Moore, Truman K. Gibson Jr., and Irvin Mollison. For more on their elite backgrounds, see Plotkin, "Deeds of Mistrust," 152–58.

20. On "racial public policy in housing," see *People v. Property*, 88, 70.

21. The defense presented an affidavit from a Woodlawn Property Owners Association president, who stated that the organization took a flawed covenant to court assuming without careful examination it would establish its legal validity (Plotkin, "Deeds of Mistrust," 171–73).

22. Robert J. Blakely with Marcus Shepard, *Earl B. Dickerson: A Voice for Freedom and Equality* (Evanston, Ill.: Northwestern University Press, 2006), 95–100. Apparently there was some controversy over who should argue the case. Jewel Rogers,

daughter of Cornelius Stradford, remembered that her father had done much of the legal work in the case and that it was his brief on behalf of the Hansberrys that "swung the case." Dickerson was added because Supreme Liberty Life was the mortgagee. She remembered that Carl Hansberry and her father were unhappy with the decision that Dickerson should argue the case. Apparently, the Hansberrys and Stradford families were close (Travis, *Autobiography of Black Chicago*, 232; Plotkin, "Deeds of Mistrust," 215 n. 154). See also "High Court Voids J. C. Covenants," ANP, no date, CAB Papers, Box 351, Folder 1.

23. "More Than Passing Victory Won in Residential Lawsuit," ANP, no date, CAB Papers, Box 305, Folder 7; "High Court Voids J. C. Covenants," ANP, no date, CAB Papers, Box 351, Folder 1; Long and Johnson, *People v. Property*, 98.

24. "Realtor Tells His Role in Covenant Case," *Chicago Defender*, November 16, 1940, 2, cited in Plotkin, "Deeds of Mistrust," 160–75.

25. Lorraine Hansberry, *To Be Young, Gifted and Black*, 51–52, cited in Plotkin, "Deeds of Mistrust," 177.

26. Plotkin, "Deeds of Mistrust," 178.

27. "Supreme Court Ruling on Residential Covenant Case Opens up Many New Homes: Hailed as Biggest Social Victory in Years," ANP, no date, CAB Papers, Box 351, Folder 1. For a more measured view of the consequences of the Hansberry decision, see Hirsch, *Making the Second Ghetto*, 30.

28. The disputed land represented twenty-seven blocks between Sixtieth and Sixty-Third Streets and between Cottage Grove and South Park ("High Court Voids J. C. Covenants," ANP, no date, CAB Papers, Box 351, Folder 1). Later, African Americans rehabilitated and modernized the properties turning a once marginal area to a showcase for black property ownership (*Some Aspects of the Negro Population of Chicago*, prepared by Frayser T. Lane, November 1948, pp. 2–3, for Housing Planners in the Privately Financed Field, Archibald Carey Jr. Papers, Box 6, Folder 36).

29. "More Than Passing Victory," CAB Papers, Box 351, Folder 1.

30. Ibid. Before the Hansberry case was ruled upon by the circuit court, Williams Pickens for the ANP wrote on "Residential Segregation by Covenant: The Menace of Private Law," Associated Negro Press (ANP), July 20, 1937, CAB Papers, Box 305, Folder 7. See also Vose, *Caucasians Only*, 56, 156. "Supreme Court Ruling on Residential Covenant Case," CAB Papers.

31. Plotkin, "Deeds of Mistrust," 99. According to Weaver, freedom of movement must be a fundamental freedom in a democratic society (Weaver, *Hemmed In*, 2). Wiese, *Places of Their Own*, 131.

32. Plotkin, "Deeds of Mistrust," 99. The historian Andrew Wiese argues that African Americans crafted their own American dream by owning single-family homes in predominantly black suburbs (Wiese, *Places of Their Own*).

33. Plotkin, "Deeds of Mistrust," 140.

34. Ibid., 142–46. The *Chicago Defender* claimed that the court case went beyond Hansberry's personal interest to represent "a battle between the races over constitutional rights." Losing the case could mean tightening racial boundaries driving up rents due to the combination of a growing population and limited space ("Judge Gives Hansberrys New Chance," *Chicago Defender*, October 23, 1937, 1, quoted in Plotkin, "Deeds of Mistrust," 163).

35. Plotkin, "Deeds of Mistrust," 99.

36. Plotkin, "Deeds of Mistrust," 101; Louis Wirth and Eleanor H. Bernert, eds., *Local Community Fact Book of Chicago* (Chicago, Ill.: University of Chicago Press Press, 1949).

37. Plotkin, "Deeds of Mistrust," 108.

38. Ibid., 109.

39. Ibid., 107–9.

40. Drake and Cayton, *Black Metropolis*, 185–86. The black social scientists go on to discuss the varied and complex positions taken by whites in neighborhoods experiencing racial transition (see ibid., 187–88; and Long and Johnson, *People v. Property*, 6). See also Plotkin, "Deeds of Mistrust," 174–75.

41. Since the seller retained title to the property, he or she could cancel the contract and retain the property if the buyer missed as little as one monthly installment. I do not have data that reveal the proportion of blacks buying with "land contracts" versus mortgages. The prevalence of land contracts was due to the difficulty black consumers had in securing mortgages. Black realtor Dempsey Travis led the fight to eliminate land contracts as a way of buying and selling property (Travis, *Black Politics*). For an excellent study of the fight against land contracts on the West Side of Chicago see Beryl Satter, *Family Properties: Race, Real Estate, and the Exploitation of Urban America* (New York, N.Y.: Metropolitan Books, 2009).

42. Schietinger, "Real Estate Transfers during Negro Invasion," 22–23, 44, 47–49, 49–50, cited by Plotkin, "Deeds of Mistrust," 105–8; Robert C. Puth, *Supreme Life: The History of a Negro Life Insurance Company* (New York, N.Y.: Arno Press, 1976), 131–32, 136–37, 139–40.

43. Plotkin, "Deeds of Mistrust," 99; Drake and Cayton, *Black Metropolis*, 744.

44. Abrams, *Race Bias*, 25.

45. Drake and Cayton, *Black Metropolis*, 114–15.

46. "University of Chicago, White Realty Owners, Lambasted in Mass Meet on Inadequate Housing: President Hutchins Tries to Defend Stand as Chicagoans Fight for Better Living Accommodations and Threaten Boycott," ANP, November 10, 1937, CAB Papers, Box 351, Folder 1, Chicago Historical Society (CHS) archives; "To Discuss Housing at Big Meeting," *Chicago Defender*, October 30, 1937; and "South Siders Gird to Fight High Rentals," *Chicago Defender*, November 6, 1937, cited by Plotkin, "Deeds of Mistrust," 169; "Race Housing Assailed at Two Meetings," *Chicago*

Defender, December 18, 1937, 6, cited by Plotkin, "Deeds of Mistrust," 170; Plotkin, "Deeds of Mistrust," 171; Drake and Cayton, *Black Metropolis*, 184.

47. Albert G. Barnett for ANP, "Cayton Resents Negro-Baiting Slur by U. of C. Magazine: Housing Expert Replies to Article Which States: 'Vigilante Committees of Whites Would Precipitate Riots and Force the Negroes from Their Community,'" ANP, November [1939], CAB Papers, Box 351, Folder 1, CHS. The number of nonwhite owners in Woodlawn tripled from 661 to 1,842 from 1940 to 1950. In the three predominantly black census tracts (623, 624, 625), the percentages of owner-occupied dwelling units were 11, 16, and 25 (Philip M. Hauser and Evelyn M. Kitagawa, eds., *Local Community Fact Book for Chicago, 1950* [Chicago, Ill.: University of Chicago Press, 1953], 175).

48. A. Barnett, "Cayton Resents Negro-Baiting Slur."

49. Ibid. Almost ten years later, Frank Horne commented on black realtor participation in "blockbusting" and developing kitchenettes in racial transitions areas (Frank S. Horne to Raymond M. Foley, "Rehabilitation Proposal of the Oakland-Kenwood Property Owners' Association, Chicago," November 25, 1947, RG 207, Box 18, Racial Relations, 1947–July 1948). See also Weaver, *The Negro Ghetto*, 273.

50. "Chicago Housing," *Chicago Defender*, November 6, 1937, cited in Plotkin, "Deeds of Mistrust," 179; Plotkin, "Deeds of Mistrust," 178–79.

51. Christopher R. Reed, *The Chicago NAACP and the Rise of Black Professional Leadership, 1910–1966* (Bloomington: Indiana University Press, 1997), 148.

52. Plotkin, "Deeds of Mistrust," 178–79. Midian Bousfield criticized the growth of "kitchenettes" without specifying the owners of such property ("Dr. Bousfield Puts Policy Barons and Kitchenette Promoters in Same Class," *Chicago Defender*, December 9, 1939, 13).

53. Plotkin, "Deeds of Mistrust," 233; "NAACP Discusses Housing Covenants," *Chicago Bee*, December 10, 1944.

54. Among them were Willis Graves and Francis Dent of Detroit, Charles Houston of Washington, D.C., Loren Miller of Los Angeles, and George Vaughn of St. Louis.

55. Vose, *Caucasians Only*, 58; Wiese, *Places of Their Own*, 128.

56. Vose, *Caucasians Only*, 60–65. Wendell Pritchett, *Robert Clifton Weaver and the American City: The Life and Times of an Urban Reformer* (Chicago, Ill.: University of Chicago Press, 2008), 128.

57. Ibid., 64.

58. The *Tovey v. Levy* case was touted in the local black press as a test case for the U.S. Supreme Court. The Levys, who were white, were charged with violating a restrictive covenant agreement in Englewood. Loring B. Moore, at a national conference of black leaders at Howard University on January 26, 1947, argued that he had a strong case in Chicago because he had testimony to emphasize the social impact of restrictive covenants on ghettoization. NAACP lawyers Thurgood Marshall and William Hastie felt the next case they chose had to be the "best possible case in which to apply

for certiorari" (a writ by higher court to review a lower court ruling; Vose, *Caucasians Only*, 151). Vose shows how the NAACP lawyers' use of sociological analysis to bolster their case against restrictive covenants anticipated their approach in *Brown v. Board of Education, Topeka, Kansas*, in 1954. Apparently "nearly 40 restrictive covenant cases are pending in local courts, awaiting the outcome of this test case" ("Chicago Has 40 Square Miles Under Restrictive Covenants, Survey Reveals Negroes Locked in 9 ¼ Square Miles Section," ANP, no date, CAB Papers, Box 351, Folder 1).

59. "The [American] Council [on Race Relations] functioned between 1944 and 1950 as a national clearing house whose purposes included 'the stimulation of research bearing upon basic factors underlying the problems of racial and cultural relations, the perfection of sound policies and techniques, experimentation with methods for evaluating the practical results of programs and procedures, together with persistent efforts to call these findings to the attention of the policy-makers and technicians in the field.'" Louis Wirth was the executive director of the American Council on Race Relations. Vose mistakenly identified Weaver as a "sociologist" (Vose, *Caucasians Only*, 162). Pritchett, *Robert Clifton Weaver*, 126–28.

60. Moore cited the evidence they gathered to suggest the *Tovey v. Levy* case was a strong case to get a certiorari. It reflected the role that social science played in supporting civil rights (Vose, *Caucasians Only*, 151–52).

61. Plotkin argued that "while in Chicago, Weaver became the leading liberal theorist on racially restrictive covenants" (Plotkin, "Deeds of Mistrust," 225). Pritchett, *Robert Clifton Weaver*, 128. Weaver prepared the pamphlet *Hemmed In* for the American Council on Race Relations in September 1945. Weaver also discussed restrictive covenants in *The Negro Ghetto*, which he wrote in 1946 and 1947 (see 228–29).

62. Long and Johnson, *People v. Property*, 8–9, 10.

63. Ibid., 38.

64. As discussed earlier, not only are they different sides of the same coin, they were sometimes the same people (Weaver, *Hemmed In*, 3–4). Sometimes the same developers had property in racially covenanted and ghetto areas (see *Memorandum: Real Estate Interests Promote Racial Hatred in Chicago*, To: Chicago Organizations Supporting Civil Liberties and Democracy, October 1944, Chicago Commons Papers, Box 29, UIC; Weaver, *Negro Ghetto*, 235).

65. Weaver, *Hemmed In*, 4–5; Weaver, *Negro Ghetto*, 237.

66. Weaver, *Hemmed In*, 5.

67. Weaver, *Negro Ghetto*, 238. See also Plotkin, "Deeds of Mistrust," 226.

68. In Chicago, over 20 percent of housing units lacked "private flush toilets," with a great majority of these located in the ghetto (Long and Johnson, *People v. Property*, 38).

69. Long and Johnson, *People v. Property*, 7; *Memorandum: Real Estate Interests Promote Racial Hatred in Chicago*, To: Chicago Organizations Supporting Civil Liberties and Democracy, October 1944, Chicago Commons Papers, Box 29, UIC.

70. Long and Johnson, *People v. Property*, 7; National Urban League, *Racial Problems in Housing*. Interracial Planning for Community Organization. Bulletin No. 2, Fall (New York, N.Y.: National Urban League, 1944), Chicago Common Papers, Box 29.

71. Long and Johnson, *People v. Property*, 83; see also 84.

72. Weaver, *Hemmed In*, 12.

73. Ibid., 6–9. Weaver made a similar argument in "Racial Tensions in Chicago," pp. 1–8, 1943, Box 750, Folder Chicago IL, I, RG 207 (see chapter 7).

74. Weaver, *Negro Ghetto*, 253–54. See also Weaver, *Hemmed In*, 11–13.

75. Weaver, *Hemmed In*, 4; Weaver, *Negro Ghetto*, 234–35, 238; Long and Johnson, *People v. Property*, 87. Hirsch makes a similar argument suggesting the decision was the "final blow to a device that was already growing unequal to the task of preserving racial homogeneity of white neighborhoods beleaguered by mounting economic and social pressures" (Hirsch, *Making the Second Ghetto*, 16; see also 29–30).

76. Weaver, *Hemmed In*, 2; Weaver, *Negro Ghetto*, 244–45. The unsuccessful effort to use state legislation to outlaw restrictive covenants continued from 1937 throughout the war years ("Fight to End Homes Bans Gains in City," *Chicago Bee*, January 28, 1945, "Memorandum: Real Estate Interests Promote Racial Hatred in Chicago"; Chicago Civil Liberties Committee, *Civil Liberties News*, August 18, 1944, RG 207, Box 750, Chicago, IL, I, NA). For the efforts to introduce two bills in Illinois House in 1944, see Long and Johnson, *People v. Property*, 100–101. See also Plotkin, "Deeds of Mistrust," 231–33.

77. "U.S. Supreme Court decision outlawing enforcement of restrictive covenants," a reprint of the *Shelley v. Kraemer* 1948 Supreme Court decision, MHPC Papers, Box 6, Folder 9; Vose, *Caucasians Only*, 207–8; Plotkin, "Deeds of Mistrust," 238–39; Philip A. Klinkner with Rogers M. Smith, *The Unsteady March: The Rise and Decline of Racial Equality in America* (Chicago, Ill.: University of Chicago Press Press, 1999), 216–17.

78. Vose, *Caucasians Only*, ix, 162, 161, 163. Robert Weaver explained how he directed the collection of social and economic data for the legal attack after he completed his manuscript for *The Negro Ghetto*. He drew upon the manuscript for a lot of the data as well as graduate research by Department of Sociology students at the University of Chicago under Louis Wirth's direction (*The Negro Ghetto*, xi–xii). Weaver wrote the preface from Hull House in Chicago. Pritchett, *Robert Clifton Weaver*, 141–143. On Charles Abrams's role in supporting the NAACP legal efforts, see A. Scott Henderson, *Housing and the Democratic Ideal: The Life and Thought of Charles Abrams* (New York, N.Y.: Columbia University Press, 2000), 150, 147.

79. [Minutes of Meeting], Part F, Tuesday morning, July 10, 1945, NAACP Residential Segregation Campaign, Roll 21, 1, quoted in Plotkin, "Deeds of Mistrust," 235; "Recommendations on Restrictive Covenants by the Race Relations Committee," Metropolitan Housing and Planning Council (MHPC) Papers, 75–104, Box 7, Folder 1, University of Illinois at Chicago, Department of Special Collections (hereafter UIC).

80. George Nesbitt, "Relocating Negroes from Urban Slum Clearance Sites," *Land Economics* 25 (August 1949): 275–88 n. 1; Plotkin, "Deeds of Mistrust," 242. See also Otis Dudley Duncan and Beverly Duncan, *The Negro Population of Chicago: A Study of Residential Succession* (Chicago, Ill.: University of Chicago Press, 1957), 106. The Duncans cited Nesbitt's comments on the racially restrictive covenant acts. They discussed the difficulty of determining what effects the Supreme Court decision had on housing availability for blacks in Chicago isolated from increased purchasing power.

81. One estimation was that in four years after *Shelley*, blacks had gained through purchase or rent 21,000 housing units in formerly all-white neighborhoods (Klinkner with Smith, *The Unsteady March*, 217; Richard Kluger, *Simple Justice: The History of Brown v. Board of Education and Black America's Struggle for Equality* [New York: Vintage Books, 1975], 255). By another calculation, African Americans in Chicago saw their housing supply double to 233,000 units (34,600 owner occupied) through expansion of the Black Belt by 1960. The black population had only increased to 800,000. "As a consequence, the vacancy rate in the ghetto had risen to 4.6 percent, the average number of persons per dwelling unit had fallen from 4.4 to 3.4, and the proportion of units in poor physical condition had dropped to a quarter of the total supply" (Brian Berry, *The Open Housing Question: Race and Housing in Chicago, 1966–1976* [Ballinger, 1979], 17; Plotkin, "Deeds of Mistrust," 241).

82. "The segregation index for Chicago was 95 in 1940, 92.1 in 1950, and 92.6 in 1960." "The segregation index is a measure of the degree to which groups are spread out in a geographical area. It is based on a calculation of what percent of the population of one group would have to move to achieve complete spatial integration with another." (Douglas S. Massey and Nancy A. Denton, *American Apartheid: Segregation and the Making of the Underclass* [Cambridge, Mass.: Harvard University Press, 1993], 47, 20; Plotkin, "Deeds of Mistrust" 241). See also Joe T. Darden, "Black Residential Segregation since the 1948 *Shelley v. Kraemer* Decision," *Journal of Black Studies* 25 (July 1995): 680–91.

83. Plotkin, "Deeds of Mistrust," 241.

84. Woodlawn, Oakland, and Park Manor, *Local Community Fact Book for Chicago, 1950*, 171, 175, 151, 163, 282–83.

85. See Robert C. Weaver, "A Tool for Democratic Housing," *Crisis* 54 (1947): 47.

86. Weaver, *Hemmed In*, 9–11. Apparently, in a court case in Michigan, it was ruled that "building restrictions which sought to maintain property values and a high-class residential character in the neighborhood" did not imply racial restrictions and therefore were acceptable (Vose, *Caucasians Only*, 7).

87. Weaver, *Hemmed In*, 12.

88. Ibid., 11–13.

89. Weaver, *Negro Ghetto*, chapter 18.

90. Ibid., 281.

91. Weaver, *Hemmed In*, 9. Charles Abrams identified "three varieties of fears, fear of losing social status, fear of losing established neighborhood associations and fear of losing investment" (Abrams, *Race Bias in Housing*, Chicago Commons Papers, Box 30, January–August 1947 Folder, UIC). "Doing away with restrictive covenants, therefore, will require more than public statements, resolutions and editorials" (Weaver, *Negro Ghetto*, 252).

92. Weaver, *Hemmed In*, 9.

93. Weaver sought to take away the "economic rationale" for racial restrictive covenants by substituting the nonracial occupancy standards (Weaver, "A Tool for Democratic Housing," 48). See also Long and Johnson, *People v. Property*, 44.

94. Weaver, "A Tool for Democratic Housing," 47.

95. Weaver, *Negro Ghetto*, 349.

96. Weaver, "A Tool for Democratic Housing," 47.

97. Ibid.

98. Without mentioning West Chesterfield, he makes reference to class exclusion in black middle-class neighborhoods during World War II. See chapter 3 on West Chesterfield (Weaver, *Negro Ghetto*, 347).

99. Ibid.

100. Weaver defined "Truly democratic neighborhoods" as "areas where many economic and all racial groups can find shelter" (ibid., 349).

101. Ibid., 348.

102. Weaver, "A Tool for Democratic Housing," 48.

103. Weaver, *Negro Ghetto*, 349.

104. Ibid., 357. Pritchett, *Robert Clifton Weaver*, 129.

105. Weaver, *Hemmed In*, 12.

106. Between 1940 and 1950, Hyde Park went from 1.1 percent to 3.2 percent black. Woodlawn went from 16.9 percent to 38.8 percent African American, with blacks concentrated in three out of twelve census tracts. In those three census tracts, they made up 98 percent or 99 percent of the population. Oakland had 22.1 percent in 1940 to 77.4 percent in 1950. Kenwood increased its black population from 0.9 percent in 1940 to 9.7 percent ten years later (*Local Community Fact Book for Chicago, 1950*, 151, 163, 171, 175; see also footnote 176).

107. Plotkin, "Deeds of Mistrust," 240–41. Weaver thought that "it is in middle-rental areas contiguous to the Black Belt and in older areas of good housing that occupancy standards have their most significant use" (Weaver, *Negro Ghetto*, 349).

108. Weaver, *Negro Ghetto*, 354–55.

109. Weaver cited the *Chicago Defender* for this information and commented with biting irony, "It is interesting to note that while the proposal of occupancy standards occasioned violent opposition in a segment of the Negro press, the actual application of such an agreement in an area of limited size brought forth optimistic comments."

He cited *Chicago Defender*, January 24 and 31, 1948, and *Pittsburgh Courier*, January 31, 1948 (Weaver, *Negro Ghetto*, 355). John Sengstacke, editor of the Chicago Defender, brought up the "occupancy covenants" in an editorial that was less than enthusiastic about Weaver's appointment as Administrator of Housing and Home Finance Agency. Pritchett, *Robert Clifton Weaver*, 215.

110. Frank S. Horne to Thomas H. Wright, November 12, 1947, RG 207, HHFA Subject, Box 18, Racial Relations, 1947–July 1948, NA.

111. Horne's comment is a rare admission by a black civic elite about black realtors' participation in blockbusting activities (Frank S. Horne to Raymond M. Foley, "Rehabilitation Proposal of the Oakland-Kenwood Property Owners' Association, Chicago," November 25, 1947, RG 207, Box 18, Racial Relations, 1947–July 1948).

112. Horne to Foley, November 15, 1947.

113. Census tract information in 1950 showed that the northern tracts 558, 559, 560 were between 88 percent and 100 percent nonwhite compared to the southern tracts 561 and 562, which were between 57 percent and 62 percent nonwhite. There was a significant difference between the median income of census tract 559, which was 100 percent nonwhite, and had a median income of $2,155 and that of census tract 562, which was 65 percent nonwhite, and had a median income of $3,142. (*Local Community Fact Book for Chicago, 1950*, 151).

114. Horne to Foley, November 15, 1947.

115. Ibid. See also Weaver, *Negro Ghetto*, 355.

116. Apparently, as early as 1946 the Mayor's Commission on Human Relations suggested to the University of Chicago that they stop enforcing racially restrictive agreements and adopt a "community conservation agreement." The university claimed it would not lead the effort to adopt class-restrictive agreements, but "they indicated that they would give aid and support to a bonafide community effort in that direction" ("Formative Work in Community Organization in the Field of Human Relations in the General Area of 47th Street to the Midway, and Cottage Grove to the Lake, Embracing a part of the Kenwood Community and all of Hyde Park," September 30, 1950, NUL Papers, III, Box 51, Chicago, 1944–1955, Library of Congress).

117. Horne to Foley, November 15, 1947; Frank S. Horne to M. R. Massey, Assistant Commissioner, FHA (Field Operations), "Occupancy Agreement of the Oakland-Kenwood Property Owners' Association, Chicago," February 9, 1948, RG 207, HHFA, Box 18, Racial Relations 1947; B. T. McGraw to M. R. Massey, FHA Assistant Commissioner, Attention: FHA Zone Commissioners, "Community Conservation Agreement adopted by the Oakland-Kenwood Property Owners' Association, Chicago, for transmittal to FHA Racial Relations Advisors, February 10, 1948, RG 207, HHFA subject, Box 18, Racial Relations 1947; "Community Conservation Agreement of the Oakland-Kenwood Property Owners' Association, Chicago, RG 207, HHFA subject, Box 18, Racial Relations 1947.

118. Vose, *Caucasians Only*, 229.

119. Between 1940 and 1950, the overall population of Kenwood increased from 29,611 to 35,705. No census tract in Kenwood had more than 26 percent black residents. "Since 1950 Negroes have moved into Kenwood in increasing numbers so that they are in the majority in all of the district up to 47th Street, and along Drexel Boulevard and Lake Park Avenue, between 47th and Hyde Park Boulevard. Many of the large single-family homes have been sold to Negro professional and business men" (*Local Community Fact Book, 1950*, 161, 162, 151).

120. Elinor Richey, "Kenwood Foils the Block-busters," *Harper's*, August 1963, 43, copy in CAB Papers, Box 351, Folder 3.

121. Richey, "Kenwood Foils the Block-busters," 43. See also Glen E. Holt and Dominic A. Pacyga, *Chicago: A Historical Guide to the Neighborhoods: The Loop and South Side* (Chicago, Ill.: Chicago Historical Society, 1979), "Kenwood" chapter, 67–72.

122. Richey, "Kenwood Foils the Block-busters," 43. Jewel Rogers was the daughter of Cornelius F. Stradford, who represented Carl Hansberry in the Supreme Court Hansberry case (see earlier).

123. Commission on Human Relations, "Formative Work in Community Organization in the Field of Human Relations in the General Area of 47th Street to the Midway, and Cottage Grove to the Lake, Embracing a part of the Kenwood Community and all of Hyde Park," September 30, 1950, p. 8, NUL Papers, III, Box 51, Chicago, 1944–1955, Library of Congress.

124. Richey, "Kenwood Foils the Block-busters," 44.

125. Ibid.

126. Ibid., 45. Kenwood resident Earl Dickerson makes similar comments at a meeting in Hyde Park in 1949 (Julia Abrahamson, *A Neighborhood Finds Itself* [New York: Harper and Brothers, 1959], 16, 300, 14).

127. "In this crisis the wealthier Negroes came to the rescue. No middle-income white buyer could afford to outbid block-busters, but a few well-to-do Negroes could" (Richey, "Kenwood Foils the Block-busters," 47).

128. Ibid., 43.

9. Selling the Negro Housing Market

1. Earl B. Schwulst, "A Banker Relates Experience in Financing Nonwhite Housing," reproduced from the *Journal of Housing*, April 1956, with permission for distribution as a Racial Relations Service Document, Racial Relations Service, Office of the Administrator, Housing and Home Finance Agency, Washington, D.C., RG 207, Box 747, General Subject—Financing.

2. Lane prepared a primary study in 1948 and followed it up with a study that had no date but used 1950 census data. His reports represent one of the early examples of

a black civic elite actively selling the Negro housing market to the real estate industry in Chicago. He was in a strategic position to know about this potential market since he worked for the Chicago Urban League in various capacities. Alternately, he directed their civic affairs or public education departments, which coordinated the League's Federation of Block Clubs and Block Beautiful contests. Lane also lived in the heart of the Black Belt, at 4722 Langley Avenue in the Grand Boulevard neighborhood. He had pushed for black-controlled redevelopment and conservation in the Douglass community, which was targeted for slum clearance and city directed redevelopment (see chapters 4 and 6; "Some Aspects of the Negro Population of Chicago," for Housing Planners in the Privately Financed Field, prepared by Frayser T. Lane, November 1948, Carey Papers, Box 6, Folder 36; Frayser T. Lane, Secretary, Public Education Department, Chicago Urban League, "Some Socio-Economic Facts on Negroes in Chicago: To Estimate Possible Home Buyers," attached to "Draft" response to Mr. Clarence Holte, Chicago Urban League [CUL] Papers, Folder 83).

3. In some of these choice spots on boulevards, blacks had owned homes for a long period including thirty years on South Parkway Avenue between Thirty-Fifth and Thirty-Ninth Streets, and for twenty years on Michigan Avenue between Forty-Third and Garfield Boulevard (Fifty-Fifth Street). This area bordered the neighborhood that Claude Barnett had targeted for black-led redevelopment and conservation for fifteen years. It was just south and west of Lake Meadows, the city's first redevelopment project (see chapter 6; Lane, "Some Aspects of the Negro Population of Chicago" and "Some Socio-Economic Facts on Negroes in Chicago: To Estimate Possible Home Buyers"). At an earlier time, Kelly Miller acknowledged the desirable residences on boulevards, although he worried that the blacks who occupied them did not have the income to maintain them (Miller, "Home Ownership by the City Negro," *Chicago Sunday Bee*, no date, clipping in Claude A. Barnett [CAB] Papers, Box 351, Folder 2).

4. Lane, "Some Aspects of the Negro Population of Chicago."

5. For the fight against black war housing bordering West Chesterfield during World War II, see chapter 3. Lane, "Some Aspects of the Negro Population of Chicago." West Chesterfield and Morgan Park carried a substantial amount of FHA-insured rental and sales housing (Robert C. Weaver, *The Negro Ghetto* [New York: Harcourt, Brace, 1948], 96). Lane's findings were also supported by an FHA analyst in late 1948. Margaret Kane mentioned two FHA-insured housing projects in Chicago: Princeton Park, which was Chicago's "largest Negro rental project with FHA insured financing" with 908 units, and Parkway Gardens, a 694-unit cooperative project that was under construction in Chicago at the time (Kane, "Opportunities in a Neglected Market," reprinted from the Fourth Quarter 1948 FHA Insured Mortgage Portfolio, Carey Papers, Box 7, Folder 43).

6. Allan F. Thornton to Guy T. O. Hollyday, Commissioner, "The Market for Housing among Minority Groups as Revealed by FHA Housing Market Studies," January 8, 1954, RG 207, Box 748, Market Demand.

7. The popular name for this elite housing development was the Rosenwald Building, after the philanthropist Julius Rosenwald who financed its construction. Lane neglected to include Princeton Park, which was built during World War II.

8. Lane, "Some Socio-Economic Facts on Negroes in Chicago."

9. James M. Geer to E. J. Kelly, District Director, "The Market for Negro Sales Housing in the Greater Metropolitan Area," September 20, 1951, attached to Roland M. Sawyer, Minority Group Housing Advisor, to George A. Bremer, Zone Commissioner, October 10, 1951, RG 207, Box 750, Chicago, Illinois. See also Thornton to Hollyday, "The Market for Housing among Minority Groups."

10. The growth of black home ownership in the Chicago SMSA went from 10 percent to 19 percent. In terms of housing units, an increase of 212 percent occurred during a period when few units were built for black occupancy and the overall rate of growth of home ownership in the city of Chicago increased only modestly, from 24 percent in 1940 to only 31 percent in 1950. The discrepancy between Geer's figures and the ones I cite earlier in the chapter has to do with scale. The figures in Table 1 are for the city of Chicago while Geer's figures cover the whole metropolitan area (Geer to Kelly, "The Market for Negro Sales Housing in the Greater Metropolitan Area"). Andrew Wiese points to the large percentage of black households living in homes they owned in Chicago's suburbs, undoubtedly, the main attraction of these locations. Black home ownership in Chicago's suburbs was 28 percent in 1940, increasing to 51 percent twenty years later (Wiese, *Places of Their Own: African American Suburbanization in the Twentieth Century* [Chicago, Ill.: University of Chicago Press Press, 2004], 123).

11. Geer to Kelly, "The Market for Negro Sales Housing in the Greater Metropolitan Area." Geer cited an analyst from the "largest Chicago Negro savings and loan company" who reported that mortgage loans from this organization were "believed to be typical of those made in the Negro market, are conventional mortgages written for 65 percent of appraised value and carry interest rates of 5 to 5½ percent. Such rates are the minimum, it is felt, to provide the necessary spread between interest income and the 3 percent interest rate paid to attract savings depositors and investors." The most well-known black-owned savings and loan company was Federal Savings and Loans, of which Robert Taylor was secretary-treasurer.

12. Margaret Kane, "Opportunities in a Neglected Market," reprinted from the Fourth Quarter 1948 FHA Insured Mortgage Portfolio, Carey Papers, Box 7, Folder 43.

13. George B. Nesbitt, Special Assistant to the Director, DSCUR, and B. T. McGraw, Deputy Assistant to the Administrator, OA, to Gordon Howard, Head, Economics Section, Planning and Engineering Branch, "Racial Aspects of Housing Market Analysis," March 12, 1954, HHFA Papers.

14. Ibid.

15. Apparently, the opponents of the Carey Ordinance for nondiscrimination in publicly aided housing in 1949 argued that blacks' "unstable job situation" made them unsuitable for "integrated housing" (Ralph Amerson to F. T. Lane, memorandum,

386 · NOTES TO CHAPTER 9

"Stability and Size of Negro Income in Chicago," January 28, 1949, Carey Papers, Box 6, Folder 39).

16. Kane, "Opportunities in a Neglected Market." See also *Housing of the Nonwhite Population, 1940–1947*, 2, 6.

17. Lane, "Some Aspects of the Negro Population of Chicago." See Thornton to Hollyday, "The Market for Housing Among Minority Groups," January 8, 1954.

18. Lane, "Some Aspects of the Negro Population of Chicago."

19. Chicago Community Survey, sponsored by the University of Chicago, was the primary vehicle for collecting and organizing decennial census data on Chicago and its metropolitan area. Weaver reported that in 1946 in north central states 38.8 percent of blacks earned between $2,000 and $2,999; 18.8 percent, $3,000 to $4,999; and 9.9 percent, $5,000 to $9,999 (Weaver, *The Negro Ghetto*, 129).

20. Lane, "Some Socio-Economic Facts on Negroes in Chicago to Estimate Possible Home Buyers."

21. On Tract 602 in Community Area No. 40, Washington Park, see *Local Community Fact Book for Chicago, 1950*, ed. Philip M. Hauser and Evelyn M. Kitagawa (Chicago, Ill.: Chicago Community Inventory, University of Chicago, 1953), 167; Lane, "Some Socio-Economic Facts on Negroes in Chicago to Estimate Possible Home Buyers."

22. Thornton to Hollyday, "The Market for Housing among Minority Groups as Revealed by FHA Housing Market Studies," January 8, 1954.

23. Lane, "Some Aspects of the Negro Population of Chicago"; Amerson, "Stability and Size of Negro Income in Chicago," January 28, 1949.

24. Lane, "Some Aspects of the Negro Population of Chicago."

25. Ibid. Lane's inclusion of "owners of kitchenette" apartments in this prosperous group is further evidence of the importance of real estate owners among the black upper and middle classes.

26. Ibid.

27. Ibid. Nesbitt and McGraw to Howard, "Racial Aspects of Housing Market Analysis," March 12, 1954. Recently, scholars have highlighted the importance of *Ebony* magazine for publicizing and normalizing black middle-class consumer tastes. Wiese, *Places of Their Own*, 148–50, 158–59. Adam Green, *Selling the Race: Culture, Community, and Black Chicago, 1940–1955* (Chicago, Ill.: University of Chicago Press Press, 2009), 129–177.

28. Lane, "Some Socio-Economic Facts on Negroes in Chicago to Estimate Possible Home Buyers"; Weaver, *The Negro Ghetto*, 137; see 136–38 for discussion on the increased standard of living for black families during World War II.

29. Nesbitt and McGraw to Howard, March 12, 1954.

30. Midwest Zone Commissioner for FHA, George A. Bremer's urgent request for this study coincided with HHFA Administrator Raymond Foley's decision on

whether or not to approve Chicago's application for slum clearance subsidies and public housing unit authorizations in 1951. Chicago's unwillingness to rehouse slum displacees who were predominantly black was an issue for Foley. Many black policy elites had called upon Foley to put pressure on Kennelly to recruit private housing developers to build for black citizens' housing needs (see chapters 4 and 5). E. J. Kelly, District Director, to George A. Bremer, Zone Commissioner, FHA, September 24, 1951, attached to Roland M. Sawyer, Minority Group Housing Advisor, to George A. Bremer, Zone Commissioner, October 10, 1951, RG 207, Box 750, Chicago, Illinois.

31. Kelly to Bremer, September 24, 1951.

32. In addition, Geer used studies of black housing markets in Detroit and New York to estimate the upmarket rental housing demand in Chicago (James M. Geer to Edward J. Kelly, Director, "The Market in the Chicago Area for Negro Rental Units Priced at $100 or More," Amendment to the Report of October 25, 1951," November 28, 1951, RG 207, Box 750, Chicago, I; "Confidential" was handwritten on the document).

33. Lane, based on his knowledge of the Michigan Boulevard Gardens tenants' housing choices and buying power, argued that Chicago had a market for 2,000 apartments comparable to the Gardens' well-appointed units. In the same report, he mentioned that there was a "market for at least 5,000 housing units for Negroes in higher rent classification" (Lane, "Some Aspects of the Negro Population of Chicago").

34. Apparently Director Kelly requested the study on short notice since the non-profit Chicago Dwellings Association "proposed a Section 207 elevator type project containing 318 units at rents ranging from $90 to $140 for Negro occupancy" (Geer to Kelly, "The Market in the Chicago Area for Negro Rental Units Priced at $100 or More," October 25, 1951).

35. Thornton to Hollyday, "The Market for Housing among Minority Groups," January 8, 1954.

36. Ibid.

37. Geer to Kelly, "The Market for Negro Sales Housing in the Greater Metropolitan Area," October 25, 1951.

38. George A. Bremer to Roland M. Sawyer, October 4, 1951, attached to Roland M. Sawyer, Minority Group Housing Advisor, to George A. Bremer, Zone Commissioner, October 10, 1951, RG 207, Box 750, Chicago, Illinois.

39. For a discussion of the "Chicago Situation," see chapter 5.

40. Roland M. Sawyer, Minority Group Housing Advisor, to George A. Bremer, Zone Commissioner, October 10, 1951, RG 207, Box 750, Chicago, Illinois.

41. Thornton to Hollyday, "The Market for Housing among Minority Groups as Revealed by FHA Housing Market Studies," January 8, 1954.

42. Ibid. Thornton's judgment was backed by African Americans flocking to suburban areas. Wiese finds that the black suburban population in Metropolitan Chicago

increased to 53,000 between 1940 and 1960. So blacks showed they would live "way out." On the other hand, due to residential segregation, Wiese also finds that 75 percent of black suburbanites lived in only seven suburbs (Wiese, *Places of Their Own*, 118). For reasons why blacks were concentrated in particular suburbs, and not others, see Lillian S. Calhoun, "Minority Home Sales Lag Despite Offers," no date, no source, CAB Papers, Box 351, Folder 2.

43. For other stereotypes about black residential behavior, see Nesbitt and McGraw to Howard, "Racial Aspects of Housing Market Analysis," March 12, 1954.

44. Thornton chronicles FHA interest in African American housing markets over time (Thornton to Hollyday, "The Market for Housing among Minority Groups as Revealed by FHA Housing Market Studies," January 8, 1954).

45. Kane, "Opportunities in a Neglected Market."

46. The data that Kane cited in 1948 to support her position that a viable black housing market needed attention were from FHA-insured housing developments for black occupancy (Kane, "Opportunities in a Neglected Market").

47. Nesbitt and McGraw to Howard, "Racial Aspects of Housing Market Analysis," March 12, 1954.

48. Nesbitt and McGraw informed their government colleagues that "subletting," "room renting," and "non-residential uses of dwellings" were due to "racially restricted housing opportunity and resultant premium prices and rents," not "racial preferences." They then assured them that "these practices will not readily transfer to new private housing, nor even to suitable standard housing in good neighborhoods, for they are quite controllable through good planning, competent management, and enforcement of proper housing and density standards" (Nesbitt and McGraw to Howard, "Racial Aspects of Housing Market Analysis," March 12, 1954).

49. Ibid.

50. This observation offers further evidence that affluent blacks valued class homogeneity even from outside the community (ibid.).

51. Ibid.

52. Ibid.

53. Ibid.

54. Frayser Lane's studies on the city's black housing market as well as an inquiry by Robert Taylor, secretary-treasurer of black-owned Illinois Federal Savings and Loan about black housing demand from Booker T. McGraw represent this local interest (Robert R. Taylor to Dr. Booker T. McGraw, February 8, 1954, attached to B. T. McGraw to Robert R. Taylor, February 11, 1954; B. T. McGraw to Robert R. Taylor, February 11, 1954, RG 207, Box 748, General Subject—Market Demand).

55. See chapter 7.

56. The League was stimulating and responding to an interest in building homes for black people that caused CUL official Frayser T. Lane to issue his reports in 1948 and the early 1950s (see earlier).

57. Taylor to McGraw, February 8, 1954.

58. The Chicago Urban League records show that between July and November 1954 Sidney Williams received four requests for information on the black private housing market in Chicago. There are no other inquiries in CUL records. It is impossible to know whether these were all the inquiries received by CUL that reflected a unique period of interest, or whether not all the inquiries were recorded. The four inquiries from Chicago builders and a New York marketing company and Williams's responses do give us a sense of the kinds of questions they asked as well as what Williams wanted to convey about the Negro housing market in Chicago (Lestre Brownlee, "Negro Home Buyers Big Factor in Chicago Area Building Boom: A Third of 15,000 Houses Built This Year Sparked by Them," *Chicago Daily News*, July 7, 1955, news clipping in CAB Papers, Box 351, Folder 3).

59. Fred Rubenstein to Urban League, July 22, 1954, Sidney Williams to Fred Rubenstein, July 26, 1954, and Fred Rubenstein to Sidney Williams, July 28, 1954, all in CUL Papers, UIC, Folder 82; Clarence L. Holte, Speciality Marketing Dept., Batten, Barton, Durstine & Osborn, Inc., to Sidney Williams, November 23, 1954, attached to "Draft" response to Mr. Clarence Holte, CUL Papers, UIC, Folder 83.

60. See chapter 7. Fred Rubenstein to Urban League, July 22, 1954, Sidney Williams to Fred Rubenstein, July 26, 1954, and Fred Rubenstein to Sidney Williams, July 28, 1954, all in CUL Papers, UIC, Folder 82; Clarence L. Holte, Specialty Marketing Dept., Batten, Barton, Durstine & Osborn, Inc., to Sidney Williams, November 23, 1954, attached to "Draft" response to Mr. Clarence Holte, CUL Papers, UIC, Folder 83.

61. Fred Rubenstein to Urban League, July 22, 1954, Sidney Williams to Fred Rubenstein, July 26, 1954, and Fred Rubenstein to Sidney Williams, July 28, 1954, all in CUL Papers, UIC, Folder 82.

62. In response to another builder's inquiry, Williams referred to "economists" who had determined that between 2,000 and 3,000 black families could afford homes costing between $15,000 to $20,000 (Sidney Williams to Nathan Malisoff, August 2, 1954, CUL Papers, UIC, Folder 82).

63. Williams to Rubenstein, July 26, 1954. Williams also suggested to another builder, Pawlow, that he "canvass the areas around 89th and Indiana, around 62nd and South Parkway and the project at 49th and Drexel to find out how many 'takers' they have had before you go too far with your proposal." These were all black middle-class areas (Sidney Williams to H. Y. Pawlow, November 23, 1954, attached to "Draft" response to Mr. Clarence Holte, CUL Papers, UIC, Folder 83). See also Nesbitt and McGraw to Howard, "Racial Aspects of Housing Market Analysis," March 12, 1954.

64. It appeared that Williams was steering Rubenstein to the upscale black housing market, and Rubenstein was more interested in the larger black home buyers' market of moderate-income clerical and skilled workers (Fred Rubenstein to Urban League, July 22, 1954; Sidney Williams to Fred Rubenstein, July 26, 1954; and Fred Rubenstein to Sidney Williams, July 28, 1954). In response to another inquiry, he emphasized the

economic insecurity of "average-income" blacks (Sidney Williams to H. Y. Pawlow, November 23, 1954, attached to "Draft" response to Mr. Clarence Holte, CUL Papers, UIC, Folder 83).

65. Clarence L. Holte, Specialty Marketing Dept., Batten, Barton, Durstine & Osborn, Inc., to Sidney Williams, November 23, 1954, attached to "Draft" response to Mr. Clarence Holte, CUL Papers, UIC, Folder 83.

66. In the records, there was a partial copy of a letter Williams wrote to H. Y. Pawlow, Hyland Builders Corporation, Chicago. Williams said it was hard to assemble the relevant facts when the spotlight was on "a matter like Lawndale area which has been receiving such press, none of which renowns to the credit of the Negro community" (Sidney Williams to H. Y. Pawlow, November 23, 1954, attached to "Draft" response to Mr. Clarence Holte, CUL Papers, UIC, Folder 83).

67. In another instance, Williams mentioned, "the improved FHA policy will enable many to make the down payment" (Sidney Williams to Clarence L. Holte, December 7, 1954, attached to "Draft" response to Mr. Clarence Holte, CUL Papers, UIC, Folder 83).

68. Ibid. Earlier, on August 2, 1954, Williams had written a similar letter to Mr. Nathan Malisoff of Courtesy Lumber Company, located at 5255 South State Street. He mentioned "trying to get Robert R. Taylor of the Rosenwald Apartments for his view, but he was out of the city." Williams said he was "attaching some straight and pure sociological details that Mr. Lane of our staff worked out" (Sidney Williams to Nathan Malisoff, August 2, 1954, CUL Papers, UIC, Folder 82). The report to which Williams referred was entitled "Some Socio-Economic Facts on Negroes in Chicago: To Estimate Possible Home Buyers." Apparently, it was an updated version of Lane's 1948 report. The updated report asserted, "Most Negro families prefer to live in the city. Many desire small private homes within city limits" ("Some Socio-Economic Facts on Negroes in Chicago: To Estimate Possible Home Buyers," attached to "Draft" response to Mr. Clarence Holte, CUL Papers, UIC, Folder 83).

69. Williams expressed his concern about the buying power of moderate-income and working-class blacks. H. Y. Pawlow, Hyland Builders Corporation in Chicago, asked Williams for "the possible number of Negro families in Chicago, both able to pay and in the market for homes around $14,000." Williams said, "Chicago's Negro community is more than 95% a working class." He reported that the economic situation of blacks due to unemployment and the curtailment of overtime meant working-class blacks could not "convert their wants into effective economic demand" like they had eighteen months earlier (Sidney Williams to H. Y. Pawlow, November 23, 1954, attached to "Draft" response to Mr. Clarence Holte, CUL Papers, UIC, Folder 83). See also Nesbitt and McGraw to Howard, "Racial Aspects of Housing Market Analysis," March 12, 1954). There was a thirteen-month recession from 1953 to 1954 that affected black incomes and employment rates (Meg Jacobs,

Pocketbook Politics: Economic Citizenship in Twentieth-Century America [Princeton, N.J.: Princeton University Press, 2005], 253).

70. Statement by George W. Snowden, Minority Group Housing Advisor, Federal Housing Administration, Before Conference of Mortgage Bankers Association, September 29, 1954—Chicago, Illinois," NUL papers III, Box 10, FHA 1956-1959.

71. However, Williams's preference for a black middle-class housing market went beyond concerns about working-class blacks' economic instability. This was the class to promote in order to convey blacks' conventional residential behavior to white audiences. In a letter to Mr. John W. Barnes of Encyclopedia Britannica Films, Inc., in Wilmette, Illinois, a northern suburb of Chicago, Sidney Williams relayed, "It has been suggested that a good short movie showing middle-class Negro people mowing and tending their lawns and keeping the exterior and interior of their homes up to standards would be useful [a] device in interpreting to the white public that there are such Negro persons and would be helpful in the over-all program of integration." Williams, who apparently knew John Barnes, asked his opinion about how much a movie like this would cost, whether Encyclopedia Britannica was interested, and who might finance such a venture (Sidney Williams to John W. Barnes, July 26, 1954, CUL Papers, Folder 82). This was not Williams first time using the media to publicize his views on blacks' housing problems. Apparently, he had his own radio show between 1945 and 1946 when he was the executive secretary of the Cleveland Urban League. Barbara Dianne Savage, *Broadcasting Freedom: Radio, War, and the Politics of Race, 1938–1948* (Chapel Hill, N.C.: University of North Carolina Press, 1999), 189–190.

72. Downs's last comment was self-interested as his agency had displaced many blacks without an adequate plan to rehouse them. The agency relied upon these black households putting pressure on bordering white neighborhoods for compensatory housing (see chapters 4 and 5).

73. The firms included Julian Black Inc., 550 E. 61st St.; Bolin Bland, 7 W. Madison; Oscar C. Brown, 4649 Cottage Grove; and Robert N. Landrum, 4805 South Park Way (Bolin V. Bland, Real Estate and Housing Editor, "Minority Housing," attached to Joseph R. Ray to Colonel Hugh Askew, Director, Director, Mortgage Finance Department, NAHB, January 31, 1955, RG 207, Box 745).

74. Wiese reports that Evanston's black population added 3,100 people, a 50 percent increase, between 1940 and 1960. During the same period, the black population in Maywood grew by 4,000. He mentions that most of the black suburban population was concentrated in the southern suburbs, which included Robbins, Phoenix, Dixmoor, and west Harvey, where blacks had lived since World War I. In the 1940s and 1950s, 1,200 new homes were constructed in Robbins. Black home ownership also increased during this period from 26 percent to 43 percent in Evanston, and 23 percent to 48 percent in Maywood. By 1960, black home ownership had grown to 58 percent in Robbins and to 79 percent in Dixmoor (Wiese, *Places of Their Own,*

118–22). A fair housing organization determined that 35,000 blacks in Chicago were "financially equipped to move to the suburbs" (Lillian S. Calhoun, "Minority Home Sales Lag Despite Offers," no date, no source, CAB Papers, Box 351, Folder 2).

75. Table 7.1: Expansion of the Nonwhite Housing Stock in U.S. Metropolitan Areas, 1950–1959 in Wiese, *Places of Their Own*, 170.

76. It appears that the National Association of Real Estate Boards encouraged "the production of new housing open to Negroes" as early as 1948 (Frank S. Horne, Assistant to the Administrator, to "Gentlemen," March 3, 1948, RG 207, HHFA Subject, Box 18, Racial Relations 1947). Robert Weaver reported on a survey put out by NAREB before 1948 about whether there was need for good Negro housing. The survey results were possibly affirming the black home buyer as "a good economic risk" (Weaver, *The Negro Ghetto*, 292).

77. Philip G. Sadler, Racial Relations, to Commissioner, PHA, "Report on Conference of National Association of Home Builders and Visit to Chicago Field Office, PHA, January 25, 1955, RG 207, Box 745. A NAHB newsletter spelled out what was at stake: "It is quite clear that, if the operative home builder does not provide a substantial volume of housing for these people by the free enterprise method, the *Federal Government will most certainly do the job at the taxpayers' expense*" (NAHB-*CORRELATOR*, March 1950, 2, 3; memo to NAHB Members from Frank Cortright, RG 207, Box 748, Market Demand).

78. There was evidence of earlier interest by home builders, but it wasn't until the mid-1950s that there was a concerted effort. As early as 1950, some members of NAHB were cognizant of a neglected minority housing market (NAHB-*CORRELATOR*, March 1950, 2, 3; memo to NAHB Members from Frank Cortright, RG 207, Box 748, Market Demand).

79. "Realtist" was the term preferred by the black real estate broker organization, in order to distinguish them from the white NAREB, which referred to its brokers as "realtors" (Conrad "Pat" Harness, Public Relations Director, NAHB, to Joseph Ray, December 29, 1953, attached to Walton Onslow, Convention Program Director, NAHB to Joseph Ray, December 29, 1953, RG 207, Box 745).

80. As far as NAHB officials were concerned, allowing "theorizing" would open the conference up to discussing the relative merits of segregated and integrated housing, which they wanted to avoid.

81. Conrad "Pat" Harness, Public Relations Director, NAHB, to Joseph Ray, December 29, 1953, attached to Walton Onslow, Convention Program Director, NAHB to Joseph Ray, December 29, 1953, RG 207, Box 745; "Outline for Round Table Conference on Housing for Minorities, National Association of Home Builders Convention, Conrad Hilton Hotel, Chicago, Illinois, Monday, January 18, 1954, North Assembly Room, 2:00 p.m.," RG 207, Box 745.

82. "Program Guide, Minority Housing Clinic, Tuesday, January 18, 1955, Conrad Hilton Hotel," RG 207, Box 745, NAHB.

83. Ray recommended enlisting the help of the white National Association of Real Estate Boards and the black National Association of Real Estate Brokers to fight the persistent obstacle of the "critical land, or site, situation." Ray recommended that builders eschew large projects for now, but concentrate instead on developing "several small projects—50 to 500 units in scattered areas rather than 1,000 or more unit in one area" (George W. Snowden to Joseph R. Ray, "NAHB Board Meeting, October 10, 1954," October 4, 1954, RG 207, Box 745). Not for publication. Report of Minority Group Housing Committee, Wallace E. Johnson, Chairman, Dow Zabolio, Co-Chairman Presiding, to NAHB Board of Directors. Meeting in New York City on Sunday, October 10, 1954. RG 207, Box 745, NAHB; "Program Guide, Minority Housing Clinic, Tuesday, January 18, 1955, Conrad Hilton Hotel, RG 207, Box 745, NAHB; "Notes on Remarks at Panel Discussion on Subject of Minority Housing, National Association of Home Builders' Annual Convention—Chicago—January.

84. NAHB-*CORRELATOR*, March 1950, 2, 3; Memo to NAHB Members from Frank Cortright, RG 207, Box 748, Market Demand.

85. The Voluntary Home Mortgage Credit Extension Program, one of the new programs to emerge from the legislation, was designed to recruit lenders willing to make FHA-insured loans under conventional terms to home buyers who were racial minorities or residents in underserved rural communities (see chapter 10).

86. This issue was regarded as sufficiently serious to warrant two sessions on "the problem of segregation." One focused on the effect on housing for minorities of the Supreme Court's *Brown* decision, while the other was titled "Problems Arising from Activity of: National Committee Against Housing Discrimination; National Association for Advancement of Colored People; National Urban League" (NAHB-*CORRELATOR*, March 1950, 2, 3; Memo to NAHB Members from Frank Cortright, RG 207, Box 748, Market Demand).

87. B. T. McGraw, Racial Relations Service, to Joseph R. Ray, Assistant to the Administrator, "Request for Official Professional Leave to Attend MBA Clinic on Financing Housing Available to Minorities, in Chicago, September 28," September 24, 1954, RG 207, Box 745, Mortgage Bankers Association of America.

88. Andrew Wiese detects a change in FHA policy as a result of the internal pressure brought by the race relations advisers it hired in 1947. Following Robert Weaver and Hortense Gabel of the National Committee Against Discrimination in Housing (NCDH), he dates this change after 1953, and credits the FHA along with the VA, despite their support for segregation, with providing substantial housing to African Americans. He calculates that approximately 300,000 new homes were acquired with FHA/VA subsidies, roughly 40 percent of all new housing going to racial minorities between 1945 and 1960 (Wiese, *Places of Their Own*, 138–40).

89. Statement by George W. Snowden, Minority Group Housing Advisor, Federal Housing Administration, before Conference of Mortgage Bankers Association, September 29, 1954—Chicago, Illinois. See also Earl B. Schwulst, "A Banker Relates

Experience in Financing Nonwhite Housing," reproduced from the *Journal of Housing*, April 1956. Beryl Satter, *Family Properties: Race, Real Estate, and the Exploitation of Urban America* (New York, N.Y.: Metropolitan Books, 2009), 43.

90. Snowden before Conference of Mortgage Bankers Association, September 29, 1954.

91. If this was not a "special program" for minority home buyers, then it is difficult to determine what Snowden meant by that term. The program largely targeted racial minorities. Ideologically, for Snowden the fact that the program was "voluntary," meant for him that it was different than direct government refinancing of minority home-buying loans, which carried an underlying compulsion, and thus represented special treatment.

92. Snowden before Conference of Mortgage Bankers Association, September 29, 1954. According to Earl Schwulst, a banker, an HHFA report said that 2.5 million private dwelling units would be needed from 1950 to 1960 to adequately house nonwhites, making the number of units needed per year closer to 250,000 than the 150,000 earlier proposed (Schwulst, "A Banker Relates Experience in Financing Nonwhite Housing," April 1956). On the follow-up between the MBA and the HHFA race relations service, see B. T. McGraw, Racial Relations Service, to Memorandum for the Record, "41st Annual Convention of the Mortgage Bankers Association," October 1, 1954, RG 207, Box 745, Mortgage Bankers Association; FHA Regional Director, Re: MBA Committee on Financing of Housing for Racial Minorities, January 31, 1955; Mortgage Bankers Association, *A Proposed Analysis of Problems and Experiences in Mortgage Financing Relating to Housing Production for Minority Groups in Selected Communities*; Mortgage Bankers Association of America, Committee on Financing of Housing for Racial Minorities, *Outline for Project Analysis* RG 207, Box 747, General Subject—Financing.

93. Wiese reported on the "deep ambivalence about residential integration" that partly shaped the "tradition of racial advancement" adhered to by southern black real estate elites (Wiese, *Places of Their Own*, 165).

94. Ray was in Memphis to dedicate the George W. Lee Homes (Housing and Home Finance Agency, HHFA-OA-No. 884, September 5, 1955, RG 207, Box 748, Press Release).

95. The United States Savings and Loan League was founded in 1893 to promote the interests of savings and loans institutions. The organization extolled the "American home," which it considered "the safeguard of American liberties." According to Henderson, "by 1939, under the leadership of Morton Bodfish . . . the League represented approximately 4,000 institutions that held 80 percent of all savings and loan assets." Bodfish, considered to be one of the most powerful lobbyists in this period, helped to influence the shaping of the Federal Home Loan Board System as well as FHA (A. Scott Henderson, *Housing and the Democratic Ideal: The Life and Thought of*

Charles Abrams [New York: Columbia University Press, 2000], 114; Kevin Fox Gotham, *Race, Real Estate and Uneven Development: The Kansas City Experience, 1900–2000* [Albany: State University of New York Press, 2002], 52, 54).

96. United States Savings and Loan League's News Release, no date. "'This is the first of a series of articles dealing with the home financing practices of savings and loan associations and Negro families" (RG 207, Box 747, General Subject—Financing). For a similar approach to Schwergel, see NAHB-*CORRELATOR*, March 1950, 2, 3; Memo to NAHB Members from Frank Cortright, RG 207, Box 748, Market Demand.

97. Dreier's comments bring to mind the debate on black locational preferences among federal housing officials in 1951 and 1954. Given other barriers than financing to settling in newer outlying neighborhoods, it is difficult to take black preferences at face value (see earlier).

98. Other observers have made this point (see Kane, "Opportunities in a Neglected Market").

99. United States Savings and Loan League's News Release, no date. "'This is the second of a series of articles dealing with the home financing practices of savings and loan associations and Negro families" (RG 207, Box 747, General Subject—Financing). Black policy elites would have been gratified to hear Dreier link citizenship with better housing. Like other housing reformers, they had been stressing the connection since the 1920s. The major difference between Dreier and them is that they did not restrict "better housing" to home ownership and also thought well-managed public housing could produce the same results (see chapter 3).

100. United States Savings and Loan League's News Release, June 22, 1955 (stamped). "This is the third of a series of articles dealing with the home financing practices of savings and loan associations and Negro families" (RG 207, Box 747, General Subject—Financing). In the HHFA files, there was a document entitled "Financial Institutions That Have Participated in the Minority Group Housing Market: Zone I and III." Interestingly, neither Union Federal Savings and Loan Association nor East Brooklyn Savings were listed. Zone I was the Northeast, and Zone III was the Midwest. Chicago had thirteen institutions, more than any other city including New York City with seven and Detroit with six. All the black-owned insurance companies were included in the thirteen institutions listed for Chicago. Mainstream financial institutions such as Chicago City Bank and Trust Co., South Side Bank and Trust Company, Merchants National Bank and Prudential Insurance Company, were also included (no date, RG 207, Box 747, General Subject—Financing).

10. Self-Help and the Black Real Estate Industry

1. Elmore Baker and William A. Occomy, "A Real Estate Program for Negroes," *Opportunity* 19, no. 2 (February 1941): 45–46.

2. Walter "Chief" Aiken, a highly successful black builder from Atlanta, was president of the National Home Builders Association "for a considerable period" (Walter H. Aiken to Franklin D. Richards, October 23, 1951, attached to Franklin D. Richards to Walter H. Aiken, November 14, 1951, RG 207, Box 748, Market Demand).

3. George S. Harris to Albert M. Cole, December 10, 1956, RG 207, Box 747, VHMCP; Joseph R. Ray to Colonel Hugh Askew, August 26, 1954, RG 207, HHFA, Box 30; Frank S. Horne to Raymond M. Foley, "Regional Meeting of National Association of Real Estate Brokers, February 8–10, 1949," February 25, 1949, RG 207, HHFA, Box 30.

4. Andrew Wiese is perhaps the first scholar to refer to a "black real estate industry" (see Wiese, *Places of Their Own: African American Suburbanization in the Twentieth Century* [Chicago, Ill.: University of Chicago Press Press, 2005]).

5. On the "real estate lobby," see Robert C. Weaver, *The Negro Ghetto* (New York, N.Y.: Harcourt, Brace, 1948), 313–16.

6. Of course, this was normal operating procedure with private businessmen serving in civic and government capacities in U.S. politics. It especially reflected the interpenetration of private elites into the government arena, which white real estate elites had perfected in the 1930s (Weaver, *The Negro Ghetto*; Kevin Fox Gotham, *Race, Real Estate and Uneven Development: The Kansas City Experience, 1900–2000* [Albany: State University of New York Press, 2002]).

7. William R. Hudgins, President, to Joseph Ray, September 30, 1954, RG 207, Box 745, ASLL Conf.

8. *The FBI's RACON: Racial Conditions in the United States during World War II*, comp. and ed. Robert A. Hill (Boston, Mass.: Northeastern University Press, 1995), 96–97.

9. The National Association of Real Estate Brokers had the same initials as the white-only National Association of Real Estate Boards. Since my study is focused on black real estate elites, NAREB refers only to the black organization in this chapter. When I mention the white organization, I spell out its name. Also, the NAREB referred to realty brokers as "realtists," whereas the white organization used the term "realtors." When I used the term "realtists," I am referring to African American real estate brokers.

10. Robert F. Weems Jr., *Black Business in the Black Metropolis: The Chicago Metropolitan Assurance Company, 1925–1985* (Bloomington: Indiana University Press, 1996), 32, 48–49.

11. Dempsey J. Travis, *An Autobiography of Black Chicago* (Chicago, Ill.: Urban Research Institute, 1981), 141.

12. Ibid., 287.

13. Robert N. Landrum was chief broker with associated brokers Elysea J. Taylor, George A. Anderson, and W. Baxter Collier Jr. This firm was a couple of blocks from

Baker and McDowell's real estate companies located on Sixty-Third Street (National Association of Real Estate Brokers Monthly News Letter, vol. 1, no. 2, March 1, 1949, RG 207, HHFA, Box 30). While Forty-Seventh Street still remained the main business district in the Black Metropolis, it is interesting that many of these real estate offices were located on or near Sixty-Third Street, which was near the periphery of the South Side ghetto. No wonder St. Clair Drake and Horace Cayton did not find any black real estate firms when they surveyed the businesses on Forty-Seventh Street between State Street and Cottage Grove Avenue in 1938 (see Table 21). However, they did find a number of black men going into the profession. They observed, "the average college-trained Negro, if he is not a professional man, is more likely to go into insurance or real estate, publishing or printing, than into the hurly-burly of retail merchandising, or he prefers a civil service job where he can immediately attain the standard of living to which he has been trained" (see Table 19, "The Ten Most Numerous Types of Negro-Owned Businesses in Chicago: 1938," Drake and Cayton, *Black Metropolis*, 450, 438, 456).

14. National Association of Real Estate Brokers, Inc. Eighth Annual Convention, Hotel St. George, Brooklyn, N.Y., October 15–19, 1955, program, Bedford Stuyvesant Real Estate Board, Inc., Hosts; Malcolm G. Martin, Convention Chairman, NAREB, to Arthur W. Viner, Executive Secretary, National Committee of the Voluntary Home Mortgage Credit Program, October 4, 1955, RG 207, HHFA, Box 30.

15. The white real estate industry was instrumental in creating and shaping federal housing policies such as FHA in the first place. National Association of Real Estate Boards, Mortgage Bankers Association, United States Savings and Loan League, and other trade organizations "advocated [for] the establishment of a federally regulated home financing system where home mortgages would be long-term, with low down payments, and amortized repayment schedules" (Gotham, *Race, Real Estate, Uneven Development*, 52).

16. The primary customers of black builders, realtors, and lenders were African Americans, although they sometimes also served whites who planned to provide housing that was intended for or open to blacks.

17. The Economy Housing program used government research and technical expertise to improve housing design, utilization of materials, and construction techniques in order "to obtain the greatest usefulness from the smallest amount of space, as well as economic utilization of material" (*Economy Housing Program*, Housing and Home Finance Agency, 1949, quoted in Donald W. Wyatt, "Better Homes for Negro Families in the South," *Social Forces* 28, no. 3 [March 1950]: 300).

18. "Conference with Mr. Leo Kirk, Federal Housing Administrator, Monday, January 31, 1949, 10:30–11:40 a.m.," typescript, pp. 5–7, RG 207, HHFA, Box 30.

19. NAREB members did recognize the invaluable role of black housing professionals who were employed as FHA racial relations advisers. As one scholar described, "The racial relations service afforded by FHA has been invaluable to communities

in analyzing the Negro market, determining the potentiality of the demand, advising community groups on land problems, organizing the support of the Negro community, and working through other facets of FHA in making available technical information and assistance" (Wyatt, "Better Homes for Negro Families in the South," 303). Wiese credited them with persuading FHA policymakers to better serve black communities, if only on a segregated basis, by insuring large black housing developments. (Wiese, *Places of Their Own*, 138–40).

20. B. T. McGraw to Frank S. Horne, "Field Trip to Chicago, Illinois—Regional Meeting of National Association of Real Estate Brokers, February 8–10, 1949. For the NAREB's statement of housing objectives, see *National Association of Real Estate Brokers Monthly News Letter*, vol. 1, no. 2, March 1, 1949, RG 207, HHFA, Box 30. See also W. D. Morison Jr. to Raymond M. Foley, March 4, 1949, and attached "Statement of Housing Objectives Adopted by the National Association of Real Estate Brokers at Chicago Regional Meeting, February 8–9, 1949, RG 207, HHFA Papers, Box 30.

21. Frank S. Horne to Raymond M. Foley, "Regional Meeting of National Association of Real Estate Brokers, February 8–10, 1949," February 25, 1949, RG 207, HHFA Papers, Box 30.

22. W. D. Morison Jr. to Raymond M. Foley, March 4, 1949, RG 207, HHFA Papers, Box 30.

23. *Economy Housing Program*, Housing and Home Finance Agency, 1949, cited in Wyatt, "Better Homes for Negro Families in the South," 300; "Conference with Mr. Leo Kirk, Federal Housing Administrator, Monday, January 31, 1949, 10:30–11:40 a.m.," typescript, pp. 5–7, HHFA Papers.

24. National Association of Real Estate Brokers, Inc., press release, August 11, 1954; George S. Harris, President, NAREB, 4459 South Parkway, Chicago, IL, to Administrator Albert M. Cole, night letter via Western Union, August 11, 1954; George S. Harris to President Dwight D. Eisenhower, telegram via Western Union, August 11, 1954, RG 207, HHFA, Box 30. Under President George S. Harris, the NAREB's headquarters was located both in the Loop and in the traditional black community at 420 E. Forty-Fifth Street.

25. HHFA, Office of the Administrator, Division of Law, "Summary of Congressional and Executive Action of Interest to the Housing and Home Finance Agency," 83rd Cong., 2nd sess., August 4, 1954, vol. 100, no. 149, August 5, 1954, no. 316, RG 207, Box 747, VHMCP.

26. Albert M. Cole to George S. Harris, August 24, 1954, attached to George S. Harris to Albert M. Cole, October 21 1954, RG 207, Box 747, VHMCP. Black insurance executive Asa T. Spaulding was named to Region 5 (HHFA press release, December 23, 1954, HHFA-OA-No. 779; Joseph R. Ray to C. L. Townes, President, National Negro Insurance Association, dispatched August 19, 1954, attached to George S. Harris to Joseph R. Ray, August 19, 1954, RG 207, Box 747, VHMCP; C. L. Townes to Joseph R. Ray, August 19, 1954, attached to George S. Harris to Joseph R. Ray, August

19, 1954, RG 207, Box 747, VHMCP; George S. Harris to Joseph R. Ray, August 19, 1954, RG 207, Box 747, VHMCP).

27. National Association of Real Estate Brokers, Inc., press release, August 11, 1954; George S. Harris, President, NAREB, 4459 South Parkway, Chicago, IL, to Administrator Albert M. Cole, night letter via Western Union, August 11, 1954; George S. Harris to President Dwight D. Eisenhower, telegram, August 11, 1954, NA.

28. George Harris wrote Cole in October 1954 about his appointment to the Subcommittee of the National Voluntary Mortgage Credit Extension Committee for Region 9 (Albert M. Cole to George S. Harris, August 24, 1954, attached to George S. Harris to Albert M. Cole, October 21 1954, RG 207, Box 747, VHMCP). Asa T. Spaulding was named to Region 5 (HHFA press release, December 23, 1954, HHFA-OA-No. 779, RG 207, Box 748, Press Release).

29. George W. Snowden to Norman P. Mason, "Nonwhite Representation on National and Regional Voluntary Mortgage Credit Extension Committees," July 30, 1954, RG 207, Box 747, VHMCP.

30. George S. Harris to Albert Cole, October 12, 1955 (President Eisenhower was copied on this letter), RG 207, Box 747, VHMCP; Albert Cole to George S. Harris, November 27, 1956, RG 207, Box 747, VHMCP.

31. George S. Harris to Albert Cole, October 12, 1955. George S. Harris to Albert M. Cole, December 10, 1956, RG 207, Box 747, VHMCP. In an earlier letter, George S. Harris had brought to Cole's attention that a VHMCP form used the term "realtor," which Harris informed him was "the trade name of an organization that discriminates in its membership." Harris requested that the term be removed from all forms or that the term "realtist" also be included (George S. Harris to Albert M. Cole, November 8, 1955, RG 207, Box 747, VHMCP).

32. Albert Cole to George S. Harris, November 27, 1956, RG 207, Box 747, VHMCP; NAREB, Office of the President, George S. Harris, "Names Submitted to Serve on National Committee of the National Voluntary Home Mortgage Credit Program," RG 207, Box 747, VHMCP. Names for the national committee included former NAREB president W. D. Morison Jr. of Detroit, Lenerte Roberts of Philadelphia, and Oscar C. Brown Sr. of Chicago. Region 9 NAREB members of the regional VHMCP from Chicago included Bolin V. Bland, 7 West Madison Street; Hazel Dorham, 4703 South Parkway; and William Y. Browne, 103 E. Forty-Seventh Street.

33. Joseph R. Ray, Informal Memorandum for: B. T. McGraw, "A Deletion of Minority Designation from Board Membership of the Voluntary Home Mortgage Credit Program," October 26, 1956, RG 207, Box 747, VHMCP.

34. HHFA, Office of the Administrator News, HHFA-OA-No. 1187, February 7, 1957, RG 207, Box 748, Press Release. For Ray's recommendations, see Joseph Ray, Racial Relations Service, to Fred B. Morrison, Executive Secretary, VHMCP, "Appointment of National and Regional Committee Members for 1957," November 21, 1956, RG 207, Box 747, VHMCP. Spaulding had been a representative from Region 5

in Charlotte, North Carolina (Arthur W. Viner, Executive Secretary, National Committee, to Joseph R. Ray, "Advisory Members of VHMCP Committees Representing Minority Groups," March 15, 1956), RG 207, Box 747, VHMCP.

35. Administrator Albert Cole to Kevin McCann, Special Assistant to the President, The White House, July 6, 1956; Albert Cole's draft of President Eisenhower's reply to Lorenzo V. Spencer, President, Consolidated Realty Board of Southern California, Inc., no date, Ninth Annual Convention of the National Association of Real Estate Brokers, Inc. Program, RG 207, HHFA, Box 30.

36. Throughout its history, the Racial Relations Service had had other names such as the Office of Racial Relations, and racial relations advisers were also referred to as racial relations officers.

37. Housing and Home Finance Agency press release, HHFA-OA-No. 915, November 5, 1955, RG 207, Box 748, Press Release.

38. Though in national circles dominated by northern-based black elites it was a minority approach, in the South where black builders were more prominent, self-help was dominant (Wiese, *Places of Their Own*, 164, 208).

39. William R. Hudgins, President, to Joseph Ray, September 30, 1954, RG 207, Box 745, ASLL Conf.

40. Joseph R. Ray to William R. Hudgins, October 22, 1954, attached to Hudgins to McGraw, December 3, 1954, RG 207, Box 745; B. T. McGraw to William R. Hudgins, November 3, 1954, attached to Hudgins to McGraw, December 3, 1954, RG 207, Box 745; B. T. McGraw to William R. Hudgins, November 3, 1954, attached to Hudgins to McGraw, December 3, 1954, RG 207, Box 745.

41. Hudgins mentioned to Ray that the League had suggested to George McAllister, director of Home Loan Bank Board (HLBB), that Dr. McGraw be appointed as a special assistant (William R. Hudgins to Joseph Ray, November 1, 1954, attached to Hudgins to McGraw, December 3, 1954, RG 207, Box 745).

42. Ibid.

43. The ASLL convention minutes reported that McGraw called upon the Home Loan Bank Board to invest more capital in minority S&Ls. Also, the role of the Federal National Mortgage Association (FNMA) and the National Voluntary Mortgage Credit Extension Committee in S&Ls secondary mortgage market was discussed (William R. Hudgins to Dr. Booker T. McGraw, December 3, 1954, RG 207, Box 745; "Minutes of American Savings & Loan League Annual Meeting," November 16–17, 1954, Los Angeles, attached to Hudgins to McGraw, December 3, 1954, RG 207, Box 745).

44. George Nesbitt supported the early slum clearance and redevelopment program in Chicago, severely criticizing black institutional elites for their opposition. Once it became clear that the city had created hardship for displaced blacks, he trained his criticism on Chicago's political regime (see chapters 4 and 5).

45. George B. Nesbitt to Racial Relations Personnel, August 12, 1954, RG 207, HHFA, Box 30

46. Nesbitt coauthored a memo with Booker McGraw in March 1954 to advise white FHA market analysts on how to interpret black residential behavior (see chapter 9) (George B. Nesbitt, Special Assistant to the Director, DSCUR and B. T. McGraw, Deputy Assistant to the Administrator, OA, to Gordon Howard, Head, Economics Section, Planning and Engineering Branch, "Racial Aspects of Housing Market Analysis," March 12, 1954).

47. George B. Nesbitt to Racial Relations Personnel, August 12, 1954.

48. George B. Nesbitt to Joseph Ray, "National Association of Real Estate Brokers, 7th Annual Convention, October 11 to 15th, 1954," August 24, 1954, RG 207, HHFA, Box 30.

49. Lenerte Roberts to "Realtist," August 20, 1954, attached to George B. Nesbitt, Special Assistant to the Director (Racial Relations), to Lenerte Roberts, National Chairman Convention Committee, NAREB, September 29, 1954, RG 207, HHFA, Box 30. Ray gave similar advice three years later at the NAREB's ninth annual mid-winter conference in Louisville, Kentucky ("Housing Outlook Facing Minorities in 1957," statement of Joseph R. Ray, Assistant to the Administrator [Racial Relations] of the Housing and Home Finance Agency presented at Mid-Winter Meeting of the National Association of Real Estate Brokers, Louisville, Kentucky, February 22–23, 1957, RG 207, HHFA, Box 30).

50. The historian Andrew Wiese finds that black self-help was more prevalent within the black real estate industry in the South, where integration was strictly prohibited. He argues that they opposed racial segregation not by proposing integration, but by seeking racial equity, and by building homes and neighborhoods that defied racial stereotypes. I contend that when black self-help took on a national presence in the hands of national black trade leaders and government officials, it became wedded to the goal of racial integration, making it a companion, however uneasy, to the principle of "open occupancy" within a racial democratic housing agenda (see Wiese, *Places of Their Own*, 164–208).

51. Interestingly, although he was certainly aware of financing problems, Weaver emphasized the problems of acquiring appropriate land sites in his 1948 classic study (Weaver, *The Negro Ghetto*, 316–18).

52. E. Franklin Frazier, "Durham: Capital of the Black Middle Class," in *The New Negro*, ed. Alain Locke (1925; New York, N.Y.: Atheneum, 1968), 333–40.

53. B. T. McGraw, Deputy Assistant to the Administrator, to Asa T. Spaulding, N. C. Mutual Life Insurance Company, June 16, 1948, RG 207, HHFA Subject files, Box 18, Racial Relations, 1947.

54. There is no indication in the records of what the NNIA response was to McGraw's proposal (B. T. McGraw, Deputy Assistant to the Administrator, to Asa T. Spaulding, N.C. Mutual Life Insurance Company, June 16, 1948, RG 207, HHFA Subject files, Box 18, Racial Relations, 1947). McGraw sent the same proposal to Warren J. Lockwood, Assistant Commissioner, FHA (Field Operations) on June 1, 1948, and to the National Negro Insurance Association, National Negro Business League, and

NAREB. See also Dave Lowery to Malcolm B. Caitlin, "Pooling Resources of Financial Institutions in order to Finance Housing for Minority Groups," May 15, 1948, and Malcolm B. Caitlin to Dr. B. T. McGraw, "Pooling Financial Resources to Finance Minority Group Housing," May 24, 1948, attached to B. T. McGraw to Warren J. Lockwood, "Pooling Devices to Finance Developments to Accommodate Minority Groups," June 1, 1948, RG 207, Box 747, General Subject—Financing.

55. A contributing factor in his success, the report suggested, was the fact that Aiken "ha[d] been building under the FHA program for homes since its beginning" ("The Role of Negro Entrepreneurs in Expanding the Privately-Financed Housing Supply Available to Non-White Families" [draft report], July 20, 1953, no author, pp. 3–6, RG 207, Box 747, General Subject—Financing). For a broader profile of Aiken, see Wiese, *Places of Their Own*, 177–79.

56. W. J. Lockwood, Assistant Commissioner, to W. H. Aiken, National Builders Association, March 24, 1950, RG 207, Box 747, GS—Financing.

57. This was the "community service" that black realtors and financial elites gave to black citizens in need of housing (Bolin V. Bland to Joseph R. Ray, June 30, 1958, attached to Ray to Bland, July 18, 1958, RG 207, Box 747, General Subject File—Financing). The complaint about financing black home purchases in white neighborhoods was a common one. Lenerte Roberts referred to it in his meeting with the FHA regional director responsible for Philadelphia ("Conference with Mr. Leo Kirk, Federal Housing Administrator, Monday, January 31, 1949, 10:30–11:40 a.m., typescript, pp. 3–5, HHFA Papers). Complaints about the need for secondary financing were also common (see J. Westbrook McPherson, Executive Director, New Orleans Urban League, to Reginald Johnson, Director, Field Services and Housing Coordinator, November 3, 1950, attached to Reginald A. Johnson to Dr. Frank Horne, November 14, 1950, RG 207, Box 751, National Urban League).

58. Joseph Ray to Bolin Bland, July 18, 1958, RG 207, Box 747, General Subject File—Financing.

59. Ray wrote to Morrison after he received a letter from Bland written two weeks earlier (Joseph R. Ray to Fred B. Morrison, July 18, 1958, attached to Ray to Bland, July 18, 1958, RG 207, Box 747, General Subject File—Financing).

60. Perhaps Bland and his associates were taking advantage of the opportunities outlined by George Nesbitt in his talk to NAREB in 1954 (George B. Nesbitt to Joseph Ray, "National Association of Real Estate Brokers, 7th Annual Convention, October 11 to 15th, 1954," August 24, 1954, RG 207, HHFA, Box 30).

61. Bolin V. Bland to Fred B. Morrison, July 2, 1958 attached to Ray to Bland, July 18, 1958, RG 207, Box 747, General Subject File—Financing; Joseph R. Ray to Bolin V. Bland, July 18, 1958, RG 207, Box 747, General Subject File—Financing. For another example see Dempsey J. Travis' efforts to launch a black-owned mortgage company in Chicago in the 1950s. Satter, *Family Properties*, 43–44, 139–141

62. Excerpt from Robert R. Taylor, "Financing Minority Group Homes," Savings and Loans News (January 1949), RG 207, Box 747, General Subject—Financing.

63. There is no record of McGraw writing directly to Moore or of Nesbitt dispensing McGraw's advice to Moore (B. T. McGraw to George Nesbitt, April 7, 1949, RG 207, Box 30; B. T. McGraw to Ernest E. Johnson, January 26, 1950, RG 207, HHFA, Box 41; B. T. McGraw to William K. Divers, Chairman, HLBB, "Field Report— Proposed Carver Savings and Loan Association," February 10, 1948, RG 207, HHFA Subject File, Box 18, Racial Relations 1947).

64. B. T. McGraw to Walter H. Aiken, June 22, 1949, RG 207, HHFA, Box 30, Racial Relations, 650; Mortimer Kaplan, Associate Chief, Actuarial and Financial Section, Division of Research and Statistics to Dr. George S. Snowden, Minority Group Housing Advisor, "FHA-insured Mortgage Investments by Major Classes of Financial Institutions Owned and Operated by Negroes," September 3, 1953, p. 1, RG 207, Box 747, General Subject—Financing.

65. "The Role of Negro Entrepreneurs in Expanding the Privately-Financed Housing Supply Available to Non-White Families" was drafted in July 1953. It's unclear whether a final report was published, but even as a draft its relevance lies in the fact that it articulated what black capital's role had been and should be in the real estate field ("The Role of Negro Entrepreneurs in Expanding the Privately-Financed Housing Supply Available to Non-White Families" [draft report] July 20, 1953, no author, pp. 1–2, RG 207, Box 747, General Subject—Financing). Most of the many examples of home builders building for black citizens were in the South and were usually in segregated communities (NAHB-*CORRELATOR*, March 1950, 2, 3; memo to NAHB Members from Frank Cortright, RG 207, Box 748, Market Demand). See also Bolin V. Bland, Real Estate and Housing Editor, "Minority Housing," attached to Joseph R. Ray to Colonel Hugh Askew, Director, Director, Mortgage Finance Department, NAHB, January 31, 1955, RG 207, Box 745. See also Donald W. Wyatt, "Better Homes for Negro Families in the South," *Social Forces* 28, no. 3 (March 1950): 297–303; and *Places of Their Own*, 169, for black developers' efforts in Atlanta and Dallas, see 184–208.

66. "The Role of Negro Entrepreneurs" (draft report), July 20, 1953.

67. According to Arnold Hirsch, "Cole's hostility toward the RRS and Horne in particular manifested itself as early as 1953 when the administrator demoted and transferred the service's top officer, making him a 'special assistant' for minority studies" (Hirsch, "Searching for a 'Sound Negro Policy': A Racial Agenda for the Housing Acts of 1949 and 1954" *Housing Policy Debate* vol. 11, no. 2 [2000]: 420–22, 428, 431; Arnold Hirsch, "Containment on the Home Front: Race and Federal Housing Policy from the New Deal to the Cold War," *Journal of Urban History* 26 [January 2000]: 173–74).

68. Joseph Ray led one of the sessions at the conference (HHFA press release, HHFA-OA-No. 847, June 2, 1955, RG 207, Box 748, Press Release).

69. Albert M. Cole to A. L. Robinson, August 25, 1955, RG 207, Program Files, Racial Relations Program, 1946–1958, Box 747, Conferences—Short Sleeve Conference with Representatives of Negro Lending Institutions.

70. HHFA press release, HHFA-OA-No. 847, June 2, 1955, RG 207, Box 748, Press Release.

71. Townes added, "It is gratifying to learn that the possibility of FHA loans being approved for minority applicants has now become more favorable under the present administration" (C. L. Townes Jr., to Albert M. Cole, June 8, 1955, RG 207, Box 748, Policy).

72. The first report was requested by George Snowden, FHA Minority Housing Advisor from HHFA's Division of Research and Statistics for a forthcoming Racial Relations Officers' Conference. The report was entitled "FHA-insured Mortgage Investments by Major Classes of Financial Institutions Owned and Operated by Negroes." A follow-up analysis of black institutions that were "active as FHA-approved mortgagees" by Mortimer Kaplan was made in October 1955 (Mortimer Kaplan, Associate Chief, Actuarial and Financial Section, Division of Research and Statistics to Dr. George S. Snowden, Minority Group Housing Advisor, "FHA-insured Mortgage Investments by Major Classes of Financial Institutions Owned and Operated by Negroes," September 3, 1953, p. 1. RG 207, Box 747, General Subject—Financing; Mortimer Kaplan to Dr. George W. Snowden, "Mortgage Activity of Major Groups of Negro Operated Lending Institutions," October 18, 1955, RG 207, Box 747, General Subject—Financing).

73. Mortimer Kaplan, Associate Chief, Actuarial and Financial Section, Division of Research and Statistics to Dr. George S. Snowden, Minority Group Housing Advisor, "FHA-insured Mortgage Investments by Major Classes of Financial Institutions Owned and Operated by Negroes," September 3, 1953, p. 1, RG 207, Box 747, General Subject—Financing.

74. Moreover, the growth of FHA-approved black mortgagees' combined assets outstripped that of the assets of comparable white lending institutions, an increase of 45 percent compared to less than 20 percent. Black mortgagees' investments also grew faster than those of comparable white firms, 80 percent compared to little over 40 percent (Mortimer Kaplan to Dr. George W. Snowden, "Mortgage Activity of Major Groups of Negro Operated Lending Institutions," October 18, 1955, RG 207, Box 747, General Subject—Financing).

75. Baker and Occomy, "A Real Estate Program for Negroes," 45–46. Exploitative "land contracts" were prevalent among black home buyers. A mortgage under any terms would be better than these financial instruments. On land contracts see Hirsch, *Making the Second Ghetto*, 32–33.

76. Baker and Occomy, "A Real Estate Program for Negroes," 45–46.

77. "Behind the veil" is a reference to Du Bois's contention that black social life must exist behind a veil because whites only saw an undifferentiated and stereotypical black social life (see his *Souls of Black Folks*).

78. A. L. Robinson, Secretary to Albert M. Cole, June 10, 1955, RG 207, Box 748, Policy.

79. Ibid.

80. Ibid. Albert Cole was grateful for Robinson's letter, although he regretted that Robinson did not voice his opinions at the meeting (Albert M. Cole to A. L. Robinson, August 25, 1955. RG 207, Program Files, Racial Relations Program, 1946–1958, Box 747, Conferences—Short Sleeve Conference with Representatives of Negro Lending Institutions). Robinson's plea may reflect the smaller capital base for black savings and loan associations compared to black insurance companies. For an examination of almost identical arguments forty years later, see my "Self-Help, Black Conservatives, and the Reemergence of Black Privatism," in *Without Justice for All: The New Liberalism and Our Retreat from Racial Equality*, ed. Adolph L. Reed (Boulder, Colo.: Westview Press, 1999).

81. HHFA press release, HHFA-OA-No. 818, March 7, 1955, RG 207, Box 748, Press Release.

82. B. T. McGraw, Racial Relations Service to Joseph R. Ray, Assistant to the Administrator, "Preliminary Report of Requested Follow-up on VHMCP Operations and Results and Proposals for Action," July 19, 1955, RG 207, Box 747, VHMCP. McGraw attempted to activate the black policy network to resuscitate what appeared to be a failing program (see Allen McDuffie, Executive Secretary to James A. Pawley, Executive Secretary, Urban League of Newark, September 19, 1955; Allen McDuffie to Reginald A. Johnson, September 29, 1955). See also Arthur W. Viner, Executive Secretary, VHMCP, to Albert M. Cole, Administrator, HHFA, "Minority group loans placed by VHMCP," September 1, 1955, attached to Allen McDuffie to Reginald A. Johnson, September 29, 1955, RG 207, Box 747, VHMCP.

83. Another reason why participation in VHMCP was slowed by minority borrowers was because they were in the "existing housing market," which used conventional financing. This was especially the case for "many displaced families" seeking "rehousing accommodations" (HHFA press release, HHFA-OA-No. 908, October 18, 1955, RG 207, Box 748, Press Release).

84. Snowden used the occasion to promote the positive features of integrated living in racially transitional areas ("Roadblock in Financing Homes for Minority Groups," *South Bend Tribune*, December 1955 news clipping in RG 207, Box 747, VHMCP). B. T. McGraw was also in attendance at the meeting. Snowden extolled the virtues of VHMCP in an unprecedented appearance he made at the Mortgage Bankers Association convention in Chicago a few months before his South Bend appearance (see chapter 9).

85. DeHart Hubbard, Racial Relations Office, to George S. Harris, President, NAREB, 4459 South Parkway, January 3, 1956. See attached list, "Suggested Points for Questionnaire to Brokers," RG 207, Box 747, Conferences.

86. Joseph R. Ray, Racial Relations Service, to Albert M. Cole, "Report of Conference on VHMCP Complaints, Detroit, Michigan, May 29, 1956," June 6, 1956. Press release from Detroit Real Estate Brokers Association, no date [received by the Racial Relations Service, June 5, 1956], both attached to Albert Cole to Senator Herbert H. Lehman, August 1, 1956, RG 207, Box 747, Conferences.

87. Joseph R. Ray to Rev. Hermes Zimmerman, March 11, 1957, RG 207, Box 747, VHMCP.

88. As a result of this controversy, mainly cosmetic changes were made in the VHMCP program. Ray suggested fewer referrals would allow "perhaps a little more attention and consideration given to minority applicants [and] will help the VHMCP" in Detroit. The Detroit brokers made other suggestions in their meeting with the Region 8 executive secretary. The new VHMCP applications were to have a space for the broker's name and contact information (Senator Pat McNamara to George H. Snowden, May 1, 1956; Albert M. Cole to Senator Pat McNamara, May 24, 1956, RG 207, Box 747, Conference—VHMCP; Joseph R. Ray, Racial Relations Service, to Albert M. Cole, "Report of Conference on VHMCP Complaints, Detroit, Michigan, May 29, 1956," June 6, 1956, attached to Albert Cole to Senator Herbert H. Lehman, August 1, 1956. RG 207, Box 747, Conferences).

89. Albert M. Cole to Senator Pat McNamara, May 24, 1956, RG 207, Box 747, Conference—VHMCP.

90. In his draft release, McGraw counted only a total of 4,317 minority loans made for minorities amounting to $41,746,000 (B. T. McGraw to Joseph R. Ray, "Draft of News Release Re Minority Group Representation on VHMCP Committees," January 25, 1957; "News for Release," Friday, February 4, 1957, RG 207, Box 747, VHMCP; HHFA, Office of the Administrator News, HHFA-OA-No. 1187, February 7, 1957, RG 207, Box 748, Press Release).

91. George S. Harris to Albert M. Cole, February 5, 1957; NAREB, "Distribution of Direct Mortgage Money from Special Fund As Stated in 1954 Housing Act," RG 207, Box 747, VHMCP.

92. Joseph R. Ray, "The VHMCP—A Source of Financing for Minority Housing," May 1958, RG 207, Box 747, Financing. The subsequent news release in July 1958, VHMCP reported serving "6109 minority families in metropolitan areas, the loans totaling approximately $60 million" (HHFA-OA-No. 58–302, July 10, 1958).

93. Wiese, *Places of Their Own*, 140.

94. In February 1957, a NAREB committee met with a committee from the Mortgage Bankers Association of America at the Conrad Hilton Hotel in Chicago (The Committee to Meet with the Mortgage Bankers Association of America to George S. Harris, President, NAREB, n.d., RG 207, HHFA, Box 30).

95. Ibid.

96. Nelson Lichtenstein, *Walter Reuther: The Most Dangerous Man in Detroit* (Urbana, Ill.: University of Illinois Press, 1995), 295. See also Meg Jacobs, *Pocketbook Politics: Economic Citizenship in Twentieth-Century America* (Princeton, N.J.: Princeton University Press, 2005), 257.

97. The Committee to Meet with the Mortgage Bankers Association of America to George S. Harris, President, NAREB, n.d., HHFA Papers.

98. Ibid.

99. It is not clear if either policy change went through. What was important was what NAREB wanted and was willing to "give up" (George S. Harris to Joseph R. Ray, March 21, 1957, Telegram: The National Association of Real Estate Brokers passed the following resolution at their Midwinter Conference, March 25, 1957, RG 207, Box 747, VHMCP).

100. "Home Lenders Oppose New Private Finance Group Plan," American Savings and Loan League news release, January 17, 1954, RG 207, Box 747, General Subject—Financing.

101. George S. Harris, "President's Message," Ninth Annual Convention of the National Association of Real Estate Brokers, Inc. Program, RG 207, HHFA, Box 30.

102. Joseph Ray explained the relationship between the racial relations officers and black interest groups in an agency press release dated November 5, 1955. The occasion for the press release was at the National Association of Real Estate Boards' 48th annual convention in New York where both Albert Cole and Joseph Ray gave addresses (Housing and Home Finance Agency press release, HHFA-OA-No. 915, November 5, 1955, RG 207, Box 748, Press Release).

103. "Housing Outlook Facing Minorities in 1957," statement of Joseph R. Ray, Assistant to the Administrator (Racial Relations) of the Housing and Home Finance Agency presented at Mid Winter Meeting of the National Association of Real Estate Brokers, Louisville, Kentucky, February 22–23, 1957, HHFA Papers; HHFA, Office of the Administrator News, HHFA-OA-No. 58–59, press release, February 21, 1958, RG 207, Box 748, Press Release. Ray later spelled out a program for NAREB to follow in regards to black housing provision (see Session of Regional Vice-Presidents, NAREB-Midwinter Conference, St. Louis, Missouri, February 21, 1958, "Program Outline for Regional Construction of New Homes 1958–1959," Joseph R. Ray, February 10, 1958).

104. Joseph R. Ray to Albert M. Cole, "9th Annual Mid-Winter Conference, National Association of Real Estate Brokers, Inc.," February 28, 1957, RG 207, HHFA, Box 30.

105. However, Ray's advocacy points to an apparent inconsistency in his position. While it was hard to distinguish between this "special assistance" and the "special pleading" that Ray earlier deplored, he was reluctant to oppose NAREB, thought the tight market required an exemption, or convinced himself this was normal government assistance that black capital required to do its job.

106. Albert Cole to Joseph Ray, "FNMA Special Assistance for Minority Group Housing," May 21, 1957, RG 207, Box 747, Conference—VHMCP. In November 1957, it was determined that 63 percent of all loans made through VHMCP went to the "lower middle income group" with incomes between $3,000 and $6,000. The prices of their homes ranged from $5,000 to $11,000 (HHFA-OA-No. 1518, November 1, 1957. RG 207, Box 747, Press Release).

Conclusion

1. James Q. Wilson, *Negro Politics: The Search for Leadership* (Glencoe, Ill.: Free Press, 1960), 185n66.

2. Adolph Reed Jr., "The Study of Black Politics and the Practice of Black Politics: Their Historical Relation and Evolution," in *Problems and Methods in the Study of Politics*, eds. Ian Shapiro, Rogers A. Smith, and Tarek E. Masoud (Cambridge: Cambridge University Press, 2004), 106–143. See also Adolph Reed Jr., *Stirrings in the Jug: Black Politics in the Post-Segregation Era* (Minneapolis, Minn.: University of Minnesota Press, 1999), 1–52.

3. Raymond A. Mohl, "The Second Ghetto Thesis and the Power of History," *Journal of Urban History* 9, no. 3 (March 2003): 251; Amanda I. Seligman, "What Is the Second Ghetto?" *Journal of Urban History* 9, no. 3 (March 2003): 273; Heather A. Thompson, "Making a Second Urban History," *Journal of Urban History* 9, no. 3 (March 2003): 294; Kenneth W. Goings and Raymond A. Mohl, eds., *The New African American Urban History* (Thousand Oaks, Calif.: Sage, 1996).

4. Arnold R. Hirsch, "Second Thoughts on the Second Ghetto," *Journal of Urban History* 9, no. 3 (March 2003): 300; Arnold R. Hirsch, *Making the Second Ghetto: Race and Housing in Chicago, 1940–1960* (New York, N.Y.: Cambridge University Press, 1983), xii.

5. Thomas J. Sugrue, *The Origins of Urban Crisis: Race and Inequality in Postwar Detroit* (Princeton, N.J.: Princeton University Press, 1996) and his *Sweet Land of Liberty: The Forgotten Struggle for Civil Rights in the North* (New York, N.Y.: Random House, 2008). Two books that represent this new scholarship include Robert Self, *American Babylon: Race and the Struggle for Postwar Oakland* (Princeton, N.J.: Princeton University Press, 2003), and Chris Rhomberg, *No There There: Race, Class, and Political Community in Oakland* (Berkeley, Calif.: University of California Press, 2004). While Self expertly employs the best methods of urban historians and urban social scientists in his examination, Rhomberg does the better job of discerning those class and generational cleavages among black political activists.

Index

Abner, Willoughby, 166, 180, 186, 370–71n94
Abrams, Charles, 367n60, 381n91
absentee landlords, 32, 95, 152
Advisory Commission on Housing, 292
AFL, 184, 186
Aiken, Walter H. "Chief," 271–72, 274–75, 396n2, 402n55
Airport Homes, 87, 161, 359n14
Alinsky, Saul D., 168, 363n43
Altgeld Gardens, 37, 43, 50, 60, 259, 323n7, 324n28
Amalgamated Butchers Union, 185
Amalgamated Meat Cutters Union, 185, 371n95
American Council on Human Rights, 292
American Council on Race Relations, 75, 76, 203, 206, 211, 215, 378n59, 378n61
American Dilemma (Myrdal), 6
American Savings and Loan League (ASLL), 259, 266, 267, 281, 290, 291, 400n43; described, 255; opposition by, 292
American Society of Planning Officials, 337n102
Anderson, George A., 396n13
ANP. *See* Associated Negro Press
antidiscrimination, xv, 15, 266, 301; self-help and, 257, 258, 291–94
Archdiocese of Chicago, 150
Arthur Rubloff & Co., 240
ASLL. *See* American Savings and Loan League

Associated Negro Press (ANP), xii, 37, 58, 63, 129, 130, 131–32, 133, 176, 196, 259, 332n69
Association of Commerce and Industry, 170–71, 363n43
Austin, J. C., 89

Back of the Yards Community, 184
Back of the Yards Neighborhood Council, 168
Baker, Elmore: proposal by, 255, 257, 259, 260, 269, 271, 280
Baker, Henry, 114
Banfield, Edward, 59
banks, 270; black owned, 259; pressure on, 268
Barnes, John W., 391n71
Barnett, Claude A., xii, 37, 130, 138, 140, 319n14, 348–49n13, 349n21, 350n27, 351n33; ANP and, 259; black leadership crisis and, 189; on black press, 176–77; on Cicero riot, 176, 177; conservation and, 384n3; on CUL, 176, 177; land-clearance program and, 135; leadership vacuum and, 177; redevelopment and, 132–38, 384n3; self-help and, 155
Bauer, Catherine, 317–18n1
Beasley, Mrs. E. W., 355n92
Beauharnais, Joseph, 167
behavior, 7; antisocial, 8, 33, 35, 39; black housing, 246; black working class, 3, 8; engendered, 250; housing and, 35; racial, 224; residential, 237

NUL and, 265; optimism of, 242; protests by, 261

black working class, 15, 41, 102; behavior/culture of, 8; displacement of, 357n106; material aid to, 13; reorganizing, 35

Bland, Bolin V., 260, 288, 391n73, 399n32, 402n60; Morrison and, 273, 274; Ray and, 272–73, 274

Blandford, John, 44

blight, 75–76, 81, 95, 125, 129, 135, 147, 149, 154, 204–5, 209, 211, 212; commercial, 17, 18; controlling, 139; economic concept of, 328n19

block associations, 92–93, 94, 140, 334n84

Block Beautiful Campaign, 92–93, 384n2

blockbusting, 110, 217, 219, 238, 259, 341n30, 355n92, 377n49, 382n111

Bodfish, Morton, 394n95

Bogue, Donald, 317n79

Bousfield, Midian, 377n52

Bremer, George A., 235, 386n30

Bridgeport Homes, 178, 187

Bristow, Judge, 196

Bronzeville, xix, 57, 67, 126, 132, 184, 260; class structure of, 14; conservation in, 138–41; migration to, 23; Negro clearance in, 85; overcrowding/congestion on, 25; public housing in, 42; radical challenge in, 10; redevelopment in, 129; slums in, 20, 108; stakeholders in, 77

Brotherhood of Sleeping Car Porters union, 16

Brown, Frank, 184, 370n89

Brown, Mrs. Sydney P., 355n92

Brown, Oscar C., Sr., 50, 51, 88, 127, 140, 259, 324n28, 328–29n20, 334n87, 355n92

Brown, Oscar, Jr., 183, 184, 185, 370n89

Brown v. Board of Education of Topeka, Kansas (1954), 181, 223, 236, 246, 378n58, 393n86

Browne, William Y., 255n92, 399n32

Browning, Alice C., 332n69, 332n70, 333n77, 333n81; the Champions and, 88, 89–92

Buchanan v. Warley (1917), 372

Bunche, Ralph, 310n17

business elites, 14, 19, 20, 100–101, 139; capital relocation and, 18; redevelopment plans and, 80

CAD. *See* Council Against Discrimination

Calloway, Nathaniel O., 366n58

Calumet Conservation and Rehabilitation Association, 352n41

capital: black, 129–32, 268–69, 347n1; investment, 18; state and, 246, 252; white, 131

Capone, Al, 367n60

Carey, Archibald J., Jr., 89, 111, 300, 313n51

Carey Ordinance, 86, 102, 104, 385n15

Cayton, Horace R., xii, 1, 10, 11, 12, 16, 22, 32, 34, 38, 44, 51, 70, 193, 200, 259, 321n37, 321n38, 329n23, 335n96, 358n3, 397n13; on black community, xi; on black housing, 33, 46; defense industry and, 316n72; on Negro clearance, 69; on residential segregation, 67; restrictive covenants and, 201–2; on social disorganization, 31, 321n33; testimony of, 23; *Tovey v. Levy* and, 203; on working-class blacks, 311n25

CCHR. *See* Chicago Commission on Human Relations

CEMV. *See* Conference to End Mob Violence

CHA. *See* Chicago Housing Authority

Champions, the, 102, 332n70, 333n73, 334n84, 335n92; black property owners and, 90–91; block associations and, 94; Browning and, 89–92; CUL and, 92–94; desegregation and, 90; homeowners/tenants and, 92;

Champions, the *(continued)*
leadership of, 334n86, 337n109; oppo-
sition by, 88, 89–90; slum clearance
and, 90, 91, 94; urban redevelopment
and, 91–92
Chicago Amalgamated Local 453, 362n32
Chicago Association of Commerce and
Industry, 170, 172
Chicago Bee, 49–50, 133, 324n23; on
Citizens Committee, 52; Jones letter
to, 51; on West Chesterfield, 48
Chicago City Bank and Trust Company,
164, 395n100
Chicago Civil Liberties Union, 89
Chicago Commission on Human Rela-
tions (CCHR), 112, 168, 169
Chicago Committee for Housing Action,
82
Chicago Community Inventory, 231
Chicago Conference on Race Relations,
319n10
Chicago Council against Racial and Reli-
gious Discrimination, 88–89
Chicago Council of Negro Organiza-
tions, 89, 331n59
Chicago Council of the Negro National
Congress, 49
Chicago Daily News, 361n28, 364n49
Chicago Defender, 23, 24–25, 63, 87,
133, 148, 149–50, 166, 217, 241, 323n8,
323n14; Barnett and, 132; *Hansberry*
and, 196; restrictive covenants and,
197, 202; Weaver and, 211, 381n109
Chicago Development Program, 61–62
Chicago Dwellings Association, 136,
387n34
Chicago Field Office (PHA), 106, 339n8,
341n34
Chicago Health Department, 24, 73
Chicago Housing Authority (CHA), xii,
26, 46, 47, 52, 56, 59, 83, 89, 106, 119,
133, 146, 181, 258–59; Board of Commissioners, 63, 314n51; FHA and, 49;
housing-based violence and, 157–58;

NAACP and, 178, 182; Nesbitt and,
105; nonsegregation policy of, 180;
occupancy policy and, 180; planning
and, 134; public housing and, 48, 54,
57, 64; racism and, 53; rejection of, 58;
slum clearance and, 339n8, 349n20;
study by, 24, 76, 122; support for, 60;
Taylor and, 320n15; Trumbull Park
and, 179
Chicago Industrial Union Housing Committee, 341n34
Chicago Land Clearance Commission
(CLCC), 83, 95, 103, 106, 108, 111, 112,
115, 124, 174; NAACP and, 114, 118;
plan by, 129; racial transition and, 110;
relocation and, 104–5, 113, 116, 117,
118, 123; relocation practices of, 104–5;
responsibility of, 349n20; slum clearance and, 110
Chicago Metropolitan Mutual Assurance
Company, 259
Chicago Plan Commission, 17, 25, 71, 81,
93, 102, 138, 331n56
Chicago Relocation Plan, 106
Chicago riot (1919), 160, 161
Chicago school of sociology, 1, 2, 4, 20,
31, 32, 147–48
"Chicago Situation," 116–18, 120
Chicago Sun-Times, 57, 59
Chicago Title & Trust Co., survey by, 242
Chicago Urban League (CUL), xii, 12, 16,
23, 44, 51, 68, 70, 73, 74, 75, 76, 95, 111,
117, 133, 165, 168, 228, 316n75, 334n87,
335n96, 336n99, 336n102, 347n5,
347n90, 352n45; Barnett and, 176, 177;
block clubs of, 92, 93, 140; Carey and,
89; the Champions and, 92–94; efforts
of, 152, 328n16; housing and, 167, 238,
239; NAACP and, 343n53; political
associations of, 170; political style of,
158; racial integration and, 175; social
base of, 92; urban renewal and, 125,
150; Williams and, 163, 170, 171, 172,
173, 174, 177, 360n19

PRESTON H. SMITH II is associate professor of politics at Mount Holyoke College.